Raphael to Renoir

Raphael to Renoir

Drawings from the Collection of Jean Bonna

EDITED BY
Stijn Alsteens, Carmen C. Bambach, George Goldner,
Colta Ives, Perrin Stein, and Nathalie Strasser

The Metropolitan Museum of Art, New York

Yale University Press, New Haven and London

This volume has been published to accompany the exhibition "Raphael to Renoir: Drawings from the Collection of Jean Bonna," held at The Metropolitan Museum of Art, New York, from January 21 to April 26, 2009, and at the National Gallery of Scotland, Edinburgh, from June 5 to September 6, 2009.

In New York, the exhibition is made possible by the Gail and Parker Gilbert Fund.

Published by The Metropolitan Museum of Art, New York

John P. O'Neill, Publisher and Editor in Chief
Barbara Cavaliere, Editor
Bruce Campbell, Designer
Peter Antony, Chief Production Manager
Salvatore Destro, Production Manager
Margaret Rennolds Chace, Managing Editor
Robert Weisberg, Assistant Managing Editor
Jayne Kuchna, Bibliographer
Jane S. Tai, Image Acquisitions and Permissions Specialist

Separations by Professional Graphics, Inc., Rockford, Illinois
Printed by Brizzolis Arte en Gráficas, Madrid
Bound by Encuadernación Ramos, S.A., Madrid
Printing and binding coordinated by Ediciones El Viso, S.A., Madrid
Typeset in Adobe Caslon Pro

Jacket illustration: Raphael, detail of *Study of Soldiers in* The Conversion of Saul (cat. 6)

Frontispiece: Jean-Antoine Watteau, detail of *Three Studies of Female Heads* (cat. 68)

Cataloging-in-Publication Data is available from the Library of Congress.

ISBN 978-1-58839-307-4 (hc: The Metropolitan Museum of Art)
ISBN 978-0-300-14207-5 (hc: Yale University Press)

Contents

Directors' Foreword

This volume, *Raphael to Renoir: Drawings from the Collection of Jean Bonna*, presents 120 of the finest drawings from the distinguished collection of M. Jean Bonna of Geneva, Switzerland. The publication and the exhibition it accompanies were planned under the stewardship of Philippe de Montebello, Director Emeritus of The Metropolitan Museum of Art.

As the title of this book reveals, the works range from the Renaissance to the late nineteenth century, and they effectively epitomize the fine quality and rich diversity of the Bonna Collection. Reaching across national boundaries, the drawings herein represent artistic schools in Italy, Northern Europe, France, and Great Britain. The works are as varied in subject matter as they are in medium and artistic styles and encompass spirited quick sketches, carefully rendered narrative scenes, arresting studies of the human figure, formal and informal portraits, detailed animal and nature studies, as well as idyllic landscapes, cityscapes, and seascapes. In addition to exceptional examples by recognized masters, the collection includes drawings of poignant content and superb aesthetic refinement by lesser-known artists.

Although most of the Bonna drawings have been previously published and individually exhibited, the great strengths and full range of these holdings seen as a whole have not been previously explored. A group of French drawings from the collection was published and exhibited in the École Nationale Supérieure des Beaux-Arts, Paris, in 2006, with a catalogue edited by Emmanuelle Brugerolles, to whom we are grateful in regard to the early stages of planning the present project.

Documentation of M. Bonna's rich holdings has been enhanced considerably by the contributions made to this catalogue by the curators of the Department of Drawings and Prints, The Metropolitan Museum of Art; the curator of M. Bonna's collection; and a number of international scholars who rank among the leading specialists in their fields. As Jean Bonna related to George Goldner, Drue Heinz Chairman of the Department of Drawings and Prints at The Metropolitan Museum of Art, in the interview that introduces him in the catalogue, he began collecting drawings some twenty years ago. M. Bonna is also an erudite collector of rare books, his collection of French literature being one of the foremost in the world. His collecting interests also extend to Old Master prints, paintings, sculpture, and the decorative arts.

The exhibition is made possible through the generosity and support of the Gail and Parker Gilbert Fund. In addition to The Metropolitan Museum of Art, New York, the selection of works in this volume will be on exhibit at the National Gallery of Scotland, Edinburgh.

Thomas P. Campbell, Director, The Metropolitan Museum of Art, New York
Michael Clarke, Director, National Gallery of Scotland, Edinburgh

Acknowledgments

We are grateful to Philippe de Montebello, Director Emeritus of The Metropolitan Museum of Art, for his warm support of this publication and the exhibition that it accompanies.

This project represents the collaboration of a team of colleagues from both inside and outside The Metropolitan Museum of Art. The curators of the Department of Drawings and Prints, The Metropolitan Museum of Art, and Nathalie Strasser, Curator of the Jean Bonna Collection, Geneva, would especially like to thank our fellow contributing authors, who are listed on the Contributors' page.

Numerous other colleagues and friends have assisted in the creation of this catalogue and the organization of the accompanying exhibition. We extend our appreciation to our colleague from the second venue of the exhibition, Aidan Weston-Lewis, Chief Curator of Italian and Spanish Art, the National Gallery of Scotland, Edinburgh. Conservation of the drawings in the Jean Bonna Collection was undertaken by Marjorie N. Shelley, Sherman Fairchild Conservator in Charge of paper conservation at The Metropolitan Museum of Art, and Véronique Strasser, Geneva.

For their work on this publication, we recognize John P. O'Neill, who oversaw every aspect of the volume; Bruce Campbell, its designer; Barbara Cavaliere, its editor; Jayne Kuchna, who researched the bibliographical elements; and Peter Antony and Salvatore Destro, who oversaw production and printing. We add special mention of the following: Novella Baroni, Christine Begley, Esther Bell, Pierre and Céline Berndt, Carole Blumenfeld, Giulio Bora, Mark Brady, Barbara Bridgers, Hans Buijs, Margaret Chace, Aileen Chuk, Ghislaine Courtet, Deanna Cross, Jean-Pierre Cuzin, Elisa Debenedetti, Martha Deese, Diane DeGrazia, David del Gaizo, Charles Dumas, Charles Ellis, Entreprise d'arts graphiques Jean Genoud, Chris Fischer, Mary Flanagan, Robyn Fleming, Achim Gnann, Patrick Goetelen, Valentine Greco, Stefaan Houtekeete, Kirstie Howard, Armin Kunz, Michael Langley, Carol Lekarew, Erik Löffler, Ricky Luna, Pietro C. Marani, Michael McAuliffe, Emil Micha, Rachel Mustalish, Stephen Ongpin, Nadine Orenstein, Pierre Pinon, Diana Pitt, Michiel Plomp, Ellen Prokop, Jan van Regteren Altena, Gregory Rubinstein, Kenneth Soehner and the staff of Thomas J. Watson Library of The Metropolitan Museum of Art, Rachel Stern, Linda Sylling, Jane Tai, Elyse Topalian, Mary Vaccaro, Emily Vanderpool, Yana Van Dyke, Marie Claire Waille, Robert Weisberg, Linda Wolk-Simon, Daniel Zolli, and Mary Zuber.

Last and foremost, our greatest acknowledgment is extended to M. Jean Bonna, whose marvelous collection was, of course, the major impetus for the entire project.

Stijn Alsteens, Carmen C. Bambach, George Goldner, Colta Ives, Perrin Stein, and Nathalie Strasser

Contributors to the Catalogue

Stijn Alsteens, Associate Curator, Department of Drawings and Prints, The Metropolitan Museum of Art, New York

Diederik Bakhuÿs, Conservateur du patrimoine, Musée des Beaux-Arts, Rouen

Carmen C. Bambach, Curator, Department of Drawings and Prints, The Metropolitan Museum of Art, New York

Emmanuelle Brugerolles, Conservateur général du patrimoine, École des Beaux-Arts, Paris

Bruno Chenique, Independent Scholar, formerly of the Villa Médicis, Rome, and the Getty Research Institute, Los Angeles

Paulette Choné, Professeur des Universités, Université de Bourgogne, Dijon

The late Philip Conisbee, Curator, National Gallery of Art, Washington, D.C.

Laurence des Cars, Conservateur en chef du patrimoine, Directrice scientifique, Agence France-Muséums - Louvre Abou Dabi, Paris

Dominique Cordellier, Conservateur en chef, Département des Arts graphiques, Musée du Louvre, Paris

Marie-Anne Dupuy-Vachey, Independent Scholar, Paris

Nicole Garnier-Pelle, Conservateur en chef du patrimoine, Musée Condé, Chantilly

George Goldner, Drue Heinz Chairman, Department of Drawings and Prints, The Metropolitan Museum of Art, New York

David Guillet, Directeur du développement culturel, Réunion des musées nationaux, Paris

Clémentine Gustin Gomez, Independent Scholar, Paris

Colta Ives, Curator, Department of Drawings and Prints, The Metropolitan Museum of Art, New York

Barthélémy Jobert, Professor, Université Paris Sorbonne - Paris IV

Alastair Laing, Curator of Pictures and Sculpture, The National Trust, London

Christophe Leribault, Conservateur en chef, Département des Arts graphiques, Musée du Louvre, Paris; Directeur, Musée Eugène Delacroix, Paris

Constance McPhee, Associate Curator, Department of Drawings and Prints, The Metropolitan Museum of Art, New York

Hélène Meyer, Conservateur du patrimoine, Palais de Compiègne, Compiègne

Jane Munro, Senior Assistant Keeper of Paintings, Drawings and Prints, The Fitzwilliam Museum, Cambridge, UK

Louis-Antoine Prat, Chargé de mission, Département des Arts graphiques, Musée du Louvre, Paris

Pierre Rosenberg, Président-directeur honoraire, Musée du Louvre, Paris

Marie-Pierre Salé, Conservateur, Musée d'Orsay, Paris

Xavier Salmon, Conservateur en chef du patrimoine, Chef de l'inspection générale des musées, Direction des musées de France, Paris

Perrin Stein, Curator, Department of Drawings and Prints, The Metropolitan Museum of Art, New York

Nathalie Strasser, Curator of the Jean Bonna Collection, Geneva

Mària van Berge-Gerbaud, Director, Fondation Custodia, Paris

Sjraar van Heugten, Curator, Van Gogh Museum, Amsterdam

Carel van Tuyll van Seeroskerken, Directeur, Département des Arts graphiques, Musée du Louvre, Paris

Interview with Jean Bonna by George Goldner

George Goldner: Jean, did you grow up in Geneva?

Jean Bonna: I was born in Geneva, where I spent all my childhood. I went to university there and received two degrees.

Goldner: Does that explain, in part, your interest in collecting French literature?

Bonna: Certainly my interest in French literature was preexistent. As you probably know, George, my book collection began earlier than my drawings collection, and it is centered, with a few exceptions, on French literature.

Goldner: What was the first thing you collected? Did you collect anything when you were very young? As a boy, did you collect tin soldiers or anything else?

Bonna: I did collect a few stamps, but very early on, I started to collect books. And I think the first book I bought was an early nineteenth-century edition of Francois Rabelais. I say that in the foreword to the first volume of my library catalogue. That was strange reading for a nine-year-old boy, but it was my first. And from then on, I bought many books. Of course, when you are twelve, you cannot buy the same things as when you are an established man. But I was always interested in books. And fifteenth-century books are very often illustrated, so that brought me to prints and then drawings.

Goldner: Do you still have the very first book you bought when you were nine?

Bonna: Yes, I still have it. And I still have another book that is quite amusing, a book written by the president of the corporation of the Bouquinistes of the Paris quays about his bookseller experience, which he gave me in March of 1957. I was eleven-and-a-half years old then, and he dedicated it to me with the inscription "To one of my good clients." So at eleven-and-a-half years old, I was already buying enough books to receive a gift from a bookseller.

Goldner: And you continued to buy books all along, until now?

Bonna: Yes, I still buy books. Of course, the difference between collecting books and drawings is that, although neither is ever totally complete, it's easier to have a collection of books that is almost complete. What I'm lacking today in the area of books is just things that are of no interest, things that cannot be found, like the first edition of Louise Labé, for instance. Maybe I'll find it one day. I did locate something even more rare, and that is the first edition of Pernette du Guillet. Today, what I mainly do with my book collection is improve it. If I find a better copy, I sell the old one. I never do that with drawings, because each drawing is unique. Sometimes I might find something more interesting than the things I have, but it's always different. You know that very well because you have been one of my best friends in building this collection. And you know that I never buy something just because it should be in the collection. I always buy things because I like them.

Goldner: Absolutely.

Jean Bonna with a selection of works in his collection, 2008

Bonna: So it makes it very difficult to resell. And in fact, I think I've only resold two drawings in my collection.

Goldner: Now tell me, you referred to how books, because they're illustrated in many cases, lead naturally to illustrations, engravings, woodcuts, and then eventually drawings. And you do have some wonderful prints in your house, which I remember very well. But you really are much more a drawings collector than a print collector.

Bonna: Yes it's true.

Goldner: I've known very few people who really collected both. I find that there are certain people who enjoy collecting prints and others who seem to collect drawings as their principal focus. So there's nothing unusual in preferring one or the other. What is it about drawings that makes you favor them as a collector more than prints, shall we say?

Bonna: I think I was led to prints by the books. I have a few very good prints, 70 to 80. And I still buy prints from time to time. Some are very rare; some are very good. But what I very quickly found quite difficult with prints is that they are extremely technical. It's not enough to like a subject. You then have to find the perfect impression. You have to find the one with the best inking, with the best sharpness of image, which is not the case with drawings. With drawings, what really seduces me is the fact that they are generally the first idea of an artist.

Even in a finished drawing, you still have this first idea that you don't have in a painting, except maybe in some modern paintings, which are of a different kind.

Goldner: With that in mind, let's turn to the drawings you select, because each collector has his or her own personal approach. For some, it seems less personal. For you, it always struck me that you have one of the most personal reactions to a drawing of any collector I know. As you say, you don't buy it for art historical reasons. So, when you open a Sotheby's or Christie's catalogue, or go to a dealer, are there certain qualities you look for? You collect most schools and centuries, so it isn't one school that you're looking for, or one period, but there's something aesthetically and emotionally that seems to attract you to particular drawings.

Bonna: Yes, although there are a few exceptions, there are two qualities that really appeal to me in a drawing, which are grace and harmony, and that is the reason the collection has a lot of representations of woodlands, a lot of landscapes, and many feminine figures. Of course, there are a few exceptions. For instance, last year I bought the drawing by Jacques Stella representing the Beheading of Saint John the Baptist, which is not really about grace and harmony.

Goldner: No, it's certainly not harmonious.

Bonna: No, there are a few exceptions. But in general, I think what appeals to me in a drawing are its grace and harmony. And if you go through the collection and if you go through the selection you have made for this show, I think it shows very well.

Goldner: I think that's very true. What was the first drawing you bought?

Bonna: Well, the first is a drawing I no longer have. I bought it when the Galerie Cailleux opened an office in Geneva in 1985. They had a little show on Hubert Robert that included a rather nice drawing called *L'Aubergiste courtisée* (*The Courted Maid*). I bought it, and that was my first drawing. The first serious drawing I bought was twenty-one years ago in January 1988, right after the stock exchange crash. There was a sale at Christie's in New York. I don't know if you remember; it was on the cover of the catalogue. It showed the heads of two horses and was sold as Cavalier d'Arpino. My curator, Nathalie Strasser, has now discovered that it's probably not by him but by his son Muzio Cesari. It's a study related to the big fresco painting called *The Battle of the Romans against the Veienti and the Fidenati*, which is in the Campidoglio in Rome. Despite this change in attribution, I still think it's a very good drawing.

Goldner: You had been collecting books for quite some time before that.

Bonna: Oh yes. I had been collecting books seriously before that for twenty years probably.

Goldner: You had the one Hubert Robert in 1985, but then in the early 1990s, you started acquiring drawings with great vigor and dedication. How did this come about?

Bonna: Well, it's difficult to say, but I would say it's the people I met. Some among them have played a very important role, and, as with all of us, the human relationship is essential. You know that you have played a very important role in the building of this collection. We did not meet immediately, but I think when we did, you had just arrived at the Metropolitan, and we soon became very good friends.

Goldner: It was 1993.

Guillaume de Digulleville, *Pélerinage de la vie humaine*, manuscript, Tours or Angers, ca. 1470; Francesco Colonna, *Hypnerotomachia Poliphili*, Venice 1499; Luca Pacioli, *Divina proportione*, Venice 1509. Collection of Jean Bonna, Geneva

Bonna: It was 1993, and I had started collecting in 1988. The first person I met was a very nice English gentleman named Richard Day. Richard was very kind to me, and we got along very well. At the beginning, I really started to listen to him, and then I met other people, and in 1993, you and I met. And that's why I'm very pleased about this show in the Metropolitan, because you have played a very important role in the development of my taste. I always choose the works I collect, but sometimes you tell me, "This is not really right. This is not good enough. This is in bad condition," and most of the time, I speak to you before buying something. I don't think one can say you buy for me, but you are a great counselor.

Goldner: In my opinion, no true collector has anyone who specifically tells him or her what to buy.

Bonna: I think that's true.

Goldner: I think what one can have is someone who gives them honest information, an analysis. But the decision always has to be made by the collector.

Bonna: The decision is definitely made by the collector.

Goldner: Otherwise, he or she is not really a serious collector.

Bonna: I fully agree with that.

Goldner: There have been occasions when I've shown you a drawing for your consideration and you've said, "It's just not my taste." And I've always answered, "Then you shouldn't buy it," because a collector has to have his own opinion, which is often different from a museum curator's.

Bonna: It's true that my taste is, as you mentioned earlier, probably rather definite.

Goldner: You are offered a great many drawings, I'm sure, as a famous collector and as someone who is very well liked by dealers and also by people in auction houses. You receive many catalogues from auctions in Paris, London, New York, and so forth. How do you go about making a decision? Is it usually that you see an image and you say "I love that," and then you make sure it's okay, and then go ahead and buy it, or is it a very slow process, and you gradually develop an interest?

Bonna: No it's not a very slow process. My collecting and my life in general have been based on very quick decisions. My judgment of people in my profession has been very quick too and generally right. When I buy something, it's extremely rare that my first impression is wrong. It is true that sometimes it takes time to buy it, sometimes you don't get it, but my decision is generally very quick, and this has probably also influenced my relationship with dealers, because of course, they prefer the kind of buyer who doesn't hesitate. I can say that my life has very often been based on very quick decisions.

Goldner: Of the different collectors I've known, most don't have real catalogues of their collection. They either wait until they have an exhibition and part of their collection appears in one that's catalogued by a museum or several museums, or they sell their collection, and Christie's and Sotheby's do what they think will be a memorable catalogue. But relatively few collectors do what you've done, which is to hire professional curators who continue to study the work every day and add information every day, update the information, and perfect knowledge of it. What does that reflect about your approach to collecting?

Bonna: I think it reflects two things, George. The first is that I don't know yet what will happen to my two collections, and I would like something of them to remain. And of course, a sales catalogue is not as good as a research catalogue. That's the first reason. The second is that it's a wonderful way to learn. When you simply buy something on the face of it and you just keep it, it's less fun than to really investigate it, to discover that it's not Giulio Campi but Antonio Campi for such and such church in Lombardy, or that something you bought thinking it was Sofonisba Anguissola is actually by her sister, or to discover something new that makes the history of art or the history of literature progress. As an intellectual, these are things that really interest me a lot. Even if the new attribution is less prestigious, it always interests me to help art history progress. And today, after I retired at the end of last year, it's to this that I devote most of my time.

When you look at the collection, and in fact when you see it every day in your house, you don't notice it. But when you see it in other surroundings, for instance when my French drawings were exhibited in Paris and Geneva, suddenly you see things in a different way. Suddenly you see that there is a line in the work and that there is a certain spirit—even if there are a few exceptions from time to time—that has guided this collection. And as you said, I'm not a museum curator, so if I don't find a good Rubens, I don't find good Rubens, and that's it—and anyway, it's impossible to find one today.

Goldner: That's very true.

Bonna: But you know there are things, for instance, the Neoclassicals or the seventeenth-century French religious drawings, which are weak in my collection because they are simply not my taste.

Goldner: You do have very good Claudes.

Bonna: Yes, I have some very good Claudes, because he is an artist I like very much, that's true, and because I found some very nice ones. I don't have a La Hyre, and I don't have a Vouet, because I never found one that appealed to me. But I have some very good Watteaus, because I love his elegance and charm.

Goldner: Perfectly understandable.

Bonna: Whereas in a museum you have to have Le Sueur and David and all the others, to show all the things that have evolved, that is not my job.

Goldner: No. As I've often said, I sometimes buy drawings for the Museum that I don't like, because we need them.

Bonna: Yes, absolutely.

Goldner: And that's one of the dividing lines with collectors. Do you find, when you live with your collection, and on different days, that there are certain parts of the collection you take pleasure in looking at? Are there days when you think, "Oh, I'm going to look at my Watteaus because they are such a marvelous group, and at my Bouchers."

Bonna: It's true, with one notable exception, the big pastel by Redon that is in the drawing room, I have arranged the rooms by schools and by periods. So it's true that one day, I will look more at my Italian drawings, which are in the drawing room. One other day, I will spend one hour or so looking at my French eighteenth-century room, where I have Watteau, Boucher, Hubert Robert. And it's true that you cannot go from one to another very quickly. Even if I have serious people coming to see the collection, unless they have all day and want to see everything, we generally choose something particular to look at, because I think it's very difficult to look at Seurat and Redon after having looked at Italian Renaissance drawings. It's a different mindset, I think.

Goldner: I've been collecting mostly for institutions for a long time, and sometimes when I'm not sleeping while I lie in bed, I think, "In 1984, I should have bought that Raphael drawing at the Chatsworth sale." And I wish I had exceeded my bid even more than I did. Are there drawings that you look back at and say, "Oh I wish I had bought that," that you think about often? I mean, we all have relatively small things that we wish we had done, but do you look back at any important drawings and say, "Ahh, I only wish I had bought that one or two." Are there such things you recall?

Bonna: I generally don't look back a lot.

Goldner: Very healthy.

Bonna: And I never did that in life in general. I've had a rather full life, and I generally look toward the future and not toward the past. That being said, there are a few things I have regretted, for instance, a Boucher, the figure of a girl seen from behind, which I missed in the sale at Christie's in 1995. I was able to buy it back in New York in 2000. About that one, I really said, "This I regret." But generally, I wouldn't say I regret things I have missed. Of course, you often have to make choices, and sometimes you think things are just too expensive or you just cannot afford them. But I think these last twenty years, I have still been able to assemble a collection that is quite representative of my taste.

Goldner: When we first met, the drawings you were buying then in the early and mid-1990s are preponderantly drawings from 1500 to 1750, and gradually you started to become interested in the nineteenth century. Was that an evolution of your taste or was it simply that in your first years of collecting, some of the earlier drawings were more available and so you started with them as a base and always intended to move more into the nineteenth century?

Bonna: I don't think I have always intended to do that. It's true that my first inclination was toward the Italian Renaissance and probably toward some French artists of the seventeenth and eighteenth centuries. That's what I bought first. I have to admit that my taste has probably evolved a bit, and perhaps drawings of those periods are more and more difficult to find. Those things have probably sometimes led me to buy nineteenth-century works, and I have also been offered things that are quite attractive.

Goldner: And also of top quality.

Bonna: Probably my taste has evolved a bit, but it has never left the figurative. I have nothing in my collection that is not figurative. I have landscapes, but I have nothing abstract, nothing in that field. Even my Picassos are figurative Picassos. I like Paul Klee, but I wouldn't include one in my collection. I think I'm still very much a collector of old masters.

Goldner: I myself share that taste, so I understand it very well.

Bonna: If you date the collection, for instance, the boundaries of the collection in terms of dates, the latest is the Balthus portrait of his wife drawn in 1943, but in terms of school, it's the landscape by Cézanne, which is really at the limit of abstraction.

Goldner: There are certain schools though that you hardly collect. You have very few British things.

Bonna: I have a few. I have five British drawings, more if you count Füseli as British.

Goldner: You have always favored the French and Italians. Is that because they simply strike a more responsive chord, because that's closer to your interest in books and literature as well, and culturally more resonant for you?

Bonna: Well, I would say so. I think it's true for the British. I have very few British drawings, because generally, they are not my taste. I just bought a very nice Gainsborough, but it's true that I have more difficulty with British artists. I have a few Northern school artists, some very good ones. The trouble with Northern schools is that they're incredibly difficult to find; good ones are incredibly difficult. They always have been. Even at the time when it was still possible to find good Italian Renaissance drawings, it was much more difficult to find good German ones like Dürer, Cranach, Schongauer, or Baldung. Recently, I found a very nice landscape by Rembrandt, but this too becomes incredibly difficult. I mean you might have one, not ten. I think I have a very nice Goltzius, maybe two.

Goldner: So it's really more a matter of what's been available at a certain quality level.

Bonna: Absolutely. I think it is. Well, maybe not for British drawings, because it's true I have maybe less of an attraction to them, although I have seen some that are fantastic, for instance, this Gainsborough portrait of a woman, which is at the Morgan Library. Fantastic. But it's true that in general, I am probably less attracted by the British or nineteenth-century Germans. For instance, at one point, I was shown a Caspar David Friedrich, which is incredibly rare, but it just did not appeal to me. And I don't have a Menzel. Earlier, I think it's simply about availability. If I find something good, I will buy it. I have a few good Northern drawings but not that many compared to what I have of Italian or French.

Goldner: Are there a few drawings with which you feel an especially close connection, not necessarily the most important?

Bonna: Of course, you have a few that are your favorites. One is *The Holy Family with Shepherds and Angels* by Parmigianino, which I think is extraordinarily moving. If I'm asked which one I would keep if I could keep only one, it's probably that one, although it's certainly not the most precious. The Raphael is probably much more valuable. But I think the Parmigianino is really close to my heart. Another drawing for which I have a great liking is *A Man in a Turban*, an early Venetian drawing that is so uniquely depicted, so precisely drawn. I love it, and when I saw it at the Salon du Dessin, it took me only a few seconds to buy it. In a minor way, the little portrait attributed to Sofonisba Anguissola but which might be by her sister, is something I like very much. Of course, my *Rest of Venus and Adonis* by Goltzius is one of my favorites. It's in my bedroom. It's really one of my preferred drawings. I also like the Seurat very much, the drawing of an old woman carrying an umbrella and the world's miseries.

Goldner: So those are the ones that make you stop most often.

Bonna: The most often, yes, and maybe also the big Redon pastel, which is one of the latest things I've bought. But I want to mention something more modest, the little pastel by Whistler. I don't know whether it will be in the show or not, but I love it. I think it's a great thing, and I simply don't understand why the Shelburne Museum that was set up by Mrs. Havemeyer sold it. So there are a few things I prefer of course, but on balance, I like all of them. If I didn't like them, as I told you earlier, I wouldn't have bought them.

Goldner: Correct me if I'm wrong, but the artists you have the greatest numbers by are perhaps Watteau, Boucher, Degas, and Gericault. Is that right?

Bonna: It's Gericault.

Goldner: But you also have several examples by the other three.

Bonna: Yes, I have several. I have nine Gericaults, I think. I love Gericault, that's true. I think I have two or three really marvelous examples. I have five works by Delacroix, four Bouchers, four Redons, four Watteaus.

Goldner: Do those represent a special preference for French drawings?

Bonna: No, I have five Parmigianinos.

Goldner: Do these represent artists who are your favorites in many ways, or is it simply that they are artists whose work you like very much and there were many good opportunities to acquire them?

Bonna: I think it's more the second case. By the way, it is probably easier to find nine Gericaults than five Parmigianinos.

Goldner: Do you have your eye out for specific artists, or is it more likely that you look for really good drawings that strike a response with you and that you're not so concerned with having work by a particular artist?

Bonna: There are probably artists of the Italian Renaissance I would like to have, like the Carracci. I have one drawing by Annibale and one by Lodovico, but I would love to have more of them. There are some pupils of Rembrandt's I'd like to have, Eeckhout, for instance. A nice Gerrit Dou is also probably something that is possible and that I'm looking for. But on balance, I think more often I am buying what I see and like.

Goldner: Some collectors reach a point where they slow down considerably, not that their collection is complete, because as you rightly said before, there is no such thing as a complete drawings collection. Is there a point at which you would anticipate saying that you probably won't add much more?

Bonna: Well, there are financial limits.

Goldner: So you imagine collecting for the rest of your life?

Bonna: Yes, I think I will. I think when you are a collector, it's a "disease" that is very difficult to cure, and I was born a collector. I think real collectors don't stop collecting. Sometimes their interests change. Sometimes they sharpen their taste. Sometimes financial conditions force them to collect other things. But when you are a collector, you continue to buy and you continue to add to your collection. Of course, the quality of what you have, the importance, the artistic importance, of what you have is crucial. But there is also one ingredient in collecting that we have not yet spoken about but that is important to me, and I think is important to any collector. It is the fact that it is yours, that you actually own it.

Goldner: Let's explore that a bit. You go to Paris very frequently, I know, as well as to many other major cities that have the greatest museums. You're a friend of curators all over the world, and can see the very best things in the very greatest collections that have ever been formed, and yet the ownership, the possession, of the things you have is special and different from that experience. Can you explain a bit, why it is, let's say, that having a Raphael in your house or several wonderful Watteaus, is in some sense different as an experience from going to the Louvre, the British Museum, the Uffizi, or any of the other great museums and seeing their examples? What is it that is so special about that sense of ownership?

Bonna: First of all, one doesn't prevent the other. You go to see exhibitions; for instance, just last week, I was in Colmar and Karlsruhe to see the Grünewald exhibition. I don't know whether you've seen it; it was absolutely marvelous. It's over, unfortunately, but you'll probably see a selection of it in Berlin. Two weeks ago, I was in Windsor to look at their Domenichinos, which was a great experience as well. It's true that I know a lot of curators around the world, and I'm well received wherever I go. I suppose that one of the reasons I am well received is because I am a collector and not only because I am simply interested, you see. If you're a collector, suddenly you become a little bit more credible, and also if you're a great scholar. Even some great scholars collect; you do; Pierre Rosenberg does. I think there is a certain additional pleasure in owning the work. You see it without having to make a special trip or a special decision. When you come back home at night, you look at your Raphael. I know my Raphael is not the best Raphael in the world but to have it in my drawing room and to be able to take a look at it and think "It's mine," is an additional pleasure. I remember, for instance, when I visited the Dürer exhibition in London about five years ago. At the end of the exhibition were two drawings by Hoffmann, one of a cat and one of a wild boar piglet that I had the occasion of buying later and that is included in this book. Of course, the first time I saw it was in a show in the British Museum. But then being able to buy it gives you a special pleasure, and this I think is the adrenaline of the quest that differentiates the collector from the amateur. I think there is something about that. It's true that I could come here and see anything at the Metropolitan Museum. I could come and ask you to see Hoffmann's *Hedgehog*, but I have to come to New York, and I have to ask you, and you will do it very kindly. But it's true that to come home at night, to open the door and look at my *Wild Boar Piglet* is a special pleasure.

Raphael to Renoir
Drawings from the Collection of Jean Bonna

1. Circle of Giovanni Bellini

Venice/Padua, ca. 1435–Venice, 1516

A Man in a Turban

Brush and brown ink, 8⅛ × 6⅛ in. (20.5 × 15.5 cm)

PROVENANCE: Private Collection, Switzerland; Katrin Bellinger Kunsthandel, Munich; acquired by Jean Bonna, 2006

EXHIBITIONS: Venice 1955, no. 8 (as attributed to Giorgione or his circle, and with the correct location); Geneva 2006–7a

BIBLIOGRAPHY: Venturi 1927, fig. 1 (as Giorgione, and erroneously as preserved in the École des Beaux-Arts, Paris); Venturi 1928, pp. 24–25, fig. 9 (as Giorgione, and erroneously as preserved in the École des Beaux-Arts, Paris); Morassi 1942, p. 123, fig. 138 (as Giorgione, and erroneously as preserved in the École des Beaux-Arts, Paris); Tietze and Tietze-Conrat 1944, p. 175, no. A715 (as not by Giorgione, and erroneously as preserved in the École des Beaux-Arts, Paris); Fiocco 1948, p. 50, no. 146a, ill. (as Giorgione, and erroneously as preserved in the École des Beaux-Arts, Paris); Coletti 1955, p. 63, pl. 93b (as Giorgione, and erroneously as preserved in the École des Beaux-Arts, Paris); Fiocco 1955, p. 16 (as Giorgione, and with correct location); Pignatti 1955, p. 136 (as Venetian School, early sixteenth century, and erroneously as preserved in the École des Beaux Arts, Paris?); Zampetti 1968, p. 102, ill. (as closely connected with Giorgione, and erroneously as preserved in the École des Beaux-Arts, Paris); Pignatti 1969, no. v27 (as close to Lorenzo Lotto, and erroneously as preserved in the École des Beaux-Arts, Paris); Pignatti 1978, no. v28 (as close to Lotto, and erroneously as preserved in the École des Beaux-Arts, Paris)

This finely executed sheet was first attributed by Adolfo Venturi to Giorgione, an attribution that was endorsed by a number of other Italian scholars. Alternative attributions to Marco Basaiti and to the circle of Lorenzo Lotto have also been proposed. Since the majority of scholars who have published it wrongly locate the drawing in the École Nationale Supérieure des Beaux-Arts, Paris, one may conclude that their opinions were based on photographs rather than study of the original.

The specific character of the figure and his turban clearly indicates that the drawing was made for a precise purpose, but no similar head can be found among the Venetian paintings of the period around 1500. The only known drawing that appears to be by Giorgione, a landscape in the Museum Boijmans Van Beuningen, Rotterdam, provides no basis for comparison, and there is no reason to relate it to the figures in *The Three Philosophers* in the Kunsthistorisches Museum, Vienna. Equally, there is no connection between the drawing and the work of Basaiti or Lotto.

Instead, the finely woven pen strokes and somewhat atmospheric effect of light and shadow bring it into the orbit of Giovanni Bellini. One thinks of relatively late works, such as the large grisaille *Pietà* in the Uffizi and the *Study of a Bull* (fig. 1) in the Gabinetto Disegni e Stampe of the Uffizi. The handling of pen strokes in the latter is quite similar, although more regular in pattern and containing somewhat greater movement. It is, therefore, not possible based on current knowledge to make an attribution to Bellini, even though it is closer to his work of about 1500 than to that of his contemporaries. The verso apparently exhibits a fragmentary outline-sketch that is only partially visible through the Japan paper lining and may represent a male profile.

GEORGE GOLDNER

Figure 1. Giovanni Bellini, *Study of a Bull.* Pen and brown ink. Gabinetto Disegni e Stampe degli Uffizi, Florence (inv. 779 Orn.)

I

2. Vittore Carpaccio

Venice, 1455/65–Capo d'Istria, 1525/26

Kneeling Figure in Prayer

Ca. 1515

Brush and wash with white gouache on blue paper,
4³⁄₁₆ × 4⅜ in. (10.6 × 11.1 cm)

PROVENANCE: Stelhi Collection, Zurich; Richard Day,
London; acquired by Jean Bonna, 1996

BIBLIOGRAPHY: Lauts 1962, p. 277, no. 52; Muraro 1977,
pp. 81–82

Vittore Carpaccio was the most original and truly Venetian draftsman of the fifteenth century. The distinctive contribution he made was his technique of drawing with a brush and wash on blue paper with rich white highlights, thereby achieving a painterly effect that is entirely Venetian in character.

This is a fine example of his use of this type of drawing. It shows a praying figure, perhaps a monk, and must have been made as a study for a figure in one of Carpaccio's paintings, given the specificity of pose and gesture. There is, however, no connection that can be made to any of his surviving paintings.

The drawing is closest in style and technique to the *Torso of a Nude Man* (fig. 2) in the Hermitage, which was probably made in connection with the *Martyrdom of the Ten Thousand* in the Gallerie dell'Accademia, Venice, painted

2

in 1515, and to the drawing of *Two Standing Men* in the Uffizi, (fig. 3), drawn in preparation for the no longer extant *Trial of Saint Stephen* of about 1515/20. The expressive character of the

figure and use of deep shadow over the faces are very similar in the Uffizi and Bonna drawings.

There is, therefore, good reason to date the Bonna Carpaccio drawing to about 1515.

GEORGE GOLDNER

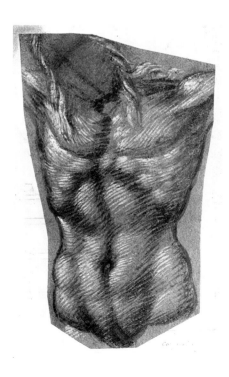

Figure 2. Vittore Carpaccio, *Torso of a Nude Man*. Brush and black ink on faded blue paper. State Hermitage Museum, Saint Petersburg (inv. OR-34846)

Figure 3. Vittore Carpaccio, *Two Standing Men*. Brush and brown wash, highlighted with white gouache, on faded blue paper. Gabinetto Disegni e Stampe degli Uffizi, Florence (inv. 1471E)

3. Lorenzo di Credi (Lorenzo di Andrea di Oderigo)

Florence, ca. 1457–Florence, 1536

The Recumbent Christ Child in the Lap of the Virgin

Ca. 1475–95

Metalpoint of two hues (probably silverpoint and lead-point), on orange-ocher prepared paper, 2⁵⁄₁₆ × 3¹⁄₁₆ in. (6 × 7.5 cm)

PROVENANCE: Jacques Petit-Hory, Paris; sale, Sotheby's, London, June 15, 1983, lot 1 (as Lorenzo di Credi); Richard Day, London, 1988; acquired by Jean Bonna, 1996

EXHIBITIONS: New York and London 1988, no. 7 (as Lorenzo di Credi); New York and London 1990, no. 4 (as Lorenzo di Credi)

BIBLIOGRAPHY: Marani 1998; Marani 1999, pp. 67–68; Marani 2000, pp. 67–68 ("Andrea del Verrocchio [or Leonardo da Vinci?]")

3

It is a testimony to the superb quality of draftsmanship of this small study in metalpoint that, although it was repeatedly published with a correct attribution to Lorenzo di Credi in very brief entries of dealer's sales catalogues during the 1980s (and was also acquired by the present owner with this attribution to Credi),[1] it has been published more recently with an upgraded attribution, as by "Andrea del Verrocchio (or Leonardo da Vinci?)," without mention of its previous history.[2] The figural vocabulary and drawing technique of the Bonna study are without doubt both strongly indebted (if in a general way) to Andrea del Verrocchio, the greatest Florentine sculptor of the second half of the fifteenth century, who was also teacher to Leonardo, Lorenzo di Credi, and a generation of Florentine artists. The style and metalpoint technique of the Bonna study are also generally evocative of the work of the 1470s by the young Leonardo, as might be expected considering Leonardo's own apprenticeship in Verrocchio's studio. But, in this case, proposals for an actual attribution to Verrocchio, or Leonardo (?), can be discarded. From among the very few drawings that can be attributed to Verrocchio himself, none of the more or less reasonably ascribed studies in metalpoint seem to resemble the Bonna sheet in the details,[3] while any possibility for the

authorship by Leonardo himself is contradicted by the fact that the areas of modeling in the delicate Bonna drawing display right-handed strokes of parallel hatching (the parallel strokes course from lower left to upper right). Leonardo ranks among the most famous left-handed artists of all time. In the exquisite Bonna study, the right-handed strokes are everywhere apparent, if one examines the drawing close-up, but are best noticeable in the lower portions of the infant's belly and leg at right.

Rather, this delicately drawn study is not only typical of the draftsmanship of Lorenzo di Credi but also closely compares to a homogeneous group of four small sheets in the Musée du Louvre, Paris (often overlooked in

Figure 4. Attributed to Lorenzo di Credi, *Enthroned Madonna and Child with Saints John the Baptist and Donatus ("The Madonna di Piazza")*. Oil on wood. Chapel of the Sacrament, Cathedral, Pistoia

the literature), which are by Credi in this author's opinion, and which are all executed in a similar technique of metalpoint on prepared paper of orange-ocher color.[4] Three of the related Louvre drawings on orange-ocher prepared paper are, in fact, of similar size to the Bonna sheet (inv. 1792, 1792bis, and 1792ter), and they also seem to bear remnants of the mounts from Giorgio Vasari's *Libro de' disegni* (album of drawings), while the fourth Louvre sheet (inv. RF 463) is of much larger dimensions and exhibits a slightly more complex technique with white gouache. Art historians acquainted with the Louvre fragments have usually attributed them to Lorenzo di Credi or his workshop, and this on quite independent grounds with respect to their opinion about the authorship of the Pistoia altarpiece, which the Bonna infant study also indubitably resembles (as will be discussed).[5] The Bonna sheet is executed in metalpoint now appearing to the eye to be of two slightly different hues, a difference that may have become accentuated as the result of oxidation. A cool gray hue (leadpoint?) seems to characterize the vibrantly energetic, repeatedly reinforced outlines of the infant's body and the outlines of the much more abstractly sketched Virgin's figure, while a slightly golden hue of metalpoint (silverpoint?) appears to predominate in the beautifully worked-up areas of shadow. The modeling of the intermediate and deepest shadows is very nuanced, done by building up layer on layer of somewhat curved parallel hatching that courses from lower left to upper right. The tonal subtlety of this parallel hatching is worthy of the young Leonardo's metalpoint drawings of the late 1470s and early 1480s, except that in the left-handed Leonardo's hatching, the parallel lines course in the opposite direction, from lower right to upper left.

The pose of the recumbent child and the sketchy indications of the Virgin's lap and arms in the Bonna drawing are much like those of the main design in the Pistoia altarpiece (fig. 4), commissioned from Andrea del Verrocchio but almost certainly painted by Lorenzo di Credi. The scholarly literature, however, is intensely divided regarding the authorship of the preliminary drawings and execution in paint of the Pistoia altarpiece, which is today installed in the Chapel of the Sacrament, on the left transept at Pistoia Cathedral but which was originally conceived for the oratory of Bishop Donato de' Medici (or "Chiesino della Madonna di Piazza"), an autonomous adjacent structure that was subsequently incorporated into the rebuilt

Cathedral in the sixteenth century.[6] According to the 1568 Giunti edition of Giorgio Vasari's *Vita* of Lorenzo di Credi, the author of the Pistoia altarpiece was Credi unequivocally, and this, one should add, is independently confirmed by a careful visual analysis of the final painting itself: "from Lorenzo's hand is a painting of Our Lady on a panel, very well executed, and which is at the corner of the great church of San Jacopo."[7] Documents from November 21, 22, and 25, 1485 suggest that the Pistoia altarpiece, which had been commissioned from Verrocchio by the executors of the will of Donato de' Medici, bishop of Pistoia (who died on December 16, 1474), was "said to be finished, or almost finished" and that Verrocchio "would have completed it more than six years ago, if he had been compensated in full."[8] But against this possibly ambiguous statement about the artist, the more decisive evidence emerges from a record of litigation initiated against Lorenzo di Credi by Verrocchio's brother Tommaso on November 5, 1490 (the great sculptor died in Venice in June 1488, leaving Lorenzo di Credi as the executor of his will and his artistic heir). It notes that Credi, while working for Andrea del Verrocchio, was being paid for "a panel of Our Lady," between November 1473 and September 1474, and that "the said Lorenzo got for the said painting of Andrea," 26 *fiorini larghi*.[9] In this author's opinion, the issue regarding the attribution of the painted Pistoia altarpiece is in favor of Lorenzo di Credi, and the documents also help pin down the date of the preliminary drawings for the altarpiece to the mid-to-late 1470s. Given that Credi painted a number of smaller-scale pictures of the Madonna and Child, in poses variant to those of the main figures in the Pistoia altarpiece, it is quite possible that the Bonna

drawing was not directly produced for the Pistoia painting and that it is later, from the 1480s or even 1490s. For on the one hand, the Bonna study seems to emanate from the general pictorial tradition of the Pistoia altarpiece, but on the other hand, it seems to conform better to the more starkly pictorial drawing style of Credi's metalpoint drawings from closer to 1500.

CARMEN BAMBACH

1. See the Sotheby's 1983 sale catalogue listed here under Provenance and Richard Day catalogues cited under Exhibitions (New York and London 1988; New York and London 1990).

2. See Marani 2000, pp. 67–68; see also Marani 1999, p. 67 ("Ginevra, collezione privata").

3. On the vexed question of Andrea del Verrocchio's authorship of drawings and for examples in metalpoint, see Bambach 2003, pp. 8–10; Carmen Bambach in New York 2003, 242–73, nos. 1–10; as well as Uffizi 212E, Florence (a study executed with Leonardo).

4. Dalli Regoli 2003, p. 85, nos. 48–51, published all four Louvre sheets as circle of Lorenzo di Credi rather than as autograph works.

5. Ragghianti Collobi 1974, vol. 1, p. 109.

6. See the summaries of evidence and historical opinions in Dalli Regoli 1966, pp. 111–12, no. 30; Gigetta Dalli Regoli in Florence 1992–93, p. 52, no. 1.5; Brown 1998, pp. 151–55, 210–11, nn. 16–38; and documents fully transcribed in Covi 2005, pp. 350–51, no. 51.

7. Vasari 1568 (1966–87 ed.), vol. 4, p. 300: "È di mano di Lorenzo una Nostra Donna in una tavola, molto ben condotta, la quale è a canto alla chiesa grande di San Iacopo di Pistoia."

8. "Dice esser facta o mancarvi poco." Archivio di Stato, Pistoia, Comune, Consigli, Provvisioni e Riforme, no. 48, fols. 111v–112r, 147v (Covi 2005, pp. 350–51, no. 51).

9. The evidence in favor of Lorenzo di Credi's authorship of the altarpiece was rightly emphasized by Gigetta Dalli Regoli in Florence 1992–93, p. 52, no. 1.5. See Archivio di Stato, Florence, Tribunale della Mercanzia (Atti in cause ordinarie, July 23, 1490–March 3, 1491), no. 1539, fols. 301r–302v (Covi 2005, pp. 286, 350, under nos. 27, 51); and for the versions of Andrea del Verrocchio's will of June 25, 1488, see Covi 2005, pp. 279–80, under no. 20. The original total amount for the contracted altarpiece to Verrocchio had been 60 *fiorini*.

4

4. Baccio della Porta (called Fra Bartolommeo after 1500)

Florence, 1472–Florence, 1517

*Landscape: Farm Buildings on a Ridge, a Haystack,
and a Flock of Birds Circling Above*

Ca. 1500

Pen and brown ink on white paper (now somewhat darkened), 5⅞ × 9¹³⁄₁₆ in. (14.9 × 25 cm)

Annotated in pen and brown ink at lower right: *And[rea] del Sarto*

Watermark: tulip with two leaves (close to Briquet 6664)

PROVENANCE: Possibly part of a large group of drawings left by Fra Bartolommeo, the artist, to Fra Paolino da Pistoia (ca. 1490–1547), convent of San Marco, Florence; possibly *suor* Plautilla Nelli (1523–1588), convent of Santa Caterina of Siena, Florence; unidentified drystamp (Lugt 1499); sale, Christie's, London, April 14, 1992, lot 81; Richard Day, London; acquired by Jean Bonna, 1996

EXHIBITION: Geneva 2006–7b, pp. 301–3

Fra Bartolommeo's pen-and-ink landscapes (a little less than sixty such sheets by him are known) rank among the earliest examples of autonomous landscapes from the Italian Renaissance, after those of Leonardo da Vinci. Like the present study, these seem to have been done mostly for the artist's pleasure, as exercises and repertories of form rather than as directly preparatory designs for paintings, unlike the vast majority of his figural drawings.[1] While the spontaneous handling of the pen and ink in many of the landscape drawings leaves no doubt that the artist worked mainly outdoors directly on the spot, a few sheets also appear to represent fanciful composites that he produced in the workshop, by borrowing motifs from one landscape drawing

for readaptation in another drawing, and he even copied selected details from Northern prints. Thus, the activity of Fra Bartolommeo as a landscape artist is unexpectedly complex. It is only recently that a prominent instance of his practice of doing composite landscapes was identified: the separate motifs of hill-town buildings in his pen-and-ink landscape drawing in The Metropolitan Museum of Art, which he then reworked in a sheet in the Louvre and which he also adapted for the background in the painting of the *Adoration of the Christ Child* in the Art Institute of Chicago.[2]

Yet Fra Bartolommeo's practices of landscape drawing, and design replication, do not seem unusual if considered within the larger

Figure 5. Fra Bartolommeo, *Landscape*. Pen and brown ink on paper. The Cleveland Museum of Art (57.498)

In contrast to that historical record, however, extremely little was known about Fra Bartolommeo's practical activity as a draftsman of landscapes until 1957, when an album of his landscape studies in pen and brown ink was rediscovered, disassembled, and sold at auction at Sotheby's, London.[7] The album pages were pasted with forty-one sheets of landscapes by Fra Bartolommeo, seventeen of which were double-sided. The 1957 rediscovery brought about a threefold increase to the known corpus of landscape drawings by the artist; the drawings are now scattered in various public and private collections. The album had been assembled in 1730 by the eminent, if at times ill-informed Florentine art historian and collector, the *cavaliere* Francesco Maria Niccolò Gabburri (1675–1742),[8] who had also made two additional volumes with pasted drawings by Fra Bartolommeo now in the Boijmans van Beuningen Museum, Rotterdam.[9] While the rarely published Bonna drawing was not part of the dismembered Gabburri album of pen-and-ink landscapes sold in 1957 (at least to judge from the condition of the album at that

context of tradition in late fifteenth-century Florentine painters' workshops. He had become the *caposcuola* (leader of the painting workshop) at his convent of San Marco, Florence, since 1504–5, following tumultuous events in his life. According to Giorgio Vasari's 1568 edition of the biography of the artist, Baccio was so moved by the sermons of Fra Girolamo Savonarola that he burned his drawings of nudes in the "bonfires of the vanities" (which took place in December 1497 and February 1498), and in 1500–1501, he renounced painting, taking his first vows in the Dominican order with the professed name of Fra Bartolommeo. He resumed his career as a painter in the autumn of 1504, at the behest of Sante Pagnini, prior of his convent at San Marco, and after having taken further vows as friar of the order.[3] The second of the two inventories drafted after Fra Bartolommeo's death in 1517 listed the contents of his studio for bequest—paintings, workshop equipment, and lay figures together with an enormous quantity of his drawings— and among these were "106 sheets of landscapes not painted in color; that is, done in pen and ink."[4] The artistic possessions in his studio, including his landscape drawings and paintings, were willed to his pupil and associate Fra Paolino da Pistoia (ca. 1490–1547),[5] the individual assessments of value for the objects having been provided by the painter Lorenzo di Credi (see cat. no. 3 for a drawing by Credi). The rich variety of items recorded in the two extant studio inventories offers a remarkable insight into Fra Bartolommeo's drawing practices, and one knows further, from Vasari's *Vita*

and other early sources, that Fra Bartolommeo's valuable artistic estate, including his drawings, then passed from Fra Paolino to the nun, *suor* Plautilla Nelli (1523–1588),[6] his pupil who had entered the neighboring convent of Santa Caterina da Siena at the Piazza San Marco, Florence, in 1537 and rose to become prioress.

Figure 6. Fra Bartolommeo, *The Temptation of Saint Anthony*. Pen and brown ink, brush and brown wash, highlighted with white gouache, on ocher washed paper. The Royal Library, Windsor (inv. 12784)

time, when it was rediscovered), it seems nevertheless precisely comparable to the nucleus of stylistically early drawings among the Gabburri sheets; a wide range of handling of the pen exists among the large group of Gabburri landscape drawings, and this argues for their having been produced during a long arc of time.[10] To this author's eye, the examples most closely related to the Bonna sheet seem datable to about 1500, or thereabouts, and share a similarly dainty, somewhat timid, although highly controlled penmanship and a mode of topographic description that presupposes the viewer's eye to be roving at a relatively far distance from the subject, although the details are minutely observed.[11] The companion sheets nearest to the Bonna drawing from the ex-Gabburri album are today in the Courtauld Gallery, London; The Cleveland Museum of Art; The Metropolitan Museum of Art (57.165 and 1972.118.239); Smith College Museum of Art, Northampton (1957:59); Barber Institute of Fine Arts, Birmingham; Art Institute of Chicago; Morgan Library & Museum, New York; and Statens Museum for Kunst, Copenhagen (Tu 4, 3a).[12] The motif of the farm buildings in the Bonna drawing is especially reminiscent of the view portrayed in the Cleveland sheet (fig. 5). Also like the Bonna sheet, these drawings do not tend to focus on the individual expressiveness or monumentality of forms in the landscape, and this again argues for an early date. The frontispiece of the now dismembered album demonstrates that the *cavaliere* Gabburri had considered all the landscape drawings in his album to have been done by Andrea del Sarto (in the case of one such study, Gabburri apparently rejected a correct, earlier attribution to Fra Bartolommeo, written in a seventeenth-century hand).[13] The Bonna drawing is annotated with an early attribution to Andrea del Sarto, at lower right (although not in Gabburri's hand), and this further connects it generally to the group of ex-Gabburri album landscapes. While many of the pen-and-ink landscape drawings from the

ex-Gabburri album seem to be based on recognizable sites in Tuscany (and two freer, somewhat later examples in this group also possibly record Venetian-style buildings),[14] extremely few of the actual designs can be connected to finished paintings. The examples number about a handful: the above-mentioned studies in The Metropolitan Museum of Art (57.165) and the Musée du Louvre (18645), adapted for the *Nativity* now in Chicago,[15] the sheet in the Courtauld Gallery (Princes Gate Collection, no. 88), in which the left part of the river landscape was used for the *Carondelet Madonna* in Besançon; the study in The Metropolitan Museum of Art (Robert Lehman Collection, 1975.1.270), in which the motif of the mountain village was adapted for the *Rape of Dinah* in the Kunsthistorisches Museum, Vienna; a lost painting by Fra Bartolommeo known from a copy by Giuliano Bugiardini; and the study in The Cleveland Museum of Art (fig. 5), in which the farm on the slope of a hill served for the *God the Father, with Saints Mary Magdalen and Catherine of Siena* in the Museo di Villa Guinigi, Lucca, which is dated 1509.[16] Given the paucity of these connections of design from drawings to paintings, the dating of Fra Bartolommeo's pen-and-ink landscapes has proved especially difficult, and thus, proposals by art historians have generally ranged from about 1495 to about 1508.[17] The papers of a number of the pen-and-ink landscapes by Fra Bartolommeo exhibit watermarks that seem datable to about 1507–8 (given that the watermark types are similar to, or the same as, those on papers bearing historical documents written in these years, but this is also a somewhat imprecise method of dating), and at least four of the ex-Gabburri album landscapes exhibit the same "tulip" watermark as the Bonna drawing.[18] A date of about 1500–1505 for the Bonna drawing and the closely related sheets from the ex-Gabburri album may be indicated not only by the delicately atmospheric use of the pen but also by the fact that several of Fra

Bartolommeo's early figural composition drawings in pen and ink include background landscapes with a very similar pen technique. Among the closest examples is *The Temptation of Saint Anthony* in The Royal Library, Windsor (fig. 6), which has been dated convincingly to about 1499 for the various independent reasons of iconography and style recently discussed by Chris Fischer.[19]

CARMEN BAMBACH

1. Fischer 1989; Rotterdam 1990–91, pp. 375–400; Ellis 1994; Paris 1994–95b, pp. 46–55.
2. The Metropolitan Museum of Art, New York, Rogers Fund (57.165), and Musée du Louvre, Paris (inv. 18645), respectively. Christie's, London, sale cat., July 11, 2001, lot 68; Ellis 2007, pp. 85–94.
3. Vasari 1568 (1966–87 ed.), vol. 4, pp. 91–93.
4. The passage in this inventory as transcribed in Knapp 1903, p. 276: "106 Fogli di paesi non coloriti cioè tochi di penna."
5. Vasari 1568 (1966–87 ed.), vol. 4, p. 103.
6. Ibid., pp. 100–101.
7. Sotheby's 1957, lots 1–41, catalogued in detail by Carmen Gronau.
8. For this history, see Gronau 1957; and Rotterdam 1990–91.
9. Fischer 1989; Rotterdam 1990–91, pp. 375–400.
10. Ellis 1994.
11. Charles Ellis has kindly endorsed this opinion (January 2, 2007).
12. These are respectively Sotheby's 1957, lots 2, 3, 7, 8, 9r, 9v, 13r, 13v, 17r, 26, 30 (catalogued by Carmen Gronau).
13. The title page to the dismembered Gabburri album of landscapes is inscribed "RACCOLTA / DI PAESI / E VEDUTE / DAL VERO. / ORIGINALI DI MANO D'ANDREA DEL SARTO." See ibid., lot 25, for the drawing annotated "di mano del Frate / Anzi di Andrea."
14. The Tuscan sites are discussed in Fischer 1989; Rotterdam 1990–91, pp. 379–400, nos. 105–12; and Paris 1994–95b, pp. 48–55. The two Venetian-style buildings were first identified in Sotheby's 1957, lots 18, 24.
15. Christie's, London, sale cat., July 11, 2001, lot 68 (catalogue entry prepared with assistance from Chris Fischer and Everett Fahy); Ellis 2007.
16. Rotterdam 1990–91, pp. 377, 393–94, no. 111, p. 399, nn. 17, 18.
17. Ibid., pp. 375–76; Ellis 1994; Paris 1994–95b, pp. 48, 52–53.
18. See watermarks noted in Sotheby's 1957, lots 13, 15, 24, 32 (the tulip type; Briquet 6664); lots 7, 8, 12, 17, 20 (the fruit type; Briquet 7386); and Rotterdam 1990–91, p. 399, n. 8.
19. Fischer in Ottawa 2005, pp. 97–99, 337, no. 17.

5. Baccio della Porta (called Fra Bartolommeo after 1500)

Florence, 1472–Florence, 1517

Study for the Virgin with Child

Ca. 1509

Black chalk and charcoal, traces of highlights in cream gouache and squaring lines in black chalk on prepared beige paper, 11 1/16 × 6 3/4 in. (28.2 × 17.2 cm)

Inscribed on recto in pen and brown ink at lower right: *342 / fra bartholomé 37*

Watermark: tulip (cf. Briquet 6662: Florence, end 15th century)

PROVENANCE: Private Collection, Switzerland; Hazlitt, Gooden & Fox, London, 1988; Private Collection, New York; Private Collection, Switzerland; Katrin Bellinger Kunsthandel, Munich; acquired by Jean Bonna, 1998

EXHIBITIONS: London 1988, no. 3; Paris 2006a, no. 2; Geneva 2006–7b, pp. 304–5

BIBLIOGRAPHY: Paris 1994–95b, p. 84

This black chalk drawing was preparatory for the altarpiece depicting the Virgin surrounded by saints that Fra Bartolommeo painted for the Florentine church of San Marco, the Dominican convent where he took orders and lived. The *Madonna with Canopy* (The Cambi Madonna) is installed in the basilica; the Virgin is surrounded by saints Benedict, Nicholas of Bari, Peter Martyr, and John the Baptist; saints Mary Magdalen and Catherine of Alexandria are kneeling at her feet. A cursory mention of the work in the *Memoriale di molte statue e picture nella città di Florentia*, published by Francesco Albertini in 1510, has allowed Chris Fischer to confirm its traditional dating (1509) and challenge the traditional view that it might have been executed about 1512–13, based on remarks in Giorgio Vasari's *Lives of the Artists*. Whatever the case, the painting dates from after the time when Fra Bartolommeo had given up painting temporarily (and perhaps drawing, from 1500–1504) and after his trip to Venice in the spring of 1508.

Some twenty studies, scattered in museum collections in Florence, Birmingham, and Rotterdam, document the genesis of this painting.[1] The important sketch of the overall composition is preserved in Birmingham (fig. 7); Fischer dated it about 1499–1500,[2] indicating that the artist might have reprised

an earlier design for the San Marco altarpiece, which would explain the evident differences between the original project and the final version. Moreover, there are preparatory drawings for several figures in the scene, such as the one in the Uffizi of Saint John the Baptist, who appears standing to the Madonna's right,[3] or the one in the Courtauld Gallery of Mary Magdalen kneeling to her left.[4] Conversely, nine sheets emanating from the Gabburri albums, today in Rotterdam,[5] and bearing annotations relative to the San Marco altarpiece, are related to other compositions by the artist (see cat. no. 4 for the history of the acquisitions by Niccolò Gabburri).[6]

Except for the Birmingham drawing, which shows the overall composition, the various known studies share a number of characteristics. The main figures were similarly drawn, as isolated motifs removed from a context, but very carefully, even if in the translation of the designs for the painting, the figures underwent some final modifications. A homogeneous technique in black chalk was used,

Figure 7. Fra Bartolommeo, *The Madonna and Child with Saints*, ca. 1509. Black chalk highlighted with yellow on gray prepared paper. The Barber Institute of Fine Arts, Birmingham (inv. BI 152658)

and in the case of the Courtauld drawing, the figure was squared to enlarge the design proportionally.

Fra Bartolommeo first began consistently using black chalk for his sketches at the same time of designing the *Last Judgment* now in the Museo di San Marco, Florence, in 1499–1500. The present drawing is an example of his characteristic use of a medium whose possibilities for modulating chiaroscuro and sfumato he explored and manipulated fluently. The dry, grainy quality of the chalk allowed him to create pictorial values, ranging from deep black through every nuance of gray, and to obtain effects of changing light that would have been impossible in pen and ink, the preferred medium of his early career.

In the present drawing, the figure's form and pose are clearly delineated, but the outline has been stumped and certain portions remain in semidarkness (see the Child, for instance); these were to be finished later, perhaps when he created the cartoon (or full-scale drawing). The existence of a cartoon for the *Cambi Madonna* is not known, even though the artist often made them, as for instance, the cartoon for Saint Catherine of Siena.[7] Comparing this drawing with the studies made nearly a decade earlier for the *Last Judgment* now in Rotterdam, one can see the extent to which he was constructing his figures in terms of volume and texture rather than from an emphasized descriptive line. The stress is clearly on the play of light in the folds of the drapery that billows around the arms in large oval gatherings. The white highlights, which can sometimes be quite pronounced in Fra Bartolommeo's drawings, are minimal here, almost invisible. The artist does not seem to have adopted them readily, and the sharp contrasts of chiaroscuro in other works yield here to a more atmospheric quality.

NATHALIE STRASSER

1. See Gabelentz 1922, nos. 64, 82, 86, 207 (Gabinetto Disegni e Stampe degli Uffizi, Florence), 304 (now in the Barber Institute of Fine Arts, Birmingham; see note 2 below), 475, 488, 495, 506, 531, 552, 562–64, 580, 746, 755, 780, 825 (now in the Museum Boijmans van Beuningen, Rotterdam). To this group should be added the study at the Courtauld Gallery (see note 4 below), which seems to correspond to Berenson 1961, no. 426A.

2. Barber Institute of Fine Arts (Berenson 1961, no. 210B; Birmingham 1986, no. 3). See also Fischer 1986, p. 90.

3. Gabinetto Disegni e Stampe degli Uffizi (inv. 395F).

4. Courtauld Gallery, London (inv. D.1978.PG.348).

5. Museum Boijmans van Beuningen (see Gabelentz 1922, nos. 544, 545, 574, 578, 579, 638, 644, 652, 658).

6. See Rotterdam 1990–91, pp. 12–13.

7. Gabinetto Disegni e Stampe degli Uffizi (inv. 1778E).

6. Raphael (Raffaello Santi)

Urbino, 1483–Rome, 1520

Study of Soldiers in The Conversion of Saul

Ca. 1515–16

Red chalk, over extensive preliminary stylus underdrawing, 12½ × 9¹¹⁄₁₆ in. (31.8 × 24.3 cm) maximum, glued onto mount and with a number of losses to the original support harmonized

Annotated in pen and brown ink on made-up support on lower right corner: *1512*

PROVENANCE: Possibly William Cavendish (1672–1729), 2nd Duke of Devonshire, Chatsworth; by descent to the 11th Duke of Devonshire; the Dukes of Devonshire and the Chatsworth Settlement Trustees (inv. 905); sale, Christie's, London, July 6, 1987, lot 11; Private Collection, United States; Katrin Bellinger Kunsthandel, Munich; acquired by Jean Bonna, 1998

EXHIBITIONS: London 1953b, no. 57; Manchester 1961, no. 50; Washington and other cities 1962–63, no. 60; Jerusalem 1977, no. 27; Richmond and other cities 1979–80, no. 59; London 1983–84, no. 156; New York 1987–88, no. 30; Paris 2006a, no. 4; Geneva 2006–7b, pp. 306–7

BIBLIOGRAPHY: *Chatsworth Raffaelles* 1872, p. 6, no. XVI; Ruland 1876, pp. 249–50, no. 5; Crowe and Cavalcaselle 1882–85, vol. 2, p. 281 (note); Dollmayr 1895, p. 266; Fischel 1898, no. 252 (as Giovanni Francesco Penni); Marabottini 1968, p. 216, ill. p. 206, fig. 15; London 1970, p. 55, under no. 77; Dussler 1971, p. 103; Shearman 1972, pp. 100–101, and nn. 37–40, fig. 63; Oberhuber 1972, pp. 133–34, no. 447; Knab, Mitsch, and Oberhuber 1983, p. 608, no. 521; Joannides 1983, p. 217, under no. 337, p. 224, no. 362; Ames-Lewis 1986, p. 134, pl. XXXVI; Jaffé 1994, [vol. 2], p. 186, no. 314; Van Tuyll 2000, pp. 277–78, under no. 249; Lorraine Karafel in New York 2002c, p. 214, under no. 23, fig. 83; Katrin Bellinger Kunsthandel 2005, p. 14, no. 4

A characteristic work of Raphael's mature period dating to about 1515–16, this justly celebrated life study portrays two Roman soldiers on horseback and another warrior, lunging on one foot and holding a spear. It was preparatory for the figural group originally seen at left in Raphael's lost cartoon, or monumental painted full-scale design on paper, for the *Conversion of Saul*, which was one of the original set of ten (completed) tapestries on the *Acts of the Apostles*, intended to decorate the lower register of the walls of the Sistine Chapel on ceremonial occasions.[1] This design would appear reversed on the final tapestry (fig 8). The subject of the composition is based on Acts 9:1–7, for on his conversion, Saul was baptized Paul and became known as the apostle of the Gentiles. The present drawing explores the design for the motif of the witnessing Roman soldiers at a small fraction of the scale of the final work (the woven tapestry, now in the Vatican Museums, measures 16 feet 2½ inches by 17 feet 8½ inches [484 by 540 cm];[2] fig. 8). Although the main soldier at center was studied from the living model, like his two companions, he was very likely posed riding on a studio prop rather than a live horse, the general form of the animal's rear being added by the artist from memory. The simply dressed figures, possibly the artist's assistants in props and workshop clothes, would be depicted in elaborate Roman military costume. A number of additional studies by the artist must have followed the present drawing in the arduous

Figure 8. Flemish weavers after Raphael's design, *The Conversion of Saul*. Tapestry. Pinacoteca, Vatican Museums, Vatican State

6

process of design. None of them is extant, not even the *modello* (a full compositional study squared in proportional scale), nor the final cartoon painted in gouache in full scale on numerous glued sheets of paper. The enormous cartoons painted on paper for the Sistine Chapel tapestries were executed between June 15, 1515, and October 20, 1516, as is established by two payment documents to Raphael for their design,[3] but the idea for this commission to Raphael by Pope Leo X de' Medici may date to as early as 1513–14. Of the original *Conversion of Saul* composition, there survives today only the final tapestry woven directly from Raphael's design in Flanders, in the workshop of Pieter van Aelst (fig. 8), which was later replicated in several copies and whose composition is also in reverse from that of Raphael's autograph drawing. While the attribution of the design of the lost cartoon (and tapestry) was questioned by some early scholars,[4] the written sources of the period leave no doubt about Raphael's authorship. For soon after Raphael's death in 1520, the cartoon of the *Conversion of Saul* was first documented as in the collection of the Cardinal Domenico Grimani, at his house in Venice, according to the guidebook of 1521 by Marcantonio Michiel ("The large cartoon of the Conversion of St. Paul was by the hand of Raphael, done for the

tapestries of the chapel"[5]), and after the death of Cardinal Grimani in 1523, it is noted to be at the house of his heir, the Cardinal Marino Grimani, in Venice, in inventories of February 26, 1526, and November 22, 1528. This cartoon was last recorded in the collection of Ferdinando II de' Medici, in Florence, in 1627.[6]

A rare instance of survival therefore, the present drawing once formed part of the fabled art collections of the dukes of Devonshire, Chatsworth (it was sold at auction on July 6, 1987), and it is best known by that provenance in the Raphael literature. To complicate matters, however, there exists a much better preserved, relatively precise copy of the Bonna drawing of ex-Chatsworth provenance, in a closely similar scale but done with a very fine, dense, and very purplish red chalk on the recto of a double-sided sheet in the Teylers Museum (fig. 9).[7] When the overall outlines of the figural designs in the two drawings are compared, it appears that the sizes and contours of the individual figures are almost identical in both drawings, but that the spacing of their forms on the respective sheets is somewhat different. Vexed questions of attribution always have existed in the case of drawings produced by Raphael in his mature career in Rome, during the period of about 1511–20, and rightly or wrongly, the doubts of scholars

Figure 10. Raphael, *Horsemen* (Study for *Lo Spasimo di Sicilia*). Red chalk over stylus underdrawing. Graphische Sammlung Albertina, Vienna (inv. 234; SR 284 R77)

usually have been motivated by the well-known fact of Raphael's frequent delegation of labor to collaborators and assistants in the workshop (Giulio Romano, Giovanni Francesco Penni, Polidoro da Caravaggio, Giovanni da Udine, and Perino del Vaga, among others). In such cases, however, it is the evidence visible in the drawings themselves that should provide the most tangible answers. Once in the collection of Queen Christina of Sweden, the Teylers Museum drawing was well regarded by the pioneering German critic of Raphael's work, J. D. Passavant, who termed it a "*dessin magistral*" in 1860,[8] and as late as 1970, the specialists I. Q. van Regteren Altena and Peter Ward-Jackson thought the Teylers Museum drawing the original and the ex-Chatsworth sheet the copy.[9] The design on the Teylers sheet is slightly more complete along the right border than is the Bonna sheet of ex-Chatsworth provenance, but it is significantly more cropped at the bottom border. The other side of the Teylers Museum sheet is tinted with a pale brown wash and offers a finished design of the kneeling Pope Julius II, a motif on the right portion of the *Mass at Bolsena* fresco (Vatican Palace), drawn in point of brush with brown ink and gray-brown wash, highlighted with white gouache, over black chalk. That verso

Figure 9. After Raphael (here attributed to Giulio Romano), *Horsemen and Running Foot Soldier*. Red chalk. Teylers Museum, Haarlem (inv. A59 recto)

drawing of belabored medium was accepted, if sometimes with trepidation, by some Raphael specialists to be a preliminary study by the master himself (by John Shearman in 1972 [as "Raphael"][10] as well as by Konrad Oberhuber in 1972 ["Kopie?"][11] and in 1983 ["Raphael oder Kopie"][12]). This view is unconvincing, given the generally weak execution of the contours and the fact that it almost exactly reproduces the design of the pertinent fresco in the Stanza di Eliodoro of the Vatican Palace, including the fictive ledge for the figure at the bottom. The verso side of the Teylers Museum sheet, therefore, is more likely a copy by the workshop of Raphael; the handling here resembles, in this author's opinion, that of drawings attributed to Giovanni Francesco Penni. In any case, the drawing in red chalk on the recto of the Teylers Museum sheet was often attributed to Raphael himself by early scholars (over the more damaged Bonna sheet of ex-Chatsworth provenance). But the tide gradually turned in 1972, as Shearman rightly made the case for the preeminence of the Chatsworth sheet (now in the Bonna Collection) by focusing attention on the fact that it displays extensive preliminary stylus underdrawing and by demonstrating that the design of the Teylers sheet seems largely derivative in its particulars.[13] To this author's eye, a firsthand examination of the Teylers Museum sheet seems to confirm that it contains an unexpectedly particularized level of detail, especially since the brutal faces of the soldiers are confidently drawn (this is not the sign of a merely sheepish copyist), since it exhibits a few, if very shallow preliminary stylus incisions (contrary to what is often stated), since it does not entirely omit passages not developed in the Bonna sheet of ex-Chatsworth provenance, and moreover, since it seems to be almost certainly by the young Giulio Romano's hand. Shearman hesitatingly mentioned an attribution to Giulio in 1972,[14] while Oberhuber in 1972 succinctly favored a seventeenth-century author, although he reversed this opinion by 1983, as he accepted the Teylers verso as possibly by Raphael or a contemporary copy.[15] The recto of the Teylers Museum sheet compares closely, in both its handling and the use of a type of a relatively purplish red chalk, to a number of undisputed drawings by the young Giulio, such as the series of twelve apostles in Chatsworth (inv. 70-81).[16]

In the case of the Bonna sheet of ex-Chatsworth provenance, the type of red chalk (a hematite of bright, saturated hue) and the bold technique of drawing with it in sweepingly broad parallel strokes over extensive preliminary stylus work that substantially differs in the outlines from the strokes in red chalk are all hallmarks precisely comparable to a number of other red chalk studies by Raphael, datable to about 1514–16. These include the measured study of one of the marble horses of the Quirinal at Chatsworth (inv. 657); the horsemen for *Lo Spasimo di Sicilia,* now in the Albertina (fig. 10), offering also an analogy of subject matter; the study of two nudes for the *Battle of Ostia,* also in the Albertina, inscribed by Albrecht Dürer as a drawing having been sent to him by Raphael in 1515; as well as the fragmentary studies for the *Charge to Peter* Sistine tapestry cartoon in the Louvre and the National Gallery of Art, Washington, D.C.[17] These are all securely accepted drawings by the master.

The compromised overall condition of the Bonna drawing of ex-Chatsworth provenance merits comment, as this aspect should not obscure the original qualities of facture by the great master. The drawing surface in the area of the main horse's buttocks and rear legs is abraded and also contains small losses in the original paper support. Thus, not unexpectedly, this portion of the drawing exhibits little outlining in red chalk and no free, preliminary stylus indentations. The poses of the three male figures, by contrast, exude an extraordinary freshness of movement; they are also better preserved. The capture of unbridled energy was a major objective for Raphael, as is vividly evident in the first layers of stylus design on the sheet, underneath the drawing surface in red chalk. Raphael laid down the entire design for the horsemen and lunging foot soldier first with a pointed instrument, very probably a metal stylus (less likely, an uninked pen), which he used to indent the paper with preliminary marks, creating numerous reinforcement lines as he blocked out the overall forms of the figures in broad strokes. He applied the stylus onto the paper with loose and long arcs of the hand, building up a multitude of indented outlines along the heads and backs of the figures. Examination of the drawing in raking light indicates the extent to which Raphael used this

profuse armature of preliminary stylus indentations to develop the arresting quality of movement that he finally achieved for the figures in the top layer of red chalk drawing. Numerous drawings by Raphael (dating from throughout his career) exhibit such preliminary stylus underdrawings.[18] This well-known practice by the master provides the final argument for this drawing's priority of design over that of the similar drawing in red chalk at the Teylers Museum, for no copyist would attempt to reinvent entirely a preliminary layer of stylus work that was intended to remain as an invisible, auxiliary support for the design of the figures, if the task was to emulate an original drawing in red chalk.

Carmen Bambach

1. For different points of view, compare Shearman 1972; Gilbert 1978, pp. 519–31; Fermor 1996; and Lorraine Karafel in New York 2002c, pp. 187–218, no. 23.
2. These measurements for the tapestry (with borders) are as published in New York 2002c, p. 211.
3. On these documents, compare most recently Shearman 1972, p. 3; Shearman 2003, vol. 1, pp. 205–6, no. 1515/6.
4. The questions of attribution regarding the *Conversion of Saul* tapestry are discussed in Shearman 1972, pp. 100–102.
5. "El cartone grande de la conversione de S. Paulo, fo de mano de Rafaelo, fatto per un di razzi della Capella." Excerpt transcribed and discussed in Shearman 2003, vol. 1, p. 714, doc. no. 1521/44.
6. Inventory of February 26, 1526: "carton grande colorito, de man di Raffaello"; inventory of November 22, 1528: "uno quadro in carta grande, conversion de San Paulo." The excerpts pertaining to works by Raphael in the two Grimani inventories of 1526 and 1528 are transcribed and discussed in Shearman 2003, vol. 1, pp. 814–15, 841–42, doc. nos. 1526/4, 1528/8.
7. See most recently Van Tuyll 2000, pp. 277–78, no. 249 (with bibliography). This sheet measures 9¾ × 9½ in. (24.6 × 24.1 cm).
8. Passavant 1860, vol. 2, p. 460, no. 299.
9. See London 1970, pp. 55–56, under no. 77.
10. Shearman 1972, p. 102, n. 40.
11. Oberhuber 1972, p. 90, no. 404, where it is catalogued among autograph Raphael drawings, though hesitantly stating ("Kopie?").
12. In Knab, Mitsch, and Oberhuber 1983, p. 599, no. 447.
13. Shearman 1972, pp. 101–2, nn. 37–40.
14. Ibid., p. 102, n. 40.
15. Oberhuber 1972, p. 134, under no. 447; Oberhuber in Knab, Mitsch, and Oberhuber 1983, p. 599, under no. 447.
16. Jaffé 1994 [vol. 2], pp. 90–93, no. 204.
17. Graphische Sammlung Albertina, Vienna (inv. 17575; SR 282 R74); Musée du Louvre, Département des Arts Graphiques, Paris (inv. 3854); and National Gallery of Art, Woodner Collection, Washington, D.C. (1993.51.2), respectively.
18. See Monbeig Goguel 1987a; Monbeig Goguel 1987b.

7. Girolamo di Romano (called Romanino)

Brescia, between 1484 and 1487–Brescia, after 1559

Two Standing Men (Study for Ecce Homo*)*

1519

Black chalk and faint traces of red chalk, 13⅜ × 9¹⁵/₁₆ in. (34 × 25.2 cm)

Inscribed on recto in pen and brown ink at lower center: *49*, and in black ink at lower right: *86* (underscored by a double line in black ink)

PROVENANCE: sale, Sotheby's, London, June 21, 1978, lot 2; Private Collection, Malibu, California; Katrin Bellinger Kunsthandel, Munich; Private Collection, Milan; Richard Day, London; acquired by Jean Bonna, 1996

EXHIBITIONS: Princeton 1981, p. 37; Trent 2006, no. 60; Geneva 2006–7b, p. 314

BIBLIOGRAPHY: Nova 1994, pp. 233–35, no. 21, fig. 44; Nova 1995, pp. 162–63, fig. 29

Figure 11. Romanino, *Ecce Homo* (detail), 1519. Fresco. Duomo cathedral, Cremona, Italy

This figural study was preparatory for one of the frescoes of the *Passion of Christ* that Romanino made for the nave of the Cremona Cathedral. He received the commission from the church administrators before August 20, 1519, and an agreement dated December 31 of that year specifies that the artist from Brescia would handle the decorations. In August 1520, however, after the first four scenes (*Christ before Caiaphas*, *The Flagellation*, *The Crown of Thorns*, *Ecce Homo*) had been finished, the project was abruptly taken away from him and given to Giovanni Antonio de Pordenone, who completed the cycle in 1522 (*Christ before Pilate*, *The Stations of the Cross*, *Christ Being Nailed to the Cross*, *The Crucifixion*, *The Lamentation*).[1]

Alessandro Nova underscored the importance of this early drawing by Romanino;[2] its dating constitutes a fixed point in the sometimes uncertain chronology of Romanino's works on paper, and its direct relation to a painting helps illuminate the working method of an artist known for his speed in executing frescoes.

The Bonna drawing, which shows the two figures standing at lower right in the *Ecce Homo* (fig. 11), is thus far the only known study for the Cremona cycle.[3] Apart from some slight variants in the position of the hands and feet, the man in the foreground appears in the fresco unchanged. The second figure, on the other hand, was completely redrawn; seen from behind in the study, he was rotated by the artist to a three-quarter frontal view, and his garments were simplified, perhaps because he appears only at the edge of the painting. Such variations were made frequently by Romanino, whose works on paper represent sources of inspiration that he sometimes treated very freely when translating the figures into paint.[4]

The different treatment of details in the two figures, as well as a comparison of the drawing with the fresco, suggests that the man in the toga in the foreground is the true subject of the Bonna preparatory study and that at this stage his companion was included only so that the artist could visualize how the former would interact as a spectator in the scene. In this foreground figure, the play of light and shadow is already defined, and the frenetic rendering of the drapery is precisely established, in straight, vigorous strokes. These indications clearly anticipate the freedom of the *pennellata* on the fresco, showing that the latter was not the result of pure improvisation. The black chalk lines, Romanino's primary medium here (the few marks in red chalk do not define the image itself), document a technique that he would later abandon in favor of red chalk or pen and ink, the preferred medium of his later sketches.[5] In the *Concert Champêtre* of about 1525,[6] the red chalk is used in a similar way—casually, with a jerky or discontinuous line for the contours but sweeping diagonally over the surface to create effects of light and shadow and to provide minimal indications of volume and space.

NATHALIE STRASSER

1. See Nova 1994, pp. 233–34.
2. In Trent 2006, no. 60. Nova assumes it was Philip Pouncey who attributed the work to Romanino when it resurfaced on the art market in 1978.
3. Maria Luisa Ferrari (1961, pls. 30, 31) did not know the present drawing. On the other hand, she mentions two studies of soldiers, one now in the Morgan Library & Museum, New York, Gift of Janos Scholz (1973.38) and the other in the Musée du Louvre, Département des Arts Graphiques, Paris (inv. 5554), which cannot be related directly to the Cremona frescoes.
4. Nova 1995, p. 160.
5. Ibid., p. 168, n. 38.
6. Morgan Library & Museum, , Gift of Janos Scholz (1973.37); Nova in Trent 2006, no. 65.

8. Andrea del Sarto

Florence, 1486–Florence, 1530

Mother and Child (Study for The Miracle of the Relics)

1510

Red chalk, traces of white chalk (various surface defects, upper right corner restored), 8¾ × 5½ in. (22.3 × 13.9 cm)

Inscribed on recto in black ink at lower left: 9

PROVENANCE: Francesco Dubini (1848–1932), Milan; Giovanni Rasini, Milan; Leonardo Mondadori, New York; Katrin Bellinger Kunsthandel, Munich; acquired by Jean Bonna, 1998

EXHIBITIONS: Paris 2006a, no. 3; Geneva 2006–7a

BIBLIOGRAPHY: Malaguzzi Valeri 1911, pp. 19–20, ill. p. 18; Morassi 1937, no. XIV; Shearman 1965, p. 365, pl. 16a; Goldner 1998, p. 29

This drawing was first published by Francesco Malaguzzi Valeri, who thought it a preliminary study for a Madonna. It was correctly related by John Shearman to the fresco cycle on the *Life of Saint Filippo Benizzi*,[1] which Andrea del Sarto executed early in his career in the *chiostrino* (narthex) of the church of the Santissima Annunziata, Florence, in 1509–10.[2] Six other studies related to this fresco cycle are known, which are now in the Uffizi, the Louvre, and The Metropolitan Museum of Art.[3]

Indeed, the fifth fresco painting in the program portrays *The Miracle of the Relics* and includes, to the left of the altar, a mother holding her child in her arms. The design of the child corresponds precisely to the figure in the present study, showing the same pose, with remarkable foreshortening, as well as the same use of chiaroscuro. The figure of the woman, on the other hand, underwent a radical transformation; her pose is sketchy, and although clearly frontal in the drawing, she is turned in profile in the final composition. A drawing of the head of a woman in the Gabinetto Disegni e Stampe degli Uffizi, Florence (inv. 270F), is generally considered the final study for the figure of the mother in the fresco. Although the margins of the present drawing seem to have been slightly damaged, the hypothesis nonetheless can be advanced that the mother's face was never depicted in its entirety—a frequent phenomenon in Andrea's studies. Dominique Cordellier noted this peculiarity in another of the artist's drawings, for the San Filippo Benizzi cycle, a quirk emulated in the work of his student Jacopo Pontormo.[4]

The concision with which Andrea del Sarto delineated the woman and situated her in space is exceptional, as is the rapport between her and her infant. Shearman suggested, apropos of the marked contrast between the cursory execution of the female figure and the meticulous rendering of the child, that the former was drawn from memory and the second from a sculpted model. It does not seem, however, that the artist necessarily used a three-dimensional prototype, as he had already fully mastered the expression of movement and plasticity. In any case, it can be said that in the drawing, the child's body in contrapposto appears to float unsupported next to the mother's breast. The artist therefore was obliged to rethink the pose of the group in the fresco by anchoring the child in his mother's arms to attain a credible compositional coherence.

Andrea del Sarto's authorship of this drawing is corroborated by the deliberate hatching and parallel red chalk lines, which are entirely characteristic of his manner when quickly and firmly defining areas of shadow or contours. These characteristics are also found in a preparatory study in the Musée du Louvre, Département des Arts Graphiques (inv. 1689) for the man standing at right in another fresco from the same cycle, *The Healing of the Possessed Woman,* in the *chiostrino* of Santissima Annunziata. Less tentative than in some of the artist's later drawings, the very visible hatching is slightly inflected to soften the chiaroscuro, as on the bust of the child, and approaches sfumato when it is used to model his face. Conversely, this way of modeling sweeps over the surface of the legs in a network of red chalk lines.

NATHALIE STRASSER

1. In 1267, Filippo Benizzi became general of the Servite order (Servi di Maria), founded in Florence in 1233.
2. Shearman 1965, pp. 198–202.
3. Gabinetto Disegni e Stampe degli Uffizi (inv. 270F, 298F, 309F, 310F), Musée du Louvre, Département des Arts Graphiques (inv. 1689), and The Metropolitan Museum of Art (1996.12), respectively.
4. Paris 1986–87, nos. 7, 85.

8

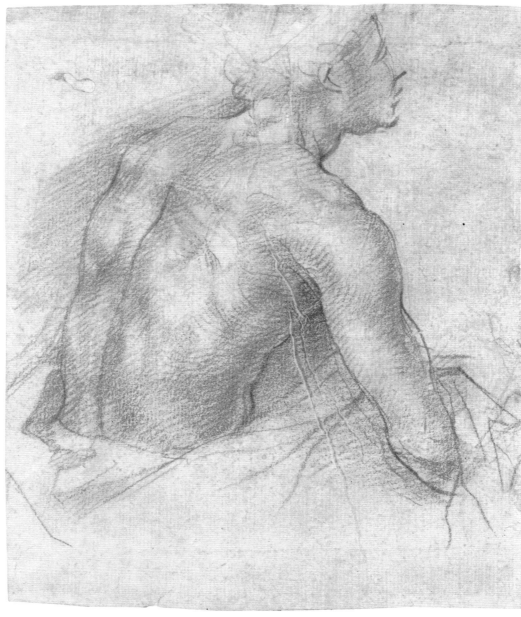

9 recto

9. Andrea del Sarto

Florence, 1486–Florence, 1530

Recto: *Half-length Study of Saint Sebastian Kneeling*

Verso: *Study of the Upper Body of a Child*

Ca. 1518

Recto: red chalk; verso: black chalk, 6⅞₁₆ × 5⅞₁₆ in. (16.2 × 13.9 cm)

PROVENANCE: Edoardo Testori, Switzerland; acquired by Jean Bonna, 1995

BIBLIOGRAPHY: Goldner 1998, pp. 29–32, figs. 4, 6

The study of Saint Sebastian on the recto was made in preparation for the kneeling figure of the saint in Sarto's altarpiece with the Holy Trinity for the church of San Gallo (fig. 12). It was preceded by a drawing in the Uffizi, Florence (6918F), which is a study from a nude studio model, whose head is covered with a turban. In the Bonna drawing, Sarto added drapery and changed the angle of the head so that it is tilted upward as in the painting. The drawing is executed with characteristic broad outlines and fine hatching for interior modeling. Although the artist already anticipated much of the final form, he turned the head more fully inward in the altarpiece and placed it in deeper shadow. The altarpiece cannot be precisely dated but appears to have been made between 1517 and 1520.

The slight black chalk study of a child on the verso may be related to the putto on the upper left in Sarto's *Charity* of 1518 in the Louvre (fig. 13).

Given these relationships, the sheet should be placed about 1518.

GEORGE GOLDNER

9 verso

Figure 12. Andrea del Sarto, *Disputation of the Holy Trinity* (Study for the church of San Gallo). Oil on wood. Galleria Palatina, Palazzo Pitti, Florence (inv. 1912. no. 172)

Figure 13. Andrea del Sarto, *Charity*, 1518. Oil on canvas (transferred from panel). Musée du Louvre, Paris (inv. 712)

10. Giovanni da Udine (Giovanni dei Ricamatori)

Udine, 1487–Rome, 1564

Study of Two Birds: at Left, a Mistle Thrush (Turdus viscivorus)
and at Right, an Alpine Chough (Pyrrhocorax graculus)

Ca. 1517–19

Brush with watercolor and gouache (motif at left); pen and medium brown ink (motif at right), 5½ × 5¾ in. (18.6 × 13.1 cm), maximum; lower left corner made up; glued onto secondary paper support

Annotated on recto in pen and brown ink by an early hand, possibly 18th century, at upper right: *46*

PROVENANCE: Charles Férault, Paris; Geneviève Aymonier-Férault, Paris, 1960; Winslow and Anna Ames, Rhode Island, dry stamp (Lugt 2602a); Alister Mathews, Bournemouth, 1972; Timothy Clifford; his sale, Sotheby's, London, July 3, 1989, lot 1 (correctly identified as by Giovanni da Udine); C. G. Boerner, New York, 1996; R. M. Light and Co., Santa Barbara, California; acquired by Jean Bonna, 1998

EXHIBITIONS: Kendal 1981, no. 1 (as attributed to Lambert Lombard); New York 1996, no. 1; Geneva 2006–7a

BIBLIOGRAPHY: Alister Mathews 1972, no. 102; Wolk-Simon 1994, p. 393, fig. 1

Animal and botanical studies fully rendered in color (especially if kept in albums as a series) are often notoriously difficult to attribute. They can seem at times to look deceptively alike, as the draftsmen of nature studies usually aimed to achieve a deliberately objective, detailed observation of the subject, sacrificing the expression of an individual artistic vision. Here, only the motif of the Alpine Chough at right, done solely in pen and brown ink, retains a significant clue to its authorship in the spidery thin outlines and confidently economic, pliant cross-hatching. Given the impersonal quality of the large main study on this sheet, it is not entirely surprising that for a long time, it was incorrectly attributed to the Flemish painter who was a native of Liège, Lambert Lombard (1505/6–1566), a mistake that probably was occasioned by the fact that this drawing was once pasted in an album of zoological drawings. The title page of this now disassembled album of clearly heterogeneous material bears an erroneous inscription stating that the drawings were commissioned by the emperor Charles V from Lambert Lombard in Brussels in 1542, although one

drawing contained therein is inscribed with a date of 1570 (Lombard died in 1566, and Charles V in 1558).[1] This album was dispersed at auction in Paris in 1952, in two large lots, one of which was purchased by the Rijksprentenkabinet, Amsterdam. By the time of its individual passage through the art market in the late 1980s, the Bonna sheet was correctly attributed to Giovanni da Udine (and in Sotheby's sale, London, July 3, 1989, lot 1), the brilliantly gifted specialist of nature studies from the Friuli region, who received varied artistic training in the North before his arrival in Raphael's workshop in Rome in about 1515.[2] This attribution to Giovanni da Udine was discussed more definitively in 1994 by Linda Wolk-Simon, who pointedly compared it to the artist's sheets in the Nationalmuseum, Stockholm.[3] As is seen in those examples and in the Bonna sheet, the juxtaposition on the same page of motifs drawn in plain monochromatic medium (pen and ink or chalk) with carefully rendered motifs worked up in color is typical of the artist.

Not noticed previously, the Bonna drawing represents the exact motif of the Mistle Thrush, although in reverse design orientation, perched on the garlands of fruits and flowers frescoed by Giovanni da Udine in the Vatican Logge (fig. 14), as assistant to Raphael. While the precise date of the commission of the Vatican Logge to Raphael remains uncertain, it is clear that the fresco cycle was executed about 1517–19; Baldassare Castiglione's letter of June 16, 1519, to Isabella d'Este in Mantua reports the paintings as being finished.[4] Further reinforcing the Roman date proposed here, the motif at the upper right portraying the Alpine Chough exhibits the same scratchy thin outlines filled with energy (as is delightfully evident on this bird's tail and feet), together with a spare use of cross-hatching to deepen some shadows (as on the neck and backside) that are found in Giovanni da Udine's drawings of the Roman period. The most salient comparisons here are to his two securely attributed and datable sheets in the Staatliche Graphische Sammlung, Munich.[5] On the verso of the latter sheet is

the inscription "*Ricamator*" (embroiderer), alluding to the early alternative name of the artist given to him after his father's profession; Giovanni da Udine himself signed "*io Zuan Ricamador pitor*."[6] Although the Bonna sheet is glued onto secondary paper support, the verso contains additional drawings of birds, which show through the paper. On the recto, the drawing at left of the Mistle Thrush, done in watercolor and gouache (very likely, over preliminary indications in leadpoint that are now erased) has suffered. Abrasion and water damage have caused pigment loss, affecting particularly the saturation of the originally very pale blue gouache on the breast and belly of the bird. This is important as a chromatic scale of intensely saturated colors characterizes the ornamental frescoes of *grotteschi* by Giovanni da Udine in the Vatican Logge. The pale blue-gray pigment in the drawing is

Figure 14. Giovanni da Udine, *Bird with Garland and Fruit* (detail). Fresco. Logge of Raphael, Vatican Palace, Vatican State

10

mostly evident now in passages close to the bird's neck and to the legs.

CARMEN BAMBACH

1. This album, its frontispiece, and its dispersal are discussed in Boon 1978, vol. 1, pp. 212–24, nos. 559–606, vol. 2, pls. 559–606.

2. On Giovanni da Udine's various apprenticeships in northern Italy before Raphael, see Bartolini 1987, pp. 19–34.

3. Nationalmuseum, Stockholm (inv. NM 389/1863; NM 384 and 385/1863; NM 390 and 387/1863); see Wolk-Simon 1994, p. 393. On the Stockholm drawings, see also Dacos and Furlan 1987, pp. 250–52, nos. 18–22; and Bjurström and Magnusson 1998, nos. 455–58.

4. The letter by Castiglione is transcribed in Bartolini 1987, p. 47.

5. Inv. 2489, 2520; Dacos and Furlan 1987, pp. 244–46, nos. 10–12; Nesselrath 1989.

6. This signature is in the *Libro dei conti* (see Bartolini 1987, p. 3); Nesselrath 1989, pp. 237–91.

11. Raffaello (Raffaellino) del Colle

Colle, ca. 1490/95–Borgo Sansepolcro, 1566

Recto: *Head of a Young Woman*

Verso: *Study of Hands*

Ca. 1530

Recto: red chalk; verso: black chalk, 11¹¹⁄₁₆ × 8⅞ in.
(29.7 × 22.5 cm)

PROVENANCE: sale, Sotheby's, London, July 2, 1984, lot
12; Private Collection, England; Thomas Williams Fine
Art, London; acquired by Jean Bonna, 2003

EXHIBITIONS: Cambridge 1985, no. 52; Paris 2006a,
no. 6

BIBLIOGRAPHY: Monbeig Goguel 1988, p. 613, fig. 919;
Wolk-Simon 1991, p. 305, n. 3; Madrid 2005–6, p. 59

Philip Pouncey first attributed this magnificent *Head of a Young Woman* to Raffaellino
del Colle,[1] an artist whose career was shaped
by contact with the leading lights of Italian
Mannerism. Arriving in Rome in 1520 (the
year of Raphael's death), he helped execute the
Sala di Costantino in the Vatican Palace, under
the direction of Giulio Romano. After the sack
of Rome in 1527, he welcomed Rosso Fiorentino
in Sansepolcro. He worked with Girolamo
Genga on the decoration of the Villa Imperiale
in Pesaro, under the commission of Francesco
Maria I della Rovere. In Naples and Rome,
he assisted Giorgio Vasari. He then went to
Florence, where he was invited by Agnolo
Bronzino in 1548 to help create the tapestries
for the duke Cosimo I de' Medici.[2] These high-
level collaborations naturally had a general
influence on his art, but they did not inform
precisely the majority of his painted output.
Several paintings, which exemplify his independent production as an artist, are preserved in
Sansepolcro and Città di Castello, two towns
near Colle, his birthplace. But these have been
underestimated, as the artist has remained in
the shadow of the great masters who were his
teachers or friends.

There surely exists a typology of female faces
in Raffaellino's work, which helped Pouncey
make his attribution, but this element of stylized form in the artist's work also makes it
difficult to connect this drawing precisely to a
finished painting. Nonetheless, two figures

display indisputable analogies with the present
drawing: the young woman crowning Truth in
the fresco *King Midas Counseled by the Vices* in
the Villa Imperiale, Pesaro (which Raffaellino
helped decorate between 1530 and 1532) and the
attendant who appears in the background of
The Purification of the Virgin in the Museo
Civico, Sansepolcro (fig. 15), which was reattributed to Raffaellino on the basis of archival
documents noting the artist's payment for it
in January 1536.[3] The verso of the Bonna
sheet reveals two hands that clearly evoke the
gesture of Christ crowning the Virgin in the
Sansepolcro *Assumption*, also in the Museo
Civico. Although traditionally dated about
1545, this latter work is cited in documents
published by David Franklin that show it was
actually commissioned in March 1526. Exactly
when the work was completed is not known,
but it can be supposed that it took no longer
than two years.[4]

With so few extant drawings by Raffaellino
del Colle, it is difficult to make comparisons
that would help date the present work more

Figure 15. Raffaellino del Colle, *The Purification
of the Virgin*, 1536. Oil on canvas. Museo Civico,
Sansepolcro, Italy

precisely.[5] Still, given its sober classicism, this
Head of a Young Woman cannot have been
drawn later than the end of 1530. For while the
paintings to which it has been related pro-
claim Raffaellino's adherence to the models of
Giulio Romano, the preparatory study clearly
demonstrates Raphael's influence. One drawing in particular illuminates the artist's debt to
the master from Urbino: the *Allegorical Figure
of Commerce* in the Louvre,[6] a red chalk drawing of one of the caryatids on the base of
The Deliverance of Saint Peter in the Stanza
d'Eliodoro, Vatican Palace. The oval of the face
in three-quarter view, the hair parted at the
top of the forehead, the depiction of the ear,
the gaze resolutely trained on the viewer, and
the straightness of the pose (perfectly suited to
a caryatid) all have their counterparts in the
present sheet. Raffaellino must have had access,
if not to the drawing, then to the fresco itself
while he assisted Giulio Romano in the Vatican.
It is therefore likely that the artist, whose
imagination was openly nourished by the rep-
ertoires of Raphael and Giulio, inserted into

11 verso (detail)

11 recto

an original composition a design largely indebted to their work.[7]

But while Raffaellino's *Head of a Young Woman* might not be particularly inventive, it nonetheless demonstrates his talents as a draftsman. The red chalk is used abundantly to mark the definitive outlines but more sparingly when defining the velvety texture of the flesh of her young face (the burgeoning shadows at the fold of the lips evoke Leonardo's *sfumato*), and forms finally disappear altogether to let the white of the paper provide the effect of light shining on the forehead and

brightening her gaze. The draftsmanship here attains a seductive degree of finish and highlights the artist's ability to use stumping, then to incorporate an important pentimento into his design, such as that on the chin line, which also entailed a subtle reworking of the background around the face. At the same time, the image avoids the metallic appearance of Raffaellino's painted works from those same years.

NATHALIE STRASSER

1. Cambridge 1985, no. 52.
2. Smyth 1971, pp. 28–32. For Raffaellino's artistic career, see Sapori 1974–76; and Dal Poggetto 1983. The most recent work on the artist is the monograph by Marco Droghini (2001).
3. Franklin 1990, pp. 150–52.
4. Ibid., pp. 149–50.
5. Linda Wolk-Simon (1991) cited five drawings, including the present *Head of a Young Girl*; Droghini (2001), without including the preceding ones, lists six sheets by Raffaellino.
6. Musée du Louvre, Département des Arts Graphiques, Paris (inv. 3877).
7. This practice was highlighted by Christopher Witcombe (1989), who noted the direct borrowings from Giulio Romano in Raffaellino's paintings.

12. Michelangelo Anselmi

Lucca, 1491–Parma, between 1554 and 1556

Allegorical Decoration with the Arms of Pope Hadrian VI

Ca. 1522–23

Red chalk over traces of stylus on paper (laid down), 12⁷⁄₁₆ × 8⁷⁄₁₆ in. (31.7 × 21.4 cm)

PROVENANCE: Paul Oppé (1878–1957), London; his sale, Christie's, London, December 5, 2006, lot 8; purchased at that sale by Jean Bonna

EXHIBITION: Edinburgh 1969, no. 3

BIBLIOGRAPHY: Washington and Parma 1984, pp. 194, 206, under no. 64; Fadda 2004, pp. 8, 19, 67, fig. 1

In his *Lives of the Artists*, Giorgio Vasari claimed that Michelangelo Anselmi was born and trained in Siena, perhaps studying under Giovanni Antonio Bazzi "Sodoma" (1477–1549).[1] In her recent monograph on Anselmi, Elisabetta Fadda confirmed that he was born in Lucca, his father having been banished from Parma, but that he might well have passed his apprenticeship in the Emilian city, to which he probably returned before 1520.[2]

The present drawing, which Philip Pouncey first attributed to Anselmi, has great similarities to a drawing formerly in Vienna that depicts the coat of arms of Pope Paul III (Alessandro Farnese)[3] as well as with the more finished drawing in the Uffizi, which also shows the pope's coat of arms in a very

elaborate arch of triumph (fig. 16).[4] Moreover, two studies by Anselmi show simple escutcheons held up by putti, one bearing the arms of the city of Parma and the second, a shield with three gourds.[5] The Bonna drawing depicts the crest of Pope Hadrian VI, "quartered at 1 and 4 in or with three crampons in vert palewise and, at 2 and 3, in argent with a sable lion." Two female figures support the escutcheon, under which a cherub crouches, presenting two blank shields. The keys of Saint Peter and the papal tiara complete the heraldic device, and framing all the elements is an arch surmounted by two other figures, possibly representing victories.

Hadrian VI (Adriaan Floriszoon Dedel) was born in Utrecht in 1459. Cardinal of Tortosa (1516) and tutor to the future Charles V, he was elected pope on January 9, 1522. Having come from Spain by ship, he was crowned in St. Peter's Basilica (Vatican Palace) on August 31, 1522, and died twenty months later, on September 14, 1523. People in Rome said of this *pontefice barbaro*, the last non-Italian pontiff until John Paul II, that he was too pious to be a pope. He labored to rein in abuses of every sort, to reform the corrupt

Figure 16. Michelangelo Anselmi, *Festival Design with the Arms of Pope Paul III Farnese*, ca. 1535. Red chalk. Gabinetto Disegni e Stampe degli Uffizi, Florence (inv. 486 Orn.)

Curia, and to balance the finances of the Holy See. The latter effort earned him the animosity of the artistic community, which found him to be a less worthy patron than his lavish predecessor, Leo X (Giovanni de' Medici).

Given this background, it is difficult to date the present drawing as from the years 1535–36, when Anselmi was depicting the Farnese coat of arms (the two drawings relating to Paul III seem to have resulted from a commission to paint the pope's coat of arms on the facade of the Palazzo Communale of Parma),[6] for it is doubtful that many people at the time thought to evoke Hadrian's memory. It therefore seems more probable that this drawing was made during Hadrian's brief papacy, even though it is unlikely that Anselmi, who was heavily occupied with his work in the church of San Giovanni Evangelista in Parma, would have traveled to Rome during those years.[7] Could the project have been commissioned by the City of Parma, which had in fact been under pontifical dominion since 1521, in the event of a visit by Hadrian VI. Moreover, the similarities between the present drawing and the two Farnese projects, while striking in composition, do not hold true for the figures. In this case, symmetry and stability predominate, whereas in the two other studies the figures are animated and odd flourishes abound (such as the two putti, their arms passing

through the keys, as in the Uffizi drawings). In the present drawing, the red chalk technique is diffuse and the shaded areas spread into full opaque surfaces, while the outlines in places are left unfinished. Diane DeGrazia compared this drawing with the frieze of putti now in Oxford,[8] which she dated toward the beginning of Anselmi's career. To this author, it seems closer to a drawing depicting a saint healing a possessed woman published by Konrad Oberhuber, who presumed a relation with the frescoes in the north transept of San Giovanni Evangelista in Parma, executed between 1521 and 1523.[9] The latter sheet can be likened to the Bonna drawing, not only in the morphology and definition of the main figure but also in the swirling draperies of the standing woman on the left and in the empty eyes of the other figures.

Two drawings, related to the Tuscan school, might constitute an iconographic precedent for Anselmi's drawing: a study for a wall decoration attributed to Jacopo Pontormo, with the coat of arms of Leo X,[10] and especially, a drawing by Baldassare Peruzzi that suggests a vague arch of triumph or wall decoration, which also depicts the escutcheon of the Medici pope held up by winged figures.[11] This type of motif, inserted in ornamental panels in the form of small cartouches, was traditional as a public display of power; on the other hand, the emphasis on the heraldic theme, which acts as the

image's true subject, seems original. Although Peruzzi was in Bologna between 1522 and 1523, busy with the San Petronio project, and although he designed Pope Hadrian VI's funeral monument in Santa Maria dell'Anima in Rome at the request of the pope's friend Cardinal Wilhelm Enckenvoert, a direct relation with Anselmi remains to be established.

NATHALIE STRASSER

1. Vasari made only brief mention of Michelangelo Anselmi: "Michelagnolo Anselmi, Sienese by origin but a citizen of Parma by adoption, being a good painter." Vasari 1568 (1912–14 ed.), vol. 8, p. 39.
2. Fadda 2004, pp. 58–59.
3. Popham 1957, Anselmi no. 15, fig. 51.
4. See Washington and Parma 1984, no. 64; and Cambridge 1985, no. 5.
5. Popham 1957, Anselmi no. 3, fig. 52, and Anselmi no. 16.
6. See Washington and Parma 1984, no. 64.
7. The hypothesis that Anselmi traveled to Rome before 1520 was advanced by Fadda (2004, pp. 62–63), based on Raphaelesque accents visible in the frescoes that the artist created for the chapel of San Mauro Abate in San Giovanni Evangelista, about 1522 and 1523.
8. DeGrazia in Washington and Parma 1984, no. 60.
9. Národní Galerie, Prague (inv. K 38104); Oberhuber 1970, p. 281, pl. 34.
10. Musée du Louvre, Département des Arts Graphiques, Paris (inv. 11159); Florence 1996–97, no. 62.
11. British Museum, London (inv. 1946-4-13-211); Frommel 1968, no. 34; Cambridge 1985, no. 42.

13. Giovanni Agostino da Lodi

Lodi (?), ca. 1470–active in Venice and Milan, ca. 1495–1520

Head of a Young Man

Ca. 1510–20

Red chalk, 4⁷⁄₁₆ × 3³⁄₁₆ in. (11.3 × 8.1 cm)

PROVENANCE: Unidentified drystamp "BB" (Lugt 346b); Jonathan Richardson (Lugt 2183); Katrin Bellinger Kunsthandel, Munich; acquired by Jean Bonna, 1995

EXHIBITIONS: New York, Paris, and London 1994, no. 1; Paris 2006a, no. 1; Geneva 2006–7b, p. 300

BIBLIOGRAPHY: Bora 1998a, pp. 110–11, fig. 4.26 (as whereabouts unknown)

A key figure among the second generation of Lombard painters who was closely influenced by Leonardo da Vinci (1452–1519), Giovanni Agostino da Lodi worked extensively in Venice from about 1500 onward, although he finally settled in Milan.[1] For this reason, and as is seen in this drawing especially, he provides an important bridge between the very diverse traditions of early sixteenth-century naturalism in northern Italy—in Milan, which were indebted to Leonardo, and in Venice,

which were shaped by Giorgione and the late work of Giovanni Bellini. Drawings by Lodi are extremely rare, however (perhaps fifteen or so may be identified), and attributions to his hand depend entirely on the relationships of drawings to signed paintings. Lodi's artistic personality has become known only in recent times, however, and this is a further complicating factor. In 1890, Wilhelm Bode first precisely individualized the work of the enigmatic painter who was later revealed to be Giovanni

13

Agostino da Lodi, and Bode at first nick-named him the pseudo Boccaccino in order to distinguish his oeuvre from that of the accomplished Cremonese painter Boccaccio Boccaccini (before ca. 1466–1523), with whom he had long been confused. In 1912, Francesco Malaguzzi Valeri put forward the identification of the pseudo Boccaccino with Lodi by calling attention to the signature inscribed on the left in the painted panel of *Saints Peter and John* (Pinacoteca di Brera, Milan), long attributed to the pseudo Boccaccino: "JOHANNES AVGUSTINVS/LAVDENSIS. P."[2] The true identity of the painter was reaffirmed further in 1972, based on the discovery of a record of payment of 1504, from a patron in Brescia,[3] and has continued to be redefined in the 1980s and 1990s with the addition of some key new works. Possibly intended as an altarpiece, Lodi's best known painting is a small panel of the *Washing of the Feet of the Apostles* in the Gallerie dell'Accademia, Venice, which is dated 1500 on the stone block of the seated Saint Peter at left, and this work offers the most concrete basis for a reconstruction of the artist's early career.[4] That dated picture of 1500, which can be compared with a few bust-length studies in

red chalk without being directly connected to it, can corroborate the very early time at which Leonardesque influences arrived in Venice. But Lodi's only signed drawing is a delicately rendered sensuous study in red chalk for a half-length figure of a woman gazing at an object in her hand, perhaps a mirror, in which case, she may be identifiable as an allegorical figure of Prudence in the Collection of Mrs. A. Alfred Taubman (fig. 17).[5] This exquisite early drawing brings together the minutely naturalistic detail of his Lombard training with subject matter of a Venetian mood.

Lodi was a prolific draftsman in his use of red chalk (a favored Leonardesque medium) and was one of the earliest disseminators of Leonardo's artistic vocabulary and ideas among Venetian painters.[6] As in Leonardo's *Last Supper* mural of about 1494–98 in the refectory of Santa Maria delle Grazie, Milan, which offered a significant source of inspiration to the artist, the expressive faces and gestures of the apostles in the Accademia *Washing of the Feet* serve as a major compositional device in creating variety and dramatic detail. The overall anatomical conception of the figures, however, is less successful in the Accademia panel, as is

particularly true of the corpus of early paintings presently attributed to the artist. By contrast, his mature drawings, of which the Bonna study is an example, seem to manifest a stunning command of the psychological dimensions of gesture, or to rely on Leonardo's words, the "motions of the mind,"[7] and it is not surprising that the primary type of extant drawings by Lodi are bust-length studies. The grandeur of psychological expression evident in Leonardo's figures of 1500–1510 immensely inspired Lodi, as is evident on comparison of his stunning study of a Herculean man in the J. Paul Getty Museum or the youth in the Kupferstich-kabinett, Dresden.[8] In stark contrast to the numerous metalpoint studies of heads on blue or gray-blue prepared paper by the earlier Milanese generations of Leonardo pupils of the 1490s, Lodi's drawings in red chalk reflect the work of the mature Leonardo (his figural models, his conception of physiognomic expression, and his innovative rendering techniques), while also retaining a veristic naturalism of detail that lies outside the intellectualized dimension of Leonardo's vocabulary but is typical of the Lombard tradition.

The Bonna study of the youth's face turned upward, which was first attributed to Giovanni Agostino da Lodi by Giulio Bora, may be proposed here as a work still later than the Getty or Dresden sheets just mentioned, datable to about 1510–20, since it combines an almost classical monumentality of form with the delicate but hard-edged details of Lombard naturalism. It seems to belong to the time of his resettlement in Milan (documents of September 7, 1510 and May 13, 1511 mention the artist as living in the city),[9] during years when his work also demonstrated a kinship with Bernardino Luini's paintings. This dating is supported further by both the physical type of the figure and the essentially pictorial style of the chalk rendering, in which his earlier precision of detail yields in rigor to a controlled calibration of tone with sfumato effects; tiny emphatic strokes of the pointy chalk (pressed hard on the paper) provide the deepest tonal accents. The youth's head especially recalls the music-making angel at bottom center of Lodi's monumental altarpiece of the *Madonna and Child with Saints John the Baptist, Peter, James, and Paul,* formerly in the oratory of San Giacomo and now in the parish church, Gerenzano, a

Figure 17. Giovanni Agostino da Lodi, *Woman Gazing into a Mirror*. Red chalk. Collection of Mrs. A. Alfred Taubman, New York

informs the young Bernardino Luini's altarpiece in the Musée Jacquemart-André, Paris, signed and dated 1507,[11] but the echoes of Luini in the Bonna sheet seem to refer to his work of about 1515–20. The figure of the angel in Lodi's Gerenzano altarpiece, although of more youthful and idealized features, is also lit in a direction similar to that of the Bonna drawing. Another work of the 1510s closely comparable to the Bonna drawing is the study in red chalk of a haggard, bearded man in bust-length profile in the Biblioteca Ambrosiana,[12] whose heightened expressionism can be likened to that of the man standing at extreme left in Lodi's painted panel of the *Road to Calvary* in the Národní Galerie, Prague.

CARMEN BAMBACH

painting that seems to breathe the Lombard sensibility for naturalistic detail into a Venetian compositional prototype reminiscent of Giorgione's Castelfranco altarpiece.[10] This hybrid Milanese-Venetian vocabulary also

1. Bora 1998a, pp. 110–12; Bora 1998b.
2. Bode 1890; Malaguzzi Valeri 1912; see also Peter Humfrey in Venice 1992, pp. 358–59, 386–87, no. 84; Schulze Altcappenberg 1995, pp. 118–20; Bora 1998a, pp. 108–11; and Bora 1998b.
3. The payment document of 1504 by a Brescian nobleman was to "Augustino de Lodi pictore"; Boselli 1972; Humfrey in Venice 1992, p. 359.
4. The lost picture is thought to have been an altarpiece for the Scuola del Sacramento, although there is no documentary confirmation of this (Humfrey in Venice 1992, pp. 368–69, no. 77; Bora 1998b, pp. 258–59).
5. This sheet in red chalk, 5½ × 5⅛ in. (13.9 x 12.9 cm), has been published previously as "whereabouts unknown." It is inscribed at the top, "joã agustin da lodi" (Provenance: Schwarz Collection; sale, Sotheby's, New York, January 16, 1986, lot 36). See Humfrey in Venice 1992, pp. 359, 386–87, under no. 84; Schulze Altcappenberg 1995, pp. 118–20; Bora 1998a, pp. 108–10, fig. 4.23; Bambach 2008, p. 60 (and n. 30), listed as "New York art market, 1986." I am indebted to Cristiana Romalli for putting me in touch with the present owner of this drawing.
6. As emphasized by Humfrey in Venice 1992, pp. 358–59.
7. "Atti mentali," "moti mentali," accidenti mentali," "intenti mentali," or "passioni dell'anima." See Codex Urbinas Latinus 1270 (Biblioteca Apostolica Vaticana), fols. 122r–127r (part 3), a manuscript compiled by Giovanni Francesco Melzi after Leonardo's notes; modern transcription in Vecce 1995, vol. 2, pp. 285–94, nos. 356–85.
8. J. Paul Getty Museum, Los Angeles (90.GB.116) and Kupferstichkabinett, Dresden (inv. C1923–140).
9. Bora 1998b, p. 265.
10. The Gerenzano altarpiece is discussed and illustrated in color in ibid., pp. 271–72, fig. 156 (without the connection to the present drawing).
11. Ibid., p. 273.
12. Biblioteca Ambrosiana, Milan (Cod. F 274, inf. 6).

14. Domenico Campagnola

Venice (?), ca. 1500–Padua, 1564

Horseman of the Apocalypse

Ca. 1550

Pen and brown ink, 12¹⁵⁄₁₆ × 9¹⁵⁄₁₆ in. (32.9 × 25.2 cm)

Inscribed on recto in pen and brown ink by French 18th-century hand at lower left: *original Dominique Campagnolle*

PROVENANCE: sale, Robinson & Foster, London, November 17, 1955, lot 61; sale, Sotheby's, London, July 9, 2003, lot 4; Katrin Bellinger Kunsthandel, Munich; acquired by Jean Bonna, 2004

EXHIBITIONS: New York and London 2004, no. 1; Paris 2006a, no. 10

BIBLIOGRAPHY: Clayton 2004, p. 320, fig. 7

This drawing by Domenico Campagnola reproduces one of the painted images in a fresco by Giusto de' Menabuoi (active between 1349 and 1390) in the apse of the Baptistery of Padua.[1] Composed of forty-three scenes, this wall decoration, executed about 1378, illustrates the vision of Saint John as it is related in the Book of the Apocalypse.[2] The drawing alludes to the opening of the second seal, described in Revelation 6:4: "And there went out another horse that was red: and power was given to him that sat thereon to take peace from the earth, and that they should kill one another: and there was given unto him a great sword."

A surprising interpretation of a medieval prototype, Domenico's *Horseman* is nonetheless not an isolated example. It is one of a series of drawings made in pen and brown ink based on the decorations of the Baptistery, twenty-two of which are known to be preserved in The Royal Library, Windsor Castle, and five more having appeared recently on the art market (one of them now in the Morgan Library & Museum, New York).[3] In addition to the scenes already noted, there is a drawing formerly in the Marignane collection, showing the angel taking Saint John by the hand at the end of his vision, as told in Revelation 22.[4]

A. E. Popham, in cataloguing the mentioned Campagnola in Windsor, stressed the naïvety of the style while rightly positing the existence of a model that was already archaic at the time they were executed.[5] Indeed, comparing the drawings to the Padua frescoes

original dominique Campagnolle

arouses the viewer's curiosity, for the awkwardness evident on certain sheets (the present horseman's right leg, for instance, being obviously too short) is in fact Domenico's literal quotation of the medieval model. On the other hand, the drawing's modernity is expressed in the abandonment of Giusto de' Menabuoi's Giottoesque vocabulary, and as faithful as the images might be to medieval iconography, the aesthetic is completely modernized. In the present drawing, the sense of movement conferred on the fleeing figures, the dynamism of the horse, and the addition of a background with its distant landscape and cloudy sky radically alter the original's severity and stiffness. Another drawing from the series, *The Archangel Michael Battles the Dragon*,[6] is particularly indicative of this process of transformation, in both the modernization of the figures and the definition of space. Moreover, that drawing suggests a familiarity with Michelangelo's *Last Judgment* of 1536–41 in the Sistine Chapel, which Domenico might have discovered

through engraved reproductions of the frescoes, such as those by Giulio Bonasone and Giorgio Ghisi that were in circulation as of the mid-1540s.

The sinuous line, use of continuous contour, and dynamic passages of hatching with curved strokes all seem characteristic of Campagnola's work of about 1550, as has been noted by Elisabetta Saccomani.[7] In this author's view, a date of about 1550, consistent with Campagnola's penmanship but late in his career, highlights the problem of what lies behind the conception and function of the entire series of drawings. It is difficult to imagine why an artist at the height of his career, whose art attests to his familiarity with the compositions of the Venetian painters with whom he had collaborated, like Titian, should suddenly take up an outmoded model and make a reinterpreted copy of it. All in all, it seems more likely that these drawings were meant for a series of engravings rather than for an album intended for some collector, even

though none of the preserved sheets shows traces of design transfer. Could the success of Albrecht Dürer's fifteen woodblock prints for his *Apocalypse* (1497–98) have inspired an aging Domenico to produce a series on the same theme? The similarity of format may not be coincidental, and one wonders if Campagnola's creation may have been determined by an infatuation with the German master's plates, which combined late Gothic tradition with a new concept of full-page art illustrations as well as a renewed vision of space and form.

Nathalie Strasser

1. Tobias B. Nickel in New York and London 2004, no. 1.
2. See Bellinati 1989, pp. 70–78.
3. Popham and Wilde 1949, nos. 161–82; Clayton 2004, figs. 9, 16, 19, 28, 33.
4. Monte Carlo 1966, no. 37.
5. Popham and Wilde 1949, p. 202.
6. Clayton 2004, fig. 19.
7. Saccomani 1980, p. 72.

15. Parmigianino (Girolamo Francesco Maria Mazzola)

Parma, 1503–Casalmaggiore, 1540

Recto: *The Holy Family with Shepherds and Angels*

Verso: *Musical Notations: "G. soli re: ♭mi / A: la . mi re/ fa: b: m/ misure / C. sol . fa. mi: d: la: sol: re. l ami : ffa. ♭mi"*

Ca. 1523–24

Pen and brown ink, brush and gray-brown wash, over some traces of black chalk; scattered traces of gray pigment (apparently oxidized leadwhite), 10¼ × 7⅜ in. (26.1 × 18.8 cm)

Watermark: "IHS" monogram surmounted by a cross (near Briquet 9641 and 9462)

Provenance: H. M. Calmann, London; Stephen Currier, New York; Private Collection, New York; Katrin Bellinger Kunsthandel, Munich; acquired by Jean Bonna, 1998

Exhibitions: New York 1965–66, no. 90; London 1988, no. 10; Parma and Vienna 2003, no. 2.3.3 (Parma), no. II.3.12 (Vienna); Paris 2006a, no. 7; Geneva 2006–7b, p. 310

Bibliography: H. M. Calmann 1964, no. 6, pl. 6; Popham 1971, vol. 1, p. 224, no. 784, vol. 2, pl. 51; Oberhuber 2003, p. 75 (Italian ed.)

While this exuberant and entirely characteristic drawing by Parmigianino has long been known in the literature as a major autograph work by the artist (discovered by the dealer Hans M. Calmann), it has rarely been seen in the original, either privately or on public display. The sheet has been cut down at all the borders, especially along the top and left, and as is often the case with Parmigianino's composition drawings, the details of the subject matter were left somewhat nebulous in the frenzy of the artist's creative outpouring. It is not precisely clear, for example, just how the main male figure at left (Saint Joseph) sits in the foreground, but his legs are stretched out to create a monumental expanse of draped form, and it is also not clear whether his body is supported by a landscape feature or a

manmade object. The composition appears to be envisioned as an *Adoration of the Shepherds*, perhaps not unlike that represented in Parmigianino's small devotional painted panel in tempera and oil that is today in a Private Collection.[1] The elegant figures in repose (especially the Saint Joseph at left) seem also evocative of the artist's *Rest on the Flight to Egypt*, another devotional panel of similar size, now in the Courtauld Gallery.[2] Like those undated paintings, the Bonna drawing has often been rightly thought by many specialists to belong in the first Parmese period of Parmigianino's career (ca. 1522–24), based on style, although some grounds may also exist for pushing it into the very early Roman years (ca. 1524–25), given that entire groups of works by the artist, none securely dated, offer

15 recto

15 verso (size reduced)

continual variations on the general themes of the Adoration of the Shepherds, the Nativity, and the Rest on the Flight to Egypt, until about 1528 or so. Parmigianino arrived in Rome in 1524, and he left there for Bologna when the Eternal City was sacked by the imperial troops of Charles V in 1527.

The figural types, compositional style, and drawing technique of the Bonna sheet seem unmistakably those of Parmigianino's pre-Roman years, and while A. E. Popham dated this work more generally, the present author greatly concurs with Lucia Fornari Schianchi in noting a more specific dating in the last part of Parmigianino's first Parmese period, that is, about 1523–24,[3] for the Bonna sheet reveals palpable echoes of Antonio Allegri "Correggio" (ca. 1490–1534), Parmigianino's master and sometime competitor in Parma, and his quick drawing style of around this same time, about

1522–24. Correggio utilized the pen-and-ink-with-wash technique with formidable virtuosity, and a datable example for the purposes of comparison with Parmigianino may be Correggio's double-sided sheet of sketches of Saints Matthew and Jerome for one of the pendentives at San Giovanni Evangelista, Parma, of about 1523, and which exhibits on the verso the *Rest on the Flight to Egypt* relating to the *Madonna della Scodella* in the National Gallery of Art, Washington, D.C. (1991.217.6b).[4] These two artists also worked in collaboration in San Giovanni Evangelista at this time. Both sides of the Washington D.C. sheet by Correggio are almost certainly closely contemporaneous in execution. In the Bonna drawing and other early examples by Parmigianino, the particularly Correggesque elements are his use of pliant, robust contours and his search for dazzling effects of movement and light, even as

the final results were often much less pictorial than those of the older master.[5] As exemplified here, in Parmigianino's early pen-and-ink drawings, the sculptural forms appear defined primarily with quickly applied gray-brown washes for subtle variations of diffused lighting, and the modeling contains little hatching with the pen (here it appears only in the deepest areas of shadow), while in his later drawings, in contrast, the modeling is done with predominantly even, graphic effects of hatching. The drawing style is nearly identical in its deployment of lighting effects and use of the pen and ink with wash to the study for the *Circumcision of Christ* in the Musée du Louvre (inv. 6390), which is by most recent accounts considered very early and preparatory for the magnificent picture of this subject in the Detroit Institute of Arts (no. 30.295), of about 1523.[6] Of the two sheets in the Louvre closely related in composition to the Bonna sheet (inv. 6393 verso and inv. 6417 recto), the sketchy, very expressive *Virgin and Child with the Infant Saint John and Other Figures* in pen and ink includes on the other side of the paper a more carefully detailed *Lamentation over the Body of the Dead Christ* (figs. 18, 19) that is exactly comparable in drawing style and technique to the Bonna sheet. Since both drawings exhibit similarly bold volumes (articulated with wash and quick, looping, greatly reinforced contours), despite their very different subject matter, the two sheets must be closely connected in time.[7] While several additional drawings of about 1523–24 can be identified—all revealing this bold pen-and-ink technique with wash and portraying male figures in similarly pronounced profile views—the most prominent comparison to the Bonna sheet is the portrait study always associated with the painting of *Galeazzo Sanvitale* in the Museo e Gallerie Nazionali di Capodimonte, Naples, which is signed and dated 1524 by the artist and whose sitter was Parmigianino's most important private patron before he went to Rome.[8]

The dainty, though vigorously done Louvre *Holy Family* sketch in red chalk (inv. 6417 recto), which is also squared for transferring the design to the final working surface, most likely was preparatory for the painted panel in oil now in the Museo Nacional del Prado, Madrid (inv. 283).[9] The Prado panel is often identified as one of the pieces Parmigianino

Figure 18. Parmigianino, *The Virgin and Child with the Infant Saint John and Other Figures.* Pen and light brown ink, brush and gray-brown wash, highlighted with white gouache on paper. Musée du Louvre, Paris (inv. 6393 verso)

Figure 19. Parmigianino, *The Lamentation over the Body of the Dead Christ.* Pen and brown ink, brush and brown wash. Musée du Louvre, Paris (inv. 6393 recto)

brought from Parma to present to Pope Clement VII de' Medici and his court, to secure patronage,[10] and it is therefore usually dated by scholars to about 1524, just about when the artist arrived in Rome.[11] The Bonna sheet must have been preparatory for a similar type of private devotional painting, such as the Prado picture. The intimate mood of the composition in the Bonna drawing is also comparable to the unfinished painted composition of a *Nativity, Adoration of the Shepherds* in the Galleria Doria Pamphili, Rome (inv. 292), another picture produced for private devotion, datable to somewhat later, about 1524–25.[12]

The early pre-Roman date of the Bonna study is further confirmed by the watermark type seen on the paper, as it is frequently found on drawings by Correggio and the young Parmigianino (it indicates a Parmese, rather than Roman origin of the paper), and this watermark type also occurs on documents from Casalmaggiore, to the north of Parma.[13] The verso of the Bonna sheet is inscribed with musical notations in the hand of the young artist (as was first recognized by Hans M. Calmann[14]). At least one more drawing exists by the young Parmigianino of exactly this date, in the late first Parmese period of about 1523–24, exhibiting the same IHS watermark (typical of Casalmaggiore), and containing musical notations and writing in his own hand (Private Collection, New York).[15] The major portion of the New York double-sided sheet is dedicated to figure studies, with the recto portraying seated and standing male nudes very likely for an *Adoration of the Shepherds*, and the verso showing seated children amidst foliage resembling motifs in the upper right of the painted panel *Saint Catherine of Alexandria* in the Städelsches Kunstinstitut, Frankfurt, of about 1523–24.[16] The fascinating account of Parmigianino's personality provided at the end of Giorgio Vasari's biography of the artist in the 1568 Giunti edition of the *Lives of the Artists* states that he delighted in playing the lute and that his musical talent with the instrument was no less than his mastery of painting.[17]

CARMEN BAMBACH

1. Illustrated and catalogued in Vaccaro 2002, pp. 136–37, no. 7.
2. Courtauld Gallery, London (inv. P.1978.PG.308); ibid., pp. 139–40, no. 9.
3. Popham 1971, vol. 1, p. 224, no. 784 (but who is often misquoted on this point); and Fornari Schianchi in Parma and Vienna 2003, p. 250, no. 2.3.3 (Italian ed.), pp. 287–88, no. II.312 (German ed.).
4. See especially Diane DeGrazia (in Washington and Parma 1984, pp. 98–101, no. 19), who rightly distinguished the date of the commission for the *Madonna della Scodella* in 1523, from the date inscribed on the frame of the picture (June 2, 1530).
5. See Béguin, Di Giampaolo, and Vaccaro 2000, pp. 64–68.
6. See Popham 1971, vol. 1, p. 136, no. 369 (for the drawing); and Vaccaro 2002, pp. 137–38, no. 8 (for the painting).
7. As already noticed in Popham 1971, vol. 1, p. 224.
8. See the seated male figure study (Devonshire Collections, Chatsworth, inv. 444) and the double-sided sheet (Private Collection, New York) whose recto relates to the decoration of the Rocca of Fontanellato and whose verso contains the portrait drawing; discussed and illustrated in London and New York 2000–2001, pp. 83, 90–91, nos. 41 (entry by Martin Clayton), 47 (entry by George Goldner).
9. See Popham 1971, vol. 1, p. 142, no. 396r.
10. As stated in Vasari's 1568 edition: "fece tre quadri, due piccoli et uno assai grande." Vasari 1568 (1966–87 ed.), vol. 4, pp. 534–36.
11. On the painting, see Vaccaro 2002, pp. 149–50, no. 14.
12. Ibid., pp. 151–52, no. 16.
13. Briquet 9462.
14. As recorded in Popham 1971, vol. 1, p. 224.
15. See Carmen Bambach in London and New York 2000–2001, pp. 98–99, no. 54.
16. Vaccaro 2002, pp. 141–42, no. 10.
17. Vasari 1568 (1966–87 ed.), vol. 4, p. 545.

16

16. Giulio Campi

Cremona, ca. 1507–Cremona, 1573

Danaë and the Golden Shower

Ca. 1545–50

Pen and brown ink, brush and brown wash, highlighted with white gouache over traces of black chalk, squared in black chalk, on ocher-prepared paper (upper right corner restored), 5 13/16 × 9¾ in. (14.8 × 24.8 cm)

Provenance: Thomas Le Claire Kunsthandel, Hamburg, 1989; Elmar W. Seibel, Boston, Massachusetts; Thomas Williams Fine Art, London; acquired by Jean Bonna, 2000

Exhibitions: New York 2000, no. 4; Paris 2006a, no. 12; Geneva 2006–7b, p. 316

Bibliography: Bora 1988, p. 17, fig. 44a; Thomas Le Claire Kunsthandel 1989, no. 2

While the exact date is undocumented, it was most likely toward the middle of the sixteenth century that one of the three Aldegatti brothers—Francesco, Agostino, or Girolamo—commissioned Giulio Campi to decorate a chamber of the family palazzo, the Aldegatti family being closely connected at the time with the ducal court of Mantua.[1] Tradition has it that Campi learned his art in Mantua from Giulio Romano,[2] the Lombard city's leading artist until his death in 1546 and that Romano was also the architect of the Palazzo Aldegatti. The iconographic program that Campi created evokes the various loves of Jupiter in a series of ten fresco paintings based on Ovid's *Metamorphoses*. Several drawings related to Campi's preparatory work for this fresco cycle are scattered in various museums and private collections. They all share the same rectangular format, dimensions, and technique (only the present drawing is squared for transfer), but not all of them are attributed to the artist himself.[3]

This study is preparatory to the scene illustrating the myth of Danaë, daughter of Acrisius, king of Argos, who locked her in a tower to ward off the prediction that she would give birth to his murderer. But the lecherous god Jupiter transformed himself into a golden rain shower to outwit the king's vigilance. The young woman's union with the divinity would produce Perseus, who later accidentally killed his grandfather with an unfortunate throw of the discus. The fresco painting, which depicts this moment of metamorphosis, is severely damaged, and the composition is no longer legible in its details. Therefore, the transposition of the rectangular format of the scene in the drawing to the rounded shape of the Mantua lunette cannot be judged.[4] The image on paper, on the other hand, has been preserved in all its freshness, including the treatment of monochromatic tones in ocher, browns, and whites. In the fully realized Bonna drawing, the figures and the ornamental elements of the composition done in antique style are coherently and harmoniously integrated, allowing for a precise understanding of Campi's artistic intentions that are no longer evident from the damaged fresco alone. As Carmen Bambach pointed out,[5] the squaring lines visible on the sheet, slightly smudged by the highlights, probably indicate that this drawing was used as a *modello* for the subsequent fresco.

Campi's manner in this drawing bespeaks the cultural influences that helped shape his art. A native of Cremona, he was imbued with Emilian culture (Correggio and Parmigianino) on the one hand and on the other, was influenced by Giulio Romano's compositions for the court of Gonzaga.[6] Most likely, it was the latter that determined the richness of the decorative vocabulary, the elaborate positioning of the figures, the "graphic solution adopted for the draperies" (as Giulio Bora put it in 1988), and even the choice of a subject in which mythological depiction is subordinated by eroticism and seduction.

Two paintings might have provided models of inspiration for Campi's conception of Danaë: a version by Correggio, realized at the request of Federico Gonzaga II in Mantua, also for a series on the theme of the loves of Jupiter;[7] and a later one by Primaticcio for the gallery of François I in Fontainebleau, which became widely known around 1543 through a print by Léon Davent.[8] From Correggio may come the imagery of the meeting of Danaë and Cupid, on either side of the golden shower that incarnates Jove's metamorphosis, as well as the heroine's gesture of grasping her drapery, which might either be covering her nakedness or revealing it. It is possible, on the other hand, that part of the idea derives from Primaticcio in that the reclining woman is seen in contrapposto and the arrangement of the narrative is in an enclosed space.

In addition to these considerations, as David Franklin noted, Campi introduced into his composition a figure directly borrowed from Polidoro da Caravaggio, who painted it in the Niobe frieze on the facade of the Palazzo Milesi in Rome (ca. 1526), a fresco decoration that was widely reproduced as an engraving upon its completion.[9] A drawing after Polidoro, from the collection of Antoine-Joseph Dézallier d'Argenville,[10] precisely shows the figure of Apollo that Campi here transcribed literally— up to and including the motif that masks his right leg—to evoke the figure of Love. Bathed in light, this adult Cupid has already entered the chamber and shot his arrow, as suggested by his open fingers and slack bow and by the fact that the arrow, having found its mark, is nowhere to be seen.

NATHALIE STRASSER

1. Renato Berzaghi (1988) established the relationship between Campi's drawings and the frescoes in the Aldegatti palazzo.
2. Baldinucci 1681–1728 (1845–47 ed.), vol. 2, p. 232.
3. *Jupiter and Callisto*, after Campi (formerly at the H. Schickman Gallery in New York); Hugo Chapman has identified a second, possibly authentic version of *Jupiter and Callisto*, sold at auction in London (Christie's, South Kensington, December 15, 1999, lot 5); *Jupiter and Mnemosyne* (Biblioteca Reale, Turin, inv. 16193); *Jupiter and Io*, Campi after Giulio Romano [?] (Royal Library, Windsor, inv. RL 0496); *Jupiter and Io*, after Campi (British Museum, London, inv. 1946-7-13-356); *Jupiter and Astéria,* formerly in the Philip Pouncey Collection (his sale, Sotheby's, New York, January 21, 2003, lot 10); Two drawings on the theme of Jupiter and Antiope document a scene that the artist probably abandoned, one in the Jean Bonna Collection in Geneva and the other, after Campi, in the British Museum (inv. 1946-7-13-355).
4. Berzaghi (1988, p. 32, n. 4) suggests that Campi conceived the cycle before seeing the space in the *stanzetta* and that he then proceeded to adjust the scenes to the dimensions of the lunettes.
5. Oral communication, October 12, 2006.
6. See Cremona 1985, p. 128.
7. See Ekserdjian 1997, pp. 279–84.
8. Zerner 1969, no. LD8.
9. See New York 2000, no. 4. Polidoro, for his part, was most likely inspired by a classical relief.
10. Musée du Louvre, Département des Arts Graphiques, Paris (inv. 6075). The Biblioteca Ambrosiana, Milan, also has two copies of the frieze (inv. F262 inf. 20, F268 inf. 40).

17. Giovanni Battista Franco (called Il Semolei)

Venice, ca. 1510–Venice, 1561

Two Figures in a Landscape

Ca. 1554

Pen and brown ink, 9¹⁵⁄₁₆ × 7⅜ in. (25.3 × 18.7 cm)

Inscribed in brown ink in the artist's hand on verso: *B.F. e vien di T.ᵃⁿᵒ*

Watermark: anchor in a circle (similar to Briquet 475: Venice, 16th century)

Stamps and marks: Peter Lely (Lugt 2092)

PROVENANCE: Sir Peter Lely (1618–1680), London; Colnaghi, London, 1955; Patrick Perrin, Paris, 1988; sale, Phillips, London, February 16, 1988, lot 122; Galerie Jean François Baroni, Paris; acquired by Jean Bonna, 2001

EXHIBITIONS: Paris and New York 2001, no. 1; Paris 2006a, no. 11

BIBLIOGRAPHY: Lauder 2004, no. 419DA

Two major artistic influences on Giovanni Battista Franco are seen juxtaposed on this sheet. On the one hand, his native region of Venice is clearly evident in his borrowings from the landscape tradition as it developed there in the sixteenth century, and on the other, the enormous impact of Michelangelo on the young artist is noticeable in the muscular male figure reclining in the foreground. According to Giorgio Vasari, in fact, Franco "resolved that he would not study or seek to imitate any other works but the drawings, paintings, and sculptures of Michelagnolo,"[1] on seeing them during his first stay in Rome at the age of twenty.

The result is a composite drawing, of a vertical format unusual for a landscape, that notably combines the rustic, steep-roofed dwellings characteristic of Venetian compositions with

17

the ancient ruins typical of the Mannerists, as in the engravings of the Fontainebleau School, the Veronese Battista del Moro, or the Dutchman Marteen van Heemskerck. As Anne Varick Lauder noted, the two figures in the scene almost literally reprise the figures of Moses and Mary Magdalen that Titian painted at the bottom of *La Gloria* of about 1554, in the Museo del Prado, Madrid. That citation is confirmed by the inscription on the verso of the drawing: "It comes from Titian." The vertical format of Titian's altarpiece no doubt has something to do with the chosen layout, but Franco nonetheless shows some inventive complexity of his own. Thus, the legs of the man encircling the female figure, which make her look more slender, create the visual effect of a disproportion between them. Also of Venetian inspiration are the fine pen strokes swaying along the hill on the left, which counterbalance the diagonal thrust of the composition created by the rays at upper right and carried forth dramatically by the slope of the landscape, the woman's arms in prayer, and the arms of the reclining old man. Franco's penmanship is surprisingly even, regardless of whether he is defining figures or landscape.

It is not easy to interpret the subject, but it might be related to a passage in the Book of Job (33:23–25) warning against the sin of pride:

"If there be a messenger with him, an interpreter, one among a thousand, to show unto man his uprightness, then he is gracious unto him, and saith, deliver him from going down to the pit. I have found a ransom. His flesh shall be fresher than a child's; he shall return to the days of his youth." The female figure can therefore be understood as an angel, or more generally as God's interpreter interceding on behalf of the ill and fallen man, her open arms establishing a link between sky and earth.

NATHALIE STRASSER

1. Vasari 1568 (1912–14 ed.), vol. 8, p. 89.

18. Girolamo Muziano

Acquafredda (Brescia), 1532–Rome, 1592

Saint Paul

Ca. 1575 ?

Black chalk and faint highlights in white chalk, on prepared pale pink paper (slight restorations on the edges, several abrasions), 15¹¹⁄₁₆ × 7¼ in. (39.8 × 18.5 cm)

Inscribed in brown ink at lower left: *Baglioni* ?

Watermark: one-headed eagle inscribed in a circle, surmounted by a crown (cf. Briquet 207 and 209: Italy, 16th century)

PROVENANCE: Private Collection, Vienna; Pandora Old Masters, New York; Private Collection, Italy; Trinity Fine Art, London; Edoardo Testori, Milan; acquired by Jean Bonna, 1999

EXHIBITION: New York 1998a, no. 3

Taco Dibbits posited a connection between this impressive drawing and the imposing altarpiece of the chapel of Saint Paul in the church of Santa Maria in Aracoeli in Rome.[1] The property of the Della Valle family, the oratory was decorated by Girolamo Muziano, who executed the painting above the altar before December 1583, and Cristoforo Roncalli (about 1553–1626), who painted the frescoes on the side walls sometime after that date.[2]

The design of the figure of Paul in black chalk, however, does not correspond by any means precisely to the one in the Santa Maria painting. There are clear variations between the initial design and the finished painting in the drapery and the position of the arms, in the addition of an attribute (the book), and especially, in the horizontal left/right reversal of the figure. Moreover, Muziano's line looks less unctuous here than in several drawings (all in red chalk) already related to the present study, such as the two versions of *Saint Jerome* in the Louvre and in Windsor Castle,[3] dated about 1580, or the *Seated Prophet* in the Morgan Library.[4] In the present drawing, the artist used a firm line to trace the contours of the figure and the drapery, superimposed over diagonal hatching that deepens the shadows, but did not stump the lines defining the garments as in the drawings mentioned above. The penetrating quality of the light and the power of the human form confer on the saint a solidity and tension that clearly demonstrate the influence of Michelangelo's late works on Muziano.

The sculptural presence of the figure in space is reminiscent of a drawing by Muziano in the Louvre,[5] a full-length portrait of a king holding the attributes of power, rendered with similar technique but on blue paper with squaring lines in red chalk. John Marciari suggested that this drawing was used by Muziano's pupil Cesare Nebbia (1536–1614) in depicting Charlemagne and Saint Louis in the apse of San Luigi dei Francesi in Rome (1572–75), frescoes that were destroyed in the eighteenth century.[6] In the two studies, black chalk is applied in large oblique swaths, and the folds of the drapery are emphasized, although the white chalk highlights are accentuated more heavily in the Paris drawing. In addition, those two figures show an evident connection with another drawing in the Louvre, attributed by Philip Pouncey to Federico Zuccaro, who supposedly based his work on the last drawing by his brother Taddeo before the latter's death in 1566.[7] Because of these comparisons, this author would situate the Bonna drawing slightly before the *Saint Paul* in Santa Maria in Aracoeli, perhaps about 1574, before Federico left Rome and Muziano's work started showing fewer affinities with the art of the Zuccaros.

John Gere and John Marciari stressed the complex artistic relations between Muziano and Taddeo Zuccaro,[8] and while the full-length figure of the apostle is a veritable topos of

engravings, the present drawing nonetheless bears a striking similarity to the etching of Saint Paul by Bartolomeo Passarotti (1529–1592), dated about 1550 or 1560,[9] and most likely based on a model by Taddeo Zuccaro. The sword that balances the figure's contrapposto, and the bulging folds and pointed flap of the drapery, are elements of both works. Although Taddeo's study for this print has not been preserved, the Morgan Library owns the one he created for the figure of Saint Peter,[10] which Passarotti also engraved.[11] As in the drawing by Muziano, the design of the figure is flipped horizontally and holds his attribute—the keys—in his left hand, which is highly unusual for traditional religious iconography but is repeated in the printed version. (For the painting in Santa Maria in Aracoeli, Muziano "corrected" the image, showing Paul holding the sword in his right hand and the book in his left.) With all due prudence, the hypothesis can be advanced that the Bonna drawing was meant to be reproduced as an engraving. Compared to Taddeo Zuccaro's *Saint Peter*, the drawing's atmospheric qualities do not seem inconsistent with a preliminary design for a print; for the Della Valle altarpiece, Muziano might well have had recourse to an earlier study. Given that Muziano was then at the height of his career and was busy with majestic commissions for Pope Gregory XIII, such a practice of self-quotation would have been understandable.

NATHALIE STRASSER

1. In New York 1998a, no. 3.
2. See Heideman 1982, pp. 69–71, 73.
3. Musée du Louvre, Département des Arts Graphiques, Paris (inv. 5109) and the Royal Library, Windsor Castle (inv. RL 0440), which are cited by Taco Dibbits in New York 1998a.
4. Morgan Library & Museum, New York (1979.6); New York 1965–66, no. 124.
5. Musée du Louvre, Département des Arts Graphiques (inv. 10850).
6. My thanks to John Marciari for having provided this information about the Louvre drawing.
7. Musée du Louvre, Département des Arts Graphiques (inv. 9061). Taddeo's drawing, in ink, is conserved at the Ashmolean in Oxford (inv. WA 1937.229).
8. See Gere 1969, pp. 49–50; and Marciari 2002, p. 117.
9. Bartsch 1803–21, vol. 18 (1818), p. 6, no. 11. This is one of six plates from the series Christ and the Apostles engraved by Passarotti.
10. Morgan Library & Museum (IV, 71b); Bohn 1988, p. 188, fig. 64.
11. Bartsch 1803–21, vol. 18 (1818), p. 3, no. 7.

19. Federico Barocci

Urbino, ca. 1535–Urbino, 1612

Head of a Young Woman in Frontal View

Ca. 1550–60

Pastel, black chalk, and traces of white chalk with stumping, on blue paper (now faded), 15⁹⁄₁₆ × 9¾ in. (39.5 × 24.7 cm)

Annotated on recto in graphite by modern hand at lower left: *420*; in graphite in modern script at lower right: (erased)

Annotated on verso in pen and dark brown ink in a 17th-century hand: *Di mano […] Andrea del Sarto*; in grayer brown ink by a different hand below: *di Andrea del Sarto*; and by same hand, a very ornate monogram below: either *GBC* or *GRC*; and in graphite by modern hand at bottom of sheet: *Andrea del Sarto (1484–1531)* and in pencil, two illegible inscriptions

PROVENANCE: John C. Schaller, San Jose, California; sale, Christie's, London, December 12, 1978, lot 2 ("attributed to Federigo Barocci"); Duke Roberto Ferretti; Kate Ganz, London, 1993; acquired by Jean Bonna, 1998

EXHIBITIONS: Washington and Parma 1984, no. 95; New York 1993, no. 3

This imposing and exquisitely rendered life-sized study in black and white chalk, with pastel, ranks among the indubitable masterpieces of the Bonna collection, notwithstanding the somewhat abraded drawing surface and the small passages of bled-through iron-gall ink at the top of the sheet. This work was first attributed to Federico Barocci in 1978, around the time of its sale at auction, and was accepted at that time by a number of scholars.[1] It was published and exhibited in 1984 with this attribution by Diane DeGrazia, who dated it to about 1556–60,[2] between Barocci's two early journeys to Rome. As is indicated by the annotations in pen on the verso of the sheet, the eighteenth-century owner of this drawing erroneously considered it to be by Andrea del Sarto (1486–1530), no doubt misled by the fact that this Florentine painter was famous for the soft sfumato rendering in his paintings and the sweet expression of his *Madonne*. An analysis of the precise historical context of this important drawing, together with its stylistic vocabulary and drawing technique, leaves little doubt in the present author's mind that the proposed attribution to the young Barocci is

correct, although this work has often been passed over in silence in the more recent literature on the artist, and although it has also been said somewhat misleadingly that the features of the face are not typical of Barocci's draftsmanship.[3] As has been observed rightly by some art historians, the serenely beautiful woman's head with downcast eyes, portrayed in a strict frontal view, of ineffable geometric purity, and bathed in an iridescent light of nearly supernatural quality, without doubt recalls the Madonnae and other holy women painted by Piero della Francesca (ca. 1415–1492), but these qualities reflect the transforming lens of Raphael's paintings.[4] While these echoes of Piero and Raphael are not surprising, given that they were the two most celebrated Central Italian painters to have been active in Barocci's native city of Urbino, the style and overall conception of the female figure in the Bonna drawing are, to this author's eye, rooted more precisely in the later Mannerist traditions of painting that emanated into Urbino from the eastern regions of upper Central Italy (the Marches and Romagna to the north). This is manifest in the work of local painters who responded in their own ways to the legacy of Raphael, such as Luca Longhi (1507–1580), from Ravenna, and more importantly, Francesco Menzocchi (1502–1574), native of Forlì, pupil of Girolamo Genga (Barocci was himself the nephew of Bartolomeo Genga, brother of Girolamo[5]). Menzocchi was an exquisitely pictorial draftsman in his own right.[6] Of direct bearing on the questions of attribution regarding the Bonna drawing, this rich artistic legacy in the regions of the Marches and Romagna was without doubt important to the formation of the young Barocci,[7] although scholars usually have paid greater attention to Barocci's direct absorption of Raphael, Correggio, and the Venetian schools—the latter through his apprenticeship with Battista Franco (the Venetian painter who worked at Urbino Cathedral ca. 1546–49) and through the artist's own early work in Pesaro. Barocci lived and worked in Pesaro in the late 1540s, under the supervision of his uncle Bartolomeo Genga. It was in 1543–44, in fact,

that Menzocchi was commissioned by the confraternity of the Oratorio della Santa Croce at Urbino to paint the triptych of the *Deposition* (now in the Pinacoteca di Brera, Milan), which was recently restored,[8] and it was in Urbino while engaged on this project that Menzocchi encountered Barocci as a young boy (less than ten years old) and "placed his firm hopes in the youngster, and urged that he apply himself wholeheartedly to painting." The words are from Barocci's biography of 1672 by Giovanni Pietro Bellori, who closely based his narrative on the artist's family papers that were gathered by Pompilio Bruni. To judge further, based on that source, the young artist was apprenticed to his teacher, the Venetian Battista Franco (ca. 1510–1561), only later, after the encounter with Menzocchi.[9] Both the soft pictorialism of the Bonna drawing and the serene Raphaelesque sweetness of the young woman's facial type, which is elegantly stylized, seem generally evocative of Menzocchi's Mannerist vocabulary of the 1540s (an example is the Virgin in his *Holy Family with Saint John the Baptist and Putti*; Bob Jones University, Greenville, South Carolina),[10] and also recall the altarpieces of the 1540s and 1550s by Luca Longhi, with whom Menzocchi was in contact.[11] Regarding the evidence of drawing technique, the medium of pastel (fabricated colored chalks) is uniquely associated in the Marches with Barocci, but Bellori's biography rightly or wrongly stated that the young artist began to use that technique when he was shown examples of monumental pastel drawings of "most divine heads" by Correggio (an artist, however, by whom no pastel drawings are extant),[12] which were brought back to Urbino by an unnamed painter who had been to Parma.[13] The style and technique of the Bonna drawing seem generally in keeping with a dating to about 1550–60 (in this author's opinion, the work could be earlier than the proposed date of ca. 1556–60 by DeGrazia), but the sheet certainly cannot postdate Barocci's frescoes of the Casino Pio IV in the gardens of the Vatican Palace, of about 1561–63. This work, therefore, would be the earliest presently known pastel drawing by Barocci.[14]

Figure 20. Federico Barocci, *Saint Cecilia with Saints Mary Magdalen, John Evangelist, Paul, and Catherine.* Pen and brown ink, brush and brown wash highlighted with white gouache. Graphische Sammlung Staatsgalerie Stuttgart (inv. 1338)

In the Bonna drawing, the head is noteworthy for its masterful command of geometry and perspectival precision (for example, the ears) while also seeming completely natural. Here, it is relevant to recall that Piero della Francesca's manuscript of *De prospectiva pingendi*, written before 1482 and containing the famous passages on the perspectival foreshortening of the human head (or "transformations"), was still among the prized possessions in the library of the Dukes of Urbino;[15] that according to Bellori, Ambrogio Barocci (the artist's father) was his first teacher of drawing and was a maker of mathematical instruments; and that Bartolomeo Genga (Barocci's uncle) was his mentor and was court architect and engineer to Duke Guidobaldo II della Rovere.[16] The artist first outlined the oval of the head with a finely pointed black chalk, positioning the features along the axes of the face and using numerous reinforcement lines. While the strokes of black chalk in the contours may be much thinner than in Barocci's later pastel drawings, this worked-over quality of the outlines is nevertheless typical. In the modeling, the individual strokes of diagonal parallel hatching from the application of the black and colored chalks—even on the smooth planes of the face—are left evident throughout the modeling, and this pronounced, relatively graphic use of the chalks is often characteristic of the young artist. Early drawings by Barocci with this more "hatched" application of the chalk include a child's head in the Nationalmuseum, Stockholm;[17] the *Madonna and Child* in the Hamburger Kunsthalle that was intended for the motif in the top register of the *Martyrdom of Saint Sebastian* altarpiece in Urbino Cathedral, of about 1557–58; the seated figure of a virtue in the Galleria Nazionale delle Marche, Urbino, possibly preparatory for the *Laetitia* fresco in the Casino Pio IV, of about 1561–63; or Barocci's figure studies in the Uffizi.[18] Despite its relatively finished appearance, the monumental Bonna drawing of the young woman's head is nevertheless a work in progress, as it represents two different ideas for the design of the hair and headdress. The artist first seems to have thought of representing the woman's hair as if emanating from behind her neck in braids gracefully resting on the front of her neckline, but that part of the design appears relatively faint and was likely erased by the artist himself, as he reconsidered the pose. This original solution is best evident at the lower left, where the drawing surface is more intact. The artist's second idea was to emphasize instead the turn of the veil and hair, as if pulled back in a gentle cascading flow, and the corresponding strokes of black chalk articulating this later thought consequently appear relatively emphatic and worked up with color.

Scholars usually agree that Barocci's first painting, the altarpiece of about 1556–60 portraying *Saint Cecilia with Saints Mary Magdalen, John Evangelist, Paul, and Catherine* in Urbino Cathedral, is indebted to Raphael's *Ecstasy of Saint Cecilia* altarpiece, now in the Pinacoteca Nazionale, Bologna, although Barocci probably relied on reproductive prints rather than on direct study of the original.[19] Barocci's preliminary composition study in Stuttgart for this first picture in Urbino Cathedral (fig. 20) was first identified by Christel Thiem in 1977,[20] and it usually has been dated to about 1555–56.[21] It portrays the female saint standing second from the left in a frontal view, with hair gathered at the top of her head, much as in the Bonna drawing and much as in Raphael's painted Saint Cecilia. In his altarpiece, Barocci would later exchange the pose of this female figure from a frontal view to a three-quarter view facing left; the painted head of Saint Cecilia at center displays hair flowing from the left side, to the back and reappearing at the right. These elements are also similar to the second and last solution in the Bonna drawing. While the Bonna drawing does not seem to be directly connected to a presently identifiable painting, it is likely that it is in the same scale as a final work, given the most recent research on Barocci's design practices.[22]

Carmen Bambach

1. This attribution in the Christie's, London, sale cat., December 12, 1978, lot 2, was accepted at the time by Diane DeGrazia and Edmund Pillsbury (written communication to this author, March 19, 2008). New York 1993, p. 10, records this as Konrad Oberhuber's attribution.
2. In Washington and Parma 1984, pp. 286–87, no. 95.
3. The latter point was made in New York 1993, p. 10.
4. The connection to Piero and Raphael was noted in Washington and Parma 1984, p. 287.
5. Bellori 1672 (1976 ed.), p. 181: "zio Bartolomeo Genga architetto del duca Guidobaldo."
6. Scrase 1991.
7. Turner 2000, p. 10, has been among the few scholars to have emphasized Francesco Menzocchi's influence on the young Barocci.
8. On Menzocchi's now restored Brera altarpiece, see Milan 2004–5.
9. Bellori 1672 (1976 ed.), p. 181: "prese ferma speranza del giovinetto, e l'esortò ad applicarsi tutto alla pittura."
10. For the suggested dating of Menzocchi's painting in the 1540s, see Forlì 2003–4, pp. 53, 58–59.
11. For particularly relevant examples by Luca Longhi, see Viroli 2000, pp. 41–54, nos. 6, 7, 12, 13, with complete catalogue entries.
12. See especially Washington and Parma 1984, pp. 36–37.
13. Bellori 1672 (1976 ed.), p. 183: "nel qual tempo capitando in Urbino un pittore, che tornava da Parma con alcuni pezzi di cartoni e teste divinissime a pastelli di mano del Correggio, Federico restò preso da quella bella maniera, la quale si conformava del tutto al suo genio."
14. As rightly emphasized in Washington and Parma 1984, p. 287.
15. Bambach 1994.
16. Bellori 1672 (1976 ed.), pp. 180–81: "padre, che lavorava di cavo e di rilievo modelli, sigilli ed astrolabii, l'indirizzò al disegno."
17. Inv. NM 409/1863; Bjurström and Magnusson 1998, no. 418.
18. Hamburger Kunsthalle, Hamburg (inv. 21054); Galleria Nazionale delle Marche, Urbino (inv. 1673); and Gabinetto Disegni e Stampe degli Uffizi, Florence (inv. 11330F, 11368F, 11405F). See Emiliani 1985, vol. 1, pp. 9, 16, 19, 23, figs. 6, 14. 24, 32, 33.
19. Ibid., pp. 4–5.
20. Thiem 1977, pp. 200–201, no. 373.
21. Turner 2000, p. 15 ("ca. 1555–56"); Edmund Pillsbury in Cleveland and New Haven 1978, p. 29, no. 1 ("ca. 1556").
22. See now Marciari and Verstegen 2008, but without mention of the present drawing.

20. Federico Zuccaro

Sant'Angelo in Vado, ca. 1541–Ancona, 1609

David Receiving Tribute from the Conquered Nations

Ca. 1566

Pen and brown ink, brown ink wash, white gouache, over faint traces of black chalk (laid down, small losses), 12¹³⁄₁₆ × 10⅜ in. (32.5 × 26.4 cm)

Inscribed in brown ink at lower center: *P. 80-5* (?)

Watermark: pilgrim in a shield (cf. Woodward 9)

Stamps and marks: Lugt 2383

Provenance: Walter Schrott, Tyrol; Thomas Le Claire Kunsthandel, Hamburg; acquired by Jean Bonna, 2006

Exhibition: Geneva 2006–7a

On September 2, 1566, the very day of his brother Taddeo's death, Federico Zuccaro wrote to Cardinal Alessandro Farnese (1520–1589), offering to take over the decorative program that Taddeo had begun in the prestigious residence that the prelate had built near Rome. The decoration of the chapel of Villa Caprarola, to which the present sheet is related, is the first drawing that Federico realized for the villa after his older brother's passing.

On September 20, from Caprarola, a certain Antinoro sent Zuccaro a plan for the cupola of the chapel,[1] conceived as a circular *tempietto* designed to fit seven rounded frescoes, along with a request for some drawings as soon as possible, which Zuccaro apparently sent. The other scenes depict *God Creating the Sun, Moon, and Stars* (in the center), *The Creation of Eve*, *The Flood*, *The Sacrifice of Isaac*, *The Crossing of the Red Sea*, and *Samuel Anointing David*. The execution of the frescoes was mainly handled by a team of assistants.[2]

The present drawing is in a rectangular format, as is another page in the artist's hand, now in the Louvre,[3] which is practically identical, save for the squaring lines inside a circle traced with a compass. The hypothesis that Antinoro might have drawn this circle himself is contradicted by the presence, in the Bonna drawing, of two curved motifs that precisely follow the circle on the Louvre version. One of the motifs is the diagonal line that marks the garments of the water bearer kneeling at the far left of the composition (a "fold" with no

true coherence to the rest), and the other is the line running from the helmet to the shoulder of the soldier standing at the right. From these elements, it can be deduced that Zuccaro first executed the Paris drawing, then outlined the central part (corresponding to the Caprarola fresco), and then made a copy before he sent it off, taking those steps in order to keep a faithful image, *a ricordo*, or perhaps to market it, naturally leaving out the squaring lines.

Four more drawings document the preparation of the tondi of the cupola; two of them, *God Creating the Sun, Moon, and Stars* and *Samuel Anointing David*, of rectangular format, are similarly framed and have squaring lines, whereas *The Creation of Eve* is now rounded.[4] *The Sacrifice of Isaac*,[5] like the Bonna drawing, has no such annotations and is lacking the underlying framework lines in black chalk that are clearly visible in the three other preparatory drawings. It follows, as James Mundy noted,[6] that Federico first conceived the entire decorative program of the vault as rectangular and then had to adapt it to the chapel's decorative schema.

The replica drawings by Zuccaro have not yet been studied systematically, but the Bonna sheet can be added to known examples. Among them are *The Virgin and the Holy Women*, preparatory to one of the niches of the chapel at Caprarola, of which John A. Gere has signaled a "drawn facsimile" in a private collection, and the two drawings, "almost indistinguishable," conserved in the Uffizi and relating to the *Sala dei Fasti Farnesiani*, also in the villa at Caprarola.[7] This seems to have been a common practice, at least with regard to the frescoes that Federico Zuccaro and his team executed in Caprarola after Taddeo's death, possibly as a consequence of the artist's commitments for the Villa d'Este in Tivoli and for the Vatican Palace, which kept him in Rome. The two versions of *David* are extremely similar, apart from the six millimeters' difference in width between the two sheets, which to this author's mind excludes the possibility that the drawing

was transferred. The draftsman's extreme talent in copying his own work is evident in the handling of the pen, which unhesitatingly reproduced each detail of the composition. The Bonna drawing is now in much better condition than the nearly identical one in the Louvre cited above; the freshness and vivacity of the white highlights and the absence of folds or squaring lines obviously make it easier to read. These two sheets, which were probably separated soon after their execution—one serving as model for the fresco and the other conserved for a yet unknown reason—highlight the destiny of two drawings made at the same time but kept independently.

The scene depicts an episode from the Old Testament related to the reign of King David and is sometimes interpreted as *Three Warriors Bringing King David Water from the Well of Bethlehem* (II. Kings 23:13–17; I. Chronicles 11:15–19). The reading seems plausible; not only does it fit with Zuccaro's composition but parallels between the kneeling knight making an offering to David and the three Magi bringing gifts to the Infant Jesus had been popular since the end of the Middle Ages. Nonetheless, it has been discarded in favor of a less frequently depicted episode, *David Receiving Tribute from the Edomites* (II. Kings 8:6–14; I. Chronicles 18:1–11), which was evoked in the poetic description of Caprarola by Ameto Orti about 1585–89.[8]

Nathalie Strasser

1. The drawing is reproduced in Gere 1970, no. 31. The identity of this assistant and second cousin of the Zuccari, Antenore Ridolfi, was established by Bonita Cleri (1993, pp. 101–5).
2. See Acidini Luchinat 1998–99, vol. 2, pp. 13–20.
3. Musée du Louvre, Département des Arts Graphiques, Paris (inv. 4469).
4. See Partridge 1999, pp. 171–75. Respectively, Allen Memorial Art Museum, Oberlin (1947.2), and Musée du Louvre, Département des Arts Graphiques (inv. 4398, 4394).
5. Musée du Louvre, Département des Arts Graphiques (inv. 4396).
6. Written communication, January 10, 2005.

20

7. See Gere and Pouncey 1983, no. 295. *The Virgin and the Holy Women*, corners rounded at the top and with squaring lines (British Museum, London, inv. 5224-4); the two studies for the *Sala dei Fasti Farnesiani*

(Gabinetto Disegni e Stampe degli Uffizi, Florence, inv. 10997F, 11195F) are squared, but the second has more ornamental details.

8. "David exigit tributa ab Idumaeis quos bello vicerat,"

cited by Partridge (1999, p. 171, n. 36). Ameto Orti was hypothetically identified as Aurelio Orsi, secretary to Cardinal Alessandro Farnese.

21. Jacopo Negretti (known as Palma il Giovane)

Venice, 1548–Venice, 1628

Saint Christopher

Ca. 1590–95

Black chalk, pen and brown ink, brush and brown wash, highlighted with white gouache, on beige laid paper (framing line in brown ink, laid down on blue cardboard with a tooled, gilded line, upper right corner incomplete), 10⁵⁄₁₆ × 8⅛ in. (26.2 × 20.6 cm)

Stamps and marks: E. J. Reynolds (Lugt 900b)

PROVENANCE: Edward James Reynolds (1876–ca. 1932), England, Saint Petersburg, and Lausanne; Anton Schmid (1904–1991), Vienna; Galerie Arnoldi-Livie, Munich; acquired by Jean Bonna, 2003

At the end of the sixteenth century, Jacopo Palma il Giovane was the primary figure of Venetian painting, following the three great masters—Titian, Veronese, and Tintoretto—who had influenced him before he reached maturity as a graphic artist. "One will never see anything as witty as his drawings," Antoine-Joseph Dézallier d'Argenville wrote in 1762; "his pen . . . is fine & light; it gives off imaginative fireworks, a vivacity of genius that has few equals. We find a small, very light wash in bister with cross-hatching in every direction: his touch, his tentative outlines, his loose draperies, are more the result of extensive practice than of natural gift."[1] A prolific draftsman, Palma made nearly one thousand drawings, some of them in preparation for an equally abundant painted output, and many others that surely allowed him to try out new formulations, and even more so to enrich and perfect a means of expression in which he excelled.

This drawing depicts Saint Christopher carrying the Christ Child on his back, a story based on the narrative by Jacopo da Voragine's *Golden Legend*, or the *Lives of the Saints*. According to Carlo Ridolfi, Palma had made a painting of this subject (now lost) for the convent of the church of Santa Maria dei Crociferi in Venice.[2] But Ridolfi also claimed that this is one of the artist's early works, which does not correspond to the later date of the present drawing. The drawing might rather call to mind Titian's fresco of about 1523 at the Palazzo Ducale, in which the saint, a powerfully rendered figure, crosses the lagoon of Venice, evoked on the horizon.

Four drawings by Palma il Giovane treat the same subject but are from different dates.[3] The earliest, from about 1580, is in the Szépmüvészeti Múzeum, Budapest (inv. 2259), while the others date from 1613 to 1615. Two of the drawings—in the Galleria Estense, Modena (inv. 780), and the Roberto Ferretti Collection—depict the figures in a natural, verdant landscape, but the fact is that all of them differ from the Bonna study in that they show Christopher bowing his head under the weight of the Christ Child on his shoulders, a feature that accentuates the expression of tenderness in the image. The Bonna drawing shows the saint as if seen from below, his face raised, in an ascendant dynamic torsion that stretches the figure diagonally, with Christ perched on the saint's shoulder, facing the viewer with fingers raised in blessing.

The markings here are ample and abundant, not yet rarefied; the modeling is done with softly subdued washes rather than deep and dark ones as in Palma's later drawings. To this author's mind, these factors suggest dating the work about 1590–95. Only a slight cast shadow is visible behind the saint's right calf, while the rest of the figure emerges from the background with no other artifice. The black chalk outlines of the figure have been reworked with pen and ink, and the technique of "commas" and "parentheses" (to rely on Mason Rinaldi's apt words)[4] that defines the musculature is evident on the torso. The contouring is accomplished mainly in brown wash, while the slightly stumped white highlights visibly reinforce the play of light that runs, with truly painterly effect, along the saint's arm and back.

NATHALIE STRASSER

1. Dézallier d'Argenville 1762, vol. 1, p. 285.
2. Ridolfi 1648 (1835–37 ed.), vol. 2, p. 379ff.; Mason Rinaldi 1984, p. 184.
3. Venice 1965a, no. 36; sale, Sotheby's, London, April 9, 1981, lot 70 (this drawing reprises the Budapest drawing, minus the wash); Elisabetta Saccomani in Bentini 1989, p. 154, pl. XLIX; Roberto Ferretti Collection (Toronto and New York 1985–86, no. 17). Finally, a drawing attributed to Palma il Giovane is in the Musée Bonnat, Bayonne (inv. RF 50937).
4. Mason Rinaldi 1972.

21

22. Jacopo Ligozzi

Verona, ca. 1550–Florence, 1627

Full-length Portrait of the Sultan Selim II with a Dragon

Between 1580 and 1585

Brush, gouache, and highlighting in gold over traces of black chalk; the background colored light blue by a later hand, 10¹³⁄₁₆ × 8⁷⁄₁₆ in. (27.5 × 21.5 cm)

Inscribed on recto at upper left: *Sultan Selim 13 Imperator de Turchi* (retraced in brown ink over another existing inscription) / *Drago* (in pen and brown ink)

PROVENANCE: Niccolò Gaddi (1537–1591), Florence (?); Edoardo Testori, Lugano; acquired by Jean Bonna, 2006

EXHIBITION: Geneva 2006–7a

Shortly after his arrival in Florence in 1577, Jacopo Ligozzi executed at least twenty-nine drawings depicting Eastern characters, in each case accompanied by an exotic or imaginary beast. Most of these drawings are now in the Uffizi[1] and were a gift to the museum by the sculptor Niccolò Bazzanti in 1867.[2] The ten additional drawings currently known to exist are scattered among various other museums and private collections.[3] Each of the Uffizi drawings is inscribed with a number in ink at the top, added to the other annotations on the off-white unprepared paper. Those sheets show minor traces of wear and are of slightly smaller dimensions than the other known drawings, which have no numbering and exhibit uniform backgrounds in colored gouache that were added later. The colors of these backgrounds range from light blue to pale green.

Originally, these drawings were probably part of an ensemble, possibly an album, which was later taken apart and dispersed. If they were drawn on commission rather than on the artist's personal initiative, they cannot be dated before Ligozzi's arrival in Florence, but the probable patron is not known. Anna Forlani Tempesti prudently suggested Francesco I de' Medici, given the late date of donation of the drawings to the Uffizi, while Lucilla Conigliello more recently proposed the eminent Florentine collector Niccolò Gaddi.[4]

This richly colored suite of drawings probably took its inspiration from a best-selling book, *Les Quatre Premiers Livres des navigations et pérégrinations orientales* by Nicolas de Nicolay, which was first published in French,

in Lyon, by Guillaume Rouille in 1567–68, illustrated with sixty etchings made about 1556 by the Fontainebleau engraver Léon Davent.[5] The book then went into a second edition in Antwerp, under the title *Les Navigations pérégrinations et voyages, faits en la Turquie*, in 1576. The first edition in Italian, *Le Navigazioni et viaggi nella Turchia*, was published in Antwerp in 1577, followed by a Venetian edition in 1580.[6] Anna Omodeo established the relationship between Ligozzi's drawings and this latter edition of Nicolay's book;[7] the illustrations by Ligozzi freely copy the French engravings. The present sultan was inspired, in fact, by Davent's *Aga Capitaine général des Janissaires*.[8] The conception of these images by Ligozzi also reveals several other cultural interests prevalent in the 1560s, such as the fascination with the costumes and customs of the Eastern world (especially Turkey) and the scientific study of botanical and zoological species. Moreover, even though one of Davent's images is of a Turkish priest holding a stag on a leash, the beast in the present drawing is actually Ligozzi's own addition.[9] Ligozzi thus matches his protagonist to an animal whose function is either symbolic, allegorical, or totemic, establishing a direct relationship between the two figures, although the ultimate meaning is sometimes obscure.

The inscription at the top of this drawing identifies the figure as Selim II, called Selim the Drunkard, an Ottoman sultan who ruled from 1566 to 1574 and was the son of Suleiman the Magnificent and Roxelane.[10] In fact, the monarch's features closely resemble those of Suleiman. The fantastic animal, its mouth open and threatening, suggests an allusion to the chivalric Order of the Dragon, which originated in the Balkans to combat the spread of Ottoman imperialism; in 1529, the Turks had even besieged the city of Vienna, to the shock of the Christian West. A fragile peace had been established in Hungary in 1562, allowing the sultan to coexist with the dragon, but the capture of Cyprus by Selim and the third Battle of Lepanto in 1571, which was won by the Holy League, remained a vivid and painful

memory for Ligozzi's contemporaries, especially for the Venetians, who never regained their former possession.

The image here fully demonstrates Ligozzi's talent for brilliant colors heightened with gold and for detailed and precise line. The artist devoted the same meticulous care to depicting the fabulous beast as he would to rendering a fish or bird that he had seen himself.[11] Such details illuminate the painter's extravagant imagination, and they also dispel the notion that his art merely reproduced the visible world. The later addition of the pale blue of the background subtly affects the presentation of the subject, but it is not possible to know when this alteration occurred, as the early history of ownership of this drawing has not been established.

NATHALIE STRASSER

1. Gabinetto Disegni e Stampe degli Uffizi, Florence (inv. 2947F–2954F and 2956F–2967F); the *Bombardiere turco* (Uffizi inv. 2955F) is now lost.
2. Forlani Tempesti 1982, p. 77.
3. Eight other drawings have (or had) a colored background, like the Bonna drawing: J. Paul Getty Museum, Los Angeles (91.GG.53); The Metropolitan Museum of Art, New York (1997.21); sale, Sotheby's, New York, January 25, 2007, lots 48–51; Trinity Fine Art, London (New York 1998b, nos. 6, 7); a drawing formerly at Hazlitt, Gooden & Fox (London 1988, no. 19) has no colored background.
4. Sale, Sotheby's, New York, January 25, 2007, p. 7.
5. See Nicolay 1989, p. 25; and Zerner 1969, no. LD 96-98.
6. For each of these editions, the engravings by Léon Davent were copied, the title changed, and the images sometimes embellished with an ornamental border. The book was also published in German (1572 and 1576), Flemish (1576), and English (1585).
7. In Florence 1965, pp. 48–51.
8. Book 3, p. 92.
9. Ibid., p. 119, after the subtitle: "Turcs, demenans vie solitaire entre les bestes."
10. Depending on whether his "precursors" are counted, Selim was considered the eleventh or thirteenth Ottoman sultan.
11. Magnificent examples can be found in the *Corpus Aldrovandino* in the Biblioteca Universitaria di Bologna, Fondo Ulisse Aldrovandi.

23. Jacopo Ligozzi

Verona, ca. 1550–Florence, 1627

Plant Study

Between 1580 and 1600

Brush and gouache on vellum, 21½ × 13⁵⁄₁₆ in.
(54.6 × 33.8 cm)

PROVENANCE: Houthakker Collection, Amsterdam;
Private Collection, New York; Katrin Bellinger
Kunsthandel, Munich; acquired by Jean Bonna, 2004

EXHIBITIONS: Paris 2006a, no. 16; Geneva 2006–7a

When the Veronese Jacopo Ligozzi arrived in Florence in 1577, in order to enter the service of Francesco I de' Medici (1541–1587), he already might have enjoyed a reputation as "scientific draftsman," earned by the drawings of animals he realized during his earlier stay in Venice, which were collected by the Hapsburg emperor Rudolph II.[1] His nature illustrations were soon noticed by Ulisse Adrovandi, the celebrated Bolognese scientist, with whom he regularly collaborated from then on. Over the next ten years, Ligozzi would execute a series of drawings depicting rare plants and strange animals, about which the Grand Duke of Florence was avidly curious.[2]

This specialty in the natural sciences, by an artist known equally for his religious and allegorical paintings, made Ligozzi a leading Italian figure in the new scientific approach to studying the world. There were many challenges in producing such images, and Ligozzi represented a particular cultural movement and political situation, that of Florence in the second half of the sixteenth century, during which time the "scientific humanism" of the Medici flourished.[3] Cosimo I (who established the first botanical garden in Pisa in 1543) and his two sons, Francesco and Ferdinando, were in fact fascinated by the projects of the eminent scientists who gravitated around the court. Such interests were not devoid of political concerns; for those bankers who had risen to power, investing capital in territorial possessions had both financial and symbolic value. The dynasty drew much of its power from land-ownership, and what better way to express the splendor of its possessions than through depiction? The Medici villas, with their gardens filled with exotic plants from the Levant, central Africa, and the New World, were a repository for displaying this new magnificence, much as the salon of the villa at Poggio a Caiano (1485–1519), which was adorned by Jacopo Pontormo's frescoes of the agricultural deities Vertumnus and Pomona.[4]

Several fundamental treatises, moreover, such as *De historia stirpium commentarii insignes* by the botanist Leonhart Fuchs (Basel, 1542) or *De humani corporis fabrica* by Andreas Vesalius (Basel, 1543), mark a turning point in the study of nature. What these books proposed, in opposition to the classical and medieval legacies of learning, was a figurative illustration of the object under study (human, vegetal, or animal), reproduced as a print.

Ligozzi's drawings sanction this modernity by giving it shape, even though many of the technical characteristics hark back to the medieval tradition of illuminated manuscripts. The preciousness of his drawings with their gold highlights, or of his zoological and botanical plates, conveys a sense of the paradox surrounding the artist, who called himself a *miniatore* (illuminator) while nonetheless also painting in large scale.[5] Ligozzi's naturalistic images oscillate between scientific studies and art objects. Is he trying to depict truth or beauty? Aldrovandi praised Ligozzi's extraordinary exactitude, so useful to a scientist, while comparing Ligozzi to the Greek painter Apelles (whose paintings, it was said, fooled his contemporaries into thinking they were real), thereby enshrining him in the pantheon of art history.

The present drawing portrays a plant of the genus *Stellaria*, found throughout the world and prized for its medicinal virtues. Realized in gouache, the depiction is characteristic of Ligozzi's work in this domain. The large dimensions of the vellum sheet allowed him to represent the plant at full scale, in an attempt to render the specimen with maximum fidelity. The arrangement, also characteristic, shows the plant and its root against a perfectly unadorned background. Here, this particular feature is hard to see because of what was most likely water damage, which caused the color to bleed onto the parchment support. It might have been this accident that led someone to retouch the veins in green, whereas Ligozzi usually rendered these elements in light tones. Despite this accident, one can see how the artist formulated his "*ritratto di pianta*" (portrait of the plant), by concentrating his efforts on depicting the specimen itself. He played with effects of lighting to contrast between the branches to detail a withered leaf and individuate its consistency, against a background devoid of any chiaroscuro. This overall process of design with chiaroscuro effects confers a "tactile reality"[6] on the objects represented, so that they emerge with a three-dimensional presence that makes the illusion more perfect.

It is difficult to date this drawing, since over a span of twenty years, Ligozzi's botanical studies did not vary significantly in technique or style.[7] His most concentrated activity in this specialty covers the ten years spent in the service of Francesco I (1577–87), the period that produced the illustrations now in the Uffizi. These latter drawings were executed on paper rather than vellum, and it therefore seems risky to consider the present drawing as one among the grand duke's commissions. It is entirely possible that the work was painted by Ligozzi later, on his own initiative, and was intended for a private collector.

Just as the Medici illustrations were not reproduced as prints, the present drawing does not seem to have been engraved. In any case, it is not included in Tobia Aldini's book *Exactissima Descriptio Rariorum Quarundam Plantarum . . . Horto Farnesiano*, published in Rome in 1625, which Conigliello related to Ligozzi's botanical images.[8] A very similar drawing, perhaps from the same album, is now in The Metropolitan Museum of Art.[9]

NATHALIE STRASSER

23

1. Österreichische Nationalbibliothek, Vienna (Cod. min. 83 and 131). About these drawings, see Essen and Vienna 1988–99, vol. 2, nos. 603, 604; Conigliello 1991; and Tongiorgi Tomasi 1993, pp. 12–14.

2. These drawings from nature, in tempera on paper, are now in the Gabinetto Disegni e Stampe degli Uffizi, Florence.

3. See Washington 2002, p. 16.

4. Florence 1990, pp. 6–7. At the end of the seventeenth century, the paintings of Bartolomeo Bimbi (1648–1730) would act as veritable inventories, attesting to the diversity of the possessions of specimens by the Medici.

5. See Paris 2005, p. 8.

6. Washington 2002, p. 40.

7. Florence 1961, p. 18.

8. See Conigliello 1994.

9. *Botanical Specimen*, gouache and watercolor on vellum, 21 x 13 ⅛ in. (53.3 x 33.3 cm), The Metropolitan Museum of Art, Promised Gift of David M. Tobey and Purchase, Rogers Fund, 2004 (2004.435).

24. Ludovico Carracci

Bologna, 1555–Bologna, 1619

Christ Adored by Carthusian Monks

Ca. 1591–92

Pen and brown ink, brush and brown ink wash (laid down, traces of creases, slight losses and tears), 14 × 9¼ in. (35.5 × 23.4 cm)

Inscribed on recto in pen and brown ink at lower right: *Baroche*; in brown ink partially erased: *L. Carraci*

PROVENANCE: Michel Gaud; his sale, Sotheby's, Monaco, June 20, 1987, lot 101; purchased at that sale by Jean Bonna

BIBLIOGRAPHY: London 1992, under no. 17; Jaffé 1994, [vol. 3], under no. 521 (reproduced in error); Brogi 2001, p. 139, under no. 29 (copy); Bohn 2004, no. 55; Loisel 2004, under no. 203

This drawing by Ludovico, the eldest of the three Carracci, depicts Christ appearing in glory before kneeling Carthusian monks. For both stylistic and iconographic reasons, it has been related to two drawings (one in Chatsworth and the other in the Ellesmere Collection)[1] that were preparatory to the fresco of Christ Bearing the Cross, which the artist executed for the church of San Gerolamo della Certosa, Bologna.[2] Although neither of these drawings corresponds exactly to the fresco, which today is in fragments, the second is closer to the final version. While Alessandro Brogi prudently related the present sheet to the painted work, the composition differs sufficiently to make one wonder whether it was an early proposal rejected by the patrons who were too attached to an established tradition (Leonora Street noted that the definitive composition is based on a century-old model, Ambrogio Bergognone's *Christ Carrying the Cross* for the Certosa of Pavia),[3] or perhaps was a preliminary design that was left undeveloped.

At present, the dating of the painting fluctuates between the end of the 1580s[4] and the years 1591–95,[5] when Ludovico was working on a commission for three other paintings for the Carthusians of Bologna: *The Preaching of Saint John the Baptist*, dated 1592, and its two pendants, *The Flagellation* and *The Crown of Thorns*, also intended for the church of San Gerolamo.[6] The posture of the adoring monk in the left foreground is reminiscent of the figure of Saint Francis kneeling in the *Holy Conversation* in the Museo Civico, Cento,[7] dated 1591, while the angel holding up the cross is similar to the one engaged in the same activity in Ludovico's *Trinity with Dead Christ* in the Vatican (about 1591–92).[8] The fluid, supple line and brilliant washes in the present drawing are typical of those years, but its state of conservation, slightly altered by what might have been too much exposure to sunlight, makes it difficult to judge the lighting effects. The drawing nonetheless can be likened to Ludovico's *Virgin and Child with Saint Anne* at the Louvre, dated about 1590–93,[9] in which the washes follow the lines indicating the folds of the garments and also work independently to deepen the creases in the draperies, as in the cloak of the kneeling woman in the Paris drawing and Christ's tunic in the Bonna composition. The small clouds, undulating and compact, that support the Virgin are also similar to the ones visible in the Bonna drawing.

The particular iconography of this drawing might well provide some further indications. In an article about a drawing by Lelio Orsi, *Christ in the Midst of Crosses*, Catherine Monbeig Goguel retraced the literary and visual origins of the motif of intertwined crosses,[10] a symbol going back to Saint Augustine that exhorts the faithful to endure their tribulations as a sign of love for Jesus Christ. While the theme is rarely depicted with the same originality as by the eccentric Orsi, Monbeig Goguel emphasized that in Italy, and especially Bologna, the motif was also included in processions imitating Christ's approach to Calvary. The allusion is also found in a print by Hans Holbein illustrating Erasmus's *Precatio Dominica*, published in Basel in 1524.[11] The vignette associates Christ followed by crossbearers—the solution adopted for the church of San Gerolamo—with the vision of God the Father in heaven, surrounded by hosts of angels.[12] In the Bonna drawing, the resurrected Christ appears to the monks, with a multitude of crosses relegated to the background.[13] It is all the more tempting to posit that Ludovico borrowed from the Holbein print, considerably reinterpreted though it might be, since another composition by Holbein from the same book seems to have inspired the above-mentioned *Preaching of Saint John the Baptist*. On a knoll, Christ teaches the Our Father prayer to his disciples, his head set against a wooded background, while the pose of the apostle in the foreground is quoted in Ludovico's painting.[14] The publisher of the *Precatio*, Johann Froben, donated a copy of his book to the charterhouse of Basel,[15] and it is tempting to surmise that Erasmus's text circulated among the Order of Saint Bruno. The Bonna drawing might well have been conceived simultaneously with the one of John the Baptist, in other words about 1591–92, and the Bolognese monks might have supplied the Holbein as a visual model when they commissioned the work. Might Ludovico have first

Baroche.

envisioned a picture of the Lord appearing before the monks, only to be asked to depict the Bearing of the Cross instead? There is nothing implausible about such a demand, especially given the oft-quoted lines by Carlo Cesare Malvasia relating the difficulties that both Ludovico and Agostino had with the prior of the Bolognese Carthusians.[16]

The copy of the present drawing preserved in the Louvre suggests the possibility that the work was in a French collection in the eighteenth century. As Perrin Stein noted,[17] Natoire reproduced Carracci's drawing but omitted the small cherub's head visible just below the cross. The modification, slight though it may be, fully clarifies the upper part of the composition.

NATHALIE STRASSER

1. Bohn 2004, nos. 53, 54.
2. Brogi 2001, no. 29.
3. Street 1972, p. 356.
4. Babette Bohn (2004, no. 55) leans toward 1588–90, which coincides with Alessandro Brogi's dating for the fresco (Brogi 2001, no. 29).
5. As of 1594, according to Catherine Loisel (communication to the author, May 24, 2006).
6. All three are now at the Pinacoteca Nazionale in Bologna; Brogi 2001, nos. 46, 47.
7. Ibid., no. 41.
8. Ibid., no. 44.
9. Musée du Louvre, Département des Arts Graphiques, Paris (inv. 7665); Bohn 2004, no. 65.
10. See Monbeig Goguel 1990, pp. 82–85; my thanks to Catherine Loisel for bringing this article to my attention.
11. Monbeig Goguel (1990, p. 83, n. 29) cites a vignette illustrating *De vera et falsa religione* by Zwingli, but to my knowledge this work includes only a border by Holbein.
12. Reproduced in Basel 1997, no. 99d.
13. Brogi (2001, p. 139) describes the drawing this way: "…il Cristo portacroce che, secondo un'intenzione ancor più visionaria e devota, appare ai certosini adoranti sull'alto di una nube."
14. Reproduced in Basel 1997, no. 99a.
15. Ibid., no. 97. This is the copy now in the Kunstmuseum, Kupferstichkabinett, Basel (inv. X.2183). After the Reformation, the Carthusians of Basel were allowed to remain in the "Klein Basel" charterhouse, so long as they did not train any novices. The last monk, a friend of Bonifacius Amerbach, died in 1564.
16. See, for example, Bologna and Fort Worth 1993–94, no. 36.
17. Musée du Louvre, Département des Arts Graphiques, Paris (inv. 15020); attributed by Catherine Loisel to Charles-Joseph Natoire; communication to the author, May 25, 2006. Regarding copies by Natoire, see Stein 2000.

25. Giovanni Battista Trotti (called Il Malosso)

Cremona, 1556–Parma, 1619

Seated Angel (*Study for* The Immaculate Conception)

1594

Black chalk, pen and brown ink, highlighted with white gouache, squared in black chalk, on blue paper, 6¾ × 5¹¹⁄₁₆ in. (17.1 × 14.5 cm)

Stamps and marks: Ch. Gasc (Lugt 543) (?); two indecipherable marks on recto

PROVENANCE: Charles Gasc Collection, Paris (?); A. F. Collection; sale, Audap, Godeau, Solanet, Paris, March 11, 1987, lot 213 (attributed to Pieter de Witte); Richard Day, London, 1987; acquired by Jean Bonna, 1996

EXHIBITIONS: New York and London 1987, no. 6; Paris 2006a, no. 17

BIBLIOGRAPHY: Tanzi 1992, p. 106, fig. 4

It was Mario Di Giampaolo who recognized this drawing, once attributed to Pietro Candido (ca. 1548–1628), as a preparatory study by Malosso for *The Immaculate Conception*, now installed on the interior entrance wall of the church of Santa Maria della Steccata in Parma (fig. 21). The painting, signed and dated 1594, was commissioned in 1591 by the brothers Teodoro and Silvio Burla, for the church of Sant'Agostino in Piacenza, and was in Parma by the turn of the twentieth century.[1]

The present sheet and a group of seven other drawings document the elaboration of the design of this canvas.[2] Two of them show the composition in its entirety;[3] four are related to the group of angels in the center and the angel playing music at right,[4] while the last one details the figures of the Virgin and God the Father.[5] These drawings, which vary widely in technique and degree of completion, display Malosso's virtuosity in first sketching out an arrangement, most often in pen and ink, then reprising and perfecting the countless figures that populate his great cycles of the heavens, and finally adding washes and highlights.

This *Seated Angel* corresponds exactly to the figure at the lower left of *The Immaculate Conception*, even though in the painting, the angel has no wings (the same omission occurred when the Venice drawing was translated into paint) and wears a crown. Much like the preliminary design at the Uffizi, the Bonna drawing was made on blue paper and bears traces

Figure 21. Il Malosso, *The Paradise* (detail), 1594. Oil on canvas. Santa Maria della Steccata, Parma

25

of squaring in black chalk. As Giulio Bora noted, this drawing displays "an extreme delicacy of tones, especially in the definition of graceful and delicate details," and underscores the care Malosso took in the final phase of his process of design.[6] The stark opposition between the white highlights and the dense pen hatching creates the effect of falling light along the diagonal arrangement of forms and plays against the color of the paper. This attains an image whose plasticity results in a

subtlety and spontaneity entirely missing from the painted version.

NATHALIE STRASSER

1. See Di Giampaolo 1974, n. 17; Adorni 1982, p. 210, n. 11; Tanzi 1992, p. 106. These authors have stated the title to be different: *Immaculate Conception, Paradise* or the *Election of the Immaculate Virgin*.
2. See Di Giampaolo 1974; Di Giampaolo 1977; Cremona 1985, p. 311, no. 2.16.3; Tanzi 1985; and Tanzi 1992.
3. Galleria Nazionale, Parma (inv. 630, 516/3).
4. Frits Lugt Collection, Paris (Byam Shaw 1983, no. 397); Gallerie dell'Accademia, Venice (inv. 244); Gabinetto Disegni e Stampe degli Uffizi, Florence (inv. 13250F); Timothy Clifford Collection (sale, Sotheby's, London, July 3, 1989, lot 35).
5. British Museum, London (inv. 1946-7-13-1287).
6. See Cremona 1985, p. 311. One may recall that although it is not the case with *The Immaculate Conception*, Trotti often delegated the execution of his paintings to his assistants, a practice that required him to create finished models.

26. Annibale Carracci

Bologna, 1560–Rome, 1609

Virgin and Child on Clouds above a City, Surrounded by Angels Playing Music

Ca. 1593

Pen and black ink, brush and brown wash (laid down, upper right corner restored), 9⅝ × 7¼ (24.5 × 18.5 cm)

Stamps and marks: William Cavendish, 2nd Duke of Devonshire (Lugt 718)

PROVENANCE: William Cavendish (1672–1729), 2nd Duke of Devonshire; Dukes of Devonshire and the Chatsworth Settlement Trustees (inv. 428); sale, Christie's, London, July 3, 1984, lot 7; Madame Eames-Gernsheim, Lausanne; acquired through Christie's, London, by Jean Bonna, 2008

EXHIBITIONS: Bologna 1956, no. 99, pl. 34 (2nd ed. of catalogue pl. 52); Newcastle-upon-Tyne 1961, no. 148; Washington and other cities 1962–63, no. 12; London 1969, no. 12

BIBLIOGRAPHY: Byam Shaw 1967, p. 102, under no. 183; Posner 1971, vol. 2, p. 34, under no. 80, fig. 80b; Malafarina 1976, fig. 75; Byam Shaw 1976, under no. 953; Jaffé 1994 [vol. 3], no. 481; Birke and Kertész 1994, under no. 2135; Oxford and London 1996–97, under no. 68; Washington 1999–2000, under no. 23; Spike 2002, p. 252, fig. 5; Harris 2005, pp. 514, 516, 524–25, n. 9; Bologna 2006–7, p. 258, under no. v.12

This drawing by Annibale Carracci is one of four known studies for the altarpiece he painted about 1593-94 for the Palazzo Caprara in Bologna (today the prefecture headquarters). The painting, now in Oxford (fig. 22)[1] was identified by Denis Mahon, who related it to the description in Giovanni Pietro Bellori's *Le vite de' pittori, scultori, et architetti moderni* of 1672, which mentions a "Madonna surrounded by angels above the town of Bologna seen from afar," executed by Annibale for the "house of Caprara."[2]

Annibale's four drawings show the recognizable landscape towers of Bologna. These appear below the Virgin, whose placement indicates that she is the city's protector. Two of the sheets are in the Albertina and come from the collection of Pierre-Jean Mariette,[3] while one of them, still in Chatsworth, formerly belonged to Sir Peter Lely.[4] Two "studio variants" are still listed as related to these sheets—one in Paris, in red chalk, and the other in Oxford.[5]

Annibale's four sheets are executed using the same technique, pen and black ink highlighted with a light wash. Three share the same dimensions; the exception is the one in the Albertina, which is slightly larger and appears to lack the rapid framing lines that the artist drew on the other three.[6] Conversely, each drawing presents noticeable differences in composition. The preservation of several studies related to a modest altarpiece is a unique phenomenon in Annibale's graphic oeuvre from before his departure for Rome (1595), a peculiarity noted by Ann Sutherland Harris, who also questioned the reasons behind such an exception.[7] The paucity of information about the circumstances surrounding the Caprara family's commission leaves no avenue to explore in search of an answer.

Historians have tried to establish a coherent sequence for these drawings but have not determined one conclusively, as none of them corresponds precisely to the final work.[8] The Bonna drawing is nonetheless unanimously held to be the first in Annibale's creative process. Here, the Virgin, surrounded by a chorus of angels, appears in a space nearly equivalent to the one occupied by the landscape beneath her. Annibale subsequently changed the scale of figure to landscape to confer greater monumentality on the Madonna, who in the painting imposes her presence above the city, which is rendered horizontally and confined to the lower margin. Such an evolution is already visible in the other preparatory sketches, each of which offers variations on the theme. While the view of the city tends to grow more distant, Annibale alternately modified the positions of the Virgin and the Child (Albertina 2136 and Chatsworth 427) and abandoned the musical angels and the putti, replacing them with two large winged figures on either side of the Madonna (Chatsworth 427 and Albertina 2135).

In the Bonna sheet, the horizontal space that divides the celestial and terrestrial spheres recalls the composition of the Bologna *Assumption of the Virgin*,[9] dated 1592. In both works, the Madonna's foot rests on the head of a putto, and the angels surrounding her hover along a rising curve. In contrast, the lower portion of the present drawing is occupied by an open landscape executed in two mediums: pen and ink for the tree in the foreground, the three tiny figures, and the city gates, and brush for the shadowy silhouette of the distant city. In the Washington D.C. *River Landscape* of about 1590,[10] a canvas that illustrates the revolution Annibale wrought on the landscape genre in Italy, he also depicted a town with hazy outlines but in very light tones. The Bonna drawing seems an attempt to reconcile the two distinct subjects, figure and landscape, using an ambitious approach that although it might have its origins in earlier Venetian experiments is quite original. The Virgin's gaze, tenderly trained on the landscape beneath her in the Bonna drawing, is also modified in the three subsequent studies, in which the attempt to equalize the two domains noticeably diminishes, only to disappear altogether in the Bologna Madonna.

NATHALIE STRASSER

Figure 22. Annibale Carracci, *The Virgin in Heaven with a View of Bologna Below*. Oil on canvas, Christ Church, Oxford (inv. JBS 183)

26

1. Christ Church Picture Gallery (Byam Shaw 1967, no. 183; Posner 1971, no. 80).
2. Bellori 1672 (1968 ed.), p. 47: "per la cappella di casa Caprari [Annibale] dipinse la Madonna in gloria di Angeli sopra la Città di Bologna veduta in lontanaza."
3. Graphische Sammlung der Albertina, Vienna (Birke and Kertész 1994, nos. 2135, 2136).
4. Collection of the Dukes of Devonshire, Chatsworth (inv. 428); Jaffé 1994, [vol. 3], no. 482.

5. Respectively: Louvre, Département des Arts Graphiques (inv. 7500; Loisel 2004, no. 461), and Christ Church Picture Gallery (Byam Shaw 1976, no. 953). A small-format work (11 × 7⅜ in. [27.8 × 18.7 cm]) in tempera on paper is considered by John Spike to be the *modello* of the Oxford painting. Brogi (in Bologna 2006–7, no. v.12) rejected this assertion.
6. Graphische Sammlung der Albertina, 12 x 8 7/8 in. (30.5 x 22.5 cm) (inv. 2135).

7. Harris 2005, p. 516.
8. See Bologna 1956, nos. 98–101; Byam Shaw 1967, p. 102; Posner 1971, vol. 2, p. 34 (which reproduces the four drawings); and Washington 1999–2000, p. 99.
9. Pinacoteca Nazionale (inv. 455); Posner 1971, no. 69.
10. National Gallery of Art, Washington, D.C. (1952.5.58); Posner 1971, no. 50.

27. Giulio Cesare Procaccini

Bologna, 1574–Milan, 1625

Female Figure Seen from Behind with Two Putti

Ca. 1610–11

Red chalk (traces of folds, and lightly foxed), 11¹⁄₁₆ × 7⁹⁄₁₆ in. (28.1 × 19.2 cm)

Inscribed on recto in pen and brown ink at upper left: *82*; flourish followed by the number *192/a*

Watermark: initials AC topped by a trefoil, in a circle

Stamps and marks: J.-F. Gigoux (Lugt 1164)

PROVENANCE: Jean-François Gigoux (1806–1894), Besançon and Paris; Private Collection, Germany; Thomas Le Claire Kunsthandel, Hamburg; acquired by Jean Bonna, 2006

EXHIBITION: Geneva 2006–7a

One aspect of Giulio Cesare Procaccini's abundant oeuvre is the existence of many drawings that have no direct relationship to his paintings. Nancy Ward Neilson emphasized that the usual correspondences of design between painting and drawing do not apply to this artist, as his drawings do not function solely as preparatory studies, even after such distinctions were clearly formulated.[1] Still, this statement does not account for what Procaccini may have intended by creating his "autonomous" sheets. Were they motifs he was working out, abandoned projects, intellectual or recreational exercises?

The present drawing illustrates this difficulty. Although it cannot be related definitively to one of Procaccini's painted works, it should be noted that the female figure—serpentine, seen from behind and with knees bent—is similar to the woman in the foreground of the *Miracle of Giovan Battista Tirone* of 1610, in Milan Cathedral.[2] But there are also several variations on that theme, as it is a *topos* in Procaccini's oeuvre from 1610 to 1620. On the other hand, the small putto on the left of the composition is reminiscent of the cherub on the springing of the vault where the artist painted *God the Father in Glory*, on the soffit of the arch of the Acerbi chapel in the church of Sant'Antonio Abate, Milan, in 1610–11.[3] In that regard, the sketch of foliage motifs at the top of the sheet suggests a decorative continuity that is unusual in Procaccini's painting, as the same Milanese work includes a figure whose arms are filled with flowers. The layout of the page, which leaves ample room for the white of the blank sheet—a magnificent arrangement, considering how crowded Procaccini's paintings and some of his drawings can be—confers an ethereal quality on the figures, which are arranged on schematically traced clouds. This work, therefore, might have been an early draft of that decoration, which was amply revised in subsequent versions.

Procaccini's style and technique in this drawing evoke the *Two Putti* in the Biblioteca Ambrosiana, which Giulio Bora dated about 1605 but which Nancy Ward Neilson placed about 1612–15.[4] One finds the same graceful execution, the rapid evocation of forms and movement, and the cursory definition of the contouring in tight lines of red chalk, while on the other hand, the reworking of the outlines is handled with great acuity. As to the facial resemblance, Neilson also cited two pen-and-ink studies of women in the British Museum and the Louvre.[5]

NATHALIE STRASSER

1. See Neilson 2004, pp. 10–11: "Giulio Cesare, disegnatore prolifico, raramente disegnava in preparazione del dipinto finito, [e] la relazione tra disegno e pittura non è più identificabile con un procedimento graduale e finalizzato a uno scopo. L'opera di Procaccini si colloca proprio nel momento iniziale di questa distinzione, prima che venissero formulate chiare definizioni." See also Rosci 1993, pp. 141–42.
2. See *Il Seicento lombardo* 1973 [vol. 2], no. 71.
3. Reproduced in New York 2002b, p. 31.
4. Biblioteca Ambrosiana, Milan (inv. F252 INF. 837). Neilson 2004, no. 50. Concerning this drawing, see also Bora in *Il Seicento lombardo* 1973 [vol. 3], no. 64; Neilson 1974, p. 59; and New York 2002a, p. 60, n. 5.
5. British Museum, London (inv. 1946-7-13-1373); and Musée du Louvre, Département des Arts Graphique, Paris (inv. 12613). Neilson 2004, nos. 20, 120; letter from Nancy Ward Neilson to Thomas Le Claire, January 12, 2005.

27

28. Domenico Zampieri (known as Il Domenichino)

Bologna, 1581–Naples, 1641

Study for The Martyrdom of Saint Andrew

Ca. 1623

Black chalk, pen and brown ink, brush with brown and gray wash highlighted with white gouache (with some oxidation), on paper originally blue (laid down on cardboard), 7½ × 9 in. (19.1 × 22.9 cm)

Inscribed on recto in pen and brown ink at lower right: *Le Dominiquain*

Stamps and marks: P.-J. Mariette (Lugt 1852)

PROVENANCE: Francesco Raspantino, Naples (?); Everhard Jabach IV (1618–1695), Paris; Anna Maria de Groote, Paris; Everhard Jabach V (1701–1721); Gerhard Michael Jabach (1721–1751), Livorno; his sale, Amsterdam, October 16, 1753, lot 410; Gerard Hoet, Netherlands; Pierre-Jean Mariette (1694–1774), Paris; his sale, Paris, November 15, 1775–January 30, 1776, lot 792; Charles-François (1693–1777), marquis de Calvière, Paris and Avignon; his sale, Christie's, Paris, December 17, 2003, lot 4; purchased at that sale by Jean Bonna

EXHIBITION: Paris 2006a, no. 18

BIBLIOGRAPHY: Py 2001, no. 231; Cavalier 2002, pp. 64–67, 68; Py 2007, p. 13, no. 231

This drawing was preparatory to a scene from the life of Saint Andrew by Domenichino, which was part of a fresco cycle painted in the apse of the church of Sant'Andrea della Valle, Rome. The frescoes were commissioned in 1621 by Cardinal Alessandro Peretti Montalto, a friend of the Bolognese pope Gregory XV, although the artist did not complete the program until 1628. Art historians remain divided about the exact chronology of the work, and one can suggest only tentatively a date of 1623 for the Bonna drawing.[1]

The posthumous inventory of Francesco Raspantino (active 1637–64), Domenichino's assistant and artistic heir in Naples, lists 178 drawings relating to the decoration of Sant'Andrea della Valle,[2] 174 of which are now in the collections of the Royal Library in Windsor Castle. Among those studies, seventeen are directly related to the fresco of the apostle's martyrdom.[3] Two of the Windsor drawings in red chalk with squaring portray the overall composition; another probably documents an early idea that Domenichino abandoned, and the others are individual studies for figures in the scene. The two Windsor red chalk drawings are particularly interesting,[4] as they show changes that the artist made to his first draft (that is, the Bonna drawing), in adapting it to the trapezoidal concave surface of the apse of the church, which was the area of the final fresco painting.

The group at the left of the composition has undergone the most revision, with a new spatial solution adopted for its translation onto a curved surface. Also visible are other divergences between the two stages of the work, such as the disappearance of certain figures that have become redundant—the standing man behind the horse, a few spectators in the background, and the small head nestled against the back of the bearded man with the large club at left. In the fresco, moreover, the bearded man has been given a new dynamic impetus and thereby, more prominence.

The Bonna drawing was executed rapidly, almost feverishly, and differs noticeably from the limpid quality of Domenichino's earlier drawings, such as the preparatory study for *The Building of the Abbey of Grottaferrata* (ca. 1608, Royal Library, Windsor),[5] which nonetheless employs a similar technique. Here, the pen traced the outlines and the brush rapidly indicated shadows, while the white highlights (which have become partially oxidized over time) show that the lighting of the scene was established by this point. The wispy clouds enliven the sky, whereas the pentimento indicating an entirely different gesture for the central soldier was a later addition, possibly by another hand. The same vivacity of execution can be found in a study for the martyrdom of Saint Andrew, also in Windsor, in which Domenichino sketched the main elements of his composition in a few impetuous pen strokes, supplemented by some rapid hatching.

At a remove of nearly twenty years, the artist chose to situate the episode in an architectural framework similar to the one he created for the *Stoning of Saint Stephen* of about 1605–7, in the Musée Condé, Chantilly, in which he also used buildings and a construction inspired by the Castel Sant' Angelo, Rome, to delimit the space in which the saint's martyrdom transpired. A beautiful drawing by Annibale Carracci, formerly in the Ellesmere Collection and now in The Metropolitan Museum of Art (1972.137.2), situates the Virgin in a landscape similarly closed off by a perpendicular wall.[6] The arrangement works in small scale proved especially convincing when Domenichino used it in a fresco of colossal dimensions, such as *The Martyrdom of Saint Andrew*.

NATHALIE STRASSER

1. See Pope-Hennessy 1948, pp. 19–21; Borea 1965, p. 184; Spear 1982, pp. 242–45; Coliva 1996, pp. 284–89.
2. See Spear 1982, p. 342.
3. Pope-Hennessy 1948, nos. 688–860 (nos. 812–829 for *The Martyrdom of Saint Andrew*).
4. Ibid., nos. 812, 813 (ill. in Coliva 1996, p. 293).
5. Pope-Hennessy 1948, no. 115.
6. See Bean 1979, no. 105.

Le Dominiquin.

28

29. Giovanni Francesco Barbieri (known as Il Guercino)

Cento, 1591–Bologna, 1666

Nude Seen from Behind

Ca. 1625–30

Pen and brown ink, 9½ × 7 in. (24.1 × 17.8 cm)

Inscribed on verso in brown ink: *610*

PROVENANCE: sale, Christie's, New York, January 10, 1990, lot 45; Hazlitt, Gooden & Fox, London; acquired by Jean Bonna, 1994

EXHIBITION: Paris 2006a, no. 19

Guercino's painted oeuvre includes several splendid female nudes, such as Susanna in the canvas *Susanna and the Elders* of about 1617 in the Museo Nacional del Prado, Madrid,[1] and in the *Landscape with Bathers*, of about 1618 in the Museum Boijmans van Beuningen, Rotterdam,[2] both created early in the artist's career. The present drawing, however, is not related to any currently known painting. For stylistic reasons, it has been compared to two drawings conserved in London and dated from the mid-1620s, one in the British Museum (inv. 1910-2-12-5),[3] showing a woman in three-quarter frontal view holding a drapery over her head, and the other in the Courtauld Gallery (fig. 23),[4] in which two seated nymphs, one seen from behind, are being spied upon by a satyr. Finally, a drawing at Hazlitt, Gooden & Fox, very similar to the Bonna sheet, might have been based on the same model.[5] The technique and penmanship in the latter work are in every way identical to the Bonna drawing.

The anatomical type of this young woman, with her rounded belly and flattened buttocks, evokes the nymphs surrounding Diana in a study in Windsor Castle dating to before 1621.[6] The draftsmanship, on the other hand, is more reminiscent of the head of Alexander the Great (also in Windsor),[7] generally dated about 1631, in which the artist distinctly renders the face using fine parallel hatching enhanced with stippling, and the garments in wide, undulating pen strokes.

In the first half of the seventeenth century, the depiction of female nudes was still restricted to certain precise biblical scenes, such as Susanna and the Elders or Bathsheba at Her Bath from the Old Testament, or to episodes from the myths featuring Venus or Diana. The present figure, captured in a state of partial undress, suggests the pose of a young woman at her toilette, but in that case, the purpose of this drawing is unclear. Moreover, as it shows only an isolated figure, the subject cannot be pinpointed definitively. What is certain is that the figure exudes an intimacy conveyed with remarkable economy, such as the

Figure 23. Guercino, *Two Nymphs and a Satyr*, ca. 1625. Pen and brown ink. Courtauld Gallery, London (inv. D.1952.RW.1346)

suggestion of chiaroscuro through simple parallel hatching and some stippling, all of which softens the light.

The date proposed for the Bonna drawing situates it well before Rembrandt's matronly female nudes in etching and drypoint from about 1660,[8] but a comparison of these works, both devoid of any aestheticized considerations, is a reminder that Guercino had an opportunity to see prints by the Dutch artist and that he expressed admiration for his work.[9]

NATHALIE STRASSER

1. Salerno 1988, no. 34.
2. Ibid., no. 51.
3. London 1991, App., no. 8.
4. Ibid., no. 203.
5. London 1988, no. 28.
6. Mahon and Turner 1989, no. 151.
7. Ibid., no. 60.
8. See Bartsch 1797, nos. 199, 200, and 202.
9. See Mahon and Turner 1989, p. xv.

29

30. Giovanni Francesco Barbieri (known as Il Guercino)

Cento, 1591–Bologna, 1666

Young Woman in Three-Quarter View, Turned to the Right and Holding a Plate

Ca. 1635–40

Pen and brown ink (laid down), 7¹¹⁄₁₆ × 6⅛ in. (19.5 × 15.6 cm)

Watermark: Latin cross on three mountains inside a circle (on the mounting paper?)

PROVENANCE: Casa Gennari, Bologna; Francesco Forni, Bologna (?); John Bouverie (ca. 1722–50), England; Christopher Hervey (d. 1786), England; Elizabeth Bouverie (d. 1798), England; Charles Noel (1781–1866), 1st Count of Gainsborough, England; by inheritance, to the counts of Gainsborough; sale, Christie's, London, November 23, 1971, lot 104; Mrs. Sally Aall (1927–2005), New York; Richard Day, London; acquired by Jean Bonna, 1993

BIBLIOGRAPHY: Cambridge, Ottawa, and Cleveland 1991, p. 225, no. 221, pl. D; London 1991, App., no. 117

This drawing evokes a contemplative universe in which time seems suspended, in contrast to Guercino's energetic and animated compositions in which his draftsmanship is distinguished by an exceptional handling of light. That quality is evident here in an arrangement that sets a cluster of dark, eccentric, bristling lines against the white of the paper and in the contrast between the nervous intensity of the technique and the stillness of the woman. The artist made no use of wash to create shadow, and while his pen sketched fine, light parallel hatching when it followed the contours of the face and neck, it became looser and more prolific for the headdress, garments, and arms. Guercino did not employ stippling, which he sometimes used to soften the contours, and did not indicate, not even summarily, the background or setting for the figure.

The drawing style and technique correspond with Guercino's works during the decade between *The Visitation* of 1632 in the Musée des Beaux-Arts, Rouen,[1] and *The Guardian Angel* of 1641 in the Museo Civico Malatestiano, Fano.[2] In the preparatory drawing for the angel in the latter composition, now in Windsor,[3] the figure is similarly elaborated with frenetic lines that avoid the outlines of the clothing; the artist used regular hatching for the face and arms. The singular cluster of lines starting

at the center of the present sheet is already visible in the preparatory drawing for *Cato Bidding His Son Farewell* of 1637,[4] although this latter drawing is heightened with a few sparingly applied brushstrokes.

Today, Guercino's drawings mainly seem subordinate to the creative process of his paintings, except for his caricatures and landscapes, which are still considered works "in their own right."[5] In the Bonna drawing, the woman's pose and headdress, and especially the platter she holds in her hands, suggest a comparison with *Salome Receiving the Head of Saint John the Baptist*, which Guercino completed in 1637, now in the Musée des Beaux-Arts et d'Archéologie, Rennes.[6] Four red chalk studies in Windsor[7] have been related to this latter painting. In one of them, the female figure is seen in three-quarter view and turned to the right (fig. 24);[8] her hands are folded over her breast, and she wears a headpiece similar to the one in the present drawing. Denis Mahon and Nicholas Turner identified that figure as Herodias, Salome's mother, who does not appear in the Rennes canvas (in which the young woman receives the saint's head on a platter from the hands of his executioner) but rather recalls an early idea of Guercino's in which Herodias is present at the scene. A painting from Guercino's studio, attributed to Ercole and Bartolomeo Gennari, reprises that composition.[9] The recto of the Windsor drawing depicts the two women at that moment, and Salome's gesture (cropped by the edge of the sheet) suggests that she was holding the platter in her hands. But if the Bonna drawing can be related to any of Guercino's planned variants, it would more logically recount the moment when Salome hands Herodias (who wears the headpiece) the head of the prophet she had ordered killed because, following Jewish law, he had condemned the adultery she committed with her brother-in-law (Matthew 14:3–12).

Two copies of this drawing are extant. One, in the Albertina, is by Francesco Bartolozzi (1727–1815), who arrived in London in 1765 to make prints from a suite of Guercino's

Figure 24. Guercino, *Standing Woman*, 1637. Red chalk. The Royal Library, Windsor (inv. RL 2789 verso)

drawings that had entered the royal collection;[10] the other, in the British Museum,[11] by Robert Shipster (active between 1794 and 1800), is dated 1794 and is based on Bartolozzi's copy rather than on the original.

NATHALIE STRASSER

1. Salerno 1988, no. 140.
2. Ibid., no. 196.
3. Mahon and Turner 1989, no. 101.
4. Ibid., no. 87.
5. Denis Mahon in Bologna 1968, p. 7; London 1991, p. 33.
6. Salerno 1988, no. 169.
7. Mahon and Turner 1989, nos. 88, 89 (recto), 89 (verso), 90. Salerno (1988, no. 169) also mentions a drawing conserved in the Szépművészeti Múzeum, Budapest (inv. 1914-113).
8. Mahon and Turner 1989, no. 89, verso.
9. Pinacoteca Civica, Cento (see Mahon and Turner 1989, pp. 53–54; and London 1991, nos. 117, 118).
10. Graphische Sammlung der Albertina, Vienna (inv. 1389); Nicholas Turner in Cento 2005, p. 21. The volume, published in London in 1764, is entitled *Eighty-two Prints, Engraved by F. Bartolozzi, & c., from the Original Pictures and Drawings by Guercino in the Collection of His Majesty*.
11. British Museum, London (inv. 1986-6-21-9).

30

31. Jacopo Vignali

Pratovecchio, 1592–Florence, 1664

Head of a Young Woman with a Coral Necklace

Ca. 1625–30

Black chalk and red chalk, various framing lines in black chalk simulating a frame (laid down), 12¹³⁄₁₆ × 8¾ in. (32.5 × 22.3 cm)

Inscribed on recto in pen and brown ink in Gabburri's hand (Lugt 2992b) at bottom center: *Vignali, 1210*; on verso, underlined once: *N. 1210*

Watermarks: paschal lamb (Central Italy, cf. Woodward 48); initials *CB*

Stamps and marks: A. G. B. Russell (Lugt 2770a)

PROVENANCE: Francesco Maria Niccolò Gabburri (1676–1742), Florence; William Kent, England (?); Gerald M. Fitzgerald; Archibald George Blomefield Russell, England; his sale, Sotheby's, London, May 22, 1928, lot 95; Heinrich Trittler, Frankfurt (?); sale, Sotheby's, London, July 5, 2000, lot 11; purchased at that sale by Jean Bonna

EXHIBITIONS: London 1925, no. 22, p. 52; London 1927, no. 3; Paris 2006a, no. 25; Geneva 2006–7a

BIBLIOGRAPHY: Byam Shaw 1983, vol. I, p. 71

The painter Jacopo Vignali devoted himself almost exclusively to sacred works, especially altarpieces. To date, only two portraits of men have been attributed to him, while a head of a woman, known through his biographer S. B. Bartolozzi's mention of it, has not been located.[1] The purpose of the present drawing therefore remains unclear, although the hypothesis that it was a detailed study for a figure in a painting seems plausible. Following common practice, Vignali might have endowed one of his figures with the features of a young woman from among his or his patron's acquaintances, as the melancholic face on the Bonna drawing possesses all the qualities of a work sketched from life. Moreover, the same face seems to reappear in the *Contratto di nozze* in the Galleria Nazionale d'Arte Antica di Palazzo Corsini, Rome (inv. 137) by Giovanni da San Giovanni (1592–1636), the center of which shows a young woman in the same pose

and wearing a similar expression. The two artists met in the studio of Matteo Rosselli (1578–1650) and knew each other well. Perhaps they took inspiration at a certain time from the same model. Moreover, a painting on copper by Vignali, the *Calendimaggio* in the Galleria Corsini, Rome (inv. 138) is considered the pendant of the *Contratto di nozze*. The dating of these two works is disputed. Giovanni Pagliarulo posited that both paintings were done in Florence in the early 1620s, while Maria Pia Mannini argued that Giovanni da San Giovanni's was painted in Rome in 1627.[2]

The attribution of the drawing to Vignali is based partly on the inscription added to the bottom of the sheet by the Florentine collector Niccolò Gabburri. It is listed in his handwritten inventory under no. 1210 as "Una testa di Donna al naturale in faccia a lapis rosso e nero, – Di mano del sud[etto] Vignali. Per alto [soldi] XI · ⅓, largo 8⅝."[3] Gabburri had an extensive knowledge of the Florentine seventeenth-century artistic milieu, which made him particularly capable of distinguishing between the works of very similar artists. The Bonna drawing possesses a refinement of technique comparable to certain drawings by Carlo Dolci, who was Jacopo Vignali's most gifted student but whose drawings display a heightened degree of finish, meticulous and polished, that the present sheet does not.

For his figure studies, Vignali favored red and black chalk, sometimes on tinted or prepared papers, much like his master, Matteo Rosselli, who used them when drawing head studies from life.[4] In fact, it was the generation preceding Vignali's that saw "a shift in [the Florentine painters'] draftsmanship, from the linearity of the *Studiolo* masters to a more tonal and coloristic handling of graphic materials."[5] The color red, used here for the flesh as well as for certain details of the young woman's hair and necklace, is the true indication for

expressing the sadness conveyed by this image. The eyes ringed in red as if by tears, arouse the viewer's sympathy, and the artist intentionally softened the chiaroscuro by his unctuous use of black chalk, animated by the hatching that marks the shadow falling on her hair.

The Frits Lugt Collection has a beautiful female head seen facing left in three-quarter view, eyes lowered.[6] This too came from Gabburri, who attributed it to Vignali. The sheet bears the number 1209 and immediately precedes the Bonna drawing in the collector's inventory. It evinces a similar approach to the face, particularly in the distinctive choice of passages in which red and black chalks are applied. Red chalk was used for the woman's face and neck, which were reworked in black to form shadows, and again for certain details, such as the ribbon in her hair. This image also seems to have been captured from life, even if the artist accentuated the contrast between lights and darks for an idealized effect. Finally, the present sheet bears a close similarity to a drawing in Berlin, *Head of a Young Man with a Mustache*,[7] which is still catalogued as by Ottavio Leoni but has a treatment of color very similar to that in the Bonna drawing.

NATHALIE STRASSER

1. Bartolozzi 1753. See also Mastropierro 1973, pp. 68, 91; and Pagliarulo 1986.
2. See Florence 1986–87 [vol. I], nos. I.117, I.125.
3. The "second" Gabburri inventory, drawn up as of 1722, is conserved in the Frits Lugt Collection, Paris (2005-A.687B).
4. See, for example, *Bust of a Man, Head Bent Forward* in the Musée du Louvre, Département des Arts Graphiques, Paris (inv. 1538).
5. Chappell 2005, p. 340.
6. Frits Lugt Collection; Byam Shaw 1983, vol. I, no. 68.
7. Staatliche Museen zu Berlin, Kupferstichkabinett (inv. KdZ 5614), black chalk and red chalk, 11 × 7⅝ in. (28 × 19.5 cm). The mount of this drawing is annotated "Matteo Rosselli?" by Philip Pouncey and "C. Dolci?" by Marco Chiarini (my thanks to Dr. Schulze Altcappenberg for providing this information).

Vivetti; 1810

32. Salvator Rosa

Arenella (Naples), 1615–Rome, 1673

Allegory of Painting

Ca. 1650

Pen and brown ink, brush and brown wash,
8¾ × 12¹⁄₁₆ in. (22.2 × 30.6 cm)

Inscribed in brown ink in the hand of the Marquis de Calvière at lower right: *Benedetto Castiglione*; in black ink: *25*

Watermark: sun in a circle (cf. Woodward 152)

PROVENANCE: Pierre Crozat (1665–1740), Paris; his sale, Paris, April 10–May 13, 1741 (?); Charles-François (1693–1777), marquis de Calvière, Paris and Avignon; his sale, Christie's, Paris, December 17, 2003, lot 15; purchased at that sale by Jean Bonna

EXHIBITIONS: Paris 2006a, no. 22; Geneva 2006–7a

Pierre-Jean Mariette's commentary in the catalogue of the April 10–May 13, 1741 Crozat auction proclaimed the attractiveness of Salvator Rosa's drawings, while stressing the artist's "immoderate" ardor, his peculiarity, and the novelty of his images.[1] That commentary prefigures the enigma posed by the intriguing drawing shown here. It was reattributed correctly to Rosa by Nicholas Schwed, on the occasion of its reappearance on the market (the attribution to Castiglione in pen and ink seems due to the marquis de Calvière and would therefore come after the Crozat auction). The figure of Painting, whose attributes are pondered by two dubious cherubs, sits in the studio in rags, chasing away the flies that cluster around some freshly painted canvases. Behind her are a bundle of clothes and some shoes, which might suggest a forthcoming departure. On the back wall are a donkey's head and a purse, both topped by a crown, elements that probably form a rebus containing the key to interpreting the work. The donkey (the pejorative Italian term is *asinaccio*) also appears in Rosa's third satire about Painting, a play he finished writing in 1649 that makes fun of an artist whose success leads him into sterile indolence.[2]

Two other drawings by Rosa offer similar allegories. They are the personifications of *Painting as a Beggarwoman* in the Royal Library, Windsor,[3] in which the woman has abandoned her brushes to beg for alms, and *Painting, Plagued by Envy* in the Staatliche Graphische Sammlung, Munich,[4] in which Envy is subject to the mockery of Envy and Indolence (also represented as a donkey). While the most obvious interpretation of these scenes is the poverty of the unknown or misunderstood painter scraping together a living from his art, Michael Mahoney suggested deciphering them as bitter observations on the state of contemporary painting, without reference to the artist's personal situation.[5] In the Bonna drawing, however, one of the canvases leaning against the wall clearly represents a self-portrait, while the rose decorating the flyswatter recalls the artist's surname. Independent by nature, Rosa did not gladly suffer the role of courtier and despised the traditional patronage system of the seventeenth century, and those character traits sometimes left him in difficult financial straits. The image therefore necessarily seems to be the lament of an artist whose only wealth was his inventiveness, represented by the works-within-a-work in the studio (none of which is recognizable in Rosa's known output). These exemplify a wide range of painterly genres and possible subjects and were all in his repertory as a painter.

The Bonna drawing has no echoes in Salvator Rosa's painted oeuvre. It is nonetheless possible to draw a parallel between the present figure in rags and the woman portrayed in his painting of *Poetry* in the Wadsworth Atheneum.[6] In 1640, the artist met his likely model, Lucrezia Paolino, who would remain his companion for the rest of his life. Soon afterward, he executed a canvas that is now lost, titled *Painting*, which Luigi Salerno situated at the beginning of the Neapolitan's satirist career.[7] The Bonna drawing seems to correspond to this late period, about 1650. It displays an almost total absence of hatching, whether on the figures or the background (except for a slight shadow in the self-portrait); a predominance of outlines, traced in a supple and sinuous line; and a light application of wash that defines the geometric surfaces of the halftones. The drawing is reminiscent of others by the artist, such as *The Lament of Jeremy and Habakkuk* in the Teylers Museum,[8] dated between 1641 and 1648, in which the two prophets and two putti are set in a simple décor formed by perpendicular planes. The linear contours with obtuse angles and the diluted, broadly applied washes reappear in a group of drawings, which Michael Mahoney dated to the early 1650s, from the collection of Livio Odescalchi (1652–1713).[9] In those works, Rosa used a cursory penmanship clearly distinct from the exploratory designs teeming with multiple reinforcements that are typical of his later drawings.

NATHALIE STRASSER

1. Mariette 1741, p. 85: "Among the curiosities, we have great admiration for the Drawings of Salvator Rosa; a brilliant ardor, though often immoderate, has led this Painter to produce new & singular themes, which pique our taste infinitely."
2. Salvator Rosa, *Satire Terza*, lines 310–15: "vedendo che più d'un l'onora / e ch'hanno facilmente esito e spaccio / le cose che dipinge e che lavora, / del faticar più non si prende impaccio / e presa la pigrizia in enfiteusi, / dolcemente diventa un asinaccio."
3. Royal Library, Windsor (inv. 6124); Mahoney 1977, no. 24.5.
4. Staatliche Graphische Sammlung, Munich (inv. 34923); ibid., no. 25.20, with some hesitation as to the attribution.
5. Mahoney 1977, nos. 24.5, 25.20.
6. Wadsworth Atheneum and Museum of Art, Hartford, Conn. (1956.159). Salerno 1963, no. 14 (*Ritratto di Lucrezia come Sibilla*). The title used here was proposed by Wendy Roworth (1989).
7. See Salerno 1963, p. 34.
8. Teylers Museum, Haarlem (inv. E-8); Mahoney 1977, no. 24.2.
9. Ibid., nos. 38.7, 38.9, and esp. no. 38.10.

Benedetto Castiglione

33. Carlo Dolci

Florence, 1616–Florence, 1687

Young Boy in Left Profile, Eyes Raised

Ca. 1645–50

Red chalk, 7½ × 5⅝ in. (19.1 × 14.4 cm)

Inscribed in pen and brown ink on verso: *Carlin Dolci*; in pen and brown ink on verso of mounting: *F. 9. / P.*; in brown ink on verso of mounting, Lugt 1420: *N. 4[5] / 7¹ᐟ² by 5³ᐟ⁴ / fiorentino, Discepolo di Jacopo Vignali.*; in pencil on verso of mounting: *Carlo Dolci*

Stamps and marks: J. Richardson (Lugt 2183, his mounting); J. Barnard (Lugt 1419, on the mounting); W. Esdaile (Lugt 2617, on the mounting)

PROVENANCE: Jonathan Richardson Sr. (1665–1745), London; John Barnard (1709–1784), London; William Esdaile (1758–1837), London; Thomas Williams Fine Art, London; acquired by Jean Bonna, 2000

EXHIBITION: London 2000, no. 6

BIBLIOGRAPHY: Fischer 2001, p. 216, under no. 146, fig. 146a

In the Florence of Ferdinando II de' Medici (1610–1670), his wife, the grand duchess Vittoria della Rovere (1622–1694), imposed on the court an intense climate of piety and austerity. Made in that setting, the paintings of Carlo Dolci typify the period's rejection of late Mannerism's elaborate and recherché aesthetic in favor of images mirroring the Counter-Reformation's demand for religious devotion and exaltation. While the last session of the Council of Trent (December 1563) was limited to the reaffirmation of the appropriateness of religious imagery and its didactic role, and to imposing the Church's strict control over it, Cardinal Gabriele Paleotti, in his *Discorso intorno alle immagini sacre e profane* (Bologna, 1582), formulated the precepts of the "new painting." According to them, painting should "imitate truth" and offer noble and moving depictions of sacred history, a program with which Carlo Dolci's pious works are in perfect harmony.

The harsh judgments pronounced on Dolci[1] should not obscure the real qualities of his painting, in which sentimentality and smoothness express genuine feelings of devotion.[2] As such, his recurrent subjects, representative of that religiosity, often relate to childhood—Christ's, naturally, but also the childhoods of John the Baptist (the patron saint of Florence) and of the martyr saints. This predilection is exemplified in his choice of a theme such as the guardian angel, to which he returned several times.

To this author's mind, the present sheet is preparatory to his first treatment of that subject, *Guardian Angel with Boy*, executed about 1645–50 (fig. 25).[3] The Bonna drawing was probably done from life, as is indicated by the young boy's contemporary garments. It was surely intended as a religious work, for the character's expression—mouth half-open, eyes staring upward, wide and moist with emotion—indicates a mystical experience, the vision of an extraordinary event. This type of figure, emblematic of Dolci's art, appears most often in three-quarter view in his early work.[4] In the Bonna drawing, the subtle mix of realistic observation (note the precise rendering of the model's clothing and hair) with a sensitive and fervent reading of his character presents one of the fundamental characteristics of Dolci's art. The use of familiar faces in paintings, moreover, was a common practice with Dolci, who, for example, used a portrait of his wife, Teresa Bucherelli, for his portrayal of Saint Agnes in the canvas now in the Collection of Mark Fehrs Haukohl, Houston.[5]

The young boy's profile is meticulously traced in a continuous line and eschews the doubled strokes typical of Dolci's earlier studies. But its definition does not yet attain the miniaturist precision evident in a drawing such as *Portrait of the Reverend Giovanni Jacopuzzi* in the Uffizi,[6] in which the hatching is blurred to engender coloristic effects produced by a very soft mix of black and red chalks. The lips are finely curled with the white showing through, while the shading and gradations of the hair,

Figure 25. Carlo Dolci, *Guardian Angel with Boy*, ca. 1645–50. Oil on panel. Lord Methuen Collection, Corsham Court, England

which correspond precisely to those of the young companion in the painting of the *Guardian Angel with Boy* in the Lord Methuen Collection (fig. 25) are defined in small, short, diagonally brushed strokes, a favorite technique of Florentine draftsmen in the first half of the seventeenth century.

NATHALIE STRASSER

1. See McCorquodale (1973, p. 477) citing Matteo Marangoni: "Non è forse egli [Dolci] il padre di tutto l'oleografia che ammorba ancora le nostre chiese, uno di quelli che hanno contribuito a creare certa falsa e morbosa sentimentalità cattolica?"
2. See Baldassari 1995, pp. 17–31.
3. Ibid., no. 55.
4. See, for example, *Bust of a Young Saint* of 1631 (ibid., no. 6).
5. Ibid., no. 133.
6. Gabinetto Disegni e Stampe degli Uffizi, Florence (inv. 1178F).

33

34. Giovanni Battista Piazzetta

Venice, 1682–Venice, 1754

Girl with a Basket of Apples

Ca. 1735

Black chalk and charcoal highlighted with white chalk on faded blue paper, 15½ × 12⅜ in. (39.4 × 31.4 cm)

Watermark: three crescents

PROVENANCE: Henry Reitlinger; sale, Sotheby's, London, December 9, 1953, lot 76; Private Collection, Great Britain; sale, Christie's, London, July 6–7, 1987, lot 23; Galerie Jan Krugier, Geneva, 1999; acquired by Jean Bonna, 2001

EXHIBITIONS: London 1953b, no. 170; Berlin, Venice, Madrid, and Geneva 1999–2000, no. 59 (Venice), no. 64 (Madrid); Paris 2006a, no. 27; Geneva 2006–7a

BIBLIOGRAPHY: Berlin, Venice, Madrid, and Geneva 1999–2000, p. 414 (German ed.)

In addition to a limited number of mid-length figure studies in preparation for his paintings, Giovanni Battista Piazzetta created several portraits and many expressive heads on paper; these works are considered to have been autonomous and intended for discerning collectors.[1] It is most likely in the latter category that the Bonna drawing can be placed. The iconography is vaguely reminiscent of the artist's painting *Girl with a Basket of Apples* of about 1740, in the Blanton Museum of Art, Austin, Texas.[2] But most likely, this drawing illustrates Piazzetta's predilection in his drawings for rendering pleasant portraits of ordinary people living in a world of simple, natural pleasures, a genre that was little exploited in Venetian artistic circles at the time. Indeed, the painterly qualities and sensuality of Piazzetta's drawn portraits ensured his vast fame.

Piazzetta used a uniform technique in these head studies, and the many sheets portraying between one and three figures constitute a homogeneous group with a great richness of expression, a "substitute for the paintings, aiming by the complexity of their texture to compete with the absolute perfection of the painted works."[3] The artist used charcoal highlighted with white, on white or blue paper. This essentially monochromatic technique played on the use of stumping to leave details vague, on the reinforcement of certain outlines in a deeper black, and on lighting effects obtained with white chalk. While the models most likely posed for the artist, "the chiaroscuro is brought to such a subtle unity of luminous vibration, so smooth an interpretation of forms, that naturalism remains subordinated to the immediate expression of purely aesthetic values."[4]

The radiant young woman in the Bonna sheet, drawn at a scale only slightly smaller than life, is striking in the freshness and immediacy of the line quality, the rapid evocation of her garments, and the invitation offered by her sidelong glance. The image evinces a certain ambiguity, for while it appears to have been captured on the spur of the moment, it exhibits an idealization identifiable in the typology repeatedly used by Piazzetta in his faces.[5] The attraction of this drawing, then, resides in the plasticity the artist conferred on the figure and the expressiveness of her pose, rendered with no attempt to smooth out the chiaroscuro effect or soften the technique. Her hand offers a basket of apples, a formula often used by Piazzetta, whose figures hold objects such as books, animals, instruments, or flowers. The gesture helps characterize the young woman, who is probably a peasant girl hoping to charm a potential buyer into acquiring her fruit.

NATHALIE STRASSER

1. Framed under glass, these drawings were almost immediately considered finished works of art, ready "to be hung on the wall like paintings" (see Pallucchini 1961, p. 54). In some cases, however, the fact that several of the models reappear in Piazzetta's paintings raises questions about the real purpose of these drawings.
2. Mariuz 1982, no. 91.
3. Ugo Ruggeri in Brussels 1983, p. 93.
4. Pallucchini 1961, p. 52.
5. Ruggeri (in Berlin, Venice, Madrid, and Geneva 1999–2000 [English ed.], no. 59) summarized the various attempts to identify the model, including the ones by George Knox (letter of January 5, 1998), on which this author's dating is based.

34

35. Giovanni Antonio Canal (known as Canaletto)

Venice, 1697–Venice, 1768

The Mausoleum of the Emperor Diocletian at Spalatro in Dalmatia

Ca. 1760–64

Pen and brown ink, brush and gray wash (laid down),
16¾ × 13⁹⁄₁₆ in. (42.4 × 34.5 cm)

Watermark: three crescents on the mounting paper

Provenance: Private Collection, England; sale,
Christie's, London, March 19, 1975, lot 21; Private
Collection, Florence; Artemis Fine Arts, London; Peter
Jay Sharp (1930–1992), New York; C. G. Boerner, New
York; acquired by Jean Bonna, 2006

Exhibitions: Venice 1982, no. 60; New York 1994,
no. 24; Geneva 2006–7a

Bibliography: *Christie's* 1975, p. 78; Links 1977, p. 82,
pl. 122; Corboz 1985, vol. 1, pp. 230–31, fig. 295, vol. 2, no.
D232; Constable 1989, no. 856; Prijatelj 1989; McCormick
1990, p. 83, fig. 71; R. M. Mason 2007

This drawing by Canaletto reproduces a print by Francesco Bartolozzi titled *Side View of the Temple of Jupiter* (fig. 26), which appeared in the publication *Ruins of the Palace of the Emperor Diocletian at Spalatro in Dalmatia* (London, 1764), a seminal work for English Neoclassicism by the Scottish architect Robert Adam (1728–1792). Adam was in Split (Spalatro) in 1757, accompanied by Charles-Louis Clérisseau (1721–1820), a French artist whose sketches from life were engraved in Venice in 1760 to illustrate this book.

Canaletto's reproduction, however, is not entirely faithful either to the Clérisseau drawing now in the Hermitage[1] or to the print by Bartolozzi that was included in the London publication (fig. 26). The Venetian artist added two wall sections to the main monument, an adjustment that provides a more accurate view of the mausoleum's octagonal form, and he modified some of the figures in the foreground. These digressions have led critics to formulate several hypotheses concerning the iconographic source and genesis of the present drawing.

J. G. Links first posited the existence of a preparatory drawing by Clérisseau, now lost, that Canaletto might have discovered at the home of the British consul Joseph Smith, as the latter not only was a patron of his but also hosted Adam during the architect's visit to Venice.[2] Bartolozzi's engraving therefore would

have already included some of Canaletto's modifications, especially with regard to the figures.[3] The theory of a lost Clérisseau drawing also found favor with Thomas McCormick. Indeed, it is hard to imagine that an engraver of reproductions like Bartolozzi would vary from his model, and the differences between the Hermitage drawing and the print (such as the slight modifications in vantage point and foreground details) make this entirely plausible.[4] On the other hand, such a drawing would not explain all the changes in Canaletto's work.

Rainer Michael Mason, noting the similarity of format between the latter and the print, concluded that Canaletto indeed reproduced the printed image but that he added details observed during his trip to Pula and Split in Dalmatia.[5] But if Canaletto went to Split, why would he have needed someone else's drawing—still less someone else's engraving? Using available iconographic models, the mediation via prints or drawings no doubt was an element of Canaletto's creative process. But it is also known that Canaletto sometimes executed precise sketches, which he annotated in order to recall the details—as in the case of *View of Westminster*

Bridge, drawn in London (see cat. no. 36) many years earlier.

This author's opinion is that Canaletto's own intellectual process and interest in architecture led him to create this particular plan of the mausoleum, which was also published in a cutaway view in *Ruins of the Palace of the Emperor Diocletian* (plate XXVI)[6] to enliven the image. This "improvement" of the model confers on it a breadth lacking in both the engraving and Clérisseau's extant drawing. Indeed, one sees that his addition of the two walls does not closely follow the rules of perspective; to the right of the cornice, two underlying parallel lines sketch out an extension, an attempt at a perspectival projection that was abandoned. The atmosphere of the drawing is also transformed by eliminating the shadows cast by the colonnade. The viewer's eye can better embrace the building, which, although falsified, appears truer to its architectural reality, while the light amply expands the surrounding space. The undulations of the pen line, which soften the sharp angles of the mausoleum, and the washes in varying tones of gray, characteristic of the artist's technique in

Figure 26. Francesco Bartolozzi (1727–1815),
Side View of the Temple of Jupiter. Engraving
and etching, pl. XXVII in Robert Adam,
*Ruins of the Palace of the Emperor Diocletian
at Spalatro in Dalmatia*, London, 1764. The
Metropolitan Museum of Art, New York,
Bequest of W. Gedney Beatty, 1941
(41.100.176)

35

the last years of his life, perfectly modulate the luminosity of the page. Thus, Canaletto did not make a simple copy. The merging of several viewpoints into a single image—and is this not what he is doing here by showing part of the monument that was hidden from Clérisseau's eye?—fits perfectly into the artist's repertoire. It is "gymnastics of the imagination"[7] at the service of an aesthetic consideration.

NATHALIE STRASSER

1. State Hermitage Museum, Saint Petersburg (inv. 11615); see McCormick 1990, p. 83, fig. 70.
2. Links 1977, p. 82.
3. "Canaletto almost certainly worked from the preparatory study for the engraving, and it is possible that the design of the figures in this reflects that of his drawing" (note by Christie's, London, written in 1975 from comments by Links, who identified the subject). My thanks to Noel Annesley for having provided this quote.
4. McCormick 1990, pp. 83–87.
5. R. M. Mason 2007, p. 12. Dalmatia remained part of Venice until 1797.
6. And, if we remain within the circles that Canaletto frequented in Venice, why not a sketch depicting the monument under a different angle, brought back to Venice by the Adam expedition?
7. See Corboz 1985, vol. 1, pp. 241–42.

36. Giovanni Antonio Canal (known as Canaletto)

Venice, 1697–Venice, 1768

Recto: *View of the Western Arch of the Westminster Bridge in London from the Terrace of Richmond House*

Verso: *Studies of Boatmen and of a Figure Leaning against a Barrier, Sketch of a Bridge*

1747

Pen and brown ink, graphite (vertical and horizontal folds), 7⅞ × 12¹¹⁄₁₆ in. (20.2 × 32.4 cm)

Inscribed on recto by the artist in pen and brown ink: *pon. nouo / Londra*; in brown ink on various facades, rooms, and chimneys: *pieª. niª. / coto / tola / cenerª. / ccº. / tole cenª. / c. / coto uechº. / ºª. / ochª. / ocª. / cº. / onª spª. / onª sporª. / tole ueª. / B / Pionº. / cotª. / Copi / B.z. / B. zaº. / B.zº. / zaleto*; in black chalk on verso: *Sopra il picolo nò …nele: N. 5. / Canaletto Venez*

Watermark: Vryheyt (Churchill 83)

PROVENANCE: Baron Karl Eduard von Liphart (1807–1891), Florence; his sale, C. G. Boerner, Leipzig, April 26, 1898, and following days, lot 186; A. W. M. Mensing (1866–1936), Amsterdam; his sale, Frederik Muller & Co., Amsterdam, October 26, 1937, lot 38; sale, Frederik Muller & Co., Amsterdam, July 23–25, 1940, lot 407; Pieter de Boer (1896–1974), Amsterdam; Stichting Collectie P. en N. de Boer, Amsterdam; sale, Christie's, London, April 7, 1995, lot 70; Edoardo Testori, Milan; acquired by Jean Bonna, 1999

EXHIBITIONS: Paris, Rotterdam, and Haarlem 1962, no. 191; Groningen and Rotterdam 1964, no. 8; Laren 1966, no. 43; New York 1998b, no. 28; New Haven and London 2006–7, no. 22

BIBLIOGRAPHY: Watson 1950; Corboz 1985, vol. 1, p. 350, fig. 425, vol. 2, no. D109; Constable 1989, vol. 1, p. 149, pl. 142, vol. 2, no. 753; Baetjer 2002, pp. 215–20, figs. 4, 5; Frankfurt 2006–7, p. 215, fig. 1

Canaletto arrived in London in May 1746 and lived there until 1755, apart from one (or possibly two) brief sojourns in his native city of Venice in 1751. Through the British consul in Venice, Joseph Smith, the artist was introduced on May 20, 1746, to Charles Lennox, the 2nd Duke of Richmond, by Thomas Hill, the duke's former tutor.[1] But it was not until the summer of 1747 that he was granted permission to draw from the vantage point of the duke's dining room.[2] This is documented by, among others, two paintings created that year showing a view of the Thames and the Whitehall district.[3]

The present drawing was made from the terrace of Richmond House looking south. On the right are two wings of the duke's residence on the banks of the river, and on the left is the final arch of the newly built Westminster Bridge.[4] Katharine Baetjer established the exact topography of this view, which until then was mistakenly considered a view of the neighboring residence of the dukes of Montagu.[5] The issue is important, since the discrepancies vis-à-vis paintings of Old Montagu House[6] led Francis Watson to cast doubt on Canaletto's abilities as a topographer and to date the drawing from after his return to Venice.[7]

Because of similarities that occur in the abbreviated notes the artist scribbled over various parts of the composition, this sheet can be related to the meticulous sketches Canaletto made in a sketchbook that is now in the Gallerie dell'Accademia,[8] which he later used for his paintings. These annotations, first written in black chalk and then traced over in pen and ink, record in shorthand the colors ash, ocher, white, yellow (in Venetian dialect: *cenere, ochra, bianco, zaleto*), the building materials old stone, brick, wooden boards, lead, tile (in Venetian dialect: *pietra vecchia, coto, tole, piombo, copi*), and the lighting effects with dark shadow (*ombra sporca*) that he saw while observing the subject. Additionally, there is an empty space at the top of the page where the building's chimney was to occupy the foreground; the artist sketched this on the wall just below as a memory prompt. These elements suggest that Canaletto carefully studied the location on-site, perhaps in view of a painting that has since been lost.[9] Finally, the scene is entirely devoid of figures, a rare occurrence in Canaletto's work, which further indicates the purpose of the drawing.

The visible economy of shading—there is very little hatching and no trace of wash—suggests that this drawing was not meant solely

36 recto

Figure 27. Canaletto, *Capriccio with Reminiscences of Westminster Bridge and Old Montagu House*, ca. 1752-55. Pen and brown ink, brown wash, brush and gray ink on traces of black chalk. Städelsches Kunstinstitut, Frankfurt-am-Main (inv. 459)

36 verso (size reduced)

for aesthetic enjoyment. In addition, the sheet both conveys architectural information and renders the particular atmosphere of the site through various details. Canaletto drew with a freer hand here than in the Venice sketchbook; his line is more supple, and the image is embellished with a boat, tree, and statue that are most likely of his own invention. On the other hand, the known variants of this motif, generally dated from after the artist's return to Venice in 1755, are certainly *capricci*. Canaletto produced at least two other versions with significant modifications, including the addition of a Renaissance portico on the wall that shuts off the composition at the center (fig. 27)[10] or else the complete removal of the bridge and transposition of the image to the Venetian lagoon.[11] Three other drawings are known, which can probably be attributed to Canaletto's followers. These also contain variants, such as the addition of windows on the building,[12] and

each of these versions includes human figures, always different.

On the verso of the drawing are two studies of boats with their boatmen (of whom it has been said that they bitterly complained about competition from the new bridge). They are sketched on-site but are not found in exactly this form in the different versions of the drawing. There is also a quick sketch of the Westminster Bridge in its entirety.

NATHALIE STRASSER

1. See Hayes 1958, p. 345, n. 27: "The best service I thought you could do him would be to let him draw a view of the river from your dining-room."
2. See Links 1982, p. 168.
3. The Trustees of the Goodwood Collection, West Sussex; Constable 1989, nos. 424, 438.
4. The first stone of Westminster Bridge was laid in 1739, and by the time Canaletto arrived in London in 1746, the penultimate arch had been completed. However, because of the collapse of a piling in 1747, the bridge was not opened to the public until 1750. The stone bridge was replaced by a metal one in 1862.
5. Baetjer 2002.
6. Watson (1950, p. 319, n. 15) notably cites the view executed by Samuel Scott about 1749 (Dukes of Buccleuch collection, Boughton House).
7. Watson 1950, p. 319: "The drawing was in all probability made after the artist's return to Italy. . . . [It throws] an interesting light on Canaletto's technical methods and, in addition, demonstrate[s] how seldom he is to be relied on as a topographer."
8. Gallerie dell'Accademia, Venice; Constable 1989, pp. 630–40.
9. Ibid., p. 581.
10. Städelsches Kunstinstitut, Frankfurt-am-Main; ibid., no. 786.
11. Victoria & Albert Museum, London; ibid., no. 786a.
12. Ibid., no. 786b (formerly George A. Simonson Collection, London), no. 786c (British Museum, London); an additional version was reproduced in *Christie's Magazine*, May–June 2005, p. 106.

37. Francesco Guardi

Venice, 1712–Venice, 1793

View of the Grand Canal in Venice with the Churches of Santa Lucia and Santa Maria degli Scalzi

Ca. 1785

Pen and brown ink, brush and brown wash over graphite (gap in center, traces of folds), 12 11/16 × 18 3/16 in. (32.4 × 46.4 cm)

Watermark: three crescents above the word *MEZANA* (cf. Heawood 875: Venice 1785), initials *GF* topped by a crown

Stamps and Marks: Sir C. Greville (Lugt 549); Count of Warwick (Lugt 2600)

PROVENANCE: Sir Charles Greville (1763–1832), England; George Guy, 4th Count of Warwick (1818–1893); Sigismond Bardac, Paris; Hendrikus Egbertus ten Cate (1868–1955), Almelo; C. G. Boerner, London, December 1964; Pieter de Boer (1896–1974), Amsterdam; Stichting Collectie P. en N. de Boer, Amsterdam; sale, Christie's, London, April 7, 1995, lot 74; purchased at that sale by Jean Bonna

EXHIBITIONS: Laren 1966, no. 102; Geneva 2006–7a

BIBLIOGRAPHY: Morassi 1973, under no. 585; Morassi 1975, no. 386; Paris 1990, under no. 80; Venice 1993, under no. 46

In contrast to most seventeenth-century artists' preference for idealized antique landscapes with ruins in bird's-eye view, the *vedute* (topographic views) of Venice depict the city as it was at the time.[1] They portray it in panoramic view, following the rational principles of objectivity and of a precise and realistic description observed from a relatively low vantage point that corresponds to the viewer's line of sight. These images differ from simple architectural perspectives; they are embellished with figures that evoke the typical life of the Venetian lagoon. In addition to the more or less faithful record they offer, the *vedute* helped forge an immutable and timeless image of Venice. The brilliant initiator of the genre is Giovanni Antonio Canal, known as Canaletto (see cat. nos. 35, 36), who practiced it from the 1720s onward and created views of great precision. He was succeeded by his nephew

Bernardo Bellotto (1721–1780). Francesco Guardi executed his first *vedute* around 1760, in a poetic idiom that bathes his works in an evanescent light and atmosphere.

The present drawing depicts a view that is also known from at least two painted versions, one in the Museo Thyssen-Bornemisza, Madrid, and the other in the Gemäldegalerie der Akademie der Bildenden Künste (fig. 28).[2] It yields interesting documentary information, especially since the area of Venice it depicts has since been transformed. In 1861, in fact, the church of Santa Lucia (shown here on the left), the Lion-Cavazza and Bragadin-Vescovi palazzi, and the Scalzi convent were all demolished to make way for the new railway station. The construction of the Scalzi Bridge in 1858, then of an embankment on the Rio dell'Isola in 1863 (the canal whose mouth is visible at right), changed the appearance of this part of

37

Figure 28. Francesco Guardi, *View of the Grand Canal in Venice with the Churches of Santa Lucia and Santa Maria degli Scalzi*, ca. 1790–93. Oil on canvas. Gemäldegalerie der Akademie der Bildenden Künste, Vienna (inv. 604)

the Cannaregio. The vantage point used here—the Fondamenta di San Simeone Piccolo, on the opposite bank of the Grand Canal—is not original. Canaletto had painted it during the years 1730–35.[3] But borrowing from previous iconographic sources was common practice with the *vedutisti*, and Canaletto himself often made use of it. Moreover, Guardi moved his angle of vision to the left, to include the church of Santa Lucia, which does not figure in his predecessor's canvas.

The relation Morassi drew between the present drawing and the Madrid painting is mainly based on the arrangement of the gondolas, but certain details portrayed in the drawing are more closely mirrored in the Vienna version, such as the woman with a parasol sitting in a gondola, the distortion of the axis of the tower of Santa Lucia, the fluttering curtain in the church door, and the compressed framing at the left of the composition.[4] Then again, this last element might be due to the sheet's having been trimmed, something that was surely done to the right-hand margin, which is missing the "side-scene" formed by a house cloaked in shadow, although it appears in both painted versions. A drawing in the

Courtauld Gallery, London,[5] shows exactly the same features at the margins and the same proportions for the buildings at right as in the present drawing. It is in fact the same sheet, but a vertical strip was removed at an unknown time and for unknown reasons.

The École des Beaux-Arts, Paris,[6] has a drawing similar to the Bonna sheet, in which the artist has reprised the same subject without the church of Santa Lucia and which because of this, has been related to a third version of this view by Guardi.[7] Such repetitions, with their slight variations, were entirely in keeping with the artist's paintings, but they also can be found in several of his drawings; for example, he twice depicted the wooden platform and staircase erected in front of Scuola Grande di San Marco at the time of Pope Pius VI's visit to Venice in 1782.[8]

Beneath the perceptive pen work, it is easy to discern the schematic annotations in black chalk that the artist used to arrange his composition. These rapid, sometimes haphazard marks were used to record the layout of the various buildings, as well as the real or imaginary placement of such movable elements as the gondolas and the figures, some with arm

raised or chest straining over an oar. The impromptu nature of the drawing is underscored by the clear rendering of the architecture and also by the curious depiction of the two churches, their facades facing the viewer—an infraction of the laws of perspective that Guardi rectified in the Madrid canvas.

Nathalie Strasser

1. The origin of these *vedute* is normally associated with the 1695 visit to Venice by Gaspar Van Wittel, or Vanvittelli (1652 or 1653–1736). See Briganti 1966, pp. 123–27.
2. Respectively, Morassi 1973, nos. 585 and 584.
3. Constable 1989, no. 260. The 1742 edition of the *Prospectus Magni Canalis Venetiarum*, engraved by Visentini after Canaletto, contains a second view of this part of the Grand Canal, as seen from the current Piazzale Roma.
4. Byam Shaw (1977, p. 13) has noted Guardi's practice of gathering elements from different drawings and integrating them in a single work.
5. The drawing was originally from the Count Anton Seilern Collection; it is now in the Courtauld Gallery (inv. D.1978.PG.389); Morassi 1975, no. 388). My thanks to Stephanie Buck, who helped establish that the two drawings were originally on the same sheet.
6. École Nationale Supérieure des Beaux-Arts, Paris (inv. 149); Morassi 1975, no. 387; Paris 1990, no. 80.
7. Morassi 1973, no. 586.
8. Morassi 1975, nos. 274, 275.

38. Francesco Guardi
Venice, 1712–Venice, 1793

Recto: *The Court of the Ridotto in San Moisè*

Verso: *Study for a Virgin of the Immaculate Conception*

Ca. 1780–85

Recto: pen and brown ink, brush and brown wash on faded blue paper; verso: black chalk, 7⁷⁄₁₆ × 6⁵⁄₁₆ in. (18.9 × 16 cm)

Provenance: Marquis de Biron, Paris; Gérard de Loriol, Geneva and Allaman; sale, Nicolas Rauch, Geneva, June 13–15, 1960, lot 208; Erich Lederer, Geneva; sale, Galerie Kornfeld, Bern, June 17, 1987, lot 120; Day & Faber, London; acquired by Jean Bonna, 1997

Exhibitions: Venice 1962, no. 77; Venice 1965b, no. 53; Pfäffikon and Geneva 1978, no. 174; Paris 2006a, no. 28; Geneva 2006–7a

Bibliography: "Il collezionista" 1960, p. 79, ill. (recto); Fiocco 1965, p. 56, fig. 59 (recto); Morassi 1975, nos. 200 (recto), 141 (verso); Binion 1976, no. 96 (verso)

This drawing has been related to a sheet in the Musée Bonnat, Bayonne (inv. 1242)[1] that depicts the portico of the *Ridotto Pubblico* as it looked after the building's renovation was completed in 1768. In 1638, Marco Dandolo had obtained special permission to open a game parlor in his palazzo, which was located between the church of San Moisè and the Grand Canal. It was to last for the duration of the carnival. The *Ridotto* (literally, the recess), a carnival to which one was required to come masked, was also the site of lively intrigues and was shut down in 1774 in the name of public morality.

This drawing by Francesco Guardi, rendered in a fluid style in ink, offers a transient view of an imposing architectural setting in which small figures move about; their outlines are summarily indicated with pen strokes, as are the elements of the rococo décor. At first glance, the activities taking place inside hardly seem compatible with the drawing's attributed date of about 1785,[2] by which time the place had long been closed to the public. But it is not impossible that the artist sketched it at that later date, perhaps with some nostalgia;[3] Guardi often improvised in his studio scenes from memory or *capricci* of his own devising.

The precise identification of the site argues against seeing the work as a *capriccio*, even though the composition is similar to the many

38 recto

38 verso (size reduced)

Figure 29. Francesco Guardi, *Charity*, ca. 1780. Oil on panel. Bequest of John Ringling, Collection of The John and Mable Ringling Museum of Art, Florida (SN190)

sottoportici (porticos) that Morassi identified as a subset of Guardi's drawn oeuvre, the "architectonic caprices."[4] The subject was treated very often by the artist, who seemed to take extraordinary pleasure in describing these isolated bits of Venice, so different from the ample panoramic *vedute* of the city (see cat. no. 37). The small specks, or *macchiette*, used to delineate the figures give these pages a curious animation. Most of these figures have their backs turned to the viewer, and therefore to the artist, whose gaze appears quite discreet.

The drawing on the verso, consistent with that of the *Ridotto*, is a fragmentary study in black chalk that has been related to two Virgins of the Immaculate Conception that Guardi had painted previously.[5] The image has been trimmed severely at the top and is hard to read. Nonetheless, one can discern a device

similar to the one the artist used to depict the *Immacolata*. Following tradition, the figure is standing on a crescent moon with right leg forward. The broken, almost ragged line is characteristic of Guardi's later graphic technique, a typical example of which, conserved in Venice (Museo Correr [inv. 7304]), is his red chalk *Study for a Saint*.[6] Most likely, the identification of the subject was based mainly on the crescent, which forms a small horn. But the position of the legs and the angular drapery point to the greatest affinities with the *Charity* in the Ringling Museum (fig. 29),[7] which has now been dated from Guardi's late period.[8]

Nathalie Strasser

1. Morassi 1975, no. 199. The Bonna and Bonnat drawings show two opposite views of the court of the *Ridotto*.

2. Pfäffikon and Geneva 1978, p. 194.

3. Two paintings, alternately attributed to Francesco and Giovanni Antonio Guardi, and another at the Metropolitan Museum depict the interior of the *Ridotto* before it was renovated (Morassi 1973, nos. 233, 235, 236).

4. Morassi 1975, nos. 532–86.

5. Morassi 1973, nos. 196, 197.

6. Morassi 1975, no. 156; Pignatti 1983, no. 542.

7. Morassi 1973, no. 214.

8. The signature and date of 1747 were revealed to be apocryphal when the work was restored.

39

39. Francesco Guardi

Venice, 1712–Venice, 1793

View of Borgo Valsugana

1778

Pen, brown and black ink, brush and India ink wash, over traces of black chalk, 12⅜ × 21¹⁄₁₆ in. (31.4 × 53.5 cm)

Inscribed in pen and brown ink on the mounting: *View of Borgo di Val di Sugana, with the castle Giovanelli, and neighbouring mountains, between Bassano and Trent*

Watermark: (large W ?), according to Byam Shaw's remarks on the back of the frame

PROVENANCE: John Strange, England (his inscription on the mounting?); Colnaghi, London; James Byam Shaw, England; Christina Byam Shaw, England; sale, Christie's, London, July 7, 1992, lot 209; sale, Sotheby's, New York, January 25, 2002, lot 70; purchased at that sale by Jean Bonna

EXHIBITIONS: London and Birmingham 1951, no. 46; Venice 1962, no. 109; Venice 1965b, no. 47; Brussels 1983, no. 110; Paris 2006a, no. 29

BIBLIOGRAPHY: Byam Shaw 1951, under no. 31, and p. 35, n. 6; Pallucchini 1951, p. 212 (as Giacomo Guardi); Parker 1956, under no. 1015; Pallucchini 1965, p. 236 (as Giacomo Guardi); Pignatti 1967, pl. LV; New York 1971, under no. 208; Rossi Bortolatto 1974, p. 84; Morassi 1975, no. 416, and pp. 61–63; New York and Richmond 1985–86, p. 42, under no. 22

This landscape is atypical of Francesco Guardi's graphic work, not only in its subject, a small town in a mountainous region, but also in its topographical peculiarities, which are quite removed from the artist's idealized views of the Venetian lagoon and *terra ferma*. It was during a trip he made in the fall of 1778 to the Val di Sole, where his family owned property, that Guardi executed this drawing, along with two others, *View of Borgo*

Valsugana Looking East[1] and *View of Levico in Valsugana*,[2] the latter annotated in his hand. Borgo Valsugana is a town in Valsugana, one of the most important valleys of northern Italy in the province of Trento. It is here observed from a distance, perhaps from Roncegno, a village some three kilometers away.[3]

The inscription added at the bottom of the image, on the mounting, is the basis for the identification of the site. It is attributed to John Strange, "British Resident" (ambassador) in Venice from 1773 to 1788,[4] a collector and patron of Guardi's.[5] A similar caption appears on a drawing made during the same voyage that has a frontal view of the Villa Loredan,[6] the diplomat's residence, which James Byam Shaw considered the pendant of the Bonna drawing.

Guardi's views are not known for their topographical precision, something for which Strange criticized him.[7] James Byam Shaw's unpublished commentary about the present drawing, which he once owned, is illuminating; having gone to the Val di Sole, a photograph of the drawing in hand, he managed to find the artist's vantage point, which suggests a certain veracity in the depiction. The author nonetheless noted that while the acacias could still be seen along the road, the dark slope to the right of the image seems to have been the draftsman's invention.[8] Despite this discrepancy, noticed nearly two centuries after the fact, this work constitutes, along with the other views of Valsugana cited above, a rare example of a Guardi drawing realized in front of the subject. This does not rule out the possibility that Guardi first might have sketched the landscape spontaneously on-site, then copied it onto this larger sheet. The curiousness of the subject nonetheless differentiates it from his

works produced in the studio, either from memory or after engravings, as was sometimes the case with Guardi's Venetian *vedute*.

On a different note, Antonio Morassi pointed out that "the precision of the drawing, the finished quality of all the details, the transparency of the sails and the luminosity of the landscape make this drawing a work complete unto itself."[9] The tight geometric marks that describe the houses of the village, contrasting with the generous washes that fill in the raised perspective of the mountains (there are analogies here with Chinese landscapes), enhance a graphic lyricism that stands out among Francesco Guardi's works on paper. The quality of these India ink washes, moreover, was the basis for the reattribution of the drawing to Guardi, after Rodolfo Pallucchini had instead affirmed that it was by his son Giacomo (1764–1835).[10]

NATHALIE STRASSER

1. Morassi 1975, no. 417 (sale, Christie's, London, July 6, 2004, lot 84).
2. Morassi 1975, no. 418 (Thaw Collection, Morgan Library & Museum New York).
3. See Venice 1962, p. 78.
4. See Byam Shaw 1951, p. 66; and Parker 1956, p. 510.
5. See Haskell 1960, pp. 268–70.
6. Morassi 1975, no. 423 (Ashmolean Museum, Oxford). A very beautiful drawing, also depicting the Loredan Villa, is in The Metropolitan Museum of Art (37.165.69); see Morassi 1975, no. 422; and Bean and Griswold 1990, no. 93.
7. See Haskell 1960, p. 269.
8. These comments were written on the back of the frame: "The dark slope in fg. R, beyond the road, seems to be an invention of the draughtsman. Acacia trees still [along] the road (R. fg) toward Trento."
9. Morassi 1975, p. 153, under no. 416: "L'accuratezza del disegno, rifinito in ogni suo particolare, la trasparenza delle velature e la luminosità del paesaggio fanno di questo foglio già un'opera pittorica compiuta."
10. "In 1778 Giacomo was only 14 years old. P[allucchini] was no doubt misled by the Indian ink wash which is unusual for Francesco, but far superior in quality to the heavy handed black ink wash of Giacomo" (commentary by Byam Shaw on the back of the frame).

40. Giovanni Domenico (Giandomenico) Tiepolo

Venice, 1727–Venice, 1804

Three Punchinellos on Horseback

Ca. 1797

Pen and brown ink, brush and brown wash, over traces of black chalk, framing line in brown ink, 14⅛ × 18¹¹⁄₁₆ in. (35.8 × 47.4 cm)

Inscribed on recto in pen and brown ink at top left: *59;* and at lower right: *Domᵒ Tiepolo f*

Watermark: letters *GAF* in a heart surmounted by leaves

PROVENANCE: sale, Sotheby's, London, July 6, 1920, one of 103 drawings in lot 41; Colnaghi, London; Richard Owen, Paris; Madame H. Lapauze, Paris; Katrin Bellinger Kunsthandel, Munich; acquired by Jean Bonna, 2002

EXHIBITIONS: Musée des Arts Décoratifs, Paris, 1921 (no catalogue); Bloomington, Stanford, and New York 1979–80, no. s32; Udine and Bloomington 1996–97, no. 59 (see also p. 188, under no. 120); Paris 2006a, no. 31; Geneva 2006–7a

BIBLIOGRAPHY: Byam Shaw 1962; Knox 1983, p. 145, no. 59; Gealt 1986a, no. 98; Gealt 1986b, no. 98

Among the series of engravings and drawings by Giandomenico Tiepolo, the one titled "*Divertimento per li Regazzi*" (*Entertainment for Children*), featuring Punchinello, is the last one made by the artist, who was seventy years old. The present drawing belongs to that group, comprising 103 drawings and a title page, which was dispersed shortly after its sale at Sotheby's in July 1920 and its exhibition at the Musée des Arts Décoratifs, Paris, in 1921.[1] By all accounts, it was begun about 1797, after Giandomenico had finished decorating the family villa in Zianigo, at the time when the republic of Venice disappeared forever, following the Napoleonic invasion.

Punchinello is a lead character in the Commedia dell'arte and was caricaturesque for his appearance and behavior. He was humpbacked, potbellied, saddled with a huge nose, and his grotesque character traits of gluttony and fecklessness left wide latitude for the

improvisational genius of the actors playing him. While he was already a frequent figure in the work of Giambattista[2] and of his son Giandomenico (in Zianigo and elsewhere), the tone of the *Divertimento*, which narrates Punchinello's adventures, joys, and sorrows from his birth to his demise, affects a notable modulation of the character by illustrating the pathetic actions of a paladin from a bygone era.

The 104 pages of the illustrated series display a uniformity of dimensions, technique, and execution, as is the case in the series of eighty-six Scenes from Contemporary Life that Giandomenico realized about 1791. The finished drawings were sketched first in black chalk, then reprised in pen and ink to sharpen the outlines of the figures and certain architectural details, and finally modeled with brown washes of varying shades. Brushed on fairly generously, these washes are jagged when their role is to emphasize the lighting of a scene and

40

abstracted to indicate distant backgrounds. Dressed and coiffed in a white costume that readily attracts light, the Punchinellos that populate these drawings always stand out amid an animated crowd of people and various animals. The draftsman was more interested in anecdotal details than in refining his forms, and he infinitely varied poses and scenes (dances, meals, games, labors, exotic voyages) with an inventiveness that often makes it difficult to interpret the subject of the work.

Despite the great attention paid to this "last masterpiece of Venetian figurative culture,"[3] the series still remains in part a mystery. On the one hand, the artist's own numbering at the top of the sheets encourages the view that they form a narrative and chronological ensemble;[4] on the other, certain inconsistencies in the story line have led some art historians to rearrange the sequence and offer new interpretations.

For instance, Marcia Vetrocq saw this as a collection of drawings using a common theme, with little concern for dramatic progression and numbered after the fact.[5] Adelheid Gealt considered the episodes interchangeable, permitting various narrations within a general framework.[6] Finally, George Knox, finding in the ensemble elements relating to the lives of Giandomenico and his father, Giambattista, saw the series as the "artistic testament" of an artist-creator at the end of his career.[7]

In addition to the shared characteristics cited above, each drawing in the series has multiple figures of Punchinello, in a troubling game of mirrors that undermines attempts to identify the hero in the masked crowd. This is true of the Bonna drawing, in which three horsemen wear identical masks with hooked noses and conical caps, and one of them holds a crop. Is he the real protagonist of the scene? The composition closely follows the motif of a slightly earlier drawing by Giandomenico,[8] in which the horsemen wear civilian clothes. There, only the man mounted on a rearing steed is shown fully lit. The transposition of

the group into masquerade costumes leads to the possibility that in the guise of entertainment, the aging artist was "using Punchinello to make fun of his contemporaries, and even more so of himself"[9]—much like Goya, who in the same period was delivering his *caprichos* for publication.[10]

NATHALIE STRASSER

1. On the entire series, see Byam Shaw 1962; Bloomington, Stanford, and New York 1979–80; Knox 1983; Gealt 1986a; Gealt 1986b; and Udine and Bloomington 1996–97. The Paris exhibition of 1921 has no accompanying publication. The catalogue of the show for the bicentennial of Giandomenico Tiepolo's death (Venice 2004) is largely devoted to the figure of Punchinello.
2. See Knox 1984.
3. Adriano Mariuz in Venice 2004, p. 55.
4. See Byam Shaw 1962.
5. Bloomington, Stanford, and New York 1979–80, pp. 19–21.
6. Gealt 1986a, pp. 15–16.
7. Knox 1983, p. 130.
8. See Udine and Bloomington 1996–97, no. 120.
9. Pierre Rosenberg in Gealt 1986b, p. 9.
10. See Stephan 1996, p. 2129.

41. Master of Liechtenstein

Documented 1549–1550

Recto: *Christ Carrying the Cross*

Verso: *The Resurrection*

Ca. 1550

Pen and brown ink, brush and brown ink, heightened with white body-color, on brown and pink prepared paper; verso: pen and black ink, heightened with white body-color and yellow watercolor, 9⁷⁄₁₆ × 12⁵⁄₁₆ in. (24 × 31.2 cm)

Inscribed on verso in pen and light brown ink in a sixteenth- or seventeenth-century handwriting at lower right: *Deis quy sta in cielo // Jaques de fletres*; inscribed in pen and dark brown ink, in the same hand below: *Asses va Quy la fortune pasz[…] / Coen [?] int Beghinnen ghestadich int Volenden[…] / / Beminde / / […] Reliose*

PROVENANCE: Private Collection, New York; acquired by Jean Bonna, 2000

EXHIBITION: Paris 2008, no. 3

This drawing is an important addition to the work of one of the most outstanding Northern artists of the mid-sixteenth century, the enigmatic Master of Liechtenstein,[1] who was named after a group of at least eleven drawings formerly in the princely collections in Vaduz and sold prior to 1950.[2] About twenty drawings[3] and one etching[4] now have been attributed to this artist, and they comprise an oeuvre that is stylistically as coherent as it is puzzling. This confusion is well exemplified by the diversity of names once associated with the Master: the Netherlandish artists Jan van Scorel, Pieter Coecke van Aelst, Cornelis Floris, and Lancelot Blondeel; the French Jean

Cousin the Elder; the Danish Melchior Lorck; the German Hermann tom Ring; and more. An additional link to Germany exists, since at least five drawings by this artist have inspired woodcuts in Virgil Solis's series *Biblische Figuren des Alten und Neuen Testaments* (Frankfurt 1560 and 1562).[5] The drawings themselves must have been made some ten years earlier, as two are dated 1549 and 1550.[6]

In many ways, the recto of the present sheet is typical of the drawings by the Master. Most of them were made on tinted paper, many—although not the present one—on sheets of a very striking red or violet hue. All the drawings depict biblical scenes.[7] This one

41 recto

is the only known representation of Christ carrying the cross, but some other scenes are known in several versions, which seems to rule out the possibility that all the drawings were commissioned by a single patron, as has been suggested.[8] The careful execution of the Master's drawings, to which the washes and highlights in white body-color lend great plasticity, certainly suggests that they were produced as finished works of art. The intricate and highly theatrical compositions and figures mainly seem to show the influence of Pieter Coecke van Aelst (the facial types, muscular bodies, and pointed feet) and possibly also a direct influence of Raphael's tapestry cartoons for the Apostle series, which were sent to Flanders in 1516 to be woven in Brussels.[9] Other peculiarities, such as the colored paper and the way the vegetation is depicted, have been explained as borrowings from artists of the Danube school. The backdrops of most of the drawings are composed of mountainous landscapes and architecture of antique inspiration.

More than the recto of the Bonna drawing, the verso offers hints at the origins and milieu of the Master of Liechtenstein that had not been noticed before.[10] The larger part of the back is occupied by a Resurrection within an ornamental border, apparently a design for a tapestry. Although this sketch is very different in style from the drawing on the recto, it most probably was made by the same hand as the rapidly drawn tuft of greenery at lower left, which is almost certainly by the artist responsible for the drawing on the recto (compare the vegetation on Calvary). It is difficult to detect any Flemish influence in the Resurrection, which is closer to Italian examples, such as certain sketches by Nicolò dell'Abate, especially some he made during his years of activity in Fontainebleau.[11] On the other hand, the strapwork used in the border design is certainly influenced by Flemish examples, most notably Cornelis Floris. The polyglotism of the inscriptions—three sayings in Italian, French, and Dutch, a French name, and two isolated words of which at least one is in Dutch—also makes it more probable that they were written by a well-traveled Fleming than by a German. At the very least, the inscriptions indicate that the sheet is more likely to have had an early history in France or Flanders than in Germany.

In fact, the mention of both dell'Abate and Floris, both of whose styles were very influential among artists at the court of Fontainebleau, should make one wonder if the Master could not have been part of its international artistic community at some point. Many of his drawings invite comparison with works by such artists as Léonard Thiry (a Fleming, but active in Fontainebleau from approximately 1535 to 1545) or with certain drawings attributed to Étienne Delaune.[12] Without intending to marginalize the influence of German art on the Master's style, it should be noted that at least some of the Master's features, such as the drooping vegetation[13] and the hollow (or black) eyes, can also be explained by his knowledge of the works made by artists at Fontainebleau. The Bonna drawing certainly attests to the complexity of the artistic personality of the Master of Liechtenstein. That stylistic complexity is one of the artist's most essential characteristics, and our inability to unravel the influences that inspired him is a tribute to his skill and originality.

Stijn Alsteens

1. On the Master of Liechtenstein, see Stuttgart 1979–80, vol. 2, pp. 170–72; Munich 1989–90, pp. 54–56; Boon 1992, vol. 1, pp. 499–503; and the literature quoted below.

2. Benesch 1930, p. 80. The artist is sometimes also called the Master of the Liechtenstein Adoration (for example, in Washington and New York 1986–87, p. 226). The Liechtenstein collection counted two Epiphanies, one now in the Frits Lugt Collection, Paris (inv. 6007; Boon 1992, vol. 1, no. 292, vol. 3, pl. 304), and an Adoration of the Shepherds, now in The Metropolitan Museum of Art, New York, Purchase, Rogers Fund (63.8); Winkler 1963, p. 35, pl. 27).

3. For drawings by the Master in addition to those mentioned in Winkler 1963, see Wegner 1970, pp. 264–65, fig. 182; and Boon 1992, vol. 1, p. 500, n. 1, under no. 292, p. 502, n. 5, under no. 293. A drawing in the sale at Christie's, Paris, March 21, 2002, lot 191, is probably a copy after a composition by the Master known in two autograph versions, both in The Metropolitan Museum of Art, New York: 63.8 (see the drawing mentioned in note 2 above) and 2007.73 (previously in the sale at Hôtel Drouot, Paris, May 23, 2007, lot 91); another variant of the composition was in the sale at Christie's, London, December 11–13, 1985, as part of lot 330 (see Boon 1992, vol. 1, p. 502, n. 5, under no. 292).

4. The probable relationship between the print and the drawings by the Master was first mentioned by Wolfgang Wegner in 1970. The print bears the unidentified monogram SAF or SA (if the F stands for fecit), which could indicate either the Master's name or that of the printmaker working after a design by the Master. Both impressions in the Rijksprentenkabinet,

Rijksmuseum, Amsterdam (inv. RP-P-1975-35, RP-P-OB-2125) have a German watermark (compare, for example, Briquet 15922). Wegner also attributes a painting to the artist in the Muzeum Narodowe w Poznaniu, Poznań (inv. 1024); Wegner 1970, pp. 265–66, fig. 185.

5. The Adoration of the Magi in the Frits Lugt Collection, Paris (inv. 6007; see note 2 above), a Circumcision of which the present whereabouts are unknown (sale, Sotheby's, London, July 5, 2000, lot 25; with Galerie Sabrina Förster, Düsseldorf, in 1992), and a drawing representing Christ among the Doctors, also in the Frits Lugt Collection (inv. 6008; Boon 1992, vol. 1, no. 293, vol. 2, pl. 305), correspond, loosely and in reverse, to woodcuts by Solis (Hollstein 1954–, vol. 66 [2006], nos. 14.109, 14.112, 19.112, ill.). It had not yet been noticed that the Adoration of the Shepherds in the *Biblische Figuren* (Hollstein 1954–, vol. 66 [2006], no. 14.111, ill.) is most closely related to the drawing mentioned in note 3 above, which was sold at auction in 1985. Many more prints in Solis's series must have been inspired by compositions by the Master of Liechtenstein, as is for instance evident in the case of Solis's *Presentation of Christ in the Temple* (Hollstein 1954–, vol. 66 [2006], no. 14.113). Joseph Meder recognized that two drawings at the university library in Erlangen (Bock 1929, nos. 485, 486) are related to the two drawings now in the Lugt Collection; two groups of ten and five drawings, also in Erlangen (Bock 1929, nos. 487–96, 497–501, ill.), are most likely also based on works by the Master. The exact relationship of these seventeen drawings with the woodcuts by Solis has not yet satisfactorily been explained (pace Stuttgart 1979–80, vol. 2, p. 170; see also Boon 1992, vol. 1, p. 502, n. 4, under no. 292).

6. Rijksmuseum, Rijksprentenkabinet (inv. RP-T-1948-384; Boon 1978, vol. 1, no. 517, vol. 2, ill. p. 198); Staatliche Graphische Sammlung, Munich (inv. 7790), inscribed "A 1550 / 20 sebtember" (Munich 1989–90, no. 43, pl. 29).

7. If accepted, the only exception in the Master's oeuvre would be the painting in Poznań (see note 4 above), which represents the Rape of Hippodamea.

8. Stuttgart 1979–80, p. 170. This is particularly obvious in the case of the two drawings in the Metropolitan Museum (see notes 2 and 3 above), which are very similar and should both be considered autograph.

9. For a direct borrowing by the Master from one of Raphael's cartoons, see John Oliver Hand in Washington and New York 1986–87, p. 227, under no. 86.

10. I am grateful to Tom Campbell, Peter Fuhring, and Catherine Jenkins for discussing the drawing with me.

11. See, for example, the drawings in the Biblioteca Marucelliana, Florence (inv. B 19; Sylvie Béguin in Modena 2005, no. 112a–c, ill.), and in the Musée du Louvre, Départment des Arts Graphiques, Paris (inv. 5877, 5839, RF 31923; Béguin in Modena 2005, nos. 221, 223, 224a, ill.).

12. See, for instance, drawings by Léonard Thiry and attributed to Étienne Delaune in the École Nationale Supérieure des Beaux-Arts, Paris (inv. 386, M 808–M 810, M 1230–M 1233; Paris, Cambridge, and New York 1994–95, nos. 32–35, 38–41, ill.).

13. Compare Held 1974, pp. 87–88, n. 24.

42. Hans Speckaert

Brussels, ca. 1540–Rome, 1577

An Unidentified Scene

Ca. 1560s

Pen and brown ink, brown-yellow wash, 8⅜ × 10⁹⁄₁₆ in.
(21.1 × 26.8 cm)

Watermark: coat of arms with letter *M* (compare
Woodward 1996, nos. 314–37)

Provenance: Sale, Sotheby Mak van Waay,
Amsterdam, April 25, 1983, lot 4; Private Collection,
United Kingdom; Thomas Williams Fine Art, London;
acquired by Jean Bonna, 2003

Exhibition: Paris 2008, no. 12

Bibliography: Široká 1995, vol. 1, no. A2; Široká 1997,
p. 138, fig. 7

Hans Speckaert played a decisive role in
the development of late sixteenth-
century Netherlandish art, although he
gained influence mainly through the works
of Bartholomeus Spranger, who became
acquainted with Speckaert's work in Rome,
where Speckaert can be supposed to have been
active since the 1560s and where he must have
died about 1577.[1] Very little is known about his
life, and very few works, if any, can be attributed to him securely. No signed drawings by
Speckaert are known,[2] and only four or five
paintings have been accepted as autograph,[3]
leaving a small group of prints after him as
the touchstones for all attributions.[4]

Nonetheless, the drawings attributed to
him generally provide a clear idea of Speckaert's
compositions and drawing style. They are dominated by robust and muscular figures in elegant
and contorted poses and are heavily inspired by
Italian examples (among others by Parmigianino,
Polidoro da Caravaggio, and the Zuccari).[5] In
addition, they are characterized by exaggerated
forms caught in imaginative lines, with heavy
washes indicating shadow in a rather general
manner and accentuated by groupings of parallel
hatching. However recognizable his style may
be, attributions are complicated by the existence of several versions of some of Speckaert's
compositions. Although it must be considered
that Speckaert himself made repetitions and
variations of some of his drawings, it is clear
that many of them are copies, a factor that

attests to his popularity and influence. At least
two renowned artists—Joseph Heintz the
Elder[6] and Hendrick de Clerck[7]—are known
to have made such copies, and in 1585, Hans von
Aachen signed a drawing that must be either a
copy after Speckaert or a composition of von
Aachen's own invention in Speckaert's style.[8]

The drawing in the Bonna collection,
which can be compared to an early drawing by
Speckaert in Stuttgart,[9] has defied all attempts
at the identification of its subject.[10] Its composition is known from three other versions, in
the Staatliche Graphische Sammlung, Munich
(fig. 30), in the Wallraf-Richartz Museum
(fig. 31), and one about which the present
whereabouts are unknown (fig. 32).[11] The
drawing in Cologne seems weaker and is possibly much later in date, but at least the drawing in Munich is of high quality and was formerly published as an authentic work.[12]
Indeed, it faithfully and sensitively reproduces
almost every pen line or brushstroke, including
the pentimenti, of the drawing in the Bonna
collection, as well as its striking yellow tinted
paper. It seems probable that it originates
from Speckaert's immediate circle. Only a
direct comparison of the drawing in Munich
with the reassured yet thin and lively lines of
the drawing under consideration here can
make clear just how subtle the distinction

between an original by Speckaert and a copy
can be.

Stijn Alsteens

1. For Speckaert, see Široká 1997, which also lists earlier
literature, and other articles referred to here. For a discussion of Speckaert's influence on Spranger, see
Oberhuber 1958, pp. 60–63, 75, where reference is made
to the drawing after Speckaert reproduced here as fig. 32.

2. A drawing in the Szépművészeti Múzeum in Budapest
(inv. 1916-34; Gerszi 1971, vol. 1, no. 227, vol. 2, ill. p. 124)
is in fact a work by Karel van Mander, and the "signature" is nothing more than an old attribution as was
recently recognized by Gerszi (in Paris 2008–9, p. 126,
under no. 60; see also Široká 1995, vol. 1, no. F15).

3. For Speckaert's paintings, see Béguin 1973 and, more
recently, Giltaij 1993, where only four are accepted.

4. Wurzbach 1906–11, vol. 2, p. 645.

5. For a discussion of the Italian influences on Speckaert's
style, see Gerszi 1968; Béguin 1973; and Široká 1995.

6. See the drawing signed and inscribed "Joseph Heintz
nach Speeckaert [. . .] Rom 85," acquired in 1996 by
The Metropolitan Museum of Art, New York, Purchase,
Anne and Jean Bonna Gift, 1996 (1996.52); Široká 1997,
pp. 138–39, fig. 8.

7. See Kloek 1997, pp. 155–56. Apart from the drawing
mentioned there (a sheet in the Rijksmuseum,
Rijksprentenkabinet, Amsterdam (inv. RP-T-1961-04;
Boon 1978, vol. 1, no. 416, vol. 2, ill. p. 160), other drawings
kept under Speckaert's name for which the authorship of
De Clerck should be considered are in the Graphische
Sammlung Albertina, Vienna (inv. 3293; Benesch 1928,
no. 285, pl. 75), in the Frits Lugt Collection, Paris (inv. 2335;
Boon 1992, vol. 1, no. 187, vol. 2, pl. 114), and formerly on
the German art market (Valentiner 1932, p. 169, fig. 134).

8. Städelsches Kunstinstitut, Frankfurt-am-Main (inv.
14268), inscribed "dasz hab ich hans von aachen

Figure 30. Anonymous artist after Hans Speckaert,
Unidentified Scene. Pen and brown ink, yellow-
green wash. Staatliche Graphische Sammlung,
Munich (inv. 7083)

Figure 31. Anonymous artist after Hans Speckaert,
Unidentified Scene. Wallraf-Richartz Museum &
Fondation Corboud, Cologne (inv. 1367)

42

gemacht zu guden gedechtniss mein guden gesellen hans holtzma[yr?] zu Venetia den 24. September a o 1585"; Schilling 1973, vol. 1, no. 1, vol. 2, pl. 1.

9. Graphische Sammlung, Staatsgalerie, Stuttgart (inv. C 83/3332); Široká 1997, pp. 134–35, fig. 1.

10. The two boys in the foreground reminded Peter Dreyer of the Christ Child and Saint John the Baptist (unpublished and undated note; copy in the archives of Jean Bonna).

11. For the drawing in Munich, see Wegner 1973, vol. 1, no. 107, vol. 2, pl. 44; and Široká 1995, vol. 1, no. C19. For the drawing in Cologne, see Široká 1995, vol. 1, no. C10. The drawing reproduced in fig. 3 was in the sale at Lempertz, Cologne, May 20, 2000, lot 894. The connection between the drawings in Munich and Cologne and the sheet in the Bonna collection was already made by Teréz Gerszi (quoted in the 1983 sale catalogue listed in the Provenance).

12. Valentiner 1932, p. 168, fig. 133. Teréz Gerszi (1968, p. 161, n. 4) has doubted the attribution, even implying that it has no relation at all to Speckaert's work.

Fig. 32. Anonymous artist after Hans Speckaert, *Unidentified Scene*. Pen and brown ink, gray wash, over a sketch in black chalk. Present whereabouts unknown

43. Hans Hoffmann

Nuremberg, ca. 1545–1550–Prague, 1591 or 1592

A Wild Boar Piglet (Sus Scrofa)

1578

Watercolor and body-color on vellum, 11¹³⁄₁₆ × 17¹⁵⁄₁₆ in. (30 × 45.5 cm)

Monogrammed and dated in pen and black ink at lower center: *Hh. / 1578.*

PROVENANCE: Private Collection; Sayn-Wittgenstein Fine Art, New York; acquired by Jean Bonna, 2004

EXHIBITIONS: London 2002–3, no. 225; Paris 2008, no. 5

Some forty years after the death of Albrecht Dürer in 1528, a renewed interest in his art resulted in what is known as the Dürer Renaissance, which originated in Nuremberg, the city where the artist worked for most of his life.[1] It is a testimony to the formidable scope of Dürer's oeuvre that the most well-known artist of that renaissance, Hans Hoffmann, based his reputation on just one aspect of Dürer's work, his depictions of plants and animals. Although Hoffmann is also known as a painter and draftsman of portraits and religious subjects, he is best remembered for his studies of those subjects.[2] Some of them are direct copies after originals by Dürer, but many, such as Hoffmann's study of a small piece of turf,[3] are variations on or works inspired by Dürer's power of observation and superior technique in the rendering of nature. Hoffmann was able to study Dürer's drawings during his years of activity in Nuremberg (where he was probably born), especially in the collections of the Imhoff family and of Paulus Praun.[4] The Imhoff Collection, assembled by the merchant Willbald Imhoff, counted two studies of a hare by Dürer, including the famous drawing in the Albertina, Vienna, still known today,[5] as well as two studies of a hare by Hoffmann. At least four other representations of hares by Hoffmann are known, including a painting he made for Rudolf II (who also owned Dürer's hare, now in the Albertina).[6] Rudolf, one of the foremost collectors in Europe around 1600, was a great admirer of Dürer, and it should therefore not be surprising that in 1585, he invited Hoffmann to his court in Prague, where the artist stayed until the end of his life.

The irresistible drawing of a wild boar piglet in the Bonna collection counts among Hoffmann's most beautiful original animal studies, comparable in quality to a study of a red squirrel in the National Gallery of Art also dated 1578 (fig. 33).[7] The same can be said of a study of a hedgehog (*Erinaceus europaeus roumanicus*) in The Metropolitan Museum of Art, which may date from about the same time (fig. 34).[8] The latter drawing is not signed, unlike the drawings of the squirrel and that of the piglet in the Bonna collection, which probably were kept framed in a cabinet of a *Wunderkammer*. One of Hoffmann's studies of a hare in the Imhoff Collection is recorded as originally "in Ebenholtz mitt silber geziehrt eingefast" (in an ebony frame, decorated with silver).[9] In addition to the marvelous and extremely detailed depiction of the fur and quills, the three animals share the "shiny amber-colored eyes" typical for Hoffmann.[10]

Especially in his studies of the piglet and the hedgehog, Hoffmann animated his works by slightly narrowing the eyes of the animals depicted, suggesting in an almost comical way a human alertness absent from the nature studies by Dürer, who tended to stress the objectivity of his observation.

STIJN ALSTEENS

1. For the Dürer Renaissance, see Mende 1996.
2. For Hoffmann, see Vienna 1985, p. 275 and passim; and Bodnár 1996 (with bibliography). For some of his portraits and head studies after Dürer, see Katrin Achilles-Syndram in Nuremberg 1994, nos. 60–65, 171.
3. The Metropolitan Museum of Art, New York (1997.20); Vienna 1985, no. 65, ill.
4. For the Imhoff Collection, see ibid., pp. 261–66, and passim; and Smith 1996 (with bibliography). For Praun, see Vienna 1985, p. 267, and passim; Achilles-Syndram in Nuremberg 1994; and Achilles-Syndram 1994.
5. Graphische Sammlung Albertina, Vienna (inv. 3073); Vienna 1985, no. 43, ill., and see also p. 132.
6. J. Paul Getty Museum, Los Angeles (2001.12); ibid., no. 49, ill. For other studies of hares by Hoffmann, see ibid., p. 132, nos. 47–49, 52, 53, ill. An unpublished copy by Hoffmann after Dürer's drawing, signed and dated 1582 and formerly in the Kunsthalle Bremen, was at Lempertz, Cologne, May 17, 2008, lot 1081.
7. Vienna 1985, no. 27, ill.
8. Another comparable study of a crouching cat was at Christie's, London, July 6, 2006, lot 67.
9. Document quoted in Vienna 1985, p. 264.
10. Ibid., p. 172, under nos. 59, 60.

Figure 33. Hans Hoffmann, *Red Squirrel*, 1578. Watercolor and gouache over traces of graphite on vellum. National Gallery of Art, Washington, D.C. (1991.182.5)

43

Figure 34. Hans Hoffmann, *A Hedgehog*. Watercolor and gouache on vellum. The Metropolitan Museum of Art, New York, Purchase, Annette de la Renta Gift, 2005 (2005.347)

44. Hendrick Goltzius

Bracht, 1558–Haarlem, 1617

The Rest of Venus and Adonis

1600

Pen and brown ink, brown wash, heightened with white body-color, on brown prepared paper, 7¹¹/₁₆ × 5 in. (19.6 × 12.7 cm)

Signed and dated in pen and brown ink at lower right: *HGoltzius* [*HG* as a monogram] / *Ao 1600*

PROVENANCE: Sale, Sotheby's, Amsterdam, November 18, 1985, lot 14; Frederick Koch, New York; sale, Sotheby's, London, November 15, 1995, lot 74; purchased at that sale by Jean Bonna

EXHIBITIONS: Philadelphia 1991–92; Paris 2008, no. 8

BIBLIOGRAPHY: Nichols 1992, pp. 27, 49, n. 86, fig. 26; Reznicek 1993, p. 217, no. K122a, fig. 34

This delicately sensual drawing is a relatively recent addition to the extensive drawn oeuvre of Hendrick Goltzius, and it surpasses that of most other sixteenth- and seventeenth-century Dutch artists in quality, number, and scope.[1] The great international fame that Goltzius enjoyed by the late 1580s, when he was not yet thirty years old, was based on his work as a virtuoso engraver, but his contemporaries also admired him for his drawings. He tried his hand at almost any genre, and he excelled both in the Northern Mannerist style of the late sixteenth century and in the realism that became the hallmark of seventeenth-century Dutch art. For inspiration, he drew on the antique, on the old masters (both Northern, such as Albrecht Dürer and Lucas van Leyden, and Italian, such as Michelangelo and Polidoro da Caravaggio), on the art of countrymen and contemporaries such as Bartholomeus Spranger and Karel van Mander, and also on studies he made from nature.

The dogs and trees in the drawing in the Bonna Collection are certainly based on studies from life,[2] but this is foremost a mythological scene, illustrating a passage from the tenth book of Ovid's *Metamorphoses* (lines 529–59), in which Venus's son, Cupid, "chanced unwittingly to graze her breast with a projecting arrow" and made her "prefer Adonis to heaven."[3] Although the goddess's "wont has always been

to take her ease in the shade, and to enhance her beauty by fostering it," she follows her mortal lover's passion for hunting, until she is tired and rests with Adonis under the shade of a "poplar, happily at hand" on a "grassy turf for couch." Merely referring to the preceding hunt by the inclusion of a horn, a spear, and four hunting dogs, Goltzius chose this moment of rest to depict how Venus "reclined upon the ground and on him, pillowing her head against his breast and mingling kisses with her words."

The Bonna drawing, dated 1600, is among several prints and drawings of mythological themes (most of them involving the goddess of love) that Goltzius started making about 1590. Among the drawings, the most exceptional are the so-called *pen-wercken* (pen works)[4] or *Federkunststücke*, some executed on parchment or canvas. Like the drawing in the Bonna Collection, they were intended as finished works of art and were the pride of some of the most celebrated collections of the period, including

that of the emperor Rudolf II. However, they differ from the Bonna drawing in technique; in the pen works, the pen imitates the hatching and the swelling lines of Goltzius's celebrated engraving style, whereas in the Bonna drawing, the pen lines mostly outline the composition, and the modeling is added with wash and white body-color, as Goltzius also did in another drawing in the Bonna Collection, an allegory of Faith, dated 1609 and drawn on prepared panel.[5]

The Rest of Venus and Adonis was a popular theme from the sixteenth to the eighteenth century, particularly for artists at the Prague court of Rudolf II, who had a particular liking for sensual subjects.[6] Goltzius must have known at least some of these works, but as Johan Bosch van Rosenthal was first to note,[7] the artist borrowed the position of Venus's arm, the intertwining of the lovers' legs, and the shaded location of their lovemaking from a pair of nymphs in an engraving by Agostino Carracci after a composition by his brother

Figure 35. Agostino Carracci after Annibale Carracci, *Omnia Vincit Amor*. Engraving. The Metropolitan Museum of Art, New York, Harris Brisbane Dick Fund, 1917 (17.3.1853)

44

Figure 36. Hendrick Goltzius, *A Pair of Lovers*. Black and red chalk on buff paper. Van Regteren Altena Collection, Amsterdam

3. The translation quoted is that of Frank Justus Miller (Ovid 1976–77, vol. 2, pp. 101–3). I see no reason to believe that Cupid's arrow is "intended to be the deadly arrow with a dull lead tip" (Reznicek 1993, p. 217, no. K122a), mentioned by Ovid in the story of Apollo and Daphne (*Metamorphoses* 1.471).

4. The Dutch word was applied to Goltzius's drawings of this type by Karel van Mander; see Van Mander 1604, fol. 285; and Van Mander 1604 (1994–99 ed.), vol. 1, pp. 400, 401. For the *pen-wercken*, see Nichols 1992; and Huigen Leeflang in Amsterdam, New York, and Toledo 2003–4, pp. 235–63.

5. Reznicek 1993, no. K95a, fig. 23.

6. See Kaufmann 1988, nos. 7.43 (by Joseph Heintz), 16.11 (by Dirck de Quade van Ravesteyn), 20.43, 20.63, and 20.90 (by Bartholomeus Spranger), ill. p. 286, under no. 22 (by Hans Strohmayer).

7. Quoted in Reznicek 1993 (see Bibliography).

8. Bartsch 1803–21, vol. 15 (1813), pp. 103–4, no. 116; DeGrazia 1979, no. 210, ill. A pair of lovers in a similar pose to that in the print occurs in another engraving by Agostino from slightly earlier (Bartsch 1803–21, vol. 15 [1813], pp. 105–6, no. 119; DeGrazia 1979, no. 191, ill.). The intertwining of the legs also occurs in a painting with a very similar composition, depicting the same subject, by Paolo Veronese, which can be dated about 1580–85 (Kunsthistorisches Museum, Vienna, inv. 1527); Pignatti 1976, vol. 1, no. 259, vol. 2, fig. 597. For another treatment of the subject by Veronese, see Pignatti 1976, vol. 1, no. 249, vol. 2, figs. 581, 582.

9. Reznicek 1961, vol. 1, no. K421, vol. 2, pl. 404. The connection with the Bonna drawing was first made in the 1985 sale catalogue (see Provenance).

10. See Nadine M. Orenstein in Amsterdam, New York, and Toledo 2003–4, p. 84; and Orenstein in Czére 2007, p. 95, under no. 27.

11. Bartsch 1803–21, vol. 15 (1813), p. 103, no. 115; DeGrazia 1979, no. 211, ill.

Annibale, or one of its many copies (fig. 35).[8] Agostino's print is dated 1599 and attests to the rapidity with which graphic works were circulated all over Europe immediately after their creation. In a sketch of two lovers in the Van Regteren Altena Collection that is dated somewhat later, Goltzius used for a second time the same pose of Venus's arm, which so wonderfully captures her abandon (fig. 36).[9] Many more examples attest to Goltzius's use of other printmakers' works as sources for his own compositions.[10] In the case of Agostino Carracci, that interest appears to have been reciprocal; in a print from 1599, the Italian artist adapted a print by Goltzius made some ten years earlier.[11]

STIJN ALSTEENS

1. For Goltzius, see Amsterdam, New York, and Toledo 2003–4; for a catalogue raisonné of his drawings, of which approximately five hundred are still known today, see Reznicek 1961; and Reznicek 1993.

2. For example, studies like that of a spaniel in the Frits Lugt Collection, Paris (inv. 262; Reznicek 1961, vol. 1, no. 414, vol. 2, pls. 295, 296; Michiel C. Plomp in Amsterdam, New York, and Toledo 2003–4, no. 61, ill.), the drawing known as *Goltzius's Dog* in the Teylers Museum, Haarlem (inv. N 74; Reznicek 1961, vol. 1, no. 415, vol. 2, pl. 300; Plomp in Amsterdam, New York, and Toledo 2003–4, no. 62, ill.), and the studies of trees, also in the Frits Lugt Collection (inv. 3084; Reznicek 1961, vol. 1, no. 402, vol. 2, pl. 348; Plomp in Amsterdam, New York, and Toledo 2003–4, no. 72, ill.), and in the Ashmolean Museum, Oxford (inv. WA 1962.17.34; Reznicek 1961, vol. 1, no. 410, vol. 2, pl. 349; Plomp in Amsterdam, New York, and Toledo 2003–4, no. 71, ill.).

45. Abraham Bloemaert

Dordrecht, ca. 1565–Utrecht, 1651

Recto: *Studies of Boys' Faces, Hands, and Drapery*

Verso: *Studies of Faces, Arms, and Drapery*

Red and black chalk, heightened with white crayon (?), on red tinted paper, framing lines in pen and brown ink and graphite, 7⁵⁄₁₆ × 9¼ in. (18.5 × 23.5 cm)

PROVENANCE: sale, Me Abraham, Béziers, September 23, 2000; acquired at that sale by Jean Bonna

EXHIBITION: Paris 2008, no. 14

BIBLIOGRAPHY: Bolten 2007, vol. 1, no. A23, vol. 2, ill. p. 503 (verso)

Abraham Bloemaert was a gifted and prolific painter,[1] but he is best loved today for his varied drawn oeuvre, which shows him capable of the enchanting eccentricities of Northern Mannerism, the clarity of observation of the best Dutch seventeenth-century artists, and an elegance akin to that of eighteenth-century French art.[2] More than 1,600 drawings by Bloemaert are known. About 500, including the recently discovered drawing in the Bonna Collection, can be termed study sheets, that is studies of heads, hands and arms, legs and feet, bodies, and draperies, many of which are double-sided.[3] The dating of these drawings is difficult; it can be assumed that many were made from life, with a model posing. Some studies are preparatory for Bloemaert's painted compositions or print designs, such as the young man lying on a sheet in the Van Regteren Altena Collection, which is a study for the dead Christ in a painted Lamentation.[4] Others only appear to be preparatory for a finished work, such as the study of a young woman kneeling like an imploring Virgin in The Metropolitan Museum of Art (fig. 37)[5] or that of a young woman in the pose of a Virgin with the Christ Child in her arms in the Frits Lugt Collection.[6]

In most study sheets, however, the artist seems to have had no specific beautiful narrative subject in mind, and these collages of heads, limbs, and drapery should be considered as part of the tradition of model sheets.[7] Prints and drawings of this kind are among the earliest known works on paper, and Bloemaert must have viewed himself in that tradition. An album consisting of such sheets is preserved in The Fitzwilliam Museum, Cambridge,[8] and was later engraved by Abraham's son Frederik and published for the first time about 1650 as a *tekenboek*, a model book meant as examples for aspiring artists (fig. 38).[9] Another album of study sheets, known as the Giroux album, was disassembled and sold in 1904, and it has been suggested that it also was made for possible publication in the form of a *tekenboek*.[10] The drawing in the Bonna Collection and many others, all in a similar technique using red or black chalk, sometimes finished with pen and brown ink, and heightened with what seems to have been white crayon,[11] originally might have been part of other such albums. However, it cannot be excluded that Bloemaert made them to accommodate collectors with a taste for such examples of pure, and superior, draftsmanship.

STIJN ALSTEENS

1. For Bloemaert as a painter, see Roethlisberger 1993, which includes a catalogue raisonné of his paintings.
2. For Bloemaert as a draftsman, see Bolten 2007, which includes a catalogue raisonné.
3. Ibid., vol. 1, nos. 809–1313, A10–A28, vol. 2, ill. pp. 322–412, 496–505.
4. Ibid., vol. 1, no. 901, vol. 2, ill. p. 351. For the painting, in the collection of Museum Boijmans Van Beuningen, Rotterdam (inv. 2062), see Roethlisberger 1993, vol. 1, no. 390, vol. 2, fig. 551.
5. Bolten 2007, vol. 1, no. 928, vol. 2, ill. p. 355.
6. Frits Lugt Collection, Paris (inv. 488); ibid., vol. 1, no. 1105, vol. 2, ill. p. 382.
7. See Saskia Sombogaart in Antwerp and Amsterdam 1999–2000, pp. 350–54, under no. 50.
8. Inv. PD 166-1963; Bolten 2007, vol. 1, p. 362, nos. 1150–1311, vol. 2, ill. pp. 391–412, and see also vol. 1, nos. 1137–49, 1312, 1313, vol. 2, ill. pp. 389–91, 412.
9. For Bloemaert's *tekenboek*, see Roethlisberger 1993, vol. 1, pp. 389–420; and Bolten 2007, vol. 1, pp. 362–97.
10. Bolten 2007, vol. 1, pp. 361–62, nos. 1093–1136, vol. 2, ill. pp. 380–88.
11. Caroline Corrigan in James et al. 1997, p. 72, figs. 82a, 82b.

Figure 37. Abraham Bloemaert, *Kneeling Female Figure with Upraised Arms*. Red chalk. The Metropolitan Museum of Art, New York, Rogers Fund, 1965 (65.131.4)

Figure 38. Frederik Bloemaert after Abraham Bloemaert, plate 16 of the first edition of the *Tekenboek*. Engraving. The Metropolitan Museum of Art, New York, The Elisha Whittelsey Collection, The Elisha Whittelsey Fund, 1949 (49.95.497)

45 recto

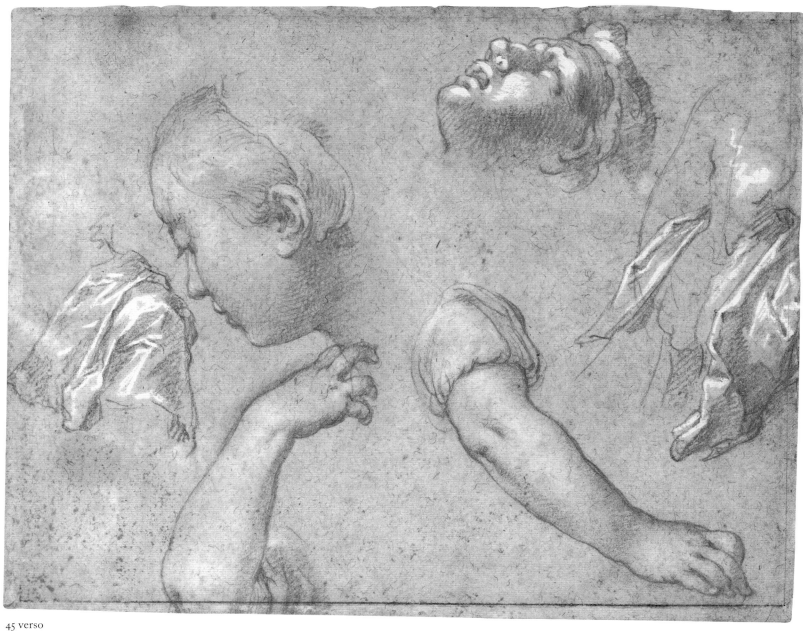

45 verso

46. Master of the Farm Landscapes

Documented 1606–1610

The Castle of Immerseel

1610

Pen and brown ink, watercolor in red, yellow-brown, and green, over a sketch in black chalk, 9½ × 18⅞ in. (24.2 × 47.9 cm)

Inscribed in pen and brown ink at lower right: *P.P. Rubens*, possibly by John Perceval; the collector's mark of *Robins* (Lugt 1433) at lower left; on verso in pen and brown ink in seventeenth-century handwriting at upper center: *dits het casteeltie van immerseel 1610*

Watermark: horn

PROVENANCE: Possibly John Perceval (1683–1748), 1st Earl of Egmont; Private Collection, United Kingdom; sale, Sotheby Mak van Waay, Amsterdam, October 29, 1979, lot 152; Richard Day, London; Sally Aall, New York; Richard Day, London; acquired by Jean Bonna, 1996

EXHIBITION: Paris 2008, no. 18

BIBLIOGRAPHY: Paris, Antwerp, London, and New York 1979–80, p. 55, under no. 19; Andrews 1985, vol. 1, p. 112, under no. D5048; Felice Stampfle in Denison and Mules 1981, p. 84, under no. 62; Stampfle 1991, p. 155, under no. 332

T his sheet is the most recent addition to a group of ten landscape drawings, most inscribed with an old attribution to Peter Paul Rubens.[1] The same annotator, possibly the collector John Perceval, 1st Earl of Egmont, incorrectly attributed to Anthony van Dyck a group of Flemish landscape gouaches in the British Museum,[2] and there is no reason we should take more seriously his identification of the artist under consideration here, whom Egbert Haverkamp Begemann and Anne-Marie Logan aptly baptized the Master of the Farm Landscapes in 1970.[3]

His drawings indeed all depict farmsteads or small castles, most of which can be located in the surroundings of Antwerp, thanks to inscriptions in seventeenth-century Flemish handwriting on the back of the sheets. By the same hand, the sheets are also dated 1606, 1609, and, as in the case of the Bonna drawings, 1610. The inscription on the latter drawing locates the castle represented in Immerseel, in present-day Wommelgem, west of Antwerp; an anonymous print from the end of the seventeenth century in Jacob Le Roy's book on

castles and manors in Brabant shows it from another side and in an even more dilapidated state (fig. 39).[4] Other sheets depict buildings in nearby Ruggeveld and Deurne,[5] in Mortsel, south of Antwerp,[6] and in Burcht and Zwijndrecht, west of the city.[7] A drawing in the Louvre does not have a seventeenth-century inscription but rather an eighteenth-century one, which locates the castle it depicts near Ypres,[8] but given the consistent location of the other buildings near Antwerp, this seems unlikely to be correct. The inscriptions on the three remaining drawings mention only the date or the house's name, not their location.[9] Other draftsmen of the beginning of the seventeenth-century made similar views of often dilapidated buildings in the Flemish countryside, for example, Jan Brueghel the Elder, whose view of the castle at Merksem, also west of Antwerp (fig. 40),[10] incidentally also bears

an inscription identifying the building and is dated 1610, but by another hand than that on the views by the Master of the Farm Landscapes.[11]

Most scholars who study these drawings have found it difficult to accept that a draftsman who was able to lend such vitality and even grandeur to the depiction of these humble buildings remains anonymous. Although Wolfgang Adler argued for an attribution to Rubens as late as 1982, Frits Lugt justly remarked in 1949 that there is neither "imitation nor influence" of Rubens's rare landscapes in the drawings of the Master of the Farm Landscapes.[12] Lugt suggested the names of artists including Gillis Peeters, Gillis d'Hondecoeter, and Jan Wildens, and "other good landscapists whose drawings are not yet well enough known."[13] A painting in the State Hermitage Museum, Saint Petersburg,

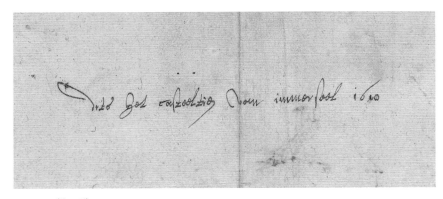

46 verso (detail)

Figure 39. Anonymous engraver, *The Castle of Immerseel.* Engraving. Frits Lugt Collection, Paris

46

Figure 40. Jan Brueghel the Elder, *The Castle of Merksem*. Pen and brown ink, watercolor. The Metropolitan Museum of Art, New York, Purchase, Anonymous Gift, in memory of Frits Markus, Louis V. Bell and Harry G. Sperling Funds, 2001 (2001.638)

Figure 41. Attributed to Marten Rijckaert, *The Castle of Immerseel*, 1627. Oil on panel. State Hermitage Museum, Saint Petersburg (inv. GE 9867)

attributed to (or monogrammed by?) one of these "forgotten" Flemish landscapists, Marten Rijckaert (fig. 41),[14] is directly connected with the Bonna drawing. Dated 1627, it depicts the building in exactly the same way, and there hardly can be any doubt that the painter used the drawing as his model. Given the discrepancy in date between the drawings by the Master and the painting and the lack of any monographic treatment of Rijckaert's oeuvre, it would be unwise for now to speculate on the possibility that Rijckaert and the Master are the same person. But certainly, the connection deserves to be studied further and may eventually lead to an identification of the Master of the Farm Landscapes.

STIJN ALSTEENS

1. This group has been repeatedly discussed, twice at length by Wolfgang Adler, in 1980 and 1982. The most recent and useful summary is Felice Stampfle's (1991, pp. 154–56, under no. 322).
2. Antwerp and London 1999, p. 60, n. 131, and p. 180, under no. 58. For the identification of the annotator, see Michiel C. Plomp in New York 2005, p. 43.
3. Haverkamp Begemann and Logan 1970, vol. 1, pp. 318–19, under no. 590. Several scholars, including Michael Jaffé (1957, p. 15), Julius Held (1986, p. 12), and Keith Andrews (1985, vol. 1, p. 113), do not think all the drawings are by the same hand, but I feel the homogeneity of the group is restored when one excludes two of the drawings listed by Andrews, which are certainly by another hand; see Andrews 1985, vol. 1, no. 5 (British Museum, London, inv. 1895.9.15.1039), for which an attribution to the Dutch artist Claes Jansz. Visscher has been proposed (in Lugt 1949, vol. 2, p. 60, under no. 1271), and no. 9 (Musée du Louvre, Département des Arts Graphiques, Paris, inv. 20209), for which see note 13 below.
4. The print is an illustration in Jacob Le Roy, *Castella & Praetoria Nobilium Brabantiae . . .* (Antwerp, 1694), p. 101; here reproduced after a later edition, published in Amsterdam in 1706 under the title *Delices de la noblesse . . .* , pl. 143. It is accompanied by the following text: "Immersel est un Château dans le Village & Seigneurie de Wommelghem, de la Majeurie de Santhove. L'un & l'autre a depuis long tems appartenu aux Comtes de Bouckhoven, & du Saint Empire de la Maison de Liere." In the 1979 sale catalogue (see Provenance), it is said of the castle, "ransacked around 1589, it remained in ruins until it was destroyed by fire in 1864." I have not been able to verify this information.
5. Kupferstichkabinett, Staatliche Museen zu Berlin, (inv. KdZ 1540), inscribed "1610 [crossed out] / de hoeve byet ruggen velt" (Hans Mielke in Mielke and Winner 1977, no. 46, ill.; Adler 1982, no. 12, fig. 40); British Museum, London (inv. 1895.9.15.1040), inscribed "dits de gastes hoef duer dueren / 1609"; Hind 1923, p. 33, no. 107; Adler 1982, no. 10, fig. 32.
6. Stedelijk Prentenkabinet, Antwerp (inv. A.XV.5), inscribed "dits de hoeve by de luijthagen / 1609"; Adler 1982, no. 8, fig. 28; Antwerp 2006, no. 3, ill.
7. Rijksprentenkabinet, Rijksmuseum, Amsterdam (inv. RP-T-1931-1), inscribed "1606 / het craejen hof te swyndrecht" (Adler 1982, no. 2, fig. 15; Antwerp 2006, no. 2, ill.); National Gallery of Scotland, Edinburgh (inv. D 5048), inscribed (twice, in two different seventeenth-century handwritings) "de hoeve bij swijndrecht" (the handwriting on the second line is that of the seventeenth-century inscriptions on the other sheets; it seems more likely that the first line was written by the artist (see Adler 1982, no. 3, fig. 19; Andrews 1985, vol. 1, p. 112, vol. 2, ill. p. 208).
8. Musée du Louvre, Département des Arts Graphiques, Paris (inv. RF 12208), inscribed "Het huys Bekelaar / in de bosselerij van / peren / A 1609"; Lugt 1949, vol. 2, no. 1272, pl. LXXIX; Adler 1982, fig. 25.
9. Kupferstichkabinett, Staatliche Museen zu Berlin (inv. KdZ 5546), inscribed "1609 / baseliers hof" (Hans Mielke in Mielke and Winner 1977, no. 45, ill.; Adler 1982, no. 9, fig. 29); British Museum, London (inv. 1895.9.15.1041), inscribed "1606" (Hind 1923, p. 33, no. 106, pl. XIV; Adler 1982, no. 7, fig. 27); Morgan Library & Museum, New York (I. 231), inscribed "dits keyzers hof" (Adler 1982, no. 11, fig. 33; Stampfle 1991, no. 322, ill.).
10. Inscribed "1610 / tkasteel van straelen bij Antwerp"; Becker 1922, no. 8, ill.
11. The handwriting is not Brueghel's, as is clear from a comparison with an undoubtedly autograph inscription on a drawing in the Frits Lugt Collection, Paris (inv. 6599; Carlos van Hasselt in London, Paris, Bern, and Brussels 1972, no. 11, pl. 20). Likewise, it is probable that the handwriting on the drawings of the Master of the Farm Landscapes is not the artist's (but see note 7 above).
12. Adler 1982, p. 22, nos. 2–13; Lugt 1949, vol. 2, p. 60, under no. 1271: "ni imitation ni influence."
13. Lugt 1949, vol. 2, p. 60, under no. 1271. It should be noted, however, that Lugt's suggestions concern as much the drawing in the Louvre belonging to the group of farm landscapes (see note 8 above), as a drawing that, in my opinion is by Lodewijk de Vadder (compare the drawing of the same subject in the Oppé sale, Christie's, London, December 5, 2006, lot 98). An attribution to D'Hondecoeter was recently also proposed by Martin Royalton-Kisch (in Antwerp and London 1999, p. 47), on the basis of a stylistic comparison with a drawing most likely by that artist in the Kupferstichkabinett, Staatliche Museen zu Berlin (inv. KdZ 11757; Bock & Rosenberg 1930, vol. 1, p. 154, vol. 2, pl. 108; Schapelhouman 1987, p. 49, under no. 31). Although the comparison is valid, the resemblance seems to this author too superficial to accept this attribution without any more evidence to support it.
14. Gritsay & Babina 2008, no. 373, ill. For Rijckaert, see, among others, De Maere and Wabbes 1994, vol. 1, pp. 342–43, vol. 2, ill. pp. 1019–20; Van Haute 1999, pp. 10–11 and passim. I am most indebted to Hans Buijs for drawing my attention to the painting in the Hermitage.

47. Hendrick Avercamp

Amsterdam 1585–Kampen, 1634

Recto: *The Outer Haarlemmerpoort in Amsterdam from the South*

Verso: *The Inner Haarlemmerpoort from the South*

After 1617–18

Pen and brown ink, brown, red and blue wash, over a sketch in black chalk; verso: pen and brown ink, 4$\frac{7}{16}$ × 11¼ in. (11.3 × 31.1 cm)

Inscribed in pen and brown ink in eighteenth- or nineteenth-century handwriting at lower right: *Geestighe Willem*; on verso in black chalk or graphite in nineteenth- or twentieth-century handwriting at lower left: *Haarlemmer Poort te Amsterdam.*; in pen and brown ink by Titus van Rijn at right: *kuiterman* [?] // *trompetter van / neptuijn // karel van gelder / Cornelia van Rijn / Titus*

PROVENANCE: Probably Rembrandt van Rijn (1606–1669), Amsterdam, and one of his auctions, Amsterdam, between summer 1656 and December 1658; Saportas and Jelgerhuis sale, Amsterdam, December 12, 1836, and following days, album X, lot 4 (as Avercamp; sold with lot 3 to Gruyter for 1 guilder 50 *stuivers*); sale, Amsterdam, April 27, 1847, and following days, album A, no. 3; Isaac Danckerts; his sale, Amsterdam, December 3-6, 1849, lot 586 (sold to De Vriend for 1 guilder); Jacob de Vos Jbsz.; his sale, Amsterdam, May 22–24, 1883, lot 7 (to Coster for 2.50 guilders); Coster Collection, Brussels; sale, Amsterdam, April 6–10, 1908, no. 85 (as Buytewech, for 225 guilders); Willem Vogelsang (1875–1954), Utrecht; J. W. Salomonson, Amsterdam and Bilthoven; Jacobus Klaver, Amsterdam, 1988; sale, Sotheby's, Amsterdam, November 8, 2000, lot 89 (as Avercamp); purchased at that sale by Jean Bonna

EXHIBITIONS: The Hague 1952, no. 12 (as Buytewech); Amsterdam 1987–88, no. 29 (as Avercamp); Amsterdam 1993, no. 23 (as Avercamp); Paris 2008, no. 16 (as Avercamp)

BIBLIOGRAPHY: Welcker 1933, nos. T462, T471 (as Avercamp); Haverkamp Begemann 1959, no. 147 (as Avercamp); Kunstreich 1959, no. 124 (as Buytewech); Welcker 1979, nos. T31.2, T462, T471; Dudok van Heel 1980 (as anonymous); Blankert 1982, p. 34, n. 25 ("attribution to Avercamp no longer accepted"); Roscam Abbing 2006, no. 48 (as attributed to Avercamp)

47 recto

47 verso

Although the Dutch artist Hendrick Avercamp may be better known as a painter of winterscapes, he was also a prolific draftsman.[1] Many of his drawings are finished, and he must have made them as independent works of art. According to an inscription on the back of a signed winter scene in the Frits Lugt Collection, which is as delicate as a miniature, it was given or sold by the artist to a collector as early as 1613.[2] A drawing like this one typically would be kept in an album, but Avercamp also must have made several drawings that were intended to be framed. One such drawing, executed in watercolor and gouache on paper, is still preserved in the Abrams collection in what appears to be its original frame.[3] With these finished drawings, Avercamp served not only a growing number of collectors who were particularly interested in works on paper but maybe also clients who preferred a cheaper drawn version on paper of an Avercamp composition to a more expensive painting.

In addition to these finished drawings, Avercamp made a great number of sketches from life. A group of more than forty such sheets is in the Royal Collections, Windsor Castle.[4] Although an eighteenth- or nineteenth-century collector preferred an attribution of the Bonna drawing to "Geestige Willem," also known as Witty Willem or Willem Buytewech, and inscribed the sheet with his name at the lower right,[5] a comparison with the drawings at Windsor confirms that it is by Avercamp, including the subtle use of watercolor and the scribbles indicating the grass. The present drawing stands out even among the artist's most important sketches from life for both its beauty and its relatively large size.

The drawing is also exceptional for Avercamp because of its topographical character, as only a few of the artist's works depict recognizable sites in Holland,[6] mostly of the small town of Kampen, in the northeastern part of the country, where Avercamp spent most of his life. He must have made his view of Amsterdam's Haarlemmerpoort, the city

Figure 42. Gerbrand van den Eeckhout, *The Outer Haarlemmerpoort in Amsterdam from the West*. Pen and brown ink, brush and watercolor, over traces of black chalk. Teylers Museum, Haarlem (inv. P* 93)

Figure 43. Reinier Nooms (called Zeeman), *The Outer Haarlemmerpoort in Amsterdam from the South*. Etching. Frits Lugt Collection, Paris (inv. 6502e)

gate on the road leading to Haarlem, during a visit to Amsterdam, perhaps prompted by the completion of the building, which was designed by the Dutch sculptor and architect Hendrick de Keyser, in 1617 or 1618.[7] The mills seen in the background at the left of the gate are located on the bulwarks called the Wester-Beer and the Boght, just north of the bulwark Slooterdijk, where Avercamp positioned himself.[8] The sinuous succession of bridges leading over the Singelgracht toward the gate is the subject of a drawing in the Teylers Museum by Gerbrand van den Eeckhout (fig. 42).[9] The gate and the bridges are seen from very much the same direction as in Avercamp's drawing (from the south) in a print by Reinier Nooms (called Zeeman) (fig. 43).[10] In the foreground

of both Zeeman's and Avercamp's views, there are washerwomen bleaching linen, but whereas those on Zeeman's print have chosen a stretch of land on the west side of the canal, those on Avercamp's drawing occupy the grounds of the same bulwark where the artist was standing while making his drawing. At the left, a man climbs the stairs leading up to the bulwark.

The verso of Avercamp's drawing shows an even more freely drawn sketch, consisting of only a few thin pen lines without any watercolor. The unassuming motif is again the Haarlemmerpoort, but now it is seen from within the city, its inner gate recognizable by the upper decoration of the portico and the chimneys on its roof.[11] Both sides of the gate are depicted in a panel in the Gemäldegalerie,

Berlin, by Jan van der Heyden (fig. 44).[12] The freedom of this second sketch has hardly any counterparts in Avercamp's work, but the verso is also remarkable for the inscription in a distinctive, somewhat labored seventeenth-century Dutch handwriting. Two of the names written on the sheet—Cornelia van Rijn, Rembrandt's third and only surviving daughter, born in 1654, and Titus, his only son, born in 1641[13]—suggest a link with the great Dutch master, and S. A. C. Dudok van Heel indeed was able to establish the handwriting as that of Titus himself.[14] In an associative manner, Titus chose a few names without much coherence to practice his penmanship. Apart from his own and his sister's name, Karel van Gelder could refer to the fifteenth-century duke of Guelders, who restored his country to independence in the beginning of the sixteenth century. "Trompetter van Neptuijn" are the first words of a poem by the great Dutch poet Pieter Cornelisz Hooft, written in 1621 and published in 1635 in the *Otia*, a volume of poetry by Rembrandt's early supporter Constantijn Huygens, to whom Hooft's poem is dedicated.[15] Titus must have found Avercamp's drawing in his father's art collection, probably during the time between Cornelia's birth and the auctions of the collection after his father's bankruptcy between Summer 1656 and December 1658.[16] The collection of art on paper contained probably several thousand drawings, by Rembrandt himself, by other contemporary artists, and by old masters.[17] Very few of these

Figure 44. Jan van der Heyden, *The Inner and Outer Haarlemmerpoort in Amsterdam from the South*. Oil on panel. Gemäldegalerie, Staatliche Museen zu Berlin (inv. 1623)

drawings can be identified today,[18] and Avercamp's sheet in fact may be the only one about which there can be hardly any doubt that it belonged to the great artist, who was so keenly interested in recording the topography of Amsterdam (see cat. no. 49).

STIJN ALSTEENS

1. For an overview of Avercamp's work as a painter and draftsman, see Welcker 1979, with a catalogue raisonné; and Blankert 1982.
2. Frits Lugt Collection, Paris (inv. 4953); Welcker 1979, no. T1, fig. XXXIX; and Brussels, Rotterdam, Paris, and Bern 1968–69, vol. 1, no. 2, vol. 2, pl. 29.
3. Amsterdam, Vienna, New York, and Cambridge 1991–92, no. 25, ill.; Plomp 2001, p. 99, fig. 78.
4. Inv. 6465, 6466, 6468–6513; Welcker 1979, nos. T135, T136, T138–82, figs. II, V, VII–X, XLIII, XLIV, XLVIII, XLIX, LIII, LIV; and C. White and Crawley 1994, nos. 240–86.
5. This attribution was probably prompted by a comparison with the style of Buytewech's spirited pen studies of young noblemen (Haverkamp Begemann 1959, nos. 49–64, 67–80, figs. 13, 14, 19–21, 32, 33, 38–41, 46, 48–51, 55, 58, 62–68).
6. Blankert 1982, p. 29. A drawing with the Paalhuis in Amsterdam is in the Frits Lugt Collection, Paris (inv. 5462; Mària van Berge-Gerbaud in Paris 2008, no. 17). In the Saportas and Jelgerhuis sale, in which the Bonna drawing was sold (see Provenance), another drawing of a site in Amsterdam came up (lot 6), described as "De Schrijershoeks Tooren, door AVERCAMP. Gekleurd" (The Schreiershoek tower, by Avercamp. Colored), which is probably identical with a drawing in the sale in Amsterdam, March 17, 1857, album I, lot 178; the drawing could also be identical to a drawing described as "Schreyerstoren en Kamperhoofd" (Schreier tower and the bulwark Kamperhoofd) in the sale at The Hague, March 29–30, 1949, lot 251, which, however, according to a note by Frits Lugt (recorded in the "fiches Hofstede de Groot" at the Rijksbureau voor Kunsthistorische Documentatie, The Hague), is not by Avercamp.
7. On the Haarlemmerpoort, see Commelin 1693, p. 221; and Neurdenburg 1930, p. 58, figs. 15, 16, pl. XI. The Haarlemmerpoort's year of completion is often given as 1618, but an alternative date is offered by Zeeman's later view, which is inscribed "1617."
8. The names of the bulwarks are quoted after Commelin 1693, p. 242.
9. Plomp 1997a, no. 127, ill. Avercamp's and Van den Eeckhout's depictions of the site agree in most of the details, and can both be considered to be accurate.
10. Hollstein 1949–2007, vol. 56 (2001), no. 25, ill. The bridge is also seen from the same point in a print in Commelin 1693, between pp. 220 and 221.
11. For a comparable view of the inner gate, see a graphite sketch by the eighteenth-century Dutch artist Jan Bulthuis in the Gemeentearchief Amsterdam (Bakker, Fleurbaay, and Gerlagh 1989, no. 300, ill.).
12. Wagner 1971, no. 20.
13. Strauss and Van der Meulen 1979, nos. 1638/8,9, 1640/5,6, 1641/4; G. Schwartz 1985, pp. 185, 293, 300.
14. Dudok van Heel 1980. For the document signed by Titus, which allowed the identification; see Strauss and Van der Meulen 1979, no. 1655/6; see also no. 1657/5.
15. Hooft 1994 (ed.), vol. 1, no. 165.1, vol. 2, p. 105.
16. Roelof van Gelder and Jaap van der Veen in Amsterdam 1999–2000, p. 54; Crenshaw 2006, pp. 75–79.
17. Roelof van Gelder and Jaap van der Veen in Amsterdam 1999–2000, pp. 37–38, 44–45, 54–55, 58–59; G. Schwartz 2006, p. 106.
18. For a drawing (now lost) by Mantegna possibly owned by Rembrandt, see Royalton-Kisch and Ekserdjian 2000.

48. Jacob Jordaens
Antwerp, 1593–Antwerp, 1678

A Moral Allegory

Ca. 1645

Red, black, and white chalk, watercolor, brush and brown ink, pen and black ink, 12⁵/₁₆ × 10⅜ in. (31.2 × 26.4 cm)

Inscribed at center left on the pages of the book: *VE / RI / TAS // DEI*, and in black chalk by the artist at lower center: *GAL. 6. Cap.*

PROVENANCE: A. F. Creswell, 1820s; by descent to Mrs. G. W. Wrangham, London; by descent to E. A. Wrangham; Day & Faber, London; acquired by Jean Bonna, 2002

EXHIBITION: Paris 2008, no. 23

BIBLIOGRAPHY: Parker 1928, p. 6, fig. 1; D'Hulst 1956, no. 213; D'Hulst 1974, vol. 1, no. A227, vol. 3, fig. 242; Held 1978, p. 730; D'Hulst 1982, pp. 308, 357, 362; Massing 1990, pp. 52, 64, 148, no. 52.c, ill.; Nora De Poorter in Antwerp 1993, vol. 1, pp. 282, 284, n. 7

This drawing by the great Flemish painter Jacob Jordaens is the least known version of an allegory of which other versions are preserved in the Albertina (fig. 45),[1] and the British Museum (fig. 46).[2] Although the main compositional elements recur in all three sheets, Jordaens tried to make their compositions as different as possible, as if in an effort to demonstrate his inventiveness. The drawings are in various degrees of finish, but all three are inscribed with a reference to the apostle Paul's Epistle to the Galatians and clearly were executed more carefully than a sketch of the same subject (fig. 47)[3] that appears to be preparatory for part of the drawing in the Bonna Collection. It has been suggested that the drawings were made as a design for a tapestry[4] or for a book illustration,[5] but no such tapestry or print is known or documented, and it seems more probable that they were produced as "ends in themselves."[6] "We must assume," remarked Julius Held in discussing the large corpus of "complete," and often watercolor, compositions on paper by the artist, "that in the Antwerp middle classes . . . there was some interest, and possibly, in a modest way, a market for such drawings. To appeal to the moral and religious convictions of these people, the drawings did not have to be as finished in every detail, as some seventeenth- and eighteenth-century drawings that were done to please collectors."[7] Indeed, it should be remembered that before becoming a famous painter and long before he became the foremost artist of the Flemish school after the death of both Peter Paul Rubens and Anthony van Dyck in 1640 and 1641, Jordaens started his career in 1615 or 1616 as a *waterverwer*, or painter in watercolor and tempera.[8]

Jordaens finished the three complete compositions representing the present allegory with a cartouche referring to the sixth chapter of Paul's Epistle to the Galatians. Although it has been noted repeatedly that this text hardly lends itself to illustration,[9] Jordaens must have been inspired by the idea expressed in the first

Figure 45. Jacob Jordaens, *A Moral Allegory*. Black and red chalk, watercolor, and body-color. Graphische Sammlung Albertina, Vienna (inv. 8457)

verse of the book's chapter, which reads: "Brethren, if a man be overtaken in a fault, ye which are spiritual, restore such a one in the spirit of meekness, considering thyself, lest thou also be tempted."[10]

Each of the drawings shows the "man overtaken in a fault," dragged along by a group of allegorical figures, representing Ignorance (with the donkey's ears), Envy (with the hair of snakes), and Deceit (with the mask),[11]

Figure 46. Jacob Jordaens, *A Moral Allegory*. Black and red chalk, brown wash, watercolor, and white gouache. British Museum, London (inv. 1895.9.15.1075)

before a preacher, who is accompanied by a peaceful seated figure with a lamb. The preacher points the mob toward an enthroned young woman holding the book of the "Truth of God," in an effort to incite them to judge the object of their fury "in the spirit of meekness." As Marian Donnelly was the first to remark, Jordaens must have drawn his inspiration for the group of Vices from the antique painting known as the *Calumny of Apelles* and described by the ancient satirist Lucian.[12] Donnelly tried to explain the drawings and several others of Jordaens's allegories as directly or indirectly influenced by the writings of John Calvin, specifically his *Institutio christianae religionis*.[13] Although it is indeed likely that it was partly Jordaens's Calvinist faith that led him to make these allegories, it should be stressed that they are not intrinsically Protestant works nor are they necessarily addressed to a Protestant public.[14] In fact, more than a religious allegory, the drawing under discussion is a *moral* one, albeit of religious inspiration, as can be expected of any moral allegory with a dating from before the Enlightenment. The words *VERITAS DEI* on the pages of the book held by the personification of Religion, which have often been used as a title for the allegory, are in fact just one of its elements.[15]

Many other elements deserve a more detailed study, such as the figure of Religion,[16] the blazing hearts or the "coals of fire" in the hands or on the heads of some of the Vices,[17] and the money pouch in the drawings in the British Museum (where Ignorance carries it around his waist) and in the Bonna Collection (in which it is carried by a putto, pointed at by another winged figure, who also appears but plays a slightly different role in the drawing in the Albertina). Indeed, close study of the iconography of most of Jordaens's "moralizing allegories or narratives taken from the Bible, with a preference for relatively obscure passages,"[18] could be a rewarding subject.[19]

One aspect of the allegory of the Bonna drawing should be discussed more fully here, and that is its central figure, who has been identified variously as the apostle Paul,[20] a Protestant preacher,[21] and a Catholic priest.[22] Certainly the identification as Paul is difficult to defend, as Jordaens himself gave the figure an entirely different appearance in paintings depicting the apostle and Barnabas at Lystra.[23] It certainly is

Figure 47. Jacob Jordaens, *A Moral Allegory*. Black chalk and watercolor. Courtesy of Jean-Luc Baroni, Ltd.

not a Protestant preacher either, for he is wearing what appears to be an alb or an ample cassock, adorned with a stola and a mozzetta, an elbow-length shoulder cape, closed in front with buttons; at the very least, this last piece of vestment is that of a Catholic cleric.[24] That cannot be said, however, of the laurel wreath that he is wearing in the Bonna drawing (but not in the drawings in the Albertina and the British Museum). Similarly crowned figures appear in paintings by both Jordaens and Rubens in the role of an Old Testament high priest,[25] but Jordaens seems also to have used the wreath to confer religious authority to preachers in contemporary clothing, as in the Bonna drawing and in a painted religious allegory in Aschaffenburg.[26] Perhaps Jordaens did so in order to lend some "neutrality" to his preacher.

Even if one accepts that his drawn religious allegories were made mainly for the artist's fellow religionists, Jordaens had reasons to be cautious, living as he did under a rule that was rather hostile toward non-Catholics. He was sentenced in the 1650s for possession of "scandalous"—or heretical—writings, but he generally seems to have been protected by his international reputation and to have professed his personal faith inconspicuously.[27] Jordaens received—and accepted—important commissions from the Catholic Church throughout his life, and even in the more private medium of drawings, he seems to have aimed at evoking a moral message inspired by his Protestant belief that would also be acceptable to Catholics.

STIJN ALSTEENS

1. D'Hulst 1974, vol. 1, no. A225, vol. 3, fig. 240.
2. Ibid., no. A226, vol. 3, fig. 241. A copy after this drawing, probably originating from Jordaens's workshop, is in the Musée des Beaux-Arts, Rennes (ibid., vol. 2, no. C42, vol. 4, fig. 519).
3. D'Hulst 1974, vol. 1, no. A228, vol. 3, fig. 243; and Ongpin 2001, no. 17.
4. Probably for the first time in Rooses 1890, p. 195.
5. Donnelly 1959, p. 363.
6. Held 1978, p. 720.
7. Ibid.
8. D'Hulst and De Poorter 1993, p. 7. For the exact meaning of the word *waterverwer*, see De Pauw-De Veen 1969, pp. 47–49.
9. For instance, in Hind 1923, p. 110, under no. 2.
10. There is no reason to consider Galatians 6:8 as Jordaens's source of inspiration (pace D'Hulst 1974, vol. 1, p. 307, under no. A225). Marian Donnelly (1959), who mistakenly believed the drawings in Vienna and London are inscribed with a reference to the first verse of Galatians 6, was the first to point out the connection between that verse and the subject of the drawings, adding that they "do not illustrate the text so much as they show . . . how the text may be used as the starting point for a moral lesson" (p. 363).
11. Compare Massing 1990, p. 148.
12. Donnelly 1959, p. 362; for the Calumny of Apelles, and Jordaens's adaptation of it, see also Massing 1990, pp. 52, 64, 148, no. 52.C. Jordaens may also have been

inspired by a passage in the preceding chapter of the Epistle to the Galatians (5:16–21), in which Paul opposes a group of vices (adultery, fornication, uncleanness, lasciviousness, idolatry, witchcraft, hatred, variance, emulation, wrath, strife, sedition, heresy, envy, murder, drunkenness, reveling, and such) to a group of virtues (love, joy, peace, longsuffering, gentleness, goodness, faith, meekness, temperance).
13. On Jordaens and Protestantism, see Held 1939, pp. 34–37; Donnelly 1959; and Tümpel 1993.
14. Compare Tümpel 1993, pp. 33–34.
15. As noted by Nora De Poorter in Antwerp 1993, vol. 1, p. 282, under no. A92: "four drawings . . . not altogether appropriately entitled *Veritas Dei*."
16. Compare the figure on the lion in Jordaens's (decidedly Catholic) *Veneration of the Eucharist* in the National Gallery of Ireland, Dublin (inv. 46; Nora De Poorter in ibid., no. A41, ill.), as well as similar figures in Otto van Veen's and Rubens's cycles of the Triumph of the Eucharist (see Vogl 1987; and De Poorter 1978).
17. Most probably "coals of fires": in Proverbs 25:22 and in Paul's Epistle to the Romans (12:20), "heaping coals of fire on your enemies' heads" means making them repentant by making them ashamed (compare the coals in Otto van Veen's *Triumph of Catholic Faith* in the Bayerische Staatsgemäldesammlung, Bamberg, as discussed in Vogl 1987, pp. 78–79).
18. Held 1978, p. 720.
19. Compare Massing 1990, p. 151, n. 24.

20. D'Hulst 1974, vol. 1, p. 307, under no. A225; Nora De Poorter in Antwerp 1993, vol. 1, p. 282, under no. A92.
21. Donnelly 1959, p. 362 ("a preacher, not a priest").
22. Tümpel 1993, p. 33 ("whose vestments are clearly those of a Catholic priest").
23. State Hermitage Museum, Saint Petersburg (inv. 491), and Akademie der Bildenden Künste, Vienna (inv. 663); R.-A. D'Hulst in Antwerp 1993, vol. 1, nos. A8, A70, ill.
24. In a painting by Jordaens in the Landesmuseum für Kunst und Kulturgeschichte, Oldenburg, Saint Dominic is similarly clothed with a mozzetta and a stola (D'Hulst 1982, ill. p. 194).
25. For examples, see the paintings by Jordaens mentioned in note 23 above, Rubens's painting *Abraham and Melchizedek* in the Musée des Beaux-Arts, Caen (inv. 172; D'Hulst and Vandenven 1989, no. 17, fig. 31), two of the tapestries in the Eucharist series (De Poorter 1978, vol. 1, nos. 7, 16, vol. 2, figs. 119–23, 125–28, 199–200, 202), and a drawing by the Flemish-inspired Dutch artist Pieter Crijnse Volmarijn in Museum Boijmans Van Beuningen, Rotterdam (inv. Jord. 8; D'Hulst 1974, vol. 2, no. D11, vol. 4, fig. 607). Usually, high priests are depicted wearing a miter, in accordance with Leviticus 8:9.
26. Bayerische Staatsgemäldesammlungen, Aschaffenburg (inv. 62988); Nora De Poorter in Antwerp 1993, vol. 1, no. A92, ill.
27. D'Hulst and De Poorter 1993, p. 16.

49. Rembrandt van Rijn

Leiden, 1606–Amsterdam, 1669

View of Sloten from the East

Ca. 1650

Pen and brown ink, brown wash on buff paper, 3¹⁵⁄₁₆ × 6⁷⁄₁₆ in. (10 × 16.4 cm)

PROVENANCE: Possibly Jan Pietersz. Zomer (1641–1724), Amsterdam; Private Collection; acquired by Jean Bonna, 2007

EXHIBITIONS: Kassel and Leiden 2006–7, no. 43 (see also p. 179, fig. 155); Paris 2008, no. 25

BIBLIOGRAPHY: Sumowski 2002, pp. 240–42, fig. 2

Rembrandt van Rijn's foremost work is in the fields of history painting and portraiture, but he excelled equally in the genre of landscape, which he explored primarily in prints and in drawings of the 1640s and early 1650s.[1] Very much as he did in his figure studies and biblical compositions from that period, he was able to lend the sites he depicted the greatest expressivity with an utmost economy

of means. This is all the more remarkable because he chose his motifs almost exclusively in the immediate surroundings of Amsterdam, where he found little more than lonely farms and manors overlooking the river Amstel, large lakes or canals, and the endless flat polders.

Although they do form a class of their own, Rembrandt's landscapes are also part of the Dutch tradition of views of the countryside around Amsterdam and Haarlem by such artists as Claes Jansz. Visscher, who published his series of etchings called *Plaisante plaetsen* [...] *ghelegen buyten de ghenoechelycke stadt Haerlem of daer ontrent (Pleasant Places Outside the Charming City of Haarlem)* as early as 1611–12.[2] However unassuming the sites depicted by Visscher and some of his contemporaries—among them Willem Buytewech and Esaias and Jan van de Velde—may seem, these prints clearly met with great success, aiming at a public of "amateurs who do not

have time to travel."[3] Rembrandt did not inscribe his drawings and prints with the names of their sites, but many of them nonetheless have appeared to be topographically correct depictions of the landscapes encountered by those walking the roads leading outside Amsterdam into the countryside—a favorite pastime of the Dutch from at least the end of the sixteenth century. Rembrandt must have taken some of his many pupils with him into the country, for numerous landscape drawings by them still exist,[4] and many other artists also followed the lead of their predecessors of Visscher's generation and produced an abundance of topographical views. One such view (cat. no. 47) by Hendrick Avercamp, almost certainly once was part of Rembrandt's personal art collection. The collector and art historian Frits Lugt made a first attempt at identifying the sites of Rembrandt's landscapes in his book *Walks with Rembrandt in and around*

49

Amsterdam (Wandelingen met Rembrandt in en om Amsterdam, Amsterdam, 1915), an attempt perfected by a team of art historians and archivists in an exhibition held in Amsterdam and Paris in 1998–99.

The present drawing, published by Werner Sumowski in 2002, is a recent addition to the corpus of Rembrandt's drawings. It is related to a sheet in the most prestigious group of his landscape drawings, that of the Duke of Devonshire (fig. 48),[5] of which the drawing in the Bonna Collection almost seems like an echo. Although a substantial number of Rembrandt drawings from the Duke's collection were sold in 1984 and 1987,[6] the larger part of the group is still preserved in the family seat in Chatsworth, Derbyshire. The drawings once were part of the acclaimed collection of Nicolaes Flinck (1646–1723), son of Rembrandt's pupil Govert Flinck.[7] The Bonna sheet most probably was not part of Flinck's collection (or at least, it is not stamped with his collector's mark, the elegant *F* seen in fig. 48). It is therefore likely that its provenance should be traced back to the other great collection of Rembrandt landscapes assembled during the artist's lifetime, that of the art dealer and collector Jan Pietersz. Zomer, who is known to have owned an album with "sixty small landscapes, outside Amsterdam, skillfully

drawn from life "[8] by Rembrandt. Both Zomer's and Flinck's collections must have originated more or less directly from Rembrandt's own, which was auctioned between 1656 and 1658 (see p. 104). The inventory of the artist's possessions indeed lists an album "full of landscapes after life by Rembrandt," "a parchment book full of landscapes drawn from life by Rembrandt," as well as a "small book full of faces, drawn by Rembrandt"—probably most of the output of landscape drawings by the artist.[9]

Both drawings depict the same road, which Frits Lugt recognized as the Sloterweg, leading from Amsterdam toward the small village of Sloten, southwest of the city.[10] In the drawings, Sloten is seen from almost the same direction, with a farm to the left of the road and other houses and the village church, surrounded by trees, to the right. But in the Chatsworth sheet, the draftsman has positioned himself on the footpath between the actual road and the small dyke or "polder ruff" (*polderkrans*) to the right,[11] whereas for the Bonna sheet, he seems to have left the footpath and be standing on the road. The drawing in Chatsworth is also made from a more distant vantage point, and it shows more of the land on both sides of the Sloterweg. To the left are two boats in a ditch separating the meadows, to which the small gate must have gained access. To the right is a larger gate that closed off a raised road leading outside the scope of the drawing. With a few minimal pen strokes, Rembrandt sketched a

Figure 48. Rembrandt van Rijn, *View of Sloten from the East.* Pen and brown ink, brown wash, on brown tinted paper. Duke of Devonshire, Chatsworth (inv. 1039)

1. For Rembrandt's landscape drawings, see, among many other publications, Amsterdam and Paris 1998–99; and Kassel and Leiden 2006–7.
2. For Rembrandt and the tradition of views of the Dutch countryside, see Bakker 1998.
3. After the omitted part of the title of Visscher's series: "liefhebbers die geen tyt en hebt om veer te reysen."
4. For Rembrandt's joint walks with pupils and the use of making landscape drawings in their artistic education, see Schatborn 2005, pp. 13–15.
5. Benesch 1973, vol. 6, no. 1237, fig. 1539; Schmitz 1998, pp. 54, 55, fig. 12; and Boudewijn Bakker, Jan Peeters, and Erik Schmitz in Amsterdam and Paris 1998–99, pp. 349, 350, ill. p. 90 and p. 351, fig. 2.
6. Sale, Christie's, London, July 3, 1984, lots 60–67; and sale, Christie's, London, July 6, 1987, lots 13–16.
7. For Flinck, see Lugt 1921, p. 169; and Schatborn 1981, pp. 16–21, 47.
8. For Zomer, see Lugt 1921, pp. 276–77; Schatborn 1981, pp. 3, 11, 21–24, 46–47, 48; and Plomp 1997b.
9. Quoted by Jaap van der Veen in Amsterdam 1999–2000, p. 150: "Een dito vol landschappen nae 't leven geteeckent bij Rembrant" (no. 244), "Een parckement boeck vol lantschappen nae 't leven van Rembrant" (no. 256), "boeckie vol gesichten geteeckent van Rembrant" (no. 259).
10. Lugt 1915, p. 149. For Rembrandt's drawings made on walks in this direction, see Bakker, Peeters, and Schmitz in Amsterdam and Paris 1998–99, pp. 303–53.
11. See Schmitz 1998, pp. 53–54.
12. Bakker, Peeters, and Schmitz in Amsterdam and Paris 1998–99, pp. 350, 352, ill. p. 141 and p. 353, fig. 3.
13. Sumowski 2002, p. 241.
14. Ibid., p. 242.

Figure 49. Rembrandt van Rijn, *View of the Church of Sloten from the East*. Pen and brown ink. Nasjonalmuseet for Kunst, Arkitektur og Design, Oslo (inv. NG.K & H.B. 15804)

cow in the polder and two figures standing on either side of the *polderkrans*. A comparison with the Bonna drawing, in which the man to the right is using a shovel, shows that they must have been fixing the dyke. The presence of the man in both views is an indication that they were most probably made on the same day, possibly within a short time. Rembrandt must have undertaken the walk to Sloten during which he made the drawings before 1654, when construction started on the nave of the village church. The dilapidated state of the church before the renovation was recorded by Rembrandt in a third drawing of Sloten, now in the Nasjonalmuseet for Kunst, Oslo (fig. 49).[12]

Despite the fact that the drawings in Chatsworth and in the Bonna Collection share the same subject, Rembrandt surprises the viewer by subtly varying composition and drawing technique. The inclusion of the boats and the gates and the rich use of wash (probably added in the studio) in the former drawing are replaced in the latter by a more focused look at the village itself and by almost imperceptible touches of brush used to provide "only discreet compositional accents in a structure of uniform lines."[13] Thus, quite different effects are achieved in two depictions of a single motif—"the pictorial and the abstract."[14]

STIJN ALSTEENS

50. Lambert Doomer

Amsterdam, 1624–Amsterdam, 1700

The Castle of Pirmil near Nantes

Ca. 1650 (?)

Pen and brown ink, brown, gray, and green wash (framing line with pen and black ink), 9³⁄₁₆ × 13¾ in. (23.4 × 36.3 cm)

Inscribed in pen and brown ink in eighteenth-century handwriting at lower right: *Doomer: fecit 1645*; signed and inscribed on verso in pen and brown ink at upper center: *Pilijemie op de bruch te Nantes / LDoomer. f. A 1645* [*LD* as a monogram]

PROVENANCE: Sale, Sotheby's, Amsterdam, December 1, 1986, lot 63; Kunsthandel Dolfijn, Amsterdam; Robert Noortman, Maastricht and London; Galerie Arnoldi-Livie, Munich, 2003; acquired by Jean Bonna, 2003

EXHIBITIONS: Paris and Amsterdam 2006–7, no. 14; Paris 2008, no. 29

BIBLIOGRAPHY: Julia Lloyd Williams in Edinburgh, New York, and Houston 1999–2001, p. 80, under no. 34; Alsteens and Buijs 2008, pp. 31, 32, 47, no. 14

Among the most endearing of Dutch seventeenth-century landscapists, Lambert Doomer is also one of the few who sought the subjects of his drawings mainly outside Holland or Italy.[1] From his trips along the Loire (1645–46)[2] and the Rhine (1663), he brought back a large number of sketches, which he kept repeating until the end of his long career, undoubtedly mainly for Dutch collectors of drawings with an interest in topography. Although most of his original sketches have been lost, Doomer's often

surprising choice of motifs is still recorded in those repetitions. More than two hundred of his views of France, Germany, and Holland are known today.

Doomer went to France in 1645 to visit two of his brothers, who had settled as merchants of wine, grain, and salt in Nantes before traveling eastward along the Loire and then back home with a fellow artist from Amsterdam, Willem Schellinks (1623–1678), who occupied himself by keeping a diary of their travels.[3] Doomer made drawings all along the way—in and between Angers, Saumur, Richelieu, Tours, Amboise, Paris, Rouen, and Le Havre—but the majority relate to his stay in Nantes and to the excursions he must have made while

50

accompanying his brothers on business trips in the surrounding region.

The Bonna drawing, which surfaced only recently, depicts the château in Pirmil (or Pillemil), on the south end of the long bridge leading toward Nantes, on the north bank of the Loire. The fourteenth-century building was already in a ruinous state when Doomer saw it, but it was demolished completely only in 1839. Some nineteenth-century views of the castle of Pirmil, including two by Joseph Mallord William Turner, who visited Nantes in 1826 (fig. 50),[4] suggest that Doomer shifted the exact position of the building in relation to the bridge from right to left. Perhaps Doomer based his drawing on a counterproof of an earlier sketch, as he is known to have done in at least some of his French views.[5] Incidentally, only the castle itself seems to be inverted, for the bridge and the skyline of the city dominated by the Saint Pierre cathedral are

drawn correctly, albeit in a somewhat simplified manner.

The style of the version under discussion here most closely resembles that of a group of repetitions probably made shortly after

Doomer's return to Amsterdam, in the later 1640s or early 1650s. (The date 1645 on the back of the drawing, in Doomer's handwriting, refers to the year when he first recorded the view.) Another version, almost identical in

Figure 50. Joseph Mallord William Turner, *The Bridge over the Loire and the Castle of Pirmil near Nantes Seen from the North.* Pen and brown ink, watercolor, and body-color over a sketch in graphite. Tate Britain, London (inv. TB CCXX Q; D 20224)

Figure 51. Lambert Doomer, *The Castle of Pirmil near Nantes Seen from the South.* Pen and brown ink and brown, gray, red, blue, and green wash on ledger paper. National Gallery of Scotland, Edinburgh (inv. D 1082)

Figure 52. Willem Schellinks, *The Castle of Pirmil near Nantes Seen from the South.* Pen and brown ink and gray wash over a sketch in graphite. Det Kongelige Bibliotek, Copenhagen (Ny Kgl. Saml., MS. 370, vol. 2)

composition, in the National Gallery of Scotland (fig. 51),[6] is one of a very large group of repetitions, made in or somewhat after 1671 and consisting of views in France, Germany, and Holland, which were dispersed at the Tonneman sale in Amsterdam on October 21, 1754, and following days. They are all executed in a slightly tamer drawing style than the earlier versions and, with few exceptions, on ledger paper, recognizable by the three parallel red lines along the upper edge. Finally, a third version is known, a sheet by Willem Schellinks (fig. 52),[7] who does not seem to have made many drawings during the trip of 1646, but

who copied several drawings by his companion back in Amsterdam.[8] The drawing is inserted in Schellinks's manuscript diary of a second trip to France, which he made in 1663.

STIJN ALSTEENS

1. The primary study on Doomer's drawings remains Schulz 1974, which includes a catalogue raisonné, complemented by the catalogue in Sumowski 1979–92, vol. 2 (1979) and by a few more additions mentioned in Alsteens and Buijs 2008, pp. 38–39, n. 40.
2. For Doomer's drawings related to his travels in France, see Alsteens and Buijs 2008, esp. pp. 31–37, and nos. 1–57. The present entry is largely based on research by Hans Buijs for that publication.

3. For an edition of this diary, as well as a French translation, see ibid., pp. 352–70.
4. London and Nantes 1997–98, no. 61, and p. 64, fig. 50. Turner's other drawing is in the Ashmolean Museum, Oxford (inv. WA 1961.20); ibid., no. 62, fig. 51.
5. See Alsteens and Buijs 2008, pp. 33–34, no. 12, and pp. 43–44, 48–50.
6. Schulz 1974, no. 81; Sumowski 1979–92, vol. 2 (1979), p. 820, no. 19; Andrews 1985, vol. 1, pp. 22–23, vol. 2, fig. 147; Julia Lloyd Williams in Edinburgh, New York, and Houston 1999–2001, no. 34, ill.; and Alsteens and Buijs 2008, p. 103, fig. c.
7. Alsteens and Buijs 2008, no. 15, ill.
8. For Schellinks' drawings, see ibid., esp. pp. 45–51.

51. Gillis Neyts

Overijse, before 1626–Antwerp (?), 1687 or later

Study of an Old Tree

1663–70 (?)

Pen and brown ink, 12⅛ × 7¾ in. (30.7 × 19.6 cm)

Inscribed in graphite at lower left: *De [...] et non [?] Breugle de Velours*; on verso in pen and brown ink in eighteenth-century handwriting at upper center: *Breughel de Velours*

PROVENANCE: Galerie de Bayser, Paris; acquired by Jean Bonna, 2001

EXHIBITION: Paris 2008, no. 20

The Flemish artist Gillis Neyts seems to have been distinctly less active as a painter than as a draftsman. With the exception of a limited group of figure studies,[1] his drawn oeuvre consists almost exclusively of landscapes executed with pen; some are imaginary, some topographically correct. The earlier drawings are all small works, many of them on vellum, meticulously executed.[2] To these should be

added more than twenty refined etchings,[3] which are similar in style and can be dated in accordance. This first manner appears to correspond to Neyts's years of activity in Antwerp, where he is documented first in 1643 and to which he must have moved as a young man from his native Overijse, a village south of Brussels.[4] Some of the early drawings include views of Antwerp and its surroundings. From

Figure 53. Gillis Neyts, *Study of a Tree*. Pen and brown ink. The Metropolitan Museum of Art, New York, Frits and Rita Markus Fund, 2005 (2005.15)

Antwerp, Neyts may have traveled to the north, because some early works include a view of the Dutch town of Dordrecht.[5] His travels also may have led to the south; at the very least, he must have spent some time in Lille, in present-day France,[6] but whether he traveled more extensively in France is uncertain (and whether he went as far as Italy even more so).[7] In 1665, he moved to Namur, in the southern part of present-day Belgium. That move seems to have been followed by a change in his drawing style, as exemplified by a group

of landscapes, of which several can be located in the surroundings of Namur. Surprisingly fresh in observation, drawn in a much looser manner than the early works, and enhanced by a restrained use of watercolor, they count among the most beautiful Flemish seventeenth-century landscape drawings.[8]

This study of gnarled and intertwining trees in the Bonna Collection, characterized by wild and sweeping lines and evidently the fruit of the artist's imagination, does not fit in either grouping. However, its attribution is ascertained by comparison with a small number of similar studies, some of which bear Neyts's signature. Two of those even share the same size as the drawing in the Bonna Collection.[9] Two other tree studies are slightly smaller—a drawing in The Metropolitan Museum of Art (fig. 53)[10] and a double-sided sheet in the National Gallery of Canada, Ottawa.[11] Four additional drawings could be viewed as horizontally extended versions of the tree studies, in which the expressive trees are set in a larger landscape; those are a double-sided sheet in the National Gallery of Scotland, Edinburgh;[12] drawings in the Klassik Stiftung Weimar[13] and in the Van Regteren Altena Collection, Amsterdam;[14] and one recently acquired by The Metropolitan Museum of Art.[15] The drawings in Amsterdam and New York are both signed and undoubtedly were made as independent works of art. The sheet in Edinburgh may have been part of a (bound?) collection of *ricordi* for the artist's own use; on one of its sides (fig. 54) is the

same composition as that of the drawing in New York (fig. 55).

Although the last four horizontal landscapes have been grouped together with the vertically oriented tree studies, the style of the former seems slightly more advanced, more overtly calligraphic,[16] and this author is inclined to date them somewhat later in the artist's career but still before the views in color that must have followed the artist's move to Namur.[17]

STIJN ALSTEENS

1. Gustot 2008, pp. 135–37, nos. D287–D329. Most of them can be found in the British Museum, London.
2. The early dating of this group is based on dated examples from the 1650s; Neyts must have worked in this style until at least 1663 (see, for example, the view of Antwerp dated 1663 in the Prentenkabinet, Museum Plantin-Moretus, Antwerp, inv. 546; Gustot 2008, no. D10).
3. Hollstein 1949–2007, vol. 14 (1956), pp. 149–59; Gustot 2008, pp. 262–63, nos. E1–E30.
4. For Neyts's biography, see Van Lerius 1880–81, vol. 2, pp. 61–75; Hymans 1920–21, vol. 2, p. 296; Courtoy 1930; Alsteens and Buijs 2008, p. 260, under nos. 73, 74; and Gustot 2008, pp. 27–34.
5. For a painted, several drawn, and one etched view of Dordrecht, see Gustot 2008, nos. P23, D28–D30, D217, E12.
6. Ibid., pp. 32–33, nos. D284, E10.
7. Alsteens and Buijs 2008, p. 257, under nos. 73, 74; Gustot 2008, pp. 138–42.
8. Ibid., pp. 108–10, D172–D213.
9. Present whereabouts unknown; see ibid., nos. D232, D233.
10. Acc. no. 2005.15; ibid., no. D231.
11. Inv. 15761; ibid., D234.
12. Inv. RSA 478; Andrews 1985, vol. 1, p. 28, vol. 2, figs. 190, 191 (as attributed to Albert Flamen); Gustot 2008,

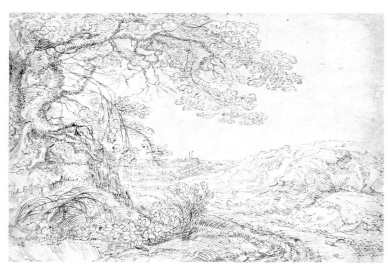

Figure 54. Gillis Neyts, *Landscape with an Old Tree to the Left*. Pen and brown ink. National Gallery of Scotland, Edinburgh (inv. RSA 478)

Figure 55. Gillis Neyts, *Landscape with an Old Tree to the Left and Figures*. Pen and brown and black ink, brown wash. The Metropolitan Museum of Art, New York, Frits and Rita Markus Fund, 2008 (2008.382)

no. D238. The attribution to Neyts was proposed in
Gordon 1988, p. 51.

13. Inv. KK 5258; Gustot 2008, no. D236.
14. Ibid., no. D235.
15. Ibid., no. D237.
16. This style is shared by some Italianate landscape drawings by Neyts (ibid., nos. D264, D265, D272–D274, D276), in some of which it is even more pronounced, and can be rather unappealing. As in the drawings in Amsterdam and New York (see notes 14 and 15 above), Neyts made extensive use of wash in these works.
17. The proposed chronology belies the assumption that Neyts signed with the Flemish form of his name ("Gillis," or "Jillis") in the first part, and with the Latinized form "Aegidius" in the later part of his career (see Joaneath Spicer in Vancouver, Ottawa, and Washington 1988–89, p. 141, under no. 43; see also Gustot 2008, p. 114): the drawing in Weimar is signed "g. Neyts. f.," whereas the stylistically identical drawings in Amsterdam and New York (see notes 14 and 15 above) are signed "Æ. Neyts f.," as are the two unlocated studies mentioned above in note 9 and those in New York and Ottawa mentioned in notes 10 and 11.

52. Jean Cousin the Elder

Soucy, ca. 1490–Paris, ca. 1560–61

Recto: *The Devastation of Job's Flocks*

Verso: *Sketch of a Scene in Perspective*

Recto: pen and brown ink, brown wash, heightened with white gouache, over traces of black chalk; verso: pen and brown ink and annotation in graphite: *J. Cousin;* on a strip of paper added vertically as a reinforcement, in pen and brown ink: *.aS* (superimposed) *.1eC* (superimposed) *.aC* (superimposed) *–a* (? superimposed) *..mag* (. . .); on a piece of paper once attached to the verso and now removed, a rebus in pen and brown ink: *comparé (vite?) quel monde est el (est tel?) que roue* (. . .), 8¹/₁₆ × 19⁷/₁₆ in. (20.4 × 49.3 cm)

PROVENANCE: Marquis de Valori (Lugt 2500); sale, Hôtel Drouot, Paris, February 13–14, 1908, lot 96 (as Jean Cousin); Private Collection, Germany; sale, Sotheby's, New York, January 21, 2003, lot 23a (as attributed to Jean Cousin the Elder); purchased at that sale by Jean Bonna

EXHIBITIONS: Paris 2006b, no. 1; Geneva 2006–7a

In the 1908 sale of the second part of the marquis de Valori's drawings collection, this sheet was described as depicting a "shepherd and his flock frightened by thunder," but as Paul Taylor of the Warburg Institute has established,[1] the subject is derived from the biblical Book of Job, in which Satan tests the righteous Job. Since God has forbidden him to lay a hand on Job, Satan destroys his flocks, attacking Job through his worldly possessions. One of Job's servants comes to tell him that "the fire of God is fallen from heaven, and hath burned up the sheep, and the servants, and consumed them; and I only am escaped alone to tell thee."[2] This servant is the shepherd standing at right, looking at the disaster while still holding a crook in his left hand. Despite this misfortune, Job, shown in the background at right, refuses to disavow God.

On the verso of the sheet is the annotation "J. Cousin," which doubtless dates back to the marquis de Valori and explains the attribution to Jean Cousin upheld by the print specialist Loys Delteil, who catalogued the works in the Valori sale. The first monograph devoted to Cousin, by A. Firmin-Didot, written when art historians knew of only one painter and draftsman by that name, does not mention this work, although one of the supplements to the 1872 edition does reference "several highly important drawings by Jean Cousin . . . owned by the marquis de Valori."[3] One year after the Valori auction, Maurice Roy, building on studies by Jules Guiffrey and Henri Monceaux,[4] demonstrated to the Académie des Inscriptions et Belles-Lettres that a distinction had to be made between Jean Cousin the Elder, who was born before 1500 and died in 1560 or 1561, and his son Jean Cousin the Younger, who was of student age in 1542 and who died in 1594 or 1595.[5] As the authors of the Sotheby's catalogue stated in 2003, the creator of the work shown here must be the older of the two masters. Indeed, we recognize, in the overall composition, his tendency to show figures in profile in the foreground and in three-quarter view in the background; to adopt a slender model for the shepherds' bodies; to align certain figures (notably the shepherd in the foreground) along diagonals, here extended by the boar's back; and, in the stylized rendering of the shepherd's hand, joining the fingers so that they appear as three-pronged claws. Moreover, the shepherd at right in the middle ground is exactly of the same type as one of the shepherds in *The Adoration of the Shepherds* at The Metropolitan Museum of Art, which had been misattributed to Jean Cousin the Younger by Charles Sterling, then later correctly attributed to Cousin the Elder by Sylvie Béguin.[6] In addition, the ram and the ox in that work are similar to the ones depicted in the present drawing; the animals' expressions, their bodies nearly parallel to the plane of the composition, are also found in one of the Saint Mammes tapestries, *Saint Mammes Preaching the Gospel to the Wild Beasts*,[7] woven in Paris between January 24, 1544, and May 1545 by Pierre Blasse (or Blacé) and Jacques Langlois from a cartoon commissioned of Jean Cousin the Elder by the cardinal of Givry on July 14, 1543.[8] There are also close similarities with the knotty tree, sitting on tentacular roots, wrapped in ivy and crowned with leaves that are partially mossy and partially hanging. In the background of another tapestry from the same series, *Saint Mammes Stands before the Governor of*

115

52 (detail)

Cappadocia,[9] the animals depicted around the
saint in his hut and those depicted *en camaieu*
on the frieze of the building that acts as the
frame for his torment also offer many similarities with the ones in Job's flock.

But the great suppleness of the forms in
space (heads of the animals in three-quarter
view, trees sinuous rather than straight) suggests
that the scene from the story of Job is later than
or perhaps contemporary with the illuminations
attributed to Jean Cousin in the *Book of Hours
of Anne de Montmorency*,[10] begun about 1549 and
completed after 1551 or with the designs for the
Book of Perspective published in Paris in 1560.

More than 7⅞ inches (20 cm) high and a
little less than 19¾ inches (50 cm) wide, this

drawing is completely pricked for its contours
to be transferred onto another support; it is,
in other words, a small cartoon. Its dimensions differ from those of the few independent paintings or stained-glass windows that
have been attributed to Jean Cousin the Elder.
Rather, the format suggests a design for wood
paneling or furniture or more likely, a *cartonetto*
for embroidery, such as that on one of the
famous *corporaliers* decorated with a *Descent
from the Cross*, the design of which is today
credited to Cousin the Elder.[11] In the mid-
sixteenth century, there were embroideries on
this scale depicting subjects from the Old
Testament. As an example, one can cite *The
Adoration of the Golden Calf* in the Musée

National de la Renaissance,[12] designed and
executed by unknown artists.[13] Documents
from 1550–51 attest that Jean Cousin the Elder
was supplying patterns for orphreys, copes, and
facings for liturgical vestments to the chapter
of the cathedral of Sens.[14] One of these documents mentions, in addition to Jean Cousin,
the name of the embroiderer Loys Guignet or
Guingnet,[15] but unfortunately, there is no
mention of the subject. Whether or not this
type of Old Testament composition, treated in
landscape format in an oblong rectangle, was
used as preparation for an embroidery, it
gained a certain fame in the work of Jean
Cousin the Younger. Two drawings in the
Wolfenbüttel Library, depicting *Joseph*

52 recto

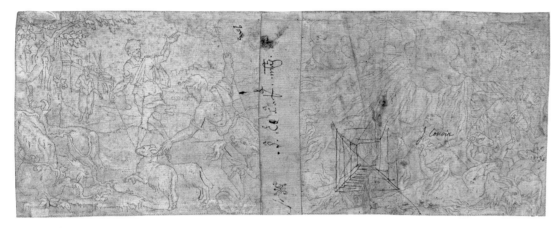

52 verso (size reduced)

Explaining Dreams and *Joseph Pulled from the Well by His Brothers*, stand as an indication of this, even though they are of smaller format.[16]

DOMINIQUE CORDELLIER

1. Oral communication quoted in the catalogue of the 2003 Sotheby's auction sale (see Provenance), p. 14.
2. Job 1:16.
3. Firmin-Didot 1872, pp. 112, 270.
4. Guiffrey (Jules) 1880; Monceaux 1884.
5. Roy 1929a.
6. Rogers Fund (61.24), 9⅞ × 15¼ in. (25.2 × 38.9 cm); Sylvie Béguin in Paris 1972–73, no. 69, ill.
7. Cathedral of Langres; Viard, Decron, and Wu 1994, ill.
8. Roy 1929b.
9. Musée du Louvre, Paris; Viard, Decron, and Wu 1994, ill. p. 101.
10. Musée Condé, Chantilly, MS 1476, fol. 78v. For the attribution to Cousin, see Myra Dickman Orth in Chantilly 2001–2, pp. 62–63; and Cécile Scailliérez in ibid., p. 67.
11. Musée National de la Renaissance, Écouen, 11⅝ × 10¼ in. (29.5 × 26.1 cm); Zerner 1996a, p. 244, ill. no. 279.
12. Inv. Ecl. 1488, 13½ × 19⅝ in. (34.2 × 50 cm).
13. Maria-Anne Privat-Savigny in Blois 2002, no. 9, ill.
14. Archives Départementales, Yonne, G. 1158, fols. 42r, 42v; cited in Roy 1929a, p. 9. A photocopy of this document was kindly provided by Danièle Véron-Denise, head curator of the Musée National du Château de Fontainebleau.
15. Fol. 42v, line 3.
16. 5⅛ × 9⅞ in. (13 × 25.2 cm); Benesch 1939–40, pp. 278–79, figs. 11, 12.

53. François Clouet

Tours, about 1515–Paris, 1572

Portrait of François II

Ca. 1556

Black and red chalk, 12¹⁵⁄₁₆ × 8¼ in. (32.9 × 20.9 cm)

Inscribed in brown ink at upper right: *le feu roi framcois 2ᵉ estam[t] / dauphim*

PROVENANCE: Probably Catherine de' Medici (1519–1589), to Christine de Lorraine (1563–1637), and Ignazio Enrico Hugford (1703–1778), Florence; Count of Sandwich, England; sale, Sotheby's, London, December 11, 1980, lot 16; Galerie Jan Krugier, Geneva; acquired by Jean Bonna, 1998

EXHIBITIONS: Paris 2006b, no. 3; Geneva 2006–7a

BIBLIOGRAPHY: Zvereva 2005, no. 41.19

Chalk portraits "of the old Court," as Michel de Marolles described them in 1672,[1] constitute a particularly coherent ensemble in French graphic works of the sixteenth century. Without being able to retrace here the complex genesis of this genre, whose origins involve a network of influences including Jean Fouquet and the German and Flemish portraitists, let us simply note that before this period, it was part of an eminently symbolic, even dynastic, tradition. Such pencil portraits were initially used as preparatory sketches to be transposed into paintings (François I had already commissioned likenesses of himself and his loved ones from Jean Clouet, François Clouet's father), but it was Catherine de' Medici, the king's daughter-in-law, who began in the 1550s to commission renowned artists to create portraits on paper of her children, close friends, and eminent courtiers, starting a fashion that lasted until the beginning of the seventeenth century.[2]

The *Portrait of François II* shown here was long considered the work of a follower of François Clouet but was recently reattributed by Alexandra Zvereva to the master himself[3]—a suggestion supported by the finesse with which the face is rendered, in which it is difficult to make out pencil marks, and by the concise depiction of the clothing and beret. Probably executed about 1556, when François was around twelve years old (he became king of France in 1559), this portrait precedes by several years another drawing by François Clouet of about 1560 (fig. 56),[4] after the young lord had acceded to the throne. Four earlier drawings conserved in Chantilly[5] also immortalize the boy's features. Added after the fact in brown ink by one of Catherine de' Medici's secretaries, the cursive writing visible on the Bonna drawing is similar to the examples gathered by Alexandra Zvereva under the rubric "Group M."[6] The presence of this caption seems to indicate that the sheet was one of several hundred portrait drawings collected by the French queen, who handed them down to her granddaughter Christine de Lorraine, Grand Duchess of Tuscany. In the eighteenth century, the collection came into the possession of the English painter Ignazio Enrico Hugford, who lived in Florence, and who then dispersed the drawings throughout Europe.

As a group, the chalk drawings created for the court of the last Valois possess a striking emotional quality. Reaching through the centuries that separate them from us, these figures train their eyes directly on the viewer, in a paradoxical inversion in which the portrait gallery contemplates its audience. The lightness of the paper support no doubt contributes to the impression of a spontaneous view, which is conveyed by the economy of means as well as by the simplicity of the pose. The young man in the present drawing, whose tragic fate it was to die barely a year after taking the throne, thus stands before us, and the frailty of his complexion, only made worse by the inscription ("the late king") that takes the place here of any

Figure 56. François Clouet, *Portrait of François II*. Black and red chalk. Bibliothèque Nationale de France, Département des Estampes et de la Photographie, Paris (Na 22 rés.)

heraldic attributes, is offered to us as a timeless testament.

NATHALIE STRASSER

1. Quoted in Adhémar 1973, p. 122.
2. Chantilly 2002–3, pp. 6–11.
3. Alexandra Zvereva, e-mail to the present author, July 6, 2005; my thanks for her gracious assistance.
4. A similar drawing is at the Fogg Art Museum, Harvard University Art Museums, Cambridge, Massachusetts (1978.21).
5. Musée Condé, Chantilly (inv. PE 571); Broglie 1971, nos. 354, 358, 359, 361.
6. Only the final "s" in the name shows some difference with this group of cursive inscriptions (Chantilly 2002–3, pp. 56–57).

le feu roi francois 2.^e estan
dauphin

53

54

54, 55. Jacques Le Moyne de Morgues

Dieppe, ca. 1533–London, 1588

54. *Peony, Spanish Iris, and Geranium*

Ca. 1555 (?)

Watercolor and gouache over black chalk underdrawing, 7⅝ × 6 1/16 in. (19.3 × 15.4 cm)

Inscribed in pen and brown ink beneath the flowers: *geranium f [. . .] le (?) yris et peonia / v* [. . .] in pen and brown ink at bottom right: *8.*

PROVENANCE: Sale, Sotheby's, New York, January 21, 2004, lot 36; purchased at that sale by Jean Bonna

EXHIBITIONS: Paris 2006b, no. 4; Geneva 2006–7a

BIBLIOGRAPHY: Denison 2006, p. 521

55. *Two Poppies, Corn Cockle, and Cornflower*

Ca. 1555 (?)

Watercolor and gouache over black chalk underdrawing, 8½ × 6¼ in. (21.5 × 15.9 cm)

Inscribed beneath the flowers in pen and brown ink: *nigella, cyanus,* and possibly *papaver rhoeas* (inscription truncated); in pen and brown ink at upper right: *2* (?)

55

PROVENANCE: Sale, Sotheby's, New York, January 21, 2004, lot 44; purchased at that sale by Jean Bonna

EXHIBITIONS: Paris 2006b, no. 5; Geneva 2006–7a

BIBLIOGRAPHY: Denison 2006, p. 521

These two drawings were part of a group of twenty-seven studies of plants, insects, birds, and fruits sold in New York in January 2004. Painted in watercolor and gouache on very fine paper, they come from a volume bound in France in the nineteenth century. The irregularity of the wire marks and chain lines on the laid paper and the watermark on a certain number of the sheets allow us to identify the support as of French origin from the 1540s. The sheets were later laid down onto paper supports, also of French manufacture, from the seventeenth century and were probably numbered at that time, but some of this numbering disappeared when the volume was bound in the nineteenth century. The annotations—in two different hands, in Latin and German— that identify the flowers seem to be from a later date.

On the first drawing, the large flower of the popular peony (*Paeonia officinalis L.*) dominates the image, concealing most of the stalk of the Spanish iris (*Iris hispanica L.*) that is placed next to the modest geranium. The artist used watercolor over black chalk and heightened the veins of the flowers and leaves in gouache, creating a subtle effect of differentiation. The second drawing, executed with a similar technique, shows three wildflowers that have grown in grainfields for centuries: the poppy (*Papaver rhoeas L.*), the cornflower (*Centaurea cyanus L.*), and the corn cockle (*Agrostemma githago L.*).

For a long time, Le Moyne was known only as a traveling companion to the Huguenots René Goulaine de Laudonnière and Jean Ribault during their 1564–65 expedition to Florida, where they hoped to establish a Protestant colony. The publisher and engraver Theodor de Bry published a book about this voyage in Frankfurt in 1591, *Brevis narratio eorum quae in Florida Americae provincia Gallis acciderunt [. . .] Anno MD LXIIII*, which includes a short narrative by Le Moyne, accompanied by captioned illustrations.[1] But it was not until 1922, and the study of fifty-nine watercolors conserved since 1856 in a sixteenth-century binding at the Victoria and Albert Museum in London, that Le Moyne was identified as the author of these botanical studies.[2] His reputation was established definitively by the discovery in 1961 of an album containing fifty watercolors of flowers, fruits, and insects, including a sonnet signed in his hand and dated 1585, which is now at the British Museum.[3]

Jacques Le Moyne—he later added de Morgues to his name—claimed to be a native of Dieppe, where he appears to have been born about 1533. Almost nothing is known of his life before the Florida expedition. Later, the religious troubles that broke out in France in 1572 (the Night of St. Bartholomew) probably forced him to immigrate to England, but he was not registered as a British subject until 1582. In 1586, he published in Blackfriars, the London neighborhood where he and many other Huguenot émigrés lived, a short work that is now very rare, *La Clef des champs*. This book of models for painters, engravers, sculptors, and

other artists, illustrated with ninety-six wood engravings of animals, birds, and plants after his own drawings, was dedicated to the mother of the writer and poet Philip Sidney.[4]

The discovery of the group of twenty-seven sheets in 2004 further establishes Le Moyne as one of the first and most talented artists from the second half of the sixteenth century when it comes to botanical or animal illustrations.[5] Several elements of these studies can be found in his later works. Although perhaps less sophisticated than the two artists who were his near-contemporaries, Joris Hoefnagel (1542–1601) in Prague and Jacopo Ligozzi (1547–1627) in Florence, Le Moyne left behind watercolors that show a heightened sense of realism in the rendering of plants. These two sheets of flower studies, extremely rich in color, bear the hallmarks of close observation but at the same time, a very natural simplicity and freshness. Compared with the studies of plants and fruits in the Victoria and Albert Museum, which are from the artist's French period (we can date the paper to about 1568), these two drawings seem much earlier, notably because of the very simple arrangement of the flowers being studied. In the Victoria and Albert album, on the other hand, each sheet depicts a single plant and each element is positioned in very balanced fashion, almost like a scientific illustration. The elegant studies of plants and fruits in the unbound album in the British Museum, dating from 1585, with their highly refined technique and bold outlines, have attained an evident perfection but remain a bit distant.[6]

The sonnet accompanying the British Museum drawings, hand-lettered by the Huguenot master calligrapher John de Bauchesne, proclaims that everything that grows and flowers is a sign of God, that "the slightest floweret shows us a Springtime of immortal colors." The verse seems to apply equally well to the simple flower of the modest geranium!

MÀRIA VAN BERGE-GERBAUD

1. On this source, which contains interesting information about the first American expeditions, see Hulton 1977, vol. 1, pp. 87–152, vol. 2, pls. 91–134.
2. Savage 1922; Savage 1923. See also Hulton 1977, vol. 1, pp. 155–62, nos. 1–33, vol. 2, pls. 17–33b.
3. Hulton 1977, vol. 1, pp. 165–73, nos. 36–86, vol. 2, pls. 35–48b.
4. Ibid., vol. 1, pp. 11–12, 186–200, nos. P1– P96, vol. 2, pls. 64–90b.

5. Among the 27 drawings sold at Sotheby's, New York, on January 21, 2004 (lots 29–55) were four studies of birds (swallow, kingfisher, yellowhammer, and jay) and six studies of plants combined with insects (dragonfly, stag beetle, butterflies, spider, ladybug, maybug, grasshopper, and caterpillar).
6. For later borrowings by other artists, see Hulton 1977, vol. 1, pp. 81–82; Gerard 1969, p. 363ff. (for the *Altera Pars* in *Hortus floridus* by Crispijn de Passe the Younger from 1614); Brenninkmeijer-De Rooij 1996, pp. 42–43, pls. 43, 44 (for the white lily by Jacques de Gheyn II from 1600).

56. Jacques Callot
Nancy, 1592–Nancy, 1635

The Bathers: View of Florence from the Porta San Niccolò

Black chalk, traces of red chalk, pen and brown ink, brush and brown wash, heightened in white gouache, 7⅝ × 13¹⁄₁₆ in. (18.8 × 33.6 cm)

PROVENANCE: Probably Israël Henriet, Paris; William Cavendish (1672–1729), 2nd Duke of Devonshire, Chatsworth, mark at lower right (Lugt 718); the Dukes of Devonshire and the Chatsworth Settlement Trustees (inv. 947); sale, Christie's, London, July 3, 1984, lot 65; John R. Gaines, Lexington, Kentucky; sale, Sotheby's, New York, November 17, 1986, lot 14; Private Collection, Switzerland; sale, Christie's, London, July 9, 2002, lot 47; purchased at that sale by Jean Bonna

EXHIBITIONS: Brussels, Rotterdam, and Paris 1949–50, no. 26 bis; Manchester 1965, no. 282; Washington and other cities 1969–70, no. 110; London 1973–74, no. 110; Paris 2006b, no. 8; Geneva 2006–7a

BIBLIOGRAPHY: Zahn 1923, p. 100, fig. 31; Lieure 1924–27, vol. 1, no. 270, fig. 73; Ternois 1954, p. 151ff., fig. 10; Glikman 1959, p. 36; Ternois 1962a, pp. 110, 120, pl. 21a; Ternois 1962b, p. 82, no. 431; Brigitte Scart in Paris 1984–85a, under no. 39; Gianvittorio Dillon in Florence 1986–87 [vol. 2], p. 200, under no. 2.147; Ternois 1992, p. 42, fig. 8; Jaffé 1993, p. 428, fig. 9; Ternois 1993, pp. 370–71, 381, n. 73; Jaffé 2002, vol. 5, no. 1605; Denison 2006, p. 512

Jacques Callot is universally acknowledged as one of the greatest landscape artists of his time, a precursor in the genre among French artists, although the foundations of his style can be traced back to his formative period at the court of the Grand Duke Cosimo II in Florence, before his return to Lorraine in 1621. This mastery is evident in the final landscapes Callot drew in Italy, most of which appear to have been engraved a few years later, after he

56

had returned to the Lorraine: the magisterial *Large Hunt*,[1] the *Four Landscapes*,[2] and the series of ten *Italian Landscapes*, more precisely titled *Diverse vedute disegnate in Fiorenza. Per Jacopo Callott*.[3] This latter series, complemented by a frontispiece and a twelfth plate (both after drawings by another artist), was published in the 1630s by Israël Henriet in Paris, and one cannot be certain that Callot made the engravings himself.[4] But if the wording of the frontispiece suggests that these are views of Italy, only one site can be identified with certainty, that of *The Bathers* (fig. 57), which depicts, with some license, Florence seen from the area around the mill at the Porta San Niccolò. This composition is also the best documented, as we know of no fewer than three preparatory sketches (all oriented in reverse) that are related to it: a very free and summary study in black chalk and brown wash in the Louvre (fig. 58);[5] the drawing in the Bonna Collection, incised for transfer but differing from the final version, both in its larger dimensions and in a number of details; and a very finished drawing in pen and brown ink, pricked for transfer and wholly identical to the

Figure 57. Jacques Callot, *The Bathers*. Etching, Musée Lorrain, Nancy (inv. L. 270)

Figure 58. Jacques Callot, *The Bathers*. Black chalk and brown wash. Musée du Louvre, Département des Arts Graphiques, Paris (inv. 25116)

print, which belonged to the engraver Israël Silvestre and was bound with the other Callot drawings from his collection in an album bound for the 6th Duke of Devonshire, around 1827 (now at the Chatsworth Library).[6] To this can be added the studies for individual bathers in the Mariette album in the Louvre[7] and in the Jullienne album in the Hermitage.[8] Taken together, these works allow us to retrace the artist's path precisely, to grasp his working method and his aesthetic concerns.

Indeed, as one progresses from sheet to sheet, one sees the artist calling on more of his technical abilities as the project came into sharper focus. In the first sketch (fig. 58), broad wash strokes describe the landscape in large masses; combined with black chalk lines, they give a cursory indication of the mill, the vegetation, and especially the figures, with large areas of the surface left untouched. Quite different from this vigorous and summary treatment—which once led scholars to attribute this drawing to Claude Lorrain[9]—is the more elaborate pen work of the present drawing. Both the mill itself and the vernacular structures springing up around it are rendered in black chalk and pen and ink down to the slightest details—chimneys, windows, balustrades, stairways, waterspouts, stonework and bricks, woodwork, and transoms—as are the vegetation and figures, most of which were no doubt studied in preliminary sketches such as the ones in the Louvre. The lighter colored wash is applied in wide swatches for the cloudy sky, but more often, a fine brush is used to go over the black chalk lines and deepen the shadows. The few white areas of the paper left in reserve indicate sections of wall exposed to the sun or the harshly lit strand, against which the silhouettes stand out. By contrast, the Chatsworth drawing is done entirely in pen and brown ink, with a dry and meticulous execution particularly suited to transfer to copperplate. However, this drawing is so different in technique and style, not only from the preceding one but from most of Callot's graphic output, that some have tried to attribute it to the engraver Israël Henriet, Israël Silvestre's uncle. Moreover, this has also been the case with the nine other sketches for the series of *Italian Landscapes* and the forty-one preparatory studies for the above-mentioned *Book of Landscapes*, with which it shares its manner of execution and its provenance.[10]

Figure 59. Domenico Cresti (called Il Passignano) *Bathers at San Niccolò*. Oil on canvas. Private Collection

The topography, which is quite approximate in the Louvre sketch (in which the only identifiable element is the outline of the mill), becomes considerably more precise in the drawing from the Bonna Collection. Indeed, the background now contains the Ponte Vecchio, in a frontal view reminiscent of the second plate in the *Caprices*,[11] and the Palazzo Vecchio, curiously placed on the banks of the Arno and depicted from an angle identical to the one used by Callot in a preparatory sketch for another plate from the *Caprices*, the *Celebration on Piazza della Signoria*.[12] This latter motif, discreetly flanked by the Duomo cupola, disappears in the Chatsworth version and in the print, but its presence here proves that the artist felt no compunctions, for so complex a composition, about reprising and merging sketches and elements taken from other recent works. Of the various successive versions of *The Bathers* known today, the present one appears to be, if not the most faithful to the actual layout of the site, at least the version that most faithfully reproduces specific details of the topography, such as those found in a drawing by Federico Zuccaro from the late 1570s (today in the Louvre), which allowed us to identify the landscape,[13] and in another by Remigio Cantagallina in the Fondation Custodia,[14] drawn about 1620. Cantagallina was a pupil of Giulio Parigi's and helped train Callot, later becoming his collaborator.[15] More generally, and in other words, the present drawing can be situated at the heart of a working method that proceeds in stages, first by enriching the composition and adding complexity, then later simplifying and paring down the detail. The Bonna drawing is therefore the most elaborate and brilliant of the series, even

if one might prefer the virtuosity of the Louvre study (fig. 58), which borders on abstraction, or the serene balance and spareness of the final version (fig. 57). Callot here proves all his skill in the layering of successive planes and the use of elaborate perspective. He also gives free rein to his penchant for observing real life, including the many picturesque details of the scene from which the print takes its title.

Among the possible sources for this work, one must naturally cite the above-mentioned drawing by Federico Zuccaro. Callot's oft-mentioned concern with fitting into the Florentine tradition of scrupulously studying nature suggests that the similarity of vantage point and composition between the two is more than simple coincidence.[16] One must also mention a painting by Domenico Cresti (called Il Passignano), signed and dated 1600, known as *Bathers at San Niccolò* (fig. 59).[17] The latter indisputably depicts the same site; the mill is easily recognized, as are the buildings flanking it and, slightly in the background, the massive outline of the Porta San Niccolò with its crenellated towers. Still, the angle chosen is different, since the view is facing the buildings that almost entirely block the perspective, leaving the nearby hills just visible in the distance. The foreground is animated and densely packed with artfully arranged figures of bathers, certain of which show a clear concern with monumentality. Unlike the mix of landscape and genre scene that characterizes Callot's drawing, it is the genre scene that is the focus of Cresti's painting, resulting in a very different compositional balance. Nonetheless, one sees in both works, although fit into a tighter space in the painting, groups of men conversing or enjoying a swim, the interplay of nude bodies and garments dropped on the ground, gestures and postures that echo each other, and even several identical elements, such as the diver. This comparison[18] makes all the more sense when one realizes that the two artists knew each other in Rome and in Florence; that Callot engraved at least one of Passignano's paintings; that he was taught by him at the Accademia del Disegno; and that, according to Baldinucci, he asked Passignano to help him with the *Foire d'Impruneta*.[19] In addition, Passignano assisted Federico Zuccaro between 1575 and 1579, when the latter was hired to finish decorating the chapel of the Duomo in Florence. Several decades later, as the master's faithful disciple, he would hand down Zuccaro's heritage to the young printmaker from Lorraine.[20]

Thus the complex nature of the Bonna *Bathers* is confirmed. It can be appreciated as one of Callot's most attractive landscapes, at once extensive and strongly architectural, exemplary for its deep space suggesting a subtle aerial perspective, and remarkable for its atmospheric qualities and its luminous poetry, anticipating Bartholomeus Breenbergh and Claude Lorrain. This refined composition also provides a framework for a scene teeming with detail and anecdote, re-created with a meticulousness that leaves room for narrative verve. Thus, the engraver's characteristic synthesis of naturalism and theatrical aesthetics is realized

in a carefully staged succession of planes, so that the view of Florence that appears in the distance, broken up by the archways of the mill, evokes a theatrical backdrop painted as a trompe-l'oeil. In one sense a genre scene, *The Bathers* also draws the viewer into the drawing, provoking his curiosity in the same way as the minuscule passersby and onlookers who, in the plate from the *Caprices*, observe from the Ponte Vecchio the naked men stretched out on the banks or up to their waists in the waters of the Arno.

EMMANUELLE BRUGEROLLES
AND DAVID GUILLET

1. Meaume 1860, no. 711; Lieure 1924–27, vol. 3, no. 353; Nancy 1992, p. 305, no. 400.
2. Meaume 1860, nos. 715–18; Lieure 1924–27, vol. 3, nos. 264–67; Nancy 1992, pp. 297–99, nos. 380–83.
3. Meaume 1860, nos. 1187–98; Lieure 1924–27, vol. 3, nos. 268–77; Nancy 1992, pp. 299–304, nos. 384–98.
4. André Félibien and Pierre-Jean Mariette say that it was made by François Collignon, who might also have been the artist of the frontispiece plate; Daniel Ternois disputes this hypothesis: "Apart from the title page, the ten other pieces can only have been engraved by Callot himself, despite the opinion advanced by some excellent authors" (Ternois in Nancy 1992, p. 299).
5. Inv. 25116; Ternois 1962b, no. 432; Nancy 1992, p. 301, no. 386.
6. Regarding this album and its history, see Jaffé 1993; for the Chatsworth drawing, see also Ternois 1962b, no. 433; note that both this drawing and the one in the Bonna collection were conserved at Chatsworth until the 1984 sale.
7. Inv. 25092, 25092 bis, 25092 ter; Ternois 1962b, nos. 491–93; Nancy 1992, pp. 301–2, nos. 387–89.
8. Ternois 1962b, nos. 442–45, apparently except for no. 444; see also Nancy 1992, p. 300, fig. 3, and p. 302, under nos. 390, 394.
9. Ternois 1992, p. 42.
10. Daniel Ternois finally disproved this hypothesis (in Nancy 1992, pp. 299–300, 306–7).
11. Meaume 1860, no. 780; Lieure 1924–27, vol. 3, no. 220; Nancy 1992, p. 199.
12. Meaume 1860, no. 858; Lieure 1924–27, vol. 3, no. 259; Nancy 1992, p. 239, no. 22. Drawing conserved at the Hessisches Landesmuseum, Darmstadt (inv. HZ 1718); Ternois 1962b, p. 46, no. 17; Nancy 1992, p. 233, fig. 1; Florence 1986–87 [vol. 2], p. 184, no. 2.134.
13. Inv. 4625; Heikamp 1967, p. 56, pl. 20; Paris 1969, p. 61, no. 75.
14. Inv. 8701; Paris 1984–85a, p. 31, no. 62, pl. 14.
15. Félibien 1725, vol. 3, p. 367; Ternois 1962a, pp. 59–60.
16. Daniel Ternois (in Nancy 1992, p. 299) does not entirely discount this hypothesis: "The meeting with Zuccaro simply might have been a coincidence."
17. Martini 1959; Joan Lee Nissman in Florence 1986–87, [vol. 1], pp. 118–19, no. 1.24.
18. Detlef Heikamp (1967, pp. 56, 66–67, n. 62) was the first to relate the works of Zuccaro, Passignano, and Callot; it is true that Passignano's canvas, the only genre scene known by this artist, remains enigmatic, so much so that Joan Lee Nissman has conjectured an as yet unidentified "specific iconography."
19. Baldinucci 1681–1728 (1767–74 ed.), vol. 14, p. 137: "The highly famous creation of *The Fair at Impruneta*, a Florentine arm and a quarter in width and more than two-thirds of that arm in height; I heard from other artists who were alive at the time that the composition and arrangement of those infinite and marvelous groupings required the assistance of the great painter Domenico Passignani." See also Bruwaert 1912, pp. 29, 82; and Nancy 1992, p. 151, n. 27, and p. 247.
20. Florence 1986–87 [vol. 3], pp. 141–42; Nancy 1992, pp. 150–51. In this regard, it is difficult to distinguish Passignano's direct influence on Callot from his role as intermediary between Callot and Federico Zuccaro.

57. Pierre Brébiette

Mandres?, 1598?–Paris, 1642

Recto: *Triton and the Women of Tanagra*

Verso: *Study of Various Figures*

Ca. 1625–35

Recto: pen and brown ink, brush and gray wash over red chalk underdrawing; verso: pen and brown ink, 9⅛ × 12¹³⁄₁₆ in. (23.1 × 32.5 cm)

Inscribed on recto in pen and brown ink at lower right: *frago*; inscribed on verso: *De juliet on doit vint pins à la boulangère*

PROVENANCE: Sale, Christie's, London, July 10, 2001, lot 93; purchased at that sale by Jean Bonna

EXHIBITIONS: Paris 2006b, no. 9; Geneva 2006–7a

BIBLIOGRAPHY: Paola Pacht Bassani in Orléans 2001–2, p. 35

Pierre Brébiette is mentioned briefly if at all in the old sources, all the key texts of the period, which even then gave imprecise information about the most basic biographical facts.[1] He has been rediscovered in recent

decades, largely through the work of Jacques Thuillier. One can now trace the major stages of his career, especially his stay in Italy from 1617 to 1625, in Rome and also in Venice, where his presence was mentioned by Pierre-Jean Mariette;[2] and thereafter his activities in Paris from 1626 until his death in 1642, a date that now has been established firmly.[3] The archives have yielded documents that reveal, beyond intuitive comparisons and stylistic analogies,

Figure 60. Pierre Brébiette, *Sea Triumph with Galatea*. Etching. Musée des Beaux-Arts, Nancy (inv. 15.855)

the circles in which he traveled: first the French artists living in Italy in the 1620s around Claude Vignon and the publisher François Langlois; then his apprentices, clients, and patrons, as well as the painters whose works he etched in his Paris studio.

Brébiette's complex and engaging artistic personality seems deeply marked—in his choice of subjects, his stylistic elegance, and even his figure types—by knowledge of the mythological and allegorical decorations that Rosso and Primaticcio created for the palace at Fontainebleau. That influence, certainly dating to his formative period, was greatly enhanced by his education in Rome, where the young artist discovered Raphael and the Carracci and embraced the study of antiquity, the spirit and forms of which imbue his work. Brébiette considered himself a painter and even represented himself as painter to the king,[4] a title disputed by neither Félibien nor Mariette (although the latter did express some reservations).[5] Still, only about ten paintings are known that are or might be attributed to him.[6] It is above all as a printmaker that he achieved posthumous renown, leaving behind more than 300 etchings, including the famous friezes (fig. 60), prized by art lovers and copied and imitated long after his death.[7] His drawings, the first catalogue of which was prepared by Thuillier, then supplemented by the monographic exhibition of his work in the Musée des Beaux-Arts, Orléans, are thus crucial to our knowledge of the artist. A large number of the known drawings can be connected to prints; some can be related to his paintings, and the status and function of others are yet to be determined. The artist generally used red or black chalk, often adding white highlights, this combination yielding refined and subtle effects of material and modeling. But there are also several studies by Brébiette in pen and wash;

their more cursory touch and livelier technique suggest that these might correspond to an early state in the compositions' evolution, but there is no proof of this. In any case, the graphic style is entirely his; the exuberant blend of meticulous execution, sensually rendered figures, visual experimentation inspired by antiquity, and an immoderate penchant for movement that caused him to be branded as "eccentric" by Mariette,[8] who deemed him "a bit too libertine, but witty"—all these characteristics relate him to the Mannerist current, although his work cannot be easily defined as such.

The drawing in the Bonna collection cannot be linked directly to any currently known work of Brébiette's, nor is its technique similar to the other pen-and-wash studies that have been identified as his. Nonetheless, its attribution is indisputable, given the abundance of characteristic motifs. Among these are the face of the leaning woman with almond eyes, contoured with no more than a stroke of gray wash; the heads of the putti with full cheeks and curving brows; the curiously bent legs; the women's figures with their pronounced muscular thighs; the open hands, their fingers splayed

in a gesture strangely devoid of grace; and the schematic rendering of the turbulent water, its rolling waves conveying a sense of agitation. In at least two instances, there are elements so similar as to border on self-plagiarism: the monstrous fish with raised tail that closes the composition on the left is very much like the ones that populate *The Toilette of Thetis* and *Triumph at Sea with Neptune*,[9] and the group of four galloping horses can be found, with variations, in the two painted versions of *The Abduction of Proserpina* (fig. 61)[10] and in a red chalk drawing in the Bibliothèque Nationale, *Pandora Modeled by Hephaestus*,[11] as well as in a print with a religious subject, *Eli Carried to Heaven in a Chariot of Fire*.[12]

More striking than these details, however numerous and significant they may be, are the composition's style and organization. The accumulation of figures might at first seem jumbled, but in fact, they are linked by the swirling flow that surrounds and unites them, evoking the power of the water gods. While the scene is strongly punctuated by several vertical motifs—such as the abovementioned fish and the two female figures, particularly the one on the right, her arms spread wide in a pose reminiscent of an abduction scene from classical antiquity—there is nonetheless a powerful horizontal movement that runs across the sheet and ensures its formal and visual coherence, a compositional strategy recalling the famous engraved friezes.[13]

In dating the work more precisely, it should be stressed that comparable plates engraved by Brébiette during his Italian sojourn are generally more serene and balanced, such as *Toilette of Thetis* and *Triumph at Sea with Neptune*,

Figure 61. Pierre Brébiette, *The Abduction of Proserpina*. Oil on canvas. Musée Municipal, Châlons-en-Champagne (inv. 861–1–38.)

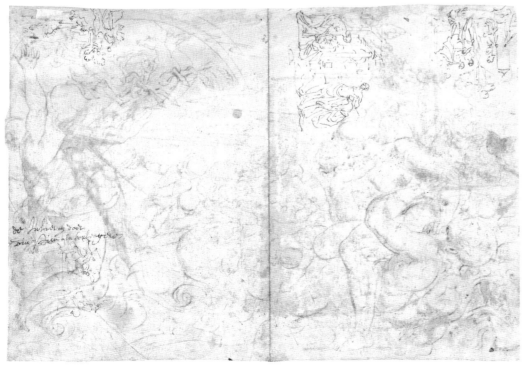

which historians agree date from about 1625, and which show the artist's attempt to achieve harmony akin to that of Raphael.[14] The more spirited character of the present composition and its apparent disorder suggest that it was among those the artist created in the late 1620s and early 1630s, after his return to Paris: the same pronounced musculature appears in drawings such as *Victims of Love* in the Musée de Beaux-Arts, Rouen;[15] and the same accumulation of putti in *Drunken Silenus*, the pendant of which is dated 1632,[16] and to an even greater extent in *Diana and Minerva Fleeing at Bacchus's Approach*, in which the cherubs are clustered on a monumental elephant, as they are here around Triton.[17]

The present drawing has recently appeared on the market and since has been identified both as an *Abduction of Tanagra* and as the *Capture of the Women of Tanagra by Triton*. This last drawn from Pausanias's *Description of Greece* is a subject rarely treated: "The women of Tanagra, as part of the mysteries of Dionysus, had gone down to the seashore to cleanse themselves, and Triton attacked them as they were bathing. The women then asked Dionysus to come to their rescue. The god heard them and triumphed over Triton after doing battle with him."[18] This interpretation helps explain the presence of the two nude women. The one on the left is certainly grappling with a triton, recognizable by his monstrous tail and athletic torso; a second male figure, of whom we see only the head, shoulders, and muscular arms, could be another triton or a second image of the same one fighting with another bather. We might also imagine that the two groups illustrate a single story that reads from right to left, from the initial aggression to final appeasement. The fact remains that there is no sign of Dionysus, to whom the women owe their safety, nor a fortiori of his battle against the sea monster. Curiously, in fact, the four horses beneath a semicircle that evokes the zodiac are more suggestive of Apollo and his chariot, except that one of the horses is ridden by a helmeted figure who holds in his hand a roughly sketched object that looks like a caduceus. Moreover, if one looks closely at the melee in which one of the two women appears at the mercy of her attacker, the one on the left seems calm, even triumphant—not through force but by the simple virtue of her charms, which reduce her adversary to silence and impotence with a hand gesture that is gracious rather than violent.

Can there be any doubt about the identification of the subject? At least two reasons suggest not. First, the composition, rendered with great vivacity in pen and wash, is neither polished nor likely to represent in its final state. Piling on motifs and figures was a favorite method of Brébiette's, and even a characteristic of his broader aesthetic, but here, they are more densely concentrated in a limited space than in almost any of his other works. The monstrous fish that closes the scene on the left is hardly visible, concealed by the group in the

foreground. The various groups of putti around the triton's tail seem to be telescoped; the one on the right, at once emblematic of an abduction scene and essential to the narrative and formal unity of the composition, was added after the fact to the best of the artist's ability, given the lack of space. The triton's head is clumsily placed next to the hooves of the horses, which are summarily sketched, while the right knee of his victim half covers one of the cherubs and her head extends beyond the frame (drawn in ink) in which it was meant to fit. The preparatory sketches of the friezes offer further examples of all these stylistic elements, as if Brébiette first had to rein in his rampant imagination to fit the imposed limits before giving it more ample space so that his creatures could arrange themselves harmoniously. Such is the case with the study for the *Sacrifice of Virginity* formerly in the Prat collection and recently given to the Louvre and with the study, also in the Louvre, for *Triumph at Sea with Neptune* (fig. 60), as well as the study in the Kupferstichkabinett, Dresden, preparatory for the second version of *The Abduction of Proserpina* (fig. 61).[19] The absence of any landscape element also tends to confirm this hypothesis: there is no distant perspective, no horizon line, no boulder acting as a repoussoir, no jetty in the foreground. The figures are alone between earth and sky with no spatial anchors, and this further accentuates the vertiginous effect of the whirlwind that seems to sweep everything along with it, again much like *The Abduction of Proserpina* in the Musée Municipal, Châlons-en-Champagne (fig. 61). As they are set against the other scenes of marine mythology (for example, fig. 60), one can imagine that at a later stage, the constituent elements of the composition were, or would have been, redistributed with a view toward narrative balance and coherence so as to conform with antique prototypes.

EMMANUELLE BRUGEROLLES AND
DAVID GUILLET

1. André Félibien (1666–88/1972, vol. 5, p. 262) insists he was born in "Mante," whereas numerous indications now lead us to think that his family came from southeast of Paris, and more specifically from Mandres (Seine-et-Marne); see Orléans 2001–2, pp. 33–35.

2. Mariette 1851–62, vol. 1 (1851–53), p. 186: "He had traveled in Italy, and he had especially stopped in Venice, struck by the beauty of the works of Paolo Veronese, several of whose paintings he engraved: these are not the least important works in his oeuvre."

3. Orléans 2001–2, pp. 34, 43.

4. Ibid., pp. 15, 28, 42, 100, no. 98, ill. p. 6. See also the *Self Portrait* of 1638, engraved by Augustin Quesnel and placed at the head of the volume *Opera diversa nunc primvm a Pietro Brebiette pictore region inventa Tabulis aeneis delineatas Anno Dom 1638* (ibid., p. 26, no. 88).

5. Félibien (1666–88/1972, vol. 5, p. 262) mentions jointly "Pierre Brébiette from Mante, & Daniel Rabel [who] painted and etched"; more articulate and explicit, Pierre-Jean Mariette (1851–62, vol. 1 [1851–53], p. 185) considers him a "painter, draftsman, and engraver," and adds: "As he found it easier to draw than to paint, he spent most of his life drawing."

6. Paola Pacht Bassani has catalogued nine paintings "gathered under the name Brébiette"; of the three other paintings published by Laura Muti (2001), she accepts only one (see Orléans 2001–2, pp. 16, 104).

7. "Nearly three hundred etchings," according to Jacques Thuillier (1996, p. 275); "between 350 and 400 pieces," according to Paola Pacht Bassani (in Orléans 2001–2, p. 47).

8. Mariette 1851–62, vol. 1 (1851–53), p. 185.

9. Orléans 2001–2, p. 55, no. 18, and p. 58, no. 22.

10. Ibid., p. 53, no. 15, ill. p. 14, and p. 88, no. 72, ill. p. 25.

11. Ibid., p. 89, no. 76.

12. Ibid., p. 86, no. 68.

13. See the *Twelve Great Friezes*, the pendants *Silenus and his Entourage Attacked by Wasps* and *Drunken Silenus*, the *Five Great Friezes* (ibid., pp. 59–61, no. 24, p. 82, nos. 59, 60, ill. pp. 83, 88, and no. 74, ill. p. 104).

14. Thuillier (1996, pp. 283, 294, n. 43) advances the hypothesis that these compositions might have influenced the young Poussin, who arrived in Rome in 1624 and who ten years later painted the four *Bacchanales* for the Cardinal de Richelieu.

15. Inv. 975-4-576; Orléans 2001–2, pp. 73–74, no. 45.

16. Ibid., pp. 82–83, no. 60.

17. Ibid., p. 80, no. 55; for a characterization of Brébiette's stylistic evolution in the 1630s, see Bassani in ibid., p. 23: "In the course of the 1630s, a more theatrical and dramatic viewpoint, a desire for a more pronounced 'sotto in su,' a taste for spectacular and dynamic bodily contortions, often in plunging view...appears more and more distinctly in Brébiette's art."

18. Pausanias's *Description of Greece* 9:1–4 (Boeotia).

19. Musée du Louvre, Département des Arts Graphiques, Paris, inv. RF 44324 (Los Angeles, Toledo, Naples, and Philadelphia 2005–6, pp. 56–57, no. 3), and inv. 20602 (Orléans 2001–2, p. 58, no. 23); Kupferstichkabinett, Dresden (Orléans 2001–2, p. 88, no. 73).

58 recto

58. Claude Lorrain (Claude Gellée)

Chamagne, Lorraine, 1604 or 1605–Rome, 1682

Recto: *Landscape with a Large Tree*

Verso: *Two Studies of a Dog*

Ca. 1640–45

Recto: pen and brown ink, brush and brown wash, heightened with white gouache, over black chalk underdrawing on blue paper; verso: red and black chalk, inscribed in pen and brown ink at right margin: *I* [?] / *primo,* 8¼ × 12¼ in. (21 × 31 cm)

Signed on recto in pen and brown ink at bottom center: *Claudio fecit*

PROVENANCE: Sale, Sotheby's, London, October 19, 1978, lot 1; Colnaghi, London; Private Collection, Chicago; C.G. Boerner, New York; acquired by Jean Bonna, 2006

BIBLIOGRAPHY: Roethlisberger 1979, pp. 25–27, figs. 34, 36

This painterly scene of a coastal landscape dominated by an ancient tree was only identified as the work of Claude Lorrain in 1978, when it surfaced on the London market in an album of mainly nineteenth-century drawings. Marcel Roethlisberger, who had published the authoritative catalogue raisonné of the drawings a decade earlier, declared it to be "one of the finest *addenda* to the *oeuvre* of Claude."[1] Although it is not connected to a known painting or print, the sheet displays many of the artist's favored themes and motifs. A lone traveler finds respite at the side of the road in the shade of a massive tree, his figure dwarfed by its massive bifurcated trunk and burgeoning foliage. He is rustic in his attire, but lacking the staff or animals that would identify him as a herdsman, he is more simply a traveler who has come around a bend and paused to take in the distant vista of the sea illuminated by the late-day sun.

As with many of Claude's drawings on blue paper, the scene was begun in pen and brown ink, over a preliminary sketch in black chalk. Brown wash was then applied in broad strokes over the foliage, barely respecting the contours of the pen-and-ink drawing below. Against these areas of shadow, which evoke the lush

58 verso (size reduced)

attractiveness of shade, the artist used white gouache to carefully pick out individual leaves caught in the sunlight, thereby giving the tree an impressive sense of volume and vigor. Further touches of white create a pale repoussoir of the stony outcropping at left and accentuate the glow of the sky along the horizon punctuated by the pen-and-ink flecks representing distant sails. While the sheet has qualities in common with Claude's plein air studies, especially in the rapid penwork of the tree,

it is ultimately a more pictorial sheet likely done in the studio as an autonomous work, judging from the expansive vista to the right and the overall sense of grandeur of the composition. As with many drawings of this type, the Bonna sheet bears a prominent signature in the center foreground.

The scene does not seem to have been intended as a setting for a specific mythological or biblical narrative. Rather, Claude created a timeless landscape conducive to reverie. A

cluster of antique buildings in the distance and the limpid late-afternoon light both evoke the passage of time, and the traveler pausing at the bend in the road likewise suggests a journey. Urban and educated patrons would have appreciated such Arcadian subjects, brimming with reverence for nature and nostalgia for times past.[2] The motif of the figure seen from the back, looking off into the unseen distance, offers the viewer someone to identify with, and by extension, a way to enter the composition. It was a device that would become a favorite of nineteenth-century Romantic artists such as Caspar David Friedrich.

At the time of its discovery, Roethlisberger considered the Bonna sheet a work of Claude's maturity, pointing to its pictorial handling and control, and suggested a date of about 1640–45. Jon Whiteley also characterized the late 1630s and 1640s as a period when Claude began to combine a range of graphic techniques to painterly effect.[3] On the verso are two light chalk sketches of resting dogs of the type that often appear in Claude's paintings as the companions of herdsmen or princes.[4]

PERRIN STEIN

1. Roethlisberger 1979, p. 27.
2. A nuanced discussion of Claude's pastoral themes can be found in London 1994, pp. 29–37.
3. Whiteley 1998, p. 130.
4. For examples, see Roethlisberger 1961, vol. 2, figs. 92, 134, 151, 154, 173, 186.

59

59. Claude Lorrain (Claude Gellée)

Chamagne, 1604 or 1605–Rome, 1682

Coastal Landscape with a Battle on a Bridge

Ca. 1655

Pen and brown ink, brown and gray wash, heightened with white gouache, over traces of black chalk, on light brown-tinted paper, framing line in pen and brown ink, 6⅞ × 9¹⁄₁₆ in. (17.5 × 23 cm)

PROVENANCE: Edward Habich, Kassel; sale, H. G. Gutekunst, Stuttgart, April 27, 1899, and days following, lot 287; D. S. Collection, Paris; sale, Hôtel Drouot, Paris, December 17, 1924, lot 142, illus. p. 33; Grosjean-Maupin Collection, Paris; Wildenstein and Company, New York; acquired by Jean Bonna, 1998

EXHIBITIONS: Paris 1925, no. 509; Paris 1948, no. 516; Munich 1983, no. 57; Paris 2006b, no. 13; Geneva 2006–7a

BIBLIOGRAPHY: Roethlisberger 1961, p. 330, under no. LV137; Roethlisberger 1968, vol. 1, pp. 288–89, no. 760, vol. 2, fig. 760; Daniel and Serebriannaya 1995, p. 87, under no. 8, ill. p. 88 (with erroneous caption); Denison 2006, p. 521

The complex technique of this magnificent drawing highlights the care that Claude Lorrain took in its execution. A preliminary sketch in black chalk, visible in the line marking the horizon, has been covered over almost entirely by the pen and ink and wash mixed with white gouache, added later. The sky is rendered in light brown washes alternating with areas heightened in white. A thick line frames the scene, although we do not know whether it was put there by the artist (who often did this on his "finished" drawings) or whether a collector added it during a subsequent mounting. A gold strip, traces of which are still visible on the edges of the sheet, might have been added at the same time.[1]

The harmonious composition is characteristic of the grand style that Claude Lorrain perfected in the 1650s. In the works he created at that time, the painter used his increasingly expressive talents as a landscape artist and his sensitivity to light effects to treat noble and serious subjects. It was during this period that he definitively established what is now known as "classical" or "ideal" landscape: an image in which nature, instead of being merely a silent witness, itself becomes the true protagonist of the historical events portrayed.

At the edge of the coast, at the far end of which we can make out a port city on a large bay, occurs a scene of rare violence in Claude's work: two armies confront each other in tumultuous battle on an arched bridge, while shepherds and their families scramble to lead their flocks to safety. Although the battle is taking place in the middle ground, the conflict is echoed not only by the landscape, in which a fierce wind bends the branches of the majestic tree at the center of the scene, but also by the execution of the drawing itself, which is characterized by many small nervous touches of white highlighting, as well as by the human and animal figures and the leaves of the trees. Everything is trembling; everything is in motion; nature itself seems to be reacting to the drama of this battle.

As Marcel Roethlisberger noted, there are many differences between this drawing and the corresponding painting, which is now in the Pushkin Museum, Moscow.[2] The large canvas was executed in 1655 for Pope Alexander VII, as is indicated by an inscription that the artist wrote on the verso of the corresponding page in his *Liber Veritatis*, the volume in which he copied nearly all his painted works in drawing form from 1635 onward. The inscription reads: *fai pp Alessandri / Claudi fecit / in V.R* (made for Pope Alexander / made by Claude / in the city of Rome) (fig 62).[3] The painting has a pendant depicting *The Rape of Europa*, created for the same patron and now also in Moscow. On the drawing in the *Liber Veritatis* made from this latter composition, the artist wrote *faict al Cardinale creato pero giusto papa* (made for the cardinal who has just been named pope). One can therefore conclude that *The Rape of Europa* was painted before its pendant.[4] Cardinal Fabio Chigi (1599–1667), an important collector and artists' patron, was elected pope in April 1655, which allows us to date the creation of these two canvases quite precisely.

It is interesting to note that, in the Habich sale at which the present drawing appeared for the first time, it was preceded by a drawing of

Figure 62. Claude Gellée, called Lorrain, *A Coastal Landscape with a Battle on a Bridge*. Pen, dark brown wash, highlighted with white, on blue paper. British Museum, London (inv. BM 143; LV 137)

the same format depicting *The Rape of Europa*, created in preparation for the Moscow canvas and today in the Kupferstichkabinett, Berlin.[5] Apparently the two drawings had remained together until the Habich collection was dispersed.

Claude was clearly pleased with these two compositions, since he executed painted versions of them that are almost identical to the originals, a rare occurrence in his oeuvre; the second version of *The Battle on the Bridge* is now in the Virginia Museum of Fine Arts, Richmond, and the one of *The Rape of Europa* is in the collection of Queen Elizabeth II.[6] Following the lead of Pierre Rosenberg, Marcel Roethlisberger suggested identifying the battle as the one in which the emperor Constantine met his rival Maxentius on the Milvian Bridge (known as the Ponte Molle) in 312 A.D. According to the historian Eusebius of Caesarea, Constantine saw a great flaming cross in the sky before the battle, bearing the words *In hoc signum vinces* (By this sign, you shall conquer). Inspired by this vision, the emperor adopted the cross as part of his blazon and scored a great victory. This hypothesis led Roethlisberger to point out the presence in the canvas of ancient armor and crowns on the heads of the two generals, details that the scale of the drawing does not allow to be included. It is important to note that such a battle, a crucial event in the Church's definitive victory, would be an especially appropriate choice for a pontiff.[7] It might be objected that one cannot see in either the painting or the drawings the victorious banner with its blazoned cross, and that Claude chose to situate his battle not on a

bridge over the Tiber near the walls of Rome but near the sea, a location that does not really conform to the historical circumstances. Michael Kitson demonstrated convincingly that, in his Virgilian works, the artist took the liberty of altering geographical facts to suit the needs of his composition, and one can imagine that he proceeded no differently in his few illustrations of historical episodes.[8] In short, it appears that he wanted to evoke the battle on the Milvian Bridge rather than depict it accurately.[9]

While the composition of the present drawing is nearly identical to that of the Moscow painting, it does differ in several details, as it also does from the version in the *Liber Veritatis*, although the latter is closer to the painting: the large tree has been moved toward the middle of the scene, which allows the artist to develop the left portion; the volume of its branches is heavier, and the port in the distance is less clearly visible. The bodies of the wounded soldiers falling from the bridge seen in both the canvas and the drawing in the *Liber Veritatis* do not appear in the Bonna drawing. Moreover, in the Bonna drawing, the figures of the herdsmen and their flocks are more monumental, so that the space of the landscape seems more limited than that in the painting. Because of these differences, Roethlisberger disputed the thesis that this is a preparatory sketch for the Chigi painting, considering it instead a slightly later variation.[10] The artist was known to reprise certain compositions in autonomous drawings. Many theories have been advanced as to the reasons for this. It may have been at the request of a friend or collector (we know that the artist was loath to part with his drawings, but several sheets with dedications inscribed on them exist). Or perhaps it was for the artist's own enjoyment, to reproduce a work that he considered particularly successful.[11] The present drawing must have been made fairly near in time to when the painting was created, in 1655.

CAREL VAN TUYLL

1. Bernadette Py at the Louvre, whom I thank for her insights, denies the possibility that this could indicate traces of mounting by Everhard Jabach (1618–1695).
2. Daniel and Serebriannaya 1995, no. 8, ill.; Marcel Roethlisberger in Munich 1983, p. 122.
3. Kitson 1978, pp. 137–38, no. 137, ill.
4. Ibid., pp. 136–37, no. 136, ill.
5. Inv. 4,537; Roethlisberger 1968, vol. 1, no. 758.
6. H. Diane Russell in Washington and Paris 1982–83, no. 44.
7. Roethlisberger 1961, vol. 1, p. 330, under no. LV137.
8. Russell in Washington and Paris 1982–83, p. 174; Kitson 1960, p. 316 (reprinted in Kitson 2000, p. 7).
9. Roethlisberger in Munich 1983, pp. 121–22.
10. Ibid., p. 122, under no. 57.
11. Kitson 1963 (reprinted in Kitson 2000, p. 77); Roethlisberger 1968, vol. 1, p. 83. For examples of drawings with dedications, see Whiteley 1998, p. 35.

60. Claude Lorrain (Claude Gellée)

Chamagne, 1604 or 1605–Rome, 1682

Landscape with View of Mount Soracte

1663

Black chalk and brown wash, framing line in brown wash, 8⅜ × 12⅝ in. (21.3 × 32.1 cm)

Signed and dated on verso: *Claudio inven / fecit Roma / 1663*

PROVENANCE: Don Livio Odescalchi (1652–1713), Rome; Odescalchi family, until 1957; H. M. Calmann; his widow, Madame H. M. Calmann; sale, Christie's, London, December 8, 1987, lot 157; acquired through Christie's, London, by Jean Bonna, 1999

EXHIBITIONS: Paris 2006b, no. 14; Geneva 2006–7a

BIBLIOGRAPHY: Roethlisberger 1968, vol. 1, pp. 39, 338, no. 906, vol. 2, fig. 906; Roethlisberger 1971, p. 9; Denison 2006, p. 521

Mount Soracte, mentioned by Horace in a famous ode (I, 9), stands roughly twenty-five miles north of Rome in the Tiber Valley. The Flaminian Way runs along its flanks, and the site, celebrated for both the beauty of its environs and its literary associations, was easily accessible to artists in Rome in the seventeenth century. Claude Lorrain depicted it in several drawings.[1] The present drawing is among the last and most majestic of these. Marcel Roethlisberger rightly considers it one of the most splendid studies from nature known to be from the artist's later period.[2]

It has been established that, in his youth, Claude drew from nature copiously and enthusiastically; his first biographer, Joachim von Sandrart, who had known him in the 1630s, reported that Claude liked to walk in the outskirts of Rome and that he spent long hours trying to "penetrate nature," observing the sky and the colors of the sunrise and sunset and drawing panoramas.[3] In oft-quoted passages, Sandrart alludes to excursions in the Roman countryside that he took with Claude, Nicolas Poussin, and Pieter van Laer, to draw and even paint "directly from nature." The many youthful drawings by Claude that clearly have been made from nature were produced during such excursions (fig. 63).[4] With advancing age and ill health—we know that he suffered from gout—the number and frequency of those walks diminished, and his drawings from nature became scarcer, although they did not disappear entirely from his work. The present drawing is a typical example of the small number of such drawings known from this later period, which count among the master's most beautiful studies.

Claude evokes a serene and grandiose nature scene with simple monumentality, in which time appears to stand still. Nothing moves except some birds in flight, who underscore the depth of the sky. Dispensing with any depiction of details, the artist sketched his view in broad strokes of black chalk, before taking up his brush and fashioning the landscape in washes of varying opacity. The result is a very painterly drawing. The strongest contrasts are concentrated in the foreground, where masses of dark rock border a luminous path that winds its way toward a thicket of shadowy trees. In the distance, the mountains are only slightly differentiated from one another through the use of transparent washes. A fortified farm, sketchily indicated at the far left, is the only reference to a human presence in this sublime landscape. The thick framing line, painted with a brush, indicates that the artist considered this study a finished, independent work.

The drawing's provenance is interesting, as it was part of an album put together either by the artist himself or by his immediate heirs. It then belonged to one of the greatest collectors of his day, Don Livio Odescalchi (1652–1713). The nephew of Pope Innocent XI, Odescalchi assembled in his Roman palazzo a huge and splendid collection of paintings, sculptures, tapestries, and drawings, the inventory of which was established in 1713–14 after the owner's death.[5] Some three hundred drawings by Claude figured among all these riches: the inventory reveals that a drawer in one of the

Figure 63. Claude Lorrain (Claude Gellée), *An Artist Drawing by a Waterfall,* ca. 1635. Black chalk, red chalk, pen, and brown wash. Teylers Museum, Haarlem (inv. S. 44)

before he acquired Queen Christina's collection.[10] The inventory lists several paintings by contemporary landscape artists such as Pierfrancesco Mola, Nicolas Poussin, Salvator Rosa, Giovanni Francesco Grimaldi, Gaspard Dughet, and especially Crescenzio Onofri. While he owned no paintings by Claude as far as is known, it is nonetheless certain that Don Livio was interested in landscape art. It is entirely possible that the so-called Wildenstein album, as well as the other two volumes of drawings by Claude inventoried as being in Odescalchi's possession in 1713, were assembled expressly for him, and that he acquired them directly from the painter's heirs.

CAREL VAN TUYLL

cabinets housing Don Livio's drawings collection contained "six fascicles of five bound sheets, with sixty-two drawings of animals and plants by Claude Gellée of Lorraine," along with "another book bound in parchment with eighty-one drawings by Claude Gellée of Lorraine" and "another book bound in parchment, oblong, with one hundred fifty-two drawings of landscapes by Claude Gellée."[6]

The drawing in the Bonna collection, still mounted on its original album sheet, is from the second of the described volumes. This volume was preserved intact in the Odescalchi collection until a fairly recent date; its dispersal began only in 1957, when Hans Calmann acquired eight drawings from the album, including this one.[7] Since the artist's death, therefore, this drawing has changed hands only three times, which partly accounts for the remarkable freshness of its state of conservation. In 1960, Georges Wildenstein acquired the rest of the album, containing sixty drawings; and later it belonged to the collector Norton Simon, who had it unbound and dispersed the drawings.

Analyzing the contents of the so-called Wildenstein album, Marcel Roethlisberger [8] noted that the ensemble of drawings composing it was representative, in both chronology

and subject, of the artist's best graphic work. He concluded that the album must have been put together by someone endowed with excellent taste and an intimate knowledge of Claude Lorrain's drawn oeuvre, and suggested that this must have been either the artist himself or at least one of his heirs immediately after his death. Whatever the case may be, it does seem that the album was intended for an eminent collector, but unfortunately it is not known who owned it from 1682, the year the artist died, to 1713, when it was first mentioned in the posthumous inventory of Don Livio Odescalchi's collection. Since Odescalchi acquired, in 1692, the nearly intact collection of artworks formerly owned by Queen Christina of Sweden (1626–1686), several authors have suggested that the queen might have been the album's first owner. But this seems highly unlikely; there is no indication that Christina of Sweden collected, or even liked, the works of Claude Lorrain—she does not figure among his patrons and owned no paintings by him—and in general, she showed little interest in landscapes, preferring instead the human figure and historical scenes.[9] On the other hand, Odescalchi clearly was very interested in landscapes, as is indicated by the inventory of his paintings drawn up in 1691, that is, one year

1. Roethlisberger 1968, vol. 1, nos. 100, 362, 906, 911.
2. Ibid., p. 39.
3. Sandrart 1675–79; English translation in Roethlisberger 1961, vol. 1, pp. 47–48. See also San Francisco and Williamstown 2006–7, for an illuminating analysis of Claude's use of nature drawings.
4. Sandrart 1675–79; English translation in Roethlisberger 1961, vol. 1, pp. 48–49, 51–52.
5. For the part of the inventory concerning the drawings, see Roethlisberger 1986, pp. 5–30; the original Italian text was published in Meijer 1984, pp. 250–54.
6. "Sei Quinternetti di carta legati assieme con sessanta due disegni rappresentati Ani mali, e Piante di Claudio Gellé Lorenese"; "Alto Libro in foglio coperto di carta pecora con ottant'uno disegni di Claudio Gellé Lorenese"; and "Altro Libro in foglio coperto di carta pecora bislungo con cento cinquanta due disegni di Paesi di Claudio Gellé." Roethlisberger 1986, p. 20; Meijer 1984, p. 250.
7. The details of the provenance are given in Roethlisberger 1968, vol. 1, p. 66; and Roethlisberger 1971, p. 6.
8. Roethlisberger 1962, pp. 10–11.
9. Roethlisberger 1968, vol. 1, p. 70; Roethlisberger 1971, pp. 7–8. For the inventories of Christina of Sweden's collection, as well as an analysis of her artistic preferences, see Montanari 1997.
10. The unpublished inventory, Inventario delli quadri dell'Ecc.ᵐᵒ Sig.ʳᵉ Pr.ᵖᵉ Don Livio 1691 li 13. Gen.°, is conserved at the Archivio Storico Odescalchi, Rome (inv. VII E 10); thanks to Dr. Marco Pizzo for his generous assistance.

60

61. Charles Le Brun

Paris, 1619–Paris, 1690

Two Draped Women, One Reclining, the Other Kneeling

Red chalk, 9¹³⁄₁₆ × 12⁷⁄₁₆ in. (25 × 31.6 cm)

PROVENANCE: Galerie Arnoldi-Livie, Munich; acquired by Jean Bonna, 2005

EXHIBITIONS: Paris 2006b, no. 15; Geneva 2006–7a

Although primarily known for his large secular decorations in the Hôtel Lambert, the Château of Vaux-le-Vicomte, and the Château of Versailles, Charles Le Brun also created many religious paintings, which he produced during two key periods in his career. The first of these was on his return from Rome in 1646, when he was assigned several commissions. Notably, there were the two "May paintings" given by the goldsmiths' guild to Notre-Dame, comprising the *Crucifixion of Saint Andrew* and *The Martyrdom of Saint Stephen*, dated 1647 and 1651 and which are still on site today.[1] There are also two works from 1653: *Christ in the Wilderness Served by Angels* and *The Feast at the House of Simon*, both intended for the Carmelites of the rue Saint-Jacques; these are now in the Louvre and the Gallerie dell'Accademia, Venice, respectively.[2] Finally, in 1654, Le Brun created for Jean-Jacques Olier, founder of the Saint-Sulpice seminary, the decorations for the chapel, along with the painting for the high altar, *The Descent of the Holy Spirit* (completed 1657).[3]

Then, toward the end of his life, sensing that he was starting to lose royal favor, Le Brun returned to religious works with two series of easel paintings. One series, from 1687, depicts scenes from the life of Moses: *Moses Defending the Daughters of Jethro* and *The Wedding of Moses and Zipporah*, both in the Galleria Estense, Modena.[4] The second series, painted between 1685 and 1689, depicts scenes from the life of Christ: *Adoration of the Shepherds* and *Christ Carrying the Cross* in the Louvre, *Jesus Raised on the Cross* in the Musée des Beaux-Arts, Troyes, and *Jesus's Entry into Jerusalem* in the Musée d'Art et d'Histoire, Saint-Étienne.[5]

The present drawing is related to the artist's earliest works, which were created about 1649–50, after his return from Italy, and illustrate episodes from the life of Moses: *The Brazen Serpent* and *Moses Striking the Rock*.[6] According to Guillet de Saint-Georges, Le Brun "twice painted the brazen serpent that Moses lifted up in the wilderness. He worked on it once for one of his closest friends, named M. Lenoir. He treated the subject a second time, for the convent of the third order of Saint Francis, in Picque-Puce [*sic*: Picpus]. M. Le Brun painted that one only in first draft and didn't have time to retouch it."[7] The smaller-format canvas, now in the City Art

Gallery, Bristol (fig. 64), served as model for one of the ten parts of the *Tapestry of the Life of Moses*, woven at the Gobelins several years later after designs by Le Brun and Nicolas Poussin. The other composition is known only through an engraving by Étienne Gantrel,[8] in which one can note several differences from the canvas in Bristol, especially in the left-hand portion.

The graphic arts department of the Louvre has several studies of individual figures for the Bristol composition, which tell us about the working method of an artist who took pains to "constantly follow nature and not do anything without [reference to] it."[9] Indeed, after a first overall sketch, Le Brun produced studies of the different motifs treated individually, such as drapery for the standing man in profile and especially, figures drawn from nude models in the poses retained for the final version.[10] The drawing in the Bonna Collection is preparatory to the group of young women in the center of the composition (fig. 64); the kneeling one weeps over her recumbent companion, who has died from a snake bite. This is clearly a study from life, and the fact that Le Brun took the trouble to depict the whole group strongly indicates that he envisioned reproducing it more completely in the painted version. The face of the kneeling woman, conveying

Figure 64. Charles Le Brun, *Moses and the Brazen Serpent*. Oil on canvas. City Art Gallery, Bristol

Figure 65. Nicolas Poussin, *Moses Striking the Rock*. Oil on canvas. State Hermitage Museum, Saint Petersburg (inv. 1117)

61

both distress and despair, seems to be the essential feature of the present drawing and corresponds to one of the artist's major preoccupations, the expression of the passions, which resulted in his lecture to the Académie Royale de Peinture et de Sculpture in 1668, later illustrated by a series of drawings engraved by Jean Audran after the artist's death.[11] The realism with which the models' poses are rendered should also be noted. Instead of stressing the details, the artist put his effort into simplifying the forms in order to make them more effective: the red chalk line is pronounced, repeated and angular for the outlines, broken for the garments' sharp folds, less insistent for the long parallel hatchings that suggest shadows and the modeling. Here is the assertion of a "realist impulse, a deliberate rejection of the linear grace that he had learned from Vouet, and even a hint of brutality"; he cultivated "more vigorous forms, a more dramatic chiaroscuro, and more emphatic movements that might even lead to a certain awkwardness . . . or limit his ability to describe anatomically plausible forms."[12]

Moreover, the poses of the two figures can be likened to those adopted by Nicolas Poussin for the group at the right of *Moses Striking the Rock*, painted for Jacques Stella and today in the Hermitage (fig. 65).[13] Executed in 1649, the painting arrived several months later in Paris, where Le Brun could have seen it, as he could have seen other canvases by Poussin then located in the capital, notably the *Sacraments* owned by Paul Fréart de Chantelou[14] as well as works sent to Parisian "art lovers," such as Jean Pointel and J. Serisier. In fact, it was during this period that Le Brun was returning to Poussin's lesson, as is shown by his conceiving an episode from the life of Moses, his "dividing up" the subject into juxtaposed groups on the canvas, and finally, his research into the expression of emotions.

Emmanuelle Brugerolles

137

1. Versailles 1963, p. 25, no. 10, and p. 27, no. 16.
2. Ibid., pp. 45–47, nos. 18, 19.
3. A version of this composition is at the Louvre; Versailles 1963, p. 63, no. 24.
4. Ibid., p. 127, nos. 44, 45.
5. Ibid., pp. 131–39, nos. 46–49.
6. Painting in the Louvre.

7. Guillet de Saint-Georges 1854, vol. 1, p. 9.
8. The hypothesis is in Beauvais 2000, vol. 1, p. 331.
9. Dézallier d'Argenville 1762, vol. 4, p. 127.
10. Beauvais 2000, vol. 1, pp. 331–34, nos. 1138–45.
11. Drawings in the Musée du Louvre, Département des Arts Graphiques; Pinault Sørensen 2000, p. 550, no. 1974, and pp. 562–63, nos. 2009–11, 2015, 2019.

12. Montagu 1992, pp. 532, 537, 540.
13. Paris and London 1994–95, pp. 419–20, no. 185.
14. Today they belong to the Duke of Sutherland and are on loan to the National Gallery of Scotland, Edinburgh (ibid., pp. 313–21, nos. 107–13).

62. Pierre Puget

Marseille, 1620–Fougette, 1694

Warship under Sail, with a Tartan on the Left and Another Vessel on the Right

Ca. 1670–85

Black chalk, gray and brown wash on vellum, framing line in pen and brown ink, 10⅞ × 16⅛ in. (27.6 × 41 cm)

Mounting from the second half of the 18th century (dry mark by the mounter ARD, Lugt 172)

Old inscription in pen and brown ink on the mounting: *Puget*; old inscriptions on the back of its original framing: *Ce précieux dessin est le plus capital des P. / que possède le ministre Louvois, qui est connu sous le nom de Michelange Tolosain*; further on: *Tolosain*; further on: *extremement rare, f. par le Puget*; further on: *Aor*

PROVENANCE: François Michel Le Tellier (1641–1691), marquis de Louvois; Pierre-François Basan (1723–1797); sale, Paris, December 1–19, 1798, lot 121; purchased at that sale by Basan fils for 90 livres; Artemis Fine Arts, New York; acquired by Jean Bonna, 2002

EXHIBITIONS: Paris 2006b, no. 16; Geneva 2006–7a

BIBLIOGRAPHY: Casselle 1982, p. 183

Pierre Puget spent most of his career in port cities, and his earliest work on naval decoration dates back to 1644. Although he had settled in Genoa in 1661, the king called him back in 1668 to oversee the decoration of ships in the Toulon dockyards. It was from that date until 1678 that Puget's output was most closely associated with the maritime world. Still, not wishing to be confined to this field, Puget contributed during those same years, as both architect and sculptor, to projects for beautifying the cities of Toulon and Marseille, even as he also worked on several marble groupings intended for Versailles. The drawings related to the world of sailing form a separate subset of his oeuvre, the typology of which was established by Klaus Herding.[1] The

artist first produced a small group of technical drawings, designed to document ship models or to record the configuration of a port. One can also attribute to him several plans for ship's decorations, among them the large *Design for the Decoration of a Warship* in the Metropolitan Museum, but there exist few such drawings in his hand.[2] However, it is the naval scenes that constitute by far the most important group. In these, Puget reveals himself to be a remarkable draftsman of boats as well as a landscape artist with a mastery of the most delicate light effects. Works of this type were generally executed on expensive supports, most often fine calfskin, occasionally parchment, and they therefore must be considered luxury works. While those naval scenes were only a side activity in Puget's career, today they account for two-thirds of the roughly 150 drawings attributed to him.[3]

This particular drawing on vellum by Puget was rediscovered only recently, but its composition is familiar; another, practically identical version is now in the Musée Bonnat (fig. 66).[4] It had been known previously through an engraving by Honoré Coussin (1698–1779), who produced several plates from naval scenes by this artist.[5] Puget sketched the composition in black chalk on a smooth vellum backing, then finished it with a brush, without any recourse to the pen.[6] The ship's main features are rendered in black ink, but the forms have been modeled using a brown wash, broadly applied for the sea and the objects in the background. Extremely precise in his depiction of the ship, the artist is also highly attentive to atmospheric effects. In particular, he managed to suggest the sea's opalescent luminosity by playing off the two tones of ink and by adding in the distance nearly transparent

Figure 66. Pierre Puget, *Warship*. Pen, black ink, and gray wash on vellum. Musée Bonnat, Bayonne (inv. RF 50911)

62

washes, which exploit vellum's specific ability to reflect light.

The bearing of the ship, which is sailing on the high seas, is observed exactly, and by introducing several particularities in the arrangement of the sails, the artist captured a sense of the moment. The mainsail has been taken up to give wind to the foresail, and the main topsail naturally takes the wind out of the foretopsail. He omitted certain details for purely decorative reasons or out of a desire to simplify; he did not depict the parrot on the bowsprit (the bowsprit should comprise two rows of sails) and neglected to draw the base of the mizzenmast. In the middle ground at left, he put in a two-masted tartan; this type of craft, which he often used as a secondary motif, was present on all the Mediterranean coasts and notably navigated off Italian shores. A warship is shown on the right, its mizzenmast oddly displaced toward the fore.[7] These small technical approximations are hardly rare in the

artist's oeuvre, and are repeated unvaryingly from one version to the next. Although the artist gave the main subject a nearly monumental presence, the vessel he depicted was nonetheless fairly modest, of the fifth or last class according to the standard classification and characteristic of ships built in the French dockyards after 1670.

Puget's earliest known naval scene is *Vessel Firing a Cannon Shot*, dated 1651.[8] He also produced simple pen and ink drawings during that period, such as *Vessels against a Colonnade in Ruins*, in which the forms are modeled by fine parallel hatching reminiscent of engravings.[9] That method was then abandoned in favor of a much more painterly approach as the artist progressively put aside the pen for the brush, which he often used alone. By 1654, his drawings were being executed in a style that hardly ever varied, making it difficult to establish a precise chronology.[10] Puget's first naval scenes date from a time when the

Toulon shipyards generated only sporadic employment, which confers a particular resonance on the grandiose visions of certain vellum drawings from this time, such as *Vessels against a Colonnade in Ruins* or *Vessels in Port near an Obelisk in Ruins*.[11] When he returned to Toulon in 1668 after spending seven years in Genoa, the king's ambitions had changed the situation, and the royal dockyards were now the site of great building campaigns. It was from this period of intense marine activity, from roughly 1670 to the beginning of the 1680s, that most of the artist's naval scenes must date. All indications suggest that his works were especially prized by those directly connected with the building of the fleet.

The present drawing belonged to François Michel Le Tellier, Marquis de Louvois (1641–1691), who, as France's Minister of War beginning in 1672, then as Colbert's successor in 1683, exerted direct authority over the Toulon dockyards. While several affectionate dedications convey that Puget reserved some of his most beautiful vellum works for his friends, it can be assumed that he also frequently gave objects of this type to his patrons. It is not impossible that he sent this one to Louvois, at the time when the latter took over for Colbert. Furthermore, an old inscription on the back of the original frame indicates that the minister owned other works by the artist. These sorts of drawings were not necessarily created for a specific person; some of the most ambitious ones include a blank cartouche intended for an eventual dedication, which was never filled in.

It was with an eye toward prestige that Colbert recommended the use of vellum by the shipyard artists, just as he required its use by the artists who created the collection of natural history drawings from the royal gardens or by the designers of emblematic devices attached to the Académie des Inscriptions et Belles-Lettres. At the same time, there was a separate tradition of naval scenes drawn on this support for private collectors; during that period, for example, Dominique Barrière (ca. 1618–1678) was drawing handsome coastal views in Rome with a very similar technique.[12] On the other hand, neither Jean-Baptiste de La Rose (1612–1687), who worked in Toulon at the same time as Puget and whose paintings of boats found favor even in the Court, nor Luca Villamage (1651–1725), who worked at the dockyard shortly afterward, seems ever to have used vellum, and it is difficult to establish exactly when its use for decorative works became prevalent in the southern French ports.[13]

The present vellum drawing also poses the issue of replicas. Between this version and the one in Bayonne, the differences are practically negligible. The artist confined himself to copying the piece very precisely, down to the movement of the waves, with only one variation in detail; the prow of the vessel is here decorated with a crest bearing the arms of France, which does not appear on the Bayonne version.

The habit of copying his best compositions was adopted early on by Puget; the Musée de Beaux-Arts, Marseille, for example, has two versions of a large vellum drawing from the mid-1650s, almost identical in format, depicting *Vessels in Marseille Harbor*.[14] There are also three similar versions of *View of a Galley* and *Two Vessels on a Calm Sea*.[15] In the same way, the composition of *A Frigate at Sea* in the Metropolitan Museum recurs in two vellum drawings now in Marseille.[16] It is quite likely that Puget executed these different replicas by very carefully transferring the composition from a prototype drawn on paper.

Puget raised the genre of naval scenes to an unparalleled level in seventeenth-century France, so much so that today he stands as a seemingly isolated figure. The question of his relations with the Italian and Dutch milieus has often been raised, and his depictions of galleys have been likened to works by Jacques Callot, Filippo Napoletano, and Stefano della Bella, whom he sometimes copied.[17] The type of vessel portrayed, along with the sense of composition and the attention to atmosphere, likens the present vellum to the works of Dutch marine artists such as Ludolf Bakhuizen or Willem Van de Velde the Younger.[18] Klaus Herding has spoken of the "port network," which allowed for exchanges between Amsterdam or London and the towns along the Mediterranean coast.[19] More likely even is that Puget came to know the art of the Northern masters through the volumes of engravings that were published in Holland and circulated throughout Europe.

But Puget's work also stands apart from that of the other marine draftsmen of his time. It has survived almost exclusively in the form of deluxe pieces, which are exceptionally plentiful but oddly lacking in any trace of variation or rough draft.[20] They are certainly related to the ambitions of a man who always aspired to a place as court artist. With his naval scenes, Puget was proclaiming his mastery of the most varied disciplines, while also showing off his competence as a painter and naval architect, exalting his prince's policies of military grandeur and finally stamping his oeuvre with the seal of luxury.

Diederik Bakhuÿs

1. Herding 1966; Herding in Toulouse 1992, p. 57; Herding in Marseille and Genoa 1994–95, esp. pp. 172–73, 177. See also Boisfleury 1972.

2. For the drawing in the Metropolitan Museum, see Herding in Marseille and Genoa 1994–95, p. 173, fig. 19. For a discussion of designs for naval decorations, see Marie-Paule Vial in Marseille and Genoa 1994–95, pp. 230–31 and nos. 99–103. The authenticity of the *Study for the Stern of the Vessel "Le Sceptre,"* at the Musée des Beaux-Arts in Angers (inv. MTC 125; Marseille and Genoa 1994–95, no. 99), has recently been challenged; see Quimper and Angers 2000–2001, no. 10.

3. Herding in Marseille and Genoa 1994–95, pp. 172–83, esp. p. 177.

4. Musée Bonnat, Bayonne, Legs Jacques Petithory (inv. RF 50911); Herding in Toulouse 1992, no. 37; Madeleine Pinault Sørensen in Marseille and Genoa 1994–95, no. 94. See also Pinault Sørensen in Rosenberg 1997, no. 166.

5. See esp. Roux 1931–55, vol. 5 (1946), nos. 7, 8. The print appeared in 1792, after the engraver's death, in *Recueil de cent vingt sujets et paysages divers, gravés a l'eau-forte par plusieurs artistes, d'après différentes maitres [. . .] dont les dessins originaux font partie de la collection du Sr Basan père à Paris* (Paris, 1792), pl. 22, fig. 2.

6. In the case of naval scenes executed after his return from Genoa, it is often in error that pen and ink is listed among the media used.

7. Heartfelt thanks to Jean Baudriot, a specialist in naval archaeology, for the many pieces of technical information that he generously provided.

8. Musée des Beaux-Arts, Marseille (inv. D. 255); Herding in Marseille and Genoa 1994–95, no. 76.

9. Musée des Beaux-Arts, Marseille (inv. D. 259); Herding ibid., no. 80.

10. The large *View of the Port of Toulon* (Musée du Louvre, Paris, inv. 32593; see Toulouse 1992, no. 35), dated 1654 and formerly in the Mariette Collection, is very similar in technique and style to the late drawings (Marseille and Genoa 1994–95, nos. 89–95).

11. Private Collection, Hamburg; Marseille and Genoa 1994–95, no. 83.

12. *Vessels and Galleys in a Bay, before a City Surrounded by Mountains*, Musée des Beaux-Arts, Besançon (inv. D. 1854); Paris 1993, no. 107.

13. For the drawings of Jean-Baptiste de La Rose, see esp. Marseille 1978; and Toulouse 1992, nos. 39, 40. For the work of Luca Villamage, author of a handsome drawing of a galley, see esp. Toulouse 1992, nos. 70, 71; and Rouen 1999, no. 104.

14. Musée des Beaux-Arts, Marseille (inv. D. 109, D. 257); ibid., nos. 85, 86.

15. Musée des Beaux-Arts, Toulouse (inv. 957.102.1); Marseille and Genoa 1994–95, no. 88. The two other versions are at the Louvre and in a Private Collection.

16. The first drawing is in The Metropolitan Museum of Art, New York (1985.103). The two others are in the Musée des Beaux-Arts (inv. D. 279) and the Musée Grobet-Labadié (inv. 521), both Marseille; Marseille and Genoa 1994–95, nos. 89–91. The first two versions are in portrait format, the third in landscape format.

17. Puget left behind a copy of a galley taken from Stefano della Bella's *Views of the Sea*, engraved by Israel Silvestre (Herding in Marseille and Genoa 1994–95, pp. 179–80, figs. 24, 25).

18. See Madeleine Pinault Sørensen in Marseille and Genoa 1994–95, pp. 202–3.

19. Herding in Toulouse 1992, p. 59, under no. 36; Herding in Marseille and Genoa 1994–95, p. 181.

20. As Madeleine Pinault Sørensen noted, the only way to imagine the variety of the preparatory work he must have done is to examine better conserved studio documents by other artists, such as the two Willem Van de Veldes, which are now in Greenwich. See Pinault Sørensen in Marseille and Genoa 1994–95, p. 203.

63

63. Charles de La Fosse

Paris, 1636–Paris, 1716

Study of a Reclining Nude

Black, red, and white chalk on light brown paper, 8¼ ×
14⁹⁄₁₆ in. (21 × 37 cm)

PROVENANCE: Galerie Arnoldi-Livie, Munich; Galerie
de Bayser, Paris; acquired by Jean Bonna, 2005

EXHIBITIONS: Paris 2006b, no. 18; Geneva 2006–7a

Charles de La Fosse spent his apprenticeship in the studio of Charles Le Brun,
whom he assisted in the decoration of the
Galerie d'Hercule in the Hôtel Lambert as
well as the seminary of Saint-Sulpice. In 1658,
he went to Rome, where for two years he
studied the work of Raphael and the art of
antiquity. His Italian sojourn then took him to
Venice, where he stayed from 1660 to 1663, a
crucial turning point in the development of his
style, which made him one of the most influential colorists in the campaign waged against
the Poussinistes. Back in Paris by 1663, he

enjoyed the patronage of Colbert and Charles
Le Brun, who sent a number of important
official commissions his way. Elected a member of the Académie in 1673, he worked
on the Tuileries and then on the Grands
Appartements of Versailles. He created decors
for a number of benefactors, such as Mlle de
Montpensier, who hired him to decorate the
chapel of the Château of Choisy, and Louvois,
who commissioned him for the grand ceiling
of the Château of Meudon. In 1690, La Fosse
decorated the London mansion of Lord
Montagu, the British ambassador to France.
At that point he was involved in every royal
building project: the Trianon, the Château of
Marly, and the church of the Invalides, the
dome of which he painted. His last major
work was the half-dome of the royal chapel at
Versailles. He also worked for many private
clients, whose houses unfortunately have been
demolished. In the early 1660s, while he was in

Figure 67. Charles de La Fosse, *Seated Servant
Holding a Jar*. Black and red chalk highlighted with
white gouache. Private Collection

Venice, he sent Colbert studies of such quality that they earned him a grant from the king, which allowed him to prolong his stay in Italy. Only 293 drawings by his hand are known today, but the inventory established after the painter's death on December 23, 1716, mentions 1,538 sheets, indicating the huge extent of his output in this area.

The present, previously unpublished drawing, which recently resurfaced in the Paris art market, unfortunately cannot be related to any known work by La Fosse, even though it must be preparatory to a painted figure, most likely for a large décor. The posture of the reclining young woman with her gaze directed upward surely is related to a mythological theme. Her attentiveness is reminiscent, with significant variations, of the pose of the muse at lower right in *The Rest of Diana* in the Hermitage or of the one in the painting of the same name in the Musée des Beaux-Arts, Rennes.

Charles de La Fosse's style is easily recognizable. He tended to favor black and red chalk, with some white chalk to add highlights and give an idea of the coloring of the planned painting. According to Dézallier d'Argenville, "La Fosse's drawings are full of color & have

the same effect as his paintings: he generally used the trois crayons technique with great artistry."[1] This technique, already used by his master Charles Le Brun, seems to date from the time of the decoration of the Château of Versailles, in other words from 1671. It was Rubens who originally mixed the three types of chalk to evoke light and color in drawings, and by the 1680s, his influence had become decisive. La Fosse, in turn, used the technique on camel-colored paper with a slightly pinkish hue and rough texture, which holds the chalk strokes rather coarsely and accentuates the coloristic effect. Here, his use of the technique attains perfection; the colors blend subtly to create a painterly effect. The white gouache is employed sparingly to add a few glints of light on the knees and arms; the black lightly shades the stomach and tops of the thighs; and the red is used to give some substance to the flesh. The perfection of the body type is effectively rendered by the modeling, the foreshortening, the narrow, well-defined waist, and the delicate joints.

The figure probably was drawn from nature, as it was in the *Two Studies of a Woman* in the École des Beaux-Arts;[2] the female

model is shown nude and undraped, which is unusual in the painter's graphic work. Contrary to habit, he devoted particular care to the depiction of her face and hair bun. Her round eyes, well rendered eyebrows, straight nose, and small mouth are scrupulously portrayed and are similar to the features of the model in a *Seated Servant Holding a Jar* in a Private Collection (fig. 67),[3] which has not been related to any currently known work.

The delicacy of this drawing naturally calls to mind the graphic works of Watteau. It should be remembered that both artists cohabited in the home of Pierre Crozat, one of the richest collectors of his day, in La Fosse's late years. This drawing, which incontestably belongs to the world of the eighteenth century, is echoed in François Lemoyne's studies for the painted vault of the Galerie d'Hercule in Versailles.

CLÉMENTINE GUSTIN GOMEZ

1. Dézallier d'Argenville 1762, vol. 4, p. 194.
2. École Nationale Supérieure des Beaux-Arts, Paris (inv. PM 901).
3. Location unknown; formerly at the Galerie Scala, Paris.

64. Joseph Werner the Younger

Bern, 1637–Bern, 1710

Apollo and Daphne

1665

Gouache on vellum laid down on copper, covered with paper on the back, framing line in gold, 5 × 5⅞ in. (12.6 × 14.8 cm)

Signed on verso in pen and brown ink on the backing paper: *JWerner, fecit. / 1665.*

PROVENANCE: William North (1678–1734), 6th Baron North, 2nd Baron Grey of Rolleston and Earl North (Lord North and Grey); his widow, Margaretta Maria de Yong (1690?–1762), Lady North, then Lady Elibank; her second husband, Patrick Murray (1703–1778), 5th Lord Elibank; his descendants; sale, Christie's, London, November 2, 1971, lot 110; Leggatt Brothers, London; Private Collection, United Kingdom; Didier Aaron, Paris; acquired by Jean Bonna, 2006

BIBLIOGRAPHY: Glaesemer 1974, no. 81

Joseph Werner was born in the Swiss city of Bern, to which he returned at the end of his life, but his career led him to Frankfurt, Rome, Paris, Augsburg, and Berlin. None of that restlessness is reflected in his exquisite miniatures on vellum, which are without any doubt the highlight of his oeuvre.[1] The best of them date from the years he spent in Paris, between 1662 and 1667, and shortly afterward. Werner was called from Italy to France by Louis XIV, for whom he made several mythological scenes and portraits, but most of his finest miniatures were made for his friend Eustache Quinault. Quinault owned at least eleven of them, all of which are described in epigrams and extensive laudatory poems, which he published in 1667 and 1671.[2] Although the work in the Bonna

Collection, signed and dated 1665 on the verso (see illustration below) cannot be traced back to the works in Quinault's collection, it is equal to them in quality.

The miniature represents the story of the nymph Daphne, daughter of the river god Peneus. As told by Ovid in the *Metamorphoses*

64 verso (detail)

64

Figure 68. Joseph Werner, *Louis XIV as Apollo next to the Slain Python*. Musée National des Châteaux de Versailles et de Trianon (inv. MV 6927²)

Figure 69. Carlo Maratti, *Apollo and Daphne*, 1681. Koninklijke Musea voor Schone Kunsten van België/Musées Royaux des Beaux-Arts de Belgique, Brussels

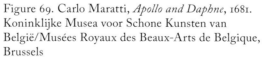

(book 1, lines 452–567),[3] Daphne is stricken by Cupid with a lead-tipped arrow that makes her flee the love of Apollo, who in his turn has been stricken by Cupid with the gold-tipped arrow that makes him passionately seek her love. After a long pursuit, Daphne sees no other way out than to ask her father to save her, and he does so by transforming her into a laurel tree. Exceptionally, Werner chose to depict the moment just before this metamorphosis takes place,[4] focusing on her and her suitor's physical beauty as well as on the ravishing landscape, rendered in the cool tones typical of the artist. The little putto at upper right is, of course, Cupid, the only one who emerges from the story as a victor. He appears in an almost identical pose in one of the miniatures Werner made for Louis XIV, which has been dated slightly earlier (fig. 68).[5]

Daphne's father, seated at lower right, is recognizable as a river god by the sculpted vase and the cornucopia that seems to have been associated with him since antiquity.[6] He stretches his arms out in a manner similar to the same figure in a painting by the Roman artist Carlo Maratti (fig. 69),[7] who was previously thought to have been one of Werner's teachers in Rome.[8] However, it does not seem likely that Maratti's Baroque painting, a commission by Louis XIV about 1680, was inspired in any way by the younger artist's miniature. Comparison of the two works highlights the classicism of Werner's composition, in which the main scene takes place in a shallow foreground and the figures move parallel to the picture plane. This classic beauty, Werner's faultless drawing, and the preciousness of the detailed execution must have appealed particularly to the aristocratic taste of his French admirers. When well preserved, as is the case of the drawing in the Bonna Collection, Werner's miniatures still hold the attraction of a gem.

STIJN ALSTEENS

1. Glaesemer 1974, nos. 63–109, 219–34.
2. The poems single out a miniature of Mount Parnassus as the most beautiful work of the collection; the work recently reappeared in the gallery J. Kugel in Paris (together with a miniature of a stormy landscape with figures of which the composition was previously known only from a pen drawing [Claude Kuhn 1987, no. 34], which is not documented in Quinault's collection). Another recently discovered miniature that may have been in Quinault's possession, depicting the death of Dido (Glaesemer 1974, no. 219F), reappeared in the sale at Sotheby's, Paris, June 25, 2008, lot 46. To Glaesemer's catalogue raisonné further can be added a *Bathing Diana* in the sale at Sotheby's, New York, January 28, 2000, lot 48.
3. For the iconography of the myth of Daphne and Apollo, see Stechow 1932, esp. pp. 34–39.
4. Among the few works of art in which the same moment is depicted is a print by the Master of the Die after Baldassare Peruzzi (Bartsch 1803–21, vol. 18 [1818], p. 198, no. 21) and paintings by Francesco Albani (Musée du Louvre, Paris, inv. 18; Puglisi 1999, no. 58), Nicola Maria Rossi, an anonymous French artist of the eighteenth century (both in the Musée Magnin, Dijon, inv. 1938 484 [Brejon de Lavergnée 1980, no. 92] and 1938 F 565 [Starcky 2000, no. 528]), and Louis de Silvestre (Schnapper 1973, p. 23, fig. 7, as Sanssouci palace, Potsdam [inv. 5641]).
5. Glaesemer 1974, no. 76; Rouen and Le Mans 2001, no. 67.
6. See, for instance, a mosaic in the House of Dionysos on Paphos (Eliades 1982, pp. 29–30). The cornucopia is also depicted in a print by the Master of the Die after Baldassare Peruzzi (Bartsch 1803–21, vol. 18 [1818], p. 197, no. 20).
7. Turner 1999, vol. 1, pp. 129–30, under no. 182.
8. Glaesemer 1974, p. 18.

65. Antoine Coypel

Paris, 1661–Paris, 1722

Orpheus Holding His Lyre

Black and red chalk with white highlights on brown paper, squaring in black and red chalk, 8¼ × 7¾ in. (21 × 19.7 cm)

PROVENANCE: R. M. Light and Co., Santa Barbara, California; acquired by Jean Bonna, 2002

EXHIBITIONS: Paris 2006b, no. 19; Geneva 2006–7a

BIBLIOGRAPHY: Garnier-Pelle 1989, p. 130, figs. 426–38

The son of the painter Noël Coypel, Antoine Coypel began training in his father's studio on Quai de la Mégisserie at an early age. In 1672, although Antoine was a mere eleven years old at the time, Colbert officially authorized him to accompany his father to Rome, where the elder Coypel served as director of the Académie de France from 1672 to 1675. It was therefore in Rome that Antoine Coypel completed his training, copying from antiquities or from Renaissance masterpieces alongside the students who had won the Prix de Rome. Once back in Paris, he began a brilliant career, becoming the champion of the Rubensistes against the Poussinistes. Along with Charles de La Fosse, Jean Jouvenet, and the Boullognes, he was representative of a transition period between the cold, austere painting of the century of Louis XIV and a lighter, more cheerful form of painting that looked forward toward the eighteenth century.

Antoine Coypel's great work, unfortunately now lost, was the decoration of the Gallery of Aeneas in the Palais-Royal, to which this drawing is related. Coypel was *premier peintre* to the Duc d'Orléans, Louis XIV's only brother; when the duke died in 1701, his son Philippe II, the future regent, almost immediately engaged Coypel to decorate the Grand Gallery of the Palais-Royal, which was forty-six meters long. Working from classical literature, Coypel chose as his theme the story of Aeneas rather than that of Hercules or Apollo. He finished the central part of the ceiling, *The Assembly of the Gods*, in the fall of 1703; the overall ceiling was completed in 1705. The ceiling was formed of a large central opening surrounded by medallions and trompe-l'oeil, for which Coypel took as his collaborator the architectural painter Philippe Meusnier. Around the central opening, the arches held six paintings at the springs of the vault. While this group of works has now been destroyed, there remain at least the oil sketches on canvas and the drawings that Coypel squared so as to enlarge them for the walls. This initial decoration of the Gallery of Aeneas was then considered complete; the windows were to be separated only by facing glass piers. This is known because in 1706, Coypel undertook to have the Gallery of Aeneas engraved, and in January 1706, the Duc d'Orléans paid his *premier peintre* for that work.

65

Figure 70. Antoine Coypel, *Aeneas Descending into the Underworld*. Oil on canvas. Musée du Louvre, Département des Peintures, Paris (inv. 3546)

Figure 71. Antoine Coypel, *Aeneas Descending into the Underworld*. Black and red chalk, highlighted with white. Städelsches Kunstinstitut, Frankfurt-am-Main (inv. 1088)

Only ten years later, toward the end of his career, Coypel returned to the Palais-Royal to complete the decorations of the Gallery of Aeneas. From 1715 to 1717, the Duc d'Orléans, now prince regent, commissioned him to create large-scale paintings to decorate the lower part of the gallery. Coypel made seven large paintings relating to the story of Aeneas, to match the theme of the ceiling and arches, but the spirit of these paintings is very different from that of the first series. While the ceiling, populated with female nudes treated in light tones, was representative of the *petit goût*, the wall decorations, filled with dramatic war scenes, exemplified the *grand goût*.

Thanks to the support of his patron, the regent Philippe, Duc d'Orléans, Coypel was lavished with honors and prestigious duties; he was named *premier peintre* to the king, director of the Académie, and keeper of the Royal Drawings. Having acquired nearly all the powers once held by Charles Le Brun, he then sought to position himself as painting's champion and saw himself as the keeper of traditional artistic values. During this period, Coypel experimented with a new palette, which was colder and more austere but also more brilliant. Unfortunately, he used materials of poor quality that were subject to rapid darkening and flaking, which completely ruined the paintings he created for the chancel of Notre-Dame in Paris and those for the Gallery of Aeneas. Because of this, most of his paintings, which also had fallen out of fashion by the end of the eighteenth century, were sent on deposit to Saint-Cloud as of 1778. As the property of Louis XVI, they were made part of

the national collections at the time of the Revolution. Among Coypel's seven large paintings at Saint-Cloud, two were put on deposit in 1803 at the Musée Fabre in Montpellier: *Aeneas and Anchises* and *The Death of Dido*; another, *Aeneas and Achates Arriving in the Temple of Dido*, was sent by the Louvre to the Musée des Beaux-Arts, Arras, in 1938. The four others, finally—*Aeneas Descending into the Underworld, Jupiter Appearing before Aeneas, The Burial of Pallas,* and *The Death of Turnus*—which had gone to the Louvre during the Revolution, remained there, but were in a very poor state of conservation.

A strong symbolic contrast can be observed between the paintings made for the gallery vault, in which one mainly sees the gods of Greco-Roman mythology seated in Olympus and where Aeneas, although ostensibly the hero of the gallery, barely appears, and the large wall paintings, which portray major scenes from Aeneas's life, including the

descent into the Underworld that Virgil recounts in Book 6 of the *Aeneid,* in which Anchises shows his son the heroes of the future city of Rome. *Aeneas Descending into the Underworld* (fig. 70)[1] is one of the largest canvases Coypel ever painted. It depicts Aeneas being led by the Sibyl of Cumae to the Elysian Fields, where he meets his deceased father Anchises. Coypel added to the scene the character of Orpheus, who does not figure in the *Aeneid* but rather in another text by Virgil, *The Georgics.* Orpheus, husband of the nymph Eurydice, inconsolable after his wife's death, weeps endlessly over her and seeks her out even in the Underworld, where his songs charm the denizens of the Elysian Fields. He finally finds her but is ordered not to gaze upon her before they leave the Underworld. Unfortunately, he is unable to resist; he turns toward Eurydice and his wife is again taken from him, this time forever. On the right of the painting, Orpheus, seated on a knoll, plays

Figure 72. Antoine Coypel, *Aeneas Descending into the Underworld.* Red chalk. Musée du Louvre, Département des Arts Graphiques, Paris (inv. RF 12349)

the harp while languid young women listen. Initially, Coypel had decided that Orpheus would be playing the violin, although this does not match the traditional iconography; we know this because one of two drawings of the overall composition, executed in trois crayons in the same orientation as the canvas (fig. 71),[2] shows Orpheus holding a violin, his head turned aside. For the second overall preparatory study in red chalk, however, Coypel

chose a lyre as the attribute of Orpheus, who is shown in a pose very similar to the one in the present drawing (fig. 72).[3] For this painting, he made about ten highly developed detail studies,[4] much like the drawing in the Bonna collection. In those studies, Coypel shows his virtuosity in the trois crayons technique, which he borrowed from the Flemish artists and which he readily used throughout his career.

Nicole Garnier-Pelle

1. Musée du Louvre, Paris, 38.5 × 75.2 cm (inv. 426); Garnier-Pelle 1989, pp. 172–73, no. 130.
2. Ibid., p. 229, no. 511, fig. 428.
3. Ibid., fig. 427.
4. Ibid., pp. 229–30, nos. 513–23, figs. 429–38.

66. Claude Gillot

Langres, 1673–Paris, 1722

Four Studies of Costumes from the Commedia dell'Arte with a Sketch of the Third

Pen and black ink, brown and orange-pink wash, blue-gray watercolor wash in the background,[1] 6 × 7^{15}/$_{16}$ in. (15.2 × 20.1 cm)

Illegible number (4?) in the upper right corner

Provenance: From an album of thirty-three drawings of studies of theatrical costumes by Claude Gillot, Galerie de Bayser, Paris; acquired by Jean Bonna, 2004

Exhibitions: Paris 2006b, no. 20; Geneva 2006–7a

Bibliography: Tonkovich 2006, pp. 469, 471, 478, no. 15, fig. 12

The theater provided Claude Gillot with his best subjects. More than a source of inspiration, it was his passion, even "a kind of religion"[2]—a religion shared at the end of the century of Louis XIV and at the beginning of the Regency by "a nebula of artists" and their new patrons, monied individuals whose taste for light entertainments distinguished them as much from the Court as from the bourgeoisie. On his arrival in Paris, Gillot discovered the brilliantly colored world of Parisian theater. From 1691 until its suppression in 1697, Gillot was able to frequent the Comédie Italienne at the Hôtel de Bourgogne. After 1697, he could see, on the stages of the theaters at the Saint-Germain and Saint-Laurent fairs, improvised Italian sketches adapted into French and plays from Evaristo Gherardi's book.[3] He made this repertoire his own, transposing into his art its whim, licentious tone, and occasional strangeness. Memories and quick sketches of the

theater, in which Gillot depicted the actors at their craft, often from comic types (especially the "fixed types" of the Gallicized Commedia dell'arte), reveal the profound originality of his aesthetic. They also show his nostalgic familiarity with the Italo-Flemish tradition of theatrical subjects (including Jacques Callot), the fashion for which he helped revive at the beginning of the eighteenth century.

The album from which the present drawing is taken was assembled in the nineteenth century and included scenes from the Commedia dell'arte, studies of theater costumes, and sketches of characters. Before its discovery, the last time such an extensive collection of Gillot's theater drawings had been publicly shown was in 1744, at the sale of the Quentin de Lorangère Collection. The catalogue of that sale mentioned "thirty drawings, mostly of various comic and theatrical costumes," "thirty others of various comic outfits," and "twenty-three drawings, mostly of comic and entertaining subjects."[4] In that catalogue, Gersaint noted Gillot's predilection for "the Comic and Theatrical side," which "makes his collection interesting & amusing." Gillot's own posthumous inventory, drawn up on May 22, 1722, had already described "a box of drawings of comic figures depicting Italian scenes" and "another box depicting various theater costumes."[5]

The Bonna drawing belonged to the largest and most homogeneous group in the album, comprising nineteen studies of theater

costumes, grouped in threes or fours and related to famous roles from the Paris stage, whether comedies, ballets, or operas. The alignment of the figures, their horizontal arrangement, and the liveliness of their poses are all typical of Gillot's manner in his costume studies. We find the same three characteristics in three drawings, now in the Louvre, for the heroic ballet *The Elements*,[6] which premiered in December 1721 at the Tuileries palace. For that show, Gillot furnished a large number of drawings, some of which Jean-François Joullain engraved and published in 1725 under the title *Nouveaux Dessins d'habillements à l'usage des ballets, opéras et comédies*.[7] The Bonna sheet, however, derives from a different impetus, notably that of the print sellers who sold portraits of the actors at the theater doors. One engraved series of this type after Gillot is known: the ten plates called *Portraits of Actors*,[8] which have often been compared with Bernard Picart's *Twelve Fashions from Italian Theater*.[9] According to Pierre-Jean Mariette, who saw these plates before the captions were added and knew the series under the title *Costumes for Theater and Ballets*, Gillot began to engrave them from his own drawings shortly before his death.[10] Left unfinished, the plates were then completed by an unknown engraver, possibly Jean Audran. The captions identifying the actors, roles, and plays in question were added at that point; in some cases, they were entirely made up, identifying actors who had begun acting only after Gillot's death.

Figure 73. Claude Gillot, *"La Torillière Senior" Costumed as the Spanish Valet in the Comedy "The Scold."* Etching. Musée d'Art et d'Histoire, Langres

Figure 74. Claude Gillot, *Standing Man in a Theatrical Costume.* Red chalk. Harvard University Art Museums, Fogg Art Museum, Cambridge, Massachusetts (1962.36)

The first and third figures in the drawing shown here refer back to two plates from the *Portraits of Actors: Fabio Costumed as the Doctor*[11] and *La Torillière Senior [sic] Costumed as the Spanish Valet in the Comedy "The Scold"* (fig. 73).[12] The Italian Fabio Sticotti (1676–1741) debuted in Paris in 1716 with Luigi Riccoboni's company, which had recently been called back by the Regent. Pierre Le Noir, called La Thorillière Jr. (1659–1731), had joined the Comédie Française as part of Molière's company in 1712, the year of Gillot's death. The caption of the print (fig. 73) mistakenly identified the actor as La Thorillière Senior, who was also an actor at the Comédie Française but had died in 1680. The second and fourth characters were not engraved. They are difficult to identify, even though the second looks somewhat like a Pierrot by Bernard Picart[13] and the fourth wears the same beret as *Ermand, of the Comédie Française, Costumed as Sganarelle in "The Doctor in Spite of Himself."*[14]

Until the album was discovered, only three drawings, figure studies in red chalk, could be related to the *Portraits of Actors*; Populus mentions a fourth in the Comédie Française library, but it has never been found. Two of those drawings, *Fabio Costumed as the Doctor*[15] and *Standing Man in a Theatrical Costume* (fig. 74), have a direct bearing on the present drawing, suggesting a complex relationship between the red chalk studies, the drawings in pen-and-ink and wash, and the prints. Like the figures in the Bonna sheet, the red chalk drawings have the same orientation as the engravings and show a similar care taken with the poses and expressions. While Fabio's costume has been simplified in the red chalk drawings—the looped knots are missing, the collar less elaborate—the costume worn by La Thorillière differs significantly from the present drawing: the actor is not wearing a fluted ruff but rather a knotted cravat; the edges of his hat are notched; the belt with little bells is gone; a dagger clasps the kind of fringed chasuble that he's wearing in place of the slashed jerkin; and his costume is spangled with bells. The pen-and-ink sketch in the background, on the other hand, matches the engraving. The drawings in the Metropolitan Museum and the Fogg Museum in Cambridge correspond more closely to the engravings than the figures in the *Four Studies* from the Bonna

Collection, in both their details and their style; they feature the same slightly constrained gestures by Fabio and the same costume for La Thorillière, despite some differences in the face. But more than anything else, they lack the vivacity and sense of irony that characterize the *Four Studies*, which led Jennifer Tonkovich to doubt the attribution of these drawings to Gillot and to suggest that they are rather, as this author also believes, studies by Audran made from engravings, perhaps in Gillot's studio. Gillot often used engraving as a direct opportunity to modify and perfect his inventions. Thus, there was probably no intermediate stage between the execution of the drawing in pen-and-ink and wash and that of the prints. The cursory pen sketch in the center, slightly behind the other figures, sets down the pentimento that inspired the engraving, toning down the exuberant fantasy of the costume and restoring to the face the jaunty and playful expression that a few too many strokes had somewhat obscured. As such, this drawing is extremely important for our understanding of Gillot's graphic process, which liberally combined improvisation and reflection.

PAULETTE CHONÉ

1. Jennifer Tonkovich mentions how rare it was for Gillot to add watercolor to the background of his figure studies, apart from brief strokes of wash—sometimes, as here, previously suggested by pen-and-ink strokes—which attach the subject to the ground. As such, she suggests that the blue-gray wash in the background might have been added by the person who gathered these drawings in an album.
2. François Moureau in Langres 1999, p. 78. On Gillot and the theater, see Dacier 1924; Dacier 1926; Moureau 1992; Tonkovich 2002; and Tonkovich 2005. Heartfelt thanks to Jennifer Tonkovich for her generous help in the writing of this entry.
3. A first version of it appeared in 1694, and the definitive version in 1700.
4. *Catalogue raisonné des diverse curiosités du cabinet de feu M. Quentin de Lorangere . . .* (Paris: chez Jacques Barois, 1744).
5. See G. Wildenstein 1923.
6. Musée du Louvre, Département des Arts Graphiques, Paris: *Four Spectres* (inv. 26768); *Four Captains* (inv. 26767); *Two Studies for Plutus and Two for Time* (inv. 26763). There are other examples of figures grouped by four on a single sheet: *Four Characters from the Commedia dell'arte* (Musée du Louvre, Département des Arts Graphiques, Paris, inv. 26755); two drawings at The Metropolitan Museum of Art (1906.1042.7, 1910.45.15); several drawings with unknown locations (sale, Piasa, Paris, March 18, 2005, lot 54; sale, Woodner Collection, Christie's, London, July 2, 1991, lot 155). Figures grouped by twos: École Nationale Supérieure

66

des Beaux-Arts, Paris (inv. M. 2541); Musée des Beaux-Arts, Dijon (inv. Alb. TH 18 fol. 18).

7. Populus 1930, nos. 394–478.

8. Ibid., nos. 21–30.

9. Jean Mariette, Paris, ca. 1696. Drawings in the Musée du Louvre, Département des Arts Graphiques, Paris (inv. 32362–32367).

10. "A series of eleven plates of costumes from theater and ballet; Gillot, who had drawn them, had begun to engrave them, but they were not yet finished upon his death" (cited in Populus 1930, p. 95). Mariette counted eleven plates; in fact there are ten, but eleven figures.

11. Populus 1930, no. 23.

12. Ibid., no. 24.

13. Musée du Louvre, Département des Arts Graphiques, Paris (inv. 32362 ter): *Jean-Joseph Geratone, aka Pierrot, in the Role of Pierrot, from the Comédie Italienne. Probable Study for the Engraved Series "Twelve Fashions from Italian Theater."* Geratone, who came to Paris in 1670, officially debuted in 1684. In 1673 he created the character Pierrot, the costume for which he borrowed from the Italian Punchinello, except for the hat. Brigitte Scart in Legrand 1997, p. 318, no. 1263.

14. Populus 1930, no. 27. The caption, added after Gillot's death, mentions Armand (1699–1755), who did not join the Comédie until 1723.

15. Red chalk and black chalk, 4⅞ × 3⅛ in. (1.24 × 7.9 cm), The Metropolitan Museum of Art, New York (1975.131.112).

67. Jean-Antoine Watteau

Valenciennes,1684–Nogent-sur-Marne, 1721

Three Studies of Men: One Seated in Three-Quarter View and Turned to the Right, Another Standing with Raised Arms, and the Third Seated and Playing the Violin

Ca. 1710–11

Red chalk, 6⅝₁₆ × 7½ in. (16 × 19 cm)

Inscribed in red chalk (almost erased) at lower right: *Watteau*

PROVENANCE: André de Hévesy, Paris; sale, Sotheby's, London, April 25, 1951, lot 69; Scharf, London; Galerie Cailleux, Paris, 1954, and again in 1957, mark at lower left (not in Lugt); H. Shickman, New York; Private Collection, New York; acquired by Jean Bonna, 2000

EXHIBITIONS: Paris 2006b, no. 21; Geneva 2006–7a

BIBLIOGRAPHY: Parker and Mathey 1957, no. 41; Eidelberg 1977, p. 127, n. 14; Margaret Morgan Grasselli in Washington, Paris, and Berlin 1984–85, p. 80; Pierre Rosenberg in Washington, Paris, and Berlin 1984–85, pp. 277, 300, and p. 276, fig. 8, p. 298, fig. 4 (detail); Grasselli 1987, pp. 105, 109–11, 117, 172–73, 175, 235, no. 62, fig. 88; Rosenberg and Prat 1996, vol. 1, pp. 158–59, no. 100

All Jean-Antoine Watteau's biographers agree about the originality of the artist's working methods, and especially his approach to drawing. Dézallier d'Argenville emphasized that Watteau "drew continually; even during his free time, walking or at leisure,"[1] while Caylus noted that he "drew without a specific goal. For he neither made sketches for nor thought out his paintings." His practice consisted of "drawing studies in a bound volume, such that he always had a large number of them readily at hand." In his studio, he asked "persons of either sex to pose for him, depending on who was available, and whom he captured in the poses that naturally occurred, preferring the simplest ones best of all;" he "changed their clothing into aristocratic outfits, sometimes rather comical ones."[2] The drawing in the Bonna Collection perfectly corresponds to Caylus's description. It shows the artist drawing from live models and seeking to capture their most characteristic poses, in spontaneous sketches made on the spur of the moment. Moreover, a slight pentimento in the right leg of the man in the center of the sheet suggests a rapid change of pose. These three figures are not looking at one another and do not form a unified group, nor are they depicted in a defined environment or space—the stool on which the musician is seated has not been drawn, and only a few lines in red chalk evoke their shadows on the ground—but rather are treated separately on the page with no apparent interrelationship. Most of the artist's attention was devoted to rendering the models' gestures and poses precisely and also to portraying their garments carefully, especially the buttons and pockets.

This unusual approach to drawing, according to Caylus, "held an infinite attraction [for Watteau]; . . . most of the time the figures he drew from nature were not destined for specific purpose."[3] Nonetheless, "when he took it into his head to create a painting, he consulted his album, choosing from it the figures that best suited him at the moment."[4] This is in fact the case with the present figures, which the artist used for three of his compositions, *Jealousy (Les Jaloux)*, now lost but engraved by Gérard Scottin; *Pierrot Content* in the Museo Thyssen-Bornemisza, Madrid, engraved by Edme Jeaurat (fig. 75); and the *Bal champêtre* in a Private Collection, engraved by Jacques Couché (fig. 76).[5] The figures on the left reappear in the first two paintings, although Watteau retained only the bust of the second concealed in the woods in the background, and the violinist reappears with the group of musicians at the left of *Bal champêtre*.

These three paintings were created at a pivotal moment in the artist's career. After a stay in Valenciennes from 1709 to 1711, during which time he painted about ten canvases with military subjects, he returned to Paris in the hope of entering the Académie Royale de Peinture et de Sculpture. On July 30, 1712, according to Pierre-Jean Mariette in his *Notes manuscrites*,[6] Watteau was admitted upon presenting his painting *Jealousy*: "His genre painting found favor . . . everyone rushed to acquire one of his works."[7] This success explains the replicas he

Figure 75. Edme Jeaurat, after Jean-Antoine Watteau, *Pierrot Content*. Engraving, École Nationale Supérieure des Beaux-Arts, Paris (inv. Est 9740)

Figure 76. Jean-Antoine Watteau, *Le Bal champêtre*. Oil on canvas. Private Collection

67

Figure 77. Jean-Antoine Watteau, *Sheet of Studies*. Red chalk. École Nationale Supérieure des Beaux-Arts, Paris (inv. 1607)

created shortly afterward: *Pierrot Content*, the *Jealous Harlequin* (now lost), and *The Foursome* in the San Francisco Museum of Art.[8] *Jealousy*, in fact, was Watteau's first open air scene of gallant life, in which various characters in fantastic costumes, playing music or theatrical roles, are brought together around an amorous intrigue. Several months later, Watteau made his first attempts at composing the *Bal champêtre* (fig. 76), generally dated 1713–14, which heralds the *fêtes galantes* of later years. In the middle of a clearing bathed in milky light, a couple made up of a dancer and a man playing castanets is accompanied by a small orchestra on the left

playing musette, oboe, and violin. The figures, however, do not seem fully integrated into the scene but rather look as if they have been placed on top of the landscape.[9] This is a consequence of the artist's favorite practice; as Caylus wrote: "When he took it into his head to create a painting, he consulted his album, choosing from it the figures that best suited him at the moment. He put them into groups, most often using a landscape background that he had already designed or prepared. It was rare for him to proceed otherwise."[10]

Whatever the case, this drawing, executed entirely in red chalk, is characteristic of the years 1710–11, the period in which Watteau was still influenced by the art of Claude Gillot. At this time, he adopted a very elongated model for his figures; the clothes are tightly fitted to the chest, a large number of vertical lines indicate the folds of the coats, and the men's thin legs all give them a svelte and elegant appearance. The lines defining the contouring are meticulous and precise, almost angular, especially in the rendering of the shoulders and knees. This technique occurs frequently in

several other drawings from the same period, notably the *Sheet of Studies* depicting two men in tricorne hats and two female heads, now in the École des Beaux-Arts (fig. 77).[11]

EMMANUELLE BRUGEROLLES

1. Antoine-Joseph Dézallier d'Argenville, in Champion 1921, p. 72.
2. Comte de Caylus, in ibid., p. 101.
3. Ibid., p. 100.
4. Ibid., p. 101.
5. Washington, Paris, and Berlin 1984–85, pp. 274–77, no. 13, and pp. 298–300, no. 24.
6. Manuscript in the Bibliothèque Nationale de France, Paris, vol. 9, fol. 193 [51].
7. Pierre-Jean Mariette, in Champion 1921, p. 67.
8. Washington, Paris, and Berlin 1984–85, pp. 274–79.
9. Pierre Rosenberg in ibid., p. 298.
10. Comte de Caylus, in Champion 1921, p. 101.
11. Paris, Sydney, and Ottawa 2003–6, pp. 53–55, no. 4.

68. Jean-Antoine Watteau

Valenciennes, 1684–Nogent-sur-Marne, 1721

Three Studies of Female Heads

Ca. 1718–19

Black, red, and white chalk and stump, brush, gray-brown wash on beige paper, 7½ × 5 in. (19 × 12.7 cm)

On verso, label with inscription: *Berlin 1910 app. Au Dr. Tuffier "44 av. Gabriel 30000 francs"*

PROVENANCE: Alfred Beurdeley, Paris, mark at lower right; Beurdeley sale, Hôtel Drouot, Paris, March 13–15, 1905, lot 275 (sold for 27,500 francs); Dr. Tuffier, Paris, 1910; Raoul Dastrac, Paris; Private Collection, France; art market, New York; Private Collection, Italy; Richard Day, London; acquired by Jean Bonna, 1997

EXHIBITIONS: Berlin 1910, no. 200 (no. 217 in enlarged edition of catalogue); Copenhagen 1935, no. 548; Paris 1950a, no. 144; Paris 1951, no. 157; London 1954–55, no. 256; Paris 1968, no. 39; Paris 2006b, no. 24; Geneva 2006–7a

BIBLIOGRAPHY: Parker and Mathey 1957, vol. 2, no. 761; Cailleux 1966, pp. i, v, n. 5; Roland Michel 1984, pp. 80, 136, 248, 277, n. 26, pl. XIV; Grasselli 1987, pp. 336–37, 354, 427, no. 256, fig. 409; Rosenberg and Prat 1996, vol. 2, p. 1084, no. 635; Denison 2006, p. 521, fig. 1

Figure 78. Laurent Cars, after Jean-Antoine Watteau, *Venetian Pleasures.* Engraving. Collection of Jean Bonna, Geneva

Figure 79. Benoît Audran II, after Jean-Antoine Watteau, *Venus Disarming Cupid.* Engraving. Collection of Jean Bonna, Geneva

The popularity of Jean-Antoine Watteau's drawings derives in large part from the originality and variety of their technique: "He most often used red chalk on white paper . . . rarely heightening his drawings in white, as the white paper background created this effect. There are many [drawings] in black and red chalk, or graphite and red chalk, which he used for the heads, hands, and flesh; sometimes he also used trois crayons."[1] This latter mix of black, red, and white chalk, whose possibilities

Watteau explored in a quite novel manner, earned him great renown among art lovers even during his lifetime. Noël Coypel and Charles de La Fosse had already made extensive use of this technique earlier, but Watteau's approach was more varied still. The Bonna drawing is surely one of the most celebrated and highly finished;[2] the artist's addition of a gray-brown wash accentuates the color effects already produced by the use of three chalks.

As was his custom, Watteau used the three studies in different compositions. The central figure was reused for one of the young women in *Venetian Pleasures*, a painting engraved by Laurent Cars (fig. 78),[3] in which she appears in the background of the composition, just beneath the feet of the statue of the Venus, and the face located at the upper left served for *Venus Disarming Cupid*, engraved by Benoît Audran II (fig. 79).[4] The beauty of such

68

a sheet—which dates to the artist's maturity, about 1718–19[5]—also resides in the mise-en-page of the motifs, which Mariette praised for "the finesse, grace, lightness, correctness, facility, and expression."[6] The three studies were undoubtedly executed at the same time, the artist studying his model successively in full-face, three-quarter view, and profile, playing off the elegant turn of her head.

EMMANUELLE BRUGEROLLES

1. Antoine-Joseph Dézallier d'Argenville in Champion 1921, p. 73.
2. This drawing was the subject of a copy, today in a private collection (Rosenberg and Prat 1996, vol. 2, p. 1084, no. 635, fig. 635b).
3. Dacier and Vuaflart 1921–29, vol. 3 (1922), pp. 9–10, no. 6.
4. Ibid., pp. 43–44, no. 87.
5. Margaret Morgan Grasselli dates this drawing about 1717–18, Marianne Roland Michel about 1715–16, and Pierre Rosenberg and Louis-Antoine Prat about 1718–19.
6. Mariette 1851–62, vol. 6 (1859–60), p. 135.

69. François Lemoyne

Paris, 1688–Paris, 1737

Study of a Young Man Serving Wine

1722–23

Red chalk on cream-colored paper, 9¹³⁄₁₆ × 6⁷⁄₁₆ in.
(25 × 16.4 cm)

PROVENANCE: Houppe Collection, Paris (as by
Antoine Watteau); Private Collection, Paris (identified
in 1951 by Jacques Wilhelm as a study by François
Lemoyne; see Bibliography); sale, Hôtel Drouot, Paris
(Maîtres Ader, Picard, Tajan) March 9, 1988, lot 43;
Private Collection, Hampton Court, Surrey; James Faber
Gallery, London; acquired by Jean Bonna, 2000

EXHIBITIONS: Paris 1950, no. 161; Paris 2006b, no. 26;
Geneva 2006–7a

BIBLIOGRAPHY: Wilhelm 1951, pp. 223–25, fig. 4;
Bjurström 1982, under no. 1054; Bordeaux 1984, p. 152,
no. 54, fig. 184 (and not fig. 182), p. 89, under no. 38; Bean
1986, p. 154, under no. 166; New York 1999, pp. 22–24,
fig. 10.2; Day & Faber 2001, p. 26, ill.; Denison 2006,
p. 512

In 1723, shortly before leaving for Italy in the company of his patron François Berger, François Lemoyne painted a large canvas depicting a hunting party resting for lunch. The work, now in the Museu de Arte de São Paolo,[1] was a concession to a genre that at the time was enjoying great success with collectors. Before 1704, Joseph Parrocel had already painted for a member of the Titon family *The Return from the Hunt* and its pendant *The Boar Hunt*, both in the National Gallery, London.[2] Between 1718 and 1720, Jean-Antoine Watteau produced a French homage to the subject, *The Halt during the Chase*, now in the Wallace Collection, London.[3] Originally a Northern theme, the subject of a meal during the hunt gained great prestige in the hands of Philips Wouwermans. By Lemoyne's time, it enjoyed enough success for him to be called on to paint a second version of his canvas, making only a few alterations that affect the landscape. This latter version, in the Alte Pinakothek, Munich (fig. 80), has not always been recognized as an authentic work by Lemoyne. Jean-Luc Bordeaux, who specializes in the artist's work, published it as a copy made by the studio. Now that it has been restored, however, the canvas displays a workmanship that suggests it might well be from the master's hand, perhaps with some help by members of his studio in rendering portions of the landscape.[4]

The Brazil canvas is of large dimensions[5] and was prepared with great care. Every figure in the composition seems to have been worked out in preliminary studies, most of them in red chalk. In 1951, Jacques Wilhelm identified several of these studies, which had been misattributed to Watteau. Since then, a few more related drawings have come to light. In 1984, Jean-Luc Bordeaux drew up an inventory. At the Louvre, the preparatory study in black chalk for the horse at the right of the composition was catalogued under the name of Adam Frans van der Meulen.[6] Like many other works by Lemoyne, it had belonged to the collector Jean-Denis Lempereur (1705–1779), a great admirer of the artist's drawings. Two other sheets might be related to the hunter seated in profile in the left foreground, who is having his glass filled. In the one mentioned in 1951 as belonging to a Private Collection in Paris,[7] the artist was

Figure 80. François Lemoyne, *A Hunting Party*. Oil on canvas. Alte Pinakothek, Munich (inv. 126)

69

primarily interested in his model's torso, right arm, and left hand; in the one from the De Lens Collection in Paris,[8] the figure is portrayed in its totality.

For the servant pouring wine for the hunter seated at the left, Jacques Wilhelm identified three studies. They help trace the changes made to the pose of this young man with the bearing of a dancer. In the study in the Nationalmuseum, Stockholm,[9] quite certainly among the first executed, he is shown in frontal view. Heavily rendered in red chalk, the drawing displays a tight, nervous line that plays on contrasts of light. The drawing in the Metropolitan Museum,[10] executed in the same medium with equal brilliance, presents two studies of the same model turned toward the left. In the small sketch at the left, the master clearly attempted to capture a posture in a few strokes. In the sketch at the right, he was more interested in the details of the garments, in the arrangement of shadows and light, and in individualizing the face. The Bonna study, the third that can be related to the young servant boy, was the last to be drawn.[11] The model is shown in the pose ultimately adopted for the painting—his body turned toward the right, holding a dish in his left hand, and his face turned to the left to ensure that the wine he's pouring with his right hand will not miss the glass being held out to him. In this superb drawing, with its perfectly mastered use of nervous lines, the strokes are lighter and less emphasized than in the preceding studies, as if Lemoyne had felt a strong need to draw this figure many times over in order to obtain the ideal image.

XAVIER SALMON

1. Bordeaux 1984, pp. 88–89, no. 38, fig. 34.
2. Amiens and Versailles 1995–96, pp. 142–45, nos. 57, 58, ill.
3. Ingamells 1989, pp. 366–70, no. P416, ill.
4. Paris, Munich, and Bonn 2005–6, p. 378, no. 84, ill. p. 277.
5. 87¾ × 72⅞ in. (223 × 185 cm).
6. Bordeaux 1984, p. 151, no. 51, fig. 179.
7. Ibid., p. 152, no. 53, fig. 180 (and not fig. 181).
8. Ibid., pp. 151–52, no. 52, fig. 181 (and not fig. 180).
9. Ibid., pp. 152–53, no. 56, fig. 182 (and not fig. 184).
10. Ibid., p. 152, no. 55, fig. 183.
11. Ibid., p. 152, no. 54, fig. 184 (and not fig. 182).

70. Hubert-François Bourguignon d'Anville (known as Gravelot)

Paris, 1699–Paris, 1773

Standing Couple

Ca. 1750–60

Black chalk with white highlights, 11⅞ × 8⁹⁄₁₆ in. (30.1 × 21.7 cm)

PROVENANCE: William Mayor (d. 1874), mark at lower right (Lugt 2799); Countess Rosebery; sale, Sotheby's, London, November 21, 1974, lot 118 (as French School, eighteenth century); Private Collection, Somerset; Day & Faber, London; acquired by Jean Bonna, 2002

EXHIBITIONS: Paris 2006b, no. 30; Geneva 2006–7a

Hubert-François Bourguignon d'Anville, known as Gravelot, is no longer in fashion. It is to the collector's credit, even taking into account that he is also a bibliophile, that he included a work by this artist in his panorama of French drawings, as the Goncourt brothers would have done. Too meticulous, too small in size, the once-popular works of the eighteenth-century vignettists have lost much of their audience, although not of their importance. Illustrative vignettes do not lend themselves well to display in temporary exhibitions; they are really intended for careful study by a connoisseur who has the privilege of holding a volume of them in his hands. The present drawing, however, which is of larger scale, should restore Gravelot's talent to its rightful place among the worthy emulators of François Boucher. Through graceful gestures, the artist shows himself capable of evoking the figures' conversation and emotions. What is difficult about the art of illustration is that it requires the same understanding of the source texts as the noble genre of historical painting. In particular, one must choose a crucial moment in the plot, the point at which an image (in the best of cases) can reveal what comes next. Along with the illustrators Charles-Nicolas Cochin and Charles Monet, Gravelot trained in the studio of Jean Restout, who is considered one of the best representatives of the Grand Manner.

Although best known for his countless small-scale drawings, which were preparatory for his illustrative vignettes, Gravelot also produced larger drawings—the present one is an example—as well as several genre paintings in the style of Jean-Siméon Chardin. When a series of such drawings surfaced in 1864, at the sale of the Comte Andreossy's collection (the count had acquired them in London about 1805, while he was there as ambassador), it elicited the astonishment of the Goncourts, who purchased several of them. "These oh so beautiful sketches," they enthusiastically wrote, "on buff-colored paper, rubbed with soft chalk, highlighted in white, and finished in black pencil, reveal a draftsman who has outdone himself and surpassed his entire oeuvre."[1] The Goncourts' purchases at that sale included *Amorous Conversation*, which hung in a place of honor in the large salon of their house in Auteuil,[2] and *Conversation*, now in the Louvre (fig. 81), which also features an elegant couple captured by the artist "in broad strokes that create powerful creases in the flowing skirts, combining stumping with thick chalk lines and leaving visible some pentimenti from the original sketch." The fact that these drawings are larger, however, should not mislead us as to their function. The grand scene from *Tom Jones*, which shares the same provenance, was squared for reduction to a vignette that is identified as having been engraved by Jean-Jacques Pasquier. What this shows is how much preparatory work Gravelot put into plates that we consider so modest.

70

Figure 81. Hubert-François Bourguignon d'Anville (known as Gravelot), *Conversation*. Black chalk highlighted with white. Musée du Louvre, Département des Arts Graphiques, Paris (inv. RF 2057)

illustrations of works such as Richardson's *Pamela* and Shakespeare's plays. It was with his flattering reputation preceding him that he returned to Paris when political events induced him to leave England. From then on, he was given the most deluxe editions to illustrate, including Boccaccio's *Decameron* in 1757, as well as the major undertakings that were the collected works of Corneille, Voltaire, and Racine.[7] But never was he so at ease as in the kind of intimate, amorous scene depicted in the present drawing.

CHRISTOPHE LERIBAULT

The small-scale preparatory drawings, which are better conserved than the larger ones because they were often bound into volumes,[3] allow us to follow the development of the vignettes (often in three or even four stages), from the initial sketch in which the figures were placed nude to the final arrangement of the décor. To save time, Gravelot would transfer his compositions from one drawing to the next by tracing over the main lines with a stylus. The geographer d'Anville, Gravelot's brother, reported that in order to arrange his compositions, the artist used three English-made mannequins "fitted with joints of flexible copper even in the fingers, and a wardrobe containing everything from street clothes to theater wear, and even a Roman toga."[4] In this exercise of precision, a great care was taken with the setting, whether a refined Rococo interior or an idyllic garden, a talent

elevated in the writings of the Goncourts to a "science where the figures would be surrounded with elegance the way gold and silver encircle the gouache on a snuffbox."[5]

Because Gravelot illustrated such a considerable number of books, it has not been possible to identify the specific engraving to which the present drawing might be related.[6] The outfit of the man is a Spanish-style fantasy, also commonly found in the works of Jean-Antoine Watteau and Jean-Honoré Fragonard. The dress worn by the female character, on the other hand, especially the shape of the sleeves, suggests that one might situate the work from after Gravelot's long stay in England (from 1732–33 to 1745), in other words in the second part of his Parisian career. Gravelot, who had immigrated to London because his future in France seemed so uncertain, gained huge success there for his

1. E. and J. de Goncourt 1880–82, vol. 2, p. 13.
2. On their purchases, see the crucial study by Elisabeth Launay (1991, pp. 312–17, ill.).
3. As such, many of the drawings by Gravelot that are now in large American public collections come from an album of more than a thousand such works, which passed from the Marquis de Fourquevaux to Emmanuel Bocher, then to Louis Olry-Roederer in Reims, where it was acquired by Rosenbach booksellers in Philadelphia; Rosenbach began dispersing it in lots in 1922. The history of this album and useful details on the artist's technique can be found in the catalogue by Kimerly Rorschach and Susan B. Taylor (Philadelphia and Houston 1985).
4. E. and J. de Goncourt 1880–82, vol. 2, p. 14. Bourguignon d'Anville 1774.
5. E. and J. de Goncourt 1880–82, vol. 2, p. 14.
6. See Hébert, Pognon, and Bruand 1968, pp. 462–650.
7. Note that the group of preparatory sketches for the volume of Racine's works, given by the Dutuit brothers to the Petit Palais in 1902 (Paris 1992–93, pp. 162–69, ill.), was recently complemented by the purchase of a group of drawings for the works of Corneille (Llanos 1998).

71. Jean-Siméon Chardin

Paris, 1699–Paris, 1779

Curiosity

1728–30

Red, black, and white chalk on beige paper, 7³⁄₁₆ × 8³⁄₈ in. (19.8 × 21.3 cm)

Inscribed in pen and brown ink at lower left: *chardin*; in pen and brown ink at upper right: *de Main / Moussard* [or *Mouffard*] *chapon p / Detin*

PROVENANCE: Du Charteaux sale, Paris, May 2, 1791, part of lot 482 ("*A Pastoral Scene* in graphite on vellum,

also by Ch. Natoire; *Curiosity*, and another drawing by Chardin, and a *Bishop* by Vassé," sold to Sollier for 8 livres); Edmond de Goncourt (1822–1896) and Jules de Goncourt (1830–1870), 1857, their mark at lower right (Lugt 1089), acquired with a *Jacquet* for 43 francs; sale, Paris, February 15–17, 1897, lot 40 (as "attributed to Chardin," sold to Marty for 70 francs); F. Gaillard; sale, Paris, March 27, 1965, lot 3 (as "Chardin?"); Pierre Monart, Compiègne, 1979; acquired through Sotheby's, London, by Jean Bonna, 1999

EXHIBITIONS: Paris 1933, no. 305 (photograph of the drawing); Paris, Cleveland, and Boston 1979, no. 140 (as "Chardin?"); Paris 2006b, no. 31; Geneva 2006–7a

BIBLIOGRAPHY: E. and J. de Goncourt 1864, p. 166 (note); E. and J. de Goncourt 1880–82, vol. 1, p. 109, ill.; E. and J. de Goncourt 1880–82/1906, vol. 1 , p. 142; E. de Goncourt 1881, vol. 1, p. 60; Mathey 1933a, pp. 9–10; Mathey 1933b, p. 82; Mathey 1964, pp. 18, 27, no. 4, fig. 4; Ananoff 1967, pp. 60–61, pl. 3; Ananoff 1979, p. 60, fig. 2; Ananoff 1983, p. 54; Rosenberg 1983a, pp. 71–75, 82–83, fig. 47; Rosenberg 1983b, p. 121; Launay 1991, pp. 251–53, no. 45, pl. 1 and fig. 99 (engraving by Edmond de Goncourt after the drawing reproduced in fig. 100); Denison 2006, p. 512

71

This drawing was etched by Edmond de Goncourt "about 1863" (fig. 82).[1] The Goncourt brothers estimated that they owned "three pure benchmarks of drawings by Chardin":[2] the *Young Man in a Tricorne*, now in the Louvre;[3] a *Portrait of an Old Man Holding a Cat*,[4] now unanimously rejected (the painting for which it was preparatory, formerly in the collection of the Baronne de Conantre, is attributed to either Joseph Ducreux[5] or

Francesco Zuccarelli[6]); and finally, the present drawing, which according to the Goncourts depicted "a man showing some children a magic lantern," or else "a man showing a curiosity to two urchins." At their posthumous auction, for which Féral father and son were the appraisers, only the first of these drawings was catalogued as being definitively by Chardin (an attribution this author rejects); the two others, along with a fourth entitled

Jacquet (*Young Lackey*), were merely "attributed" to the artist.

The drawing in the Bonna collection was restored to Chardin by Jacques Mathey and Alexandre Ananoff, and with good reason. Indeed, it shows clear similarities to both *The Vinaigrette* and *Man Pouring a Drink*, two drawings in the Nationalmuseum, Stockholm, for which the attribution to Chardin dates to the first half of the eighteenth century. It has

Figure 82. Edmond de Goncourt, after Jean-Siméon Chardin, *Curiosity.* Etching. Bibliothèque Nationale de France, Département des Estampes et de la Photographie, Paris (Ef 407a rés.)

Let us conclude with a quotation from Edmond de Goncourt.[12] It concerns the interpretation of the pen-and-ink inscription that can be read on the drawing, and it is cited here with all due reserve: this inscription "is perhaps—although trimmed off by the knife of the mounter Glomy—an invitation from the painter to a friend, which he wrote on his own drawing, inviting him to come dine on chicken the next day at the Plat d'Etain." And let us stress the extreme scarcity of drawings by Chardin; fewer than ten are known to this day. Chardin took up chalk again in the final years of his career to create his admirable pastels. Among these was one he exhibited at the Salon of 1779: a *Jacquet*! [13]

PIERRE ROSENBERG

the same slightly hesitant line, the same kind of reworking in black chalk, the same way of planting the figures firmly on the ground. And there is more. The Goncourts barely mention their fourth drawing, the *Jacquet* "drawn on the same paper as *Curiosity* and mounted on the same old mount."[7] The present location of this drawing is unknown, but a trace of it remains thanks to an etching by Edmond de Goncourt (fig. 83),[8] which confirms that *Jacquet* and *Curiosity* are by the same hand. This *Jacquet* is a preparatory study for a figure in a small *Genre Scene*, signed and dated 1730 and recently put up for sale (fig. 84).[9] The canvas is surprising, and this writer hesitated a long time before accepting its attribution.[10] Why can we now attribute the work to Chardin?

There are several reasons. For one, the water spaniel visible at the left of the painting is identical to the one that figures in a large eponymous canvas, also signed and dated 1730, currently in a Private Collection in Paris.[11]

The work in the Bonna collection figures among Chardin's last drawings. From that point on, the artist would paint directly from nature or from models, with his subject before him, without making use of preparatory sketches. Unlike the artists of his generation, who all drew abundantly and referred to their studies when executing their paintings (following the principles they had learned at the Académie), Chardin, having come to understand the nature of his genius, stopped using drawings.

1. Engraving in two states (Adhémar and Lethève 1955, p. 247, no. 9, *Montreur d'images*).
2. E. and J. de Goncourt 1864, p. 165.
3. Inv. RF 2055; Launay 1991, p. 254, no. 47, fig. 102.
4. Ibid., p. 277, no. 73, fig. 126.
5. See Mathey 1964, p. 29, figs. 13, 14.
6. Sale, Christie's, South Kensington, July 6, 2005, lot 187.
7. From the same Du Charteaux sale in 1791 (see Provenance); E. de Goncourt 1881, vol. 1, p. 60; sale, Paris, February 15–17, 1897, lot 41.
8. Adhémar and Lethève 1955, p. 247, no. 10; see also Launay 1991, p. 253, no. 46, fig. 101.
9. Sale, Christie's, London, December 8, 2004, lot 48.
10. Paris, Cleveland, and Boston 1979, no. 141 (as "Chardin?"); Rosenberg and Temperini 1999, no. 51, ill.
11. Rosenberg and Temperini 1999, no. 50, ill.
12. E. de Goncourt 1881, vol. 1, p. 60.
13. Part of no. 55 in the Salon *livret*.

Figure 83. Edmond de Goncourt, after Jean-Siméon Chardin, *Jacquet.* Etching. Bibliothèque Nationale de France, Département des Estampes et de la Photographie, Paris (Ef 407a rés.)

Figure 84. Jean-Siméon Chardin, *Genre Scene.* Oil on canvas. Private Collection

72, 73. Jean-Siméon Chardin

Paris, 1699–Paris, 1779

72. *Portrait of a Young Girl*

1777

Pastel, 17¾ × 14¾ in. (45.1 × 37.5 cm)

Signed in black chalk at lower left: *chardin / 1777*

73. *Portrait of a Young Boy*

1777

Pastel, 17¾ × 14¾ in. (45.1 × 37.5 cm)

Signed in black chalk at lower right: *chardin / 1777*

PROVENANCE: Princess Mathilde Bonaparte (1820–1904), 1862 (not included in the posthumous sale of her collection on May 17–21, 1904); M. Foulon de Vaulx, 1907 and again in 1933; Mr. and Mrs. Lester F. Avnet; Wildenstein and Company, New York, ca. 1985; Private Collection, Japan; Matthiesen Fine Art, London; Sayn-Wittgenstein Fine Art, New York; acquired by Jean Bonna, 2002

EXHIBITIONS: Paris, Salon of 1777 (part of no. 50, *Three Studies of Heads*, pastel); Paris 1907, nos. 75, 76; Paris 1936b, nos. 49, 50; West Palm Beach 1969, nos. 11, 12; New York 1979, nos. 6, 8; London 1983, p. 55; Paris 2006b, nos. 32, 33; Geneva 2006–7a

BIBLIOGRAPHY: Dayot and Vaillat 1907, p. 1, nos. 2, 3, pls. 2, 3; Guiffrey (Jean) 1907, p. 102; Guiffrey (Jean) 1908, p. 77, nos. 125, 126; Furst 1911, p. 136; G. Wildenstein 1933, pp. 204, 205, nos. 656, 667, figs. 205, 207; G. Wildenstein 1963, pp. 219–20, nos. 376, 377, fig. 173 (*Portrait of a Young Boy*); G. Wildenstein 1969, p. 227, nos. 376, 377a, pls. 62, 63, and fig. 173; Cailleux 1975, p. 294; Paris, Cleveland, and Boston 1979, p. 374, under no. 139; Rosenberg 1983b, p. 114, nos. 198, 199, ill.; Whiteley 1983, p. 506, fig. 70 (*Portrait of a Young Boy*); Roland Michel 1994, p. 98, ill. pp. 100, 101; Rosenberg and Temperini 1999, p. 114, nos. 198, 199, ill.; Matthiesen Fine Art 2003, pp. 11–30, figs. 1, 2; Denison 2006, p. 512

On December 13, 1862, the Goncourt brothers[1] paid a visit to Princess Mathilde, the daughter of Jérôme Bonaparte and, consequently, Napoleon's niece. As usual, they showed their customary bitterness, misogyny, contempt, and arrogance: "We saw all sorts of knickknacks. The place is cluttered with the kinds of objects that only a woman could consider art [sic], including a fake pastel by Boucher and some fake pastels by Chardin."[2] It is not known where or from whom the princess acquired these "fake pastels"

nor what became of them while she was alive. In any case, they are not listed in the catalogue of her posthumous sale and do not seem to have been mentioned again before 1907.

The harshness shown by the Goncourts is all the more unjustified in that the two pastels, along with a *Head of an Old Man*, now lost, were quite certainly exhibited by Chardin at the Salon of 1777. This is confirmed by two drawings by Gabriel de Saint-Aubin (1724–1780) in the margins of his copy of the Salon *livret*.[3] Reviewers of the Salon were extremely favorable, praising these works for their "free skillful touch, full of effect"[4] and their "warmth and . . . freedom."[5]

Some have wondered what led Chardin to devote himself almost exclusively to pastel and to the portrait beginning in 1771. Most likely, the artist chose this new medium for reasons of health; the binders and lead-based pigments necessary for oil painting burned his eyes, leading to slow paralysis and progressive blindness. The powders of pastel did not have the same effect. As for the choice of portraits—it was the combination of medium and genre in which Maurice-Quentin de La Tour and Jean-Baptiste Perronneau, and before them Rosalba Carriera, had distinguished themselves—it confirms Chardin's desire late in life to climb a rung on the hierarchy of genres. That hierarchy, which is still so poorly understood today, placed works of "invention" at the top and relegated still lifes and genre scenes to secondary status. For it was universally thought at the time that the latter subjects required the artist only to copy what was before his eyes and did not call upon him to exercise his imagination.

Chardin's favorite model for these pastels was himself. Apart from his second wife, Françoise-Marguerite Pouget (and Rembrandt), the models for his other pastels, expressive head studies, have not been identified. Such is the case with the *Young Girl* and *Young Boy* in the Bonna Collection, to which

Philip Conisbee devoted a fine monographic study in 2003.[6] The first wears in her hair a delicate blue ribbon somewhat reminiscent of the ones in *Self-Portrait with Spectacles, Self-Portrait with Easel*, and *Portrait of Mme Chardin*, all three in the Louvre. The boy, who is younger than the girl, is seated on a chair, while his companion seems to be posed standing. He is wearing a curious hat decorated with a large, charcoal-gray feather that casts a shadow over his forehead. Neither one is looking at the viewer.

In his essay on Chardin, Charles-Nicolas Cochin (1715–1790) had already made the point that, when the artist switched over to pastel, he "did not use it for his usual subjects but rather to create life-sized head studies. He made several of them, of various characters, young people, old people, and others. He had great success in the medium because of his skill and his loose style—or at least so it appeared, for it was the fruit of much reflection, and he was not easily satisfied. These pieces clarified his sense of grandeur and what he might have accomplished in the genre of historical painting had he pursued it. And I do not believe it can be denied that, if he had treated it from the same angle as Caravaggio, he would have succeeded handsomely."[7]

PIERRE ROSENBERG

1. For the drawing in the Bonna collection that belonged to them, see cat. no. 71.
2. E. and J. de Goncourt 1851–65/1989, vol. 1, p. 902.
3. Bibliothèque nationale de France, Département des Estampes et de la Photographie, Paris.
4. *Mercure de France*, October 1777.
5. *Année littéraire*, 1777.
6. See Matthiesen Fine Art.
7. Manuscript at the Bibliothèque Municipale, Rouen. See Cochin 1780/1875–76.

74

74. Jean-Étienne Liotard

Geneva, 1702–Geneva, 1789

Greek Dancer

Ca. 1738–42

Red and black chalk on parchment, 3 × 2⅛ in. (7.6 × 5.4 cm)

Drawing acquired in sharkskin case lined in red velvet with two small copper clasps; originally backed with a piece of a playing card (8.1 × 5.5 cm) featuring orange hearts over a background of white and yellow stripes

PROVENANCE: Miss C. L. K. Adye; sale, Sotheby's, London, June 26, 1969, lot 51 (*A Frankish Woman from Galata*), color ill., frontispiece, and black-and-white ill., p. 34 (reproduction reversed); Hans Calmann, London; Norton Simon, Santa Monica, California; John Goelet; Richard Day, London; acquired by Jean Bonna, 2001

EXHIBITIONS: Geneva and Paris 1992, p. 278, no. 39 (as location unknown), ill. p. 88; Paris 2006b, no. 36; Geneva 2006–7a; Paris 2008, no. 33

This elegant young woman figures in a counterproof in black and red chalk now in the Bibliothèque Nationale (fig. 85). In the counterproof, she naturally appears in reverse, but in full length and with the graceful gestures of a dancer with castanets held one in each hand and her arms spread. The present half-length portrait, therefore, might well be the truncated original of the counterproof. The parchment seems in fact to have been trimmed on all four sides around the bust of the model,[1] probably in order to mount it in the case in which it was purchased. This hypothesis is corroborated by the position of the arms, which appear arbitrary in this format.

Although the title of the counterproof identifies the model as a Greek dancer, she wears the sumptuous costume that Jean-Étienne Liotard often depicted in his portraits of women from Smyrna and Constantinople: a hat made of brocaded cloth decorated with pearls or gems; a dress with long, open sleeves, belted at the waist by a double metal buckle; and a very low-necked corsage of white, semitransparent muslin, ornamented with jewels sewn onto the fabric. The model for this drawing has been identified mistakenly as the one in *Frankish Woman from Galata and Her Slave*, now in the Fondation Custodia, Paris.[2] While their respective costumes bear some resemblance to each other, these are surely two different young women, if only because of their eye color; the eyes of the woman in the present drawing are light colored, and those of the woman in the Fondation Custodia drawing are dark.

Traveling with the great British tourist William Ponsonby, the future Lord Bessborough, whom he had met in Rome, Liotard arrived in Constantinople in May 1738, after several stops along the Italian and Sicilian coasts (Capri, Messina, Syracuse), followed by stopovers in Malta, the Cycladic islands of Mílos, Páros, and Ios, and finally Smyrna. The artist's stay in the Levant, where he remained until 1742, yielded pastels and drawings that bear witness to his fascination with the East. His many drawings from nature give a Westernized but objective image of the East, unlike the imaginary *turquerie* created in Europe during the Rococo era. Seduced by the novelty of this shimmering exoticism, Liotard drew copiously, with a predilection for young female models wearing rich traditional costumes.

For these drawings from models, Liotard usually adopted the same layout—a full-length figure in three-quarter view with shadow on the ground—and the same mix of black and

red chalk, which was well suited for rendering physical materials and contrasts of light and dark. In this "portrait," he skillfully alternated the different tonalities: from deep black for the hair and embroideries to pale gray for certain details of dress; from thick reds in the folds of the garment to pinks for the chest and face, subtly shading these colors onto the pearls to give them greater brilliance. Liotard was a virtuoso miniaturist, and he took great care in rendering the slightest facial features and details of costuming; he used a personally developed pointillistic technique, which is particularly evident in the modeling of the face. That heightened concern with the rendering of

minute details yielded an image of exquisite delicacy and purity, attaining a degree of clarity that is substantially muted in the counterproof.

HÉLÈNE MEYER

1. Geneva and Paris 1992, p. 278, no. 39.
2. Red and black chalk, 8 × 9⅞ in. (20.4 × 25 cm), Frits Lugt Collection, Paris (inv. 1931-6); the comparison was suggested in the catalogue for the sale at Sotheby's, London, June 26, 1969, lot 51.

Figure 85. Jean-Étienne Liotard, *Greek Dancer with Castanettes.* Counterproof in black and red chalk, graphite. Bibliothèque Nationale de France, Département des Estampes et de la Photographie, Paris (B6c fol. 32 rés.)

75. François Boucher

Paris, 1703–Paris, 1770

Study of a Young Boy Uncorking a Bottle

Ca. 1735

Two different red chalks, heightened with white on buff-colored paper, 11⅝ × 11⁷⁄₁₆ in. (29.5 × 21.9 cm)

Signed (?) at lower right, in red chalk: *f boucher*

PROVENANCE: Anonymous sale, Hôtel Drouot, Paris (Maîtres Couturier and Nicolay), December 13, 1989, lot 46; Galerie Arnoldi-Livie, Munich; acquired by Jean Bonna, 1996

EXHIBITIONS: Munich 1995, no. 4; New York and Fort Worth 2003–4, no. 24; Paris 2006b, no. 38; Geneva 2006–7a

BIBLIOGRAPHY: Galerie ArnoldiLivie 1990, no. 31

In 1735, François Boucher had not yet come to specialize in a particular genre and produced any type of painting that his clients requested: mythological scenes, pastorales,

and even *scènes galantes*. In the series of four paintings that might have been intended for the Duc de Richelieu—*Le Bonheur au village* and *La Halte à la fontaine,* both in the Alte Pinakothek, Munich; *Le Retour de marché,* in the Chrysler Museum, Norfolk, Virginia; and *L'Heureux pecheur,* in the Frick Art Museum, Pittsburgh[1]—he treated the theme of a village pastorale that perfectly suited his talents; an idyllic landscape replete with memories of his stay in Italy is the setting for a group of peasants engaged in their daily activities or in an amorous intrigue. The artist also explored this type of subject in a tapestry series entitled Fêtes italiennes (Italian Village Scenes), for which he provided two sets of four paintings. The first series, woven in 1736, depicts figures frolicking in a landscape that still abounds with umbrella pines, broken columns, and

remnants of an ancient temple.[2] The second series, woven about 1744, features scenes of young aristocrats being served by domestics, a good example of which is *The Collation.*[3] Finally, on the theme of outdoor recreation, Alastair Laing noted[4] that Boucher apparently created a group, most likely made up of three compositions—illustrating a picnic, a dance, and a meal during the hunt—that today are known only through painted copies.[5] Early auction catalogues mention these works as designs for fans intended for the czarina, a hypothesis that so far has little documentation to support it.

Preparatory studies exist for most of these canvases, usually devoted to individual figures, and these allow us better to situate the drawing in the Bonna Collection. Thus, for *Le Bonheur au village,* there are several drawings,

75

Figure 86. François Boucher, *Standing Servant*. Red chalk highlighted with white. Nationalmuseum, Stockholm (inv. 2927/1863)

notably *Man Kissing a Servant* and *Standing Servant* in the Nationalmuseum, Stockholm (fig. 86),[6] which can be dated about 1735 and which bear stylistic similarities to the present work—the same angular stroke for defining the outlines, the same use of copious hatching in red chalk to place shadows around the figure,

and finally, the same attention to the depiction of the garments.

The *Young Boy Uncorking a Bottle* surely must have been intended for a scene of a meal, but *The Collation*, woven in 1744, shows no such figure and is dated too late with respect to the style of the drawing. It seems more likely that this drawing was related to the series that is now lost, for which there are either painted copies or preparatory sketches. The picnic scene,[7] in particular, was preceded by several red chalk studies very similar in technique to the Bonna sheet, such as *The Group of Gentlemen* in the Musée des Beaux-Arts, Orléans, *The Valet* in a private collection, and *Seated Young Woman* in the Metropolitan Museum.[8] The present figure, however, is almost certainly related not to the picnic scene but to the *Meal during the Hunt*, currently known through a painted copy.[9] And indeed, on the right of the copy, there is a man in a tricorne hat plunging his hand into a basket of provisions containing bottles of wine and in front of him, a boy uncorking a bottle in a very similar pose.

The theme of a meal during the hunt was especially popular at the time, from works such as Watteau's famous *The Halt during the Chase* in the Wallace Collection, paintings by Joseph Parrocel, Carle Van Loo, and Jean-François de Troy now in the National Gallery and the Louvre, to *The Hunting Breakfast* by François Lemoyne, now in the Museu de Arte de São Paulo.[10] Comparison with the latter work is all the more interesting since the Bonna collection contains studies for two of its figures, a young man serving wine (see cat. no. 69) and a hunter seen from behind.[11] The elegance of

the gestures and the fluidity of the outlines of these drawings, which have often led scholars to attribute them to Watteau, stand in contrast to the realism of the present sheet. Here, Boucher was breaking with his master's lessons and adopting a more direct approach to the subject drawn from life, which in some ways is reminiscent of the art of Abraham Bloemaert, which Boucher discovered during his time in Italy.[12] This effort at realism in portraying everyday domestic chores often can be found in the artist's work, notably in *Le Déjeuner* in the Louvre, painted in 1739, for which Boucher executed a superb *Study of a Valet with Coffeepot* in the Art Institute of Chicago.[13]

EMMANUELLE BRUGEROLLES

1. New York, Detroit, and Paris 1986–87, pp. 166–71, no. 27, figs. 118–20.
2. *L'Opérateur* and *La Curiosité* (woven together), *La Bohémienne, Les Chausseurs*, and *Les Filles aux raisins* (woven together), and *La Pêcheuse* (ibid., pp. 328–39, nos. 86–89).
3. The three other compositions are *Le Jardinier, La Danse*, and *La Musique*; ibid.
4. New York and Fort Worth 2003–4, p. 86, no. 24.
5. Ibid., p. 86, no. 24, and see also p. 234 (notes).
6. Inv. 2928/1863, 2927/1863; New York, Detroit, and Paris 1986–87, p. 170, figs. 121, 122.
7. Private Collection; Washington and Chicago 1973–74, p. 30, fig. 10.
8. Ibid., pp. 30–32, no. 23, figs. 11, 12.
9. Sale, Palais d'Orsay, Paris, December 14, 1979, lot 40, under the name of Étienne Jeaurat; the comparison and the hypothesis were suggested in New York and Fort Worth 2003–4, p. 86, no. 24.
10. Paris, Munich, and Bonn 2005–6, p. 378, fig. a.
11. Paris 2006b, pp. 138–39, no. 27.
12. Regarding Boucher's drawn copies after Bloemaert, see Shoolman Slatkin 1976.
13. Inv. RF 926; New York, Detroit, and Paris 1986–87, pp, 182–85, no. 33, fig. 132.

76. François Boucher

Paris, 1703–Paris, 1770

Study of a Young Woman Viewed in Full Length,
Her Right Arm Resting on a Plinth

1761

Black chalk with stump, heightened in white on brown
paper, 20 11/16 × 15 9/16 in. (52.5 × 39.5 cm)

Signed or inscribed in black chalk at lower right: *f.*
Boucher 1761

PROVENANCE: Posthumous sale of the collection of M.
de Bourlamaque, former cavalry captain, rue de la Perle,
Paris (Pierre Remy), March 22, 1770, and following days,
lot 22 (*Une femme debout, appuyée sur un piédestal* and
two other drawings); sale, Christie's, Monaco, July 2,
1993, lot 100 (Desrouges sale, Paris, December 17, 1924,
lot 125, listed erroneously in PROVENANCE); Katrin
Bellinger Kunsthandel, Munich, 1994; acquired by Jean
Bonna, 1997

EXHIBITIONS: New York, Paris, and London 1994,
no. 31; New York and Fort Worth 2003–4, no. 51; Paris
2006b, no. 41; Geneva 2006–7a

BIBLIOGRAPHY: Ananoff 1966, pp. 130–31, no. 455,
fig. 85; Versailles 2004, p. 130, under no. 60

In the 1750s, François Boucher was at the
height of his career and enjoying great success for his village scenes, *scènes galantes*, and
studies of women. Despite this, he seems to
have returned to religious painting around
that time, under the influence of Madame de
Pompadour, with *The Adoration of the*
Shepherds, dated 1750 and now in the Musée
des Beaux-Arts, Lyon,[1] as well as with *The Rest*
during the Flight to Egypt of 1757, painted for
the château of Bellevue and now in the
Hermitage.[2] He also treated subjects from
ancient history, such as in his frontispiece for
an edition of Corneille's tragedy *Rodogune*, for
which he made two preparatory studies that
are now in the Morgan Library, New York.[3]
This project, etched in 1759 by Madame de
Pompadour herself with the help of Boucher
and Charles-Nicolas Cochin on the "north"
press (that is, in her apartments in the north
wing of the Palais de Versailles),[4] illustrates
a passage from Scene 4 of Act V, in which
Rodogune indicates the dying Cleopatra:
"Lord, see how her eyes / Grow so confused,
maddened, and wild." Several years later, in
1764, Cochin, then secretary of the Académie,
commissioned from Boucher a *Clemency of*
Titus[5] for the gallery of the château of Choisy,[6]
envisioned to hang alongside works by Carle
Van Loo, Joseph-Marie Vien, and his student
Jean-Baptiste Deshays. That same year, the artist created a composition showing *Hecuba and*

Cassandra before the Statue of Minerva, now
lost but known through two compositional
studies of the complete work in Princeton
University and the Ackland Art Museum,
Chapel Hill, as well as a sketch now in a
Private Collection.[7] Finally, Boucher provided
his son-in-law Jean-Baptiste Deshays with
sketches illustrating various episodes of *The*
Iliad, intended to serve as cartoons for
tapestries woven at the Beauvais factory
beginning in 1761.[8]

It is in the context of this return to grand
subjects taken from ancient history that we
must situate the drawing in the Bonna collection. Initially, it was considered preparatory to
the frontispiece of *Rodogune* and related to the
studies in the Morgan Library,[9] and indeed,
we find the same type of woman shown full-
length next to an architectural element from
antiquity, dressed in an ample fringed costume
and wearing a large turban. However, the date
of 1761, written on the drawing, excludes a
relation with the frontispiece, which was
engraved in 1759. Alastair Laing suggested that
it might be a study of Briseis, intended for one
of the cartoons for the tapestries executed by
Deshays, *The Wrath of Achilles*, which in fact
depicts a devastated Briseis leaving the hero's
tent.[10] However, the young woman in the
present drawing is in an interior setting, with
her right arm resting on a plinth and in a fairly
different posture, which suggests that it was
intended for a different composition, possibly
one preceding Achilles's wrath, for which
Boucher might have drawn preparatory studies.

Whatever the case, the Bonna drawing fits
perfectly with Boucher's studies of women
from that time; alongside the nudes in sensual
and voluptuous poses so prized by connoisseurs, he represented figures inspired by
ancient history and exemplifying the *grand*
goût. Some of these were preparatory for
Hecuba and Cassandra (1764), notably *The Two*
Followers of Hecuba and an *Old Woman*
Leaning on a Bas-Relief, respectively in the
Collection of Jeffrey E. Horvitz (fig. 87)[11] and
in a Private Collection (fig. 88).[12] *Young*

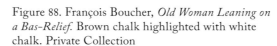

Figure 87. François Boucher, *The Two Followers of*
Hecuba. Black chalk highlighted with white chalk.
Collection of Jeffrey E. Horvitz, Boston (DF 32)

Figure 88. François Boucher, *Old Woman Leaning on*
a Bas-Relief. Brown chalk highlighted with white
chalk. Private Collection

76

Woman in Classical Dress in the Morgan Library[13] is also part of this series, although it is difficult, as with the Bonna drawing, to relate it to any currently known work. As he often did in the 1760s, the artist here adopted a very painterly technique, mixing different chalks on colored papers and using stumping and white highlights to accentuate the effects of light and shadow. The monumentality of these full-length figures is reinforced by the ampleness of the drapery with its deep folds and by the emphatic black chalk strokes that define the outlines.

EMMANUELLE BRUGEROLLES

1. New York, Detroit, and Paris 1986–87, pp. 245–49, no. 57.
2. Ibid., pp. 279–82, no. 68.
3. Acc. no. 104a; Washington and Chicago 1973–74, pp. 103–4, no. 80.
4. Etching reproduced in ibid., fig. 41.
5. Ultimately, Boucher did not execute these compositions, as Louis XIV had asked him for four paintings in a wholly different spirit (Michel 1993, p. 499; Alastair Laing in Cambridge and other cities 1998–2000, p. 232, no. 62).
6. Michel 1993, pp. 499, 522.
7. For the two drawings, see Anne L. Schroder in Gilham and Wood 2001, no. 28, n. 2; and Versailles 2004, p. 128.

The painted sketch is mentioned in the catalogue for the sale of the Jean de Jullienne Collection, March 30, 1767, Paris, lot 271, now in a Private Collection in Hamburg (Versailles 2004, p. 128, no. 59).
8. See New York and Fort Worth 2003–4, p. 144, no. 51; and Sandoz 1977, p. 84, no. 70.
9. The relation was established at the time the drawing was sold at Christie's, Monaco, on July 2, 1993, lot 100.
10. Sandoz 1977, p. 84, nos. 70, 71.
11. Versailles 2004, p. 130, no. 60.
12. Jacoby 1992, p. 255, fig. 22.
13. Acc. no. 1983; Paris and New York 1993–94, p. 126, no. 55.

77. François Boucher

Paris, 1703–Paris, 1770

Bust of a Young Woman in a Shift with Her Hair Tied Up, Seen from Behind

Ca. 1740

Black, red, and white chalk on fawn paper, 11⁵/₁₆ × 9⁵/₁₆ in. (28.7 × 23.6 cm)

Inscribed in black chalk at bottom left: *Boucher*

PROVENANCE: Lionel Lucas (1822–1862), mark at bottom right (Lugt 1733a); his nephew Claude Lucas; sale, Christie's, London, December 9, 1949, lot 62; purchased at that sale by Agnew's, London; Barbara Astor (née Colonsay; d. 1980), Viscountess Ward of Whitley; sale, Christie's, London, July 4, 1995, lot 133; sale, Christie's, New York, January 24, 2001, lot 106; purchased at that sale by Jean Bonna

EXHIBITIONS: New York and Fort Worth 2003–4, no. 59; Paris 2006b, no. 39; Geneva 2006–7a

BIBLIOGRAPHY: Lugt 1956, p. 241, no. 1733a (as the only French drawing in this select but little-known collection); Ananoff 1976, vol. 1, pp. 272, 351, nos. 153/1 and 237/9, figs. 502, 708; Denison 2006, p. 512

In the François Boucher tercentenary exhibition held in the Frick Collection, New York, in 2003, this author published this drawing as preparatory for one of the handmaidens in the lost cartoon for the Beauvais tapestry of *The Toilette of Psyche*, first woven in 1741.[1] But this study was also used for one of the handmaidens for another mythological figure—Diana—in an unpublished painting, *Diana Accusing Callisto* by a student or follower of Boucher (fig. 89). This picture once served as the ceiling of a room in a castle in Northern Ireland, its nudities painted over so as not to offend the Puritan sensibilities of that community. It also appears to be one of the rare instances of a painting for which Boucher supplied the idea to one of his former pupils or followers as well as a drawing or drawings such as this for an individual figure or figures in it.

The artist conceived a first draft in red chalk,[2] followed by a large and elaborate compositional drawing in black chalk that was in no lesser collections than those of Randon de Boisset and Gaspard de Sireul, and later in that of Mr. and Mrs. Robert Scheiner.[3] In the painting, the composition has been truncated on the right, and there are also a number of other changes, leaving open the possibility that Boucher made a second drawing closer to the painting as executed, and that the first drawing,

Figure 89. Student or Follower of François Boucher, *Diana Accusing Callisto*. Oil on canvas. Private Collection

not having been used in the studio, was thus in a good state of preservation and available to a collector.

The truncation of the original design on the right necessitated the introduction of a new figure to close the composition on the right side, and Boucher introduced a seated handmaiden holding two hounds on a leash, her back to the viewer so that her gaze is directed at Diana. It may be because this figure was a late addition that the present study was needed. She is essentially the figure on the right of the tapestry *The Toilette of Psyche*, in reverse. In the painting, the ribbons that tie her hair are red; in the tapestry, they are blue; and in the present drawing, they are not colored in at all. The artist also may have made a full-length study of the figure, which corresponds perhaps to lot 172 in Sireul's posthumous sale.[4] The compositional drawing was not specifically dated by Boucher specialist Regina Shoolman Slatkin, when she borrowed

it in 1973 for the exhibition "François Boucher in North American Collections: 100 Drawings," but she placed it among other works of the 1740s.[5] Colin Bailey placed it in that same decade when he reproduced it in his 1991 catalogue *The Loves of the Gods*.[6] As *The Toilette of Psyche* was first woven in 1741, it is evident that the present drawing should be dated at the beginning of the decade. To identify the author of Diana and Callisto from among the artists who had left Boucher's studio by that time, is not easy. The task is made more difficult by the amount of restoration that the painting had to undergo to remove the overpainting. An attribution will perhaps only be found once the painting is exhibited publicly. If so, that would more probably be from the figures of Diana's nymphs rather than the repoussoir figure on the right, whose dependence on Boucher, and on the present drawing, is total.

ALASTAIR LAING

1. Ananoff 1976, vol. 1, p. 310, no. 191/6, fig. 603; Colorno 1998, pp. 181–82, ill. p. 65, fig. 4; Bremer-David 1997, p. 109, color ill. p. 108.
2. The drawing was consigned to Sotheby's in February 2004 but seems never to have been put up for sale. It measures 6 × 8⅜ in. (14.9 × 21.1 cm).
3. Washington and Chicago 1973–74, no. 45; the drawing was subsequently auctioned at Christie's, London, December 8, 1976, lot 110.
4. This author cited this in New York and Fort Worth 2003–4, no. 59, as a possible provenance for the present drawing, which sounds, on further reflection, more like a drawing for the entire figure.
5. See note 3 above.
6. Paris, Philadelphia, and Fort Worth 1991–92, pp. 418, 421, fig. 5.

78. Charles-André (known as Carle) Van Loo

Nice, 1705–Paris, 1765

Perseus Rescuing Andromeda

Ca. 1762

Pen and brown ink over sketch in black chalk, brown wash, heightened with white gouache on brown paper, 13⅜ × 18¾ in. (34 × 47.6 cm)

Inscribed in pen and brown ink at lower right: *C vanloo*

PROVENANCE: Ange-Laurent de La Live de Jully (1725–1779), 1762; sale, Hôtel Drouot, Paris, March 31, 2000, lot 59; purchased at that sale by Jean Bonna

EXHIBITIONS: Paris 2006b, no. 42; Geneva 2006–7a

BIBLIOGRAPHY: Dandré-Bardon 1765, p. 66; Nice, Clermont-Ferrand, and Nancy 1977, p. 149, under no. 459

Shortly after Carle Van Loo's death, a catalogue of his works, drawn up by his friend and first biographer, the Aix painter Michel-François Dandré-Bardon, was published, preceded by the text of Dandré-Bardon's eulogy of Van Loo, which had been presented at the

Académie.[1] Among the many writings that the celebrity of the king's *premier peintre* inspired, this work is of incalculable value when it comes to understanding his oeuvre. More than two centuries later, however, it is not so simple to reconstruct that oeuvre; the exhibition catalogue devoted to Van Loo in 1977,[2] still considered authoritative, mentions more than one hundred paintings or drawings that have been lost or whose whereabouts are unknown. Although he enjoyed great renown in his lifetime, the "Chief Painter of Europe," as Grimm dubbed him, found himself pushed aside in his final years by the emergent current of neoclassicism. But thanks to various discoveries made in the art market and in the domain of scholarship, the corpus of Van Loo's work has continued to grow richer.

The present drawing, formerly classed among the lost works,[3] until now was known only

through an engraving (fig. 90). Announced both in *L'Avant-coureur* of July 19, 1762, and in the *Mercure de France* of the following month,[4] it was cited with five other prints as examples of a new engraving technique developed by Pierre-Gustave Floding and François-Philippe Charpentier that faithfully reproduced wash drawings. Executed by Charpentier to imitate brown wash and in the same orientation as the drawing, the print was dedicated to the Marquis de Marigny, whose crest of arms it bears.[5] This shows how much importance Van Loo ascribed to the original drawing, which he must have considered sufficiently finished to allow it to be engraved for the Superintendent and whose technique lent itself well to the new method of printmaking. In addition, the drawing was mentioned by Dandré-Bardon as having been in the collections of Ange-Laurent de La Live de Jully, a major Parisian collector of

78

Figure 90. François-Philippe Charpentier, after Carle Van Loo, *Perseus and Andromeda*. Engraving. Institut National d'Histoire de l'Art, Collection Jacques Doucet, Paris (inv. 100425)

Figure 91. Carle Van Loo, *Perseus Rescuing Andromeda*. Oil on canvas. State Hermitage Museum, Saint Petersburg (inv. GE 1230)

eighteenth-century French drawings and paintings, and the caption in the margin of the print, which reads "from the cabinet of Monsieur de La Live," confirms the provenance.

The rediscovery of this drawing some thirty years after the 1977 exhibition constitutes a major event, all the more so since it is a preparatory sketch for the painting in the Hermitage (fig. 91).[6] It is no surprise that this canvas is in Russia, as several important works by Van Loo were purchased in the eighteenth century by Catherine the Great, either directly from their owners such as Madame Geoffrin (*Spanish Concert* and *Spanish Reading*) or through sales of prominent Paris collections, such as the Marquis de Marigny's (*The Sultanas*, formerly in the bedchamber of Madame de Pompadour in Bellevue) or the Comte de Baudoin's (*The Rest of Diana*). This particular painting was acquired for the empress by Denis Diderot between 1769 and 1774. Moreover, there exists yet another drawing (current location unknown) of the same subject and in a similar technique but of smaller dimensions, which might also relate to the genesis of the composition.[7]

Considered by his contemporaries to be one of the greatest draftsmen of his century, Van Loo displayed a marked predilection for red chalk, which he used especially for nudes and figure studies. He also used black chalk when drawing portraits. But pen and ink or wash were reserved for his finished compositions, such as the present *Perseus Rescuing Andromeda*. This technique is therefore one of the rarest in the artist's repertoire and was employed for drawings that were directly preparatory to paintings. In this case, there are several notable differences between the brilliant final canvas, dated 1735–40, and this magnificent and highly powerful study. The vigor of the emphatic pen strokes and the accents of

gouache, as well as the barely sketched allusion on the left to a landscape, make up for the artist's hesitations, which can be divined in several pentimenti still visible beneath the thickness of the gouache. These indecisions, which are reflected in variations eventually adopted in the painting, mainly concern the placement of the figures and their poses: Perseus's right arm holding the sword and the positioning of his shield, Andromeda's face and the angle of her legs.

Although a symbol of French Rococo—of which he was, along with his rival François Boucher, one of the major representatives—Van Loo, in his capacity as a painter of historical works, favored noble subjects celebrating the virtues of courage and heroism. With the exception of a few rare portraits, *scènes galantes*, "Turkish scenes," and decorative compositions, his repertoire abounds in serious religious subjects and mythological epics, brilliantly tempered by an elegant and graceful style all his own. As in the text of the legend, Perseus, wearing the helmet of Hades and the winged sandals, brandishing in his two hands a shield decorated with Medusa's head and a fearsome sword, swoops like an angel onto the dragon with a striking foreshortening that indicates the artist's familiarity with Italian art. There is no lack of models for this oft-depicted subject, from Paolo Veronese in the Farnese, Gallery, Rome (now in the Louvre) through Van Loo's contemporaries François Lemoyne (1723, Wallace Collection, London), Charles-Antoine Coypel (1727, the Louvre), or Edme Bouchardon, one of whose drawings presents a composition that is noticeably analogous to Van Loo's (in the Louvre).[8] The freedom with which this work is rendered shows the natural ease of the painter, who depicted the rhythm and dynamism of the action with consummate skill. Despite the dramatic force of the scene,

underscored by the monstrous maw of the dragon in the foreground and the bound Andromeda's terrified expression, the composition remains both dazzling and elegant, in the spirit of the "grand style."

HÉLÈNE MEYER

1. Dandré-Bardon 1765, pp. 53–69 ("Liste des principaux ouvrages de Carle van Loo").
2. Nice, Clermont-Ferrand, and Nancy 1977.
3. Ibid., p. 149, no. 459.
4. *Mercure de France*, August 1762, p. 159: "The pieces engraved by Monsieur Charpentier are: 1. *Perseus and Andromeda*, after M. Wanloo, *Premier Peintre* to the King; dedicated to M. the Marquis de Marigny, printed with two plates on a folio of Elephant paper. Its price is 4 livres"; Roux 1931–55, vol. 4 (1940), p. 203, no. 3.
5. 13½ × 18¾ in. (34.4 × 47.6 cm); at lower left: *C. Vanloo prim. Pictor Regis invenit.*; at lower right: *F. P. Charpentier B. Sculpsit*; on either side of the cartouche bearing the crest of arms of the marquis de Marigny: *PERSEE ET ANDROMEDE / A Monsieur le Marquis De Marigny / Conseiller du Roi en ses Conseils, Commandeur de Ses Ordres, Directeur et Ordonnateur / Général de ses Bâtimens, Jardins, Arts, Académies et Manufactures Roïales*; below this to the left: *Tiré du Cabinet de Monsieur De la Live*; at right: *Par son très humble et très obéissant Serviteur Charpentier*; at center: *A Paris chez Charpentier graveur, rue Clos Georgeot, Bute St. Roch, chez Mr. La Male Chirurgien et chez Bligny, Cour du Manège aux Thuilleries*, Jacques Doucet collections, Institut National d'Histoire de l'Art, Paris (inv. 10042); Nice, Clermont-Ferrand, and Nancy 1977, p. 149, no. 459.
6. Oil on canvas, 28¾ × 36¼ in. (73 × 92 cm), inv. GE 1230; Nice, Clermont-Ferrand, and Nancy 1977, p. 36, no. 37; Nemilova 1982, p. 127, no. 39.
7. Sale, Hôtel Drouot, Paris, March 11–12, 1858, collection of A. Mouriau, former captain in the service of Belgium, lot 171: "Loo (CARLEVAN). Mythology. Andromeda attached to the boulder is rescued by Mercury, aided by Cupid. Lively finishing in pen over graphite lines, washed in sepia. At left the master's signature"; 16 × 10¾ in. (40.5 × 27.3 cm).
8. Edme Bouchardon, *Persée delivrant Andromède*, red chalk, 9¾ × 15 in. (24.9 × 38.1 cm), Musée du Louvre, Département des Arts Graphiques, Paris (inv. 24690).

Je vous promets de mieux — GEORGE D'ANDIN — Vivre a l'avenir

79

79. Jean-Baptiste Marie Pierre

Paris, 1714–Paris, 1789

Scene from George Dandin

Ca. 1754–55

Pen and black ink, brush and gray wash, heightened with white gouache, over black chalk, on blue paper, 8¹¹⁄₁₆ × 10⅝ in. (22.7 × 28.9 cm)

Signed in pen and brown ink at lower right: *Pierre*

Inscribed in pen and dark brown ink below image at lower left: *Je vous promets de mieux*, and at lower right, *Vivre a l'avenir*, and in pen and black ink at center of lower margin: *GEORGE D'ANDIN*

PROVENANCE: Léon Decloux; his sale, Hôtel Drouot, Paris, February 14–15, 1898, lot 134; L[eboeuf] de M[ontgermont]; his sale, Galerie Georges Petit, Paris, June 16–19, 1919, lot 271; purchased at that sale by Georges Petit; Marcel Razsovich, Saint-Germain-en-Laye, 1929; by descent to Eric Audemars, Alençon; André Fabius, Paris, ca. 1950; by descent to Fabius Frères, Paris; Katrin Bellinger Kunsthandel, Munich; acquired by Jean Bonna, 2005

EXHIBITION: Paris 1929, no. 182

BIBLIOGRAPHY: New York and London 2005–6, pp. 126, 223, under no. 49

Born into a successful family of jewelers, Jean-Baptiste Marie Pierre was trained as a history painter and became one of the most able decorators in large scale of his generation. The numerous commissions for paintings, ceilings, and altarpieces he executed in the 1740s and 1750s display a sober elegance, recalling the style of Pierre Subleyras (1699–1749). These accomplishments found recognition in prestigious appointments, first as *premier peintre* to the duc d'Orléans in 1752 and then as *premier peintre du roi* and director of the Académie

Figure 92. Jean Sauvé, after Pierre Brissart, *George Dandin*, 1682. Engraving. New York Public Library, John Davis Batchelder Collection

Royale in 1770. Like many of his fellow academicians, especially François Boucher who preceded him as director, Pierre did not let the hierarchy of genres restrict his realm of activity. In addition to his work for the crown and the church, he lent his fluid and captivating manner to the production of prints, genre paintings, ornament, and illustration.

Using gray wash and white gouache to painterly effect, Pierre here presented the moonlit final scene of Molière's comedy *George Dandin*. Angelique de Sotenville, daughter of impoverished provincial nobility, has been forced to marry the wealthy peasant George Dandin to save her family from financial ruin. She has no intention, however, of remaining faithful to a man she considers beneath her station. Dandin repeatedly tries to expose her dalliance with the vicomte de Clitandre to her parents. When he finally catches her outside with her lover in the middle of the night, he sends for her parents, but not before she comes up with a ruse to switch places and accuse him instead. Her parents believe her story and force Dandin to kneel before his duplicitous wife and pledge "to behave better in the future."[1]

From at least the beginning of the twentieth century to the beginning of the twenty-first, the drawing remained together with Pierre's two other depictions of plays by Molière: *Le Misanthrope* in the Morgan Library, New York, and *Le Sicilien* in a Private Collection, London.[2] As no prints or paintings relating to the compositions survive, the series has elicited a certain amount of speculation as to its function and date. Olivier Aaron and Nicolas Lesur, who are preparing a catalogue raisonné on the artist, have stressed Pierre's association with Parisian theatrical productions at different points in his career, from an early

collaboration with Jean-Nicolas Servandoni (1695–1766),[3] to an active involvement in the duc d'Orléans's private theater on the faubourg Saint-Martin in the mid-1750s.[4] Stylistically, it is to this later period of involvement that Pierre's theater subject drawings seem to date.[5] Charles Collé, a dramatist occasionally in the employ of the duc d'Orléans, described the theater in January 1754 in his *Journal et mémoires*, as featuring décor "faites sur les dessins et conduits par M. Pierre." In April, he elaborated, "[l]es decorations sont faites avec une intelligence et un goût supérieurs. M. Pierre, premier peintre de M. le duc d'Orléans, m'a donné les dessins, et a conduit toute la besogne; et tout le monde est convenu qu'il avoit fait un petit chef-d'œuvre."[6] Over the same few months that Collé refers to his work for the faubourg Saint-Martin theater, Pierre would have had the opportunity to see many of the plays he illustrated performed at the Comédie Française (*Le Misanthrope*, January 4, 1754; *George Dandin*, February 11, 1754; and *Don Japhet*, February 24, 1754).[7]

Even for those who did not frequent the theater, reading Molière was a popular pastime in the eighteenth century—if the title of Jean-François de Troy's *Reading from Molière* is anachronistic[8]—and Pierre could hardly have been unaware of the success of the 1734 edition illustrated by Boucher, which was reprinted approximately every five years.[9] Indeed, earlier engraved illustrations of *George*

Figure 93. François Joullain, after Charles Coypel, *George Dandin*, 1726. Etching and engraving. Bibliothèque National de France, Département des Estampes et de la Photographie, Paris (D6-7 fol. 77)

Figure 94. Laurent Cars, after François Boucher, *George Dandin*, 1734. Etching and engraving. The Metropolitan Museum of Art, New York, Harris Brisbane Dick Fund, 1942 (42.24)

Dandin provide a compelling context for Pierre's drawing, and they suggest that he may have intended his Molière drawings as models for engravings. Pierre Brissart's design for the 1682 edition[10] (fig. 92) established the final scene, with George Dandin on bended knee as the conventional moment to illustrate. Charles Coypel, who was Pierre's predecessor as *premier peintre* of the duc d'Orléans and was likewise involved with theater, designed a suite of five prints illustrating scenes from different Molière comedies in 1726.[11] For *George Dandin*, he envisioned the same scene as a shallow horizontal tableau (fig. 93). Boucher's design for the 1734 edition of Molière's *Oeuvres* (fig. 94) includes the same six characters but depicts a slightly earlier moment in the story, as Monsieur and Madame de Sotenville approach to find George Dandin clutching a torch and locked out of his own house. When Pierre illustrated the play some twenty years later, he went back to the recognizable final scene with George Dandin on bended knee. The stage-like presentation recalls Coypel's scene, although certain elements—the balcony, the moon, and the cypresses—show an awareness of Boucher's print.

Seen against this survey of George Dandin prints, Pierre's drawing can be proposed as a model for a never-executed print, probably intended to be part of a suite of Molière prints in the vein of Coypel's 1726 project rather than a book illustration.[12] Given his involvement with the theater, his conception of the scene may well owe something to a performance he attended, or contributed to, but such connections will have to remain hypothetical.

PERRIN STEIN

1. "Je vous promets de mieux vivre à l'avenir"; Molière, *George Dandin* (Paris: Gallimard, 2002), p. 115 (act 3, scene 7).
2. The three are illustrated together in New York and London 2005–6, p. 126. A sheet of similar format and technique but of slightly larger dimensions and depicting a scene from Paul Scarron's comedy *Don Japhet d'Arménie* is in the British Museum, London (New York and London 2005–6, pp. 126–27, no. 49).
3. Olivier Aaron and Nicolas Lesur discovered in the Archives Nationales, Paris, a letter revealing that Pierre had collaborated with Servandoni on projects of theater décor before leaving on his Roman sojourn (e-mail correspondence, September 22, 2004).
4. E-mail correspondence, September 10, 2004.
5. New York and London 2005–6, p. 126, no. 49.
6. Collé 1748–72/1967, vol. 1, pp. 410, 416.
7. Lancaster 1951, p. 776. I would like to thank Esther Bell for her research on these productions.
8. Christophe Leribault in Ottawa, Washington, and Berlin 2003–4, no. 25, pp. 168–69.
9. Cohen 1912, pp. 712–16.
10. Molière, *Les Oeuvres de Monsieur de Molière: Reveuës, corrigées & augmentées, enrichies de figures en taille-douce* (Paris, 1682), vol. 4, facing p. 213.
11. The set was announced in the *Mercure de France* in July 1726; see Lefrançois 1994, pp. 425–30, nos. D29–D33.
12. He himself had etched a similar series after Subleyras's paintings of Les Contes de la Fontaine during his student years in Rome; see Paris and Rome 1987, pp. 173–93.

80. Claude-Joseph Vernet

Avignon, 1714–Paris, 1789

Coast View with Fishermen

1754

Pen, brown ink, gray and brown wash on cream paper, 14⅞ × 21¼ in. (37.8 × 54 cm)

Signed and dated on a stone at lower right: *J. Vernet f. / 1754*

PROVENANCE: Ducs d'Harcourt, until 1935; Wildenstein and Company, New York; acquired by Jean Bonna, 1999

EXHIBITIONS: London 1993, no. 43; Paris 2006b, no. 43; Geneva 2006–7a

The critical interest that Claude-Joseph Vernet's work arouses today is a far cry from mirroring his former reputation, when he was the most famous painter of landscapes and seascapes in Europe in the second half of the eighteenth century. Moreover, the attention he does receive has been strongly influenced by the commentaries of Diderot, who, like all his contemporaries, saw Vernet almost exclusively as a painter, the creator of canvases that combined a striking fidelity to nature with a powerful ability to inspire reverie. His graphic work has never met with the same enthusiasm. The first serious research into Vernet's drawings dates back only about thirty years, and even this has had little direct consequence; still today, the field remains largely unexplored.[1]

The drawings now attracting the most notice are studies executed during his stay in Italy, from 1734 to 1753—works treated with wide swatches of brown wash, such as *View of the Port of Naples*, which extend Gaspar van Wittel's (1653–1736) tradition of plein-air execution, or else drawings of greater density and detail that mix inks of different colors, such as *Ruins of the Roman Colosseum*.[2] All those drawings were intended for his personal use and probably figured in the group of more than 700 sheets dispersed after his death. Many studies of that type are now at the Albertina, and while they have rarely been researched, they are nonetheless enough to class Vernet among the most important landscape draftsmen of the eighteenth century. The drawings for collectors, on the other hand, form in his drawn oeuvre an ensemble the importance of which has not yet been measured but which seems to have occupied a considerable place in his career.

Given its scale, energy, and the care lavished on its painterly effect, the present drawing is one of the most ambitious that the artist is known to have made. The black chalk sketch is visible in spots, beneath the pen-and-ink lines that precisely define the outlines and make only limited use of hatching. The delicacy of the outlining is comparable to what is found on the studies of the port of Naples[3] or certain drawings for collectors, probably made in Italy, such as *Fishermen and Boatmen near the Port of Genoa*.[4] Wide brushstrokes of gray wash were then applied before the ink was completely dry. They are warmed in places with a few touches of brown wash, the interplay of the two tones alternating darker and lighter areas with impeccable rigor. To make certain motifs stand out in the foreground and strengthen the effect of depth, the artist added some darker accents with the tip of his brush. In particular, these accents bring out the boulder and the tree, which he has then reworked energetically in pen, with an almost black ink. This way of distributing light and shadow helps give the work a radically different character from studies made directly from the subject, in which the foreground is often left empty and most of the effect is concentrated on the middle ground. Still, it is highly unlikely that this sheet was made to work out the arrangement of a painting, as the artist never liked preparing his canvases with compositional studies. An examination of his drawings confirms what he himself said: "I am not in the habit of making sketches for my paintings, and I never have been. My custom is to compose the painting I have to create directly on the canvas and to paint it immediately, in the heat of my imagination."[5] In this regard, his method was entirely personal and

differs from the approach used by Adrien Manglard (Lyon, 1695–Rome, 1760), who for a time was his teacher in Rome and who left detailed studies relating to his paintings.[6] Nor would Vernet's method be followed by Pierre-Jacques Volaire (1729–ca. 1802), his main assistant from 1754 to 1762, by whom we also have preparatory drawings in which he precisely works out the relationship between the figures and their surroundings.[7]

Conceived somewhat on the model of his paintings, this large wash drawing belongs with the works on paper that Vernet created specifically for buyers. The first drawings of this type date from his sojourn in Italy, when the artist would sell them to English tourists. He continued to produce them long after his return to France, and the account books in which he noted commissions and payments preserve traces of several such transactions.[8] The date shown here under the signature could read either 1734 or 1754. The earlier date is impossible to reconcile with such an ambitious piece, and moreover, Vernet's earliest known drawing dates from 1737.[9] This piece was therefore created in 1754, at a time when Vernet was working in the south of France on his first views of the French ports, which the Marquis

de Marigny had commissioned from him for the king the previous year and which were to occupy him until 1765. The artist spent part of the month of January 1754 in Bandol to sketch the *View of the Gulf of Bandol: Tuna Fishing*.[10] He then returned to Marseille, where much of the year was spent painting the two large views of the port that were exhibited at the salon the following year,[11] and in September, the painter moved with his family to Toulon. Despite the considerable amount of work that the execution of the king's paintings required, Vernet accepted a large number of private commissions during that period. His account books record a long list of easel paintings ordered by gentlemen, provincial merchants, and a number of visiting foreigners. Few of the entries from that time concern drawings; nonetheless, Vernet noted that in Marseille in 1754, the "Maltese Count Prezziosi," who commissioned him to paint several canvases, also "asked for two drawings" on behalf of the Chevalier de Valabres.[12] The present drawing could well be one of these, but it might also be one of the four drawings that Vernet sold at around the same time to a Parisian merchant named Rémy on behalf of his brother.[13] It is likely that a work of such strong decorative qualities

Figure 95. Claude-Joseph Vernet, *Le Retour de Pêche*. Etching. Bibliothèque Nationale de France, Département des Estampes et de la Photographie, Paris

VUE PROCHE DE GÊNES.

Figure 96. François Godefroy, after Claude-Joseph Vernet, *View near Genoa*. Engraving. Musée Calvet, Avignon (inv. I 66-67)

80

was designed from the outset to be placed in a frame. It might have been conceived as a pendant, as many drawings of this type are one of a pair, following a principle that had been earning Vernet great success in painting since the late 1730s.[14] Indeed, another version of this drawing has come to light recently as part of a pair,[15] adding weight to the theory that the Bonna sheet likewise once had a pendant. The date inscribed on both of those newly discovered sheets, however, has been read as 1734, the year Vernet arrived in Rome.

The present drawing is solidly arranged around the motif of the tree cutting diagonally across the composition. The overall layout relates it to relatively early pieces such as *The Marina of Anzia*, which was Vernet's reception piece at the Academy of Saint Luke in Rome in 1743.[16] But it bears an especially striking

similarity of conception with *Le Retour de Pêche*, one of the very few etchings Vernet ever produced, which dates from the end of his Italian sojourn (fig. 95).[17] While the print is in a vertical format, its pictorial organization is based on similar motifs: a composition solidly weighted to the left side, a boulder in the foreground with a knotty tree whose branches spread all the way to the upper edge, and figures of fishermen who are, as here, vigorously rendered, with a slightly angular penmanship explicitly reminiscent of Salvator Rosa.[18] During Vernet's entire stay in Italy, Rosa's art was one of his great references, and several collectors ordered paintings from him that were composed in the master's manner. The influence of the Neapolitan painter can also be seen in the style of his drawings: the *Study of Trees with Figures*, signed *Vernet f.t Ro.mae*, now in

the Musée des Beaux-Arts, Orléans, makes explicit reference to Rosa's graphic technique.[19] It is very much in the context of this filiation, claimed long after his return to France, that we must understand the energetic penmanship and the typology of figures in the present work. At the same time, especially when compared with the etching, the drawing shows how much Vernet had moved away from the Neapolitan's tortured compositions after he returned to France. With a sense of recession built around a series of frontally seen planes opening onto a peaceful maritime vista, the present composition is much more classical in nature.

François Godefroy (1743–1819) made an engraving from this composition in reverse orientation, titled *View near Genoa* (fig. 96).[20] The print surely was executed at a fairly late date, long after the drawing had left the artist's studio, as the engraver only began signing his name to plates in the 1760s. It carries the indication *Jos. VERNET pinx.*, but the term "pinx" in this context does not necessarily imply the existence of a painting. Moreover, the watchtower linked to the shore by a small stone bridge belongs to a repertoire of picturesque architectural motifs that bear only a vague resemblance to the structures scattered over the Ligurian coastline, and the title of the engraving was probably invented by its publisher, Basan, who followed what had become standard practice among print publishers in the second half of the century who supplied spurious captions to market their products.[21] With its elegant little tower, the arcaded structure that can be glimpsed behind the branches, and the group of fishermen pushing a little boat to the sea—a motif he often used in both painting and drawing[22]—Vernet composed an idealized image of the Italian coast highly appreciated by connoisseurs of his day.

DIEDERIK BAKHUŸS

1. The first general study devoted to Vernet's drawings was done by Philip Conisbee for the retrospective organized in London in 1976 (London 1976, nos. 50–64 and figs. 4–11). The exhibition in Paris (1976–77) repeated some of the same drawings shown in London but included a number of works incorrectly attributed to the artist. No. 66 is by Pierre-Jacques Volaire (1716–1803); no. 77 is the work of an imitator, and nos. 79–93 are by a later artist.
2. *View of the Port of Naples*, Musée du Louvre, Paris, inv. RF 117; (London 1976, no. 56; Paris 1976–77, no. 65); *Ruins of the Roman Colosseum*, Private Collection (London 1976, no. 62).
3. See, for example, in addition to the *View of the Port of Naples* (see note 2 above), *Bateaux dans le port de Naples* in the Courtauld Gallery, London (inv. 1952. RW. 1798; London 1976, no. 63), or several sheets in the Graphische Sammlung Albertina, Vienna, such as *Palais de Donn'Anna à Naples* (inv. As no. 51); London 1976, no. 58).
4. Musée du Louvre, Paris, inv. 33258; Paris 1976–77, no. 67.
5. Lagrange and Montaiglon 1856, p. 150, cited in Manoeuvre and Rieth 1994, p. 26.
6. The Musée des Beaux-Arts, Rouen, notably has a *View of the Port* (inv. 868.5.12), preparatory to a canvas now in the Palazzino Buoncompagni-Ludovisi, Rome; see Maddalo 1982, p. 138, no. 74 (drawings), ill.
7. The Louvre notably has a large preparatory drawing (inv. RF 3936) for a painting at the château of Compiègne, *Moonlight Seen from Vesuvius* (Paris 1976–77, no. 66, catalogued as being by Joseph Vernet but correctly identified by Philip Conisbee).
8. The account books, conserved at the Musée Calvet in Avignon and published by Léon Lagrange, mention several orders for drawings "in India ink," which the artist began receiving in 1737; see Lagrange 1864, p. 322, no. 3, and pp. 324–25, no. 32.
9. This is *View of the Gardens of the Villa Mattei*, now in Hessisches Landesmuseum, Darmstadt (London 1976, fig. 8).
10. Paris, Salon of 1755, no. 101.
11. Paris, Salon of 1755, nos. 98, 99.
12. Lagrange 1864, p. 339, no. 158.
13. Ibid., pp. 78, 362, no. 73.
14. Let us cite, among many other examples of drawings conceived as pendants, *The Banks of the River* and *The Seashore*, in the sale at Christie's, New York, January 9, 1991, lot 59.
15. Sale, Sotheby's, Paris, June 19, 2007, lot 24; acquired by Jean-François Heim; Paris; see Galerie Jean-François Heim 2008, pp. 14–15.
16. Accademia di San Luca, Rome; Ingersoll-Smouse 1926, vol. 1, no. 77, pl. IX, fig. 17; Conisbee 1973, p. 791, fig. 16.
17. Ingersoll-Smouse 1926, vol. 2, no. 1320, pl. CXXXVII, fig. 320; see Conisbee 1973, p. 791, fig. 18; and London 1976, no. 65. Richard Campbell has contributed some specific information about the dating of this plate: see Baltimore, Boston, and Minneapolis 1984–85, no. 30.
18. For the matter of Vernet's relations with Salvator Rosa, which is evident even in the titles of his paintings mentioned in the salon booklet, see Conisbee 1973.
19. Musée des Beaux-Arts, Orléans; London 1976, no. 64; Paris 1976–77, no. 64.
20. Ingersoll-Smouse 1926, vol. 2, no. 1276, pl. CXXXII, fig. 297. The Musée Calvet in Avignon has an impression of this print that seems, on the other hand, to be missing from the collection of the Bibliothèque Nationale de France, Département des Estampes, Paris; see Arlaud 1976, no. 191.
21. Lagrange (1864, pp. 219–20) was the first to note the multitude of spurious locations invented by publishers of prints made from the artist's works.
22. The motif appears, for instance, in the painting *The Departure for Fishing* (Ingersoll-Smouse 1926, vol. 1, no. 272; sale, Christie's, New York, May 25, 1999, lot 144) or in the drawing *The Departure of the Fishermen* (Marius Paulme sale, Galerie Georges Petit, Paris, May 13–15, 1929, lot 256).

81. Jean-Baptiste Greuze

Tournus, 1725–Paris, 1805

Pouting Girl

Ca. 1760–65

Red chalk, 11⅜ × 8¼ in. (28.9 × 21 cm)

PROVENANCE: Possibly N. A. [Durand] sale, April 17, 1825, lot 132, which Jean Martin and Charles Masson (see Bibliography) relate to the engraving by Louis-Marin Bonnet; Galerie de Bayser, Paris; acquired by Jean Bonna, 2003

EXHIBITIONS: Paris 2006b, no. 50; Geneva 2006–7a

BIBLIOGRAPHY: Martin and Masson 1908, under no. 632; Ongpin 2003, under no. 35

The son of a master roofer, Jean-Baptiste Greuze was born in Tournus, on the border of Burgundy. He was trained in Lyon by a local painter, Charles Grandon (ca. 1691–1762), and he arrived in Paris about 1750. For several months he studied with Charles Natoire, until the latter was appointed director of the Académie de France in Rome. The young Greuze made rapid progress and soon was noticed. At that point, there occurred the sort of event with which the artist's career seems to have been studded. Accused of employing others to help execute his paintings, he was summoned to do the portrait of Louis de Silvestre, director of the Académie Royale de Peinture et de Sculpture, in front of the other academicians. Greuze passed the test brilliantly, as is witnessed by the painting now at the Alte Pinakothek in Munich.[1] The artist was elected to the Académie in 1755 as a genre painter, upon presentation of that portrait and several other canvases, and henceforth was allowed to show his works at the Salon des Artistes Vivants, which earned him considerable success, especially for his genre scenes.

81

Figure 97. Jean-Baptiste Greuze, *The Reading from the Bible*. Oil on canvas. Private Collection

execution and knowing how to derive a handsome profit from them.[5] In addition to his large compositions, for which he entered into an exclusive contractual arrangement with one engraver, he had a number of individual figures turned into prints. These prints were often derived from his paintings of genre scenes. Their most accomplished and expressive faces were reprised and widely distributed, thereby increasing the success of the paintings as well. So it was that in 1766 Greuze published a volume titled *Têtes de différents caractères* (*Heads of Different Character Types*), engraved by Pierre-Charles Ingouff (1746–ca. 1780?). As such, Greuze was responding, a century after the fact, to Charles Le Brun's famous 1668 lecture on the expression of emotions, the publication of which was of particular relevance in the second half of the eighteenth century, largely due to the influence of the Philosophes and the naturalists. In 1766, Diderot devoted a chapter of his *Essay on Painting* to the expression of emotions.[6] Two years later, the same year that Greuze was elected to the Académie, the Comte de Caylus inaugurated a Prize for Expressive Head Studies. In 1772, Johann Caspar Lavater published his first research into physiognomy.[7] While reviving Le Brun's approach, Greuze also acted as a pioneer by extending the investigation of human facial

Exhibited at the Louvre in the fall of 1755, *The Reading from the Bible*, now in a Private Collection, shows an old woman and a mother with her six children grouped around a table in a rustic setting, listening as the father of the family reads from the Bible (fig. 97). That composition, which exalts the benefits of family life, is characteristic of Greuze's moralistic and sentimental painting style. The profile of the girl shown kneeling in the right foreground presents some similarities with the present *Pouting Girl*, especially her passive expression and her pretty cap with its fluted frills. At the same time, it is difficult to consider the drawing in the Bonna Collection as a preparatory study for the painting. The drawing's highly finished character and firmness suggest that it was done later in the artist's career. Furthermore, it can be related stylistically to the next drawing (cat. no. 82), dated 1765 or slightly before; both have the same way of contouring the cheeks by crosshatching the lines of red chalk.

The literature about Greuze lists a certain number of "pouting" children. Ange Laurent de La Live de Jully (1725–1779), a major collector of the artist's work and one of his early supporters—he owned *The Reading from the Bible*, along with two other canvases shown at the Salon of 1755—owned a *Pouting Boy* that since has been lost.[2] In July 1777, the *Mercure de France* announced that a *Pouting Boy* based on Greuze's work recently had been woven at the Gobelins.[3] What has become of about ten

paintings, either on wood or canvas and titled either *Pouting Girl* or *The Pretty Pouting Girl*, is not known.[4] While a link between these lost works and the present red chalk drawing cannot be established, this drawing nonetheless can be related to the many expressive head studies that the artist drew, often with the intent of having them engraved.

From very early on, in fact, Greuze became involved in distributing his works in the form of prints, always keeping a close eye on their

Figure 98. Louis-Marin Bonnet, after Jean-Baptiste Greuze, *The Pouting Girl*. Engraving. Musée Greuze, Tournus

Figure 99. Attributed to Pierre-Alexandre Wille, after Jean-Baptiste Greuze, *Head of a Young Woman Wearing a Bonnet*. Black chalk. Private Collection

expressions to children. The expressions his models adopted are not as extreme as the ones used to illustrate the lecture by Louis XIV's first painter; rather than archetypes, Greuze offered expressions that radiate naturalness, such as the one displayed by this little girl, who is at most twelve years old. The pout playing about her lips gives her a slightly scornful look and offers a tableau that is both charming and amusing. The same contrast between the girl's serious expression and childish demeanor had been exploited by the sculptor Jacques-François Saly (Valenciennes, 1717–Paris, 1776) in his bust *Girl with Braids*, sometimes called *Pouting Girl*, which was exhibited at the Salon of 1750. Numerous replicas were made of this figure—one of the most popular images of the eighteenth century—in addition to engravings for young artists to use as models.[8]

The *Pouting Girl* from the Bonna Collection was engraved in the manner of a red chalk drawing by Louis-Marin Bonnet (1736–1793) (fig. 98)[9] at the end of 1766, the same year that *Têtes de différents caractères* was published. While he did not invent chalk-manner engraving—that discovery belongs to Jean-Charles François—Louis-Marin Bonnet, along with Gilles Demarteau, greatly contributed to its refinement. Among the many

engravings he created using that technique, there are four plates after Greuze, whose large head studies lent themselves especially well to this type of reproduction. The engraving of *Pouting Girl*, in the same orientation and in almost the same dimensions as the drawing, captures the childish countenance with great fidelity, except for the light pentimenti visible under the girl's chin.

A drawing in black chalk, which recently surfaced on the art market, seems to be a version derived from the present *Pouting Girl* (fig. 99).[10] The slight elongation of the face and the bonnet give the model a more placid expression and a less juvenile appearance. This might be a replica, done by Pierre-Alexandre Wille (1748–1821), the son of the engraver Jean-Georges Wille[11] and a student of Greuze's from 1761 to 1763. Wille engraved a number of plates from his teacher's works, and Greuze's influence can be seen throughout his career. The drawing in question might be yet one more proof of Wille's talents as an imitator.

MARIE-ANNE DUPUY-VACHEY

1. On this painting, see most recently Pierre Rosenberg in Paris, Munich, and Bonn 2005–6, no. 55.
2. La Live de Jully sale, Paris, March 5, 1770, lot 109; Martin and Masson 1908, no. 433.

3. For other paintings with the same title, see Martin and Masson 1908, nos. 434–36.
4. Ibid., nos. 437, 631, 632; no. 438 must correspond to the painting now at the Art Institute of Chicago and attributed to a follower of Greuze (1933.1079), also known by the title *Child with Bread and Butter*, which cannot be related to the present drawing.
5. On this subject, see notably Griffiths 1980; and Arquié-Bruley 1981.
6. Diderot, *Essais sur la peinture*, 1766/1984, pp. 39–52.
7. On the posterity of Charles Le Brun's lectures, see Montagu 1994 and Pinault Sørensen 2000.
8. Paris, Salon of 1750, no. 147. On this bust, see most recently Bent Sørensen in Versailles, Munich, and London 2002–3, no. 224.
9. 11 × 8¾ in. (28.1 × 22.2 cm); signed at lower right: *Bonnet Sculpt.*, at left: *C [sic] reuze delin.*; at upper right above the first line: *No. 176*, corresponding to the number in the catalogue Bonnet drew up of his own plates (see Hérold 1935, no. 176). The Greuze scholar Edgar Munhall has confirmed in a written communication (July 18, 2002) that the quality of the drawing disproves any inference that it is a copy based on an engraving. Moreover, careful examination of the sheet leads him to affirm that no counterproof was made of it and that it didn't serve for making tracings. Munhall also mentions a drawing nearly identical to the present one (11 × 8 in. [27.8 × 20.3 cm]; Private Collection, France), as well as the existence of a copy, likely based on the Bonnet engraving, carrying the annotation "Pouting Girl" at bottom center and a false signature "J. B Greuze" at lower right.
10. 11¾ × 8⅞ in. (30 × 22.6 cm); Ongpin 2003, no. 35.
11. To whom the volume *Têtes de différents caractères* after Greuze was dedicated.

82. Jean-Baptiste Greuze

Tournus, 1725–Paris, 1805

Head of a Smiling Young Woman

Ca. 1765

Red chalk, 15⅝ × 12³⁄₁₆ in. (39.7 × 30.9 cm)

PROVENANCE: M. G. T. de Villenave (1762–1846), Paris; sale, Paris [Alliance des Arts], mark at lower left (Lugt 61), December 1, 1842, lot 646; purchased at that sale by E. Marcille; sale, Paris, March 4–7, 1857 (several numbers describe heads of young women in red chalk: nos. 121, 123, 124, 127, 129, 130, 133); sale, Sotheby's, New York, January 28, 1999, lot 69; Agnew's, London; acquired by Jean Bonna, 1999

EXHIBITIONS: New York and Los Angeles 2002, no. 31 and p. 112; Paris 2006b, no. 51; Geneva 2006–7a

This very lovely head of a woman fits into a series of drawings that Edgar Munhall has related to *The Spoiled Child*, a painting exhibited at the Salon of 1765 (no. 111) and belonging at the time to the duc de Choiseul-Praslin. It has been in the Hermitage since 1923 (fig. 100).[1] The composition portrays a child in a rustic interior. Instead of eating his soup, he is giving the dog his spoon to lick, while his mother, rather than getting angry, looks on indulgently, her head cocked slightly to one side. The expression on her face conveys

a certain amusement at her son's shenanigans. Along with *Silence!*[2] a canvas that might be its pendant, *The Spoiled Child* bears witness to period attitudes in matters of childrearing. Jean-Baptiste Greuze's works often reflected those attitudes, either to illustrate and promote new pedagogical methods or, as here, to denounce the culpable laxity of a mother who is unwittingly prejudicing her child's future. The opposite example, of a responsible mother assuming her duties as a disciplinarian, had been depicted by Greuze several years earlier

Figure 100. Jean-Baptiste Greuze, *The Spoiled Child.* Oil on canvas. State Hermitage Museum, Saint Petersburg (inv. 5725)

Figure 101. Jean-Baptiste Greuze, *A Seated Woman Smiling and Raising her Eyes.* Red, black, and white chalk. State Hermitage Museum, Saint Petersburg (inv. Port 80-3-1, no. 44)

in *The Maternal Reprimand.* The work has a very similar composition to the 1765 painting, but this time with a little girl feeding the dog under her mother's reproving eye.[3]

Munhall traced very precisely the process by which *The Spoiled Child* was developed,

which attests to the attentiveness with which Greuze prepared each of his works. There are three known studies for the figure of the mother.[4] In the first, the artist attempted to fix the model's pose, seen full-length and seated. She is a fleshy woman with a generous décolleté, drawn in trois crayons with a fairly rapid line (fig. 101).[5] Her facial expression was also treated in individual studies. The red chalk drawing in the Bonna collection is the closest to the painted version. The almost life-sized figure is slimmer, and her headwear, a pretty bonnet tied on the top of her head with floating sidepieces, is carefully detailed. She seems to be looking toward the child, whereas in the painting her gaze is lost in space, reinforcing the mother's indolent nature. In the same way, the smile in the drawing does not yet have the same palpable indulgence as in the final version.

The drawing in the Albertina is one of the artist's most accomplished and most famous (fig. 102).[6] The combination of trois crayons, the effect of the stumping and black chalk, and the white highlights give it a particularly lively character. The very finished appearance of the drawing, the rounder shape of the head, the model's delighted, almost childlike expression, and the work's slightly smaller dimensions all indicate that it could not have been done later than the present drawing. As Munhall suggested, the Bonna sheet likely was created once the painting was finished, and the artist decided to take up again the motif of the mother's face as the subject of an independent work, as he often seems to have done.

Finally, one must mention a reprise of the composition drawn in wash after the painting,[7] intended as a model for engraving, a process that Greuze often used. Issued in 1772, the print by Pierre Maloeuvre and Jacques-Philippe Le Bas after *The Spoiled Child* helped popularize a composition that had not elicited very favorable comments from Diderot when it was exhibited at the Salon of 1765. We know that the philosopher was an unconditional admirer of Greuze for a good decade. *The Village Bride,* painted in 1761 and now at the Louvre, or *Filial Piety* (*The Paralytic*), executed in 1763 and now in the Hermitage, inspired particularly enthusiastic remarks from him: "This Greuze is really the man for me."[8] But their relationship declined progressively until

Figure 102. Jean-Baptiste Greuze, *Head of a Smiling Young Woman.* Red, black, and white chalk. Graphische Sammlung Albertina, Vienna (inv. 12771)

the "affair" of *Septimus Severus Reproaching Caracalla,* the painting with which the artist was elected to the Académie Royale de Peinture et de Sculpture in 1769 as a genre painter and not, as he had hoped, a history painter.[9] The harsh words Diderot addressed to the painter during the salon of 1765—"My dear friend Greuze, I do not care for your *Spoiled Child....* The painting is devoid of interest"[10]—give a fair indication of the misunderstandings to come. Nonetheless, a few details managed to win the critic's favor: the "very beautiful" child's head, the "charming colors" of the mother's. And Diderot continued: "Her headpiece does not seem to fit her head, and keeps her from looking fully rounded." No such problems occur with the present drawing, which is masterfully executed and magnificently composed.

MARIE-ANNE DUPUY-VACHEY

1. 26⅛ × 22 in. (66.5 × 56 cm), State Hermitage Museum, Saint Petersburg (inv. 5725).

2. 24¾ × 20 in. (62.8 × 50.8 cm), Her Majesty the Queen, London; see Colin Bailey in Ottawa, Washington, and Berlin 2003–4, no. 69.

3. 18 × 13½ in. (45.7 × 34.3 cm), pen and brown ink, gray and brown wash, Sterling and Francine Clark Art Institute, Williamstown, Massachusetts (1955.1660). Another version, in pen and gray wash over black chalk, was reproduced in New York and Los Angeles 2002, p. 22, fig. 12.

4. In a letter to Jean Bonna, Edgar Munhall (March 11, 2003) mentions a rather vulgar copy after the mother's head (Private Collection, France), which can in no case be considered a study for the painting.

5. 15¼ × 11 in. (38.9 × 28.1 cm), State Hermitage Museum, Saint Petersburg; see New York and Los Angeles 2002, no. 30.

6. 13½ × 10¼ in. (34.2 × 26 cm), Graphische Sammlung Albertina, Vienna (inv. 12771.)

7. 17¾ × 13⅜ in. (45 × 34 cm), Graphische Sammlung Albertina, Vienna. An inscription on the mounting specifies: "This drawing was engraved by Maloeuvre under the direction of Le Bas"; New York and Los Angeles 2002, no. 33.

8. Diderot, *Salon de 1763*, 1984 (ed.), p. 233. On the relations between the painter and the critic, one can consult Edgar Munhall in Paris 1984–85b, pp. 217–20.

9. On "the *Septimus Severus* affair," see Tournus 2005.

10. Diderot, *Salon de 1765*, 1960 (ed.), p. 150.

83. Jean-Baptiste Greuze

Tournus, 1725–Paris, 1805

Recto: *Head of a Young Girl*

Verso: *Study of a Woman and a Child*

Ca. 1770 (?)

Two different red chalks, 15⅛ × 11⅞ in. (38.4 × 30.2 cm)

PROVENANCE: Henry S. Reitlinger (1882–1950); sale, Sotheby's, London, April 14, 1954, lot 311; Lansing W. Thoms, Saint Louis, Missouri, 1985; Private Collection, Missouri, until 2003; Day & Faber, London; acquired by Jean Bonna, 2003

EXHIBITIONS: Saint Louis 1961; Toronto, Ottawa, San Francisco, and New York 1972–73, no. 58, pl. XIV; Paris 2006b, no. 52; Geneva 2006–7a

BIBLIOGRAPHY: Aaron 1985, p. 100, and p. 19, fig. 3; Denison 2006, p. 521

Jean-Baptiste Greuze's painted genre scenes are underappreciated, and have been since the nineteenth century. Their moralizing tone and the grandiloquent, declamatory gestures of his figures are no longer in step with the times. Conversely, Greuze's drawings have never failed to inspire admiration. His works in red chalk in particular are visually seductive, and as Pierre Rosenberg has pointed out: "Few drawings seem better to summarize an essential aspect of Greuze's talent than this head of a young girl with her sensual mouth."[1] Neither a preparatory study for a painting nor a drawing made for engraving, this portrait seems rather to have been executed as an independent work, for the delectation of collectors who had begun avidly seeking out Greuze's drawings even during the artist's lifetime.

Two different hues of red chalk, reddish-brown and orange-red, describe the childish face and evoke the velvety quality of the skin.

The firm and decisive lines nonetheless let the white of the paper show through in spots. These areas left in reserve allow the artist to suggest the light shining on the locks of her hair and illuminating her forehead, the bridge of her nose, and her cheeks. The model's age is difficult to determine. She is not the little village girl with plump cheeks and set expression found in many of the master's paintings and in the volume *Têtes de différents caractères* (*Heads of Different Character Types*), engraved in 1766. One can divine a hint of flirtatiousness in the narrow ribbon that ties back her hair. Yet she is not the type of young girl with languid, sorrowful looks that Greuze so enjoyed portraying, such as the one staring out at the viewer from the famous *Broken Pitcher* of 1777, now at the Louvre. The long lock of hair floating above the model's right shoulder conveys a sense of movement that contrasts with her calm pose, which is underscored by the proud bearing of her head. The loose bangs—a hairstyle that rarely occurs in the artist's work—casts a shadow of mystery over her eyes, which stare fixedly, as if in fascination.

The power that emanates from this *Head of a Young Girl* and the way she stands out from the sheet give the drawing a sculptural character reminiscent of marble statues of vestals. Moreover, the ambiguous sensuality emanating from the portrait calls to mind several of the master's canvases. One might think of the adolescent girl in *Virtue on the Brink* (*La Vertu chancelante*), painted about 1775 and now in the Alte Pinakothek, Munich,[2] or, for its more blatant eroticism, the *Two Sisters* portrayed

83 verso (size reduced)

nude in a painting that can be dated to 1770.[3] Without being able to state that the present drawing is from the same period, one can nonetheless relate it to a series of studies mentioned by Edgar Munhall and inspired by antiquity, probably made before or right after Greuze's 1769 election to the Académie Royale de Peinture et de Sculpture.

The recent discovery of a sketch on the verso argues for caution in attempting to date the work. The sketch shows a subject in red chalk, rapidly executed with an energetic, supple, and discontinuous line, which illustrates another aspect of the artist's talents: his virtuosity in arranging a composition, situating the

83 recto

figures in space. Despite the summary character of the sketch, we can clearly distinguish a seated woman clasping a child tightly against her. The child seems to be holding an object in his right hand, possibly a toy trumpet, and lifting it to his face. This same wooden toy is held by the child who figures in the canvas *Silence!*, which the artist exhibited at the Salon of 1759 and is today in the collection of Her Majesty Queen Elizabeth II of England.

The woman, her legs folded, seems to be seated on a low stool or bench, as we find in several of Greuze's compositions that are set in modest interiors. She might be related to one of those "rustic Madonnas," to borrow Colin Bailey's expression,[4] who illustrate family virtues in the artist's painted genre scenes. Although he frequently depicted mothers or wet nurses taking care of children, it has not been possible to relate this study directly to any known painting. However, it can be related to a group of a woman sitting in a low chair, leaning toward a small boy holding a porringer, situated at right of the engraving by Jacques-Philippe Le Bas after *Shelling Peas* (1757), and in *The Dry Nurses*, a canvas shown at the Salon of 1765.[5] Even so, these comparisons do not allow us to establish a precise date, given the gap of almost ten years that might separate the recto from the verso.

MARIE-ANNE DUPUY-VACHEY

1. Toronto, Ottawa, San Francisco, and New York 1972–73, p. 164, no. 58.
2. On this painting, see David Mandrella in Paris, Munich, and Bonn 2005–6, no. 57.
3. Current location unknown; on this painting and its preparatory drawings, see New York and Los Angeles 2002, no. 59.
4. Colin Bailey in Ottawa, Washington, and Berlin 2003–4, p. 258.
5. This latter work is known today only through Jean-Baptiste Tilliard and Pierre-Charles Ingouf's engraving and through the painted copy now in the Nelson-Atkins Museum of Art, Kansas City. Munhall in fact considers this painting a copy; see New York and Los Angeles 2002, p. 115.

84. Jean-Honoré Fragonard

Grasse, 1732–Paris, 1806

Park of an Italian Villa

Ca. 1760–62

Pen, brown ink, brown and gray wash, touches of watercolor over black chalk underdrawing, traces of a framing line in black ink visible on bottom and right edges, 7⁹⁄₁₆ × 9¾ in. (19.2 × 24.7 cm)

Old inscription in pen and black ink at lower right, scratched out and now almost illegible: [*frago?*]

PROVENANCE: Count Grégoire Stroganoff (1829–1910), Rome (Lugt 550); Gilbert Lévy (1884–1944); sale, Hôtel Drouot, Paris (Maîtres Ader, Picart, Tajan), May 6, 1987, lot 30; Baskett and Day, London; Private Collection; Katrin Bellinger Kunsthandel, Munich; acquired by Jean Bonna, 1997

EXHIBITIONS: New York 1997, no. 26; Paris 2006b, no. 47; Geneva 2006–7a

BIBLIOGRAPHY: Sotheby's, London, sale cat., July 2, 1997, under no. 69

The chronology of Jean-Honoré Fragonard's landscapes has long been a particularly thorny question. The artist practiced the genre throughout his career, using different techniques. His aptitude for varying styles is well known, and elements that would help date the works are scarce. Scholarship over the past thirty years nonetheless has allowed us to clarify a large number of problems. The present work is part of a group of drawings that share a common style, technique, and format. Eunice Williams, who has closely studied several of these drawings, suggests that they might have been the first landscapes the artist created in pen and wash, around 1760.[1]

Winner of the Grand Prize in Painting in 1752, Fragonard was allowed to prolong his training in Paris for a time and did not go to the Académie de France in Rome until the last days of December 1756. His earliest landscape drawings are from a little later, and in most cases, they were drawn in red chalk and made from nature; notably, there is a drawing depicting part of the Colosseum ruins, dated 1758, and also the studies made in Tivoli during his sojourn at the Villa d'Este in the summer of 1760.[2] Even as he was creating these famous works, however, Fragonard also produced landscapes in other techniques. According to Williams, his first landscapes in ink were done slightly after the study for *The Stalled Cart*, dated 1759,[3] which is one of his first masterpieces in pen and wash but is not a landscape per se. They do not seem to have been conceived a priori as drawings for buyers, and in some cases, their technique shows a remarkable freedom. The artist chose to work on fairly small sheets of paper; the drawing covers nearly the entire surface in a profusion of pen strokes that combine inks of different colors and are often mixed with dabs of watercolor. None of these early wash landscapes seems to have been inspired by an actual site, unlike many of the red chalk works from the same period. *Temple in a Garden*, now in the Baltimore Museum, seems to be the starting point for the series.[4] This work has been compared with *Wooded Landscape with Figures*,[5] formerly in the Collection of Dr. Francis Springell; with a *Halt in the Forest*,[6] which appeared on the New York art market in 1977; and with *Statue in a Park*, formerly in the Cailleux Collection.[7] The *Wooded Landscape with Figures near a Torrent*[8] is also related to

84

Figure 103. Jean-Honoré Fragonard, *Scene in a Park.* Pen and brown ink, brush and brown wash, and colored washes. The Cleveland Museum of Art (25.1006)

this group, but it depicts a wilder form of nature, whereas the other works generally take as their settings gardens decorated with mills, balustrades, or sculptures. The *Scene in a Park* [9] in the Cleveland Museum of Art (fig. 103) is considered the other great milestone in this grouping. It has the same density of layout, obstructed perspective, and somewhat frenetic pen work that characterize the other drawings. The fluidity of the rendering and more nuanced distribution of the washes, however, indicate greater facility with the medium, and we must therefore consider it one of the last pieces in this series of loose experiments. Williams suggested dating this work about 1760–61, but there is no reason not to situate it a little later, about 1762.[10] It nonetheless remains very difficult to evaluate precisely how long it took the artist to create the entire series, and the last works were probably done after his return to Paris in September 1761.

Rediscovered more recently, the Bonna drawing easily fits into this group. The fact that the black chalk is barely visible should not mislead us. As in the other sheets, it is certainly present as a pervasive undercurrent, allusive and dense, although subsequently masked by the washes. In the present case, it is especially noticeable in the areas that the brush did not pass over, notably under the greenery of the pines. The pen strokes are often very rapid and suggest the volume of foliage, sometimes with a kind of frothing effect, sometimes by small zigzagging touches, although this latter pen work is not as widely used here as it is in the other landscapes from the series. The artist then highlighted the effects of color by using a brush, but he hardly indulged in the brilliant chromatic interplays that Hubert Robert produced in the same period, even though the two artists often drew side by side about 1758–60. Fragonard here put a blue-green wash in the foreground combined with several tones of brown ink. Certain strokes must have been mixed with watercolor, as the dress of the woman standing at the left and some of the

flowers in the foreground indicate a pinkish hue that originally might have been more pronounced.

Fragonard took pleasure in counteracting the relatively modest format of the sheet by endowing his composition with heroic monumentality. The small figures at left who seem to be pointing at people on the terrace lend the park its majestic scale. The nobility of the décor, however, does not imply solemnity, and the setting even retains a certain character of prosaic familiarity, expressed in the heap of planks and garden implements stacked haphazardly in the foreground. While it was probably executed after Fragonard's return to Paris, this is nonetheless the drawing in the series that is perhaps the most laden with Italian reminiscences, with its umbrella pines, large garden populated with statues, and walls covered in vegetation. Fragonard was returning here, albeit in smaller format, to the idealized visions of grand villa gardens depicted in such famous red chalk drawings as *The Game of Paddles* or *The Seesaw* in the Städelsches Kunstintitut, Frankfurt, which were probably drawn at the end of his stay in Italy.[11]

In the many landscapes in wash that he created after this, Fragonard progressively abandoned the richness of chromatic interplay that one can appreciate here, as he would also turn away from a picturesque profusion of elements. In its place, he developed a much more synthetic vision, which can be seen both in the organization of the composition and in his attempts to pull together and unify the effects produced by the washes. This evolution resulted in drawings heightened with touches of heavily diluted bistre ink, such as the ones that can be dated precisely from his second stay in Italy, where he returned in 1773–74 in the company of Pierre-Jacques Onésyme Bergeret de Grancourt.[12] Fragonard then used this technique to create some of his greatest works on paper, such as *The Shaded Avenue*[13] in the Petit Palais, Paris. In comparing the present drawing with a study of smaller dimensions

such as *Gardens of an Italian Villa*[14] in the National Gallery of Art, Washington, D.C., which must be from about a dozen years later, one can measure fully the shift in style. The subject is similar but the way he renders it is airier, more transparent, and while the later drawing is hardly devoid of lyrical accents, it possesses neither the slightly chaotic ardor nor the almost dreamlike quality that distinguished the first landscapes produced with this technique.

DIEDERIK BAKHUŸS

1. See the entry by Eunice Williams on this drawing in New York 1997, no. 26.
2. *The Hermit's Court in the Colosseum* was acquired by the Sterling and Francine Clark Art Institute, Williamstown, Massachusetts. Many drawings are now in the Musée des Beaux-Arts et d'Archéologie, Besançon (Paris and New York 1987–88, nos. 24, 25, 27–30, 32–35; Washington, Cambridge, and New York 1978–79, nos. 62–68, 70–72; Besancon 2006–7.
3. Art Institute of Chicago (1936.4); Washington, Cambridge, and New York 1978–79, no. 3; Rome 1990–91, no. 27. The work is signed *fragonard Romae 1759*. Its reversed composition is repeated in the famous painting at the Louvre, formerly in the La Caze Collection (Paris and New York 1987–88, no. 20; Rome 1990–91, no. 28).
4. Robert Gilmore Jr. Collection, Baltimore Museum of Art; Washington, Cambridge, and New York 1978–79, no. 4.
5. Ibid., under no. 4; see also Sotheby's, London, *The Springell Collection: Old Master Drawings*, sale cat., June 3, 1986, lot 83.
6. Washington, Cambridge, and New York 1978–79, under no. 4.
7. See Paris 1983, no. 22; Paris 1987, no. 44.
8. Private collection; Tokyo and Kyoto 1980, no. 91.
9. Cleveland Museum of Art (25.1006); Washington, Cambridge, and New York 1978–79, no. 5; Massengale 1979, p. 270.
10. This later dating was suggested by Jean-Pierre Cuzin and Pierre Rosenberg in Rome 1990–91, no. 81.
11. Städelsches Kunstinstitut, Frankfurt-am-Main (inv. 1234, 1235); Paris and New York 1987–88, nos. 14, 15; Rome 1990–91, pp. 63–64, under no. 13.
12. Rome 1990–91, nos. 153–55, 163–66.
13. Musée du Petit Palais, Paris (inv. Dutuit 966); Paris and New York 1987–88, no. 186; Rome 1990–91, no. 165.
14. National Gallery of Art, Samuel H. Kress Collection, Washington, D.C. (1963.15.17); Rome 1990–91, no. 163.

85

85. Hubert Robert

Paris, 1733–Paris, 1808

Architectural Capriccio with the Port of Ripetta and the Pantheon

1760

Pen and gray ink, brush and gray wash and watercolor, over black chalk underdrawing, 12½ × 18⅟₁₆ in. (31.7 × 45.8 cm)

Signed and dated above the fountain: *1760 / H. / ROBERTI / D. ROMAE*

PROVENANCE: Pierre-Jean Mariette (1694–1774), mark at lower right (Lugt 2097); sale, Paris, November 15, 1775–January 30, 1776, lot 1344 (with another drawing depicting *The Temple of Tivoli*); purchased at that sale by Alexandre-Joseph Paillet (1743–1814); possibly Harenc de Presle; sale, Paris, April 30, 1795, lot 125; John, Lord Northwick; sale, Sotheby's, London, July 5, 1921, lot 44, ill.; Mrs. M. Rosenthal; Wildenstein and Company, New York; acquired by Jean Bonna, 2002

EXHIBITIONS: Washington 1978–79, no. 21 (color ill. p. 10); Paris 2006b, no. 49; Geneva 2006–7a

BIBLIOGRAPHY: Shoolman Slatkin 1980; Washington, New York, Minneapolis, and Malibu 1981–82, under no. 105, ill.; Paris 1984–85b, under no. 101; Paris 1985, under no. 37; Guy Bauman in New York 1985–86, under no. 146; Roland Michel 1987, p. 119; Catherine Boulot and Jean-Pierre Cuzin in Rome 1990–91, under no. 83; Sophie Join-Lambert in Tours and Toulouse 2000, pp. 182, 184, under no. 43, fig. 43d; Paris 2000, under no. 54

At the time he wrote the entry on Hubert Robert for the *Abecedario*, Pierre-Jean Mariette—who considered Robert a better draftsman than a painter—said of his drawings: "Everyone has asked him for some, especially the ones where he added a little color." He expressed concern that the talented watercolorist was in danger of succumbing to too great a facility, and added: "He also made several colored drawings for me, and I have every reason to be pleased with his fine manner."[1] The collector must have entered into contact with the artist shortly after the latter returned from Italy in 1765, as he was able to acquire some of the best drawings Robert brought back with him from Rome. The present

Figure 104. Hubert Robert, *The Port of Rome Embellished with Various Modern and Ancient Monuments.* Oil on canvas. Kunstmuseum Liechtenstein, Vaduz (inv. 511)

Figure 105. Hubert Robert, *The Port of Rome Embellished with Various Modern and Ancient Monuments.* Oil on canvas. École Nationale Supérieure des Beaux-Arts, Paris (inv. 7635)

drawing was one of those. In the tradition of the *capriccio* that Giovanni Paolo Panini (1691–1765) helped popularize, Hubert Robert depicted the Pantheon in a reinvented setting. The temple had long been one of the most admired monuments of ancient Rome; debates around the revival of antiquity in the mid-eighteenth century elevated its fame even further, while the majestic simplicity of its forms made it a paradigm of classical grandeur. The Pantheon figured frequently in Robert's imaginary landscapes, notably in watercolors produced during his stay in Rome.[2] Here, he placed it in an idealized setting inspired by the river port of Ripetta, which was located several hundred meters downstream from the Castle Sant'Angelo. A hitherto unnoticed inscription in a cartouche over the artist's signature gives the date of the sheet as 1760.

The composition of the drawing was repeated, with noticeable revisions, in a canvas painted the following year and dedicated to the artist's great patron, Étienne-François de Stainville, the Duc de Choiseul (1719–1775); it is now in the collections of the Prince of Liechtenstein (fig. 104).[3] Since he saw it as the culmination of what he had learned during his years in Rome, the painter must have asked Choiseul for the temporary use of the painting after his return to Paris. He executed a replica with no major variations, which he presented for his candidacy to the Académie Royale de Peinture et de Sculpture on July 22, 1766. It earned him the very rare privilege of being received and elected a member on the same

day. This second version, now in the École des Beaux-Arts, Paris, was exhibited at the Salon of 1767 under the title *The Port of Rome Embellished with Various Modern and Ancient Monuments* (fig. 105).[4] In 1782, Hubert Robert reprised the main motifs of this landscape for a painting with a different composition, now at the Palazzo Barberini in Rome.[5] In some respects—the placement of the Pantheon and several details of the quay—its composition is closer to the one of the present drawing than to the 1761 painting. Finally, a small painting of the same subject, now lost, figured in the posthumous sale of Pierre-Jacques Onésyme Bergeret de Grancourt (1715–1785) in 1786.[6]

The Choiseul painting is one of the most ambitious works Robert created during his Italian sojourn. The richness of the workmanship and the evocative forcefulness of the layout reveal the artist as a brilliant rival to Panini, whose teachings he had followed in Rome. The genre of architectural landscapes, a favorite since the seventeenth century, was undergoing a resurgence in popularity at the time; not only did it still afford a poetic and fantasized image of antiquity, but now it was also linked to ongoing archaeological developments and scientific debates. *The Port of Rome Embellished with Various Modern and Ancient Monuments* had a pendant in Choiseul's collection, an *Architectural Landscape with a Port Decorated with Buildings*, now in the Musée des Beaux-Arts, Dunkerque.[7] While the first painting fits into a genre that is inseparable from the name Panini, the second borrows its

composition from Giambattista Piranesi's *Ponte Magnifico*,[8] and in this regard, the two canvases summarize the twin sources from which the painter was seeking to establish his style.

Hubert Robert had arrived in Rome in 1754 at the age of twenty-one, following his patron, the Comte de Stainville, who had gone there to take up his post as French ambassador. The latter's support earned him the special favor of being allowed to take courses at the Académie de France even though he had not competed for the Grand Prize, and five years later, to obtain a place there as a full *pensionnaire*. Very close to Jean-Honoré Fragonard, who arrived in 1756, Robert also became friends about 1760 with the enigmatic Jean-Robert Ango (?–1773), who had begun frequenting the milieu of the Académie de France around that time.

Numerous drawings have been related to the genesis of the Choiseul painting. The variety in their techniques, formats, and degrees of completion shows the whimsy with which the artist designed his compositions, sometimes abandoning an idea from one drawing to the next, then picking it up again several drawings later.

It is probably in small pen and wash sketches that Robert initially developed his composition. Several are known that almost certainly come from disassembled notebooks. They show the ease with which the draftsman put together various motifs, inventing and recomposing in a spirit that owes more to the visionary fantasies of Piranesi than to Panini's

Figure 106. Hubert Robert, *The Port of Ripetta and the Pantheon*. Pen and wash. Private Collection

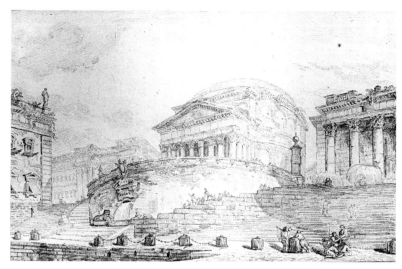

Figure 107. Jean-Robert Ango, *The Port of Ripetta and the Pantheon*. Red and black chalk. Musée des Beaux-Arts, Rouen (inv. 964.4.1)

ingenious juxtapositions. In one such quick sketch, the artist envisioned the port of Ripetta joined with the Pantheon, viewed almost at eye level, with a large fountain placed in an arched niche that has been hollowed out of the quay rotunda (fig. 106).[9] This design element was abandoned in the present drawing but returns in the painting. A large red and black chalk drawing in the Musée des Beaux-Arts, Rouen, once passed for the second step in the process of fine-tuning the subject (fig. 107).[10] It was assumed to be a preparatory sketch for the watercolor shown here, whereas it is in fact a copy of it. The style of the hatching, the schematic outlines of the figures, and the fact that the arrangement is identical down to the slightest details with the Mariette drawing suggest that Catherine Boulot and Jean-Pierre Cuzin are correct in attributing it to Ango.[11] For all intents and purposes, the Mariette watercolor developed the original design, but with a much more elaborate technique that is ultimately indistinguishable from the "colored drawings" made during that same period for a paying clientele. That Robert should do this is hardly surprising, for the artist often drew little distinction between preparatory sketches and clean copies intended for sale. Moreover, several watercolors from the Roman period, collected by Mariette, served as a point of departure for paintings; the composition of the *Architectural Landscape with the Pantheon* in the Hermitage[12] was reprised for a painting in the Pushkin Museum, Moscow,[13] just as the canvas depicting the Villa Madama, now in the

Hermitage,[14] surely proceeds directly from the magnificent watercolor dated 1760 and now in the Albertina.[15]

One can relate two more drawings to the conception of the 1761 painting. Marianne Roland Michel noted a *capriccio* inspired by the Capitoline square, in pen and wash, dated 1761 and now at the Musée des Beaux-Arts in Poitiers.[16] In addition, there exists a much larger watercolor on which the date, now quite faded, could be read as 1758, but which appears to be less directly related to the final arrangement.[17] A wash drawing of similar composition but in circular format, which the abbé de Saint-Non engraved in 1766 for the series *Griffonis*,[18] is probably from a later date.

The authoritative layout and delicate nuances of the present drawing bear witness to the increased mastery of watercolor Robert had acquired by 1760, which moreover is confirmed by other works, such as the *Villa Madama* in the Albertina. This becomes particularly evident when one compares it to *Architectural Landscape with the Pantheon* in the Hermitage, executed two years earlier. Robert devised several handsome lighting effects, with extended shadows that stretch down the steps and along the walls. He did not repeat these effects in the painting, which has more diffuse light. With a great architectonic sensibility, he enveloped all of the buildings in a delicately faded red monochrome that calls to mind the warm tones of brick but also suggests the erosion of centuries, discreetly reinforced by the detail of the dilapidated

balustrades. In this regard, the drawing, much more than the two versions of the painting, expresses the poetry of ruins that Diderot lamented not finding in the artist's reception piece.[19] As is typical of Robert's use of watercolor, a painterly evocativeness warms and livens what essentially remains a drawing; outlines in pen and ink are visible everywhere, supplemented by a network of lines in gray ink that are applied with the tip of the brush. The artist restricted his palette to a few tones of watercolor, and that discretion in chromatic effects helps give the work its character of idealized melancholy.

A concern for archeological correctness led Robert to show the Pantheon without the pinnacles that were added behind the pediment around 1660—which, until their demolition in 1883, were familiarly known as "Bernini's donkey ears." Panini often had operated the same way,[20] as did Piranesi.[21] The artist opted for a view that is more oblique than in his original sketch. The composition of the painting remains faithful to this principle, but the effect of a view from below is attenuated to bring out more of the monument and display it more largely in the space. Robert moved it to the right and reconstructed it by punctuating its lateral facades with a row of pilasters. In the painting, the temple rises before a huge Doric peristyle directly inspired by Bernini's colonnade in Saint Peter's Square, which already accompanied the central motif in some of the drawings mentioned earlier. Here, the temple is framed by two buildings whose Corinthian columns echo the row of the portico. The façade of the palace that ends the composition on the left evokes the Palazzo dei Conservatori built on the Capitol by Michelangelo and Giacomo della Porta; in the painting, the artist depicted it more precisely. The foreground gives a fairly faithful rendering of the port of Ripetta, which was built at the beginning of the eighteenth century and, with its circular terrace lined with rostral columns, its stairways, and its fountain, was one of the most picturesque sites on the banks of the Tiber, until it was demolished at the end of the nineteenth century.

This oblique view of the Pantheon above the quay of Ripetta constitutes one of Robert's most majestic scenographic inventions. The imposing placement dramatizes the presence of the monument and accentuates its colossal nature, and gives rise to an especially effective interplay between the rotundity of the temple and a piece of baroque urbanism that employs a complex variety of curves and exedrae. Designed primarily as an exercise in architectural composition, mixing structures from various periods, the drawing leaves only limited space for the picturesque animation of the port itself, which in the painting, plays an important role. With its groups of figures in Roman costumes and its boats from which jars of olive oil and barrels and bundles of other

merchandise have been unloaded, it offers a prosaic counterpoint, anchored in the present, to the heroic grandeur of the architecture, thus permitting the juxtaposition of opposing registers that is intimately linked to Robert's vision of city life. The image of an idealized Rome, at once immemorial, historical, and living, is already contained in the present watercolor, which offers a particularly poetic meditation on the unity of the Eternal City, the center of architecture par excellence.

DIEDERIK BAKHUŸS

1. Mariette 1851–62, vol. 4 (1857–58), p. 414.
2. The monument notably appears in a watercolor that can be dated to 1758, now in the State Hermitage Museum, Saint Petersburg (inv. 43727); see Rome 1990–91, no. 5.
3. Guy Bauman in New York 1985–86, no. 146; Catherine Boulot and Jean-Pierre Cuzin in Rome 1990–91, no. 83.
4. Musée du Louvre, Paris (inv. 7635), on deposit in the École Nationale Supérieure des Beaux-Arts, Paris, since 1872 (inv. MRA 123); Marianne Roland Michel in Paris 1984–85b, no. 101; Sophie Join-Lambert in Tours and Toulouse 2000, no. 43.
5. Galleria Nazionale d'Arte Antica di Palazzo Barberini, Rome; Paris 2000, no. 54.
6. Sale, Paris, April 24–29, 1786, lot 85. The work was described as a première pensée (first draft) of his reception piece.
7. Musée des Beaux-Arts, Dunkerque, legs Coffin, 1887 (inv. P. 527); Marianne Roland Michel in Rome, Dijon, and Paris 1976, no. 176; Roland Michel in Paris 1984–85b, no. 102.
8. Antiquità romane, pt. 1 (1753), pl. 7.
9. Le Port de la Ripetta et le Panthéon, formerly Galerie Cailleux, Paris; Paris 1985, no. 37.
10. Washington, New York, Minneapolis, and Malibu 1981–82, no. 105, pl. 69; Roland Michel 1987, p. 119. The drawing's authenticity was maintained even recently (Tours and Toulouse 2000, under no. 43).
11. For the suggested attribution to Ango, with which I entirely agree, see Rome 1990–91, under no. 83. A counterproof of the drawing was destroyed in Warsaw during the Second World War; see Sawicka and Sulerzyska 1960, p. 46, pl. 22.
12. See note 5 above. The work is clearly contemporary with its pendant, dated 1758, an Architectural Landscape with the Colosseum (inv. 43726); Paris 1985, under no. 5, fig. 5a.
13. Pushkin Museum, Moscow (inv. 1077).
14. State Hermitage Museum, Saint Petersburg (inv. 5649); Rome 1990–91, no. 53.
15. Graphische Sammlung Albertina, Vienna (inv. 12431); ibid., no. 52.
16. Marianne Roland Michel in Paris 1984–85b, under no. 101.
17. Paris 1975, no. 28 (not ill.); Marianne Roland Michel in Paris 1984–85, under no. 101; Roland Michel 1987, p. 119.
18. Cayeux 1963, pp. 339–40. It was described as "The first draft of the painting on which M. Robert was accepted into and elected a member of the Royal Academy of Painting in Paris, 1766."
19. Diderot, Salon de 1767, 1995 (ed.), pp. 348–49.
20. This is the case, for instance, in a painting in the Palais du Luxembourg, Paris, Preacher Amid Roman Ruins Enlivened with Figures, with the Pantheon and the Statue of Flora (Paris, Piacenza, and Brunswick 1992–93, no. 21).
21. Scenographia Panthei, ejusque pronai . . . , from Il Campo Marzio dell'antica Roma (1762); see Ficacci 2000, p. 412, no. 507, ill.

86. Henry Fuseli (Johann Heinrich Füssli)

Zurich, 1741–Surrey, 1825

A Fashionable Young Woman (A Lady Walking)

Ca. 1792

Graphite, pen and brown ink, brush and watercolor on white paper, 12¾ × 8½ in. (32.8 × 21.1 cm)

PROVENANCE: Possibly Eliza Frances Ward Wainewright (1794–1847), wife of Thomas Griffiths Wainewright; Harriet Jane Moore (1801–1884), who placed the drawing in an album and inscribed the page "Mrs. Wainwright's"; sale, Christie's, London, April 14, 1992, lot 14; Maurice Rheims, Paris; Jean-Claude Vrain, Paris; acquired by Jean Bonna, 2006

EXHIBITION: Geneva 2006–7a

Using fluid pen lines over graphite, Henry Fuseli described a beautiful young woman moving through a summer landscape. He finished his drawing with blue and gray washes, with touches of pink on the lips, cheeks, and arms. This subtle use of color, combined with the fine detailing of face and costume, indicates a work carefully conceived. Previously unknown to scholars, *A Fashionable Young Woman* came to light in 1992, in an album assembled by Harriet Jane Moore

(1801–1884), whose family had been friends with Fuseli for forty years.[1] The image of a woman with elaborately dressed hair and holding up her gown closely resembles a drawing of the early 1790s in the Kunsthaus, Zurich, identified by Gert Schiff as a representation of the artist's wife (fig. 108).[2] Changes to the hair and face in the Bonna watercolor indicate that a different sitter has been depicted. During the first half of the 1790s, Fuseli drew a large number of fantastically coiffed women.[3] This work is one

Figure 108. Henry Fuseli, *Mrs. Fuseli Taking a Walk* (*Mrs. Fuseli beim Spaziergang*), ca. 1790-95. Ink and wash. Kunsthaus, Zurich (inv. 1914/27)

of the gentlest; here, the sense of erotic menace so often present in such works is subdued.

At first glance, the full-length figure and the landscape setting seem simply to denote an admiring response to the new sort of Romantic portraiture launched at the Royal Academy in 1790 by Thomas Lawrence's *Elizabeth Farren*.[4] Fuseli's subject similarly turns her head to gaze at the viewer from a windswept landscape and stands before a low horizon line. Her costume differs, however, since she wears no cloak but a white chemise, gathered at the waist with a wide silk sash tied in a large bow. Conveying a taste for naturalness and simplicity, this dress had been popularized in the late 1780s by noblewomen such as Georgiana, Duchess of Devonshire.[5] More characteristic of the early 1790s are the skin tight sleeves, exaggerated fichu puffed out over the chest, elaborate hairstyle, and ruffled confection of a cap, all of which suggest careful study of the fashion plates that appeared monthly in publications such as the *Journal de la mode et du goût*.[6]

As has been noted, the features of the woman in the Bonna drawing differ from those of Sophia Rawlings, whom Fuseli had

married in 1788. The eyes are larger and more widely set, the nose broader, and the hair strikingly dark. In the related drawing in Zurich (fig. 108), the artist's wife is distinguished by a pointed nose, distinct beauty mark, and light powdered hair. A more likely candidate for Fuseli's dark-haired subject is Mary Wollstonecraft (1759-1797), the radical feminist writer who became his friend and admirer in the late 1780s. A portrait print of Wollstonecraft in the National Portrait Gallery, London (fig. 109), published in 1798, resembles the woman in the Bonna drawing, and contemporary sources attest that Wollstonecraft had become deeply infatuated with the artist by 1792. She pursued him with long adulatory letters and went so far as to adopt fashionable dress in place of her formerly unkempt toilette. When this failed to attract the artist, she approached his wife and begged to be allowed to move into their household.[7] When Sophia Fuseli rejected this proposal and forbade future visits, Wollstonecraft departed for France. It is conceivable that the artist responded to this dramatic episode by casting his wife and his admirer as rival beauties in two similar drawings.

With this context in mind, the erotic subtext clearly woven into the details of *A*

Fashionable Young Woman begins to make sense. The elegantly draped left hand holding a pair of limp gloves represents compliant femininity of the sort Fuseli idealized in illustrations for Johann Caspar Lavater's *Essays on Physiognomy*.[8] The woman's left hand in the drawing accords with this ideal, but her right hand transgresses it. Held behind her back, it tensely twists the fabric of her skirt into a sexually suggestive arrangement of folds. Fuseli may have derived this gesture from an emblematic print in the British Museum by Jost Amman (fig. 110) that he knew and used elsewhere. The print shows a coquette lifting her skirt before a flock of tiny winged fools who fight to possess a dovecote symbolizing her favors.[9] William Godwin, later Wollstonecraft's husband, described her conflicted feelings at this time: "It was in vain that she enjoyed much pleasure in [Fuseli's] society. . . . Her ardent imagination was continually conjuring up pictures of the happiness she should have found, if fortune had favoured their more intimate union."[10]

A Fashionable Young Woman presents a subject whose upright posture and cool expression convey composure but whose flushed cheeks and cloaked gesture suggest desires barely controlled. Her simple white gown indicates a

Figure 109. John Chapman (British, active 1792–1823), *Mary Wollstonecraft*, 1798. Stipple engraving. National Portrait Gallery, London (1966-04-26)

Figure 110. Jost Amman (Swiss, 1539-1591), *Der Buler Narzheit*. Woodcut from *Stam und Dapenbuch*, Frankfurt, 1579. British Museum, London (1925-12-13-231/159.c.12, leaf 54 recto)

taste for natural simplicity, but her exaggerated coiffure and cap mark her as a follower of fickle fashion and, not coincidentally, mimic the pointed shape and dangling tassel of a foolscap. Mary Wollstonecraft's attraction to Fuseli drove her to act in ways that contradicted her declared devotion to high-minded principle, and the conflicting demands of reason and passion lie at the heart of the Bonna drawing.

CONSTANCE C. MCPHEE

1. Martin Butlin, in the introduction to the sale cat., Christie's, London, April 14, 1992.
2. Schiff 1973, no. 1090.
3. Ibid., nos. 1046–19; Cambridge, New York, and Los Angeles 1998, no. 11.
4. *Elizabeth Farren*, oil on canvas, The Metropolitan Museum of Art, New York; the connection is noted in Christie's, London, sale cat., April 14, 1992, p. 28.
5. Ribeiro 1984, pp. 153–55, traces the origin of this costume to the French court.
6. Schiff 1973, p. 231, singles out a costume plate published in this journal in October 1791, but similar details appear in many plates published 1790–91.
7. Knowles (1831, vol. 1, pp. 161–69), Antal (1956, pp. 146–48), and Weinglass (1982, pp. 82–83, 85, 143) all indicate that Mary Wollstonecraft's passions, though intense, remained platonic, and Fuseli never offered her more than friendship.
8. Fuseli's illustrations for Lavater are discussed in Antal 1956, p. 32; and Schiff 1973, nos. 507, 972.
9. Schiff 1973, no. 1044, shows how Fuseli borrowed Amman's dovecote and fools for another erotic drawing of the early nineties.
10. *Memoirs of the Author of A Vindication of the Rights of Women* (1798), quoted in E. C. Mason 1951, pp. 147–48.

87. Pierre-Adrien Pâris

Besançon, 1745–Besançon, 1819

View of the Temple of Vesta at Tivoli

Ca. 1772

Red chalk, 21¼ × 15¾ in. (54 × 40 cm)

PROVENANCE: Estate of Eleanor Bostwick, New York; Michel Castellino, Geneva; acquired by Jean Bonna, 2006

This impressive drawing of the Temple of Vesta at Tivoli drenched in sunlight and rising over a diagonal repoussoir of lush foliage is as puzzling as it is beautiful. Despite its resemblance to the many plein-air studies made in Tivoli by young French artists in the 1760s and 1770s, Pierre-Adrien Pâris's view is in reverse of the actual site. In fact, when the sheet is seen in the context of drawings of the same motif by Pâris's contemporaries, a range of practices much more complex than previously assumed begins to come into focus.

After studying architecture in Paris with Louis-François Trouard, Pâris left for Rome in 1771 in the official capacity of tutor to Trouard's son, Louis-Alexandre. He also supplemented his income by instructing Piranesi's son Francesco in architecture and by supplying drawings for the abbé de Saint-Non's *Voyage pittoresque ou Description des royaumes de Naples et de Sicile*. During this time, he made many excursions in Rome and the surrounding countryside in the company of the young architects and painters studying at the Académie de France, where he himself was eventually

granted a place. The impressive productivity of this period can be appreciated in Pâris's precise architectural studies in pen and wash as well as his picturesque views in chalk, which were assembled into portfolios and brought him renown as well as commissions upon his return to France.[1]

Tivoli was perhaps the most popular destination for the young *pensionnaires.* The site boasted a spectacular cascade, several Roman ruins, and the gardens and buildings of the Villa d'Este. During his first Italian sojourn, Pâris visited Tivoli on at least two occasions and made numerous drawings, both architectural and picturesque.[2] In a journal Pâris kept during this time, he recorded a stay in Tivoli in late May 1772 in the company of a large group of painting and architecture students. He even specifically described, on May 24, 1772, walking to the cascade and making a view of the Temple of Vesta as seen from a charming vantage point across the torrent, where one could see on the side the other temple, which had been made into a church.[3]

However tempting it is to conclude that this is the drawing Pâris described in his journal, there remains the simple problem of its reverse direction. The Bonna sheet therefore must have been drawn from (or over) a counterproof of another drawing, and the closest parallel is a drawing in black chalk, of the

same composition and scale, but in reverse (the correct) direction (fig. 111). Published in 1921 and 1963 as by Jean-Honoré Fragonard,[4] then sold in New York in 2005 as by Claude-Joseph Vernet,[5] the sheet is in fact by François-André Vincent (1746–1816) and compares closely to a signed and dated landscape in the Frits Lugt Collection.[6] Drawings from the same vantage point are also known by Jean-Simon Berthélemy (1743–1811) (fig. 112)[7] and Joseph Benoît Suvée (1743–1807) (fig. 113),[8] and in both cases, counterproofs also survive.[9] In his journal, Pâris mentioned exchanging counterproofs of Tivoli drawings with Berthélemy,[10] and he apparently also made copies of quite a number of Berthélemy's compositions.[11]

Perhaps the most likely scenario for the Bonna sheet is that Pâris had a counterproof of Vincent's black chalk view of Tivoli (fig. 111) upon which he based his freehand copy. Another possibility is that he made a freehand copy directly from Vincent's drawing, and a counterproof of that copy exists below the Bonna drawing. However, aside from a few faint red chalk lines that can be seen beneath the drawing in a few areas, there is little visual support for the latter theory.

The fact that extremely close versions of this composition exist by at least five different artists suggests that in addition to embarking on sketching excursions together and

Figure 111. Here attributed to François-André Vincent, *The Temple of Vesta at Tivoli*. Black chalk. Private Collection, New York

Figure 112. Jean-Simon Berthélemy, *The Temple of Vesta at Tivoli*. Red chalk. Graphische Sammlung Albertina, Vienna (inv. 12-946)

Figure 113. Joseph Benoît Suvée, *The Temple of Vesta at Tivoli*. Red chalk. Groeningemuseum, Bruges (inv.0000.GR01873.11)

occasionally drawing side-by-side before the motif, it was also common practice among *pensionnaires* in the 1770s to make and exchange counterproofs and to copy one another's landscape drawings. Judging from the quality of these examples by Vincent, Berthélemy, Suvée, and Pâris, a good-spirited competitiveness must have fueled these exercises, which all display a bravura technique and a convincing naturalism—the typical hallmarks of the work of an inspired artist sketching *en plein air* with speed and dexterity.

PERRIN STEIN

1. The majority are held in the Bibliothèque d'Étude et de Conservation, Besançon. See Pinon 2007.
2. Ibid., p. 254.
3. "Je suis allé faire une vue du temple prise de l'autre coté du torrent d'ou elle est charmante surtout a peindre car le temple y devient trop petit on voit a coté l'autre temple dont on a fait une eglise." In "Journal de mon voyage d'Italie, commencé le 19 septembre 1771," Bibliothèque d'Étude et de Conservation, Besançon, Fonds Pâris, MS 6, pp. 187–88.
4. See Ananoff 1961–70, vol. 2 (1963), p. 114, no. 870, and vol. 3 (1968), addenda, p. 329, fig. 527. The drawing was also illustrated as "attributed to Fragonard" in Paris and New York 1987–88, p. 103, under no. 27, fig. 4 (correct caption with fig. 3).
5. Lillian Rojtman Berkman estate sale, Sotheby's, New York, January 28, 2005, lot 500.
6. F. A. Vincent, *Dessinateurs dans un paysage près de Tivoli*, black chalk, 10½ × 15¾ in. (26.7 × 39.9 cm), inscribed in pen and ink at lower left, "Vincent. F. Tivoly. 1773" (inv. 1974-T.23).
   The attribution of the sheet sold in 2005 was also made independently by François Borne, who purchased the sheet at auction. The attribution was also confirmed, based on a photograph, by Jean-Pierre Cuzin (e-mail communication, October 3, 2007).
7. Volle 1979, p. 110, no. 130.
8. Bruges and Enschede 2007–8, pp. 160, 162, no. 66. I would like to thank Jean-Pierre Cuzin for bringing this sheet to my attention.
9. For the Suvée, see ibid., pp. 160, 163, no. 67. For the Berthélemy, see Cornillot 1957, no. 87 (as Jean-Jacob Guerne, following the inscription of Pâris); and Besançon 2006–7, p. 61, under no. 16, fig. 6b.
   Another version in red chalk is in the Indiana University Art Museum, Bloomington (81.63.2), under an unlikely attribution to Jean-Laurent Legeay. I would like to thank Pierre Rosenberg for bringing this drawing to my attention.
10. "Berthelemi en a fait une du grouppe de cipres qui est au millieu du jardin et qui est charmant. Il m'en a donné la contre epreuve pour une des mienne[s]." In "Journal de mon voyage d'Italie" (see note 3 above), p. 187 (entry for May 23, 1772).
11. Compare, for example, Pâris's *Vue de la villa Negroni à Rome*, Bibliothèque d'Étude et de Conservation, Besançon, Fonds Pâris, vol. 480, no. 80, and *Vue de la partie des jardins Colonna où sont déposés les restes d'un édifice antique*, vol. 476, no. 68, to Berthélemy's *L'Escalier de la villa Negroni* and *La Terrasse de la villa Colonna*, Musée des Beaux-Arts, Valence (see Volle 1979, pp. 111–12, nos. 132–33, figs. 94, 95).

87

88. Francisco de Goya y Lucientes

Fuendetodos, 1746–Bordeaux, 1828

Double-sided sheet of drawings from Album B ("Madrid Album")

Recto, 65: *Cantan para el q.e lo hizo (They sing for the one who made it up)*

Verso, 66: *Sueña de un tesoro. (She dreams of a treasure)*

1796–97

Brush, ink, and wash on laid paper with partial watermark: fleur-de-lis, 9¼ × 5¹³⁄₁₆ in. (23.5 × 14.7 cm)

Numbered on recto, *65*, by the artist in brush and gray ink at top right: *65*; numbered by the artist's son Javier in pen and black ink at top center: *8*.

Numbered on verso, *66*, by the artist in brush and gray ink at top left: *66*; numbered by the artist's son Javier in pen and black ink at top center (partially trimmed): *7*.

PROVENANCE: Javier Goya y Bayeu, 1828; Mariano Goya y Goicoechea, 1854; Federico de Madrazo and/or Ramón Garreta y Huerta, ca. 1855–65; Paul Lebas, Paris; sale, Hôtel Drouot, Paris, April 3, 1877, lot 63; Collection Vazier; Private Collection, Lille, by 1970; Wildenstein and Company, New York; acquired by Jean Bonna, 2001

EXHIBITION: Paris 1970, no. 2

BIBLIOGRAPHY: Gassier and Wilson 1971, nos. 425, 426, ill. pp. 162, 174; Gassier 1973, pp. 46–47, 132, nos. B.65, B.66, ill. pp. 97–98; Gassier 1983, p. 65

Goya launched his career by painting public churches, designing tapestries, and making portraits of the rich and well positioned, but at the age of fifty, after suffering a near-fatal illness that left him deaf, he began to give rein to private and often bitter thoughts that he expressed frequently and powerfully in prints and drawings.

Goya is known to have filled eight albums with ink-drawn inventions that, although they appear casually drawn, are much more than spur-of-the-moment sketches; each is a carefully scripted tableau, individually staged, one to a page. The second of Goya's drawing albums, and perhaps the most dramatic in its demonstration of the artist's development, was probably begun in Andalusia in 1796 and completed the following year in Madrid; thus, it is called the Madrid Album, or Album B. Its more than ninety drawings on double-sided sheets started out in a relatively lighthearted mood that disturbingly soured midway through the album as amusing lads and maidens morphed into oafs

and harlots. Goya's ink-laden brush thus framed his first battery of attacks on the perilous foibles of Spanish culture, which evolved into the sharply satirical suite of eighty etchings he published in 1799, *Los Caprichos.*

The comparison of page 65 of the Madrid Album with page 27 (fig. 114) vividly represents the transformation that took place in Goya's imagery. Although compositional elements remain consistent in both drawings (the overlapping figures in a loosely triangular arrangement presented close to the picture plane), the pictorial space has become compressed. Tonal contrasts are now much bolder, and the introduction of a dark backdrop contributes a stifling atmosphere to the crowded scene. Far

from a lovers' duet, the apparently raucous performance of the mixed trio is distasteful even to the composer, identified by the artist as "the one who made it up" in one of the terse titles he began to attach to such drawings at this time. The harsh, exaggerated features and postures of Goya's figures must be owed to his familiarity with contemporary English and French caricature.

She dreams of a treasure, on page 66 of the Madrid Album, introduced two themes that Goya pursued further in the etchings of *Los Caprichos*, dreams and foolishness of young women. The dreamer here, who may imagine discovering her fortune, nonetheless must wake to find her finger in the chamber pot.

Figure 114. Francisco de Goya y Lucientes, *Duet at the Clavichord*, page 27 from Album B ("Madrid Album"), 1796–97. Brush and ink wash. Museo Nacional del Prado, Madrid

Figure 115. Francisco de Goya y Lucientes, *Tantalo (Tantalus)*, plate 9 of *Los Caprichos (The Caprices)*, 1797-98. Etching and aquatint from the first edition (1799). The Metropolitan Museum of Art, New York, Gift of M. Knoedler & Co., 1918 (18.64)

cantan para el q.^e lo hizo

88 recto

Sueña de un tesoro.

88 verso

Her figure, draped in white and outlined against her bedsheets, appears to float in a mist that is made of the gray wash Goya came to rely upon for scene setting and that he re-created in his etchings with grained aquatint. The female figure, stretched out before us dreaming, smiling, or swooning, perhaps dying, with her head thrown back, attracts attention in a great number of Goya's works, sometimes, as she does in plate 9 (*Tantalo*, or *Tantalus*, fig. 115) of the *Caprichos*, calling to mind the artist's most famous model, the Duchess of Alba.

COLTA IVES

89. Pierre-Paul Prud'hon

Cluny, 1758–Paris, 1823

Head of Love, from The Union of Love and Friendship

1792

Black chalk, stumping, and heightening in white gouache, framing line in pen and black ink, on yellowed paper, 15³⁄₁₆ × 10¹³⁄₁₆ in. (38.5 × 27.5 cm)

PROVENANCE: E. Marcille; Chévrier-Marcille; Didier Aaron & Cie, Paris; acquired by Jean Bonna, 2002

EXHIBITIONS: Paris 1874, no. 175; Paris 1922, no. 101 (erroneously as no. 217 by Jean Guiffrey [see Bibliography] and by Sylvain Laveissière in Paris and New York 1997–98, no. 26); Paris 1958, no. 3 (*Étude pour la Tête de l'Amour*); Dijon 1959, no. 46; Paris and New York 1997–98, no. 26; Paris 2006b, no. 56; Geneva 2006–7a

BIBLIOGRAPHY: Guiffrey (Jean) 1924, pp. 14–15, no. 30; Elderfield and Gordon 1996, p. 29, ill.

Pierre-Paul Prud'hon exhibited in the Paris salon for the first time in 1791, with a single drawing;[1] two years later, in 1793, he showed his first true salon painting, *The Union of Love and Friendship*, now in the Minneapolis Institute of Arts (fig. 116).[2] With that allegory—the most elevated form of history painting, according to Johann Joachim Winckelmann—Prud'hon hoped to prove himself from the outset as a history painter. Unfortunately there were no reviews of his work; the canvas had arrived late at the salon, as he had not managed to finish it in time. By now, however, its critical fortunes allow one to appreciate the importance of the work, as Sylvain Laveissière has quite justly underscored.[3] In the painting, Prud'hon already gave an indication of his visual sources, reflecting his years in Rome—ancient statuary and the great sixteenth-century masters Leonardo, Raphael, and Correggio—and of his deep aspirations, those of a painter of human poetry in search of his personal truth. The first allegory in a career that would produce many, it inaugurated a long series of works (which stand alongside his revolutionary subjects) treating the recurrent theme of human passions grappling with the torments of love, in some cases brought back to reason, in others seducing innocence, suffering remorse, or incarnated by Psyche abducted by the zephyrs.

Moreover, this work indeed seems to be the one the artist was counting on to earn him acceptance into the Académie Royale de Peinture et de Sculpture, following his return from Rome in 1789. A letter of October 20, 1789,[4] from Prud'hon to his first teacher in Dijon, François Devosge, in fact tells us that he had begun "a composition with four figures" with precisely this in mind—a composition that Laveissière identified as *Cupid Seducing Innocence under the Promptings of Pleasure, with Repentance in Their Wake* (ca. 1809, Private Collection, United States). But the need to earn a living with more salable paintings led him to undertake a less ambitious composition, which was, according to Laveissière, none other than *The Union of Love and Friendship*.

Prud'hon was paid a yearly wage by Pierre Didot (1761–1853), a Parisian printer and bookseller better known as Didot the Elder, to create drawings as book illustrations, and he spent his time working on those rather than finishing his painting.[5] In fact, this canvas, which Prud'hon no doubt intended to complete some day, was still in the artist's studio when he died. Several preparatory drawings preceded the development of the composition: a study for the two main figures in the Musée Condé, Chantilly;[6] another for the drapery on the figure of *Friendship* in the Albertina, Vienna;[7] and the last for the *Head of Love* in the École des Beaux-Arts, Paris (fig. 117).[8]

While the latter, sketched rapidly and leaving the hair and shoulders unfinished, was a *première pensée*, the drawing in the Bonna Collection, which reprises in full the features of Love's face in the canvas, stands as a finished drawing, typical of the kind of work Prud'hon intended for engraving and illustrations. The finished quality of the composition, its use of the full sheet, the perfection of its execution, and the refinement of its technique leave no doubt about its function. Recalling the artist's wish to engrave his compositions

Figure 116. Pierre-Paul Prud'hon, *The Union of Love and Friendship*. Oil on canvas. Minneapolis Institute of Arts (64.50)

203

Figure 117. Pierre-Paul Prud'hon, *Head of Love.* Black and white chalk on blue paper. École Nationale Supérieure des Beaux-Arts, Paris (inv. 1493)

Figure 118. Barthélemy Roger, after Pierre-Paul Prud'hon, *Head of Love.* Lithograph. Bibliothèque Nationale de France, Département des Estampes et de la Photographie, Paris (DC 115 t.1 fol. 30)

spent time with his friend Antonio Canova. His interest in and taste for antiquities is also evident in the many sketches in his Roman notebooks.

Moreover, in the Bonna drawing, the legibility of the composition, the way the forms are simplified, the schematic delineation of light and dark zones created by letting the paper show through in certain areas, and the precise details made possible by an utter mastery of technique all contribute to the development of an extremely purified (some have called it primitivistic) style. Indeed, Prud'hon cannot have been indifferent a decade later to the radical aesthetic concepts of the post-David generation, which advocated a return to Greek simplicity.

HÉLÈNE MEYER

himself, Edmond de Goncourt described Prud'hon's working method: "He labored to obtain on paper the sharpness and stippling of engraving. . . . The drawings he made at the time served him as models to give to engravers . . . as a kind of line engraving, as it were."[9]

Executed by Barthélemy Roger, the print after this drawing (fig. 118) was published by Noël with the caption "Study. / After the original painting by Prud'hon," indicating that the drawing was made from the painting.[10] Moreover, the print bears the words "Deposited at the Bibliothèque Impériale," allowing us to date it no earlier than 1804. It has been associated with a series of about fifteen other expressive head studies, engraved by various hands (Roger, Prud'hon *fils*, Noël, Girard, Cazenave) after Prud'hon's works, which were issued by different publishers and intended for use in teaching drawing.

Taken to its highest point of finish, this drawing exhibits a subtle technique in which the white gouache highlights are diluted by wash and the stumping of the black chalk gives the outlines of the face a vaporous quality. These sfumato effects, which can also be seen in the painting owing to its (perhaps intentional) state of incompletion and the limited use of color in favor of grisaille, constitute a veritable homage to Leonardo, whom Prud'hon had

called "the Homer of painting." Laveissière pointed out, in fact, how indebted this work is to Leonardo, even down to the iconography: isn't the union of Love and Friendship also the union of painting (Leonardo, Correggio) and sculpture—an interpretation buttressed by the contrast between the colors of Friendship's attributes (the drapery and wreath of flowers) and the marmoreal appearance of Love with his classical contrapposto. The softness of the modeling, the sensual charm of the face with its reserved smile, the elegance of the hairstyle—all these attributes constitute so many Correggio-like elements in Prud'hon's style that he earned the nickname Correggio.

Like a direct reference to antiquity, the face of Love, an androgynous figure of supernatural perfection, is the expression, in the drawing even more than in the painting, of an ideal of classical beauty that refers back to the canons of Greek art. During his years in Rome, from 1784 to 1788, Prud'hon was immersed in a milieu that had been evolving rapidly since the 1760s; from archaeological excavations to the publication of new treatises on aesthetics, the city was enjoying renewed prominence, embodied by Johann Joachim Winckelmann and Raphael Mengs, both active in the neoclassical reform. In addition to David, who exhibited *The Oath of the Horatii* in 1785, the young Prud'hon

1. *La Génie de la Liberté et de la Sagesse*, 1791, Fogg Art Museum, Harvard University Art Museums, Cambridge, Massachusetts (1943.890); Paris and New York 1997–98, p. 67, fig. 23a.
2. Oil on canvas, 5¾ × 4½ in. (14.6 × 11.4 cm), Minneapolis Institute of Arts (64.50); Paris and New York 1997–98, pp. 69–71, no. 25, ill.
3. Ibid., pp. 65–66, 68–71.
4. Letter in the Musée des Beaux-Arts, Dijon (inv. 196 Pr 22); Lamarre and Laveissière 2003, pp. 263–64.
5. Paris and New York 1997–98, p. 68.
6. Black chalk heightened with white chalk on blue paper, 22⅞ × 17⅜ in. (58 × 44 cm), Musée Condé, Chantilly (inv. 488); Paris and New York 1997–98, p. 65, fig. 25a.
7. Black chalk heightened with white chalk on blue paper, 13¼ × 10¾ in. (33.8 × 27.4 cm), Graphische Sammlung Albertina, Vienna (inv. 24202); Paris and New York 1997–98, p. 69, no. 24, ill. p. 68.
8. Black chalk heightened with white chalk on blue paper, 11⅛ × 8¾ in. (28.2 × 22.1 cm), École Nationale Supérieure des Beaux-Arts, Paris (inv. 1493); Paris and New York 1997–98, p. 71, fig. 26a.
9. E. de Goncourt 1876, p. 276.
10. At upper right: No. 2 (2nd state); at lower left: *Prud'hon Del*; at lower right: *Roger Sculp.*; lower middle: *ETUDE Déposée à la Bibliothèque Impériale. D'Après le Tableau Original de Prud'hon Représentant l'Amour et l'Amitié Gravé par Roger / A Paris, chez A. Noël Graveur et Md. D'Estampes, Rue St. Jacques N° 16 au Pont des Arts*, Bibliothèque Nationale de France, Département des Estampes et de la Photographie, Paris (DC 37 fol. vol. 1 fol. 29); E. de Goncourt 1876, pp. 282–83, no. 168.

90. Jean-Auguste-Dominique Ingres

Montauban, 1780–Paris, 1867

Portrait of an Unidentified Woman

1816

Graphite on wove paper, 8¹⁄₁₆ × 6⅛ in. (20.5 × 15.5 cm)

Signed and dated in graphite at lower left: *Ingres Del / à Rome / 1816*

PROVENANCE: Possibly from the collection of Prince Camillo Massimo (1770–1840), Rome; Colnaghi, London, 1971; David Carritt / Artemis, London, 1972; Thomas Williams Fine Art, London; acquired by Jean Bonna, 2005

EXHIBITIONS: Paris 2006b (not in catalogue); Geneva 2006–7a

BIBLIOGRAPHY: *Artemis* 1972, pp. 20–21; Naef 1974; Naef 1977–80, vol. 4, no. 166, pp. 304–5, ill.

Jean-Auguste-Dominique Ingres had been living in Rome for a decade when he drew this young woman's portrait. He had completed his term as a *pensionnaire* of the French Academy at the Villa Medici in 1810 and decided to stay on in Italy, where he had secured a number of commissions from his fellow countrymen. However, with the definitive fall of the French in 1815, and the repatriation of his protectors, fewer and fewer opportunities came the artist's way, and he fell on hard times. During the five years he remained in Rome, before moving to Florence in 1820, Ingres relied almost entirely upon his production of pencil portraits to support himself and his wife, Madeleine, whom he married in December 1814. Indeed, if we may judge from the large number of likenesses the artist drew at this time, it would appear that many of the travelers who resumed their grand tours after Napoleon's defeat regarded a sitting with Ingres as an essential experience in their Roman itinerary.

This portrait dated 1816, having escaped much notice in the literature on Ingres until Hans Naef published the work in 1980, is now so far removed from its subject that the identity of the demure young lady portrayed is unknown.[1] Indeed, her features (wide-set almond-shaped eyes, aquiline nose, and tiny mouth) are scarcely distinctive, as they typify many of the artist's female subjects, and the sitter is presented in an oft-chosen pose, the two-thirds length figure, turned slightly to the side yet gazing directly outward. The young woman probably was seated for the study but may as well have been standing, given the straight fall of her gown and cape; what her impossibly long right arm and gloved hand rest on is unclear.

Like so many of Ingres's graphite portraits of this period, this one displays a remarkable delicacy in the modeling of the subject's face (accents distributed in the sheerest of tones), distinctly at odds with the sketchy delineation of her simple dress. But it is in the exquisite framing of that dreamy face with a wreath of corkscrew curls, echoed in the frilly trimming of her collar, that Ingres captured the young lady's charms most effectively.

Ingres customarily penciled portraits on tablets fabricated of wood pulp board wrapped with a close-grained wove paper. The board provided handy support to the draftsman, who might be seated or standing and could hold the tablet at any convenient angle. Inevitably, the paper became separated from its backing and became trimmed in the process of removal. A tablet in the standard size of 215 by 165 millimeters was the likely support for the present drawing, which now measures about a centimeter less than that in each dimension.[2]

COLTA IVES

1. According to dealers handling the drawing, it is said to have come from the family estate of Prince Camillo Massimo, who was married to princess Christine von Sachsen (1775–1837). However, Ingres's cataloguer, in comparing the subject to a portrait of the princess, found no resemblance between the two sitters to establish an identity. See Naef 1977–80, vol. 4, no. 166, pp. 304–5, ill.
2. The present drawing measures approximately the same as Ingres's portrait of Lady Mary Cavendish-Bentinck, also drawn in 1816 (21.9 × 17.2 cm; The Metropolitan Museum of Art, New York [43.85.6], which retains the full drawing face-sheet plus raw edges of the folded flaps. See Marjorie B. Cohn's study of Ingres's drawing materials in Cambridge 1967, pp. 241–49.

90

91. Jean-Auguste-Dominique Ingres

Montauban, 1780–Paris, 1867

Female Nude, in Frontal View, Her Hands Bound behind Her Back;
Study for Angelica and Roger

1867

Graphite, 5¼ × 3⁷⁄₁₆ in. (13.4 × 8.7 cm)

Signed in graphite at lower left: *Ingres;* annotated in graphite at mid-height at right: *venus danse / devant mars;* annotated on verso in pen and brown ink, showing through the sheet: *Ingres. Croquis pour Angélique et Roger*

Inscribed on mounting with cartouche in handwriting: *J. A. D. Ingres perfeciebat 5 janvier MDCCCLXVII*

PROVENANCE: Philippe Burty (1830–1890)[1]; Victor Gille; sale, Hôtel Drouot, Paris, May 6, 1927, lot 4 (as *Andromeda* [*sic*] *Enchained*); sale, Hôtel Drouot, Paris, November 24, 1995, lot 70 (ill., with same title); purchased at that sale by Jean Bonna

EXHIBITIONS: Paris 1867, no. 132; Paris 2006b, no. 58; Geneva 2006–7a

BIBLIOGRAPHY: Delaborde 1870, p. 209

During the summer of 1817, while he was in Rome, Jean-Auguste-Dominique Ingres received a letter from the comte de Forbin commissioning him to create an "overdoor" decoration for the throne room at the château of Versailles, as a pendant to a *Rinaldo and Armida* assigned to Pierre-Jacques Onésyme Bergeret de Grancourt. It was probably Ingres who then suggested the subject of *Roger Rescuing Angelica*, from Canto 10 of Ariosto's *Orlando Furioso*. The work was shown at the Salon of 1819 and was poorly received, the critics as usual reproaching Ingres for his "Gothicism" and his taste for the painters of the first quattrocento. The harsh Auguste Hilarion, comte de Kératry (1769–1859), even mistook the subject Ingres had treated for Perseus and Andromeda, an error repeated by specialists at the auctions where this drawing appeared. The painting was sent to the Musée du Luxembourg in 1824 and is now in the Louvre (fig. 119).

There are relatively few preparatory drawings for the painting,[2] even though it was reproduced in several successive versions, which are now in the National Gallery, London; the Musée Ingres, Montauban; and the Museu de Arte, São Paulo. A small canvas in the Detroit Institute of Arts, the authenticity of which is still contested, does in fact depict Perseus and Andromeda; the female figure is shown in a pose fairly similar to the one in the present drawing, but her head is turned to the left. Finally, an undisputed oil sketch, now in the Fogg Art Museum, presents the same female figure, with a variation in the position of her head.

Ingres's first drawings of the overall composition, now in the Musée Ingres,[3] show Angelica in a nearly frontal position. It was only in a slightly later drawing, now in the Fogg Art Museum (fig. 120),[4] that Ingres portrayed the young heroine in a pose similar to the one in the Bonna drawing. This latter sheet, which Ingres revised long after the fact,[5] shows almost no variation from Angelica in the Fogg drawing, simply a few differences in the treatment of her hair. But the figure's pose eventually was abandoned for one used in the various painted versions of the subject: an Angelica with her arms raised level to her head and chained to a boulder at the right.

It is amusing to note that Ingres, who was prey to lifelong insecurities, repeatedly revised the same subject in order to "perfect" it. But the desire to revisit his works and ameliorate them was plainly underscored by the artist himself, who in 1859 defended his numerous repetitions—in painting, drawing, and watercolor—of the themes he liked best: "People have pointed out to me, and perhaps rightly, that I repeat my compositions too many times, instead of making new works. Here is the reason: it seemed to me that most of these works, which I like because of the subject matter, were worth improving with a little retouching."[6]

LOUIS-ANTOINE PRAT

1. According to Paris 1867, no. 132.
2. Vigne 1995, nos. 1300, 1322.
3. Ibid., nos. 1300, 1301.
4. Cambridge 1980, no. 24, ill.
5. Nine days before his death on January 14, 1867, in fact, according to the inscription on the cartouche! Only one later drawing by Ingres is known, a copy after Giotto dated January 8 and now at the Musée Ingres, Montauban (Vigne 1995, no. 4368).
6. Delaborde 1870, p. 108.

91

Figure 119. Jean-Auguste-Dominique Ingres, *Roger Rescuing Angelica*. Oil on canvas. Musée du Louvre, Département des Peintures, Paris (inv. 5419)

Figure 120. Jean-Auguste-Dominique Ingres, *Roger Rescuing Angelica*. Drawing. Fogg Art Museum, Cambridge, Massachusetts (1943.859)

92

Théodore Gericault

Rouen, 1791–Paris, 1824

92. *Study for* The Italian Family

Ca. 1816–17

Graphite and chalk on laid paper, 5⅛ × 6¹⁵⁄₁₆ in. (13 × 17.6 cm)

Inscribed at lower left: *Léopold Robert*

PROVENANCE: Private Collection, France; sale, Hôtel des Ventes, Neuilly-sur-Seine, December 7, 2004, lot 15; Neal Fiertag, Paris; W. M. Brady & Co., New York; acquired by Jean Bonna, 2005

93. *The Italian Family*

Ca. 1816–17

Watercolor and gouache over Conté crayon on wove paper, 8¹³⁄₁₆ × 6¾ in. (22.4 × 17.2 cm)

Annotated on the support sheet: *Gericault* and *15*

PROVENANCE: *Album amicorum*, now disassembled, containing works by several artists, given in 1834 as a gift to the son of a Marshal of the Empire. According to one of the last owners, this drawing came from the collection of the painter Alexis-Nicolas Pérignon (1785–1864), a student of Girodet and subscriber to Gericault's tomb by Antoine Etex; Private Collection, Paris; Galerie de Bayser, Paris; acquired by Jean Bonna, 2001

EXHIBITIONS: Paris 2006b, no. 60; Geneva 2006–7a

BIBLIOGRAPHY: Bazin 1987–97, vol. 4 (1990), pp. 136–37, no. 1200; Whitney 1997, p. 69, no. 87

*T*he Italian Family is an intriguing composition depicting a mother seated on a low wall, gripping a staff in one hand while holding the body of her young male child with the other. Is he sleeping? Is he dead? Another of her children sits at her side, his head turned toward this strange scene, his left hand raised to his mouth in a gesture that at first glance seems pensive or meditative. In fact it is

neither; he is simply eating a grape, a bunch of which he holds in his right hand. The banality of his action undercuts the strange atmosphere of the drawing, which appears to take place on a Roman street. Like a stage set, the two columns in the background seem to indicate that beyond them, there is nothing.

Subjects drawn from daily life were very dear to Théodore Gericault at the time he made this drawing. During his stay in Rome (1816–17), the artist broke the promise he had made to himself to come up with a style and themes that his teacher Pierre Guérin could finally approve—in other words, ones worthy of treatment by a historical painter[1]—and instead found topics in the lives of ordinary Italians. Gericault did not hesitate to adopt such picturesque subjects, which, according to the aesthetic hierarchy then in force, were considered the province of genre painting and therefore minor.

93

Figure 121. Théodore Gericault, *The Italian Family*, also called *The Poor Family*. Oil on paper backed with canvas. Graphische Sammlung, Staatsgalerie, Stuttgart (inv. 2793)

Many extant drawings by Gericault treat the theme of a poor Italian family reduced to begging in the streets. His Zurich notebook, for instance, contains a magnificent example showing a woman sitting on the ground, her arms around her young child. Such drawings can be considered the starting points of the figural group that Gericault then developed, adding more characters as he went along. The artist transcended the more banal meaning of this scene, injecting it with deeper significance.

One must realize the essential aim of Gericault's approach: starting with a genre scene, he worked to subtly transform it into an allegory. The first to recognize this approach was Wheelock Whitney, at the Gericault colloquium in 1991.[2] Commenting on preparatory sketches related to *The Italian Family*, a painting now in the Staatsgalerie, Stuttgart (fig. 121), he arrived at some provocative hypotheses. His comments were based on an analysis of several drawings in which Gericault seems to have been thinking of the traditional motif of the Three Fates, the guardians of life and destiny, which the artist superimposed onto the tableau

of his destitute Italian family. More than a simple genre scene, then, the composition can be seen as the work of a history painter in perfect control of symbols and allegories.[3]

In this regard, it is worth pausing a moment to consider the motif of the staff, which is also found in both the Bonna preparatory drawing shown here and in the painting at the Staatsgalerie, Stuttgart. In 1844, true to his tendency to note any subject liable to edify the masses, David d'Angers wrote: "In the cemeteries of the Vendée region, I saw old gravestones on which a staff had been carved. The new gravestones do not have this sign—too bad for the new generation! They should have carved a staff without a tow-rope: it would have been a symbol that the journey was over, a sign of labors finished, as tombstones in Pompeii show sailors folding the sails. In the mountains, I saw three women taking shelter under a single coat. It would be the motif of a group of Three Fates: the one in the middle holding a staff, the second weaving the thread, and the third holding the scissors with which to cut the thread."[4] In Gericault's watercolor, the thread

of life hangs above the child with his head thrown back, whose outstretched body might suggest either sleep or death—both, no doubt, since as he often did, Gericault is here cultivating a purposely ambiguous image. The viewer's uneasy response is therefore a function of the painter's subtle thought process.

The theme of the family is in fact recurrent in Gericault's work. A magnificent illustration exists from as early as 1810–12, in a drawing from the Zoubaloff notebook depicting a father, a mother, and their four children taking shelter at the foot of an antique column.[5] The family was clearly important to Gericault. Could he have been referring to his own? That is quite possible, and if such is the case, it remains to be decoded. But this romance might also, and especially, be an allusion to the first post-Revolutionary generation, when the status of the family and the place of the individual in society were completely redefined by the new political and social order. Might not the motifs of father, mother, and children in Gericault's work be a metaphor for another triangle, which would be called "Past, Present, and Future"? In any case, that is the exact message of *The Raft of the Medusa*, Gericault's monumental canvas in which he addresses the question of our fate on this earth.

BRUNO CHENIQUE

1. Bruno Chenique in Flers 2000, p. 36.
2. On November 14, 1991, in the Louvre. His talk was entitled "Scenes of Everyday Italy." Unfortunately it was not included in the published proceedings of the colloquium (*Géricault* 1996).
3. Whitney 1997, pp. 63–70.
4. Bruel 1958, vol. 2, p. 187.
5. Eight studies for a family and various subjects, graphite, brush, and brown wash, 5¾ × 7½ in. (14.7 × 19 cm), Musée du Louvre, Département des Arts Graphiques, Paris, Carnet Zoubaloff, p. 46; Bazin 1987–97, vol. 2 (1987), p. 398, no. 221.

94

94. Théodore Gericault

Rouen, 1791–Paris, 1824

Entwined Couple

Ca. 1816–17

Graphite, Conté crayon, pen and black ink, heightened in white gouache on tan paper, 7⅝ × 9½ in. (19.4 × 24.2 cm)

Stamp of the Coutan-Hauguet Collection at lower right: (Lugt 464)

PROVENANCE: Louis-Joseph-August Coutan (1779–1830); by inheritance to his widow, Madame Coutan (1788–1838), née Lucienne Hauguet; her brother Ferdinand Hauguet (d. 1860); his son Maurice-Jacques-Albert Hauguet (1819–1883); his wife, Madame Hauguet (1842–1883), née Marie-Thérèse Schubert; her sister, Madame Gustave Milliet (b. 1844), née Henriette Schubert; posthumous sale of Coutan-Hauguet Collection, Hôtel Drouot, Paris (Maître Escribe, appraiser; Haro Brothers, specialists), December 16–17, 1889, part of lot 208 (?); Paul Vercier Collection, Le Havre (according to Lorenz Eitner); Hazlitt, Gooden & Fox, London; acquired by Jean Bonna, 1996

EXHIBITIONS: Paris 2006b, no. 61; Geneva 2006–7a

BIBLIOGRAPHY: Lorenz Eitner in Matthiesen Fine Arts 1993; pp. 204, 205, fig. 5; Eitner 1996, pp. 381, 389, n. 24, fig. 14; Bazin 1987–97, vol. 7 (1997), p. 284, no. 2767

While the man's face and genitals are hidden, the sex of his partner is revealed. Stretching from behind her neck to her left breast, an area of shadow acts as a temporary refuge for the man's head. The obvious relaxation of his body seems to indicate that their pleasurable tussle has just ended. Attentive but somehow absent, the woman seems to be waiting for her partner's virility to reawaken.

The scene is simple and true to life. The sketch of a canopied bed barely indicates that this is a mythological scene. The subject is imbued with realism, accentuated by the

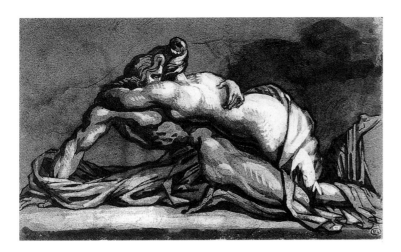

drawings will be consigned to a fire lit by some local priest, on the pretext of nudity or some other more or less diabolical or cabalistic sign. Imagine having a country and a family, being Gericault, only to have fate toy like this with your dreams of glory and your entire existence of work and struggle!"[1]

For our great delectation as voyeurs and aesthetes, several canvases and drawings apparently managed to escape the brazier that Huet so dreaded.[2] Gericault's sensuality, not yet dampened by moralistic strictures, preserved its vital energy by overstepping iconoclastic bounds.

BRUNO CHENIQUE

graphic treatment of the bodies—empty areas and white highlights for the woman, hatching and visibly heavier lines for the man. In the hands of Théodore Gericault, black and white act as colors in the service of the flesh and of the differences between the sexes.

Familiar to Gericault scholars only since 1993, the Bonna drawing belongs to an important series of erotic drawings that have gradually come to light (see fig. 122), following decades of the prudery that Paul Huet remarked upon during an excursion through

Normandy in 1857: "I wanted to tell you about Mortain, as I said I would. Thanks to a suit brought by the family, two or three old women now own a few canvases by Gericault and several hundred drawings. You can imagine how eager I was to get a glimpse of those lost sketches by our great painter. But I have to admit that our attempts were in vain. Those old harpies, incapable of judging or appreciating the works that fortune has thrust into their hands, will not allow anyone to see them, I'm told. At the first chance they get, those

1. Paul Huet to his wife, Vire, October 1, 1857, in Huet 1911, p. 224; drawing, Conté crayon, pen, brown ink wash, and white gouache on blue paper, 5⅜ × 8⅜ in. (13.5 × 21.3 cm), Musée du Louvre, Département des Arts Graphiques, Paris (inv. RF 29483r).
2. For example, *Le Trio érotique*, oil on canvas, J. Paul Getty Museum, Los Angeles, and *L'Accouplement*, black chalk drawing, now in a Private Collection (sale, Sotheby's, New York, October 29, 2002, lot 5).

95. Théodore Gericault

Rouen, 1791–Paris, 1824

Recto: *Montmartre Landscape: 23 Rue des Martyrs*

Verso: *Étude pour la Course des chevaux libres, la Mossa*

1817–18

Recto: Conté crayon, watercolor, gouache, and brown ink wash on parchment; verso: Conté crayon and white chalk on a scumbling of red chalk, 8⅜ × 11³⁄₁₆ in. (21.3 × 28.4 cm)

Signed on verso in reverse orientation from the drawing: *Gericault*

Stamp from the Coutan-Hauguet collection on both sides: (Lugt 464)

PROVENANCE: Louis-Joseph-August Coutan (1779–1830); by inheritance to his widow, Madame Coutan (1788–1838), née Lucienne Hauguet; her brother Ferdinand Hauguet (d. 1860); his son Maurice-Jacques-Albert Hauguet (1819–1883); Madame Hauguet (1842–1883), née Marie-Thérèse Schubert; by inheritance to her sister, Madame Gustave Milliet (b. 1844), née Henriette Schubert;

Wildenstein Collection, New York; sale, Sotheby's, London, December 6, 1978, lot 310; Wildenstein and Company, New York; acquired by Jean Bonna, 2003

EXHIBITIONS: New York 1949, no. 61; London 1953a, no. 78; Winterthur 1953, no. 150; New York 1955, no. 137; New York 1956, no. 56; New York 1959a, no. 1; Rome and Turin 1961, no. 164 (Rome, pl. 164, recto and verso), no. 157 (Turin, pl. 40, recto and verso); Saint Louis 1962, no. 18; Corpus Christi 1970, no. 15; New York 1982, p. 104, ill. p. 58 (recto); Paris 2006b, no. 62; Geneva 2006–7a

BIBLIOGRAPHY: Berger 1952, p. 106, no. 24, ill. (verso); Eitner 1953, pp. 80–81; Eitner 1954, p. 168; "In the Galleries" 1956; M. Schwartz 1959, ill. (recto); Berger 1968, p. 47, no. 28, ill.; Bazin 1987–97, vol. 4 (1990), p. 120, no. 1146 (recto), no. 1339 (verso); Linda Muehlig in Sievers 2000, p. 131, ill. p. 132, figs. 1, 2; Chenique 2001, p. 184, n. 78; Denison 2006, p. 521

This magnificent drawing, dominated by three saturated hues in stark opposition—brown for the ink, white and blue for the gouaches—has always been considered an Italian landscape from 1816–17. The jolting contrasts, the extraordinary interplay of light and shadow, and a certain geometric treatment of the architectural shapes lead to that conclusion. However, this author suggests slightly modifying the dating to late 1817 or the spring of 1818, that is, on Gericault's return to France to live with his aging father in a house owned by Colonel Bro at 23 rue des Martyrs. The change might seem unimportant to anyone not familiar with the subtle difficulties involved in dating certain of Gericault's works;

95 recto

biographers have long tried (and are still trying, with varying success) to situate these
works in the master's oeuvre, based on their
own observations about the stylistic evolution
of his paintings and drawings.

The house depicted here is therefore not in
Italy but in Paris and more specifically, in
Montmartre. Gericault devoted a whole series
of drawings to the urban layout of this neighborhood located at the foot of the famous hill.
Several years later, real estate speculations by
some developers, some of whom were friends
of the artist, would earn the area the nickname
New Athens. In 1817–18, those large-scale

Figure 123. Théodore Gericault,
View of the Hill of Montmartre.
Black chalk, brown ink, and
watercolor. Collection Jan
Krugier and Marie-Anne
Krugier-Poniatowski, Geneva

95 verso (size reduced)

Gericault's own home, which in 1824, on the painter's death, was lived in by the famous singer Béranger and the liberal deputy Manuel, two friends of Colonel Bro.[4] A lithograph in the Bibliothèque Nationale de France by Jean-Jacques Champin and Claude Regnier (fig. 124), published in 1834, attests that it is indeed the same house (now demolished), drawn more or less from the same angle.[5]

One may now wonder if this strange dreamlike landscape, modeled by light and shadow using a technique that Gericault employed in his portraits, has the symbolic value of an actual self-portrait, and even if it is a veritable manifesto of Romanticism.

BRUNO CHENIQUE

1. Paris 1991–92, p. 123.
2. Gericault produced two other broad views of the Montmartre landscape in pen and ink, one in the École Nationale Supérieure des Beaux-Arts, Paris, 8½ × 10½ in. (21.5 × 26.7 cm) (inv. 973; Paris and Cambridge 1997–98, no. D82); and another in a Private Collection, 8¼ × 6⅛ in. (21.1 × 15.4 cm; Bazin 1987–97, vol. 5 [1992], p. 230, no. 1709).
3. Miquel 1987, p. 223.
4. "We like to know where great artists lived and where they died. And in this regard, it is worth noting that the apartment where Gericault died, in the house on the rue des Martyrs at no. 21 [sic], . . . was inhabited immediately afterward by Béranger." Blanc 1845, p. 432, n. 1.
5. On this subject, see Chenique 2001. Another drawing in the Smith College Museum of Art, Northampton, Massachusetts (pen and ink, 11¼ × 8½ in. [28.6 × 21.5 cm]), apparently portrays the same house on the rue des Martyrs.

developments had not yet begun, and Gericault shows the neighborhood in its semi-urban state, when it was still located on the fringes of the capital in a country-like setting. A more expansive view of the district is shown in a related drawing in the Collection of Jan Krugier and Marie-Anne Krugier-Poniatowski (fig. 123),[1] whose stylistic parentage with the Bonna drawing is at once close and distant. Gericault set down a panorama of the Montmartre hill, taking care to respect several significant details such as the telegraph pole and the mill as well as a large building at the extreme right of that sheet that would be worth trying to identify.[2]

Starting with realistic observation, Gericault managed to render the very essence of the landscape, in other words, its soul—or, to put it another way, the mysterious ungraspable side of nature. This true, "purely aesthetic" pleasure in fact presents the antithesis of a classical landscape, which translates its subject with readability and order. Better still, this is the quintessence of a Romantic landscape and of its aesthetic of the sublime—an emotive landscape, or, as Pierre Miquel nicely put it, "a masterpiece of violence and anguish."[3]

The drawing in the Bonna collection belongs to this same vein, apart from the fact that the fascinating ambiguity of this drawing rests on the idea not of a panorama but of a close-up, of the aesthetic of the fragment. Rather than being diluted, attention instead is focused on a few trees and buildings that are fairly ordinary in themselves but whose sentimental and even historical interest soon becomes apparent. Here again, there is no action, no subject, only a magnificent invitation to pure contemplation. And in reality, the place is not so insignificant, since it shows

Figure 124. Jean-Jacques Champin and Claude Regnier, *Houses of the Most Celebrated Personages in France since 1790 until Today: the House of Gericault, Béranger and Manuel*, 1834. Lithograph. Bibliothèque Nationale de France, Département des Estampes et de la Photographie, Paris (DC 211b)

96 recto

96. Théodore Gericault
Rouen, 1791–Paris, 1824

Recto: *Half-Length Portrait of a Young Boy*

Verso: *Studies of a Young Boy*

Ca. 1818–19

Graphite, pen and brown ink and wash, 7⅛ × 5¾ in. (18.1 × 14.6 cm)

PROVENANCE: Christopher Powney, London; Private Collection; sale, Hôtel Drouot (Gros & Delettrez, appraisers), Paris, April 11, 2005, lot 11; Galerie de Bayser, Paris; acquired by Jean Bonna, 2005

EXHIBITIONS: London 1968, no. 35; Paris 2006b, no. 63; Geneva 2006–7a

BIBLIOGRAPHY: Eitner 1983, p. 347, n. 212; Bazin 1987–97, vol. 5 (1992), p. 281, no. 1831 (recto), no. 1832 (verso)

There was a time, not so long ago, when reactionary art historians who despised Théodore Gericault dared claim that he was not a portraitist worthy of the term.[1] The four studies that appear on the recto and verso of this magnificent pen-and-ink drawing give ample proof of the artist's mastery of portraiture.

Fierce is no doubt the adjective that first comes to mind when considering the triangular face of this young boy. On the verso, three studies made from life (two of which have been cropped) examine the model in profile; his hair, upper lip, small chin, and almond eye have caught the draftsman's particular

96 verso

attention. His hands, rapidly sketched, did not receive the same care. Gericault seems to have been concerned less with depicting the model's features perfectly than with capturing his firey inner personality. Here is a child of about eight or ten, attentive and no doubt quite intelligent.

On the recto, Gericault took a completely different approach. He omitted the hands and arms of the child and solidly defined the limit of this new half-length portrait with a triple line in ink that almost looks like the base of a statue. On this base rest two shoulders and a broad white collar, from which emerge the neck and small face of a young boy, magnificently sketched in pen and ink and heightened with ink wash. The change is radical. This entanglement of lines, of areas of light and shadow, yields a psychological portrait in which several emotional states seem to be conjoined. There is a certain fierceness, as stated above, but the figure's authoritative quality is

conveyed mainly by the thick eyebrows and the closed mouth that seems to express some unknown bitterness. The left half of the face and neck is plunged in shadow. When the result is compared to the initial studies, it becomes clear that the model's inwardness, or melancholy, is marked much more strongly and is quite striking.

The existence of this drawing has been known to Gericault scholars only since 1968. Germain Bazin reproduced it for the first time in 1992, which gives an idea of how little commentary it has received. When the sheet came to light, it was suggested that the young model might be Olivier Bro, the son of Gericault's friend and neighbor, on the basis of a possible resemblance with a portrait of young Bro in the Collection of M. A. K. Solomon (fig. 125). Bazin did not even bother to mention this hypothesis, which can be eliminated by even a quick examination of the two faces. If one had

to establish a resemblance with a painted work that might be considered the definitive version, it is quite obviously, as Lorenz Eitner indicated, with the one now in the Musée de Tessé (fig. 126).[2] Bazin was excessively harsh when he wrote about this painted portrait (again in 1992): "This likeness of a small boy with his melancholy face makes for a very pretty picture, but its technique, which makes great use of transparencies, renders it unlike Gericault and bears no similarity with the paintings previously studied as authentic and forming a coherent whole. As such, there is no reason to consider this painting one of the artist's works, likable though it might be."[3] Bazin's rejection must be taken apart and negated. In fact, everything about this "pretty picture" suggests the authentic hand of the painter of the *Raft of the Medusa*. Bazin is unfortunately bound by an ultraclassical view, which aims to deny Gericault's Romanticism and label him a

Figure 125. Théodore Gericault, *Portrait of Olivier Bro as an Infant*. Oil on canvas. Collection M. A. K. Solomon, Cambridge

Figure 126. Théodore Gericault, *Portrait of a Young Boy*. Oil on canvas. Musée de Tessé, Le Mans (inv. 10.265)

painter indentured to the Grand Manner. Such a portrait, on the contrary (and the preparatory sketches attest to this), is in some ways the quintessence of Gericault's art. Hence, the profound unease of someone like Bazin, who does not like and probably cannot like this artist who was far too revolutionary for him in every sense of the word.[4]

The identity of the young boy in the Le Mans portrait poses another problem. In 1971, Eitner noted a certain resemblance with the portrait of the above-mentioned Olivier Bro and suggested dating the Le Mans canvas from 1817–19.[5] In 1978, Philippe Grunchec accepted Eitner's hypothesis (while still cataloguing the painting under the simple title *Portrait of a Child*) but found the model older. He therefore suggested dating it later, about 1821–23, stressing, and rightly so, a shared palette between the Le Mans portrait and the famous series of mental patients.[6] In 1983, Eitner again postulated the resemblance with Olivier Bro, accepted Grunchec's remarks, and this time suggested dating the four drawn studies about 1819[7] and the Le Mans portrait about 1820, or two years after the portrait of young Bro with a dog, which Eitner dates from about 1818.

The dryness or subtleties of these debates attest to the difficulties scholars still face in trying to date certain of the artist's works

precisely. Concerning this painted head of a young boy, Eitner again stressed a "liveliness and intimacy of characterization rare in Gericault's work, particularly in his portraits before 1820."[8] It would be more accurate to say that all Gericault's portraits exude an extraordinary psychological truth, which reached its acme in the portraits of mental patients. Grunchec's suggestion of a stylistic comparison with that series is therefore highly interesting, even if, here again, the dating of those five portraits is subject to much debate and includes anywhere from 1819 to 1823.

In 1991, Henri Zerner made an excellent summary of this debate, which is worth quoting: "Recent authors seem to agree with Eitner in recognizing the face of little Olivier Bro in the head from Le Mans, apparently ignoring the fact that Olivier Bro had steely blue-gray eyes, while the child in Le Mans has distinctly brown eyes. But in the final account, it matters little, because what is most striking is the contrast between our desire for identification and the lingering uncertainty surrounding it. Is the Le Mans painting a portrait, even an unfinished one, possibly even a mere study? Shouldn't we rather liken it to an expressive head study? A visitor to the exhibition [Jean-Claude Lebensztejn] remarked to me that this boy was a good candidate for the later paintings of mental patients, a kind of madman

before the fact. If the identities of these children are so uncertain, it is because Gericault was interested only in their gazes, in a temporary movement of emotion, or else in a certain expressive emptiness, and not in the permanent physiognomic traits that are essential to making an identification. Still, he is working from a model, and the vessel of those emotions is an individual. Hence our desire to identify him, but also the uncertainty into which this throws us."[9]

The four pen-and-ink studies, with which Zerner seems unfamiliar, respond in part to these interesting remarks. The painting in Le Mans is therefore not an unfinished portrait, nor a study, and still less a simple sketch. It is a completely finished, thought-out, sophisticated portrait. A simple and attentive comparison between the painted portrait and the pen-and-ink portrait (recto) allows a better grasp of the artist's approach. If there is something here reminiscent of an expressive head study, it is not in the sense meant by Charles Le Brun and the famous contest sponsored by the École des Beaux-Arts. While Gericault began by observing reality, it was not to create an ideal type but rather a face of very subtle expressiveness. In the painted version, he willfully accentuated the model's inwardness, giving him a thoughtful, or perhaps pensive or wistful, look—or, if he is insane, then he is so as any child would be who is forced to confront the insanity of the world on a daily basis. If this young boy (who to this day remains anonymous) is not a monster in the sense that Michel meant about Louise Vernet and the Dedreux children,[10] he nonetheless remains terribly affecting. This is not simply a child, as Françoise Dolto would have said, but above all a person. "Gericault portrays the budding inwardness of childhood," Michel wrote, "genesis of the self, premise of the cogito, formation of the subject."[11] If we feel some unease, then, it was intentionally planned and subtly developed by the painter, in order to communicate to us and do violence to our conventions.

BRUNO CHENIQUE

1. "Gericault was always lacking in taste in his faces, the bearing of the heads, and also in his execution"; Dimier 1914, p. 59. "For it does no honor to Gericault, nor give proof of much critical acumen, to devote too much attention to these ambiguous faces with their eyes widened by the worst kind of pathos, just as it does him no

justice to praise him as the author of the Dedreux portraits, created with a lax brush style, . . . and we cannot
view without some discomfort the portrait of the little
Louise Vernet, the bizarre product of a Michelangelo
who has strayed too close to the doll shelf. These errors,
which usually end up being expunged from the catalogues of the old masters, occupy too much place in
Gericault's"; Thuillier 1978, p. 6.

2. Paris 1991–92, p. 120, no. 139, fig. 197.
3. Bazin 1987–97, vol. 5 (1992), p. 103.
4. This paradox, which merits further study, was confirmed
   for me over the past few years by several of his close
   associates or by collectors of Gericault.
5. See Los Angeles, Detroit, and Philadelphia 1971–72,
   p. 114, no. 72.
6. Grunchec 1978, p. 123, no. 233.

7. Eitner 1983, p. 347, n. 212.
8. Ibid., p. 205; Eitner 1991, p. 280.
9. Zerner 1996b, p. 330.
10. Régis Michel in Paris 1991–92, p. 108.
11. Ibid.

97. Théodore Gericault

Rouen, 1791–Paris, 1824

Three Horses in a Stable

Ca. 1822–23

Watercolor heightened with white over traces of black
chalk on wove paper, mounted on Japanese paper,
12⁹⁄₁₆ × 18½ in. (31.9 × 47 cm)

PROVENANCE: Private Collection, Luxembourg;
Galerie Eric Coatalem, Paris; acquired by Jean Bonna,
2004

The well-muscled forms of men and horses
figure prominently in Théodore Gericault's
art, for he was exceptionally skilled in their
sculptural rendering. An ardent sportsman, he
enjoyed devoting much of his art to picturing
horses—running, jumping, and rearing, as
well as working and resting—beginning with
his earliest efforts in the studio of Carle Vernet,
himself a talented painter of horses. It is
thought that when Vernet, in 1813, received an

assignment to paint the animals in the stables
at Versailles, his pupil worked beside him on a
portrait of seven steeds belonging to Lord
Seymour. The canvas remained one of
Gericault's favorites, and after his untimely
death in a riding accident at the age of thirty-
three, it was hung in his funeral room.[1]

Although his painting of *Seven Horses in
Front View*, as well as the contemporary
Twenty-Four Horses in Rear View, display
their subjects lined up like collectors' items, it
became Gericault's practice generally to depict
single or groups of horses in more realistic sit-
uations and settings. While in Italy (1816–18),
he pictured the wild races of the Barberi
horses, and in England (1820–21), he painted
the derby at Epson Downs. But for him, the

more routine workaday aspects of equine life
seem always to have held greater appeal.

Particularly in the early 1820s, as if recalling
the dark warmth of the stalls at Versailles,
Gericault repeatedly pictured horses in or near
their stables, their sleek bodies shown, as they
are in this drawing, from the side or at an
angle from the rear, silhouetted against stone
or rough wood walls.[2] These compositions vary
in medium between oil, watercolor, and litho-
graphic ink. Comparable in many ways to the
Bonna drawing is the watercolor now in The
Cleveland Museum of Art (fig. 127), centered
on three horses of different colors held tightly
within the picture frame and a narrow foreground. Although the horses' postures and
activities vary greatly between the two pictures,

Figure 127. Théodore Gericault,
Fighting Horses, ca. 1820. Watercolor
over graphite. The Cleveland Museum
of Art (1929.13)

97

both works in the familiar gold/brown palette exhibit dynamic brushstrokes that describe the scenes with stunning brevity yet precision. Here, as he always did, Gericault found in each animal unique and distinguishing characteristics, which he presented with great sensitivity and care. This is a special aspect of the artist's genius and was recognized by the scholar Lorenz Eitner, who observed that the features of Gericault's horses were "individualized to a degree normally reserved for human portraiture."[3]

Colta Ives

1. The painting, *Seven Horses in Front View*, formerly in the Cottier-Inglis collection, is now in a Private Collection in England. See Paris 1991–92, no. 26, fig. 64.

2. See, for example: *Two Posthorses at the Entrance to a Stable*, ca. 1822–23, oil on canvas, Musée du Louvre, Paris; *Interior of a Stable*, watercolor, British Museum, London; *Dappled Draught Horse Being Shod*, 1822–23, graphite and wash, Museum of Fine Arts, Boston; *Brown Bay Tethered in a Stable*, watercolor over graphite, Musée du Louvre, Département des Arts Graphiques, Paris; and similar compositions among the artist's lithographs of the same period. Closest to the Bonna drawing in subject matter are: *Draught Horses in a Stable*, watercolor, Private Collection (Bazin 1987–97, vol. 7 [1997], no. 2585); the pendant oil paintings *Three Horses in a Stable* and *Horses in a Stable*, formerly in the Collection of Général de Brack (Grunchec 1978, nos. 238, 239); and *Three Horses in a Stable*, watercolor over graphite, Morgan Library & Museum, New York.

3. Eitner 1983, p. 38. According to the Parisian art dealer Eric Coatalem, from whom Mr. Bonna purchased this drawing, its attribution to Gericault was confirmed by Mr. Eitner, who placed its date about 1822–23.

98. Ferdinand-Victor-Eugène Delacroix

Paris, 1798–Paris, 1863

Study of a Standing Moroccan, Frontal View

1832

Charcoal and red chalk heightened with watercolor on ivory paper, 13⅞ × 9⁷⁄₁₆ in. (35.3 × 23.9 cm)

PROVENANCE: Stamp of the artist's studio at lower left (Lugt 838a); probably Achille Arosa sale, Hôtel Drouot, Paris, May 6, 1891, lot 105 (125 francs to P.-A. Chéramy [?]); probably P.-A. Chéramy sale, Galerie Georges Petit, Paris, May 5–7, 1908, lot 330 (280 francs to Delaunay); Galerie de la Scala, Paris; acquired by Jean Bonna, 2000

EXHIBITIONS: Paris 2006b, no. 65; Geneva 2006–7a

BIBLIOGRAPHY: Denison 2006, p. 521

Ferdinand-Victor-Eugène Delacroix's voyage to North Africa in 1832 is well known. It is documented in the letters he sent to his friends and family, the notebooks he filled with jottings and sketches, and the drawings he made while there, not to mention all the subsequent works inspired by his journey, which were most often based on specific episodes from the trip.[1] Scholars have combed through the archives at length—Delacroix went to Africa as part of an official diplomatic mission—and have added information of their own to the available documentation.[2] Several years ago, for instance, the discovery and publication of a manuscript in which the artist recounts his voyage nearly twenty years after the fact finally shed new light on Delacroix's Moroccan experience.[3]

During his trip, Delacroix produced an abundance of documents, both written and drawn, which he executed (as his friend Philippe Burty later noted) "on horseback, in an Arab tent, in the streets of Meknes, or in the palace of Abd el Rahman."[4] Two of the drawings in the Bonna Collection are from this group (*Study of a Standing Moroccan, Frontal View* and *Arabs in Morocco*, cat. no. 99). Indeed, it is worth differentiating when these studies were made, as they also correspond to different stages in Delacroix's assimilation of his experience of Morocco. At first, the artist drew from life, sketching rapidly (and sometimes secretly), taking written notes in which he described what he saw, indicating the color

of a garment and his emotional responses, so that he could later revisit the moment. In the evenings, he organized his initial impressions, completing his sketches with watercolor or transforming them into more polished and individualized drawings. It was from this mass of words and pictures that Delacroix later took the subjects of his Moroccan works, beginning during his quarantine in Toulon and then in Paris. In Toulon, he produced an album of eighteen watercolors as a thank you for the sponsor of his trip, Comte de Mornay; in them, he depicted memorable characters or episodes from the voyage that had just ended. In Paris, he produced still more Moroccan watercolors. To these, he would later add, beginning in 1834, the canvases that made him one of the acknowledged masters of Orientalism—paintings such as *Women of Algiers* of 1834, in the Musée du Louvre, Paris; *The Sultan of Morocco amidst His Guards* of 1845, in the Musée des Augustins, Toulouse; and *Fanatics of Tangiers* of 1838, in the Minneapolis Institute of Arts.

Delacroix made all his drawings in the Bonna Collection for his personal use, and they therefore remained in his storage boxes until the posthumous sale of his estate (all three bear his stamp). They correspond to three different stages in his efforts to appropriate and mature his grasp of Moroccan reality; *Study of a Standing Moroccan, Frontal View* was probably executed at the beginning of his stay, while the drawing *Arabs in Morocco* (cat. no. 99) dates from the end of the trip.

From the moment he arrived in Tangiers, Delacroix tirelessly recorded what he saw. In fact, the process began even before his disembarkation in Morocco; while still on board the frigate *La Perle*, he drew several magnificent landscapes of the Spanish and Moroccan coastlines. Those drawings were made sometimes in notebooks such as the ones conserved in the Louvre, sometimes on loose sheets, as with *Study of a Standing Moroccan*; the former allowed Delacroix to capture scenes on the fly, while the latter were used in more tranquil

Figure 128. Ferdinand-Victor-Eugène Delacroix, *Study of a Moor*. Black chalk and watercolor. Nationalmuseum, Stockholm (inv. NM 71/1915)

circumstances. The artist's letters to his friends and family from early in his stay give precious information about that period. For instance, he wrote to Félix Feuillet de Conches, who worked at the Ministry of Foreign Affairs, that he was "in a country that is quite new to me and abundantly picturesque. One would need a long stay here to convey adequately even a fraction of the strange and remarkable things to be seen."[5] Soon afterward, once he had become more settled, Delacroix confided to his close friends Jean-Baptiste Pierret and Félix Guillemardet: "I am gradually insinuating myself into the customs of the country, so as to be able to draw many of these Moorish figures quite freely. They have very strong prejudices against the noble art of painting, but a few coins slipped here and there settle their scruples."[6] About two weeks later, he confessed to the painter Théodore Gudin that he had been "above all surprised by the extreme simplicity of their dress and at the same time by the variety of ways in which they arrange the articles that compose it."[7] And he wrote to

Henri Duponchel, the director of the Opéra, who had lobbied to get him included in the Mornay mission: "Their dress is quite uniform and very simple, and yet the various ways of arranging it confer on it a kind of beauty and nobility that leave one speechless. I plan to bring back enough sketches to give some idea of these gentlemen's appearance. Moreover, I shall bring back actual specimens of most of their articles of dress. I'll gladly ruin myself for this purpose, and for the sake of the pleasure you will get from seeing them."[8]

The Moor that Delacroix drew in this study is very similar to the one portrayed in another drawing in the Nationalmuseum, Stockholm (fig. 128), dated February 16, 1832, in other words at the beginning of his sojourn in Tangiers. In both cases, a model (who had probably been slipped a few coins) poses stiffly, either sitting or standing, which allowed Delacroix to depict his garments in great detail. The technique of both drawings is identical, charcoal and red chalk heightened with watercolor on ivory paper. As Arlette Sérullaz pointed out, the combination of red chalk and black crayon is fairly rare in Delacroix's work and was used only during his time in Morocco.[9] In his *Memoir of a Journey to Morocco*, Delacroix noted "the whiteness [that] predominates in

these costumes and beautifully offsets the black or bronze-colored faces. Ordinarily, a caftan in a brightly colored cloth, such as scarlet, sulfur yellow [*sic*], or pale blue, falls to slightly below the knee and is covered by a similarly shaped caftan in white percale or damask, which affords a glimpse of the one underneath only through a few openings near the bottom because of the irregularity of the folds draped from the waist and the sleeves; these latter are wide and pull up at the slightest movement, leaving the arm free and entirely exposed. On this blindingly white overgarment, which gives only a glimpse of the clothes beneath, he wears silk cords in bright colors, which are strung across the chest and support either a sword or a dagger hanging from the side, or else a kind of bag or sabretache in finely wrought leather. A very narrow belt in finely worked leather or velvet, red, yellow, or light green in color, cinches the waist with military elegance. Sometimes, other cords hang from this belt, twisting as they hold a powder horn that is highly awkward to carry but that produces a very graceful effect. The legs are bare and the feet shod in slippers that are always yellow and of very old style, which go up to the instep like the footwear of the ancients."[10]

BARTHÉLÉMY JOBERT

1. For a summary, see Paris 1994–95a.
2. See in particular the facsimile edition of Delacroix's four travel diaries from Morocco, in the Musée du Louvre, Paris, and the Musée Condé, Chantilly, with two volumes of supplementary texts (*Le Voyage au Maroc* 1992).
3. See Beaumont-Maillet, Jobert, and Join-Lambert 1999.
4. Preface to the catalogue of the posthumous sale of Delacroix's estate, Hôtel Drouot, Paris, February 22–27, 1864, p. xiii. The sale revealed Delacroix's genius as a draftsman to the public, which until then had been unaware of this aspect of his talent. The artist had exhibited or sold only very finished watercolors (which bore some similarity to his paintings) and had given some of his less "polished" drawings only to close friends and family members. Most of the Moroccan drawings, which he had kept for himself mainly for private documentation, were dispersed after his death; this notably includes the notebooks, some of which were subsequently disassembled.
5. Delacroix to Félix Feuillet de Conches, January 25, 1832, in Delacroix, *Letters*, 2001 (ed.), p. 182.
6. Delacroix to Jean-Baptiste Pierret and Félix Guillemardet, February 8, 1832, ibid., p. 183. In another letter to Pierret of February 29, Delacroix spoke of "what a wretched Moor looked like, begging for a handful of coppers a couple of days ago" (ibid., p. 188).
7. Delacroix to Théodore Gudin, February 23, 1832, ibid., p. 184.
8. Delacroix to Henri Duponchel, February 23, 1832, ibid., pp. 185–86.
9. Arlette Sérullaz in Paris 1994–95a, p. 138 (entry for *Seated Moor* in the Nationalmuseum, Stockholm).
10. Beaumont-Maillet, Jobert, and Join-Lambert 1999, pp. 98–99.

99. Ferdinand-Victor-Eugène Delacroix

Paris, 1798–Paris, 1863

Arabs in Morocco

1832

Conté crayon, brown wash, and watercolor, 10⅝ × 16¹⁵⁄₁₆ in. (27 × 43 cm)

Inscribed in Conté crayon at lower left: *3 juin Dimanche*, followed by *fen.* (?); above the figure in crayon, in graphite to the right of the central figure: *double tour sur / la tête*

PROVENANCE: stamp of the artist's studio (Lugt 838a); probably the artist's posthumous sale, Hôtel Drouot, Paris, February 22–27, 1864; stamp of the Maurice Gobin Collection at lower left; Galerie de Bayser, Paris; acquired by Jean Bonna, 2000

EXHIBITIONS: Paris 2006b, no. 66; Geneva 2006–7a

BIBLIOGRAPHY: Denison 2006, p. 521

Ferdinand-Victor-Eugène Delacroix made this drawing at the end of his Moroccan journey. It is unusual in more ways than one: first, because he used a large-format sheet for a series of rapid notes and sketches juxtaposed with no apparent interconnection, as in a sketchbook, and second, because of the presence of very diverse techniques and effects, from watercolor to graphite, with one figure entirely in color and another rendered in a simple wash over Conté crayon. The patches of watercolor at the upper right, which look thoroughly improvised, add to the impression that this is a sheet of studies from life. There is a

contradiction between its appearance as a simple sheet of sketches and the large format. Was Delacroix forced to use this sheet for lack of other paper, having exhausted the supplies he brought from France, or did he intentionally make a "false" sheet of sketches from life?

By this time, Delacroix was aiming to recapitulate and summarize his experiences in Morocco rather than create new studies of a country that he had been exploring and extensively depicting for five months. He suggested as much in a letter he wrote to the critic and journalist Auguste Jal on June 4 (one day after drawing *Arabs in Morocco*), the tone of which

shows a marked difference from his earlier letters: "Fame, here, is a meaningless word; everything inclines one to delightful indolence; nothing suggests that this is not the most desirable
state in the world. Beauty lies everywhere about
one. It drives one to despair, and painting, or
rather the frantic desire to paint, seems the
greatest of follies. You have seen Algiers, and you
can imagine what the natives of these regions
are like. Here, there is something even simpler
and more primitive; there is less of the Turkish
alloy; I have Romans and Greeks on my door-
step; it makes me laugh heartily at David's
Greeks, apart, of course, from his sublime skill
as a painter. I know now what they were really
like."[1] Rather than the enthusiastic discovery
of a new land and foreign civilization that he
had evoked in his letters of February and March,
here Delacroix is stressing the "living antiquity"
that Morocco revealed to him, a theme that
would become increasingly prominent in his
writings as his journey progressed.

Arabs in Morocco most likely derives from
this latter impulse. Techniques and subjects are
jumbled together, but the whole maintains a
certain balance, both in the use of color and in
the arrangement of motifs on a sheet that is
completely filled, leaving almost no empty space.
These figures might have been drawn in a
moment of relaxation or they might be studies
made at various times during his stay. Whatever
the exact nature of this drawing, which remains
difficult to establish, it displays the artist's clear
interest in the Moroccan types who caught his
attention, as each of these figures evokes a specific individual. Except for the barely sketched
character seen from behind (second from left,
at top), these figures can be divided into three
distinct groups: three women studied in frontal
view (at upper right and just below, and at lower
left), four busts or heads of Arabs in burnooses,
in profile or full-face (in the right-hand part),
and finally two Arabs seated or semireclining.
The last two are extensively heightened in

watercolor, while the others are drawn in
Conté crayon and simply touched up with
wash in the heads and, in one case, the feet.

The three female figures can be related to
a passage in Delacroix's *Memoir of a Journey to
Morocco*. He first described some houses in the
fields, which "looked like fortresses without
windows and even without a door. The one
egress is always masked so carefully or made
so small that one would scarcely notice it: it
looks as though the owner himself would have
to break into his home." He then went on to
say: "The women in the streets are like those
houses. They are walking bundles: from beneath
the massive wrapping wound all around them,
all you can see are two eyes that help them
find their way and the tips of their fingers,
which they use to hold up a large piece of this
shroud to cover the rest of their face. This use
of the veil throughout the Orient—leaving
aside the fact that it makes the women look
slightly grotesque—does have something

rather intriguing about it. One is free to imagine that beneath those envelopes, these creatures are actually quite enticing, when they pass nearby with the one allure they have at their disposal, that dark and expressive glance that the heavens have given almost all of them."[2]

The other figures on this sheet, men in burnooses, are much less strongly typed and appear instead as simple silhouettes, as in many of Delacroix's drawings from this trip. It is another matter entirely for the two magnificent seated figures, on which the artist has merely applied a few touches of watercolor—white and black, blue, red, green, and brown—with great subtlety and remarkably fine brushwork. What makes them all the more singular on this sheet is that they are the only two that appear truly finished. Delacroix adopted a favored motif from his trip to Morocco, one that he would later reprise in the works in watercolor and oil that he executed after his return to France. Sketched when Delacroix was on the verge of leaving Morocco, works such as this one in the Bonna Collection act as a kind of final punctuation to his voyage of discovery, the consequences of which would mark his subsequent career profoundly.

BARTHÉLÉMY JOBERT

1. Delacroix to Auguste Jal, June 4, 1832, in Delacroix, *Letters*, 2001 (ed.), pp. 193–94.
2. Beaumont-Maillet, Jobert, and Join-Lambert 1999, pp. 124–25.

100. Ferdinand-Victor-Eugène Delacroix

Paris, 1798–Paris, 1863

Fuchsias in a Pot

1855

Watercolor over Conté crayon, 11¹³⁄₁₆ × 7½ in. (30 × 19 cm)

Inscribed in Conté crayon in the artist's hand at upper left: *le bout des pédoncules rouges*; in graphite at middle right: *vif*

PROVENANCE: François de Verninac, Delacroix's nephew; Verninac sale, Paris, December. 8, 1948, lot 11 (sold for 120,000 francs); Maurice Gobin, his collection stamp at lower right and on the mounting at lower left (Lugt 1124a); sale, Hôtel Drouot, Paris, March 31, 2000, lot 124; purchased at that sale by Jean Bonna

EXHIBITIONS: Paris 1963, no. 480; Paris 2006b, no. 68; Geneva 2006–7a

I witnessed Eugène Delacroix first try his hand at painting flowers. He had studied botany in his childhood, and his prodigious memory still retained it. But botany had not made much of an impact on him as an artist, and its meaning was revealed to him only when he set out attentively to reproduce the plant's form and color. I caught him in an ecstasy of delight in front of a yellow lily whose beautiful architecture—that was the word he used—had just revealed itself to him. He quickly set to painting it, seeing that at every moment his model, as it blossomed in the water, changed color and pose. He thought he had finished his painting, and the result was marvelous, but the next day, when he compared art to nature, he was dissatisfied and retouched it. The lily had completely changed. The lobes of the perianth had curved outward; the stamens had grown more pale; the color of the flower had grown more intense, its golden yellow having turned orange; the stem was stiffer and straighter; and the leaves, which had drawn in more tightly, seemed narrower. This too was a kind of harmony, but not the same. The following day, the plant was beautiful in still an entirely different way. It was becoming more and more *architectural*. The flower dried out and showed its inner organs more fully; its shapes became *geometrical*—that too was Delacroix's word. He saw the skeleton begin to emerge, and the beauty of this skeleton charmed him. We had to take the sheet away from him to keep him from turning it from a study of a plant in splendid full bloom into one of a plant that belonged in the herbarium."[1]

As always when she spoke of Delacroix, George Sand, in this text written toward the end of her life and after the painter's death, here rendered a living, intimate, and very revealing portrait, which helps provide a better understanding of the Bonna study of fuchsias. First, she indicated that Delacroix began studying and depicting flowers during one of his three stays at Nohant, which took place in the summers of 1842, 1843, and 1846. The purpose of those stays was to get him out of Paris and away from the arduous task of decorating the libraries of the Chambre des Députés and the Palais du Luxembourg. They also gave him the opportunity to paint for himself, as he confided to his friend Frédéric Villot in June 1842: "The strange thing is that I fled Paris to take a rest from working, and here I am back at work! The difference, though, is that here I can work on whatever I feel like, and there's shade so that I can take a rest and walk around, which you don't find in Paris."[2] At the time, he was painting *Education of the Virgin* for the church of Nohant, but it is entirely possible that he also became interested in flowers in this same period. Sand was a passionate botanist who maintained a garden and, as she mentioned, a herbarium. The painter's rental in 1844 of a country home in Champrosay on the edge of the Sénart forest (he purchased it in 1858) encouraged him to study nature, as did his extensive trips in the provinces and abroad beginning in the 1840s.[3] Although Paris remained his primary residence, Delacroix had often traveled outside the capital even in his youth, spending time in the forest of Boixe, where his mother owned property, or at his brother's in the Touraine, or with his relations

Figure 129. Ferdinand-Victor-Eugène Delacroix, *Bouquet of Flowers*. Oil on canvas. Musée Ingres, Montauban (inv. M.N.R. 162; D.51.3.2)

the Batailles or Bornots at the Valmont abbey in Normandy, or with his cousins the Rieseners in Frépillon, not far from the city. By the 1840s, Delacroix had even more opportunities for such trips, which fulfilled both his increasingly acute desire to get away from Paris and his need to take care of himself because of worsening health.

The drawings and paintings of flowers that Delacroix executed during that period—including the series of five great paintings from 1848–49, two of which were sent to the Salon of 1849 and the other three to the Exposition Universelle of 1855—illustrate the artist's return to still life, which he had more or less abandoned after the *Still Life with Lobster* of 1826–27.[4] According to his friend Frédéric Villot, who stayed in Champrosay in 1833,[5] Delacroix began painting several canvases (studies or full-scale works), which he left unfinished.[6] He later returned to the subject via studies from life, such as the present

drawing, in which he created a kind of basic vocabulary for himself. *Fuchsias in a Pot* is therefore analogous to *Study of Flowers with a Branch of Fuchsia* and *White Daisies and Zinnias* in the Louvre, which are usually dated 1849–55,[7] during the period when Delacroix was working on his great flower paintings, such as the *Bouquet of Flowers* in the Musée Ingres, Montauban (fig. 129). Those drawings are not so easy to date with precision, but the provenance of *Fuchsias in a Pot* in the Bonna collection nonetheless suggests that it was drawn fairly late, in September 1855, while Delacroix was staying with his cousins the Verninacs in the Périgord; in his *Journal* he noted that during his stay he drew several landscapes and spent time in the garden.[8] It is also possible that the fuchsias were drawn a bit earlier, in Nohant, Champrosay, or somewhere else. Like most of Delacroix's drawings, the present one was not exhibited in his lifetime. Very loosely rendered, retaining a certain measure of incompletion, it either remained in the artist's storage boxes or, more likely in this case, was given to a close friend or family member as a token of affection or friendship.

Here is the artist studying and appropriating these flowers, which he sketched in crayon before applying watercolor, following a practice that he commonly used even in the studio. In this way, they become not so much an artistic subject as an interplay of shapes and colors. A letter addressed to his friend the painter Constant Dutilleux gives a better grasp of this working method. Delacroix first commented on two old master paintings that Dutilleux had mentioned to him: "They show great talent; the brushwork is particularly remarkable; their only fault seems to be that which is common to almost all works of this sort, painted by specialists: the study of details, highly elaborated, somewhat detracts from the effect of the whole. Since the artist, in carrying out his work, proceeded not so much by broad local division of line and colors as by an extremely

careful rendering of the various parts, those objects which in the picture serve, as it were, as background to each of these too lovingly emphasized details, eventually fade out, and the consequent dispersal of interest rather spoils the general effect." He then added, in reference to his own work: "As it happens, I have been working in exactly the opposite way to the two works in question, and I have subordinated details to the whole as far as possible. I tried to get away from the convention that seems to condemn anyone who paints flowers to reproduce the same vase with the same columns of fantastic draperies to serve as background or provide contrast. I have tried to paint bits of nature as we see them in gardens, only assembling within the same frame and in a fairly probable manner the greatest possible variety of flowers."[9] It therefore seems impossible to consider *Fuchsias in a Pot* a preparatory study to a particular painting. More concerned with the overall impression produced by these flowers than with their details, Delacroix was working here without a defined goal, absorbing a portion of nature that he would later idealize in a more polished work.

BARTHÉLÉMY JOBERT

1. Sand, *Lettres*, 2005 (ed.), pp. 94–95.
2. Delacroix to Frédéric Villot, June 14, 1842, in Delacroix, *Correspondance*, 1936–38 (ed.), vol. 1 (1936), p. 110.
3. See the summary in Pomarède 1998.
4. On Delacroix's flower paintings and drawings, see most recently Margret Stuffmann in Karlsruhe 2003–4, pp. 81–85. For a political interpretation of the flower paintings from 1848–49, a discussion of which would exceed the limits of the present entry, see Clark 1982, pp. 124–41.
5. Note by Villot in the catalogue of his sale, February 11, 1865; cited in Johnson 1986, p. 258.
6. See Johnson 1986, pp. 258–60, nos. 492–97.
7. Inv. RF 3440; see the entry by Arlette Sérullaz in Paris and Philadelphia 1998–99, p. 137, no. 35.
8. For the trip to the Périgord, see Delacroix, *Journal*, 1981 (ed.), pp. 535–39.
9. Delacroix to Constant Dutilleux, February 6, 1849, in Delacroix, *Letters*, 2001 (ed.), p. 287.

101

101. Victor Hugo

Besançon, 1802–Paris, 1885

New Year's Card 1855

Pen and brown ink, brush and brown wash, gold paint,
Prussian blue and white gouache on wove paper,
3⁷⁄₁₆ × 7 ½ in. (8.8 × 19 cm)

Mounted on wove paper: 20 × 31 cm (sight)

Incorporated within the design: *Victor Hugo /
Jersey / 1855*

Initialed in pen and ink at lower right: *V.H.*

Inscribed in pen and brown ink on the mount: *A la
charmante fée de Saumaurez Cottage / Victor Hugo / 1er
janvier 1855*[1]

PROVENANCE: Private Collection; Librairie Jean-
Claude Vrain, Paris; acquired by Jean Bonna, 2006

EXHIBITION: Lausanne 2008, no. 39

Fearing reprisals on account of his vehe-
ment political views, Victor Hugo fled
France after Louis–Napoléon's coup d'état in
1851 and thereafter spent twenty years in mostly
voluntary exile. He traveled briefly through
Brussels and London, finally taking refuge on
the islands of the English Channel, first Jersey,
then Guernsey. He spent three years on Jersey,
from August 5, 1852, to October 31, 1855, on an
isolated property overlooking the sea at the
edge of the town of Saint-Hélier. His days
there were filled with swimming, gardening,
walking on the beach, and writing visionary
poetry. He also found time to smuggle off the
island hundreds of copies of his invective pam-
phlet *Napoléon-le-Petit* and to engage in the
latest craze imported from America, Table-
Turning or Spiritism, an after-dinner entertainment designed to conjure the dead.

Although daringly experimental drawings
frequently flowed from Hugo's pen alongside
his vast literary output, few were produced in
1852 and 1853, when he was engaged in intense
writing activity. The following year, he renewed
his practice of pictorial free association, enclos-
ing fantastic scribbles in letters to friends and
sending on New Year's Day his so-called visiting card, which often included, as this one
does, the letters of his name and the numerals
of the year entwined with ornamental motifs
or elements of a brooding landscape. In this
New Year's Card of 1855, the blocky letters of
the artist's name, interlaced with the ciphers
for "Jersey" and "1855," meander into trees, and
arch over a view of distant buildings bathed in
a chilly, blue mist, this bleak expanse recalling
the situation of his house, Marine Terrace,
near the windswept beach, Fort Elizabeth, and
an ancient breakwater.[2]

229

"Here, in winter," Hugo wrote from Jersey to Émile Deschanel, in December 1853, "Everything is somber, dark, violent, terrible, tempestuous, severe. The rain pours down my windowpane like a stream of silver; all nature plunges with frenzy into the tumult, and I have little to do but storm like the wind and roar like the sea."[3] Yet, a year later, in January 1855, when sending a New Year's greeting to the same addressee, Hugo revealed his eventual embrace of the vagaries of his outpost: "I am working almost night and day; I am sailing in a sea of poetry, I am faint with excess of light. . . . I have wedded the sea, the hurricane, a vast sandy shore, sadness, and the starry canopy of heaven."[4]

COLTA IVES

1. Although we were unable to identify with any certainty "la charmante fée," or "charming fairy," to whom Hugo dedicated this drawing, I wish to thank graduate assistant Esther Bell for her indefatigable efforts. Her correspondence with Alexandra Müller at the Maison de Victor Hugo in Paris prompted Hugo scholar Sheila Gaudon's suggestion that the New Year's card recipient might be Josephine Nicole, a good friend of the Hugo family, living in Jersey in 1855. The rare book dealer Jean-Claude Vrain thought the recipient might be Madame Paul Maurice.

2. Another visiting card that incorporates the words "Victor Hugo, Jersey, 1855" was included in the exhibition "Drawings by Victor Hugo," held at Victoria and Albert Museum, London (see London 1974, no. 28).

3. Hugo to Émile Deschanel, December 11, 1853, in Hugo, *Letters*, 1898/2002 (ed.), p. 122.

4. Hugo to Émile Deschanel, Marine Terrace, January 14, 1855; ibid., p. 130.

102. Jean-François Millet

Gruchy, 1814–Barbizon, 1875

The Well at Gruchy

After 1854

Black chalk, stumping, brown-gray wash, heightened in white chalk (fixed), traces of erasure (on the steps), framing line in black chalk on vellum with watermark (watermark truncated and not identified), 13 15/16 × 11 1/16 in. (35.4 × 28.1 cm)

Signed in black chalk at lower right: *J. F. Millet*

PROVENANCE: Probably Feral sale, Hôtel Drouot, Paris, March 12, 1874; Stephen Mitchell, Esq., Stirlingshire; sale, Christie's, London, November 24, 1933, lot 81; James Connell & Sons, Glasgow; Isabel K. Mitchell, Stirlingshire; sale, Christie's, New York, February 28, 1991, lot 62; Private Collection, New York; acquired by Jean Bonna, 2000

EXHIBITIONS: Paris 2006b, no. 79; Geneva 2006–7a

BIBLIOGRAPHY: Alexandra Murphy in Boston 1984, p. 80

In June 1854, Jean-François Millet left Barbizon to spend the summer at his native home in Gruchy, near Gréville in Normandy. In a letter to his brother written at the end of that summer, he reported having produced several painted studies and nearly sixty drawings: "I haven't been working as much as I'd wanted—not that I've deliberately wasted my time, but whether one likes it or not, it's tiring to work outdoors! . . . I've nonetheless begun several painted studies, and to date I've made about sixty drawings, which will help me recall what I've seen. They're mostly sketches, but the kind that will prove very useful once I'm back."[1]

The covered well adjoining a structure that served as a barn or stables, located opposite the Millet farm on the other side of the path, was one of the painter's favorite subjects during his stay. He made several sketches of this structure from direct observation, which can be dated from the summer of 1854,[2] as well as a series of finished drawings that are more difficult to date (between the fall of 1854 and 1865–66), which he made later in the studio at Barbizon, based on memory and a loose interpretation of those initial sketches. It is known from the artist's correspondence that, once back from Normandy, he asked Alfred Sensier to procure him enough drawing paper to cover his feverish inspiration (Sensier sent him thirty sheets):[3] "Tell no one I've returned [from Gruchy], so that I can have time to do some drawings. . . . / I began some painted studies, but mainly made a large number of sketches—about a hundred of them—all as memory prompts, as I said. All that time I was like a man having a nervous breakdown. With so much to do, I would have liked to do it all in half an hour, and I most bitterly regretted what I couldn't bring back with me."[4] The nostalgia for this stay in Normandy was still with him: "I feel like someone transplanted," he continued, and it shows through in the drawings from this series, even the ones made subsequently.

This drawing is among the more elaborate compositions that Millet created in the studio after his return. He executed numerous variants based on the subject of the well, either without human figures, as with the well in the snow, the framing of which is identical to that of the drawing in the Musée des Beaux-Arts, Lyon,[5] or with figures, as here. In the early 1860s, he reworked the subject to give a wider view of the buildings, notably in two virtually identical drawings now in the Museum of Fine Arts, Boston,[6] and the Musée Fabre, Montpellier.[7] The farm woman standing in front of the well, filling two copper jugs from a wooden bucket while geese mill around the farmyard, is a recurrent motif in Millet's work from the years 1850–60;[8] the most polished variations are the painting made in 1859 for Alfred Feydeau, one of the artist's main patrons,[9] and the pastel from 1866–68 originally in the Émile Gavet Collection, called *The Woman at the Well*.[10] Étienne Moreau-Nélaton thought to identify the young farm girl pouring water as a portrait of the artist's sister, Émélie, but beyond specifics, she is characteristic of the type of peasant woman

in Millet's drawings from the years 1850–60, at a midpoint between realism and bucolic idealization.

This scene of rural life reflects the artist's observation of nature (a 1914 photograph of the site shows just how precisely he rendered the well house, fig. 130) and also shows the influence of seventeenth-century Flemish and Dutch genre scenes, which Millet knew from engravings and which he took as inspiration, all the while laying claim to a naive realism: "You know the first drawing I made in the country, with no teacher, no model, no guide: it is still here in my studio, and since then I've never done anything different."[11]

The drawing in the Bonna collection is related to a painting attributed to Millet, formerly in the Constantin A. Ionides Collection and now at the Victoria and Albert Museum, London, which is of identical composition, apart from a few small variations of detail. Still, it should be considered that this is not so much a preparatory study as it is a handsome work of fairly large format, executed for a collector or for exhibition. In the 1850s and 1860s, when his standing at the salon was still tentative—his paintings were not always accepted and were sometimes the subject of controversy—Millet regularly sold drawings to collectors in France and abroad; the ones executed in black chalk were already gaining an appreciative audience. "We have a voracious appetite for your drawings,"[12] Campredon wrote in 1853, for instance, referring to Eugène Atget, Georges Beugniet, and himself. The present drawing, acquired in 1874 by the Scottish connoisseur Stephen Mitchell (1789–1874), a Glasgow tobacco merchant and the founder of the Mitchell Public Library, shows that foreign collectors also took an interest in Millet's drawings, even during the artist's lifetime.

MARIE-PIERRE SALÉ

Figure 130. *The Well House*, photograph taken in 1914, reproduced in Étienne Moreau-Nélaton, *Millet raconté par lui-même* (Paris, 1921), vol. 3, fig. 310

1. Jean-François Millet, signed handwritten letter, undated [1854], Gréville, Musée d'Orsay, Paris, in the Musée du Louvre, Département des Arts Graphiques, Paris, É. Moreau-Nélaton bequest, 1927 (bs. 12 l. 50); Moreau-Nélaton 1921, vol. 2, p. 15.
2. *Well of the Stables at Gruchy*, 1854, black chalk on beige wove paper, 9⅝ × 6⅛ in. (24.4 × 15.7 cm), Museum of Fine Arts, Boston, Edwin E. Jack Fund, 1961 (61.626); *Well of the Stables at Gruchy*, Conté crayon on paper, 17¼ × 12½ in. (43.8 × 31.8 cm), stamp of the studio sale at lower right (sale, Christie's, London, November 17, 1995, lot 96; prior sales, Hôtel Drouot, Paris, June 21, 1974, no. 52, and Versailles, April 18, 1982, no. 56).
3. Jean-François Millet to Alfred Sensier, signed handwritten letter, undated [September 27, 1854], Musée d'Orsay, Paris, in the Musée du Louvre, Département des Arts Graphiques, Paris, É. Moreau-Nélaton bequest, 1927 (bs. bl 12. l. 50); and Sensier to Millet, September 26, 1854, Paris, copy by Étienne Moreau-Nélaton from a signed and dated handwritten letter, Musée d'Orsay, Paris, in the Musée du Louvre, Département des Arts Graphiques, Paris, É. Moreau-Nélaton bequest, 1927 (AR 47), p. 60.
4. Jean-François Millet to Campredon, signed handwritten letter, undated [1854], in Moreau-Nélaton 1921, vol. 2, p. 16.
5. *The Well at Gruchy*, charcoal and pastel, Musée des Beaux-Arts, Lyon (inv. B1209); reproduced in Moreau-Nélaton 1921, vol. 3, fig. 257.
6. *House with a Well at Gruchy*, pastel over black chalk heightened with pen and ink on darkened cream wove paper, 12½ × 17 in. (31.8 × 43.2 cm), signed lower right, "J F. Millet," Museum of Fine Arts, Boston, gift of Quincy Adams Shaw through Quincy Adams Shaw, Jr., and Mrs. Marian Shaw Haughton, 1917 (17.1496).
7. Musée Fabre, Montpellier, Alfred Bruyas bequest, formerly Théodore Rousseau Collection, Conté crayon and pastel on paper, 14¾ × 18⅛ in. (37.5 × 46 cm).
8. There is notably a glass-plate negative from 1862, now in the Bibliothèque Nationale de France, Département des Estampes et de la Photographie, Paris, and several sketches, including the one at the Museum of Fine Arts, Boston (76.433), and the ones at the Musée d'Orsay, Paris (inv. RF 11226, RF 5697), as well as engravings. On this subject, see Moreau-Nélaton 1921, vol. 2, pp. 70, 78; Paris 1975–76, no. 175; and Boston 1984, nos. 94, 95.
9. Reproduced in Moreau-Nélaton 1921, vol. 2, pp. 70, 78.
10. Black chalk and pastel, 44 × 34.5 cm., Musée d'Orsay, Paris, Alfred Chauchard bequest, 1906 (inv. RF 3969); another version is owned by the Fukuoka Broadcasting Corporation, Fukuoka.
11. Remarks by Millet, undated, quoted in Sensier 1881, p. 40.
12. Campredon to Jean-François Millet, October 19, 1853, Paris, copy by Étienne Moreau-Nélaton from a signed and dated handwritten letter, Musée d'Orsay, Paris, in the Musée du Louvre, Département des Arts Graphiques, Paris, É. Moreau-Nélaton bequest, 1927 (AR 44), p. 9.

103

103. Jean-François Millet

Gruchy, 1814-Barbizon, 1875

Cottages near Vichy

Ca. 1866–68

Pen and brown ink, watercolor over graphite on laid paper, 7¼ × 9½ in. (18.1 × 24.1 cm)

Stamped in black ink at lower right: J.F.M. (Lugt 1460); stamped on verso: *Vente Millet* and inscribed in graphite: *No 10*; inscribed in pen and brown ink: *387*

PROVENANCE: Atelier Millet sale, Hôtel Drouot, Paris, May 10–11, 1875, lot unknown (probably between lots 70 and 102); private collection, Paris and Gers; sold, Hôtel des Ventes, Nice, April 8, 2006; Sayn-Wittgenstein Fine Art, New York; acquired by Jean Bonna, 2006

Although Jean-François Millet is better known for the peasants he pictured than he is for the landscapes in which they figure, his devotion to the beauty of the French countryside is evident in the meadows, streams, and shaded glades he depicted. The artist strove to glorify the good people who labored day after day in fields and farms, but the quiet dignity he meant them to impart often eludes us, and they may stand strangely lifeless in the midst of more alluring scenery.

It was only well on in Millet's career that features of the landscape began to displace those of human figures in his art, a shift in focus stimulated by periodic travel in the regions of Vichy and the Auvergne. On account of his wife's illness, he and she spent a month every summer during the three years 1866–68, taking the curative waters at Vichy. Those excursions produced an abundance of penciled, penned, and watercolored sketches, some in little notebooks, others on larger notepads, all in appreciative response to the shapes and textures of newly discovered terrain.

In letters to his nine children and their guardians back home in the village of Barbizon,

233

Millet sometimes complained that he had little time to draw on account of the weather, or the spa's too-rigid regimen. But, in the most productive of his summers, 1866, he wrote that he had done eighty sketches, many of which would serve as models for later pastels and paintings.

Perhaps because of the confining schedule at Vichy, Millet developed there a rapid, free-hand scrawl that captured the freshness of scenery he observed on walks and carriage rides. To his lively sketches (so admirably composed they could be studio works long in preparation), he often added, probably back in his rooms, a rich array of watercolor greens and browns.

One may discern in drawings such as this strands of the enthusiasms Millet shared with his friends and fellow painters Théodore Rousseau and Narcisse Diaz, who admired the graphic shorthand of Renaissance artists of the Danube school, the intense realism of the old Dutch landscape masters, and the brilliant simplicity of Japanese color woodcut prints.[1] In turn, Millet's energetic and heartfelt appraisals of humble nesting grounds like this became the stuff that Van Gogh admired.

COLTA IVES

1. Millet had begun collecting Japanese prints by 1863.

104. Théodore Chassériau

Sainte Barbe de Samana (Santo Domingo), 1819–Paris, 1856

Portrait of Berthe de Prailly as a Child, Bust in Three-Quarter View

1841

Graphite and stumping, 5⅜ × 4⁹⁄₁₆ in. (13.6 × 11.6 cm)

Signed in graphite at upper left: *Th. Chassériau*

PROVENANCE: Remained in the sitter's family until 1991; Galerie de Bayser, Paris; acquired by Jean Bonna, 1999

EXHIBITIONS: Paris, Strasbourg, and New York 2002–3, no. 50; Paris 2006b, no. 70; Geneva 2006–7a

BIBLIOGRAPHY: Sandoz 1974, p. 36, fig. 10; Sandoz 1986, no. 234A, ill. (erroneously as no. 233); Prat 1988, p. 17, no. 73; Prat 1996, pp. 575, 579, n. 11; Prat 2003, p. 123

portraitist's art, according to Chassériau's style and method.

The portrait of little Berthe certainly bespeaks obligations of friendship, or perhaps, as will be seen, of ambition. The child's mother, Hortense Chevandier de Valdrome, was, as Léonce Bénédite tells us, "the sister of Chassériau's close friend Paul Chevandier. In 1834, she had married the Baron [*sic*] de Prailly, president of the civil court of Nancy. She maintained a long correspondence with [the prominent theologian] Père Lacordaire that lasted several years."[1] It is known that this couple and their daughter Berthe were in Rome in 1840, the year Chassériau left for Italy in the company of Henri Lehmann, "one of Ingres's most orthodox students."[2] One unexpected outcome of this Italian excursion was the end of Chassériau's friendship with the painter Paul Chevandier de Valdrome (1817–1877).[3] It is not known how these two artists met, but their friendship is documented

Seated in an armchair, or perhaps a simple wooden chair, the back of which Théodore Chassériau quickly sketched, little Berthe de Prailly, the future wife of the comte de Guichen, looks the viewer straight in the eye. One does not know whether to smile at the beauty of this innocent little girl or to melt in admiration for a model who embodies what is surely the ne plus ultra of children's portraits and of innocence as fantasized by adults. In order to arrive at this brilliant result, Chassériau first accentuated the softness of the child's face by playing on the contrast between the white paper and the graphite, which can be either tender (Ingres-like might be more accurate) or frenetic. The repeated strokes that define the volumes of the dress, the shadows in the background, and that strange, intentionally unfinished hand, in addition to the tight cropping, all contribute toward making this drawing the quintessence of the

Figure 131. Théodore Chassériau, *Portrait of the Countess de Prailly and her Daughter Berthe.* Graphite. Private Collection

Figure 132. Théodore Chassériau, *Bust Portrait of Berthe de Prailly as a Child.* Graphite on blue paper. Private Collection

104

by 1838 at the latest, when Chevandier met Théophile Gautier in Chassériau's studio.[4] That same year, they were close enough that Chevandier, already in Rome, could confide in Chassériau about his emotional trials: "You tell me of your sorrows, my poor friend, and I too have suffered cruelly, so cruelly that it has dried out my heart."[5]

From the time Chassériau and Lehmann arrived in Rome, in early July 1840, Chevandier joined the two students of Ingres, and in mid-July, all three left for Naples. Lehmann sent Marie d'Agoult an account of his journey with Chassériau, calling him "an immense genius, I believe. His noble and unorthodox understanding of the slightest event, gesture, object, and generally of all things in life, makes this clear to me. I have faith in him as a man and as a painter."[6] The ensuing events would prove extremely cruel for the true believer. As Lehmann later told it, Chassériau stole from

him the idea that he had been nurturing since deciding to go to Rome: to have the honor of portraying the very famous, and at the time highly visible, Père Lacordaire. And indeed, as soon as Chassériau returned to Rome in early September, he used his privileged relations with Chevandier and his sister Hortense to arrange a meeting with Lacordaire and convince the theologian to let *him* paint his portrait, which Lacordaire accepted on September 8.[7] The very next day, Chassériau told his brother that he would soon be back in Paris. Everything therefore went very quickly, perhaps too quickly. It is probably no coincidence that in the several days preceding his departure from Rome, Chassériau also made sure to execute a magnificent portrait of the Countess Hortense de Prailly and her daughter Berthe, signed, dated, and dedicated "to Monsieur / Are Chevandier / T. Chasseriau / Rome 1841" (fig. 131). Louis-Antoine Prat, who recently discovered the

work, has provided this description: "The seductive thing about this drawing . . . is both the beauty of its composition and its extraordinary elegance of line, which in no way undermines the realism of the portrayal. The interplay of the mother's hands with those of the little girl, as they cover and overlap each other, is reminiscent of Ingres's boldest visual inventions. . . . Contrasting with the frail young mother's pensive, slightly stiff face and its border of braids is the open expression on little Berthe de Prailly, who must have particularly attracted the artist since he made two other portraits of her in graphite, both in private collections."[8]

In one of these, the special attention Chassériau devoted to little Berthe (fig. 132), with her disconcerting and tender innocence, might well be interpreted as an attempt to seduce the girl's mother, and perhaps even more so, her grandfather, Hortense's father,

Anatole Chevandier. In 1839, the dedicatee of the drawing had recommended that the Ministry of the Interior purchase *Susanna at Her Bath* (*Suzanne au bain*), an ambitious and monumental canvas that Chassériau had exhibited at the salon that same year.[9] Ultimately, Berthe's shining innocence cannot make up for the execrable reputation Chassériau gained during his time in Rome. His relationship with Hortense de Prailly, again according to Lehmann, bordered on the inappropriate, and the countess "continued to receive M. C[hassériau]" merely for her brother's sake.[10] As it happens, Chassériau had a falling out with the Chevandier family not long afterward, on April 23 and September 27, 1841.[11]

If placed in the context of his Roman sojourn, then, it is curious to note that the Bonna drawing, however sweet it may appear, has behind its creation an infinitely "Chassériesque" episode, or rather, a strange alchemy that combines a fabulous sensuality of line with extremely dubious intentions on the part of an "immense" young artist of twenty-one.

BRUNO CHENIQUE

1. Bénédite 1931, vol. 1, p. 155.
2. Prat 2003, p. 117.
3. On this artist, see Foucart-Walter 1991.
4. Gautier, *Correspondance*, 1991 (ed.), p. 175.
5. Paul Chevandier to Théodore Chassériau, November 25, 1838, Rome, quoted in Bénédite 1931, vol. 1, p. 93. The "cruel" individual responsible for Chassériau's own heartache was Clémence Monnerot, the future wife of Arthur de Gobineau (Bénédite 1931, vol. 1, p. 101); see Chenique 2002, p. 174, col. 3.
6. Henri Lehmann to Marie d'Agoult, undated [August 19, 1840, Naples], Comte Hauteclocque archives, from a transcription kindly provided by Ch.-F. Dupêchez; see also Joubert 1947, p. 113; and Chenique 2002, p. 179, col. 1.
7. Chenique 2002, p. 179, col. 2.
8. Prat 1996, p. 575.
9. Chenique 2002, p. 175, col. 2.
10. Henri Lehmann to Marie d'Agoult, Rome, March 2, 1841, Comte Hauteclocque archives, from a transcription kindly provided by Ch.-F. Dupêchez; see also Joubert 1947, p. 153, who dates the letter March 11; and Chenique 2002, p. 180, col. 3, p. 181, col. 1.
11. Chenique 2002, p. 182, col. 2, p. 183, col. 2.

105. Édouard Manet

Paris, 1832–Paris, 1883

Madame Loubens

1878–82

Pastel on canvas, 17½ × 21¹/₁₆ in. (44.5 × 53.5 cm)

Signed at lower right: *E. Manet*

PROVENANCE: Édouard Manet studio, stamp of the studio at lower right: *E. M.* (Lugt 880); Madame Édouard Manet (1830–1906), née Suzanne Leenhoff, Paris; Mrs. Thomas Alexander Scott, née Anna Dyke Riddle, Philadelphia, acquired December 10, 1883; Mrs. Thomas Alexander Scott (d. 1901); her daughter Mrs. Mary D. Scott (d. 1905); her son Clement B. Newbolt Jr.; his wife, Anna Newbolt; Private Collection; Wildenstein and Company, New York; acquired by Jean Bonna, 2003

EXHIBITIONS: Paris 1884, no. 135; Philadelphia 1905, no. 362; Paris 2006b, no. 81; Geneva 2006–7a

BIBLIOGRAPHY: Duret 1902, no. 14; Duret 1919, no. 14; Duret 1926, p. 287, no. 14; Moreau-Nélaton 1926, vol. 2, p. 64, fig. 271; Tabarant 1931, p. 473, no. 36; Jamot and G. Wildenstein 1932, vol. 1, p. 172, no. 436, ill., vol. 2, p. 215, fig. 453; Tabarant 1947, p. 398; Rouart and Orienti 1970, p. 114, no. 337; Rouart and D. Wildenstein 1975, vol. 2, p. 16, no. 40; Philadelphia 1985, pp. 15, 30, n. 87; B. E. White 1996, ill. p. 41

The Loubenses were close family friends of the Manets. Madame Loubens had already posed once for Édouard Manet in the inaugural masterpiece of New Painting, *Music in the Tuileries Gardens* (1862), now at the National Gallery, London. She can be seen in the left foreground, seated next to Madame Lejosne. In addition to the pastel in the Bonna Collection,[1] there is a second pastel of her by Manet, which Manet's widow gave the sitter after the artist's death.[2] Edgar Degas, who had met Madame Loubens through the Manets, also painted her portrait, posing her with Madame Lisle.[3] Before the painting, he made a drawn sketch (this and the painting are in the Art Institute of Chicago) and a preparatory study in pastel and charcoal, now in The Metropolitan Museum of Art (fig. 133).[4]

Although pastel was enjoying a resurgence of favor in Impressionist circles, Manet did not take it up for the first time until 1874, in *Madame Manet on a Blue Sofa*, now in the Musée d'Orsay, Paris. He began using pastel more frequently at the end of the 1870s, a choice that Théodore Duret ascribed to the fact that the painter, already weakened by illness, found the technique less tiring: "Pastel allowed him to indulge in relatively easy work, which he enjoyed because it offered the pleasant company of the women posing for him."[5]

Figure 133. Hilaire-Germain-Edgar Degas, *Portrait of Madame Loubens*. Charcoal and pastel, with touches of red and black chalk on beige paper. The Metropolitan Museum of Art, New York, Rogers Fund, 1918 (19.51.4)

Indeed, the present pastel should be included in the series of female portraits that Manet realized between 1878 and 1882, some of which were exhibited at the gallery of the newspaper

105

La Vie moderne in April 1880, an indication of how important the artist now considered the technique. Perhaps Manet hoped that these lighter works would win him popular success, but that still eluded him. These portraits of sophisticated "Parisian Women," dominated by the likenesses of *Irma Brunner* of about 1880, now in the Musée d'Orsay, and *Méry Laurent*, whom he portrayed in pastel seven times, were the pretext for brilliant formal exercises. The painter used these models as an excuse to intensify the freshness and smoothness of this precious technique. The kind of psychological exploration evident in Degas's use of the

medium for the most part was completely foreign to Manet's approach.

While a perfect example of the artist's seductive pastel portraits, *Madame Loubens* also subtly stands apart from them. The context of its creation reveals the iconographic and psychological key to the work; at its origin is the model's unstable health. Étienne Moreau-Nélaton alludes to this relation between illness and the portrait in his monograph on Manet: "A lady friend who had been confined by illness summoned the artist to her bedside: Madame Loubens shines forth in a symphony of whites."[6] On a more dramatic note, Adolphe Tabarant

added: "Episode of serious illness nearly carried off this old friend of the Manets."[7] For this pastel, then, Manet left his studio and had his friend pose in bed, in the comfort of her convalescent garments. The artist transcended the slightly forced intimacy of the scene with the nervousness of his pastel strokes and some splendid gradations of whites mixed with blues and grays, one of the painter's favorite chromatic variations. The work's intimate and refined character, moreover, is not entirely foreign to the spirit of eighteenth-century pastel portraits of women; a slight retro aura hovers over the present drawing. The position of the woman's hand on her face echoes that in Manet's other pastel of the same model as well as the two portraits of Marguerite de Conflans (now in the Smith College Museum of Art, Northampton, Massachusetts, and the Oscar Reinhart Collection, Winterthur).[8] But in light of the circumstances, what is retained most is the slightly distant languor of the pose and of the pastel strokes. This bittersweet note establishes a dialogue between Manet and Degas, with respect to the same model (see fig. 133), concerning the unvarnished transcription of the truth about individuals and their

emotions. *Madame Loubens* thus demonstrates a rare aspect of Manet as pastel artist and portraitist in which the elegance of an affectionate tribute conceals the anxiety of a painful memory.

Finally, it should be noted that *Madame Loubens* was among the first of Manet's works to enter an American collection; on the advice of her cousin Mary Cassatt, Anna Riddle Scott bought it directly from Manet's widow in December 1883.

LAURENCE DES CARS

1. Archives, Lochard photograph no. 153 (January 1884); Étienne Moreau-Nélaton, unpublished catalogue of Manet's works, n.d. [1906], no. 376, manuscript conserved in the Bibliothèque Nationale de France, Département des Estampes et de la Photographie, Paris.
2. Rouart and D. Wildenstein 1975, vol. 2, no. 41.
3. Executed between 1869 and 1872; Lemoisne 1946–49, vol. 1, no. 265.
4. Lemoisne 1946–49, vol. 1, no. 267.
5. Duret 1926, p. 175.
6. Moreau-Nélaton 1926, vol. 2, p. 64.
7. Tabarant 1947, p. 398.
8. Rouart and D. Wildenstein 1975, vol. 1, nos. 203, 204.

106. Sir Edward Burne-Jones

Birmingham, 1833–London, 1898

Study for Minerva in The Call of Perseus

Ca. 1885

Black and white chalk on brown paper, 17¹¹⁄₁₆ × 9¼ in. (45 × 23.5 cm)

Inscribed at lower right: *EBJ / to / AG*

PROVENANCE: Given by the artist to Helen Mary (or Ann) Gaskell; thence by descent to Mrs. Robert Beloe, 1975; sale, Sotheby's London, July 10, 1995, lot 105; purchased at that sale by Jean Bonna

EXHIBITIONS: London, Southampton, and Birmingham 1975–76, no. 160; Geneva 2006–7a

Sir Edward Burne-Jones made this delicate nude study in chalks in preparation for *The Call of Perseus* (fig. 134), a late oil painting now in the Staatsgalerie, Stuttgart. The latter belongs to one of the artist's most important cycles, commissioned in 1875 by the conservative politician Arthur James Balfour, for his London drawing room. Allowed to determine the subject matter, Burne-Jones chose the adventures of the classical hero Perseus, deriving the series from *The Earthly Paradise*, a narrative poem by his friend William Morris.[1] The artist worked on the cycle for more than twenty years and produced many drawings in the process.[2] The Bonna nude study is one of the finest, demonstrating the subtle mastery of the artist's mature draftsmanship and recording his altered conception of the goddess Minerva in the final version of the composition.

Figure 134. Edward Burne-Jones, *The Call of Perseus*, begun late 1880s. Oil on canvas. Staatsgalerie, Stuttgart (inv. 3103)

Figure 135. Edward Burne-Jones, *The Call of Perseus*, 1877. Gouache. Southampton City Art Gallery, England (inv. 100)

Shortly after receiving the commission for the *Perseus Cycle*, Burne-Jones established its basic components in watercolor.[3] Between 1877 and 1885, he went on to paint a set of gouache cartoons, now at the Southampton City Art Gallery, England.[4] In the gouache version of *The Call of Perseus* (fig. 135), the goddess wears classical armor and heavy draperies, revealing

careful study of the Elgin marbles and admiration for the Phidian ideal. At the time of the artist's death in 1898, the final oil version of the composition (fig. 134) remained unfinished in his studio.[5] Even in this state, it is clear that Burne-Jones intended to transform Minerva from a solid and imposing physical presence to an ethereal, otherworldly being. The Bonna

Figure 136. Edward Burne-Jones, *Study for Minerva (Athena) in* The Call of Perseus, 1876–77. Graphite. The Fitzwilliam Museum, Cambridge (inv. 2012)

Study for Minerva records how he carefully adjusted the goddess's pose and physique in order to transform her appearance and interaction with Perseus.

The alterations made to Minerva stand out when one compares the Bonna drawing to an earlier nude study for the goddess in the Fitzwilliam Museum, Cambridge (fig. 136).[6] In that work of 1876 or 1877, the model's physique is robust, with broad hips and full breasts, and her head tilts forward over her outstretched arm. These elements support the goddess's heavily armored form in the gouache and establish her divine dominance over the hero. When Burne-Jones began to rework *The Call of Perseus* in oil, sometime after 1885, he brought Minerva and Perseus closer in scale, and the Bonna study demonstrates how he adjusted the goddess's appearance to that end. Choosing a slimmer, smaller-breasted model, he turned her torso toward the viewer, straightened her spine, and raised her head, to create a space between chin and shoulder. When incorporated into the Stuttgart oil, these changes made Minerva less imposing. Although still taller than Perseus, she now is closer to him in mass, a transformation aided by substituting close-fitting garments, and a gauze skirt for the heavy breastplate and drapery. At this final stage, Burne-Jones was willing to depart from details of Morris's text, faithfully incorporated into earlier versions of the composition.[7] The shift accords with his aesthetic development in the late 1880s away from classicism toward a Symbolist approach to form.

Technically, Bonna's *Study for Minerva* displays a masterful handling of black and white chalks against the brown middle tone of the paper, with volume expressed through subtle shifts of light and shadow. This was a skill hard-won, considering Burne-Jones's lack of academic training. He had abandoned divinity studies at Oxford in 1855, shortly before taking his final exams, to become a follower of Dante Gabriel Rossetti.[8] Only in the 1860s, urged by his friend George Frederick Watts, did Burne-Jones adopt a rigorous regime of sketching

from the nude and classical sculpture.[9] This practice eventually produced a level of graphic skill as fine as any artist of his generation and, by the 1880s, his long-held admiration for Michelangelo was evident in chalk drawings of elongated, spiritualized nudes.[10] *Study for Minerva* belongs to this group and demonstrates a natural propensity for expressive line, applied to the goddess's elegant form.

Constance C. McPhee

1. Burne-Jones 1904, vol. 2, p. 60; Balfour 1930, p. 233. Balfour's house, at 4 Carlton Gardens, near the end of Carlton Terrace, no longer stands. Morris wrote *The Earthly Paradise* in 1865, in which the Perseus legend is retold in "The Doom of King Acrisius." He asked Burne-Jones to design woodcut illustrations for the text, but technical problems kept them from the 1868–70 publication (New York, Birmingham, and Paris 1998–99a, p. 116; and Wood 1998, p. 45).
2. Many are in the Birmingham City Museum and the Fitzwilliam Museum, Cambridge (Löchner 1973, pp. 98–108; Nantes, Charleroi, and Nancy 1992, pp. 115–16; and Birmingham 2007, pp. 56, 77).
3. The watercolors are in Tate Britain, London (Harrison and Waters 1973, p. 119; New York, Birmingham, and Paris 1998–99a, p. 222).
4. Burne-Jones displayed the set framed in his studio (New York, Birmingham, and Paris 1998–99a, p. 222; New York, Birmingham, and Paris 1998–99b, nos. 1–10).
5. After Balfour, the oils went as a group to the Huntington Hartford Collection, New York, then the Staatsgalerie, Stuttgart (Löchner 1973, pp. 98–108, figs. 7–14; New York, Birmingham, and Paris 1998–99a, p. 222).
6. Nantes, Charleroi, and Nancy 1992, pp. 115, 164, no. 99.
7. Morris's text is quoted in Löchner 1973, pp. 42–43.
8. Burne-Jones attended classes at several London art schools, but Rossetti's suspicion of academic structure kept his early studies to a minimum; see Wood 1998, p. 20.
9. Burne-Jones 1904, vol. 1, p. 260, vol. 2, p. 294; Robertson 1931, p. 84; Harrison and Waters 1973, pp. 41–42; Toronto 2000, p. 77.
10. New York, Birmingham, and Paris 1998–99a, pp. 153–55.

107. James McNeill Whistler

Lowell, Massachusetts, 1834–London, 1903

Variations in Violet and Rose

1885–86

Pastel and charcoal on brown paper, laid down on card, 10¼ × 7 in. (26 × 17.8 cm)

Signed: the artist's butterfly monogram

PROVENANCE: The artist to H. Wunderlich & Co., New York, 1888; Mr. and Mrs. H. O. Havemeyer, 1889; by descent to Electra Havemeyer Webb, 1929; her gift to the Shelburne Museum, Vermont, 1960; sale, Sotheby's, New York, December 5, 1996, lot 9; purchased at that sale by Jean Bonna

EXHIBITIONS: London 1886, no. 21 (*Variations in Violet and Rose*); New York 1889, no. 46 (*Pink and Violet*); Boston 1904, no. 124 (*The Greek Slave Girl*); New York 1961; Geneva 2006–7a

BIBLIOGRAPHY: Kay 1886, p. 2; *New York Herald*, March 2, 1889; *Havemeyer Collection* 1931, p. 438; Havemeyer 1961/1993, p. 331, n. 290; Muller 1976, p. 138, fig. 315; Weitzenhoffer 1986, pp. 55, 159, fig. 13; MacDonald 1995, p. 402, no. 1079, ill.

James McNeill Whistler drew lightly draped female models throughout his career but never to finer effect than in *Variations in Violet and Rose*. The work dates to 1885 or 1886 and

belongs to a series of classically inspired pastels made after the artist returned to London in 1880, after a fourteen-month sojourn in Venice. In Italy, he had experimented freely with brilliant pastels on brown paper and had created landscapes that responded to the changing elements of sky, water, and reflected light.[1] When exhibited at the Fine Art Society in 1881, these drawings elicited critical acclaim and found ready buyers.[2] It is not surprising that Whistler soon focused his newfound affinity for color on another favorite subject, the female form. Retaining the basic dynamic of pastels on brown paper, he now selected lighter shades and abandoned the subdued tonality he had employed in previous decades.[3] The titles Whistler chose for *Variations in Violet and Rose*, and a series of related works of the 1880s, emphasize both the centrality of color and their non-narrative character.[4]

In *Variations in Violet and Rose*, Whistler used color in an abstract manner comparable to music, the sister art evoked by its title.[5]

After defining the model's form with black chalk lines, he laid down areas of tone. Medium pink mixed with white was used for the draped robe and the model's cap, turquoise blue for the hanging underdrape and robe covering the left thigh, and violet over pale orange for the bands across the breasts. The flesh of the arms is mainly pale pink, and the neck and face are a light yellow. White strengthens the cascade of drapery next to the right leg and enlivens the background. Whistler then added numerous unblended touches: pale orange on the arms, plum on the left hand, pink, blue and white across the cheek, and brown and orange to define the hair and features. Notes of purple and turquoise enliven the space around the upper body and are set against the warm brown of the paper (which has darkened over time). The effect is one of singing color.

The drawing is not entirely devoid of traditional subject, however, since the model wears attire recognizably inspired by the antique: a short-sleeved gown with bands crossed over

Figure 137. Terracotta statuette of a standing woman, Greek, probably Boeotian, late 4th–early 3rd century B.C. The Metropolitan Museum of Art, New York, Rogers Fund, 1909 (09.221.28)

the breasts and a cap, or head-wrap. In her left hand, she holds a sketchily indicated palm-shaped fan. These elements evoke an ancient setting so effectively that the drawing's first owners, Mr. and Mrs. H. O. Havemeyer, called it *The Greek Slave Girl* when they lent it to the Whistler memorial exhibition in Boston in 1904.

By the 1880s, Whistler's focus on *Japonisme* had abated, and he again was looking carefully at classical sources. Most important to *Variations in Violet and Rose* are those small-

scale Hellenistic molded terracotta known as tanagra figurines (after an important discovery site in Boeotia), which the artist had studied since the 1860s.[6] Many of the finest examples depict standing women wrapped in flowing robes, naturalistically posed, often painted in pastel shades (fig. 137). As miniature variations of the late classical style associated with the sculptor Praxiteles, they translated monumental marble into a living vernacular. The figurines began to enter the British Museum by the 1850s, and a number were collected by Whistler's friends, the Ionides family, who displayed them in their Holland Park mansion.[7] *Variations in Violet and Rose* exhibits an informal classicism characteristic of tanagras, and its tonality pays tribute to theirs.[8]

In his famous "Ten O'Clock" lecture of 1885, delivered close to the time that he drew *Variations in Violet and Rose*, Whistler declared Praxitelean sculpture to be the first great achievement of "Art" and evoked that "sunny morning, when [Art], with her glorious Greek relenting . . . yielded up the secret of repeated line, as, with his hand in hers, together they marked, in marble, the measured rhyme of lovely limb and draperies flowing in unison."[9] The artist's brightly hued pastels of the mid-1880s take delight in describing flesh and limb simultaneously echoed and revealed by translucent fabric. Wrought with repeated bright touches over black chalk, these drawings use color to embody measured rhyme.

CONSTANCE C. MCPHEE

1. MacDonald 2001, pp. 36–63; Myers 2003, pp. 49–55.
2. MacDonald 2001, pp. 99–110; Kenneth Myers (2003, p. 50) says Whistler called these pastels "totaly [*sic*] new and of a brilliancy very different from the customary watercolor."
3. Up to 1880, Whistler generally used black and white chalks on brown paper for figure studies, except for color drawings for the "Six Projects," unrealized murals begun in 1867. His colored pastels of the 1880s are distinct as finished works intended for exhibition and sale.
4. See MacDonald 1995, nos. 1070, 1074, 1076, 1078, 1080–1, all either sold directly to collectors or exhibited in London at the Dowdeswell Galleries (May 1886) or the Society of British Artists (Winter Exhibition, 1885–86 and 1886–87).
5. Whistler's title for his 1886 Dowdeswell exhibition, "'Notes'–'Harmonies'–'Nocturnes,'" used musical terms as did the titles of many works shown.
6. Washington 1984, p. 108; Richard Dorment (in London, Paris, and Washington 1994–95, p. 92) notes that by the late sixties Whistler was studying both tanagras and the Elgin marbles in the British Museum.
7. Dakers 1999, p. 111, mentions Alexander Ionides displayed his tanagras in the antiquities room at no. 1 Holland Park, in "a temple-like cabinet . . . [of] ebony with gilded recesses," designed by Walter Crane. While a student in Paris, Whistler met Alexander's sons, Luke and Alecco, and later became close to the whole family in London. He created a photograph album of the Ionides's tanagras that is now in the University of Glasgow; see Washington 1984, pp. 49, 108.
8. David Park Curry (in Washington 1984, p. 49) suggests the flaking paint of ancient tanagras may have influenced Whistler's pastel technique.
9. Whistler 1888/1908, p. 28; quoted in MacDonald 1995, no. 1078.

108. Hilaire-Germain-Edgar Degas

Paris, 1834–Paris, 1917

A Woman in Abruzzese Costume

Ca. 1856–57

Graphite on paper, 13⁹⁄₁₆ × 8⁹⁄₁₆ in. (34.4 × 21.7 cm)

Inscribed in graphite at upper right: *Abruzzes / turban mêlé de / verts jaune rouge / jupe vert émeraude / pardessus velours grenat*

Degas studio sale stamp at lower left: Lugt 658

PROVENANCE: Estate of the artist; sale (Degas Atelier Sale IV), Galerie Georges Petit, Paris, July 2–4, 1919, lot

68a, ill. p. 64; Joseph Durand-Ruel, Paris; sale, Sotheby's, London, June 22, 1993, lot 1; Galerie Jan Krugier, Geneva; acquired by Jean Bonna, 1999

EXHIBITIONS: Paris 1955, no. 12; Paris 1960, no. 18; New York 1994a, ill. p. 7; Zurich and Tübingen 1994–95, no. 22; Berlin, Venice, Madrid, and Geneva 1999–2000, no. 101 (Berlin), no. 117 (Venice); Paris 2006b, no. 82; Geneva 2006–7a

Ah! Comme le doute et l'incertitude me fatiguent!" (Ah! How doubt and uncertainty tire me!)[1] This annotation by Hilaire-Germain-Edgar Degas was emphatically scribbled at the top of a page of a notebook he used during his visit to Italy between 1856 and 1859. Self-doubt and exasperation—frequently on more than just an artistic level—periodically assailed him during his sojourn, and yet this

Degas

Figure 138. Hilaire-Germain-Edgar Degas, *Woman of Mola Gaeta*. Graphite. Private Collection

remarkably assured drawing clearly proclaims his confidence as a draftsman.

On the same page where he wrote the somewhat despondent comment cited above, Degas also drew a faint sketch of the head of an Italian woman in profile and a more highly worked study in watercolor of a seated woman in a brightly colored costume. These are among a number of similarly rapidly executed sketches of Italian women that he made in his notebooks throughout the period[2] and occasionally produced as independent watercolor studies.[3]

By the time Degas began to explore what has been called the "folklore genre"[4] at the end of the 1850s, the subject was commonplace and had been taken up notably by successive generations of French painters in the nineteenth century. His interest in such picturesque motifs was ultimately short-lived, yet he conducted his research into various Italian regional types and costume with characteristic thoroughness. In common with other nineteenth-century artists,[5] Degas was struck by the timeless features of the people, who seemed so familiar to any student of the masters of the Italian Renaissance. In Perugia, he wrote, it was as if the women had walked directly out of a

painting by Perugino, and he wondered, "Is this an illusion?"[6]

This beautiful, heavy-lidded woman in Abruzzese costume is among Degas's most consciously studied drawings of regional types. Leaning on a plinth or pedestal, her hand on her hip and foot poised on its base, the model looks away with a stare that is both melancholic and defiant. In this, she recalls some of Degas's other female sitters at this time, notably his sisters, Thérèse and Marguérite, and his young Bellelli nieces in Florence.

Although it has been suggested on the basis of the inscription that Degas may have made this drawing during an unrecorded visit to the Abruzzo,[7] a mountainous region northeast of Rome, it is more likely that he drew it in the more formal surroundings of his studio in the capital. Rare were those who, like Berlioz in 1830, actively sought out this remote region, much less allowed their "poetic impressions"[8] of the place to fuel their art. This hypothesis is supported by the relatively formal nature of the model's pose and by the fact that a similar pencil drawing of a woman from Mola Gaeta (fig. 138), with which this drawing was paired at Degas's posthumous sale in 1919,[9] was inscribed by the artist as having been drawn in Rome, although the latter should be treated with caution, since Degas applied the inscription at a much later date, as a general reminder that the drawing was executed in Italy at some point between 1856 and 1858.[10]

Toward the end of his stay in Italy, in the summer of 1858, Degas wrote in one of his carnets that he had begun to tire of the *mode éternelle* for scenes of picturesque Italian country people,[11] and his ambivalence toward the folkloric genre is already apparent in this drawing. On one level, he reveals himself as a worthy successor of Ingres by the attention he devoted to rendering the embroidery of the bodice, decorations of the sleeves, loosely draped necklace, and fringed headdress on the illuminated left-hand side of the woman's body, although his interest in this decorative detail appears comparatively halfhearted and is not sustained as far as her right side, which slips into the broad hatching of the shadow. Undoubtedly, much of the seriousness of this study derives from the absence of color, without which Degas evoked the vivid contrasts of pomegranate reds, yellow, and greens in a few hastily

inscribed notes at the top right corner of the drawing. Such complementary visual and verbal *riccordi* are found extensively elsewhere in the notebooks he used during this period (and indeed elsewhere in his oeuvre), as Degas felt compelled to supplement a drawn description with ideas for compositions and subject matter, vital additional information on pictures, people, and places seen, and details of colors and meteorological effects and natural phenomena that were not recordable in images alone, such as the *sillon de bronze* left by the foam trail of a boat in the silver-blue sea at Velletri[12] or the subtlest gradations of gray that he observed in the Neapolitan sky during a return visit in 1860.[13]

Like his rare paintings of Italian women, such as *The Old Italian Women* of 1857 in The Metropolitan Museum of Art and the *Beggar Woman* of 1857 (fig. 139), which can be described more properly as character studies midway between genre and portraiture, this drawing combines an accurate study of a particular physiognomy with a studied expression of distanced neutrality, in an enigmatic partnering of the recognizable and the unknowable that was to become characteristic of Degas's representations of women.[14]

Jane Munro

Figure 139. Hilaire-Germain-Edgar Degas, *Beggar Woman*. Oil on canvas. City Museum and Art Gallery, Birmingham, England (inv. P44'60)

1. Reff 1976, Carnet 8, p. 32. Reff dated the use of the notebook to between October 1856 and July 1857.
2. See, for example, ibid., Carnet 7, pp. 4, 21, Carnet 8, pp. 35, 57v, 58, and Carnet 9, p. 21.
3. See Lemoisne 1946–49, nos. 16–18; and Brame and Reff 1984, nos. L9, L10.
4. Bezzola 1994, p. 280.
5. As, for example, the British painter, Thomas Uwins (1782–1857), who in a letter to his brother from Castellamare in October 1825, noted that so little had changed in the manner and habits of the people that he found himself "surrounded by figures such as have furnished models for Rafaelle and Michael Angelo"; Uwins 1858/1978, vol. 1, p. 263.
6. "Toutes les femmes ressemblent à des Pérugin! Est-ce une illusion." Reff 1976, Carnet 11, p. 66.
7. Sotheby's, London, sale cat., June 22, 1993, under lot 1.

8. Belioz claimed that his opera *Harold in Italy* had been influenced in part by the "poetic impressions" he had gained during his wanderings in the Abruzzo. See Cairns 1987, p. 174.
9. In the fourth studio sale, Galerie Georges Petit, Paris, July 2–4, 1919, lot 68b; sale, Sotheby's, London, June 22, 1993, lot 3.
10. See Henri Loyrette in Paris, Ottawa, and New York 1988–89, p. 65. The full inscription reads "Mola di Gaëta / Rom."
11. "Je ne suis pas fou de ce pittoresque italien qui est connue—Mais ce qui est touchant n'est plus du genre. C'est une *mode* éternelle"; Reff 1976, Carnet 11, p. 94.
12. "Velletri la mer d'un bleu argenté. le bâteau laisse une trace bouillonnante dans le milieu de laquelle . . . un sillon de bronze"; ibid., Carnet 18, p. 111.
13. "Je n'oublierai jamais ce gris nacré et ce vert somber et

puissant des arbres. Un soir avant dîner revenant par Ste Lucie ciel estompé . . . gris perle, au dessus dans toute sa hauteur dégradé très insensiblement dans un ton bleu gris nuancé d'améthyste"; ibid., Carnet 19, p. 16.
14. Mari Kálmán Meller (1988, p. 198) has commented at length on the duality that Degas exploited in his work throughout his life, in particular in his dance paintings. Or, as Max Liebermann wrote in the year of Degas's death: "Nicht Positives—Nur Suggestives." See Liebermann 1918, p. 11.

109. Hilaire-Germain-Edgar Degas

Paris, 1834–Paris, 1917

Portrait of Adelchi Morbilli

Ca. 1857

Graphite on wove paper, 9⁷⁄₁₆ × 6⁷⁄₁₆ in. (24 × 16.4 cm)

Stamped on recto with the marks of the artist's estate in red ink at lower left: Degas (Lugt 658); verso: *Atelier / Ed. Degas* (Lugt 657)

Inscribed on verso in blue pencil (underlined): *Ph 1797*

PROVENANCE: Estate of the artist; sale (Degas Atelier Sale III), Galerie Georges Petit, Paris, April 7–9, 1919, part of lot 93 (*Portraits d'hommes. Trois dessins à la mine de plomb, en un cadre*; sold for 5,700 francs), ill.; probably purchased from that sale by Lucien Mellerio (1879–1943), Paris and Stresa; his daughter, Hélène Mellerio, Paris; sale, Étude Tajan, Paris, June 20, 2001, lot 17; C. G. Boerner, New York; acquired by Jean Bonna, 2006

EXHIBITIONS: New York 2002a, no. 31; Geneva 2006–7a

BIBLIOGRAPHY: Raimondi 1958, pp. 149, 150, and Quadro IV (Family Tree); Boggs 1962, pp. 11, 87–88, n. 49, p. 125; Boggs 1963, pp. 274–75; Loyrette 1991, pp. 85–86; New York and London 2002, under no. 37, ill.

One can easily imagine Edgar Degas directing one of his relatives toward a chair in order to position him or her for a portrait sitting. Throughout his career, he made the most of models he found closest at hand in order to exercise his fascination with human features and forms. Particularly early in his career, it seems that any special gathering of Degas family members might serve to launch a new effort, for as his sister Marguerite reported, when Edgar celebrated the New Year 1864 with the Mussons (family on his mother's side) in Bourg-en-Bresse, "He took with him a lot of pencils and paper in order to draw, to do their portraits, and to sketch Didy's hands in all their aspects."[1]

Degas's visits to Naples, where his paternal grandfather had settled and established his career as a banker, presented frequent opportunities for the artist to study his kinfolk. The Bonna portrait of his cousin Adelchi Carlo Diodato Morbilli (1837–1913), the youngest son of his aunt Rosa and Giuseppe Morbilli, Duca di Sant'Angelo e Frosolone, was almost certainly made during Degas's first trip to Italy, and probably sometime between August and October 1857. Like most of the family portraits he produced, this one remained in Degas's hands until his death. At the time of his estate sale in 1919, it appeared framed in a triptych that included another study of the sitter and a penciled portrait of Adelchi's elder brother, Alfredo (fig. 140).[2] Pictures of the two brothers flanked a portrait of their mother in another framed triptych auctioned from the artist's estate later the same year.[3]

Adelchi was nineteen years old when his slightly older cousin captured him seated sideways in a wooden chair, his left leg crossed over his right and with a riding crop held in his hand.[4] The two similar drawings must have been made at the same sitting; the later one, seemingly drawn at a greater distance, shows more of the figure, including Adelchi's ankle and part of his foot, raised on a level with the chair seat and the tail of his loosened jacket. The subject's pose was shifted slightly, his left arm brought forward, although he remains seated at an angle to his chair, in a nonchalant pose rather like those Degas employed in later portraits of the painters Gustave Moreau, Édouard Manet, and James Tissot. Every feature in the second version is more crisply defined, including the sitter's expression, which seems to have hardened, perhaps out of impatience with the duration of the posing session.

At this early stage of his career, the artist was influenced particularly by the great portrait masters Rembrandt and Ingres, one of whose pupils, Louis Lamothe, was for a time, his teacher. Degas met Ingres in 1855, visited

245

109

Figure 140. Hilaire-Germain-Edgar Degas, *Pencil Portraits of Adelchi and Alfredo Morbilli*, mounted together in one frame, as illustrated in the catalogue to the sale of Degas's estate, Galerie Georges Petit, Paris, April 7–9, 1919, lot 93

Figure 141. Jean-Auguste-Dominique Ingres, *Bust of a Man* (Noël-Thomas-Joseph Clérian), 1814. Graphite with white chalk. Private Collection, formerly Collection of Edgar Degas

him on more than one occasion, and maintained a lifelong admiration for his work. Degas's personal art collection included twenty paintings by Ingres, and more than eighty of his drawings, which represented for the younger artist the ideal of draftsmanship.[5]

A drawing from Degas's own collection, such as that of Noël-Thomas-Joseph Clérian (fig. 141), exemplifies the characteristics of Ingres's graphic style that his follower strove to emulate in his brisk handling of Adelchi Morbilli's suited torso and sensitive description of his face. Degas's natural reserve and moody temperament always seeped into his portraits, whether of himself or others, and so

the openness of Ingres's smooth faces was seldom translated. It is perhaps Rembrandt's influence: the secret depths suggested in his thoughtful portraits, whether painted, drawn, or darkly etched, which inspired the shadowy aspects of the portrait seen here.

COLTA IVES

1. Marguerite De Gas (in Paris) to the Musson family (in New Orleans), December 31, 1863, Tulane University Library, New Orleans, quoted in Paris, Ottawa, and New York 1988–89, p. 55.
2. In the third studio sale, Galerie Georges Petit, Paris, April 7–9, 1919, lot 93, ill. The portrait of Adelchi at the far right of the triptych was sold at Étude Tajan, Paris, June 20, 2001, lot 16, and later offered for sale by its purchaser, Jean-Luc Baroni; see his dealer catalogue (New York and London 2002, no. 37).
3. In the fourth studio sale, Galerie Georges Petit, Paris, July 2–4, 1919, lot 102. The watercolor portrait showing Adelchi standing at left in the triptych entered the collection of Mr. and Mrs. Nathan Halpern, New York, and was sold at Christie's, New York, November 3, 2004. A small pencil sketch once thought to picture the head of Adelchi Morbilli was owned by John Rewald before it appeared on the London art market in 1960. Jean Boggs soon after identified the sitter as Alfredo Morbilli (Boggs 1962, pp. 87–88, n. 49).
4. Adelchi Morbilli maintained residence in Naples, marrying in 1877 and becoming director of the Banca Nazionale.
5. See New York 1997–98, vol. 1, and vol. 2, nos. 615–720.

110. Hilaire-Germain-Edgar Degas

Paris, 1834–Paris, 1917

Head of a Woman and a Seated Dancer

Ca. 1879

Pastel and black chalk heightened with white chalk on pink laid paper, slightly faded, 18¹¹⁄₁₆ × 12⁵⁄₁₆ in. (47.5 × 31.3 cm)

Stamp of Degas studio sale at lower left: Lugt 658

PROVENANCE: Estate of the artist; sale (Degas Atelier Sale III), Galerie Georges Petit, Paris, April 7–9, 1919, lot 209, no. 1; Georges Viau (ca. 1855–1939), Paris; Franz Koenig; his sale, Sotheby's, New York, January 23, 2001, lot 39; Private Collection, United States; Sayn-Wittgenstein Fine Art, New York; acquired by Jean Bonna, 2003

EXHIBITIONS: Washington 1984–85, no. 26; Martigny 1993, no. 38; Detroit and Philadelphia 2002–3, pp. 113, 291, pl. 124; Paris 2006b, no. 83; Geneva 2006–7a

BIBLIOGRAPHY: Rivière 1922–23, pl. 75; Pečírka 1963, p. 24, pl. 23; *Degas' Drawings* 1973, p. viii, pl. 48

This arresting sheet is composed of preparatory studies for two of the dancers in *The Dance Lesson*, dated about 1879, now in the National Gallery of Art, Washington, D.C. (fig. 142). The painting, exhibited at the fifth Impressionist exhibition in 1880, is generally thought to be the first in a series of about twenty friezelike compositions depicting

Figure 142. Hilaire-Germain-Edgar Degas, *The Dance Lesson*. Oil on canvas. National Gallery of Art, Washington, D.C. (1995.47.6)

Figure 143. Hilaire-Germain-Edgar Degas, *Two Seated Dancers*. Pastel. Museum of Art, Providence, Rhode Island (59.111)

dancers in an oblong-shaped room that Edgar Degas executed in oils and pastels from the 1880s to the first years of the twentieth century (see cat. 112).[1] In preparation for those works, Degas made over one hundred drawings of the individual dancers who populate their elongated, consciously constricted spaces, the majority on a scale far larger than in the finished paintings and pastels.[2]

The studies on this sheet are for two of the three principal figures in the Washington D.C. painting, in which they occupy the middle ground: at the top, the standing dancer adjusting the ribbon of her dress, her head profiled against the suffused light of the window, and, below, the seated dancer beside her, whose pose and glance draw the eye to the dancers who occupy the furthest extremities of the composition.

Apparently unconnected on the sheet, each figure nevertheless assumes the same directional position as in the Washington D.C. painting. The different degrees of finish in each study signal their relative importance as formal elements in the painting. The luminous—and voluminous—expanse of tutu continues the diagonal perspectival axis established by the double bass on the floor, while the sharply outlined features of the standing dancer, cameoed in *contre-jour*, define the upper limits of the canvas. As Jean Sutherland Boggs pointed out, the standing dancers in some of these frieze-like canvases seem to bend forward deliberately, as if to avoid the low headroom of the canvas edge,[3] and in the slight outline reprise of the dancer's head in the top left of the present drawing, Degas seems to explore its relationship to the receding line of the uppermost compositional space. The head itself, as Ronald

Pickvance noted, has been "breathed-on . . . Watteau-like"[4] to a (now slightly faded) pink paper and worked up in an astonishingly bold range of colored chalks, from the aubergine cloud that encircles the head to the subtlest touch of pink that models the ear and the slight contours of turquoise around the nose, a combination that has proved resolutely resistant to photographic reproduction.

By contrast, the head of the seated dancer on the lower part of the sheet was sketched in the most summary of outlines. Instead, Degas concentrated on fixing the position of the body and on modeling the dancer's skirts. Ironically, it is this faceless figure whose identity has been established convincingly by George Shackelford as an English dancer called Nelly Franklin,[5] whom Degas referred to in an inscription as "unhappy Nelly."[6] That Degas was dissatisfied with his efforts on this sheet is suggested by the alterations he made to the figure in the final canvas, in which she sits upright, if hunched, on the chair, itself angled slightly more to the left. On the other hand, as if not to give up entirely on the potential of the pose, Degas reused the seated figure in a number of other works, notably in the pastel *Three Dancers Preparing for Class* in The Metropolitan Museum of Art, in which she appears head-to-head with another seated dancer.

As Shackelford noted, the seated dancer in the Washington D.C. painting is a composite, pairing the lower half of the dancer in this sheet with the right-hand figure in a pastel study for the same painting in the Museum of Art, Providence, Rhode Island (fig. 143).[7] In the Bonna drawing, she is shown engaged in a more vigorous activity, bending over to adjust a slipper or to rub her foot, in a pose that would

become a favorite subject of Degas's in the 1880s.[8] For the Washington picture, however, her more upright position better served his compositional purposes, by providing a continuum between the vertical of the chair leg and that of the wall, while the compressed muslin of the skirt forms an impenetrable barricade that further isolates the dancer on the extreme left, slumped to the floor in exhaustion and/or ennui.

Degas included the figure of a seated dancer in several of his very earliest dance paintings, such as the *Foyer de danse à l'Opéra* of 1872, in the Musée d'Orsay, or *La Répétition de danse* of 1874, in The Burrell Collection, Glasgow.[9] In classroom scenes, the resting figures sit in contrast to the dancers actively engaged in classroom exercises. However, from the 1880s onward, Degas gradually isolated such figures, so that, even when they appear in groups of two or three, they turn their backs on one another. In this way, the seated dancer gradually became among his most expressive compositional vehicles. Slumped, scratching, yawning, or bending over, feet splayed, she conveys an awkwardness borne of fatigue and sometimes despair—the very contradiction of her dazzling onstage presence.

A number of authors have shown how wittily and potently Degas used apparently insignificant pictorial accessories to formal and expressive ends—a watering can to lighten the compositional gravitas of dancers at the barre, for example as in *Two Dancers at the Barre* of about 1876–67, in The Metropolitan Museum of Art,[10] or in a still life of a jug and copper pot to echo the curves and color of a woman washing in *The Tub* in the Musée d'Orsay.[11] In the case of the seated dancer, the tutu—an extension of

the dancer's anatomy rather than a "prop" in the strictest sense—became central to Degas's enterprise. Toward the end of his life, Degas claimed that his dance subjects merely provided him with "un prétexte à peindre de jolies étoffes" (a pretext for painting pretty fabrics).[12]

However, in his later works—his pastels, in particular—the dancers' muslin skirts unify the compositions coloristically through their properties of light diffusion and saturation and allow Degas to give full rein to his coloristic fantasy. Elsewhere, as in this drawing and the related painting, it is clear that he felt no obligation to paint these "pretty fabrics" attractively. Instead, the tutu becomes an assertive formal element, a figure-deforming covering on the

dancer's well-honed body that engulfs or isolates her and cocoons her in a protective shell from which she emerges as if in a kind of parody of a classical Venus Anadyomène.

JANE MUNRO

1. Jill DeVonyar and Richard Kendall (in Detroit and Philadelphia 2002–3, p. 283, n. 60) list ten paintings in oils on this theme, each measuring about 38 × 88 cm; see Lemoisne 1946–49, nos. 625, 820, 894, 900, 902, 905, 941, 996, 1107, and 1394. They add (in Detroit and Philadelphia 2002–3, p. 110) that there are around a further ten in the same format in pastel or charcoal.

2. As DeVonyar and Kendall point out (in Detroit and Philadelphia 2002–3, p. 113), this is a testimony both to the sustained importance of drawing in Degas's working practice and to the seriousness with which he executed these preliminary studies, many of which he signed and sold during his lifetime as independent works of art.

3. Jean Sutherland Boggs in Paris, Ottawa, and New York 1988–89, p. 574; see also cat. 112.

4. See Martigny 1993, p. 70.

5. See Washington 1984–85, p. 88.

6. Degas's drawing of her of about 1880 is inscribed "Unhappy Nelly / ça m'est égal"; Brame and Reff 1984, no. 107. See also Detroit and Philadelphia 2002–3, p. 219.

7. See Washington 1984–85, p. 88.

8. For a full discussion of the role of the seated dancer, in what Richard Thomson has described as the "cuboid" pose, see Thomson 1995, p. 16ff.

9. Lemoisne 1946–49, nos. 298, 430.

10. Ibid., no. 408; Manchester and Cambridge 1987, p. 48.

11. Lemoisne 1946–49, no. 872; Gary Tinterow in Paris, Ottawa, and New York 1988–89, pp. 446–48, no. 271.

12. Vollard 1924, pp. 109–10.

III. Hilaire-Germain-Edgar Degas

Paris, 1834–Paris, 1917

A Woman Bent over a Basin, Washing Her Neck

Ca. 1887–90

Black chalk over charcoal, highlighted with white on laid paper, 24⁷⁄₁₆ × 18½ in. (61.4 × 47 cm)
Watermark: MICHALLET

Stamped in red ink at lower left: *degas* (Lugt 658); on verso in red ink: *Atelier / Ed. Degas* (Lugt 657)

Inscribed on verso in blue pencil: *Ph 797*

PROVENANCE: Estate of the artist; sale (Degas Atelier Sale II), Galerie Georges Petit, Paris, December 11–13, 1918, lot 306, ill. (sold for 4,600 francs); Madame Langweil, Paris; André Noufflard (1885–1968), Paris; Private Collection, France; Sayn-Wittgenstein, New York; acquired by Jean Bonna, 2006

EXHIBITION: Geneva 2006–7a

BIBLIOGRAPHY: Rivière 1922–23, pl. 44; Lemoisne 1946–49, vol. 3, no. 919, ill. p. 535; Pečírka 1963, p. 56, pl. 50; *Degas' Drawings* 1973, p. viii, pl. 81

Edgar Degas's enduring fascination with the human figure led him to venture beyond the panorama of Parisian public life to enter the city's most private domains. As he strove to represent the female body with greater truth, women engaged in the intimate rituals of the bath became regular themes. "The nude has always been represented in poses which presuppose an audience, but these women of mine are honest, simple folk,

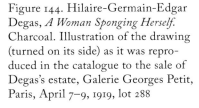

Figure 144. Hilaire-Germain-Edgar Degas, *A Woman Sponging Herself.* Charcoal. Illustration of the drawing (turned on its side) as it was reproduced in the catalogue to the sale of Degas's estate, Galerie Georges Petit, Paris, April 7–9, 1919, lot 288

Figure 145. Hilaire-Germain-Edgar Degas, *Two Studies of a Woman Bathing.* Charcoal. Illustration in the catalogue to the sale of Degas's estate, Galerie Georges Petit, Paris, July 2–4, 1919, lot 159

unconcerned by any other interests than those involved in their physical condition," Degas reported to the English writer George Moore in 1886, about the time he made this drawing, which he declared should appear "as if you looked through a key-hole."[1]

Degas's interest in monumental depictions of the female bather can be traced back to his youth, when he took the trouble to persuade a school friend's father to lend to the 1855 Exposition Universelle Ingres's great painting the "Valpinçon" *Bather*, now in the Louvre. It was not until the late 1870s that Degas himself began to devote much effort to portraying nude bathers, but it became a theme that he would continue to explore for some thirty years.

The uncommon, unpretentious pose always caught Degas's eye. In the early 1860s, he painted a seated nude with her head thrown forward, her hair obscuring a view of her face, in his composition *Scene of War in the Middle Ages* in the Musée d'Orsay, and in the years that followed, he frequently captured ballerinas bent over their tutus or their toe shoes to show only the tops of their heads. In the 1880s, when he portrayed private dialogues between bathers and their washbasins, he found many occasions to present a figure kneeling, sitting, squatting, or standing (as she is here), and reaching behind her bowed head to scrub her neck.

Although unconnected, so far as is known, to any one pastel or painting, the Bonna drawing is closely related to two other charcoal drawings, of similar size, that quite likely were done at the same time (figs. 144, 145).[2] This, the most detailed drawing of the three, presents a figure solidly built but faceless, an unknown individual who stands in for countless women engaged day after day in a mundane task. Her supple right arm, her shoulder, and her back are beautifully sculptural, and quite apart from any other aspect of the drawing, deserve admiration.

COLTA IVES

1. Moore 1891, p. 318.
2. The drawing reproduced in figure 144 was sold in the third sale of Degas's studio, Galerie Georges Petit, Paris, April 7–9, 1919; the drawing reproduced in figure 145 was sold in the fourth sale, Galerie Georges Petit, July 2–4, 1919, and more recently was auctioned at Sotheby's, London, February 6, 2007, lot 110. Neither is listed in Lemoisne's catalogue raisonné.

112. Hilaire-Germain-Edgar Degas

Paris, 1834–Paris, 1917

Three Dancers

Ca. 1895–1905

Charcoal on tracing paper, laid down, with traces of blue paint on the right-hand figures, 18¾ × 15³⁄₁₆ in. (47.7 × 38.5 cm)

PROVENANCE: Estate of the artist; sale (Degas Atelier Sale II), Galerie Georges Petit, Paris, December 11–13, 1918, lot 282; Lucien-Marcel Bing; Lee A. Ault (1915–1996), 1937; Frank Perls (1910–1975), Beverly Hills, California; M. H. Feheley, Toronto; his sale, Sotheby's, London, June 28, 1972, lot 4; Private Collection; Wildenstein and Company, New York; acquired by Jean Bonna, 2000

EXHIBITIONS: Los Angeles 1957, Paris 2006b, no. 84; Geneva 2006–7a

BIBLIOGRAPHY: Alexandre 1918, ill. p. 11; Rivière 1922–23, pl. 48; R. Huyghe and L. Huyghe 1953, pl. 38; *Degas' Drawings* 1973, p. ix, pl. 88

With minor variations in pose, these figures form the pivotal grouping in three friezelike dance compositions that Edgar Degas executed between about 1898 and 1905.[1] It is generally agreed that *Dancers in the Waiting Room*, in the Fondation E. G. Bührle, Zurich (fig. 146) precedes by at least seven years the two versions of the composition in pastel, *Dancers*, in the Wallraf-Richartz Museum, Cologne, and *The Dancers* in the Toledo Museum of Art, both of which adopt the same elongated format and use the shaft of light from the slightly opened door to divide the composition between the uninhabited space on the left and the overlapping figures of preening dancers on the right.[2] The two drawings are also executed in charcoal and pastel on tracing paper, a combination of media and support that Degas came to relish in the 1890s for the flexibility it allowed him to revise and rework figure groups, individual poses, and compositions.

Degas made a large number of preparatory drawings of dancers in singles and in groups for his elongated paintings, in a sequence that is extremely difficult to reconstruct.[3] Although the precise date of the Bonna drawing, like that of the Zurich painting, remains uncertain, the schematic rendering of the heads and heavily outlined contours of the limbs are not inconsistent with his drawing style in the early part of the 1890s.[4] Certainly, the slight adjustments that he made to the direction of the heads of the two dancers on the extreme left, who in the finished compositions turn to face in the opposite direction, away from the unoccupied terrain and toward the cluster of dancers in the far extremities of the room, suggest that this drawing may have been made at an early stage in the evolution of the sequence.[5] On the other hand, two closely related drawings of dancers grouped exactly as they are in this sheet, only partially (fig. 147) and fully (fig. 148) dressed in tutus, have been convincingly dated on stylistic grounds to about 1900–1905, implying that Degas may have chosen to maintain this grouping until a

Figure 146. Hilaire-Germain-Edgar Degas, *Dancers in the Waiting Room*. Oil on canvas. Fondation E. G. Bührle, Zurich

relatively late stage in the evolution of the compositions.

As a result of this fine-tuning of the dancers' positions, the group's sense of inwardness and self-sufficiency is enhanced, as they seem to become absorbed in adjustments to their costumes. Of the three, only the dancer fluffing out her tutu on the right is retained with minimal changes in the finished compositions. In fact, Degas included a figure of a dancer

arranging the airy volume of her tutu, gently bending forward into the spectator's space as she does so,[6] in several of his earliest dance paintings, such as *The Dance Class* of 1874, in The Metropolitan Museum of Art, New York, and *La Répétition de danse* of about 1874, in The Burrell Collection, Glasgow Museums.[7] Here, as in these earlier paintings, this dancer occupies, if not center stage, nevertheless a key position at the meeting point of two

converging diagonals. Like her ancestors, she invites the viewer to explore the deepest recesses of the compositional space.

In 1903, Degas famously told his American patron Louisine Havemeyer that his reason for painting ballet subjects was to find again "the combined movement of the Greeks."[8] In fact, the present drawing and the related compositions all depend on a distinct classical prototype, that of the dancing female figures known

Figure 147. Hilaire-Germain-Edgar Degas, *Three Dancers*. Charcoal heightened with white. Collection Dr. Morton and Toby Mower, Beaver Creek, Colorado

Figure 148. Hilaire-Germain-Edgar Degas, *Three Dancers*. Charcoal heightened with white. Private Collection

as the Three Graces, the daughters of Zeus who performed at the feasts of the gods, of which Degas would have known many representations in paintings and sculpture both in Paris and during his stay in Italy.[9] In the mid-1870s, he freely interpreted this prototype in another grouping, *Petites Paysannes se baignant à la mer vers le soir* of 1875–76, in a Private Collection,[10] albeit in a more abandoned and less lyrically rhythmic tempo than in his later dance compositions. The comparatively large scale of the figures in this and related drawings is echoed and enhanced in the final compositions, where they take their place in a relatively compressed space, thus emphasizing their friezelike arrangement and kinship to classical bas-reliefs.[11]

In their pared-down nakedness, divested of the identifying attributes of their profession (without knowledge of the final composition would we even recognize them as dancers?), these three figures testify to the formalist and analytical nature of Degas's art in the last years of the nineteenth century. This, in part, is the art that he described to Paul Valéry as an "art savant," one in which a painting was the result of a "series of operations."[12] Each of the "Graces," as individual participants in this "Dance to the Music of Time," is carefully calibrated in relation to the other, their awkwardly splayed elbows interlinked to form a self-contained dynamic that is in constant evolution as Degas incorporates the group into the final composition. As Gauguin recognized, Degas's dancers were "not women, they are machines moving with graceful lines and marvelous balance, arranged with all the pretty artificiality of the Rue de la Paix."[13] Their anonymous, decontextualized presence and their partially obscured faces underline their quasi-mechanical nature as formal components, almost as if Degas were rotating the individual figures to "feel" their three-dimensional possibilities with his eyes. In this way, he put himself, not his dancers, to work, responding to his self-exhortation in a notebook used between 1877 and 1883 "to study a figure or an object from every angle."[14]

The first recorded owner of this drawing was Marcel Bing, son of the well-known connoisseur of Japanese art and promoter of Art Nouveau Siegfried Bing (1838–1905). An accomplished jeweler, Marcel owned a total of ten drawings by Degas, nine of which were lent by his heirs to the 1924 Degas retrospective held at the Galerie Georges Petit in Paris[15]; he bequeathed several important drawings by the artist to the Louvre.

JANE MUNRO

1. For the role of the frieze-like composition in Degas's work, see cat. no. 110.
2. Lemoisne 1946–49, nos. 996, 998, 997.
3. The drawings closest to the present sheet were sold in the Degas Atelier Sale II, Galerie Georges Petit, Paris, December 11–13, 1918, lots 276, 341; Degas Atelier Sale III, Galerie Georges Petit, April 7–9, 1919, lots 172, 231; and Degas Atelier Sale IV, Galerie Georges Petit, July 2–4, 1919, lot 149.
4. See, for example, *Three Nude Dancers*, Private Collection (Degas Atelier Sale II, Galerie Georges Petit, December 11–13, 1918, lot 284; London and Chicago 1996–97, p. 263, no. 75).
5. Degas maintained the positions of the dancers in this drawing in another, more worked up, pastel showing the same figures in tutus (Lemoisne 1946–49, no. 999bis; formerly in the collection of Mr. and Mrs. Block, Chicago). I am grateful to Suzanne McCullagh of the Art Institute of Chicago for her efforts to trace this drawing.
6. Jean Sutherland Boggs, in discussing the monumental proportions of the figures in relation to the tight space of the canvas, describes this figure as inclining her head, "pour éviter 'd'accrocher' le haut de la toile." Boggs in Paris, Ottawa, and New York 1988–89, p. 574.
7. Lemoisne 1946–49, nos. 397, 430.
8. Havemeyer 1961/1993, p. 256.
9. See Detroit and Philadelphia 2002–3, pp. 244–45.
10. Lemoisne 1946–49, no. 377.
11. Ibid., no. 999bis (fig. 148), is clearly marked with horizontal lines at top and bottom, suggesting that Degas clearly established for himself the height restrictions of the compositional space in the preparatory phase. According to Renoir, who believed Degas, not Rodin, to be first among contemporary sculptors, Degas had executed a bas-relief sculpture, "beau comme l'antique," which he had, however, so neglected that it was left "tomber en poussière"; see Vollard 1924, p. 63, note.
12. Valéry 1938, p. 75.
13. Gauguin, *Intimate Journals*, 1923/1985 (ed.), p. 65.
14. Reff 1976, vol. 1, p. 134, Carnet 30, p. 65.
15. Paris 1924, nos. 2, 57, 65, 93, 100, 111, 170, 184, 187.

113. Paul Cézanne

Aix-en-Provence, 1839–Aix-en-Provence, 1906

Wooded Landscape

Ca. 1895

Graphite and watercolor, 12 11/16 × 19 in. (32.2 × 48.3 cm)

PROVENANCE: Ambroise Vollard, Paris; sale, Hôtel Drouot, Paris, March 6, 1940, lot 10; Galerie Bernheim-Jeune, Paris (purchased by Montag, May 26, 1940); Private Collection; Galerie Jan Krugier, Geneva; acquired by Jean Bonna, 2000

EXHIBITIONS: Paris 2006b, no. 85; Geneva 2006–7a

BIBLIOGRAPHY: Rewald 1983, no. 465, ill.; Berlin, Venice, Madrid, and Geneva 1999–2000, p. 398, ill.

"The trees were his only true friends." This reminiscence by Joachim Gasquet,[1] who befriended the solitary master from Aix from the late 1880s through the 1890s, is amply confirmed by the many depictions of trees in Paul Cézanne's works on paper and on canvas. Dozens of works attest to Cézanne's love for the vitality and monumentality of those shaded masses, from a few spare lines on the pages of a sketchbook suggesting leaves or branches to magnificently polished oil paintings—such as *Great Pine near Aix*,[2] in the Hermitage, which was painted in Bellevue in the same period as the Bonna watercolor, or *The Big Trees*,[3] in the National Galleries of Scotland, Edinburgh, which depicts undergrowth the artist observed during an outing from his studio in Lauves late in his career. It was Cézanne's custom to stop and draw a clump of trees on the side of a path, or to make some preliminary open air studies of trees in the area around Auvers, accompanied by Camille Pissarro, or to paint the groves of the Jas de Bouffan, his family's property until 1899, or to study the dappled light and shadow in a patch of undergrowth, or to penetrate more deeply into the untamed forests along the Tholonet road and into the lush park of Château Noir. Joseph Ravaisou, a young painter from Aix who knew Cézanne toward the end of his life, noted in his interesting memoir of the aging master: "He was, moreover, a voluptuary in art. He loved Nature with a passion, perhaps exclusively; he painted so as to prolong in himself the joy at living among the trees."[4]

The Bonna collection's *Wooded Landscape* is characteristic of the many watercolors Cézanne painted, with modest ambitions but with evident fascination for the chiaroscuro in a wooded landscape, the interplay of light and shadow he saw at the edge of a forest, and the moment when motifs created by the trunks, the branches, and the luminous dance of the leaves become visible. He was often intrigued by branches with unusual shapes, such as the slightly curved ones on the present sheet, which call to mind the masterful *Twisted Tree and Cistern in the Park of Château Noir*,[5] now in the Pearlman Foundation, to cite a particularly striking example.

Cézanne began by lightly sketching the main lines in graphite and indicating a few shadows. He then traced the massive outlines of the trunks and branches in a relatively dark tone, after which he added the translucent shapes of the leaves by gradually layering on wash. Here, he demonstrated great mastery of the wash technique, all the more so since he had to let each layer dry before applying the next. One fully experiences the vitality of nature in the rhythmic and interlacing shapes of the branches and in the luminosity of the lighter surfaces in wash that represent the foliage. Just above is the sky, barely suggested. As always with Cézanne, the white of the paper—which here shows through nearly half the sheet—plays a positive, dynamic role, as it introduces a feeling of daylight at the edge of the forest and enlivens the subject of the watercolor. As stated above, Cézanne, who "loved Nature," was also "a voluptuary in art." Highly sensitive to the natural forms that profoundly attracted him, he was able to create an abstract motif of color, light, and shadow that, to modern eyes, almost has a life of its own, independent of the depiction of nature.

The Bonna watercolor was probably produced during one of the walks that Cézanne took almost daily in the countryside around Aix. In the 1890s, he was still living at the Jas de Bouffan (until the property was sold in 1899), but it was not unusual for him also to rent a cabin in the Bibémus quarry or even a room in the nearby Château Noir, where he stored his painting supplies. After his first major exhibition in Paris in 1895, organized by the dealer Ambroise Vollard, Cézanne, true to his temperament, distanced himself from society and retired to the abandoned Bibémus quarry or the private grounds of the Château Noir. The precise spot that inspired this watercolor is impossible to identify. It might be somewhere along the Tholonet road, one of the painter's habitual haunts. That country road, linking Aix to the village of Le Tholonet at the foot of Mont Sainte-Victoire, skirts the Château Noir and its wooded park, a place where Cézanne often worked, enjoying his solitude among the trees, as this beautiful watercolor attests.

PHILIP CONISBEE

1. Gasquet 1926.
2. Rewald 1996, no. 761.
3. Ibid., no. 904.
4. Ravaisou 1907.
5. Rewald 1983, no. 532.

113

114. Odilon Redon

Bordeaux, 1840–Paris, 1916

Spring

1883

Charcoal, oiled charcoal, black pastel or Conté crayon, erasure, grattage, and stumping, 13 × 14⅝ in. (33 × 37.1 cm)

Signed at lower left: *ODILON REDON*

PROVENANCE: Émile Hennequin, Paris, 1887; Edmond Picard, Brussels; E. Picard sale, Le Roy, Brussels, March 26, 1904, lot 95; André Bonger, Almen, 1904; Madame Bonger, Almen; Jacques Seligman, New York, ca. 1952; Germain Seligman, New York, ca. 1959; Eugene Victor Thaw, New York, before 1978; Alice M. Kaplan, New York; Sayn-Wittgenstein Fine Art, New York; acquired by Jean Bonna, 2003

EXHIBITIONS: Brussels 1890, no. 4; The Hague 1892, no. 26; Paris 1894, no. 4; The Hague 1894, no. 36; Rotterdam 1907, no. 36; Amsterdam 1909, no. 41; Paris 1926b, no. 178; New York, Cleveland, and Minneapolis 1951–52, no. 25, ill. (*Profil sur un fonds de feuillage*); Lawrence 1958, no. 20; New York 1959b, no. 75, pl. LXXVI; New York 1989, no. 33; Chicago, Amsterdam, and London 1994–95, no. 82, p. 164, fig. 74; Paris 2006b, no. 88; Geneva 2006–7a

BIBLIOGRAPHY: Bacou 1956, vol. 1, pp. 105, 124, n. 3; Bantell 1981, no. 53; A. Wildenstein 1992–98, vol. 1 (1992), p. 102, no. 239; Denison 2006, p. 521

In the early 1880s, emerging from a long period of withdrawal in Peyrelebade, Odilon Redon began seeking recognition for his work. His first one-person exhibitions were held in Paris, following the publication in 1879 of his volume of lithographs *In the Dream*. In April and May 1881, a dozen charcoal drawings were exhibited at the galleries of *La Vie moderne*,[1] and in February 1882, a group of twenty-nine charcoal drawings and prints was shown at the office of *Le Gaulois*.[2] These two exhibitions[3] show how the themes of Redon's *noirs* (works in black) were beginning to evolve in the early 1880s; alongside his hybrid and frightening creatures, he began drawing faces with peaceful profiles, such as the *Head of a Young Girl* in the Museum of Fine Arts, Gifu,[4] the *Head of a Roman* in the Rijksmuseum Kröller-Müller, Otterlo,[5] and *Profile of Light* in the Musée d'Orsay (fig. 149),[6] which he also reworked for his lithographed series.[7] *Spring*, which was exhibited for the first time with Les Vingt in 1890, belongs to this period of renewal, which

coincided with the new happiness the painter found after his marriage to Camille in 1880. The profile, which stands out against a vegetal background, shows not only a fascination with plant physiology and hybridization but also a reminiscence of fifteenth- or early sixteenth-century Italian works by Piero della Francesca, Sandro Botticelli, or Antonio Pisanello (more than ancient intaglios or profiles), and in fact, Redon had the opportunity to study Pisanello's *Portrait of a Princess of the House of Este* (Ginevra d'Este), which the Louvre acquired in 1893.[8] Redon's title can be understood as an acknowledgment of his portrait's indebtedness to and loose analogy with the Renaissance allegories. Redon was normally quite cautious about the titles of his works, as he emphasized in a text dedicated to André Bonger, the future owner of *Spring*: "Applying a title to designate one of my drawings is sometimes adding too much, so to speak. A title is justified only when it is vague, indeterminate, and even intentionally ambiguous. My drawings *inspire* and cannot be defined. They do not determine anything. Like music, they place us in the ambiguous sphere of the indeterminate."[9]

Spring belonged to two, possibly three, of the artist's most illustrious collectors, enlightened connoisseurs who very early on—nearly twenty years before Gustave Fayet or Robert de Domecy—were able to appreciate the *noirs*, at a time when most critics completely misunderstood them. A letter from Edmond Picard to Redon suggests that the drawing's first owner, or at least addressee, was Émile Hennequin. A journalist and early champion and admirer of Redon's, as well as a faithful friend in difficult times, Hennequin met Redon at the 1882 exhibition of his charcoal drawings at *Le Gaulois*; the artist, who was still in a fragile emotional state, was touched by the critic's laudatory review of it. It appears Hennequin agreed to let *Spring* go, or to exchange it: "Next, my young friend Émile Hennequin has authorized me to sell the drawing *Spring*, which you wished to own, and has offered instead to choose another one from my storage boxes,"[10] Redon wrote to Picard, who indeed wanted

the drawing: "I would be delighted to own the drawing *Spring*," he told Redon. "Kindly let me know your price."[11] He also selected it as one of the works by Redon exhibited at the Vingt show in 1890: "[Octave] Maus and I have already chosen, from among my drawings, those that could go to the XX. We have settled on *The Beheaded*, the frontispiece of *Le Juré*, which hasn't yet been exhibited, *Spring*, and the drawing from *Le Juré* that I have in an album. . . . Please let me know if you find this acceptable."[12] A prominent figure in French and Belgian Symbolist circles, Edmond Picard was already collecting works by Félicien Rops, and it was owing to his precocious interest in Redon that the latter's works were shown in Belgium. Two years earlier, Picard had commissioned a series of lithographs to illustrate his dramatic monologue *Le Juré*,[13] which appeared in Brussels in 1887. One plate from this series, showing the "dramatic and grandiose figure of a druidic priestess," is not unlike *Spring*. The drawing then went to the Dutchborn Bonger, who acquired it at the dispersal

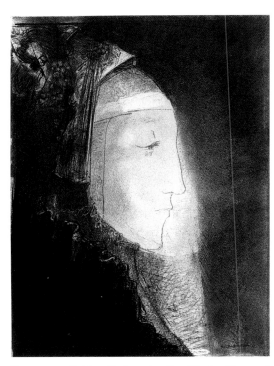

Figure 149. Odilon Redon, *Profile of Light*. Charcoal heightened with white. Musée d'Orsay, located in the Musée du Louvre, Département des Arts Graphiques, Paris (inv. RF 36816)

of the Picard collection in 1904. It was through the intermediary of Émile Bernard that this collector of Vincent van Gogh and Paul Cézanne made Redon's acquaintance in the fall of 1890. He became one of the artist's greatest collectors, buying both directly from him and, as in this case, at public auction. Their close friendship was a source of moral, even more than material, support for Redon.[14]

Redon had worked almost exclusively in charcoal since the early 1860s. His very particular technique set him apart from others working in charcoal (mainly laborious salon artists) and from their canonical approach to the medium, as taught in such contemporary treatises as the ones by Gustave Fraipont, Karl Robert, and Maxime Lalanne.[15] In an article for the Belgian periodical *L'Art moderne* in August 1894, "Confidences of an Artist" (dedicated to Picard, one of the few to appreciate the difficult art of the *noirs*), Redon described his exclusive use of charcoal: "Around 1875, my inspiration came only in crayon, in charcoal, that volatile, impalpable powder that flees under the hand. And the medium, because it offered me a better means of expression, remained with me. This lackluster material, which has no inherent beauty, was a great help with my explorations of chiaroscuro and the invisible. It is a medium deprecated and neglected by artists. It should be said, however, that charcoal leaves no room for lightness; it is full of gravity and one can only use it successfully in the same spirit. Nothing that does not stimulate the mind can produce worthwhile results in charcoal."[16] *Spring*, like the other great charcoal drawings from the 1880s, also transmits Redon's admiration for Rembrandt, whose work he studied in Holland with "veneration"[17] for the way the Dutch master's faces emerge from shadows. Moreover, Redon preferred tinted paper instead of flat white for his charcoal drawings, which allowed him to obtain a more subtle chiaroscuro— although sadly, as in this case, the corrosion of the sheets over time has slightly falsified our ability to appreciate that accomplishment.

After 1900, leaving charcoal and his *noir* period behind—as he put it, they had become "impossible" for him—Redon returned to color, exploring the theme of faces emerging from vegetation. Those sumptuous pastels with their flowered backgrounds thus appear to be the culmination of the images he began creating in the 1880s.

MARIE-PIERRE SALÉ

1. "Charcoals by Odilon Redon," at *La Vie moderne*, April–May 1881.
2. "Odilon Redon: Charcoals and Prints," at *Le Gaulois*, February 1882.
3. See the reconstitution of these two exhibitions proposed in Druick and Zegers 1994a, pp. 128–29, 134–35.

4. Charcoal (A. Wildenstein 1992–98, vol. 1 [1992], no. 253).
5. Conté crayon and charcoal (ibid., no. 26).
6. Ibid., nos. 266, 267.
7. Mellerio 1913, p. 94, no. 39, and p. 102, no. 80.
8. Musée du Louvre, Paris (Inv. RF 766).
9. "On Oneself: Some Notes by Odilon Redon," dedicated "To Monsieur Bonger, my friend and a faithful admirer of my art," May 1909; published in Mellerio 1913, p. 65.
10. Odilon Redon to Edmond Picard, signed and dated handwritten letter, October 18, 1887, Paris, in the catalogue of the Alphonse Dupont sale, Hôtel Drouot, Paris, December 3–4, 1958, no. 259.
11. Edmond Picard to Odilon Redon, signed and dated handwritten letter, June 28, 1887, Brussels, in Bacou 1960, p. 155; this letter appears to have been written before the preceding one: either Picard had already been assured of owning the drawing or the date on one of the letters is incorrect.
12. Edmond Picard to Odilon Redon, signed and dated handwritten letter, December 12, 1889, Brussels; ibid., pp. 161–62.
13. *Le Juré, monodrame en cinq actes: Sept Interprétations originales par Odilon Redon et deux portraits* (Brussels, 1886); seven plates printed in 100 copies on Japanese vellum by Becquet (Paris [1887]), pl. VI (Mellerio 1913); the illustrations also appeared in 1887 as an album, pl. VI (Mellerio 1913, p. 102, no. 80, pl. XVIII). Preparatory drawing for pl. VI, charcoal, signed upper left (A. Wildenstein 1992–98, vol. 1 [1992], no. 238).
14. On Bonger and Redon, see esp. Bacou 1956, vol. 1, pp. 106–11.
15. Lalanne 1875; Fraipont 1896; Robert 1908. On Redon's technique, see Stratis 1994.
16. Redon 1894, quoted in Mellerio 1913, p. 18.
17. Ibid.

115. Odilon Redon

Bordeaux, 1840–Paris, 1916

Sailing Boat with Two Passengers (La Barque)

Ca. 1900

Pastel on wove paper, 23 1/16 × 19 in. (58.5 × 48.2 cm)

Signed in graphite at lower right: *ODILON REDON*

PROVENANCE: Madame Pierre-Étienne-Henri Goujon (1884–1971), née Lily Reinach, Paris; by descent to a private collector (as of 1995); Wildenstein and Company, New York; acquired by Jean Bonna, 2006

BIBLIOGRAPHY: Cassou 1972, pp. 22–23, fig. 1; A. Wildenstein 1992–98, vol. 3 (1996), pp. 325, 353, no. 1955, and frontispiece

Believing black to be the most important color in any artist's palette, Odilon Redon devoted most of his career to working in monochromatic graphic media: etching (in the 1860s), charcoal (in the 1870s), and lithography (in the 1880s). When he discovered the charms of color by adopting oil paints and pastels in the 1890s, his art brightened considerably, but it retained, nonetheless, an air of dusky mystery.

Having passed a lonely childhood, probably buried in storybooks, Redon remained personally withdrawn, while as an artist, he became resolutely independent. He purposefully bypassed the contemporary world of the Impressionists and Realists and ventured instead to explore the world beyond everyday vision, preferring to surrender to his dreamy imagination.

There were recurring themes in his art and oft-repeated symbols such as the knight, the

winged horse, and the devil. At the time of this pastel's creation, Redon had become drawn to the subject of a solitary boat, sailing on an open sea, bearing only two or three passengers.[1] The significance of marine voyages to Redon has been linked with his parents' crossing of the Atlantic Ocean, from New Orleans to France, in 1840, when his Creole mother was pregnant; the artist later expressed regret that he had not been born then, at sea, "a place without a country, above an abyss."[2]

Because some of the passengers in the roving boats he depicted are crowned with golden halos, they have been associated with the Virgin Mary or Saint Mary Magdalen.[3] But Redon repeatedly denied specific interpretations of his pictures and refused to be identified with Catholicism, Buddhism, or any of the mystical movements that were popular in Paris in the late 1890s, although he associated with important members of groups, like the Rose+Croix, and indeed there was a surge of religious imagery in his work at the time.

Redon maintained an eclectic attitude toward spiritual beliefs and steadfastly created pictures in which there was an atmosphere of the miraculous. Of all things, he declared himself committed to "the charm of the vague," and in that respect, he appears to have allied himself with the Symbolist poets.

Colta Ives

1. See A. Wildenstein 1992–98, vol. 3 (1996), nos. 1921–59.
2. Redon's autobiographical statement of 1898, first published in Mellerio 1913, p. 50, and quoted in Druick and Zegers 1994b, p. 105.
3. See Leeman 1994, p. 231. See also *The Golden Legend of Jacobus de Voragine,* translated and adapted by Granger Ryan and Helmut Ripperger (New York, 1941), p. 363, according to which, a pregnant woman on a storm-tossed ship invoked the Magdalen and vowed to dedicate her child to the saint's monastery, if it were saved.

116. Odilon Redon

Bordeaux, 1840–Paris, 1916

Portrait of Geneviève de Gonet at about the Age of Three

1906–7

Pastel on gray-coated canvas, lines of the face in brown pastel, framing lines in graphite pencil visible on lower and left edges, 19¾ × 18 in. (50.2 × 45.7 cm)

Signed and dated at lower right: *1907 – Odilon Redon*

Provenance: Marquis Jean de Gonet; his sale, Christie's, New York, November 11, 1997, lot 131 (unsold); estate of the marquis de Gonet, Paris; acquired by Jean Bonna, 1999

Exhibitions: Paris 1956–57, no. 104, pl. xlvi; Paris 2006b, no. 89; Geneva 2006–7a

Bibliography: Mellerio 1923, p. 136; Bacou 1956, vol. 1, p. 152; Berger 1965, p. 211, no. 400; A. Wildenstein 1992–98, vol. 1 (1992), p. 56, no. 109; Denison 2006, p. 521

During the years 1895 to 1900, Odilon Redon turned away from his *noirs,* having, as he put it, "embraced color." Beginning mainly after 1900, he became more assured as a portraitist and supported himself with commissions from the close circle of learned connoisseurs of his works: Ernest Chausson, André Mellerio, Gustave Fayet, Arthur Fontaine, Robert de Domecy, and André Bonger. The portrait of his son Arï in the Art Institute of Chicago (fig. 150) can be considered the prototype of Geneviève de Gonet's portrait and of the few portraits of children from 1900–1910;[1] in its wake, Redon also drew, always in half-length and in either frontal view or profile, the daughters of Fayet, the children of Domecy, and the Mellerio family.[2]

At the turn of the century, Redon completely overhauled the genre of pastel portraiture by freeing it from the formulas of worldly academicism and from Impressionism,[3] both of which had been influenced by eighteenth-century precedents. In his pastels, he made no attempt to create a realistic illusion of flesh and clothing. He invented an intermediate genre between pastel and chalk portraits, reminiscent of those executed in trois crayons by old masters he admired. By leaving part of the face unfinished, he gave his portraits a subtle character, at once archaic and modern. In 1898, the critic Mellerio, who several years later wrote the first catalogue raisonné of Redon's work, underscored the incomparable refinement of the artist's portraits of children.[4] As

Figure 150. Odilon Redon, *Portrait of Arï Redon.* Pastel on paper, ca. 1898. Art Institute of Chicago (1950.130)

with his finest portraits from the beginning of the century, that of Geneviève de Gonet stands out from a background of abstract and luminous flowers, which Redon himself compared to a stained-glass window. Commenting on the colors radiating from these portraits, which he considered "Redon's cardinal originality," Marius-Ary Leblond wrote in 1907: "In his particular adoration of flora, the rose window of the universe, he sees flowers floating in the sky, much as the ancient painters of the Madonna and Child, from Giotto to Da Vinci, saw little angels. . . . All those skies, composed of violets, mauves, lustrous bronzes that deepen the headiness of the velvety spaces, and blues that are at once interstellar and earthly, are spangled and sparkle like comets and nebulas—it's a cosmogony of flowers."[5]

About 1906, Gustave Fayet (1865–1925), a collector of modern art and a notable patron of Redon's, introduced Jean de Gonet to the artist. Fayet, who was the future owner of Fontfroide abbey, was a native of the Languedoc and a childhood friend of Gonet's. Trained as a lawyer but a dilettante by reputation, Jean-Louis-Marie-Gabriel, comte, then (upon the death of his brother Étienne) marquis de Gonet (1872–1925), was an informed music lover with a passion for opera and the esoteric. He was also an occasional poet, who published in the early 1920s under the pseudonym Pierre Terme and who later wrote a play about Redon called *The Thorns of Odilon Redon*.[6] He divided his time between Paris— his apartment on the boulevard de Courcelles was not far from Redon's studio—and his property near Béziers, Domaine de la Présidente. The marquis de Gonet became a regular at the gatherings in Fontverault, where Fayet brought together

close friends of Redon's such as Ricardo Viñes (1875–1943), a Spanish pianist of Catalan origin who was interested in astrology and spiritism.

Redon's unpublished account books confirm that this portrait was purchased in June 1907 from the artist,[7] who registered it this way: "Mlle de Gonet as child. Her portrait, imaginary background, intricate pattern like illusion of stained-glass window." This, along with the portrait of the marquis's wife,[8] was one of the first works by Redon that Gonet acquired. He pursued his collection of Redons, which is inseparable from the two men's deep friendship, until 1910; some fifteen paintings and pastels have now been catalogued, among them a version of *Apollo's Chariot*.[9] This group remained with the heirs of the marquis de Gonet until the estate was dispersed in New York in 1997.

Born in 1904, Jeanne-Geneviève was the first of five children resulting from the marriage of Jean de Gonet and Henriette Malric-Cazes, of the Pereire family, in June of that year.[10] Redon had been the marquis's witness at the wedding, and this portrait of his child attests to the closeness of their relations.

Although his work was gaining recognition by that time, and although his portraits were prized by refined connoisseurs and their friends, Redon did not pursue a career as a professional portraitist; he was never the kind of worldly painter who lived on commissions, portraying children all dressed up for their sittings in ribbons and bows to show off their parents' social standing. As with the drawing of Geneviève de Gonet, his portraits after 1900 attest not only to his artistic and technical evolution but also to the privileged bonds of friendship he enjoyed

with exceptional personalities, which to him remained a source of great pride.

Marie-Pierre Salé

1. A related work is *Portrait of a Little Girl*, a drawing known through an old photograph in the Druet papers, now in the Bibliothèque Nationale de France (DC 354a f°; A. Wildenstein 1992–98, vol. 4 [1998], no. 2566).
2. *Simone Fayet with a Doll*, 1906, pastel (ibid., vol. 1 [1992], no. 93); *Simone Fayet at Her Communion*, 1908, pastel (ibid., no. 94); *Iseult Fayet*, 1908, pastel (ibid., no. 95); *Profile of a Young Domecy*, 1898 (ibid., no. 729); *Portrait of Jeanne Roberte de Domecy*, 1905 (ibid., no. 725); *Marcel Mellerio* (ibid., no. 108).
3. Mary Cassatt (1844–1926), *Portrait of Louise Aurore Villeboeuf*, 1902, pastel on paper, 28¾ × 23⅝ in. (73 × 60 cm), signed and dated at lower left, "Mary Cassatt. 1902," Musée d'Orsay, Paris, gift of L. A. Villeboeuf, 1978 (inv. 36822).
4. Mellerio 1898.
5. Leblond 1907, p. 160; Marius-Ary Leblond was the collective pen name of the journalists and writers Marius Athenas and René Merlo, collectors of Redon who championed his work.
6. Terme 1921; Terme 1922.
7. Bibliothèque Littéraire Jacques Doucet, Paris, manuscript collection, gift of Arï Redon.
8. A. Wildenstein 1992–98, vol. 4 (1998), no. 2564.
9. The catalogued works that belonged to the Marquis Jean de Gonet are *Apollo's Chariot*, oil on canvas, acquired from the artist in 1908 (ibid., vol. 2 [1994], no. 867); *Black Pegasus*, oil on canvas, acquired in 1910 (ibid., no. 982); *Saint George and the Dragon*, oil on wood (ibid., no. 1273); *Portrait of the Marquise de Gonet*, pastel, 1907 (ibid., vol. 4 [1998], no. 2564); *A Buddha or Person Asleep*, ca. 1910, mixed media on cardboard (ibid., no. 2579); *The Sermon*, ca. 1905, oil on wood (ibid., no. 2596); *The Wheel of Fortune*, oil on cardboard (ibid., no. 2606); *Flowers*, pastel (ibid., no. 2642); *The Boat*, oil on panel (ibid., no. 2657). This list was established based on the artist's catalogue raisonné and the auction catalogue from the sale of the Gonet Collection, Christie's, New York, November 11, 1997.
10. On the genealogy of the Gonets, see Salvaing 1996, pp. 40–45.

117

117. Pierre-Auguste Renoir

Limoges, 1841–Cagnes-sur-Mer, 1919

Nude Bathers Playing with a Crab

Ca. 1897–1900

Pastel on laid paper, 17¹¹⁄₁₆ × 24 in. (45 × 61 cm)

Signed in graphite at lower right: *Renoir*

PROVENANCE: The artist to Ambroise Vollard, Paris, ca. 1897–1900; Édouard Jonas, Paris; Ohana Gallery, London; Edgar William and Bernice Chrysler Garbisch; sale, Christie's, June 28, 1968, lot 68; purchased at that sale by Arthur Murray, Honolulu, thence by descent; Sayn-Wittgenstein Fine Art, New York; acquired by Jean Bonna, 2006[1]

EXHIBITIONS: London 1956, no. 53; Geneva 2006–7a

Pierre-Auguste Renoir began painting with broken brushstrokes in the late 1860s and famously devoted much of his art to depicting the pleasures of life in Paris, yet he often doubted the direction his career had taken. His uncertainty, perhaps fueled by the lack of traditional artistic training, led him to reform his art and, after 1877, to refuse further participation in the Impressionists' exhibitions. During the 1880s, he traveled widely and studied old masters, as if to make up for the fact that

while many of his contemporaries trained under pupils of Ingres, he was apprenticed to a decorator of porcelain.

After working four years (1884–87) on a canvas to demonstrate a newfound control of pictorial compositions and the contours of the figures within them, Renoir presented his monumental painting *The Bathers*, now in the Philadelphia Museum of Art. It was followed by many more pictures of young, healthy women frolicking in the water, but none quite so

Figure 151. Pierre-Auguste Renoir, *Bathers Playing with a Crab*, ca. 1897. Oil on fabric. The Cleveland Museum of Art

Figure 152. Pierre-Auguste Renoir, *Bathers with a Crab*, ca. 1890–99. Oil on canvas. Carnegie Museum of Art, Pittsburgh

(figs. 151, 152).[3] The pastel differs from the paintings in several ways, most notably in the postures of the nudes and their arrangement, which allow for more open areas in the drawn composition, enhancing its airiness and luminosity that is conveyed primarily through the blending of opalescent colors in the then almost forgotten medium of Watteau, Boucher, and Fragonard.

COLTA IVES

firmly sculptural as his first demonstration piece. Like his friend Paul Cézanne, Renoir was determined to revive the tradition of grand bather paintings, not, it turns out, in a formal classical mode but rather in the softened, luminous style of Impressionism to which he eventually returned and which happily accorded with the rococo motifs he had copied onto cups and plates during his youth. He always loved the vivacity and rosy prettiness of François Boucher's and Jean-Honoré Fragonard's young women and confessed going back again and again to the former's *Bath of Diana* of 1742, now in the Louvre, "as one returns to one's first love."[2]

Like the large *Bathers* painting in Philadelphia, the Bonna pastel depicts a triangular arrangement of three nudes seen from the front, side, and back, all of which are brought close to the picture plane. It is an alluring group, recalling the mythical trio of goddesses from which Paris had to select the loveliest. But this is a much more down-to-earth ensemble and highly animated, in which one beauty acts the tease and the mood is all playfulness.

The drawing may be situated in time somewhere between Renoir's execution of two paintings of nearly the same composition and size, both dating from about 1890 to 1900

1. The vendors stated that the work is recorded and illustrated in the Vollard archives. They provided a transcript of a letter dated March 7, 2006, from Pascal Perrin at the Wildenstein Institute, Paris, in which it was stated that François Daulte had studied the pastel when it was in the Garbisch Collection and had wished to include it in the sixth volume of his catalogue raisonné of Renoir's pastels, watercolors, and drawings. M. Perrin stated also that a counterproof printed from the pastel by Auguste Clot was in the collection of Baron Petiet.
2. Vollard 1919, p. 20.
3. Another closely related small painting is illustrated in Vollard 1918, no. 85, along with another related drawing, no. 73. The painting was sold at Sotheby's, New York, May 16–17, 1979, lot 231. A black and white chalk drawing of the three bathers in the Bonna drawing is identified as "location unknown" and illustrated in Argencourt 1999, vol. 2, p. 534.

118. Paul Gauguin

Paris, 1848–Atuona (Marquesas), 1903

Two Tahitian Women: Study for Women by the Sea

Ca. 1895–1900

Conté crayon and charcoal, 16 15/16 × 12 in. (43 × 30.5 cm)

PROVENANCE: Richard Zinser, Forest Hills, New York; Albert Gordon, New York; Kate Ganz, London; acquired by Jean Bonna, 1998

EXHIBITIONS: Paris 2006b, no. 96; Geneva 2006–7a

BIBLIOGRAPHY: Denison 2006, p. 521

This large study can be related to three paintings from Paul Gauguin's second and final stay in the South Seas, which began in 1895 and ended with the artist's death in the Marquesas Islands on May 8, 1903. Of these, the drawing has the most in common with *Women by the Sea* (fig. 153), of which two versions exist.[1] There are, in fact, a study and an arrangement of the two Tahitian women's faces that are extremely close to the final canvas. The latter was in a lot of ten paintings that Gauguin sent to Ambroise Vollard in October 1900; these were shown at the posthumous exhibition organized by that dealer in 1903. The Bonna drawing, notably the primary face, can also be related to the *Three Tahitians* in the National Gallery of Scotland, Edinburgh (fig. 154),[2] which for many years was thought to be from 1897 but which must now be dated 1899. A second drawing can also be added to this coherent group of works, showing only the more finished face and bearing an inscription to Daniel de Monfreid that reads: "My dear Daniel / Here is the head of the model / in this state it does not / show what I had intended / Let me know your thoughts / Cordially / Paul Gauguin."[3]

Figure 153. Paul Gauguin, *Women by the Sea*, 1899. Oil on canvas. State Hermitage Museum, Saint Petersburg (inv. GE 8979)

Figure 154. Paul Gauguin, *Three Tahitians*, 1899. Oil on canvas. National Gallery of Scotland, Edinburgh (inv. NGS 2221–W.573)

The drawing in the Bonna Collection and the ensemble of works with which it is associated are highly representative of the intellectual and stylistic inflection that Gauguin imprinted on his art during his South Seas sojourn. The ethnographic scrupulousness with which he treated daily life and Polynesian religion are here pushed into the background to make room for the more conceptual, and more directly Symbolist, type of vision summarized in Gauguin's painted manifesto

Where Do We Come From? What Are We? Where Are We Going?, made in 1897 and now in the Museum of Fine Arts, Boston. From that point on, Gauguin's search for the best way to express myth would lead him to view forms through the prism of purification and monumentality. The economy of this strong simple drawing is an element of that new draftsmanship. It is a reminder that Gauguin's final aesthetic reinvention presides over the harmonious natural encounter of Symbolist

ambitions and the perennial nature of classical expression.

LAURENCE DES CARS

1. G. Wildenstein 1964, nos. 582, 583.
2. Ibid., no. 573.
3. Paul Gauguin, *Head of a Young Woman*, drawing in grease pencil and stumping, signed; sale, Nicolas Rauch, Geneva, June 13–15, 1960, lot. 482, ill. This author is indebted to Nathalie Strasser for providing this information.

119. Vincent van Gogh

Zundert, 1853–Auvers-sur-Oise, 1890

Recto: *Houses in a Landscape*

Verso: *Houses in the Countryside in the Snow*

1890

Conté crayon and stumping, 9¼ × 12⁵⁄₁₆ in. (23.5 × 31.3 cm)

PROVENANCE: Paul Ferdinand Gachet, Auvers; Paul Gachet, Auvers, until 1905; Wildenstein and Company, New York, 1955; Ernesto Blohm, Caracas, until 1970; Private Collection, Germany; Katrin Bellinger Kunsthandel, Munich; acquired by Jean Bonna, 2004

EXHIBITIONS: Paris 1905, no. 23; New York 1955, no. 108; Paris 2006b, no. 97; Geneva 2006–7a

BIBLIOGRAPHY: Faille 1928, vol. 3, p. 179, no. 1648; Faille 1970, p. 555, no. 1648 (recto and verso); Hulsker 1996, p. 441, nos. 1913, 1914

The drawings on the recto and verso of this sheet are part of a group of about sixty sketches executed by Vincent van Gogh in March and April 1890, in Saint-Rémy. The majority of these have rural subjects, a theme that is central to the work of van Gogh, who

throughout his life remained fascinated by the countryside and the harsh existence of the peasants. He grew up in North Brabant province in the southern Netherlands, and his youth was deeply marked by the countryside around his native village of Zundert. The drawings in this group are inspired very broadly by his memories of the Brabantine countryside, which he readily evoked during his stay in Saint-Rémy.

119 recto

119 verso (size reduced)

Figure 155. Vincent van Gogh, *Reminiscence of the North*. Oil on canvas. Van Gogh Museum, Amsterdam (inv. F 1593r JH 1906)

Van Gogh chose to pursue an artistic career in 1880, and when in April 1881, he went to live with his parents in the Brabantine village of Etten, he devoted himself passionately to illustrating the lives of the local peasantry. He often portrayed them sowing, digging, or harvesting grain, humble labors of the fields that comprise one of the recurrent themes of his work. Van Gogh was also fascinated by the cottages in which these people lived, eloquent testaments to their difficult and simple lives and also refuges in which the inhabitants felt safe. That is why he likened *The Cottage*,[1] which he painted in Nuenen in April and early May 1885, to a wren's nest;[2] later, he would call these cottages "little human nests."[3]

These rural themes naturally became less prominent during the two years van Gogh spent in Paris, from March 1886 to February 1888, a period that saw him develop into one of the most modern artists of his time, but they would reappear definitively in his work from Arles. The sowing of crops is the subject is several of his most ambitious drawings. And during an excursion to Saintes-Maries-de-la-Mer in May 1888, he made several large studies depicting the picturesque cottages found in the fishing village.

At the end of 1888, van Gogh began showing the first signs of his illness, thought to be a form of epilepsy, and in May 1889, he committed himself to the Saint-Paul-de-Mausole

Institute in Saint-Rémy. When his health permitted, he continued drawing and painting in the confines of the former convent, venturing outdoors if he felt well enough. But on several occasions, severe seizures kept him from working for long periods at a stretch. The last and most dramatic bout of illness occurred on February 22, 1890, and he did not recover until the end of April. As often when he was depressed, van Gogh was besieged by melancholic thoughts of his native village. During an earlier crisis, he had been assailed by specific childhood memories; this time, his recollections inspired him to produce a series of five paintings that he entitled Reminiscences of the North (fig. 155).[4]

While van Gogh used that label only for the paintings, clearly it applies just as well to the large group of drawings that includes the present one. These drawings show, for instance, farm workers at their labors, Brabantine cottages, and couples or families strolling about. The weather is typical of the Northern countries, the landscapes drenched with rain, the cottages and fields buried in snow. The vegetation, on the other hand, is Provençal, with its cypress and pine trees. The paintings date from March and April 1890, and the drawings were probably made at around the same time.

The two images in the Bonna Collection drawing are perfectly representative of the series. One side of the sheet shows a group of

five cottages under a heavy, overcast sky. Snow covers the landscape and the picturesque cottages whose chimneys emit trails of smoke, signs of life that van Gogh often added. A woman in front of a cottage holds a shovel, probably to clear the snow from the path leading from the house to the road. The peasant shoveling is a frequent motif in van Gogh's work, especially when the artist was going through a difficult period, as was the case at the time. It has been maintained, with some justification, that peasants digging symbolize the harsh existence of humankind, for as the Bible says: "In the sweat of thy face shalt thou eat bread" (Genesis, 3:19).[5] Does the woman shoveling snow also symbolize the difficult human condition? This is less certain. It seems more likely that she was added to highlight the harsh winter conditions. Two strollers are walking along the road, canes in hand, looking like many of the figures in the drawings from this group—gangling gait, stocky silhouettes, debatable anatomy, and yet possessing great expressive power.

On the recto of the sheet is another group of cottages, this time without snow. In front of the last two is a haystack. The sky is cloudy but not as dark as it is depicted on the verso. This time, van Gogh did not add any figures.

The two drawings on the Bonna sheet also show the same characteristics in technique as several others in the series, which are on simple sheets of wove paper, about 24 by 32 centimeters in dimension, and are executed in Conté crayon. Some are also done in graphite and sometimes in black chalk. In this sheet only graphite was used. It should be noted that in many places, the outlines have been stumped, which creates seductive gradations of gray.

Sjraar van Heugten

1. Oil on canvas, May 1885, Van Gogh Museum, Amsterdam (on permanent loan from the Vincent van Gogh Fondation) (F 83 JH77; inv. s 87 V/1962).
2. Vincent van Gogh to Theo van Gogh, in Van Gogh, *Letters*, 2000 (ed.), vol. 2, p. 386, letter 411.
3. Ibid., p. 397, letter 418.
4. Ibid., vol. 3, p. 261, letter 629.
5. Kōdera 1990, pp. 67–68, "'In the sweat of thy face shalt thou eat bread': diggers in the oeuvre of Van Gogh."

120. Georges Seurat

Paris, 1859–Paris, 1891

Woman in a White Bonnet

1882–85

Conté crayon on Michallet paper (vertical watermark at right edge), 12½ × 10¹⁄₁₆ in. (31.8 × 25.6 cm)

PROVENANCE: Édouard Vuillard; Jacques Salomon, Paris; Wildenstein and Company, New York; acquired by Jean Bonna, 2002

EXHIBITIONS: Paris 1926a, no. 135; Paris 1936a, no. 115; Paris 1957, no. 42; Paris 2006b, no. 98; Geneva 2006–7a

BIBLIOGRAPHY: Kahn 1928, pl. 114; Hauke 1961, vol. 2, p. 100, no. 502, and vol. 1, p. 269 (photograph of the exhibition at Galerie Paul Rosenberg, Paris, in 1936); Herbert 1962, p. 189, no. 163, ill. p. 184; Kahn 1928/1971, p. xviii, pl. 134; Zimmermann 1991, p. 127, no. 249, ill. p. 129

Figure 156. Georges Seurat, *The Orange Seller*, signed and dated *Seurat, 1881*. Conté crayon and traces of white chalk on laid paper. Musée d'Orsay, located in the Musée du Louvre, Département des Arts Graphiques, Paris (inv. RF 31207)

In the 1880s, Georges Seurat turned his back on his academic training, and his style evolved toward a kind of naturalism. Robert L. Herbert studied this evolution and the corpus of drawings that displays it.[1] The painter had been in the habit of sketching street scenes from life ever since his early years, but at this point, they became the main subject of his independent crayon drawings—women in profile, passersby in rear view, modest street professions such as the orange seller (fig. 156),[2] nannies, concierges, and other ordinary people. These black-and-white works are related to the artistic and literary naturalism of the period by their social significance and their choice of modern subjects—the lives of working people or, conversely, of stern bourgeoisie and elegant Parisians. *Woman in a White Bonnet* fits into this series and evokes the studies of young nannies in bonnets and white aprons. In this case, the bonnet does not have the long black ribbon that characterizes nannies, but the apron indicates a "menial job" in the city, perhaps that of a chambermaid. Michael F. Zimmermann discussed these silhouettes from 1882 to 1885 as an ensemble and returned the current figure to the gallery of (mostly female) "Parisian passersby."[3]

This link with contemporary naturalism is quite removed from the demands of illusionistic realistic depiction, especially when concerned with the seamier side of life. Seurat's eclectic references combine the cursory outlines of popular prints (which he collected), the drawings of Jean-François Millet (which he greatly admired), and the etchings of Rembrandt (in which he pondered the use of chiaroscuro and the infinite possibilities of monochrome),[4] as well as the engravings and drawings of Honoré Daumier. Indeed, certain figures in his black drawings are more like caricatures, such as *Woman with a Muff* from about 1884, now in

the Art Institute of Chicago.[5] In fact, there is nothing in French drawing that truly compares to Seurat's works in black, not even Redon's *noirs* in charcoal, which explore a different path (see cat. no. 114) Seurat used the rough texture of Ingres paper to create his values; Conté, an artificial composite crayon, is not powdery like charcoal, does not require stumping, and allows for deep blacks and light grays, with whites, as in the bonnet here, showing through uncovered areas of the paper. More than the naturalism of the subjects, the critics of the time noted the poetry of the drawings, the paradox (as his disciple Paul Signac put it) of those "whites and blacks . . . more luminous and more colored than many paintings."[6]

The present drawing once belonged to Édouard Vuillard, although the archives do not give more precise information about when the painter acquired it or received it as a gift. Vuillard, who was a great admirer of Seurat, owned another drawing by him, *The Anchors*,[7] which Thadée Natanson reproduced in his study of Seurat for *La Revue blanche* in 1900.[8] In that study, Natanson admired the artist's primitivism and the black drawings, which he already interpreted as the most modern of forms.

MARIE-PIERRE SALÉ

1. Paris and New York 1991–92, pp. 73–78.
2. Gift of the Baronne Eva Gebhardt-Gourgaud, 1965.
3. Zimmermann 1991, nos. 240–47, ill. pp. 128, 129.
4. On Seurat's sources and his personal documentation, see Paris and New York 1991–92, App. C, pp. 427–28.
5. Herbert 1962, no. 612.
6. Signac 1911/1978, p. 109. On Seurat's drawings, see New York 2007–8.
7. Herbert 1962, no. 698, study for *The Channel of Gravelines, Evening* (Herbert 1962, no. 210). This author is indebted to Mathias Chivot for kindly undertaking this research in the Vuillard archives.
8. Natanson 1900, p. 614.

Bibliography

Aaron 1985
Olivier Aaron. *Dessins insolites du XVIII⁰ français*. Paris, 1985.

Achilles-Syndram 1994
Katrin Achilles-Syndram. *Die Kunstsammlung des Paulus Praun: Die Inventare von 1616 und 1719*. Quellen zur Geschichte und Kultur der Stadt Nürnberg 25. Stadtarchiv Nürnberg. Nuremberg, 1994.

Acidini Luchinat 1998–99
Cristina Acidini Luchinat. *Taddeo e Federico Zuccari: Fratelli pittori del Cinquecento*. 2 vols. Archivi arte antica. Milan and Rome, 1998–99.

Adhémar 1973
Jean Adhémar. "Les Portraits dessinés du XVI⁰ siècle au Cabinet des Estampes." *Gazette des beaux-arts*, 6th ser., 82 (September 1973), pp. 121–98.

Adhémar and Lethève 1955
Jean Adhémar and Jacques Lethève. *Inventaire du fonds français après 1800*. Vol. 9. Cabinet des Estampes, Bibliothèque Nationale, Paris. Paris, 1955.

Adler 1980
Wolfgang Adler. *Jan Wildens: Der Landschaftsmitarbeiter des Rubens*. Fridingen, 1980.

Adler 1982
Wolfgang Adler. *Landscapes*. Vol. 1 of *Landscapes and Hunting Scenes*. 2 vols. Corpus Rubenianum Ludwig Burchard 18. London and Oxford, 1982.

Adorni 1982
Bruno Adorni, ed. *Santa Maria della Steccata a Parma*. Parma, 1982.

Alexandre 1918
Arsène Alexandre. "Essai sur Monsieur Degas." *Les Arts*, no. 166 (1918), pp. 2–24.

Alister Mathews 1972
Alister Mathews. *Drawings & Watercolours*. Catalogue no. 79, Spring 1972. Bournemouth, 1972.

Alsteens and Buijs 2008
Stijn Alsteens and Hans Buijs. *Paysages de France dessinés par Lambert et les artistes hollandais et flamands des XVI⁰ et XVII⁰ siècles*. Paris, 2008. Index and errata available at http://www.fondationcustodia.fr/publicaties/paysages_index.pdf

Ames-Lewis 1986
Francis Ames-Lewis. *The Draftsman Raphael*. New Haven, 1986.

Amiens and Versailles 1995–96
Versailles: Les Chasses exotiques de Louis XV. Exh. cat. by Xavier Salmon. Musée de Picardie, Amiens, October 14, 1995–January 14, 1996; and Musée National des Châteaux de Versailles et de Trianon, February 15–May 12. Paris, 1995.

Amsterdam 1909
Catalogus der tentoonstelling van werken van Odilon Redon. Larensche Kunsthandel, Amsterdam, May 7–14, 1909. Amsterdam, 1909.

Amsterdam 1987–88
Dossier Rembrandt: Documenten, tekeningen en prenten / The Rembrandt Papers: Documents, Drawings and Prints. Exh. cat. by S. A. C. Dudok van Heel et al., with contributions by Peter Schatborn and Eva Ornstein-van Slooten. Museum Het Rembrandthuis, Amsterdam, October 17, 1987–January 4, 1988. Amsterdam, 1987.

Amsterdam 1993
Tekeningen van oude meesters: De verzameling Jacobus A. Klaver. Exh. cat. by Marijn Schapelhouman and Peter Schatborn. Rijksprentenkabinet, Rijksmuseum, Amsterdam, May 8–July 25, 1993. Zwolle, 1993.

Amsterdam 1999–2000
Rembrandt's Treasures. Exh. cat. edited by Bob van den Boogert. Museum Het Rembrandthuis, Amsterdam, September 25, 1999–January 9, 2000. Zwolle and Amsterdam, 1999.

Amsterdam and Paris 1998–99
Landscapes of Rembrandt: His Favourite Walks. Exh. cat. by Boudewijn Bakker, Mària van Berge-Gerbaud, Erik Schmitz, and Jan Peeters. Gemeentearchief, Amsterdam, September 30–November 29, 1998; and Institut Néerlandais, Paris, December 17, 1998–February 14, 1999. Bussum, 1998.

Amsterdam, New York, and Toledo 2003–4
Hendrick Goltzius (1558–1617): Drawings, Prints and Paintings. Exh. cat. by Huigen Leeflang et al. Rijksmuseum, Amsterdam, March 7–May 25, 2003; The Metropolitan Museum of Art, New York, June 23–September 7; and Toledo Museum of Art, October 18, 2003–January 4, 2004. Zwolle, 2003.

Amsterdam, Vienna, New York, and Cambridge 1991–92
Seventeenth-Century Dutch Drawings: A Selection from the Maida and George Abrams Collection. Exh. cat. by William W. Robinson. Rijksprentenkabinet, Rijksmuseum, Amsterdam, February 23–April 28, 1991; Graphische Sammlung Albertina, Vienna, May 16–June 30; Pierpont Morgan Library, New York, January 22–April 22, 1992; and Fogg Art Museum, Harvard University, Cambridge, Massachusetts, October 10–December 6. Lynn, Mass., 1991.

Ananoff 1961–70
Alexandre Ananoff. *L'Oeuvre dessiné de Jean-Honoré Fragonard (1732–1806): Catalogue raisonné*. 4 vols. Paris, 1961–70.

Ananoff 1966
Alexandre Ananoff. *L'Oeuvre dessiné de François Boucher (1703–1770): Catalogue raisonné*. Paris, 1966.

Ananoff 1967
Alexandre Ananoff. "Chardin: Il Reste sûrement plus de quatre dessins." *Connaissance des arts*, no. 180 (February 1967), pp. 60–63.

Ananoff 1976
Alexandre Ananoff, with Daniel Wildenstein. *François Boucher*. 2 vols. Lausanne, 1976.

Ananoff 1979
Alexandre Ananoff. "Les Chardin de la collection Goncourt." *L'Oeil*, no. 290 (September 1979), pp. 60–61.

Ananoff 1983
Alexandre Ananoff. *Ce qu'il faut connaître de la peinture et du dessin ancien*. Paris, 1983.

Andrews 1985
Keith Andrews. *Catalogue of Netherlandish Drawings in the National Gallery of Scotland*. 2 vols. Edinburgh, 1985.

Antal 1956
Frederick Antal. *Fuseli Studies*. London, 1956.

Antwerp 1993
Jacob Jordaens (1593–1678). Exh. cat. by R.-A. d'Hulst, Nora De Poorter, and Marc Vandenven. Koninklijk Museum voor Schone Kunsten, Antwerp, March 27–June 17, 1993. 2 vols. Antwerp, 1993.

Antwerp 2006
Verbeeld land: De provincie Antwerpen in tekeningen, 1600–1900. Exh. cat. by Bob Daems. Koningin Fabiolazaal, Antwerp, June 16–September 3, 2006. Antwerp, 2006.

Antwerp and Amsterdam 1999–2000
Anthony van Dyck as a Printmaker. Exh. cat. by Carl Depauw and Ger Luijten, with contributions by Erik Duverger et al. Museum Plantin-Moretus / Stedelijk Prentenkabinet, Antwerp, May 15–August 22, 1999; and Rijksprentenkabinet, Rijksmuseum, Amsterdam, October 9, 1999–January 9, 2000. Antwerp and Amsterdam, 1999.

Antwerp and London 1999
The Light of Nature: Landscape Drawings and Watercolours by Van Dyck and His Contemporaries. Exh. cat. by Martin Royalton-Kisch. Rubenshuis, Antwerp, May 15–August 15, 1999; and British Museum, London, September 18–December 5. London, 1999.

Argencourt 1999
Louise d'Argencourt, with Roger Diederen, and with contributions by Alisa Luxenberg et al. *European Paintings of the Nineteenth Century*. 2 vols. Cleveland Museum of Art. Cleveland, 1999.

Arlaud 1976
Pierre Arlaud. *Catalogue raisonné des estampes gravées d'après Joseph Vernet*. Avignon, 1976.

Arquié-Bruley 1981
Françoise Arquié-Bruley. "Documents notariés inédits sur Greuze." *Bulletin de la Société de l'Histoire de l'Art Français*, 1981 (pub. 1983), pp. 125–54.

Artemis 1972
Artemis 71–72: Consolidated Report, Annual General Meeting, 27 October 1972. Luxembourg, 1972.

Bacou 1956
Roseline Bacou. *Odilon Redon*. 2 vols. Geneva, 1956.

Bacou 1960
Roseline Bacou, ed. *Lettres de Gauguin, Gide, Huysmans, Jammes, Mallarmé, Verhaeren . . . à Odilon Redon*. Paris, 1960.

Baetjer 2002
Katharine Baetjer. "A Drawing by Canaletto of Richmond House Terrace." *Metropolitan Museum Journal* 37 (2002), pp. 213–22.

Bakker 1998
Boudewijn Bakker. "A Booke Fulle of Landscapes Drawne from Life: Art and Reality in Rembrandt's Landscapes." In Amsterdam and Paris 1998–99, pp. 15–39.

Bakker, Fleurbaay and Gerlagh 1989
Boudedwijn Bakker, E. Fleurbaay, and A. W. Gerlagh. *De verzameling Van Eeghen: Amsterdamse tekeningen, 1600–1950.* 2nd ed. Publikaties van het Gemeentearchief Amsterdam 16. Zwolle and Amsterdam, 1989. [1st ed., 1988.]

Baldassari 1995
Francesca Baldassari. *Carlo Dolci.* Turin, 1995.

Baldinucci 1681–1728 (1767–74 ed.)
Filippo Baldinucci. *Notizie dei professori del disegno da Cimabue in qua.* 6 vols. in 5. Florence, 1681–1728. 1767–74 ed.: Edited by Domenico Maria Manni. 21 vols. Florence, 1767–74.

Baldinucci 1681–1728 (1845–47 ed.)
Filippo Baldinucci. *Notizie dei professori del disegno da Cimabue in qua.* 6 vols. in 5. Florence, 1681–1728. Repr., edited by Ferdinando Ranalli. 7 vols. Florence, 1845–47. [Repr., 1974–75.]

Balfour 1930
Arthur James Balfour. *Chapters of Autobiography.* London, 1930.

Baltimore, Boston, and Minneapolis 1984–85
Regency to Empire: French Printmaking, 1715–1814. Exh. cat. by David Becker et al. Baltimore Museum of Art, November 1, 1984–January 6, 1985; Museum of Fine Arts, Boston, February 6–March 31; and Minneapolis Institute of Arts, April 17–June 23. Baltimore and Minneapolis, 1984.

Bambach 1994
Carmen C. Bambach. "On '*la testa proportionalmente degradata*': Luca Signorelli, Leonardo, and Piero della Francesca's *De Prospectiva Pingendi.*" In *Florentine Drawing at the Time of Lorenzo the Magnificent: Papers from a Colloquium Held at the Villa Spelman, Florence, 1992,* edited by Elizabeth Cropper, pp. 17–43. Villa Spelman colloquia 4. Bologna, 1994.

Bambach 2003
Carmen C. Bambach. "Introduction to Leonardo and His Drawings." In New York 2003, pp. 3–30.

Bambach 2008
Carmen C. Bambach. "Drawings in Dresden: Newly Identified Works by Italian Masters." *Apollo* 167 (January 2008), pp. 54–61.

Bantell 1981
Linda Bantell. *The Alice M. Kaplan Collection.* New York, 1981.

Bartolini 1987
Elio Bartolini. *Giovanni da Udine.* [Vol. 3], *La vita.* Udine, 1987.

Bartolozzi 1753
Sebastiano Benedetto Bartolozzi. *Vita di Jacopo Vignali: Pittor fiorentino.* Florence, 1753.

Bartsch 1797
Adam Bartsch. *Catalogue raisonné de toutes les estampes qui forment l'oeuvre de Rembrandt et ceux de ses principaux imitateurs.* 2 pts. in 1 vol. New ed. Vienna, 1797.

Bartsch 1803–21
Adam Bartsch. *Le Peintre graveur.* 21 vols. Vienna, 1803–21.

Basel 1997
Hans Holbein d. J.: Die Druckgraphik im Kupferstichkabinett Basel. Exh. cat. by Christian Müller. Kunstmuseum Basel, May 14–September 7, 1997. Basel, 1997.

Bazin 1987–97
Germain Bazin. *Théodore Géricault: Étude critique, documents et catalogue raisonné.* 7 vols. Paris, 1987–97.

Bean 1979
Jacob Bean. *Seventeenth Century Italian Drawings in The Metropolitan Museum of Art.* New York, 1979.

Bean 1986
Jacob Bean, with Lawrence Turčić. *Fifteenth–Eighteenth Century French Drawings in The Metropolitan Museum of Art.* New York, 1986.

Bean and Griswold 1990
Jacob Bean and William Griswold. *Eighteenth Century Italian Drawings in The Metropolitan Museum of Art.* New York, 1990.

Beaumont-Maillet, Jobert, and Join-Lambert 1999
Eugène Delacroix. *Souvenirs d'un voyage dans le Maroc.* Edited by Laure Beaumont-Maillet, Barthélemy Jobert, and Sophie Join-Lambert. Paris, 1999.

Beauvais 2000
Lydia Beauvais, with a contribution by Madeleine Pinault Sørensen and the assistance of Véronique Goarin and Catherine Scheck. *Charles Le Brun, 1619–1690.* 2 vols. Inventaire général des dessins. École française. Département des Arts Graphiques, Musée du Louvre, Paris. Paris, 2000.

Becker 1922
Felix Becker. *Handzeichnungen alter Meister in Privatsammlungen: Fünfzig bisher nicht veröffentliche Originalzeichnungen des XV. bis XVIII. Jahrhunderts.* Leipzig, 1922.

Béguin 1973
Sylvie Béguin. "Pour Speckaert." In *Album Amicorum J. G. van Gelder,* edited by J. Bruyn, Jan A. Emmens, E. De Jongh, and D. P. Snoep, pp. 9–14. The Hague, 1973.

Béguin, Di Giampaolo, and Vaccaro 2000
Sylvie Béguin, Mario Di Giampaolo, and Mary Vaccaro. *Parmigianino: The Drawings.* Archivi di arte antichi. Turin, 2000.

Bellinati 1989
Claudio Bellinati. "Iconografia e teologia negli affreschi del Battistero." In *Giusto de' Menabuoi nel Battistero di Padova,* pp. 41–82. Trieste, 1989.

Bellori 1672 (1968 ed.)
Giovanni Pietro Bellori. *Le vite de' pittori, scultori et architetti moderni.* Rome, 1672. 1968 ed.: Quaderni dell'Istituto di Storia dell'Arte della Università di Genova 4. Genoa, 1968.

Bellori 1672 (1976 ed.)
Giovanni Pietro Bellori. *Le vite de' pittori, scultori et architetti moderni.* Rome, 1672. 1976 ed.: Edited by Evelina Borea. I millenni. Turin, 1976.

Bénédite 1931
Léonce Bénédite. *Théodore Chassériau: Sa Vie et son oeuvre.* 2 vols. Paris, 1931.

Benesch 1928
Otto Benesch. *Die Zeichnungen der niederländischen Schulen des XV. und XVI. Jahrhunderts.* Beschreibender Katalog der Handzeichnungen in der Graphischen Sammlung Albertina 2. Vienna, 1928.

Benesch 1930
Otto Benesch. [Review of Bock 1929.] *Belvedere* 9 (1930), pp. 75–82.

Benesch 1939–40
Otto Benesch. "Jean Cousin Fils dessinateur." *Prométhée* 20 (December 1939–January 1940), pp. 271–80.

Benesch 1973
Otto Benesch. *The Drawings of Rembrandt.* Edited by Eva Benesch. 6 vols. London, 1973.

Bentini 1989
Jadranka Bentini, ed. *Disegni della Galleria Estense di Modena.* Modena, 1989.

Berenson 1961
Bernard Berenson. *I disegni dei pittori fiorentini.* 3 vols. Milan, 1961.

Berger 1952
Klaus Berger. *Géricault et son oeuvre.* Translated by Maurice Beerblock. Vienna, 1952.

Berger 1965
Klaus Berger. *Odilon Redon: Fantasy and Color.* Translated by Michael Bullock. New York, 1965.

Berger 1968
Klaus Berger. *Géricault et son oeuvre.* Paris, 1968.

Berlin 1910
Ausstellung von Werken französischer Kunst des XVIII. Jahrhunderts. Exh. cat. Königliche Akademie der Künste, Berlin, January 26–March 6, 1910. Berlin, 1910.

Berlin, Venice, Madrid, and Geneva 1999–2000
Linie, Licht und Schatten: Meisterzeichnungen und Skulpturen der Sammlung Jan und Marie Anne Krugier-Poniatowski. Kupferstichkabinett, Staatliche Museen zu Berlin, May 29–August 1, 1999; Peggy Guggenheim Collection, Solomon R. Guggenheim Foundation, Venice, September–December; Museo Thyssen-Bornemisza, Madrid, February 2–May 14, 2000; and Musée d'Art et d'Histoire, Geneva, Summer. Berlin, 1999. English ed., *The Timeless Eye: Master Drawings from the Jan and Marie-Anne Krugier-Poniatowski Collection.* Berlin, 1999. Spanish ed., *Miradas sin tiempo: Dibujos, pinturas y esculturas de la colección Jan y Marie-Anne Krugier-Poniatowski.* Madrid, 2000.

Berzaghi 1988
Renato Berzaghi. "Uno sconosciuto ciclo mantovano di Giulio Campi: Gli Amori di Giove in Palazzo Aldegatti." *Verona illustrata,* 1988, pp. 31–36.

Besançon 2006–7
Les Fragonard de Besançon. Exh. cat. by Pierre Rosenberg and Claudine Lebrun Jouve. Musée des Beaux-Arts et d'Archéologie, Besançon, December 8, 2006–April 2, 2007. Milan and Besançon, 2006.

Bezzola 1994
Tobia Bezzola. "Portrait und Genre." In Zurich and Tübingen 1994–95, pp. 278–301.

Binion 1976
Alice Binion. *Antonio and Francesco Guardi: Their Life and Milieu; with a Catalogue of Their Figure Drawings.* Outstanding Dissertations in the Fine Arts. New York, 1976.

Birke and Kertész 1994
Veronika Birke and Janine Kertész. *Die italienischen Zeichnungen der Albertina: Generalverzeichnis.* Vol. 2. Veröffentlichungen der Albertina 34. Vienna, 1994.

Birmingham 1986
Master Drawings in the Barber Institute. Exh. cat. by Hamish Miles and Paul Spencer-Longhurst. Barber Institute of Fine Arts, Birmingham, November 20–December 12, 1986. London, 1986.

Birmingham 2007
Hidden Burne-Jones: Works on Paper by Edward Burne-Jones from Birmingham Museums and Art Gallery. Exh. cat. by John Christian, Elisa Korb, and Tessa Sidey. Birmingham Museums and Art Gallery, April 4–July 1, 2007. London, 2007.

Bjurström 1982
Per Bjurström. *French Drawings: Eighteenth Century.* Drawings in Swedish Public Collections 4. Nationalmuseum. Stockholm, 1982.

Bjurström and Magnusson 1998
Per Bjurström and Börje Magnusson. *Italian Drawings: Umbria, Rome, Naples.* Drawings in Swedish Public Collections 6. Stockholm, 1998.

Blanc 1845
Charles Blanc. *Histoire des peintres français au dix-neuvième siècle.* Paris, 1845.

Blankert 1982
Albert Blankert. "Hendrick Avercamp." In *Frozen Silence: Hendrick Avercamp, 1585–1634, Barent Avercamp, 1612–1679; Paintings from Museums and Private Collections,* pp. 15–36. Exh. cat. by Albert Blankert et al. Waterman Gallery, Amsterdam, March 13–April 18, 1982. Amsterdam, 1982.

Blois 2002
Parures d'or et de pourpre: Le Mobilier à la cour des Valois. Exh. cat. by Jacques Thirion et al. Château de Blois, June 15–September 30, 2002. Paris and Blois, 2002.

Bloomington, Stanford, and New York 1979–80
Domenico Tiepolo's Punchinello Drawings. Exh. cat. by Marcia E. Vetrocq. Indiana University Art Museum, Bloomington, September 2–October 6, 1979; Stanford University Museum of Art, November 13–December 30; and Frick Collection, New York, January 22–March 30, 1980. Bloomington, 1979.

Bock 1929
Elfried Bock. *Die Zeichnungen in der Universitätsbibliothek Erlangen.* 2 vols. Die Kataloge der Prestel-Gesellschaft, 1 Erlangen. Frankfurt-am-Main, 1929.

Bock and Rosenberg 1930
Elfried Bock and Jakob Rosenberg. *Die niederländischen Meister: Beschreibendes Verzeichnis sämtlicher Zeichnungen.* 2 vols. Berlin, 1930.

Bode 1890
Wilhelm Bode. "Un maestro anonimo dell'antica scuola lombarda (Il Pseudo Boccaccino)." *Archivio storico dell'arte* 3 (1890), pp. 192–95.

Bodnár 1996
Szilvia Bodnár. "Hoffmann, Hans." In *The Dictionary of Art,* edited by Jane Turner, vol. 14, pp. 626–27. New York, 1996.

Boggs 1962
Jean Sutherland Boggs. *Portraits by Degas.* California Studies in the History of Art 2. Berkeley, 1962.

Boggs 1963
Jean Sutherland Boggs. "Edgar Degas and Naples." *Burlington Magazine* 105 (June 1963), pp. 273–77.

Bohn 1988
Babette Bohn. "Bartolommeo Passarotti and Reproductive Etching in Sixteenth-Century Italy." *Print Quarterly* 5, no. 2 (June 1988), pp. 115–27.

Bohn 2004
Babette Bohn. *Ludovico Carracci and the Art of Drawing.* Turnhout, 2004.

Boisfleury 1972
Sabine de Boisfleury. "L'Oeuvre dessiné de Pierre Puget." Master's thesis, École du Louvre, Paris, 1972.

Bologna 1956
Mostra dei Carracci: Catalogo critici dei disegni. Exh. cat. edited by Denis Mahon. Translated by Maurizio Calvesi. Palazzo dell'Archiginnasio, Bologna, September 1–November 25, 1956. Bologna, 1956. [2nd ed., Bologna, 1963.]

Bologna 1968
Il Guercino (Giovanni Francesco Barbieri, 1591–1666): Catalogo critico dei dipinti. Exh. cat. edited by Denis Mahon. Palazzo dell'Archiginnasio, Bologna, September 1–November 18, 1968. Bologna, 1968.

Bologna and Fort Worth 1993–94
Ludovico Carracci. Exh. cat. Museo Civico Archeologico and Pinacoteca Nazionale, Bologna, September 25–December 12, 1993; and Kimbell Art Museum, Fort Worth, January 22–April 10, 1994. Bologna, 1993.

Bologna and Rome 2006–7
Annibale Carracci. Exh. cat. edited by Daniele Benati and Eugenio Riccòmini. Museo Civico Archeologico, Bologna, September 22, 2006–January 7, 2007; and Chiostro del Bramante, Rome, January 25–May 6. Milan, 2006.

Bolten 2007
Jaap Bolten. *Abraham Bloemaert, c. 1565–1651: The Drawings.* 2 vols. [The Netherlands], 2007.

Boon 1978
Karel G. Boon. *Netherlandish Drawings of the Fifteenth and Sixteenth Centuries.* 1 vol. in 2. Catalogus van de Nederlandse tekeningen in het Rijksmuseum te Amsterdam / Catalogue of the Dutch and Flemish Drawings in the Rijksmuseum 2. The Hague, 1978.

Boon 1992
Karel G. Boon. *The Netherlandish and German Drawings of the XVth and XVIth Centuries of the Frits Lugt Collection.* 3 vols. Paris, 1992.

Bora 1988
Giulio Bora. "Maniera, 'idea' e natura nel disegno cremonese: Novità e precisazioni." *Paragone* 39, nos. 459–461–463 (May–June–September 1988), pp. 13–38.

Bora 1998a
Giulio Bora. "The Leonardesque Circle and Drawing." In *The Legacy of Leonardo: Painters in Lombardy, 1490–1530,* pp. 92–120. Milan, 1998.

Bora 1998b
Giulio Bora. "Giovanni Agostino da Lodi." In *The Legacy of Leonardo: Painters in Lombardy, 1490–1530,* pp. 251–74. Milan, 1998.

Bordeaux 1984
Jean-Luc Bordeaux. *François Le Moyne and His Generation, 1688–1737.* Neuilly-sur-Seine, 1984.

Borea 1965
Evelina Borea. *Domenichino.* Florence, 1965.

Boselli 1972
Camillo Boselli. "Nuovi documenti sull'arte veneta del secolo XVI nell'archivio della famiglia Averoldi di Brescia." *Arte veneta* 26 (1972), pp. 234–36.

Boston 1904
Oil Paintings, Water Colors, Pastels, and Drawings: Memorial Exhibition of the Works of Mr. J. McNeill Whistler. Exh. cat. Copley Hall, Boston, February–March 1904. Boston, 1904.

Boston 1984
Jean-François Millet. Exh. cat. by Alexandra R. Murphy, with contributions by Susan Fleming and Chantal Mahy-Park. Museum of Fine Arts, Boston, March 28–July 1, 1984. Boston, 1984.

Bourguignon d'Anville 1774
Jean-Baptiste Bourguignon d'Anville. "Éloge de M. Gravelot." In *Le Nécrologe des hommes célèbres de France.* Paris, 1774.

Brame and Reff 1984
Philippe Brame and Theodore Reff, with Arlene Reff. *Degas et Son Oeuvre: A Supplement.* New York, 1984.

Brejon de Lavergnée 1980
Arnauld Brejon de Lavergnée. *Dijon, Musée Magnin: Catalogue des tableaux et dessins italiens (XVᵉ–XIXᵉ siècles).* Inventaire des collections publiques françaises 24. Paris, 1980.

Bremer-David 1997
Charissa Bremer-David. *French Tapestries and Textiles in the J. Paul Getty Museum.* Los Angeles, 1997.

Brenninkmeijer-De Rooij 1996
Beatrijs Brenninkmeijer-De Rooij. *Roots of Seventeenth-Century Flower Painting: Miniatures, Plant Books, Paintings.* Leiden, 1996.

Briganti 1966
Giuliano Briganti. *Gaspar van Wittel e l'origine della veduta settecentesca.* Rome, 1966.

Briquet
C. M. Briquet. *Les Filigranes: Dictionnaire historique des marques du papier des leur apparition vers 1282 jusqu'en 1600.* 4 vols. 2nd ed. Leipzig, 1923. [Repr., New York, 1966.]

Brogi 2001
Alessandro Brogi. *Ludovico Carracci (1555–1619).* 2 vols. Pittori d'Italia 3. Ozzano Emilia, Bologna, 2001.

Broglie 1971
Raoul de Broglie. "Les Clouet de Chantilly: Catalogue illustré." *Gazette des beaux-arts,* 6th ser., 77 (May–June 1971), pp. 259–336.

Brown 1998
David Alan Brown. *Leonardo da Vinci: Origins of a Genius.* New Haven, 1998.

Bruel 1958
André Bruel, ed. *Les Carnets de David d'Angers.* 2 vols. Paris, 1958.

Bruges and Enshede 2007–8
Bruges, Paris, Rome: Joseph Benoît Suvée et le néoclassicisme. Exh. cat. by Sandra Janssens and Paul Knolle. Groeningemuseum, Bruges, October 19, 2007–January 6, 2008; and Rijksmuseum Twenthe, Enschede, February 2–May 5. Ghent, 2007.

Brussels 1890
"Les Vingt: VIIᵉ Exposition anuelle des Vingt." Brussels, February 1890.

Brussels 1983
Dessins vénitiens du XVIIIᵉ siècle. Exh. cat. by Alessandro Bettagno et al. Palais des Beaux-Arts, Brussels, April 15–June 5, 1983. Brussels, 1983. [English ed., *Masterpieces of Eighteenth-Century Venetian Drawing.* New York, 1983.]

Brussels, Rotterdam, and Paris 1949–50
Le Dessin français de Fouquet à Cézanne. Exh. cat. Palais des Beaux-Arts, Brussels, November–December; Museum Boymans, Rotterdam, December 25, 1949–February 6, 1950; and Musée de l'Orangerie, Paris, February–March 1950. Brussels, 1949.

Brussels, Rotterdam, Paris, and Bern 1968–69
Dessins de paysagistes hollandais du XVIIᵉ siècle de la collection particulière conservée à l'Institut Néerlandais de Paris. Exh. cat. by Carlos van Hasselt. Bibliothèque Albert Iᵉʳ, Brussels, October 22–November 24, 1968; Museum Boymans-van Beuningen, Rotterdam, December 1, 1968–January 12, 1969; Institut Néerlandais, Paris, February 1–March 16; and Musée des Beaux-Arts, Bern, April 1–May 11. Brussels, 1968.

Bruwaert 1912
Edmond Bruwaert. *Vie de Jacques Callot: Graveur lorrain, 1592–1635.* Paris, 1912.

Burne-Jones 1904
Georgiana Burne-Jones. *Memorials of Edward Burne-Jones*. 2 vols. London, 1904.

Byam Shaw 1951
James Byam Shaw. *The Drawings of Francesco Guardi*. London, 1951.

Byam Shaw 1962
James Byam Shaw. *The Drawings of Domenico Tiepolo*. London, 1962.

Byam Shaw 1967
James Byam Shaw. *Paintings by Old Masters at Christ Church, Oxford*. London, 1967.

Byam Shaw 1976
James Byam Shaw. *Drawings by Old Masters at Christ Church, Oxford*. 2 vols. Oxford. 1976.

Byam Shaw 1977
James Byam Shaw. "Some Guardi Drawings Rediscovered." *Master Drawings* 15, no. 1 (Spring 1977), pp. 3–15.

Byam Shaw 1983
James Byam Shaw. *The Italian Drawings of the Frits Lugt Collection*. 3 vols. Institut Néerlandais, Paris. Paris, 1983.

Cailleux 1966
Jean Cailleux, ed. "L'Art du dix-huitième siècle." *Burlington Magazine* 108 (April 1966), suppl., pp. i–v.

Cailleux 1975
Jean Cailleux. "Les Artistes français du dix-huitième siècle et Rembrandt." In *Études d'art français offerts à Charles Sterling*, edited by Albert Châtelet and Nicole Reynaud, pp. 287–305. Paris, 1975.

Cairns 1987
David Cairns, ed. and trans. *A Life of Love and Music: The Memoirs of Hector Berlioz, 1803–1865*. London, 1987.

Cambridge 1967
Ingres Centennial Exhibition, 1867–1967: Drawings, Watercolors and Oil Sketches from American Collections. Exh. cat. by Agnes Mongan and Hans Naef. Fogg Art Museum, Harvard University, Cambridge, Massachusetts, February 12–April 9, 1967. Cambridge, Mass., 1967. [With a "Technical Appendix" by Marjorie B. Cohn, pp. 241–49.]

Cambridge 1980
Works by J.-A.-D. Ingres in the Collection of the Fogg Art Museum. Exh. cat. by Marjorie B. Cohn and Susan L. Siegfried. Fogg Art Museum, Harvard University, Cambridge, Massachusetts, October 19–December 7, 1980. Fogg Art Museum Handbooks 3. Cambridge, Mass., 1980.

Cambridge 1985
The Achievement of a Connoisseur, Philip Pouncey: Italian Old Master Drawings. Exh. cat. by Julien Stock and David Scrase. Fitzwilliam Museum, Cambridge, October 15–December 15, 1985. Cambridge, 1985.

Cambridge and other cities 1998–2000
Mastery and Elegance: Two Centuries of French Drawings from the Collection of Jeffrey E. Horvitz. Exh. cat. edited by Alvin L. Clark Jr., with Margaret Morgan Grasselli, Jean-François Méjanès, and William W. Robinson; foreword by Pierre Rosenberg. Harvard University Art Museums, Cambridge, Massachusetts, December 5, 1998–January 31, 1999; Art Gallery of Ontario, Toronto, February 20–April 18; Musée Jacquemart André, Paris, May 1–June 25; National Gallery of Scotland, Edinburgh, July 9–September 5; National Academy of Design, New York, October 8–December 12; and Los Angeles County Museum of Art, February 24–April 14, 2000. Cambridge, Mass., 1998.

Cambridge, New York, and Los Angeles 1998
Fuseli to Menzel: Drawings and Watercolors in the Age of Goethe from a German Private Collection. Exh. cat. by Hinrich Sieveking and John Gabriel. Busch-Reisinger Museum, Harvard University Art Museums, Cambridge, Massachusetts, April 4–June 7, 1998; Frick Collection, New York, June 23–August 30; and J. Paul Getty Museum, Los Angeles, September 15–November 29. Munich and Cambridge, Mass., 1998.

Cambridge, Ottawa, and Cleveland 1991
Guercino: Master Draughtsman. Works from North American Collections. Exh. cat. by David M. Stone. Arthur M. Sackler Museum, Harvard University Art Museums, Cambridge, Massachusetts, February 15–March 31, 1991; National Gallery of Canada, Ottawa, May 3–June 16; and Cleveland Museum of Art, August 27–October 13. Cambridge, Mass., and Bologna, 1991.

Casselle 1982
Pierre Casselle. "Pierre-François Basan: Marchand d'estampes à Paris (1723–1797)." In *Mémoires* (Fédération des Sociétés Historiques et Archéologiques de Paris et d'Île de France) 33 (1982), pp. 99–185.

Cassou 1972
Jean Cassou. *Odilon Redon*. Gli impressionisti. Milan, 1972.

Cavalier 2002
Odile Cavalier, with Marie-Odile Jentel. *L'Empire de Mars et des muses: La Collection du marquis de Calvière, lieutenant-général des armées du Roi, 1693–1777*. Musée Calvet, Avignon. Paris and Avignon, 2002.

Cayeux 1963
Jean de Cayeux. "Introduction au catalogue critique des *Griffonis* de Saint-Non." *Bulletin de la Société de l'Histoire de l'Art Français*, 1963 (pub. 1964), pp. 297–384.

Cento 2005
Nel segno di Guercino: Disegni dalle collezioni Mahon, Oxford e Cento / Guercino as Master Draughtsman: Drawings from the Mahon Collection, the Ashmolean Museum at Oxford, and the City of Cento. Exh. cat. Pinacoteca Civica, Cento, May 28–July 31, 2005. Cento, 2005.

Champion 1921
Pierre Champion. *Notes critiques sur les vies anciennes d'Antoine Watteau*. Paris, 1921.

Chantilly 2001–2
L'Art du manuscrit de la Renaissance en France. Exh. cat. by Valérie Auclair et al. Musée Condé, Château de Chantilly, September 26, 2001–January 7, 2002. Paris and Chantilly, 2001.

Chantilly 2002–3
Les Clouet de Catherine de Médicis: Chefs-d'Oeuvre graphiques du Musée Condé. Exh. cat. by Alexandra Zvereva. Musée Condé, Château de Chantilly, September 25, 2002–January 6, 2003. Paris and Chantilly, 2002.

Chappell 2005
Miles Chappell. "Reform and Continuity in Later Florentine Drawing." *Master Drawings* 43, no. 3 (Fall 2005), pp. 339–48.

Chatsworth Raffaelles 1872
The Chatsworth Raffaelles: A Series of . . . Reproductions of the Raffaelle Drawings in the Collection of the Duke of Devonshire at Chatsworth. London, 1872.

Chenique 2001
Bruno Chenique. "Géricault et ses cercles politiques de la rue des Martyrs." In *La Nouvelle Athènes: Haut lieu du Romantisme*, edited by Bruno Centorame, pp. 172–84. Collection Paris et son patrimoine. Paris, 2001.

Chenique 2002
Bruno Chenique. "La Vie de Théodore Chassériau (1819–1856): Essai de biochronologie, 1819–1843." In Paris, Strasbourg, and New York 2002–3, pp. 163–86.

Chicago, Amsterdam, and London 1994–95
Odilon Redon: Prince of Dreams, 1840–1916. Exh. cat. by Douglas W. Druick et al. Art Institute of Chicago, July 2–September 28, 1994; Van Gogh Museum, Amsterdam, October 20, 1994–January 15, 1995; and Royal Academy of Arts, London, February 16–May 21. Chicago, Amsterdam, London, and New York, 1994.

Christie's 1975
Christie's Review of the Season. London, 1975.

Clark 1982
Timothy J. Clark. *The Absolute Bourgeois: Artists and Politics in France, 1848–1851*. [New ed.] Princeton, 1982. [1st ed., London, 1973.]

Claude Kuhn 1987
Claude Kuhn. *Handzeichnungen alter Meister*. Basel, 1987.

Clayton 2004
Martin Clayton. "Drawings by Domenico Campagnola after Giusto de' Menabuoi's Apocalypse Frescoes." *Master Drawings* 42, no. 4 (Winter 2004), pp. 315–32.

Cleri 1993
Bonita Cleri. "Officina familiare.'" In *Per Taddeo e Federico Zuccari nelle Marche*, pp. 95–108. Exh. cat. Palazzo Fagnani, Sant'Angelo in Vado, September 18–November 7, 1993. Sant'Angelo in Vado, 1993.

Cleveland and New Haven 1978
The Graphic Art of Federico Barocci: Selected Drawings and Prints. Exh. cat. by Edmund P. Pillsbury and Louise S. Richards. Cleveland Museum of Art, February 15–March 26, 1978; and Yale University Art Gallery, New Haven, April 11–June 4. [Cleveland], 1978.

Cochin 1780/1875–76
Charles-Nicolas Cochin. "Essai sur la vie de Chardin." [1780.] Edited by Ch. Beaupaire. In *Precis analytique des travaux de l'Académie des Sciences, Belles-Lettres et Arts de Rouen* 73 (1875–76), pp. 417–41.

Cohen 1912
Henry Cohen. *Guide de l'amateur de livres a gravures du XVIIIᵉ siècle*. 6th ed. Edited by Seymour de Ricci. Paris, 1912. [Repr., Breuil-en-Vexin, 1973.]

Coletti 1955
Luigi Coletti. *Tutta la pittura di Giorgione*. Milan, 1955.

Coliva 1996
Anna Coliva. "Sant'Andrea della Valle." In *Domenichino, 1581–1641*, pp. 284–97. Exh. cat. Palazzo Venezia, Rome, October 10, 1996–January 14, 1997. Milan, 1996.

Collé 1748–72/1967
Charles Collé. *Journal et mémoires de Charles Collé sur les hommes de lettres, les ouvrages dramatiques et les événements les plus mémorables du règne de Louis XV, 1748–1772*. 3 vols. Geneva, 1967. [Repr. of ed. edited by Honoré Bonhomme. Paris, 1868.]

"Il collezionista" 1960
"Il collezionista." *Sele arte* (Studio di Storia dell'Arte, Florence) 8 (July–September 1960), pp. 75–80.

Colorno 1998
Gli arazzi dei Farnese e dei Borbone: Le collezioni dei secoli XVI–XVII. Exh. cat. edited by Giuseppe Bertini and Nello Forti Grazzini. Palazzo Ducale, Colorno, September 19–November 29, 1998. Milan, 1998.

Commelin 1693
Casparus Commelin. *Beschrijvinge van Amsterdam . . . .* Amsterdam, 1693.

Conigliello 1991
Lucilla Conigliello. "Pesci, crostacei e un'iguana per l'imperatore Rodolfo II." *Paragone* 42, nos. 493–495 (March–May 1991), pp. 22–29.

Conigliello 1994
Lucilla Conigliello. "Jacopo Ligozzi negli orti farnesiani." *Paragone* 45, nos. 529-531-533 (March–July 1994), pp. 184–90.

Conisbee 1973
Philip Conisbee. "Salvator Rosa et Claude-Joseph Vernet." *Burlington Magazine* 115 (December 1973), pp. 789–94.

Constable 1989
William George Constable. *Canaletto: Giovanni Antonio Canal, 1697–1768.* 2 vols. Repr. of 2nd ed., with supplement and additional plates. Oxford, 1989.

Copenhagen 1935
Exposition de l'art français au XVIIIᵉ siècle. Exh. cat. Charlottenborg Exhibition Hall, Copenhagen, August 25–October 6, 1935. Copenhagen, 1935.

Corboz 1985
André Corboz. *Canaletto: Una Venezia immaginaria.* 2 vols. Milan, 1985.

Cornillot 1957
Marie-Lucie Cornillot, ed. *Collection Pierre-Adrien Pâris, Besançon.* Inventaire general des dessins des musées de province 1. Paris, 1957.

Corpus Christi 1970
Romantic Art at the Time of Beethoven. Exh. cat. Art Museum of South Texas, Corpus Christi, March 14–April 28, 1970. Corpus Christi, 1970.

Courtoy 1930
F. Courtoy. "Gilles Nyts peintre de Namur, au XVIIᵉ siècle." *Namurcum: Chronique de la Société Archéologique de Namur* 7, no. 1 (1930), pp. 12–16.

Covi 2005
Dario A. Covi. *Andrea del Verrocchio: Life and Work.* Arte e archeologia 27. Florence, 2005.

Cremona 1985
I Campi e la cultura artistica cremonese del Cinquecento. Exh. cat. edited by Mina Gregori. Santa Maria della Pietà, Vecchio Ospedale, and Sala Manfredini, Museo Civico, Cremona, April 27–July 31, 1985. Milan, 1985.

Crenshaw 2006
Paul Crenshaw. *Rembrandt's Bankruptcy: The Artist, His Patrons, and the Art Market in Seventeenth-Century Netherlands.* New York, 2006.

Crowe and Cavalcaselle 1882–85
J. A. Crowe and G. B. Cavalcaselle. *Raphael: His Life and Works; with Particular Reference to Recently Discovered Records, and an Exhaustive Study of Extant Drawings and Pictures.* 2 vols. London, 1882–85.

Czére 2007
Andrea Czére, ed. *In Arte Venustas: Studies on Drawings in Honour of Teréz Gerszi. Presented on Her Eightieth Birthday.* Budapest, 2007.

Dacier 1924
Émile Dacier. "Les Scènes & figures théâtrales de Claude Gillot." *Revue de l'art ancien et moderne* 45 (January–May 1924), pp. 44–56.

Dacier 1926
Émile Dacier. "Les Scènes & figures théâtrales de Claude Gillot." *Revue de l'art ancien et moderne* 49 (January–May 1926), pp. 280–94.

Dacier and Vuaflart 1921–29
Émile Dacier and Albert Vuaflart. *Jean de Jullienne et les graveurs de Watteau au XVIIIᵉ siècle.* 4 vols. Paris, 1921–29.

Dacos and Furlan 1987
Nicole Dacos and Caterina Furlan. *Giovanni da Udine.* [Vol. 1], *Giovanni da Udine: 1487–1561.* Udine, 1987.

Dakers 1999
Caroline Dakers. *The Holland Park Circle: Artists and Victorian Society.* New Haven, 1999.

Dalli Regoli 1966
Gigetta Dalli Regoli. *Lorenzo di Credi.* Raccolta pisana di saggi e studi 19. [Milan], 1966.

Dalli Regoli 2003
Gigetta Dalli Regoli, ed. *Verrocchio, Lorenzo di Credi, Francesco di Simone Ferrucci.* Cabinet des Dessins, Musée du Louvre, Paris. Milan and Paris, 2003.

Dal Poggetto 1983
Paolo Dal Poggetto. "Raffaellino del Colle tra Marche, Toscana ed Umbria (1525–1545 c.)." In *Urbino e le Marche prima e dopo Raffaello,* pp. 414–39. Exh. cat. edited by Maria Grazia Ciardi Duprè Dal Poggetto and Paolo Dal Poggetto. Palazzo Ducale and church of San Domenico, Urbino, July 30–October 30, 1983. Florence, 1983.

Dandré-Bardon 1765
Michel-François Dandré-Bardon. *Vie de Carle Vanloo.* Paris, 1765.

Daniel and Serebriannaya 1995
Sergei Daniel and Natalia Serebriannaya. *Claude Lorrain: Painter of Light.* Bournemouth and Saint Petersburg, 1995.

Day & Faber 2001
Day & Faber. *European Drawings, 1570–1870.* London, 2001.

Dayot and Vaillat 1907
Armand Dayot and Léandre Vaillat. *L'Oeuvre de J.-B.-S. Chardin et de J.-H. Fragonard.* Paris, [1907].

Degas' Drawings 1973
Degas' Drawings. New York, 1973.

DeGrazia 1979
Diane DeGrazia Bohlin. *Prints and Related Drawings by the Carracci Family: A Catalogue Raisonné.* National Gallery of Art. Washington, D.C., 1979.

Delaborde 1870
Henri Delaborde. *Ingres: Sa vie, ses travaux, sa doctrine d'après les notes manuscrites et les lettres du maître.* Paris, 1870.

Delacroix, *Correspondance*, 1936–38 (ed.)
Eugène Delacroix. *Correspondance générale d'Eugène Delacroix.* Edited by André Joubin. 5 vols. Paris, 1936–38.

Delacroix, *Journal*, 1981 (ed.)
Eugène Delacroix. *Journal, 1822–1863.* Edited by André Joubin. Revised ed. by Régis Labourdette. Collection Les Mémorables. Paris, 1981.

Delacroix, *Letters*, 2001 (ed.)
Eugène Delacroix. *Selected Letters, 1813–1863.* Edited and translated by Jean Margaret Stewart. Boston, 2001.

Denison 2006
Cara D. Denison. "Suite francaise: Dessins de la collection Jean Bonna." [Review of Paris 2006b.] *Master Drawings* 44, no. 4 (Winter 2006), pp. 520–21.

Denison and Mules 1981
Cara D. Denison and Helen B. Mules, with the assistance of Jane V. Shoaf. *European Drawings, 1375–1825.* Pierpont Morgan Library. New York, 1981.

De Pauw-De Veen 1969
Lydia De Pauw-De Veen. *De begrippen "schilder", "schilderij" en "schilderen" in de zeventiende eeuw.* Verhandelingen van de Koninklijke Vlaamse Academie voor Wetenschappen, Letteren en Schone Kunsten van België, Klasse der Schone Kunsten, vol. 31, no. 22. Brussels, 1969.

Detroit and Philadelphia 2002–3
Degas and the Dance. Exh. cat. by Jill De Vonyar and Richard Kendall. Detroit Institute of Arts, October 18, 2002–January 12, 2003; and Philadelphia Museum of Art, February 16–May 11. New York, 2002.

Dézallier d'Argenville 1762
Antoine-Joseph Dézallier d'Argenville. *Abrégé de la vie des plus fameux peintres, avec leurs portraits gravés en taille-douce, les indications de leurs principaux ouvrages, quelques réflexions sur leurs caractères et la manière de connoître les dessins et les tableaux des grands maîtres.* 4 vols. Paris, 1762. [Repr., 2 vols. Geneva, 1972.]

Diderot, *Essais sur la peinture*, 1766/1984
Denis Diderot. "Essais sur la peinture: Pour faite suite au Salon de 1765." [1766.] In Denis Diderot, *Essais sur la peinture: Salons de 1759, 1761, 1763,* edited by Gita May and Jacques Chouillet, pp. 11–79. Paris, 1984.

Diderot, *Salon de 1763*, 1984 (ed.)
Denis Diderot. *Salon de 1763.* 1984 ed.: Denis Diderot. "Salon de 1763." In *Essais sur la peinture: Salons de 1759, 1761, 1763, 1765,* edited by Gita May and Jacques Chouillet, pp. 171–255. Paris, 1984.

Diderot, *Salon de 1765*, 1960 (ed.)
Denis Diderot. *Salon de 1765.* 1960 ed.: Denis Diderot, *Salons.* Vol. 2. Edited by Jean Seznec and Jean Adhémar. Oxford, 1960.

Diderot, *Salon de 1767*, 1995 (ed.)
Denis Diderot. *Salon de 1767.* 1995 ed.: Denis Diderot, *Ruines et paysages: Salons de 1767,* edited by Else-Marie Bukdahl, Michel Delon, and Annette Lorenceau. Salons 3. Collection Savoir. Lettres. Paris, 1995.

Di Giampaolo 1974
Mario Di Giampaolo. "Per il Malosso disegnatore." *Arte illustrata,* no. 57 (March 1974), pp. 18–35.

Di Giampaolo 1977
Mario Di Giampaolo. "A Drawing by Malosso at Oxford and Some Additions to His Oeuvre." *Master Drawings* 15, no. 1 (Spring 1977), pp. 28–31.

Dijon 1959
Pierre-Paul Prud'hon, 1758–1823: Les Premières Étapes de sa carrière. Commémoration du deuxième centenaire. Exh. cat. by Pierre Quarré and Monique Geiger. Musée des Beaux-Arts, Dijon, 1959. Dijon, 1959. [2nd ed., 1973.]

Dimier 1914
Louis Dimier. *Histoire de la peinture au XIXᵉ siècle (1793–1903).* Paris, 1914.

Dollmayr 1895
Hermann Dollmayr. "Raffaels Werkstätte." *Jahrbuch der Kunsthistorischen Sammlungen des Allerhöchsten Kaiserhauses* 16 (1895), pp. 231–363.

Donnelly 1959
Marian C. Donnelly. "Calvinism in the Work of Jacob Jordaens." *Art Quarterly* 22, no. 4 (Winter 1959), pp. 356–66.

Droghini 2001
Marco Droghini. *Raffaellino del Colle.* "La valle dorata" 3. [Fermignano], 2001.

Druick and Kort Zegers 1994a
Douglas W. Druick and Peter Kort Zegers. "In the Public Eye." In Chicago, Amsterdam, and London 1994–95, pp. 120–74, 395–402.

Druick and Kort Zegers 1994b
Douglas W. Druick and Peter Kort Zegers. "Taking Wing, 1870–1878." In Chicago, Amsterdam, and London 1994–95, pp. 74–117, 389–95.

Dudok van Heel 1980
S. A. C. Dudok van Heel. "Schrijfoefeningen van Titus van Rijn (1641–1668)." In *Amstelodamum: Maandblad voor*

de kennis van Amsterdam 67, no. 1 (January–February 1980), pp. 3–7.

Duret 1902
Théodore Duret. *Histoire d'Édouard Manet et de son oeuvre.* Paris, 1902.

Duret 1919
Théodore Duret. *Histoire d'Édouard Manet et de son oeuvre, avec un catalogue des peintures et des pastels.* New ed. Paris, 1919.

Duret 1926
Théodore Duret. *Histoire d'Édouard Manet et de son oeuvre, avec un catalogue des peintures et des pastels.* 4th ed. Paris, 1926.

Dussler 1971
Luitpold Dussler. *Raphael: A Critical Catalogue of His Pictures, Wall-Paintings, and Tapestries.* London, 1971. [Translated from the German ed., Munich, 1966.]

Edinburgh 1969
Italian Sixteenth Century Drawings from British Private Collections. Exh. cat. by Yvonne Tan Bunzl and Keith Andrews. Merchants' Hall, Edinburgh, August 23–September 13, 1969. Sponsored by the Edinburgh Festival Society. Edinburgh, 1969.

Edinburgh, New York, and Houston 1999–2001
The Draftsman's Art: Master Drawings from the National Gallery of Scotland. Exh. cat. by Colin Bailey et al. National Gallery of Scotland, Edinburgh, April 9–June 13, 1999; Frick Collection, New York, December 12, 2000–February 25, 2001; and Museum of Fine Arts, Houston, March 20–June 8. Edinburgh, 1999.

Eidelberg 1977
Martin P. Eidelberg. *Watteau's Drawings: Their Use and Significance.* Outstanding Dissertations in the Fine Arts. New York, 1977.

Eitner 1953
Lorenz Eitner. Review of *Géricault und sein Werk,* by Klaus Berger. *Zeitschrift für Kunstgeschichte* 16 (1953), pp. 80–82.

Eitner 1954
Lorenz Eitner. [Letter to the Editor.] *Art Bulletin* 36, no. 2 (June 1954), pp. 167–68.

Eitner 1983
Lorenz Eitner. *Géricault: His Life and Work.* London, 1983.

Eitner 1991
Lorenz Eitner. *Géricault: Sa Vie, son oeuvre.* Translated by Jeanne Bouniort. Art et artistes. Paris, 1991.

Eitner 1996
Lorenz Eitner. "Erotic Drawings by Gericault." *Master Drawings* 34, no. 4 (Winter 1996), pp. 375–89.

Ekserdjian 1997
David Ekserdjian. *Correggio.* New Haven, 1997.

Elderfield and Gordon 1996
John Elderfield and Robert Gordon. *The Language of the Body: Drawings by Pierre-Paul Prud'hon.* New York, 1996. [French ed., *La Poésie du corps: Dessins de Pierre-Paul Prud'hon.* Paris, 1997.]

Eliades 1982
G. S. Eliades. *Das Haus des Dionysos: Die Villa mit dem Mosaiken von Nea Paphos.* 2nd ed. Paphos, 1982.

Ellis 1994
Charles S. Ellis. "The Landscape Drawings of Fra Bartolommeo." Ph.D. diss., University of Chicago, 1994.

Ellis 2007
Charles S. Ellis. "Observations on a Picture by Fra Bartolommeo." *Paragone* 58, no. 689 (July 2007), pp. 85–94.

Emiliani 1985
Andrea Emiliani. *Federico Barocci (Urbino, 1535–1612).* 2 vols. Bologna, 1985.

Essen and Vienna 1988–89
Prag um 1600: Kunst und Kultur am Hofe Kaiser Rudolfs II. Exh. cat. Kulturstiftung Ruhr, Villa Hügel, Essen, October 6–30, 1988; and Kunsthistorisches Museum, Vienna, November 24, 1988–February 26, 1989. 2 vols. Freren, 1988.

Fadda 2004
Elisabetta Fadda. *Michelangelo Anselmi.* Archivi di arte antica. Turin, 2004.

Faille 1928
Jacob-Baart de la Faille. *L'Oeuvre de Vincent Van Gogh: Catalogue raisonné.* 4 vols. Paris, 1928.

Faille 1970
Jacob-Baart de la Faille. *The Works of Vincent Van Gogh: His Paintings and Drawings.* Amsterdam, 1970.

Félibien 1666–88/1972
André Félibien. *Entretiens sur les vies et sur les ouvrages des plus excellens peintres anciens et modernes.* 5 vols. Paris, 1666–88. Repr., 5 vols. in 3. Geneva, 1972.

Félibien 1725
André Félibien. *Entretiens sur les vies et sur les ouvrages des plus excellens peintres anciens et modernes; avec la vie des architectes.* 6 vols. New ed. Trévoux, 1725. [Repr., Geneva, 1972.]

Fermor 1996
Sharon Fermor. *The Raphael Tapestry Cartoons: Narrative, Decoration, Design.* London, 1996.

Ferrari 1961
Maria Luisa Ferrari. *Il Romanino.* Antichi pittori italiani. Milan, 1961.

Ficacci 2000
Luigi Ficacci. *Giovanni Battista Piranesi: The Complete Etchings / Gesamtkatalog der Kupferstiche / Catalogue raisonné des eaux-fortes.* Cologne, 2000.

Fiocco 1948
Giuseppe Fiocco. *Giorgione.* I grandi artisti italiani. Bergamo, 1948.

Fiocco 1955
Giuseppe Fiocco. "Il mio Giorgione." *Rivista di Venezia,* 1955, no. 1.

Fiocco 1965
Giuseppe Fiocco. *Guardi.* Milan, 1965.

Firmin-Didot 1872
Ambroise Firmin-Didot. *Étude sur Jean Cousin, suivie de notices sur Jean Leclerc et Pierre Woeiriot.* Paris, 1872. [Repr., Geneva, 1971.]

Fischel 1898
Oskar Fischel. *Raphaels Zeichnungen Versuch einer Kritik der Bisher veröffentlichen Blätter.* Strasbourg, 1898.

Fischer 1986
Chris Fischer, ed. *Disegni di Fra Bartolommeo e della sua scuola.* Gabinetto Disegni e Stampe degli Uffizi 66. Florence, 1986.

Fischer 1989
Chris Fischer. "Fra Bartolommeo's Landscape Drawings." *Mitteilungen des Kunsthistorischen Institutes in Florenz* 33, nos. 2–3 (1989), pp. 301–42.

Fischer 2001
Chris Fischer. *Central Italian Drawings: Schools of Florence, Siena, the Marches and Umbria.* Statens Museum for Kunst. Copenhagen, 2001.

Flers 2000
Jean-Victor Schnetz, 1787–1870: Couleurs d'Italie. Exh. cat.

edited by Laurence Chesneau-Dupin, with contributions by Michel Caffort, Bruno Chenique, Valérie Collardeau, Stéphane Guégan, and Alain Jacobs. Musée du Château de Flers, 2000. Cabourg, 2000.

Florence 1961
Mostra di disegni di Jacopo Ligozzi (1547–1616). Exh. cat. by Mina Bacci and Anna Forlani [Tempesti]. Gabinetto Disegni e Stampe degli Uffizi, Florence, 1961. Gabinetto Disegni e Stampe degli Uffizi 12. Florence, 1961.

Florence 1965
Anna Omodeo. *Mostra di stampe popolari venete del '500.* Exh. cat. Gabinetto Disegni e Stampe degli Uffizi, Florence, 1965. Gabinetto Disegni e Stampe degli Uffizi 20. Florence, 1965.

Florence 1986–87
Il Seicento fiorentino: Arte a Firenze da Ferdinando I a Cosimo III. 3 vols. [Vol. 1], *Pittura;* [vol. 2], *Disegno / incisione / scultura / arti minori;* [vol. 3], *Biografie.* Exh. cat. Palazzo Strozzi, Florence, December 21, 1986–May 4, 1987. Florence, 1986.

Florence 1990
"Flora e Pomona": L'orticoltura nei disegni e nelle incisioni dei secoli XVI–XIX. Exh. cat. edited by Lucia Tongiorgi Tomasi and Alessandro Tosi. Gabinetto Disegni e Stampe degli Uffizi, Florence, October–December 15, 1990. Florence, 1990.

Florence 1992–93
Maestri e botteghe: Pittura a Firenze alla fine del Quattrocento. Exh. cat. edited by Mina Gregori, Antonio Paolucci, and Cristina Acidini Luchinat. Palazzo Strozzi, Florence, October 16, 1992–January 10, 1993. Cinisello Balsamo, 1992.

Florence 1996–97
L'officina della maniera: Varietà e fierezza nell'arte fiorentina del Cinquecento fra le due repubbliche (1494–1530). Exh. cat. edited by Alessandro Cecchi and Antonio Natali. Galleria degli Uffizi, Florence, September 28, 1996–January 6, 1997. Florence and Venice, 1996.

Forlani Tempesti 1982
Anna Forlani [Tempesti]. "Jacopo Ligozzi nel Gran Serraglio." *FMR* (Italian ed.), March 1982, pp. 72–103.

Forlì 2003–4
Francesco Menzocchi: Forlì, 1502–1574. Exh. cat. edited by Anna Colombi Ferretti and Luciana Prati. Pinacoteca Civica, Forlì, 2003–4. Ferrara and Forlì, 2003.

Foucart-Walter 1991
Élisabeth Foucart-Walter. "Paul Chevandier de Valdrome: *Paysage, plaine de Rome.*" In Musée du Louvre, *Nouvelles Acquisitions du Département des Peintures (1987–1990),* edited by Jacques Foucart, pp. 137–39. Paris, 1991.

Fraipont 1896
Gustave Fraipont. *Le Fusain: Figure—Paysage.* Paris, 1896.

Frankfurt 2006–7
Von Tizian bis Tiepolo: Venezianische Zeichnungen des 15. bis 18. Jahrhunderts aus der Graphischen Sammlung im Städel Museum. Exh. cat. by Julia Schewski-Bock. Städel Museum, Frankfurt am Main, November 3, 2006–January 28, 2007. Petersberg, 2006.

Franklin 1990
David Franklin. "Raffaellino del Colle: Painting and Patronage in Sansepolcro during the First Half of the Sixteenth-Century." *Studi di storia dell'arte,* no. 1 (1990), pp. 145–70.

Frommel 1968
Christoph Luitpold Frommel. *Baldassare Peruzzi als Maler und Zeichner.* Beiheft zum Römischen Jahrbuch für Kunstgeschichte 11. Vienna and Munich, 1968.

Furst 1911
Herbert Furst. *Chardin*. London, 1911.

Gabelentz 1922
Hans von der Gabelentz. *Fra Bartolommeo und die Florentiner Renaissance*. 2 vols. Leipzig, 1922.

Galerie Arnoldi-Livie 1990
Galerie Arnoldi-Livie. *70 Nordeuropäische Meisterzeichnungen, 1500–1920*. Munich, 1990.

Galerie Jean-François Heim 2008
Galerie Jean-François Heim. *Selection of Master Drawings and Paintings, XVIIth Century to XXth Century*. Catalogue 16. Paris, 2008.

Garnier-Pelle 1989
Nicole Garnier[-Pelle]. *Antoine Coypel, 1661–1722*. Paris, 1989.

Gasquet 1926
Joachim Gasquet. *Cézanne*. New ed. Paris, 1926. [1st ed., 1921.]

Gassier 1973
Pierre Gassier. *Francisco Goya, Drawings: The Complete Albums*. Translated by Robert Allen and James Emmons. New York, 1973.

Gassier 1983
Pierre Gassier. *Goya: A Witness of His Times*. Translated by Helga Harrison. Seacaucus, N.J., 1983.

Gassier and Wilson 1971
Pierre Gassier and Juliet Wilson. *Goya: His Life and Work*. London, 1971.

Gauguin, *Intimate Journals*, 1923/1985 (ed.)
Paul Gauguin. *The Intimate Journals of Paul Gauguin*. Translated by Van Wyck Brooks. Preface by Émil Gauguin. London, 1923. Repr., Pacific Basin Books. London, 1985.

Gautier, *Correspondance*, 1991 (ed.)
Théophile Gautier. *Correspondance générale*. Edited by Claudine Lacoste-Veysseyre and Pierre Laubriet. Vol. 5, *1852–1853*. Geneva, 1991.

Gealt 1986a
Adelheid Gealt. *Domenico Tiepolo: The Punchinello Drawings*. New York, 1986.

Gealt 1986b
Adelheid Gealt. *Gian Domenico Tiepolo: Dessins de Polichinelle*. Arcueil, 1986.

Geneva 2006–7a
"Le Choix d'un regard: Dessins de la collection Jean Bonna." Musée d'Art et d'Histoire, Geneva, December 7, 2006–March 4, 2007. [Included the drawings shown at the École Nationale Supérieure des Beaux-Arts, Paris, from February 14 to April 23, 2006, in "Suite française: Dessins de la collection Jean Bonna" (see Paris 2006b).]

Geneva 2006–7b
La Renaissance italienne: Peintres et poètes dans les collections genevoises. Exh. cat. edited by Michel Jeanneret and Mauro Natale. Fondation Martin Bodmer, Geneva, November 25, 2006–April 1, 2007. [Milan], 2006.

Geneva and Paris 1992
Dessins de Liotard: Suivi du catalogue de l'oeuvre dessiné. Exh. cat. by Anne de Herdt. Musée d'Art et d'Histoire, Geneva, July 17–September 20, 1992; and Musée du Louvre, Paris, October 15–December 14. Paris and Geneva, 1992.

Gerard 1996
Robert A. Gerard. "Woutneel, de Passe and the Anglo-Netherlandish Print Trade." *Print Quarterly* 13, no. 4 (December 1996), pp. 363–76.

Gere 1969
John Arthur Gere. *Taddeo Zuccaro: His Development Studied in His Drawings*. London, 1969.

Gere 1970
John Arthur Gere. "The Lawrence-Phillipps-Rosenbach 'Zuccaro Album.'" *Master Drawings* 8, no. 2 (Summer 1970), pp. 123–40.

Gere and Pouncey 1983
John Arthur Gere and Philip Pouncey. *Italian Drawings in the Department of Prints and Drawings in the British Museum*. [Vol. 5], *Artists Working in Rome, c. 1550 to c. 1640*. 2 vols. London, 1983.

Géricault 1996
Géricault. Edited by Régis Michel. 2 vols. Louvre conférences et colloques. Proceedings of a conference organized by the Musée du Louvre, Paris, and the Musée des Beaux-Arts, Rouen, 1991. Paris, 1996.

Gerszi 1968
Teréz Gerszi. "Unbekannte Zeichnungen von Jan Speckaert." *Oud Holland* 83, no. 2 (1968), pp. 161–80.

Gerszi 1971
Teréz Gerszi. *Netherlandish Drawings in the Budapest Museum: Sixteenth-Century Drawings. An Illustrated Catalogue*. 2 vols. Amsterdam and New York, 1971.

Gilbert 1978
Creighton E. Gilbert. "The Usefulness of Comparisons between the Parts and the Set: The Case of the Cappella Paolina." In *España entre el Mediterráneo y el Atlantico: Granada, 1973; Actas del XXIII Congreso Internacional de Historia del Arte*, vol. 3, pp. 519–31. Granada, 1978.

Gilham and Wood 2001
Carol C. Gilham and Carolyn H. Wood, with contributions by Carolyn M. Allmendinger et al. *European Drawings from the Collection of the Ackland Art Museum*. Chapel Hill, 2001.

Giltaij 1993
Jeroen Giltaij. "Een 'uytnemend fraey' schilderij van Hans Speckaert." In *Vorm geven aan veelzijdigheid: Opstellen aangeboden aan Wim Crouwel ter gelegenheid van zijn afscheid als directeur van Museum Boymans-van Beuningen*, pp. 14–25. Rotterdam, 1993.

Glaesemer 1974
Jürgen Glaesemer. *Joseph Werner, 1637–1710*. Oeuvre-katalogue Schweizer Künstler 3. Zurich, 1974.

Glikman 1959
Alexandr Semenovich Glikman. *Zhak Kallo / Jac. Callot*. Leningrad, 1959.

Goldner 1998
George R. Goldner. "Two New Drawings by Andrea del Sarto." *Master Drawings* 36, no. 1 (1998), pp. 29–32.

E. de Goncourt 1876
Edmond de Goncourt. *Catalogue raisonné de l'oeuvre peint, dessiné et gravé de P.-P. Prud'hon*. Paris, 1876.

E. de Goncourt 1881
Edmond de Goncourt. *La Maison d'un artiste*. 2 vols. Paris, 1881. [Repr., Collection Textes et documents. Dijon, 2003.]

E. and J. de Goncourt 1851–65/1989
Edmond and Jules de Goncourt. *Journal: Mémoires de la vie littéraire*. Edited by Robert Ricatte. Vol. 1, *1851–1865*. Collection Bouquins. Paris, 1989.

E. and J. de Goncourt 1864
Edmond and Jules de Goncourt. "Chardin." *Gazette des beaux-arts* 16 (February 1864), pp. 144–67.

E. and J. de Goncourt 1880–82
Edmond and Jules de Goncourt. *L'Art du dix-huitième siècle*. 2 vols. 3rd ed. Paris, 1880–82.

E. and J. de Goncourt 1880–82/1906
Edmond and Jules de Goncourt. *L'Art du dix-huitième siècle*. 2 vols. 3rd ed. Paris, 1880–82. New ed. 3 vols. Bibliothèque Charpentier. Paris, 1906.

Gordon 1988
George Gordon. [Review of Andrews 1985.] *Master Drawings* 26, no. 1 (1988), pp. 49–52.

Grasselli 1987
Margaret Morgan Grasselli. "The Drawings of Antoine Watteau: Stylistic Development and Problems of Chronology." 2 vols. Ph.D. diss., Harvard University, Cambridge, Mass., 1987.

Griffiths 1980
Antony Griffiths. "Greuze et ses graveurs." *Nouvelles de l'estampe*, nos. 52–53 (1980), pp. 9–11.

Gritsay and Babina 2008
Natalya Gritsay and Natalya Babina. *Seventeenth- and Eighteenth-Century Flemish Painting*. State Hermitage Museum Catalogue. Saint Petersburg and New Haven, 2008.

Gronau 1957
Carmen Gronau. Preface and and catalogue entries in Sotheby's 1957.

Groningen and Rotterdam 1964
18e eeuwse Venetiaanse tekeningen. Exh. cat. by Francesco Valconover. Pictura, Groningen, May 27–July 4, 1964; and Museum Boymans-Van Beuningen, Rotterdam, July 29–September 13. N.p., 1964.

Grunchec 1978
Philippe Grunchec. *Tout l'oeuvre peint de Gericault*. Les Classiques de l'art. Paris, 1978.

Guiffrey (Jean) 1907
Jean Guiffrey. "L'Exposition Chardin—Fragonard." *Revue de l'art ancien et moderne* 22 (July–December 1907), pp. 93–106.

Guiffrey (Jean) 1908
Jean Guiffrey. *Catalogue de l'oeuvre de J. B. Siméon Chardin (1699–1769)*. Paris, 1908.

Guiffrey (Jean) 1924
Jean Guiffrey. "L'Oeuvre de Pierre-Paul Prud'hon." *Archives de l'art français* 13 (1924).

Guiffrey (Jules) 1880
Jules Guiffrey. "La Famille de Jean Cousin: Peintre et verrier du seizième siècle." *Mémoires de la Société des Antiquaires de France* 41 (1880; pub. 1883), pp. 141–62.

Guillet de Saint-Georges 1854
Guillet de Saint-Georges [Georges Guillet]. "Charles Le Brun." In *Mémoires inédits sur la vie et les ouvrages des membres de l'Académie Royale de Peinture et de Sculpture, pub. d'après les manuscrits conservés à l'École Impériale des Beaux-Arts*, edited by Louis Dussieux, Eudoxe Soulié, Philippe de Chennevières, Paul Mantz, and Anatole de Montaiglon, vol. 1, pp. 1–72. Paris, 1854.

Gustot 2008
Pierre Gustot, with Sabine van Sprang. *Gillis Neyts: Un Paysagiste brabançon en Vallée Mosane au XVIIe siècle*. Monographies du Musée Provincial des Arts Anciens du Namurois 36. Namur, 2008.

The Hague 1892
"Tentoonstelling van schilderijen en teekeningen van eenigen uit de 'XX' en uit Association pour l'Art in den Haagschen Kunstkring." Haagsche Kunstkring, July 1892.

The Hague 1894
"Odilon Redon." Haagsche Kunstkring, May–June 1894.

The Hague 1952
Hollandse tekeningen rond 1600. Exh. cat. Rijksbureau voor Kunsthistorische Documentatie, The Hague, July 20–August 11, 1952. The Hague, 1952.

Harris 2005
Ann Sutherland Harris. "The Drawings of Annibale Carracci." [Review of Washington 1999–2000.] *Master Drawings* 43, no. 4 (Winter 2005), pp. 512–26.

Harrison and Waters 1973
Martin Harrison and Bill Waters. *Burne-Jones.* London, 1973.

Haskell 1960
Francis Haskell. "Francesco Guardi as *Vedutista* and Some of His Patrons." *Journal of the Warburg and Courtauld Institutes* 23 (1960), pp. 256–76.

Hauke 1961
César M. de Hauke. *Seurat et son oeuvre.* 2 vols. Les Artistes & leurs oeuvres: Études et documents. Paris, 1961.

Van Haute 1999
Bernadette van Haute. *David III Ryckaert: A Seventeenth-Century Flemish Painter of Peasant Scenes.* Pictura nova 6. Turnhout, 1999.

Havemeyer 1961/1993
Louisine W. Havemeyer. *Sixteen to Sixty: Memoirs of a Collector.* New York, 1961. 1993 ed.: Edited by Susan Alyson Stein. New York, 1993.

Havemeyer Collection 1931
H. O. Havemeyer Collection: Catalogue of Paintings, Prints, Sculpture and Objects of Art. Portland, Maine, 1931.

Haverkamp Begemann 1959
Egbert Haverkamp Begemann. *Willem Buytewech.* Amsterdam, 1959.

Haverkamp Begemann and Logan 1970
Egbert Haverkamp Begemann and Anne-Marie S. Logan. *European Drawings and Watercolors in the Yale University Art Gallery, 1500–1900.* 2 vols. New Haven, 1970.

Hayes 1958
John Hayes. "Parliament Street and Canaletto's Views of Whitehall." *Burlington Magazine* 100 (October 1958), pp. 341–49.

Hébert, Pognon, and Bruand 1968
Michèle Hébert, Edmond Pognon, and Yves Bruand. *Inventaire du fonds français: Graveurs du dix-huitième siècle.* Vol. 10. Département des Estampes, Bibliothèque Nationale, Paris. Paris, 1968.

Heideman 1982
Johanna Elfriede Louise Heideman. *The Cinquecento Chapel Decorations in S. Maria in Aracoeli in Rome.* Amsterdam, 1982. [Originally presented as the author's Ph.D. diss., Rijksuniversiteit te Utrecht, 1982.]

Heikamp 1967
Detlef Heikamp. "Federico Zuccari a Firenze, 1575–1579." *Paragone* 18, no. 205 (March 1967), pp. 44–68.

Held 1939
Julius S. Held. "Malerier og tegninger af Jacob Jordaens i Kunstmuseet." *Kunstmuseets aarsskrift* (Statens Museum for Kunst) 26 (1939), pp. 1–43.

Held 1974
Julius S. Held. "A Protestant Source for a Rubens Subject." In *Liber Amicorum Karel G. Boon*, edited by Dieuwke de Hoop Scheffer, Carlos van Hasselt, and Christopher White, pp. 78–95. Amsterdam, 1974.

Held 1978
Julius S. Held. [Review of D'Hulst 1974.] *Art Bulletin* 60, no. 4 (December 1978), pp. 717–32.

Held 1986
Julius S. Held. *Rubens: Selected Drawings.* [2nd ed.] Mount Kisco, N.Y., 1986.

Herbert 1962
Robert L. Herbert. *Seurat's Drawings.* New York, 1962.

Herding 1966
Klaus Herding. "Schiffszeichnungen im Werk von Pierre Puget." *Zeitschrift für Kunstgeschichte* 29, no. 2 (1966), pp. 133–48.

Hérold 1935
Jacques Hérold. *Louis-Marin Bonnet (1736–1793): Catalogue de l'oeuvre gravé.* Publication de la Société pour l'Étude de la Gravure Française. Paris, 1935.

Hind 1923
Arthur M. Hind. *Catalogue of Drawings by Dutch and Flemish Artists Preserved in the Department of Prints and Drawings in the British Museum.* Vol. 2. London, 1923.

H. M. Calmann 1964
H. M. Calmann. *Catalogue: Dealer in Old Master Drawings.* London, 1964.

Hollstein 1949–2007
F. W. H. Hollstein et al. *Hollstein's Dutch and Flemish Etchings, Engravings, and Woodcuts, ca. 1450–1700.* 71 vols. Amsterdam, 1949–2007.

Hollstein 1954–
F. W. H. Hollstein et al. *Hollstein's German Engravings, Etchings and Woodcuts, 1400–1700.* 73 vols. to date. Amsterdam, 1954–.

Hooft 1994 (ed.)
P. C. Hooft. *Lyrische poëzie.* Edited by P. Tuynman and Gerrold P. van der Stroom. 2 vols. Amsterdam, 1994.

Huet 1911
René-Paul Huet. *Paul Huet (1803–1869), d'après ses notes, sa correspondance, ses contemporains.* Écrits d'amateurs et d'artistes. Paris, 1911.

Hugo, *Letters*, 1898/2002
Victor Hugo. *The Letters of Victor Hugo: From Exile, and after the Fall of the Empire.* Edited by Paul Meurice. Boston, 1898. Repr., Honolulu, 2002.

Hulsker 1996
Jan Hulsker. *The New Complete Van Gogh: Paintings, Drawings, Sketches.* Amsterdam and Philadelphia, 1996.

D'Hulst 1956
R.-A. D'Hulst. *De tekeningen van Jakob Jordaens: Bijdrage tot de geschiedenis van de XVII'-eeuwse kunst in de zuidelijke Nederlanden.* Verhandelingen van de Koninklijke Vlaamse Academie voor Wetenschappen, Letteren en Schone Kunsten van België, Klasse der Schone Kunsten 10. Brussels, 1956.

D'Hulst 1974
R.-A. d'Hulst. *Jordaens Drawings.* 4 vols. Monographs of the Nationaal Centrum voor de Plastische Kunsten van de XVI^de en XVII^de Eeuw 5. London, 1974.

D'Hulst 1982
R.-A. d' Hulst. *Jacob Jordaens.* London, 1982.

D'Hulst and De Poorter 1993
R.-A. d'Hulst and Nora De Poorter. "Chronology." In Antwerp 1993, vol. 1, pp. 7–21.

D'Hulst and Vandenven 1989
R.-A. d'Hulst and Marc Vandenven. *Rubens: The Old Testament.* Corpus Rubenianum Ludwig Burchard 3. London, 1989.

Hulton 1977
Paul Hulton. *The Work of Jacques Le Moyne de Morgues: A Huguenot Artist in France, Florida, and England.* 2 vols. London, 1977.

R. Huyghe and L. Huyghe 1953
René Huyghe and Lydie Huyghe. *Edgar-Hilaire-Germain Degas (1834–1917).* Le grand art en livres de poche 9. Paris, 1953.

Hymans 1920–21
Henri Hymans. *Oeuvres de Henri Hymans; études et notices relatives à l'histoire de l'art dans les Pays-Bas.* Edited by Fanny Hymans-Cluysenaar. 4 vols. Brussels, 1920–21.

Ingamells 1989
John Ingamells. *The Wallace Collection: Catalogue of Pictures.* [Vol. 3], *French before 1815.* London, 1989.

Ingersoll-Smouse 1926
Florence Ingersoll-Smouse. *Joseph Vernet, peintre de marine, 1714–1789: Étude critique, suivie d'un catalogue raisonné de son oeuvre peint.* 2 vols. Paris, 1926.

"In the Galleries" 1956
[G. D.] "In the Galleries: Drawings." *Arts* 31 (October 1956), p. 54.

Jacoby 1992
Beverly Schreiber Jacoby. "Boucher's Late Brown Chalk Composition Drawings." *Master Drawings* 30, no. 3 (Autumn 1992), pp. 255–86.

Jaffé 1957
Michael Jaffé. "A Sheet of Drawings from Rubens' Second Roman Period and His Early Style as a Landscape Draughtsman." *Oud Holland* 72 (1957), pp. 1–19.

Jaffé 1993
Michael Jaffé. "Quelques Dessins de Chatsworth: Questions de provenance ou d'attribution." In *Jacques Callot (1592–1635): Actes du colloque organisé par Le Service Culturel du Musée du Louvre et la ville de Nancy, à Paris et à Nancy, les 25, 26 et 27 juin 1992*, edited by Daniel Ternois, pp. 423–43. Paris, 1993.

Jaffé 1994
Michael Jaffé. *The Devonshire Collection of Italian Drawings.* 4 vols. [Vol. 1], *Tuscan and Umbrian Schools*; [vol. 2], *Roman and Neapolitan Schools*; [vol. 3], *Bolognese and Emilian Schools*; [vol. 4], *Venetian and North Italian Schools.* London, 1994.

Jaffé 2002
Michael Jaffé. *The Devonshire Collection of Northern European Drawings.* 5 vols. Archives of Art pre-1800. Turin, 2002.

James et al. 1997
Carlo James et al. *Old Master Prints and Drawings: A Guide to Preservation and Conservation.* Translated and edited by Marjorie B. Cohn. Amsterdam, 1997.

Jamot and G. Wildenstein 1932
Paul Jamot and Georges Wildenstein. *Manet.* 2 vols. L'Art francais. Paris, 1932.

Jerusalem 1977
Old Master Drawings: A Loan from the Collection of the Duke of Devonshire. Exh. cat. I. M. Cohen Gallery, Israel Museum, April–July 1977. [In English and Hebrew.] Jerusalem, 1977.

Joannides 1983
Paul Joannides. *The Drawings of Raphael, with a Complete Catalogue.* Berkeley, 1983.

Johnson 1986
Lee Johnson. *The Paintings of Eugène Delacroix: A Critical Catalogue.* Vols. 3 and 4, *1832–1863: Movable Pictures and Private Decorations.* Oxford, 1986.

Joubert 1947
Solange Joubert. *Une Correspondance romantique: Madame d'Agoult, Liszt, Henri Lehmann*. Paris, 1947.

Kahn 1928
Gustave Kahn. *Les Dessins de Georges Seurat (1859–1891)*. 2 vols. Paris, 1928.

Kahn 1928/1971
Gustave Kahn. *The Drawings of Georges Seurat*. Translated by Stanley Appelbaum. New York, 1971.

Karlsruhe 2003–4
Eugène Delacroix. Exh. cat. Staatliche Kunsthalle Karlsruhe, November 1, 2003–February 1, 2004. Sonderausstellung des Landes Baden-Württemberg. Heidelberg, 2003.

Kassel and Leiden 2006–7
Rembrandt's Landscapes. Exh. cat. by Christiaan Vogelaar and Gregor J. M. Weber, with contributions by Boudewijn Bakker et al. Translated by Lynn Richards, Jaco Rutgers, and Ruth Koenig. Gemäldegalerie Alte Meister, Staatliche Museen Kassel, June 22–September 6, 2006; and Stedelijk Museum De Lakenhal, Leiden, October 6, 2006–January 7, 2007. Zwolle, Kassel, and Leiden, 2006.

Katrin Bellinger Kunsthandel 2005
Katrin Bellinger Kunsthandel. *Master Drawings, 1985–2005*. London, 2005.

Kaufmann 1988
Thomas DaCosta Kaufmann. *The School of Prague: Painting at the Court of Rudolf II*. Chicago, 1988.

Kay 1886
Charles de Kay. "Whistler: The Head of the Impressionists." *Art Review* 1, no. 1 (November 1886), pp. 1–3.

Kendal 1981
Sixteenth and Seventeenth Century Italian Drawings. Exh. cat. Abbot Hall Art Gallery, Kendal, Cumbria, May 2–June 21, 1981. Kendal, 1981.

Kitson 1960
Michael Kitson. "The 'Altieri Claudes' and Virgil." *Burlington Magazine* 102 (July 1960), pp. 312–18. [Reprinted in Kitson 2000, pp. 1–17.]

Kitson 1963
Michael Kitson. "The Place of Drawings in the Art of Claude Lorrain." In *Studies in Western Art: Acts of the Twentieth International Congress of the History of Art, New York, 1961*, vol. 3, *Latin American Art, and the Baroque Period in Europe*, pp. 91–112. Princeton, 1963. [Reprinted in Kitson 2000, pp. 59–75.]

Kitson 1978
Michael Kitson. *Claude Lorrain: Liber Veritatis*. London, 1978.

Kitson 2000
Michael Kitson. *Studies on Claude and Poussin*. London, 2000.

Kloek 1997
Wouter Th. Kloek. "Hans Speckaert and the Many Copies after His Drawings." *Bolletino d'arte* 100 (1997), suppl., *Fiamminghi a Roma, 1508–1608: Atti del convegno internazionale, Bruxelles, 24–25 febbraio 1995*, edited by Nicole Dacos, pp. 149–60.

Knab, Mitsch, and Oberhuber 1983
Eckhart Knab, Erwin Mitsch, and Konrad Oberhuber, with Silvia Ferino-Pagden. *Raphael: Die Zeichnungen*. Veröffentlichungen der Albertina Wien 19. Stuttgart, 1983.

Knapp 1903
Fritz Knapp. *Fra Bartolommeo della Porta und die Schule von San Marco*. Halle, 1903.

Knowles 1831
John Knowles, ed. *The Life and Writings of Henry Fuseli*. 3 vols. London, 1831.

Knox 1983
George Knox. "Domenico Tiepolo's Punchinello Drawings: Satire, or Labor of Love?" In *Satire in the Eighteenth Century*, edited by J. D. Browning, pp. 124–46. Publications of the McMaster University Association for Eighteenth-Century Studies 10. New York, 1983.

Knox 1984
George Knox. "The Punchinello Drawings of Giambattista Tiepolo." In *Interpretazioni veneziane: Studi di storia dell'arte in onore di Michelangelo Muraro*, edited by David Rosand, pp. 439–46. Venice, 1984.

Kōdera 1990
Tsukasa Kōdera. *Vincent Van Gogh: Christianity versus Nature*. Oculi 3. Amsterdam, 1990.

Kunstreich 1959
Jan S. Kunstreich. *Der "Geistreiche Willem": Studien zu Willem Buytewech (1591–1624)*. Arbeiten des Kunsthistorischen Instituts der Universität Kiel 3. Kiel, 1959.

Lagrange 1864
Léon Lagrange. *Joseph Vernet et la peinture au XVIIIᵉ siècle*. Paris, 1864.

Lagrange and Montaiglon 1856
Léon Lagrange and Anatole de Montaiglon. "Joseph Vernet: Pièces et notes pour servir à l'histoire de ses tableaux des ports de France." *Archives de l'art français* 4 (1855–56; pub. 1856), pp. 139–63.

Lalanne 1875
Maxime Lalanne. *Le Fusain*. 5th ed. Paris, 1875.

Lamarre and Laveissière 2003
Christine Lamarre and Sylvain Laveissière, eds. *Les Prix de Rome des États de Bourgogne: Lettres à François Devosge, 1776–1792*. Musée des Beaux-Arts, Dijon. Dijon, 2003.

Lancaster 1951
H. Carrington Lancaster. "The Comédie Française, 1701–1774: Plays, Actors, Spectators, Finances." *Transactions of the American Philosophical Society*, n.s., 41, pt. 4 (December 1951), pp. 593–849.

Langres 1999
Claude Gillot (1673–1722): Comédies, sabbats et autres sujets bizarres. Exh. cat. by Paulette Choné et al. Musée Saint-Didier, Langres, July 2–September 27, 1999. Langres, 1999.

Laren 1966
Oude tekeningen: Een keuze uit de verzameling P. en N. de Boer. Singer Museum, Laren, June 18–September 18, 1966. Laren, 1966.

Lauder 2004
Anne Varick Lauder. "Battista Franco, c. 1510–1561: His Life and Work with Catalogue Raisonné." 4 vols. Ph.D. diss., Corpus Christi College, University of Cambridge, 2004.

Launay 1991
Élisabeth Launay. *Les Frères Goncourt: Collectionneurs de dessins*. Paris, 1991.

Lausanne 2008
Victor Hugo: Dessins visionnaires. Exh. cat. Fondation de l'Hermitage, Lausanne, February 1–May 18, 2008. Milan and Lausanne, 2008.

Lauts 1962
Jan Lauts. *Carpaccio: Paintings and Drawings*. London, 1962.

Lawrence 1958
Profiles and Perspectives in Nineteenth Century French Art.

Exh. cat. by Klaus Berger. Museum of Art, University of Kansas, Lawrence, January 14–February 26, 1958. Lawrence, 1958.

Leblond 1907
Marius-Ary Leblond [pseud.]. "Le Merveilleux dans la peinture: Odilon Redon." *Revue illustrée* 1 (1907), pp. 155–60.

Leeman 1994
Fred Leeman. "Redon's Spiritualism and the Rise of Mysticism." In Chicago, Amsterdam, and London 1994–95, pp. 215–36, 406–8.

Lefrançois 1994
Thierry Lefrançois. *Charles Coypel: Peintre du Roi (1694–1752)*. Paris, 1994.

Legrand 1997
Catherine Legrand, ed., with the assistance of Varena Forcione, Véronique Goarin, and Catherine Scheck. *De Pagnest à Puvis de Chavannes*. Inventaire général des dessins. École française 13. Cabinet des Dessins, Musée du Louvre. Paris, 1997.

Lemoisne 1946–49
Paul-André Lemoisne. *Degas et son oeuvre*. 4 vols. Les Artistes & leurs oeuvres: Études et documents. Paris, 1946–49. [Repr., New York, 1984.]

Van Lerius 1880–81
Théodore Van Lerius. *Biographies d'artistes anversois*. Edited by Pierre Génard. 2 vols. Uitgave (Maatschappij der Antwerpsche bibliophilen), 8, 11. Antwerp, 1880–81.

Liebermann 1918
Max Liebermann. *Degas*. 7th ed. Berlin, 1918.

Lieure 1924–29
Jules Lieure. *Jacques Callot*. 2 pts. in 5 vols. Paris, 1924–29.

Links 1977
J. G. Links. *Canaletto and His Patrons*. London, 1977.

Links 1982
J. G. Links. *Canaletto*. Oxford, 1982. [Repr., Paris, 2005.]

Llanos 1998
José de los Llanos. "Voltaire, Gravelot et les oeuvres de Corneille." *Collections parisiennes*, no. 2 (May 1998), pp. 32–44.

Löchner 1973
Kurt Löchner. *Der Perseus-Zyklus von Edward Burne-Jones*. Stuttgart, 1973.

Loisel 2004
Catherine Loisel. *Ludovico, Agostino, Annibale Carracci*. Inventaire général des dessins italiens 7. Cabinet des dessins, Musée du Louvre, Paris. Paris, 2004.

London 1886
"Notes"—"Harmonies"—"Nocturnes." Exh. cat. Dowdeswell Galleries, London, May 1886. London, 1886.

London 1925
Catalogue of an Exhibition of Italian Art of the Seventeenth Century. Exh. cat. Burlington Fine Arts Club, London, 1925. London, 1925.

London 1927
Catalogue of a Loan Exhibition of Drawings of the XVII. & XVIII. Centuries: The Magnasco Society. Exh. cat. Warren Gallery, London, 1927. London, 1927.

London 1953a
The Art of Drawing, 1500–1950. Exh. cat. Wildenstein and Company, London, May 14–July 4, 1953. London, 1953.

London 1953b
Drawings by Old Masters. Exh. cat. by Karl Theodore Parker and James Byam Shaw. Diploma Gallery, Royal

Academy of Arts, London, August 13–October 25, 1953. London, 1953.

London 1954–55
European Masters of the Eighteenth Century. Exh. cat. Royal Academy of Arts, London, Winter Exhibition, 1954–55. London, 1954.

London 1956
Renoir: An Exhibition of Paintings from European Collections in Aid of the Renoir Foundation. Exh. cat. Marlborough Fine Art, London, May–June 1956. London, 1956.

London 1968
Exhibition of Early Drawings. Exh. cat. Christopher Powney, London, July 9–26, 1968. London, 1968.

London 1969
Old Master Drawings from Chatsworth. Royal Academy of Arts, London, July 5–August 31, 1969. London, 1969.

London 1970
Drawings from the Teyler Museum, Haarlem. Exh. cat. by I. Q. van Regteren Altena and Peter W. Ward-Jackson. Victoria & Albert Museum, London, 1970. London, 1970.

London 1973–74
Old Master Drawings from Chatsworth: A Loan Exhibition from the Devonshire Collection. Exh. cat. by James Byam Shaw. Victoria & Albert Museum, London, 1973–74. London, 1973.

London 1974
Drawings by Victor Hugo. Exh. cat. by Pierre Georgel. Victoria & Albert Museum, London, 1974. London, 1974.

London 1976
Claude-Joseph Vernet, 1714–1789. Exh. cat. by Philip Conisbee. Iveagh Bequest, Kenwood House, London, June 4–September 19, 1976. London, 1976.

London 1983
La Douceur de vivre: Art, Style and Decoration in XVIIIth Century France. Exh. cat. Wildenstein and Company, London, June–July 1983. London, 1983.

London 1983–84
Drawings by Raphael from the Royal Library, the Ashmolean, the British Museum, Chatsworth, and Other English Collections. Exh. cat. by John Arthur Gere and Nicholas Turner. British Museum, London, October 13, 1983–January 15, 1984. London, 1983.

London 1988
European Drawings: Recent Acquisitions. Exh. cat. Hazlitt, Gooden & Fox, London, November 23–December 9, 1988. London, 1988.

London 1991
Drawings by Guercino from British Collections, with an Appendix Describing the Drawings by Guercino, His School and His Followers in the British Museum. Exh. cat. by Nicholas Turner and Carol Plazzotta. British Museum, London, May 17–August 18, 1991. London, 1991.

London 1992
Drawing in Bologna, 1500–1600. Exh. cat. Courtauld Institute Galleries, University of London, June 18–August 31, 1992. London, 1992.

London 1993
"Cabinet des dessins: French Master Drawings, XVIth–XIXth Century." Wildenstein and Company, London, June 3–July 30, 1993.

London 1994
Claude: The Poetic Landscape. Exh. cat. by Humphrey Wine. National Gallery, London, January 26–April 10, 1994. London, 1994.

London 2000
Old Master Drawings: Recent Acquisitions. Exh. cat.

Thomas Williams Fine Art, London, June 27–July 14, 2000. London, 2000.

London 2002–3
Albrecht Dürer and His Legacy: The Graphic Work of a Renaissance Artist. Exh. cat. by Giulia Bartrum, with Günter Grass, Joseph L. Koerner, and Ute Kuhlemann. British Museum, London, December 5, 2002–March 23, 2003. London, 2002.

London and Birmingham 1951
Eighteenth Century Venice. Exh. cat. by F. J. B. Watson. Whitechapel Art Gallery, London, January 3–March 14, 1951; and Museum and Art Gallery, Birmingham, March 21–April 18. London, 1951.

London and Chicago 1996–97
Degas: Beyond Impressionism. Exh. cat. by Richard Kendall. National Gallery, London, May 22–August 26, 1996; and Art Institute of Chicago, September 28, 1996–January 5, 1997. London and Chicago, 1996.

London and Nantes 1997–98
Turner on the Loire. Exh. cat. by Ian Warrell. Tate Gallery, London, September 30, 1997–February 15, 1998; and Musée du Château, Nantes, June 13–September 14. London, 1997.

London and New York 2000–2001
Correggio and Parmigianino: Master Draughtsmen of the Renaissance. Exh. cat. by Carmen C. Bambach, Hugo Chapman, Martin Clayton, and George R. Goldner. British Museum, London, October 6, 2000–January 7, 2001; and The Metropolitan Museum of Art, New York, February 5–May 6. London, 2000.

London, Paris, and Washington 1994–95
James McNeill Whistler. Exh. cat. by Richard Dorment and Margaret MacDonald, with contributions by Nicolai Cikovsky Jr., Ruth Fine, and Geneviève Lacambre. Tate Gallery, London, October 13, 1994–January 8, 1995; Musée d'Orsay, Paris, February 6–April 30; and National Gallery of Art, Washington, D.C., May 28–August 20. London, 1994.

London, Paris, Bern, and Brussels 1972
Flemish Drawings of the Seventeenth Century from the Collection of Frits Lugt, Institut Néerlandais, Paris. Exh. cat. by Carlos van Hasselt. Victoria & Albert Museum, London, February 9–March 26, 1972; Institut Néerlandais, Paris, April 14–May 28; Kunstmuseum Bern, June 8–July 23; and Royal Library of Belgium, Brussels, September 30–November 8. [Paris, 1972.]

London, Southampton, and Birmingham 1975–76
Burne-Jones: The Paintings, Graphic and Decorative Work of Sir Edward Burne-Jones, 1833–1898. Exh. cat. Hayward Gallery, London, November 5, 1975–January 4, 1976; Southampton Art Gallery, January 24–February 22; and City Museum and Art Gallery, Birmingham, March 10–April 11. London, 1975.

Los Angeles 1957
"Sculpture Past and Present." University of California, Los Angeles, 1957.

Los Angeles, Detroit, and Philadelphia 1971–72
Géricault. Exh. cat. by Lorenz Eitner. Los Angeles County Museum of Art, October 12–December 12, 1971; Detroit Institute of Arts, January 23–March 7, 1972; and Philadelphia Museum of Art, March 30–May 14. Los Angeles, 1971.

Los Angeles, Toledo, Naples, and Philadelphia 2005–6
Passion for Drawing: Poussin to Cézanne. Works from the Prat Collection. Exh. cat. by Pierre Rosenberg, with contributions by Louis-Antoine Prat and Bruno Ferté. Los Angeles County Museum of Art; Toledo Museum of Art; Naples Museum of Art, Naples, Florida; and Philadelphia

Museum of Art. Exhibition circulated by Art Services International, 2005–6. Alexandria, Va., 2005.

Loyrette 1991
Henri Loyrette. *Degas.* Paris, 1991.

Lugt
Frits Lugt. *Les Marques de collections de dessins & d'estampes.* Amsterdam, 1921. *Supplément.* The Hague, 1956.

Lugt 1915
Frits Lugt. *Wandelingen met Rembrandt in en om Amsterdam.* 2nd ed. Amsterdam, 1915.

Lugt 1921
Frits Lugt. *Les Marques de collections de dessins & d'estampes.* Amsterdam, 1921.

Lugt 1949
Frits Lugt. *Inventaire général des dessins des écoles du Nord, publié sous les auspices du Cabinet des Dessins. École flamande.* 2 vols. Musée du Louvre, Paris. Paris, 1949.

Lugt 1956
Frits Lugt. *Les Marques de collections de dessins & d'estampes. Supplément.* The Hague, 1956.

MacDonald 1995
Margaret F. MacDonald. *James McNeill Whistler: Drawings, Pastels, and Watercolours. A Catalogue Raisonné.* New Haven, 1995.

MacDonald 2001
Margaret F. MacDonald. *Palaces in the Night: Whistler in Venice.* Aldershot, 2001.

Maddalo 1982
Silvia Maddalo. *Adrien Manglard (1695–1760).* Rome, 1982.

Madrid 2005–6
Rafael: Retrato de un joven. Exh. cat. by Mauro Natale. Museo Thyssen-Bornemisza, Madrid, October 18, 2005–January 15, 2006. Madrid, 2005.

De Maere and Wabbes 1994
Jan De Maere and Marie Wabbes. *Illustrated Dictionary of Seventeenth Century Flemish Painters.* Edited by Jennifer A. Martin. 3 vols. Brussels, 1994.

Mahon and Turner 1989
Denis Mahon and Nicholas Turner. *The Drawings of Guercino in the Collection of Her Majesty the Queen at Windsor Castle.* The Italian Drawings at Windsor Castle. Cambridge, 1989.

Mahoney 1977
Michael Mahoney. *The Drawings of Salvator Rosa.* 2 vols. Outstanding Dissertations in the Fine Arts. New York, 1977.

Malafarina 1976
Gianfranco Malafarina. *L'opera completa di Annibale Carracci.* Classici dell'arte 87. Milan, 1976.

Malaguzzi Valeri 1911
Francesco Malaguzzi Valeri. "Due nuove mostre di antichi disegni." *Rassegna d'arte* 11 (January 1911), pp. 18–22.

Malaguzzi Valeri 1912
Francesco Malaguzzi Valeri. "Chi è lo 'Pseudo Boccacino.'" *Rassegna d'arte* 12 (1912), pp. 99–100.

Manchester 1961
Old Master Drawings from Chatsworth. Exh. cat. City Art Gallery, Manchester, July 19–September 10, 1961. Manchester, 1961.

Manchester 1965
Between Renaissance and Baroque: European Art, 1520–1600. Exh. cat. City Art Gallery, Manchester, March 10–April 6, 1965. Manchester, 1965.

Manchester and Cambridge 1987
The Private Degas. Exh. cat. by Richard Thomson.

Whitworth Art Gallery, Manchester, January 20–February 28, 1987; and Fitzwilliam Museum, Cambridge, March 17–May 3. London, 1987.

Van Mander 1604
Karel van Mander. *Het schilder-boeck, waer in voor eerst de leerlustighe ieught den grondt der edel vry schilderconst in verscheyden deelen wort voorghedraghen.* Haarlem, 1604.

Van Mander 1604 (1994–99 ed.)
Karel van Mander. *The Lives of the Illustrious Netherlandish and German Painters, from the First Edition of the Schilder-Boeck (1603–1604), Preceded by the Lineage, Circumstances and Place of Birth, Life and Work of Karel van Mander, Painter and Poet, and Likewise His Death and Burial, from the Second Edition of the Schilder-boeck (1616–1618).* Edited by Hessel Miedema. 6 vols., Doornspijk, 1994–99.

Manoeuvre and Rieth 1994
Laurent Manoeuvre and Emmanuel Rieth. *Joseph Vernet, 1714–1789: Les Ports de France.* Arcueil, 1994.

Marabottini 1968
Alessandro Marabottini. "I collaboratori." In *Raffaello: L'opera, le fonti, la fortuna*, edited by Mario Salmi, vol. 1, pp. 199–302. Novara, 1968.

Marani 1998
Pietro C. Marani. "Un disegno inedito di ambito Verrocchiesco." In *"Tutte le opere non son per istancarmi": Raccolta di scritti per i settant'anni di Carlo Pedretti*, edited by Fabio Frosini, pp. 237–41. Immaginare l'Europa. Rome, 1998.

Marani 1999
Pietro C. Marani. *Leonardo: Una carriera di pittore.* Milan, 1999. [French ed., *Léonard de Vinci: Une Carrière de peintre.* Paris, 1999.]

Marani 2000
Pietro C. Marani. *Leonardo da Vinci: The Complete Paintings.* New York, 2000. [Translation of Marani 1999.]

Marciari 2002
John Marciari. "Girolamo Muziano and the Dialogue of Drawings in Cinquecento Rome." *Master Drawings* 40, no. 2 (Summer 2002), pp. 113–34.

Marciari and Verstegen 2008
John Marciari and Ian Verstegen. "'Grande Quanto l'Opera': Size and Scale in Barocci's Drawings." *Master Drawings* 46, no. 3 (Autumn 2008), pp. 291–321.

Mariette 1741
Pierre-Jean Mariette. *Description sommaire des dessins des grands maistres d'Italie, des Pays-Bas et de France, du cabinet de feu M. Crozat. Avec des réflexions sur la manière de dessiner des principaux peintres.* Paris, 1741.

Mariette 1851–62
Pierre-Jean Mariette. *Abecedario de P. J. Mariette et autres notes inédites de cet amateur sur les arts et les artistes. Ouvrage publié d'après les manuscrits autographes, conservés au Cabinet des Estampes de la Bibliothèque Impériale.* Edited by Philippe de Chennevières and Antoine de Montaiglon. 6 vols. Archives de l'art français. Paris, 1851–62.

Mariuz 1982
Adriano Mariuz. *L'opera completa del Piazzetta.* Classici dell'arte 108. Milan, 1982.

Marseille 1978
La Peinture en Provence au XVIIe siècle. Exh. cat. Musée des Beaux-Arts, Marseille, July–October 1978. Marseille, 1978.

Marseille and Genoa 1994–95
Pierre Puget: Peintre, sculpteur, architecte, 1620–1694. Exh. cat. Centre de la Vieille Charité, Musée des Beaux-Arts, Marseille, October 28, 1994–January 30, 1995; and Palazzo Ducale, Genoa, March 4–June 4. Marseille and Paris, 1994. [Italian ed., *Pierre Puget (Marsiglia, 1620–1694): Un artista francese e la cultura barocca a Genova.* Milan, 1995.]

Martigny 1993
Degas. Exh. cat. by Ronald Pickvance. [In English and French.] Martigny, Fondation Pierre Gianadda, June 19–November 21, 1993. Martigny, 1993.

Martin and Masson 1908
Jean Martin and Charles Masson. *Catalogue raisonné de l'oeuvre peint et dessiné de J.-B. Greuze, suivi de la liste des gravures exécutées d'après ses ouvrages.* Paris, 1908. [First published in Camille Mauclair, *Jean-Baptiste Greuze.* Paris, 1906.]

Martini 1959
Alberto Martini. "Un singolare dipinto del Passignano." *Paragone*, no. 109 (January 1959), pp. 55–58.

E. C. Mason 1951
Eudo C. Mason. *The Mind of Henry Fuseli: Selections from His Writings.* London, 1951.

R. M. Mason 2007
Rainer Michael Mason. "Canaletto en Dalmatie." *Art Passions*, no. 11 (September 2007), pp. 8–12.

Mason Rinaldi 1972
Stefania Mason Rinaldi. "Disegni preparatori per dipinti di Jacopo Palma il Giovane." *Arte veneta* 26 (1972), pp. 92–110.

Mason Rinaldi 1984
Stefania Mason Rinaldi. *Palma il Giovane: L'opera completa.* Milan, 1984.

Massengale 1979
Jean Montague Massengale. "Drawings by Fragonard in North American Collections." [Review of Washington, Cambridge, and New York 1978–79.] *Burlington Magazine* 121 (April 1979), pp. 270–72.

Massing 1990
Jean Michel Massing. *Du texte à l'image: La Calomnie d'Apelle et son iconographie.* Strasbourg, 1990.

Mastropierro 1973
Franca Mastropierro. *Jacopo Vignali: Pittore nella Firenze del Seicento.* Definizioni critiche 6. Milan, 1973.

Mathey 1933a
Jacques Mathey. "Étienne Jeaurat (1699–1789)." *Old Master Drawings*, no. 29 (June 1933), pp. 8–10.

Mathey 1933b
Jacques Mathey. "Jeaurat, Cochin, Durameau et les dessins de Chardin." *Bulletin de la Société de l'Histoire de l'Art Français*, 1933, pp. 82–86.

Mathey 1964
Jacques Mathey. "Les Dessins de Chardin." *Albertina-Studien*, nos. 1–2 (1964), pp. 17–31.

Matthiesen Fine Art 1993
Matthiesen Fine Art. *Fifty Paintings, 1535–1825, to Celebrate Ten Years of Collaboration between the Matthiesen Gallery, London, and Stair Sainty Matthiesen, New York.* London and New York, 1993.

Matthiesen Fine Art 2003
Matthiesen Fine Art. *Chardin's têtes d'études au pastel.* With an essay by Philip Conisbee. London, 2003.

McCormick 1990
Thomas J. McCormick. *Charles-Louis Clérisseau and the Genesis of Neo-Classicism.* New York and Cambridge, Mass., 1990.

McCorquodale 1973
Charles P. McCorquodale. "A Fresh Look at Carlo Dolci." *Apollo* 97 (May 1973), pp. 477–88.

Meaume 1860
Édouard Meaume. *Recherches sur la vie et les ouvrages de Jacques Callot, suite au peintre-graveur français de M. Robert-Dumesnil.* 2 vols. Paris, 1860.

Meijer 1984
Bert W. Meijer. *I grandi disegni italiani del Teylers Museum di Haarlem.* Milan, 1984.

Meller 1988
Mari Kálmán Meller. "Exercises in and around Degas's Classrooms. Part I." *Burlington Magazine* 130 (March 1988), pp. 198–215.

Mellerio 1898
André Mellerio. "La Femme et l'enfant dans l'oeuvre d'Odilon Redon." *L'Estampe et l'affiche*, February 15, 1898.

Mellerio 1913
André Mellerio. *Odilon Redon.* Paris, 1913.

Mellerio 1923
André Mellerio. *Odilon Redon: Peintre, dessinateur et graveur.* Paris, 1923.

Mende 1996
Matthias Mende. "Dürer Renaissance." In *The Dictionary of Art*, edited by Jane Turner, vol. 9, pp. 445–47. New York, 1996.

Michel 1993
Christian Michel. *Charles-Nicolas Cochin et l'art des Lumières.* Bibliothèque des Écoles Françaises d'Athènes et de Rome 280. Rome, 1993.

Mielke and Winner 1977
Hans Mielke and Matthias Winner. *Peter Paul Rubens: Kritischer Katalog der Zeichnungen. Originale, Umkreis, Kopien.* Zeichnungen alter Meister im Berliner Kupferstichkabinett (Staatliche Museen Preussischer Kulturbesitz). Berlin, 1977.

Milan 2004–5
Francesco Menzocchi, pittore "raro e mutevole": Il trittico urbinate della "Deposizione," 1544. Brera mai vista. Exh. cat. by Maria Teresa Fiorio, Matteo Ceriana, Matteo Mazzalupi, and Isabella Righetti. Pinacoteca di Brera, Milan, October 2004–January 2005. Milan, 2004.

Miquel 1987
Pierre Miquel. *Le Paysage français au XIXe siècle.* Vol. 6, *Art et argent, 1800–1900.* L'École de la nature. Maurs-la-Jolie, 1987.

Modena 2005
Nicolò Dell'Abate: Storie dipinte nella pittura del Cinquecento tra Modena e Fontainebleau. Exh. cat. edited by Sylvie Béguin and Francesca Piccinini. Foro Boario, Modena, March 20–June 19, 2005. Cinisello Balsamo, 2005.

Monbeig Goguel 1987a
Catherine Monbeig Goguel. "Style et trace sous-jacent dans les dessins de Raphael." In *Le Dessin sous-jacent dans la peinture: Colloque VI, 12–14 septembre 1985; infrarouge et autres techniques d'examen*, edited by Hélène Verougstraete-Marcq and Roger van Schoute, pp. 99–101. Document de travail (Université Catholique de Louvain). Institut Supérieur d'Archéologie et d'Histoire de l'Art 23. Louvain-la-Neuve, 1987.

Monbeig Goguel 1987b
Catherine Monbeig Goguel. "Le Trace invisible des dessins de Raphael: Pour une problematique des techniques graphiques a la Renaissance." In *Studi su Raffaello: Atti del congresso internazionale di studi (Urbino—Firenze 6–14 aprile 1984)*, edited by Micaela Sambucco Hamoud and Maria Letizia Strocchi, pp. 377–89. Urbino, 1987.

Monbeig Goguel 1988
Catherine Monbeig Goguel. "Il disegno italiano nel

Cinquecento." In *La pittura in Italia: Il Cinquecento*, vol. 2, pp. 593–614. Rev. ed. Milan, 1988.

Monbeig Goguel 1990
Catherine Monbeig Goguel. "Le Dessin du Christ avec les croix retrouvé." In *Lelio Orsi e la cultura del suo tempo: Atti del convegno internazionale di studi, Reggio Emilia—Novellara, 28–29 gennaio 1988*, edited by Jadranka Bentini, pp. 79–93. Bologna, 1990.

Monceaux 1884
Henri Monceaux. "Les Cousin de Sens." *L'Art* 36 (1884), pp. 106–9.

Montagu 1992
Jennifer Montagu. "Les Oeuvres de jeunesse de Charles Le Brun: L'Influence de Simon Vouet et d'autres." In *Simon Vouet: Actes du colloque international, Galeries Nationales du Grand Palais, 5–6–7 février 1991*, edited by Stéphane Loire, pp. 531–43. Rencontres de l'École du Louvre. Paris, 1992.

Montagu 1994
Jennifer Montagu. *The Expression of the Passions: The Origin and Influence of Charles Le Brun's "Conférence sur l'Expression Générale et Particulière."* New Haven, 1994.

Montanari 1997
Tomaso Montanari. "Il Cardinale Decio Azzolino e le collezioni d'arte di Cristina di Svezia." *Studi secenteschi* 38 (1997), pp. 187–264.

Monte Carlo 1966
Catalogue de l'exposition de dessins italiens du XVe au XVIIIe siècles de la collection H. de Marignane. Exh. cat. Palais des Congrès, Monte Carlo, May 29– June 4, 1966. Monte Carlo, 1966.

Moore 1891
George Moore. *Impressions and Opinions.* New York, 1891.

Morassi 1937
Antonio Morassi. *Disegni antichi dalla collezione Rasini in Milano.* Milan, 1937.

Morassi 1942
Antonio Morassi. *Giorgione.* Milan, 1942.

Morassi 1973
Antonio Morassi. *Guardi: Antonio e Francesco Guardi.* 2 vols. Profili e saggi di arte veneta [11]. Venice, 1973.

Morassi 1975
Antonio Morassi. *Guardi: Tutti i disegni di Antonio, Francesco e Giacomo Guardi.* Venice, 1975.

Moreau-Nélaton 1921
Étienne Moreau-Nélaton. *Millet raconté par lui-même.* 3 vols. Paris, 1921.

Moreau-Nélaton 1926
Étienne Moreau-Nélaton. *Manet raconté par lui-même.* 2 vols. Paris, 1926.

Moureau 1992
François Moureau. *De Gherardi à Watteau: Présence d'Arlequin sous Louis XIV.* Collection Bibliothèque de l'âge classique 4. Paris, 1992.

Muller 1976
Nancy C. Muller. *Paintings and Drawings at the Shelburne Museum.* Shelburne, Vt., 1976.

Munich 1983
Im Licht von Claude Lorrain: Landschaftsmalerei aus drei Jahrhunderten. Exh. cat. by Marcel Roethlisberger, with contributions by Eva-Maria Marquart, Christian Lenz, and Erich Steingräber. Haus der Kunst, March 12– May 29, 1983. Munich, 1983.

Munich 1989–90
Niederländische Zeichnungen des 16. Jahrhunderts in der Staatlichen Graphischen Sammlung München. Exh. cat. by Holm Bevers. Staatliche Graphische Sammlung, Munich, November 22, 1989–January 21, 1990. Munich, 1989.

Munich 1995
Sehnsucht zur Kindheit: Kinderdarstellungen in der Romantik und ihre Vorläufer. Exh. cat. Galerie Arnoldi-Livie, Munich, 1995. Munich, 1995.

Muraro 1977
Michelangelo Muraro. *I disegni di Vittore Carpaccio.* Corpus Graphicum 2. Florence, 1977.

Muti 2001
Laura Muti. "Segnalazione di altri dipinti di Pierre Brébiette." In *Per l'arte, da Venezia all'Europa: Studi in onore di Giuseppe Maria Pilo*, edited by Mario Piantoni and Laura De Rossi, [vol. 2,] *Da Rubens al contemporaneo*, pp. 375–78. Monfalcone, 2001.

Myers 2003
Kenneth Joseph Myers. "The Freer Gallery of Art Pastels." In *Whistler and His Circle in Venice*, pp. 49–55. Exh. cat. by Eric Denker et al. Corcoran Gallery of Art, Washington, D.C., February 8–May 5, 2003; and Grolier Club, New York, September 17–November 22, 2003. London, 2003.

Naef 1974
Hans Naef. "L'Ingrisme dans le monde." *Bulletin du Musée Ingres*, no. 36 (December 1974), pp. 37–38.

Naef 1977–80
Hans Naef. *Die Bildniszeichnungen von J.-A.-D. Ingres.* 5 vols. Bern, 1977–80.

Nancy 1992
Jacques Callot, 1592–1635. Exh. cat. by Paulette Choné et al. Musée Historique Lorrain, Nancy, June 13–September 14, 1992. Paris, 1992.

Nantes, Charleroi, and Nancy 1992
Burne-Jones, 1883–1898: Dessins du Fitzwilliam Museum de Cambridge. Exh. cat. Musée des Beaux-Arts, Nantes, May 7–July 27, 1992; Palais des Beaux-Arts, Charleroi, September 5–October 15; and Musée des Beaux-Arts, Nancy, October 20–December 21. Nantes, 1992.

Natanson 1900
Thadée Natanson. "Un Primitif d'aujourd'hui: Georges Seurat." *La Revue blanche*, April 15, 1900, pp. 609–14.

Neilson 1974
Nancy Ward Neilson. Review of *Il Seicento lombardo*, vol. 3, *Catalogo dei disegni, libri, stampe, Milano, Pinacoteca Ambrosiana. Master Drawings* 12, no. 1 (Spring 1974), pp. 57–60.

Neilson 2004
Nancy Ward Neilson. *Giulio Cesare Procaccini disegnatore.* La pittura in Italia. Seicento—Settecento 2. Busto Arsizio, 2004.

Nemilova 1982
Inna Sergeevna Nemilova. *La Peinture française du XVIIIe siècle, Musée de l'Ermitage: Catalogue raisonné.* [In Russian, with summary in French.] Leningrad, 1982.

Nesselrath 1989
Arnold Nesselrath. "Giovanni da Udine disegnatore." *Bollettino: Monumenti, Musei e Gallerie Pontificie* 9, no. 2 (1989), pp. 237–91.

Neurdenburg 1930
Elisabeth Neurdenburg. *Hendrick de Keyser: Beeldhouwer en bouwmeester van Amsterdam.* Amsterdam, [1930].

Newcastle-upon-Tyne 1961
The Carracci: Drawings and Paintings. Hatton Gallery, Newcastle-upon-Tyne, November–December 1961. Newcastle-upon-Tyne, 1961.

New Haven and London 2006–7
Canaletto in England: A Venetian Artist Abroad, 1746–1755. Exh. cat. by Charles Beddington, with essays by Brian Allen and Francis Russell. Yale Center for British Art, New Haven, October 19–December 31, 2006; and Dulwich Picture Gallery, London, January 24–April 15, 2007. New Haven, 2006.

New York 1889
"Notes"–"Harmonies"–"Nocturnes." Exh. cat. H. Wunderlich & Co., New York, March 1889. New York, 1889.

New York 1949
Drawings through Four Centuries. Exh. cat. Wildenstein and Company, New York, June–November 1949. New York, 1949.

New York 1955
Timeless Master Drawings. Exh. cat. Wildenstein and Company, New York, November 16–December 31, 1955. New York, 1955.

New York 1956
For the Connoisseur: Watercolors and Drawings through Five Centuries. Exh. cat. Wildenstein and Company, New York, September 24–October 31, 1956. New York, 1956.

New York 1959a
Contrasts in Landscape: Nineteenth and Twentieth Century Paintings and Drawings. Exh. cat. Wildenstein and Company, New York, 1959. New York, 1959.

New York 1959b
Great Master Drawings of Seven Centuries. Exh. cat. M. Knoedler and Company, New York, October 13–November 7, 1959. New York, 1959.

New York 1961
"The Electra Havemeyer Webb Memorial Exhibition." The Metropolitan Museum of Art, New York, 1961.

New York 1965–66
The Italian Renaissance. Exh. cat. by Jacob Bean and Felice Stampfle. The Metropolitan Museum of Art, New York, November 8, 1965–January 9, 1966. Drawings from New York Collections 1. New York, 1965.

New York 1971
The Eighteenth Century in Italy. Exh. cat. by Jacob Bean and Felice Stampfle. The Metropolitan Museum of Art, New York, January 30–March 21, 1971. Drawings from New York Collections 3. New York, 1971.

New York 1979
"French Pastels." Wildenstein and Company, New York, 1979.

New York 1982
Art in Early XIX Century France. Exh. cat. Wildenstein and Company, New York, April 21–May 28, 1982. New York, 1982.

New York 1985–86
Liechtenstein: The Princely Collections: The Collections of the Prince of Liechtenstein. Exh. cat. The Metropolitan Museum of Art, New York, October 26, 1985–May 1, 1986. New York, 1985.

New York 1987–88
Drawings by Raphael and His Circle: From British and North American Collections. Exh. cat. by John Arthur Gere. Pierpont Morgan Library, New York, October 9, 1987–January 3, 1988. New York, 1987.

New York 1989
Barnard Collects: The Educated Eye. Exh. cat. Salander O'Reilly Galleries, New York, September 28–October 31, 1989. New York, 1989.

New York 1993
Heads and Portraits: Drawings from Piero di Cosimo to Jasper Johns. Exh. cat. Jason McCoy, New York, May 6–June 12, 1993. Catalogue / Kate Ganz Ltd 9. London and New York, 1993.

New York 1994a
Edgar Degas: Drawings. Exh. cat. Marc de Montebello Fine Art, New York, April 29–June 10, 1994. New York, 1994.

New York 1994b
European Master Drawings from the Collection of Peter Jay Sharp. Exh. cat. by William L. Barcham et al. National Academy of Design, New York, May 25–August 28, 1994. New York, 1994.

New York 1996
Selected Drawings. Exh. cat. C. G. Boerner, New York, January 9–26, 1996. New York, 1996.

New York 1997
Old Master Drawings. Exh. cat. W. M. Brady & Co., New York, May 8–31, 1997. Presented in association with Katrin Bellinger Kunsthandel. Munich and New York, 1997.

New York 1997–98
The Private Collection of Edgar Degas. Exh. cat. [Vol. 1, essays], by Ann Dumas, Colta Ives, Susan Alyson Stein, and Gary Tinterow; [vol. 2, summary catalogue], compiled by Colta Ives, Susan Alyson Stein, and Julie A. Steiner, with Ann Dumas, Rebecca Rabinow, and Gary Tinterow. The Metropolitan Museum of Art, New York, October 1, 1997–January 11, 1998. New York, 1997.

New York 1998a
An Exhibition of Italian Old Master Drawings and Oil Sketches. Exh. cat. Pandora Old Masters, New York, January 27–February 14, 1998. New York, 1998.

New York 1998b
An Exhibition of Old Master Drawings, Prints and Paintings. Exh. cat. Newhouse Galleries, New York, May 6–15, 1998. Trinity Fine Art Catalogue 14. London, 1998.

New York 1999
Eighteenth-Century French Drawings in New York Collections. Exh. cat. by Perrin Stein and Mary Tavener Holmes. The Metropolitan Museum of Art, New York, February 2–April 25, 1999. New York, 1999.

New York 2000
W. M. Brady & Co. and Thomas Williams Fine Art. *Old Master Drawings*. Exh. cat. W. M. Brady & Co., New York, May 10–June 2, 2000. New York and London, 2000.

New York 2002a
Old Master Drawings. Exh. cat. C. G. Boerner, New York, January 21–February 8, 2002. Neue Lagerliste 116. New York, 2002.

New York 2002b
Procaccini in America. Exh. cat. by Hugh Brigstocke. Hall & Knight, New York, October 15–November 23, 2002. London and New York, 2002.

New York 2002c
Tapestry in the Renaissance: Art and Magnificence. Exh. cat. by Thomas P. Campbell, with contributions by Maryan W. Ainsworth et al. The Metropolitan Museum of Art, New York, March 14–June 19, 2002. New York, 2002.

New York 2003
Leonardo da Vinci: Master Draftsman. Exh. cat. edited by Carmen C. Bambach, with contributions by Carmen C. Bambach et al. The Metropolitan Museum of Art, New York, January 22–March 30, 2003. New York, 2003.

New York 2005
Peter Paul Rubens: The Drawings. Exh. cat. by Anne-Marie S. Logan, with Michiel C. Plomp. The Metropolitan Museum of Art, New York, January 15–April 3, 2005. New York, 2005.

New York 2007–8
Georges Seurat: The Drawings. Exh. cat. by Jodi Hauptman, with essays by Karl Buchberg et al. Museum of Modern Art, New York, October 28, 2007–January 7, 2008. New York, 2007.

New York and Fort Worth 2003–4
The Drawings of François Boucher. Exh. cat. by Alastair Laing; foreword by Pierre Rosenberg. Frick Collection, New York, October 8–December 14, 2003; and Kimbell Art Museum, Fort Worth, Texas, January 17–April 18, 2004. New York, 2003.

New York and London 1987
An Exhibition of Old Master Drawings. Exh. cat. E. J. Landrigan, New York, November 17–21, 1987; and Richard Day, London, December 8–18. London, 1987.

New York and London 1988
An Exhibition of Old Master Drawings. Exh. cat. E. J. Landrigan, New York, November 7–11, 1988; and Richard Day, London, December 6–16. London, 1988.

New York and London 1990
European Drawings and Manuscripts, 1480–1880. Exh. cat. Verdura, New York, November 5–20, 1990; and Richard Day, London, December 11–21. London, 1990.

New York and London 2002
An Exhibition of Master Drawings. Exh. cat. by Stephen Ongpin. Adam Williams Fine Art, New York, May 1–31, 2002; and Asian Art Gallery, London, July 1–12. Presented by Jean-Luc Baroni. London, 2002.

New York and London 2004
Master Drawings, 2004. Exh. cat. Jack Kilgore & Co., New York, May 5–14, 2004; and Colnaghi, London, July 3–9. Presented in association with Katrin Bellinger Kunsthandel. London, 2004.

New York and London 2005–6
French Drawings from the British Museum: Clouet to Seurat. Exh. cat. by Perrin Stein; introduction by Martin Royalton-Kisch. The Metropolitan Museum of Art, New York, November 8, 2005–January 29, 2006; and British Museum, London, June 29–November 26. New York and London, 2005.

New York and Los Angeles 2002
Greuze: The Draftsman. Exh. cat. by Edgar Munhall, with an essay by Irina Novosselskaya. Frick Collection, New York, May 14–August 4, 2002; and J. Paul Getty Museum, Los Angeles, September 10–December 1. London, 2002.

New York and Richmond 1985–86
Drawings from the Collection of Mr. & Mrs. Eugene Victor Thaw. Part II. Exh. cat. by Cara D. Denison et al. Pierpont Morgan Library, New York, September 3–November 10, 1985; and Virginia Museum of Fine Arts, Richmond, February 17–April 13, 1986. New York, 1985.

New York, Birmingham, and Paris 1998–99a
Edward Burne-Jones: Victorian Artist-Dreamer. Exh. cat. by Stephen Wildman and John Christian, with essays by Alan Crawford and Laurence des Cars. The Metropolitan Museum of Art, New York, June 4–September 6, 1998; Birmingham Museums and Art Gallery, October 17, 1998–January 17, 1999; and Musée d'Orsay, Paris, March 1–June 6. New York, 1998.

New York, Birmingham, and Paris 1998–99b
The Perseus Series: Sir Edward Coley Burne-Jones. Exh. cat. by Anne Anderson and Michael Cassin. The Metropolitan Museum of Art, New York, June 1–September 6, 1998; Birmingham Museums and Art Gallery, October 17, 1998–January 17, 1999; Musée d'Orsay, Paris, March 1–June 6. Southampton, 1998.

New York, Cleveland, and Minneapolis 1951–52
Odilon Redon, 1840–1916: Pastels and Drawings. Exh. cat. Jacques Seligmann & Co., New York, October 22–November 10, 1951; Cleveland Museum of Art, November 29, 1951–January 20, 1952; and Walker Art Center, Minneapolis, February 1–March 1. [New York], 1951.

New York, Detroit, and Paris 1986–87
François Boucher, 1703–1770. Exh. cat. by Alastair Laing and Pierre Rosenberg. The Metropolitan Museum of Art, New York, February 17–May 4, 1986; Detroit Institute of Arts, May 27–August 17; and Galeries Nationales du Grand Palais, Paris, September 19, 1986–January 5, 1987. Paris, 1986. [English ed., New York, 1986.]

New York, Paris, and London 1994
European Master Drawings. Exh. cat. Hazlitt, Gooden & Fox, New York, May 1994; Galerie de Bayser, Paris, June; and Hazlitt, Gooden & Fox, London, July. Presented in association with Katrin Bellinger Kunsthandel. Munich and London, 1994.

Nice, Clermont-Ferrand, and Nancy 1977
Carle Vanloo: Premier Peintre du Roi. Exh. cat. by Marie-Catherine Sahut. Musée Chéret, Nice, January 21–March 13, 1977; Musée Bargoin, Clermont-Ferrand, April 1–May 30; and Musée des Beaux-Arts, Nancy, June 18–August 15. Nice, 1977.

Nichols 1992
Lawrence W. Nichols. "The 'Pen Works' of Hendrick Goltzius." *Philadelphia Museum of Art Bulletin*, Winter 1992, pp. 4–56. [Published in conjunction with the exhibition "A Masterpiece in Focus: Goltzius's *Without Ceres and Bacchus Venus Would Freeze*," at the Philadelphia Museum of Art, November 16, 1991–February 2, 1992.]

Nicolay 1989
Nicolas de Nicolay. *Dans l'empire de Soliman le Magnifique*. Edited by Marie-Christine Gomez-Géraud and Stéphane Yérasimos. Paris, 1989.

Nova 1994
Alessandro Nova. *Girolamo Romanino*. Archivi di arte antica. Turin, 1994.

Nova 1995
Alessandro Nova. "The Drawings of Girolamo Romanino. Part I." *Burlington Magazine* 137 (March 1995), pp. 159–68.

Nuremberg 1994
Das Praunsche Kabinett: Kunst des Sammelns, Meisterwerke von Dürer bis Carracci. Exh. cat. by Katrin Achilles-Syndram et al. Germanisches Nationalmuseum, Nuremberg, March 3–May 15, 1994. Nuremberg, 1994.

Oberhuber 1958
Konrad Oberhuber. "Die stilistische Entwicklung im Werk Bartholomäus Sprangers." Ph.D. diss., Universität Wien, 1958.

Oberhuber 1970
Konrad Oberhuber. "Drawings by Artists Working in Parma in the Sixteenth Century." *Master Drawings* 8, no. 3 (Autumn 1970), pp. 276–87.

Oberhuber 1972
Konrad Oberhuber. *Raphaels Zeichnungen*. Vol. 9, *Entwürfe zu Werken Raphaels und seiner Schule im Vatikan, 1511/12 bis 1520*. Berlin, 1972.

Oberhuber 2003
Konrad Oberhuber. "Parmigianino disegnatore." In Parma and Vienna 2003, pp. 71–81.

Ongpin 2001
Stephen Ongpin. *Old Master and Nineteenth Century Drawings*. Colnaghi. London, 2001.

Ongpin 2003
Stephen Ongpin. *Old Master and Nineteenth Century Drawings*. Jean-Luc Baroni. London, 2003.

Orléans 2001–2
Pierre Brébiette (1598?–1642): Seule la peinture. Exh. cat. by Jacques Thuillier, Paola Pacht Bassani, and S. Kespern. Musée des Beaux-Arts, Orléans, October 17, 2001–January 20, 2002. Orléans, 2001.

Ottawa 2005
Leonardo da Vinci, Michelangelo, and the Renaissance in Florence. Exh. cat. edited by David Franklin. National Gallery of Canada, Ottawa, May 29–September 5, 2005. Ottawa, 2005.

Ottawa, Washington, and Berlin 2003–4
The Age of Watteau, Chardin, and Fragonard: Masterpieces of French Genre Painting. Exh. cat. edited by Colin Bailey. National Gallery of Canada, Ottawa, June 6–September 7, 2003; National Gallery of Art, Washington, D.C., October 11, 2003–January 11, 2004; and Gemäldegalerie, Staatliche Museen zu Berlin, February 8–May 9. New Haven, 2003.

Ovid 1976–77
Ovid. *Metamorphoses.* Translated by Frank Justus Miller. 2 vols. Vols. 3 and 4 of *Ovid in Six Volumes.* Loeb Classical Library. Cambridge, Mass., 1976–77.

Oxford and London 1996–97
Drawings by the Carracci from British Collections. Exh. cat. by Clare Robertson and Catherine Whistler. Ashmolean Museum, Oxford, December 10, 1996–March 31, 1997; and Hazlitt, Gooden & Fox, London, April 9–May 9. Oxford and London, 1996.

Pagliarulo 1986
Giovanni Pagliarulo. "Jacopo Vignali." In Florence 1986–87, [vol. 3], pp. 183–87.

Pallucchini 1951
Rodolfo Pallucchini. "La pittura veneziana del settecento alla Whitechapel Gallery di Londra." *Arte veneta* 5 (1951), pp. 209–14.

Pallucchini 1961
Rodolfo Pallucchini. *Piazzetta.* Les plus grands artistes italiens. Milan, 1961.

Pallucchini 1965
Rodolfo Pallucchini. "Note alla mostra dei Guardi." *Arte veneta* 19 (1965), pp. 215–36.

Paris 1867
Catalogue des tableaux, études peintes, dessins et croquis de J.-A.-D. Ingres, peintre d'histoire, sénateur, membre de l'Institut, exposés dans les galeries du Palais de l'École Impériale des Beaux-Arts. Exh. cat. École Impériale des Beaux-Arts, Paris, 1867. Paris, 1867.

Paris 1874
Exposition des oeuvres de Prud'hon, au profit de sa fille. Exh. cat. by Eudoxe Marcille and Camille Marcille. École des Beaux-Arts, Paris, May 4–July 4, 1874. Paris, 1874.

Paris 1884
Exposition des oeuvres d'Édouard Manet. Exh. cat. École des Beaux-Arts, Paris, 1884. Paris, 1884.

Paris 1894
Exposition Odilon Redon. Exh. cat. Galerie Durand-Ruel, Paris, March 29–April 14, 1894. Paris, 1894.

Paris 1905
Salon des Artistes Indépendants, Paris, March 24–April 3, 1905.

Paris 1907
Exposition Chardin et Fragonard. Exh. cat. Galerie Georges Petit, Paris, June–July 1907. Paris, 1907.

Paris 1922
Exposition P.-P. Prud'hon. Exh. cat. Palais des Beaux-Arts de le Ville de Paris (Petit Palais), May–June 1922. Paris, 1922.

Paris 1924
Exposition Degas . . . : Peintures, pastels et dessins, sculptures, eaux-fortes, lithographies et monotypes. Exh. cat. Galerie Georges Petit, Paris, April 12–May 2, 1924. Paris, 1924.

Paris 1925
Exposition du paysage français de Poussin à Corot. Exh. cat. by Henry Lapauze, Camille Gronkowski, and Adrien Fauchier-Magnan. Musée du Petit Palais, Paris, May–June 1925. Paris, 1925.

Paris 1926a
Les Dessins de Seurat (1859–1891). Exh. cat. Galerie Bernheim-Jeune, Paris, November 29–December 24, 1926. Paris, 1926.

Paris 1926b
Odilon Redon: Exposition rétrospective de son oeuvre. Exh. cat. Musée des Arts Décoratifs, Paris, March 1926. Paris, 1926.

Paris 1929
Le Théatre à Paris (XVIIᵉ–XVIIIᵉ siècles). Exh. cat. Musée Carnavalet, Paris, March 19–May 4, 1929. Paris, 1929.

Paris 1933
Exposition Goncourt. Exh. cat. Galerie de la Gazette des Beaux-Arts, Paris, 1933. Paris, 1933.

Paris 1936a
Exposition Seurat (1859–1891). Exh. cat. Galerie Paul Rosenberg, Paris, February 3–29, 1936. Paris, 1936.

Paris 1936b
Exposition de portraits français de 1400 à 1900. Exh. cat. with preface by Claude Roger-Marx. André J. Seligmann, Paris, June 9–July 1, 1936. Paris, 1936.

Paris 1948
Chefs-d'Oeuvre de l'art alsacien et de l'art lorrain. Exh. cat. Musée des Arts Décoratifs, Paris, October–November 1948. Paris, 1948.

Paris 1950a
Cent Portraits de femmes: Du XVᵉ siècle à nos jours. Exh. cat. Galerie Charpentier, Paris, 1950. Paris, 1950.

Paris 1950b
Chefs-d'Oeuvre des collections parisiennes. Exh. cat. edited by Jacques Wilhelm. Musée Carnavalet, Paris, November–December 1950. Paris, 1950.

Paris 1951
Le Dessin français de Watteau à Prud'hon. Exh. cat. by Jean Cailleux. Galerie Cailleux, Paris, April 1951. Paris, 1951.

Paris 1955
Degas dans les collections françaises. Exh. cat. by Daniel Wildenstein. Galerie de la Gazette des Beaux-Arts, Paris, 1955. Paris, 1955.

Paris 1956–57
Odilon Redon. Exh. cat. Musée de l'Orangerie, Paris, October 1956–January 1957. Paris, 1956.

Paris 1957
Seurat. Exh. cat. Musée Jacquemart-André, Paris, November–December 1957. Paris, 1957.

Paris 1958
Pierre Paul Prud'hon, 1758–1823: Exposition organisée pour le 200ᵉ anniversaire de la naissance du peintre. Exh. cat. Musée Jacquemart-André, Paris, October 15–December 1, 1958. Paris, 1958.

Paris 1960
D'Ingres à nos jours: Aquarelles, pastels et dessins. Exh. cat. Jean-Claude & Jacques Bellier, Paris, 1960. Paris, 1960.

Paris 1963
Mémorial de l'exposition Eugène Delacroix. Exh. cat. by Maurice Sérullaz. Musée du Louvre, Paris, May–September 1963. Paris, 1963.

Paris 1968
Watteau et sa génération. Exh. cat. Galerie Cailleux, Paris, March–April 1968. Paris, 1968.

Paris 1969
Dessins de Taddeo et Federico Zuccaro. Exh. cat. by John Arthur Gere and Roseline Bacou. Cabinet des Dessins, Musée du Louvre, Paris, 1969. Paris, 1969.

Paris 1970
Goya: Dessins, gravures, lithographies. Exh. cat. Huguette Berès, Paris, November–December 1970. Paris, 1970.

Paris 1972–73
L'École de Fontainebleau. Exh. cat. with an introduction by Sylvie Béguin. Galeries Nationales du Grand Palais, Paris, October 17, 1972–January 15, 1973. Paris, 1972.

Paris 1975
Tableaux et dessins anciens. Exh. cat. Didier Aaron, Paris, October 2–31, 1975. Paris, 1975.

Paris 1975–76
Jean-François Millet. Exh. cat. Galeries Nationales du Grand Palais, Paris, October 17, 1975–January 5, 1976. Paris, 1975.

Paris 1976–77
Joseph Vernet, 1714–1789. Exh. cat. Musée de la Marine, Paris, October 15, 1976–January 9, 1977. Paris, 1976.

Paris 1983
Rome, 1760–1770: Fragonard, Hubert Robert et leurs amis. Exh. cat. by Marianne Roland Michel. Galerie Cailleux, Paris, February 15–March 26, 1983. Paris, 1983.

Paris 1984–85a
Dessins français du XVIIᵉ siècle. Exh. cat. Cabinet des Dessins, Musée du Louvre, Paris, October 26, 1984–January 28, 1985. Paris, 1984.

Paris 1984–85b
Diderot et l'art, de Boucher à David: Les Salons, 1759–1781. Exh. cat. Hôtel de la Monnaie, Paris, October 5, 1984–January 6, 1985. Paris, 1984.

Paris 1985
Oeuvres de jeunesse, de Watteau à Ingres. Exh. cat. by Marianne Roland Michel. Galerie Cailleux, Paris, June 3–July 12, 1985. Paris, 1985.

Paris 1986–87
Hommage à Andrea del Sarto. Exh. cat. by Dominique Cordellier. Cabinet des Dessins, Musée du Louvre, Paris, October 23, 1986–January 26, 1987. Paris, 1986.

Paris 1987
Aspects de Fragonard: Peintures, dessins, estampes. Exh. cat. by Marianne Roland Michel. Galerie Cailleux, Paris, September 23–November 7, 1987. Paris, 1987.

Paris 1990
Les Dessins vénitiens des collections de l'École des Beaux-Arts. Exh. cat. École Nationale Supérieure des Beaux-Arts, Paris, May 3–July 15, 1990. Paris, 1990.

Paris 1991–92
Géricault. Exh. cat. by Régis Michel, Sylvain Laveissière, and Bruno Chenique. Galeries Nationales du Grand Palais, Paris, October 10, 1991–January 6, 1992. Paris, 1991.

Paris 1992–93
Fragonard et le dessin français au XVIIIᵉ siècle dans les collections du Petit Palais. Exh. cat. Musée du Petit Palais, Paris, October 16, 1992–February 14, 1993. Paris, 1992.

Paris 1993
Dessins français du XVIIᵉ siècle dans les collections publiques françaises. Exh. cat. Musée du Louvre, Paris, January 28–April 26, 1993. Paris, 1993.

Paris 1994–95a
Delacroix: Le Voyage au Maroc. Exh. cat. Institut du Monde

Arabe, Paris, September 27, 1994–January 15, 1995. Paris, 1994. [English ed., *Delacroix in Morocco*. New York and Paris, 1994.]

Paris 1994–95b
Fra Bartolommeo et son atelier: Dessins et peintures des collections françaises. Exh. cat. by Chris Fischer. Musée du Louvre, Paris, November 17, 1994–February 13, 1995. Paris, 1994.

Paris 2000
Settecento, l'Europe à Rome: Chefs-d'Oeuvre de la peinture du XVIIIᵉ siècle des collections de la Galerie Nationale d'Art Ancien du Palais Barberini. Exh. cat. by Lorenza Mochi Onori. Mairie du Vᵉ arrondissement, Paris, September 27–December 13, 2000. Rome, 2000.

Paris 2005
Ligozzi. Exh. cat. by Lucilla Conigliello. Musée du Louvre, Paris, January 26–June 25, 2005. Drawing Gallery 7. Milan and Paris, 2005.

Paris 2006a
Dessins italiens de la collection Jean Bonna. Exh. cat. by Nathalie Strasser. École Nationale Supérieure des Beaux-Arts, Paris, February 14–April 23, 2006. Carnet d'études 4. Paris, 2006.

Paris 2006b
Suite française: Dessins de la collection Jean Bonna. Exh. cat. edited by Emmanuelle Brugerolles, with Joëlla de Couëssin. École Nationale Supérieure des Beaux-Arts, Paris, February 14–April 23, 2006. Paris, 2006. [The drawings in this show were exhibited at the Musée d'Art et d'Histoire, Geneva, from December 7, 2006, to March 4, 2007, in "Le Choix d'un regard: Dessins de la collection Jean Bonna" (see Geneva 2006–7a).]

Paris 2008
Dessins nordiques des collections Jean Bonna & Frits Lugt. Exh. cat. by Stijn Alsteens et al. Exposition-dossier (Fondation Custodia) 9. Hôtel Turgot, Paris, March 27–May 4, 2008. Paris, 2008.

Paris 2008–9
Renaissance et maniérisme aux Pays-Bas: Dessins du Musée des Beaux-Arts de Budapest. Exh. cat. by Teréz Gerszi. Musée du Louvre, Paris, October 8, 2008–January 12, 2009. Paris, 2008.

Paris and Amsterdam 2006–7
Tour de France, 1646: Le Val de Loire en dessins / De Loire vallei getekend door Rembrandts tijdgenoten. Exh. cat. by Erik Spaans. Institut Néerlandais, Paris, October 5–December 3, 2006; and Museum Het Rembrandthuis, Amsterdam, December 16, 2006–February 11, 2007. Paris, 2006.

Paris and Cambridge 1997–98
Géricault: Dessins & estampes des collections de l'École des Beaux-Arts. Exh. cat. École Nationale Supérieure des Beaux-Arts, Paris, November 25, 1997–January 25, 1998; and Fitzwilliam Museum, Cambridge, March 26–May 24. Paris, 1997.

Paris and London 1994–95
Nicolas Poussin, 1594–1665. Exh. cat. by Pierre Rosenberg and Louis-Antoine Prat. Galeries Nationales du Grand Palais, Paris, September 27, 1994–January 2, 1995; and Royal Academy of Arts, London, January 19–April 9. Paris, 1994.

Paris and New York 1987–88
Fragonard. Exh. cat. by Pierre Rosenberg. Galeries Nationales du Grand Palais, Paris, September 24, 1987–January 4, 1988; and The Metropolitan Museum of Art, New York, February 2–May 8. New York, 1988. [French ed., Paris, 1987.]

Paris and New York 1991–92
Seurat. Exh. cat. by Robert L. Herbert. Galeries Nationales du Grand Palais, Paris, April 9–August 12, 1991; and The Metropolitan Museum of Art, New York, September 24, 1991–January 12, 1992. Paris, 1991. [Eng. ed., *Georges Seurat, 1859–1891*. New York, 1991.]

Paris and New York 1993–94
Le Dessin français: Chefs-d'Oeuvre de la Pierpont Morgan Library. Exh. cat. by Cara D. Denison. Musée du Louvre, Paris, June 1–August 30, 1993; and Pierpont Morgan Library, New York, September 15, 1993–January 2, 1994. Paris and New York, 1993. [English ed., *French Master Drawings from the Pierpont Morgan Library*. New York, 1993.]

Paris and New York 1997–98
Pierre Paul Prud'hon. Exh. cat. by Sylvain Laveissière. Galeries Nationales du Grand Palais, Paris, September 23, 1997–January 12, 1998; and The Metropolitan Museum of Art, New York, March 2–June 7. New York, 1998. [French ed., *Prud'hon, ou Le Rêve du bonheur*. Paris, 1997.]

Paris and New York 2001
Galerie Jean François Baroni. *Sélection de dessins anciens et du XIXᵉᵐᵉ siècle / A Selection of Old Master Drawings and XIXth Century*. Exh. cat. Salon du Dessin, Paris, March 28–April 2, 2001; and International Fine Art Fair, New York, May 11–16. Paris, 2001.

Paris and Philadelphia 1998–99
Delacroix: Les Dernières Années. Exh. cat. by Arlette Sérullaz, Vincent Pomarède, and Joseph J. Rishel. Galeries Nationales du Grand Palais, Paris, April 7–July 20, 1998; and Philadelphia Museum of Art, September 10, 1998–January 3, 1999. Paris, 1998. [English ed., *Delacroix: The Late Work*. Philadelphia, 1998.]

Paris and Rome 1987
Subleyras, 1699–1749. Exh. cat. edited by Olivier Michel and Pierre Rosenberg. Musée du Luxembourg, Paris, February 20–April 26, 1987; and Accademia di Francia, Villa Medici, Rome, May 18–July 19. Paris, 1987.

Paris, Antwerp, London, and New York 1979–80
Rubens and Rembrandt in Their Century: Flemish and Dutch Drawings of the Seventeenth Century from the Pierpont Morgan Library. Exh. cat. by Felice Stampfle. Institut Néerlandais, Paris, April 5–June 10, 1979; Koninklijk Museum voor Schone Kunsten, Antwerp, June 22–September 9; British Museum, London, September 27, 1979–January 13, 1980; and Pierpont Morgan Library, New York, April 3–July 31. New York, 1979.

Paris, Cambridge, and New York 1994–95
The Renaissance in France: Drawings from the École des Beaux-Arts, Paris. Exh. cat. by Emmanuelle Brugerolles and David Guillet. École Nationale Supérieure des Beaux-Arts, Paris, September 23–November 6, 1994; Fogg Art Museum, Harvard University Art Museums, Cambridge, Massachusetts, February 4–April 9, 1995; and The Metropolitan Museum of Art, New York, September 12–November 12. Cambridge, Mass., 1995.

Paris, Cleveland, and Boston 1979
Chardin, 1699–1779. Exh. cat. edited by Pierre Rosenberg. Galeries Nationales du Grand Palais, Paris, January 29–April 30, 1979; Cleveland Museum of Art, June 6–August 12; and Museum of Fine Arts, Boston, September 11–November 19. Cleveland, 1979. [French ed., Paris, 1979.]

Paris, Munich, and Bonn 2005–6
Poussin, Watteau, Chardin, David: Peintures françaises dans les collections allemandes, XVIIᵉ–XVIIIᵉ siècles. Exh. cat. edited by Pierre Rosenberg, with David Mandrella. Galeries Nationales du Grand Palais, Paris, April 18–July 31, 2005; Haus der Kunst, Munich, October 5, 2005–January 8, 2006; and Kunst- und Austellungshalle der Bundesrepublik Deutschland, Bonn, February 3–April 30. Paris, Munich, and Bonn, 2005.

Paris, Ottawa, and New York 1988–89
Degas. Exh. cat. by Henri Loyrette, Michael Pantazzi, Gary Tinterow, and Jean Sutherland Boggs. Galeries Nationales du Grand Palais, Paris, February 9–May 16, 1988; National Gallery of Canada, Ottawa, June 16–August 28; and The Metropolitan Museum of Art, New York, September 27, 1988–January 8, 1989. Paris, 1988. [English ed., New York and Ottawa, 1988.]

Paris, Philadelphia, and Fort Worth 1991–92
Les Amours des Dieux: La Peinture mythologique de Watteau à David. Exh. cat. by Colin Bailey et al. Galeries Nationales du Grand Palais, Paris, October 15, 1991–January 6, 1992; Philadelphia Museum of Art, February 23–April 26; and Kimbell Art Museum, Fort Worth, May 23–August 2. Fort Worth and Paris, 1991. [English ed., *The Loves of the Gods: Mythological Painting from Watteau to David*. New York and Fort Worth, 1992.]

Paris, Piacenza, and Brunswick 1992–93
Pannini. Exh. cat. by Michael Kiene. Musée du Louvre, Paris, October 15, 1992–February 15, 1993; Museo Civico, Piacenza, March 15–May 15; and Herzog Anton-Ulrich Museum, Brunswick, June 15–August 15. Les Dossiers du Musée du Louvre, Exposition-dossier du Département des Peintures 41. Paris, 1992.

Paris, Rotterdam, and Haarlem 1962
Le Dessin italien dans les collections hollandaises. 2 vols. Exh. cat. Institut Néerlandais, Paris, March–April 1, 1962; Museum Boymans-Van Beuningen, Rotterdam, April 14–June 3; and Teylers Museum, Haarlem, June 10–July 22. Paris, 1962.

Paris, Strasbourg, and New York 2002–3
Chassériau: Un Autre Romantisme. Exh. cat. by Stéphane Guégan, Vincent Pomarède, Louis-Antoine Prat et al. Galeries Nationales du Grand Palais, Paris, February 26–May 27, 2002; Musée des Beaux-Arts, Strasbourg, June 19–September 21; and The Metropolitan Museum of Art, New York, October 21, 2002–January 5, 2003. Paris, 2002. [English ed., *Théodore Chassériau, 1819–1856: The Unknown Romantic*. New York, 2002.]

Paris, Sydney, and Ottawa 2003–6
François Boucher et l'art rocaille dans les collections de l'École des Beaux-Arts. Exh. cat. École Nationale Supérieure des Beaux-Arts, Paris, October 16–December 21, 2003; Art Gallery of New South Wales, Sydney, March 5–May 1, 2005; and National Gallery of Canada, Ottawa, September 16, 2005– January 1, 2006. Paris, 2003.

Parker 1928
Karl Theodore Parker. "Some Drawings by Rubens and His School in the Collection of Mrs. G. W. Wrangham." *Old Master Drawings*, no. 9 (June 1928), pp. 1–6.

Parker 1956
Karl Theodore Parker. *Catalogue of the Collection of Drawings in the Ashmolean Museum*. Vol. 2, *Italian Schools*. Oxford, 1956. [Repr., 1972.]

Parker and Mathey 1957
Karl Theodore Parker and Jacques Mathey. *Antoine Watteau: Catalogue complet de son oeuvre dessiné*. 2 vols. Paris, 1957.

Parma and Vienna 2003
Parmigianino e il manierismo europeo. Exh. cat. by Lucia Fornari Schianchi and Sylvia Ferino-Pagden. Galleria Nazionale, Parma, February 8–May 15, 2003; and Kunsthistorisches Museum, Vienna, June 4–September 14. Milan, 2003. [German ed., *Parmigianino und der europäische Manierismus*. Milan, 2003.]

Partridge 1999
Loren Partridge. "Federico Zuccari at Caprarola,

1561–1569: The Documentary and Graphic Evidence." In *Der Maler Federico Zuccari: Ein römischer Virtuoso von europäischem Ruhm; Akten des internationalen Kongresses der Bibliotheca Hertziana, Rom und Florenz, 23.–26. Februar 1993*, edited by Matthias Winner and Detlef Heikamp, pp. 159–84. Munich, 1999.

Passavant 1860
Johann David Passavant. *Raphael d'Urbin et son père Giovanni Santi*. 2 vols. Paris, 1860.

Pečírka 1963
Jaromir Pečírka. *Drawings: Edgar Degas*. London, 1963.

Pfäffikon and Geneva 1978
Venezianische Kunst in der Schweiz und in Liechtenstein. Exh. cat. Seedamm-Kulturzentrum, Pfäffikon, June 18–August 27, 1978; and Musée d'Art et d'Histoire, Geneva, September 8–November 5. Zurich and Milan, 1978.

Philadelphia 1905
Catalogue of the Second Annual Philadelphia Water Color Exhibition. Pennsylvania Academy of the Fine Arts, Philadelphia, April 3–29, 1905. Philadelphia, 1905.

Philadelphia 1985
Mary Cassatt and Philadelphia. Exh. cat. by Suzanne G. Lindsay. Philadelphia Museum of Art, February 17–April 14, 1985. Philadelphia, 1985.

Philadelphia 1991–92
"A Masterpiece in Focus: Goltzius's *Without Ceres and Bacchus Venus Would Freeze*." Philadephia Museum of Art, November 16, 1991–February 2, 1992. [Exh. cat. published in Nichols 1992.]

Philadelphia and Houston 1985
Eighteenth-Century French Book Illustration: Drawings by Fragonard and Gravelot from the Rosenbach Museum & Library. Exh. cat. by Kimerly Rorschach and Susan B. Taylor. Rosenbach Museum & Library, Philadelphia, May 15–July 28, 1985; and Museum of Fine Arts, Houston, September 27–December 1. Philadelphia, 1985.

Pignatti 1955
Terisio Pignatti. *Giorgione*. Verona, 1955.

Pignatti 1967
Terisio Pignatti. *Disegni dei Guardi*. Florence, 1967.

Pignatti 1969
Terisio Pignatti. *Giorgione*. Venice, 1969. [English trans., *Giorgione: Complete Edition*. London, 1971.]

Pignatti 1976
Terisio Pignatti. *Veronese*. 2 vols. Venice, 1976.

Pignatti 1978
Terisio Pignatti. *Giorgione*. 2nd ed. Milan, 1978.

Pignatti 1983
Terisio Pignatti. *Disegni antichi del Museo Correr di Venezia*. Vol. 3. Cataloghi di raccolte d'arte, n.s., 18. Vicenza, 1983.

Pinault Sørensen 2000
Madeleine Pinault Sørensen. "Les Dessins consacrés à l'expression des passions." In Beauvais 2000, vol. 2, pp. 543–70.

Pinon 2007
Pierre Pinon. *Pierre-Adrien Pâris (1745–1819): Architecte, et les monuments antiques de Rome et de la Campanie*. Collection de l'École Française de Rome 378. Rome, 2007.

Plomp 1997a
Michiel C. Plomp. *The Dutch Drawings in the Teyler Museum*. Vol. 2, *Artists Born between 1575 and 1630*. Haarlem, 1997.

Plomp 1997b
Michiel C. Plomp. "Jan Pietersz. Zomer's Inscriptions on

Drawings." *Delineavit et Sculpsit*, no. 17 (March 1997), pp. 13–27.

Plomp 2001
Michiel C. Plomp. *Les Collectionneurs hollandais de dessins au XVIIIᵉ siècle*. [Vol. 1] of *Collectionner, passionnément*. Exh. cat. Teylers Museum, Haarlem, December 16, 2001–February 17, 2002; and Institut Néerlandais, Paris, February 28–April 28, 2002. Paris, 2001. [Dutch ed., *18ᵈᵉ-eeuwse Hollandse verzamelaars van tekeningen en hun collecties*. Vol. 1 of *Hartstochtelijk verzameld*. Paris and Bussum, 2001.]

Pomarède 1998
Vincent Pomarède. "Le Sentiment de la nature." In Paris and Philadelphia 1998–99, pp. 117–22.

De Poorter 1978
Nora De Poorter. *The Eucharist Series*. 2 vols. Corpus Rubenianum Ludwig Burchard 2. London and Philadelphia, 1978.

Pope-Hennessy 1948
John Pope-Hennessy. *The Drawings of Domenichino in the Collection of His Majesty the King at Windsor Castle*. The Italian Drawings at Windsor Castle. London, 1948.

Popham 1957
Arthur Ewart Popham. *Correggio's Drawings*. London, 1957.

Popham 1971
Arthur Ewart Popham. *Catalogue of the Drawings of Parmigianino*. 3 vols. The Franklin Jasper Walls Lectures, 1969. Pierpont Morgan Library, New York. New Haven, 1971.

Popham and Wilde 1949
Arthur Ewart Popham and Johannes Wilde. *The Italian Drawings of the XV and XVI Centuries in the Collection of His Majesty the King at Windsor Castle*. London, 1949.

Populus 1930
Bernard Populus. *Claude Gillot, 1673–1722: Catalogue de l'oeuvre gravé*. Publication de la Société pour l'Étude de la Gravure Française. Paris, 1930.

Posner 1971
Donald Posner. *Annibale Carracci: A Study in the Reform of Italian Painting around 1590*. 2 vols. Kress Foundation Studies in the History of European Art. London, 1971.

Prat 1988
Louis-Antoine Prat. *Théodore Chassériau, 1819–1856: Dessins conservés en dehors du Louvre*. Cahiers du dessin français 5. Paris, 1988.

Prat 1996
Louis-Antoine Prat. "Quelques Feuilles réapparues de Théodore Chassériau." In *Hommage au dessin: Mélanges offerts à Roseline Bacou*, edited by Maria Teresa Caracciolo, pp. 572–843. Rimini, 1996.

Prat 2003
Louis-Antoine Prat. "Théodore Chassériau: Un Séjour italien (1840–1841)." In *Maestà di Roma, da Napoleone all'unita d'Italia, d'Ingres à Degas: Les Artistes français à Rome*, pp. 116–25. Exh. cat. Accademia di Francia, Villa Medici, Rome, March 7–June 29, 2003. Milan and Rome, 2003.

Prijatelj 1989
Kruno Prijatelj. "Canalettov crtez Dioklecijanova mau-zoleja u Splitu." In *Studije o umjetninama u Dalmaciji*, vol. 5, pp. 100–107. Zagreb, 1989.

Princeton 1981
Princeton Alumni Collections: Works on Paper. Exh. cat. Art Museum, Princeton University, April 26–June 21, 1981. Princeton, 1981.

Puglisi 1999
Catherine R. Puglisi. *Francesco Albani*. New Haven, 1999.

Py 2001
Bernadette Py. *Everhard Jabach collectionneur (1618–1695): Les Dessins de l'inventaire de 1695*. Paris, 2001. [Based on a manuscript inventory of Jabach's collection in the Bibliothèque Centrale, Musées Nationaux, Paris (MS no. 8).]

Py 2007
Bernardette Py. "Everhard Jabach: Supplement of Identifiable Drawings from the 1695 Estate Inventory." *Master Drawings* 45, no. 1 (2007), pp. 4–37.

Quimper and Angers 2000–2001
Desseins d'artistes: Les Plus Beaux Dessins français des musées d'Angers. Exh. cat. Musée des Beaux-Arts, Quimper, November 22, 2000–February 26, 2001; and Musée Pincé, Angers, May–September. Paris and Angers, 2000.

Ragghianti Collobi 1974
Licia Ragghianti Collobi. *Il libro de' disegni del Vasari*. 2 vols. Florence, 1974.

Raimondi 1958
Riccardo Raimondi. *Degas e la sua famiglia in Napoli, 1793–1917*. Naples, 1958.

Ravaisou 1907
Joseph Ravaisou. *Lou Cadet d'Ais*. 1907.

Redon 1894
Odilon Redon. "Confidences d'artiste." *L'Art moderne*, no. 34 (August, 25 1894), p. 268ff.

Reff 1976
Theodore Reff. *The Notebooks of Edgar Degas: A Catalogue of the Thirty-eight Notebooks in the Bibliothèque Nationale and Other Collections*. 2 vols. Oxford, 1976. [Repr., New York, 1985.]

Rewald 1983
John Rewald. *Paul Cézanne, the Watercolours: A Catalogue Raisonné*. London, 1983.

Rewald 1996
John Rewald, with Walter Feilchenfeldt and Jayne Warman. *The Paintings of Paul Cézanne: A Catalogue Raisonné*. 2 vols. New York, 1996.

Reznicek 1961
E. K. J. Reznicek. *Die Zeichnungen von Hendrick Goltzius, mit einem beschreibenden Katalog*. 2 vols. Orbis Artium, Utrechtse kunsthistorische studiën 6. Utrecht, 1961.

Reznicek 1993
E. K. J. Reznicek. "Drawings by Hendrick Goltzius, Thirty Years Later: Supplement to the 1961 *Catalogue Raisonné*." *Master Drawings* 31, no. 3 (Autumn 1993), pp. 215–78.

Ribeiro 1984
Aileen Ribeiro. *Dress in Eighteenth-Century Europe, 1715–1789*. London, 1984.

Richmond and other cities 1979–80
Treasures from Chatsworth: The Devonshire Inheritance. A Loan Exhibition from the Devonshire Collection. Exh. cat. Virginia Museum of Fine Arts, Richmond, September 11–October 21, 1979; Kimbell Art Museum, Fort Worth, November 17–December 30; Museum of Art, Toledo, January 27–March 2, 1980; Witte Memorial Museum, San Antonio, March 22–May 4; New Orleans Museum of Art, May 24–July 6; and California Palace of the Legion of Honor, San Francisco, July 26–September 7. Organized by the International Exhibitions Foundation. Washington, D.C., 1979.

Ridolfi 1648 (1835–37 ed.)
Carlo Ridolfi. *Le maraviglie dell'arte; ovvero, Le vite degli illustri pittori veneti e dello stato*. 2 vols. Venice,

1648. 2nd ed. Edited by Giuseppe Vedova. Padua, 1835–37. [Repr., Bologna, 2000.]

Rivière 1922–23
Henri Rivière. *Les Dessins de Degas reproduits en fac-simile.* Les dessins des grands artistes français: Degas. Paris, 1922–23.

Robert 1908
Karl Robert. *Le Fusain sans maitre: Traité pratique et complet sur l'étude du paysage au fusain.* Paris, 1908.

Robertson 1931
W. Graham Robertson. *Time Was: The Reminiscences of W. Graham Robertson.* London, 1931.

Roethlisberger 1961
Marcel G. Roethlisberger. *Claude Lorrain: The Paintings.* 2 vols. Yale Publications in the History of Art 13. New Haven, 1961.

Roethlisberger 1962
Marcel G. Roethlisberger, ed. *Claude Lorrain: The Wildenstein Album.* Paris, 1962.

Roethlisberger 1968
Marcel G. Roethlisberger. *Claude Lorrain: The Drawings.* 2 vols. California Studies in the History of Art 8. Berkeley, 1968.

Roethlisberger 1971
Marcel G. Roethlisberger. *The Claude Lorrain Album in the Norton Simon, Inc., Museum of Art.* Los Angeles, 1971.

Roethlisberger 1979
Marcel G. Roethlisberger. "Additional Works by Goffredo Wals and Claude Lorrain." *Burlington Magazine* 121 (January 1979), pp. 20–28.

Roethlisberger 1986
Marcel G. Roethlisberger. "The Drawing Collection of Prince Livio Odescalchi." *Master Drawings* 23–24 (Spring 1986), pp. 5–30.

Roethlisberger 1993
Marcel G. Roethlisberger, with Marten Jan Bok. *Abraham Bloemaert and His Sons: Paintings and Prints.* 2 vols. Aetas Aurea 11. Doornspijk, 1993.

Roland Michel 1984
Marianne Roland Michel. *Watteau: An Artist of the Eighteenth Century.* London, 1984.

Roland Michel 1987
Marianne Roland Michel. *Le Dessin français au XVIIIᵉ siècle.* Fribourg, 1987.

Roland Michel 1994
Marianne Roland Michel. *Chardin.* Paris, 1994.

Rome 1990–91
J. H. Fragonard e H. Robert a Roma. Exh. cat. edited by Catherine Boulot, Jean-Pierre Cuzin, and Pierre Rosenberg. Accademia di Francia, Villa Medici, Rome, December 6, 1990–February 24, 1991. Rome, 1990.

Rome and Turin 1961
L'Italia vista dai pittori francesi del XVIII e XIX secolo. Exh. cat. Palazzo delle Esposizioni, Rome, February–March 1961; and Galleria Civica d'Arte Moderna, Turin, April 20–May 25. Rome, 1961.

Rome, Dijon, and Paris 1976
Piranèse et les Français, 1740–1790. Exh. cat. Accademia di Francia, Villa Medici, Rome, opened May 11, 1976; Palais des États de Bourgogne, Dijon, July 10–September 15; and Hôtel de Sully, Paris, October 4–November 15. Rome, 1976.

Rooses 1890
Max Rooses. *Jordaens' Leben und Werke.* Stuttgart, 1890.

Roscam Abbing 2006
Michiel Roscam Abbing, ed. *Rembrandt 2006: New Rembrandt Documents.* Leiden, 2006.

Rosci 1993
Marco Rosci. *Giulio Cesare Procaccini.* Mensili d'arte 13. Soncino, 1993.

Rosenberg 1983a
Pierre Rosenberg. *Chardin: New Thoughts.* The Franklin D. Murphy Lectures 1. Helen Foresman Spencer Museum of Art, University of Kansas. Lawrence, Kans., 1983.

Rosenberg 1983b
Pierre Rosenberg. *Tout l'oeuvre peint de Chardin.* Les Classiques de l'art. Paris, 1983.

Rosenberg 1997
Pierre Rosenberg, ed. *La Donation Jacques Petithory au Musée Bonnat, Bayonne: Objets d'art, sculptures, peintures, dessins.* Paris, 1997.

Rosenberg and Prat 1996
Pierre Rosenberg and Louis-Antoine Prat. *Antoine Watteau, 1684–1721: Catalogue raisonné des dessins.* 3 vols. Paris, 1996.

Rosenberg and Temperini 1999
Pierre Rosenberg and Renaud Temperini. *Chardin: Suivi du catalogue des oeuvres.* Collection Grandes Monographies. Paris, 1999.

Rossi Bortolatto 1974
Luigina Rossi Bortolato. *L'opera completa di Francesco Guardi.* Classici dell'arte 71. Milan, 1974.

Rotterdam 1907
"Peintures, pastels, dessins et lithographies par Odilon Redon." Kunstzaal Reckers, Rotterdam, May 1907.

Rotterdam 1990–91
Fra Bartolommeo, Master Draughtsman of the High Renaissance: A Selection from the Rotterdam Albums and Landscape Drawings from Various Collections. Exh. cat. by Chris Fischer. Museum Boymans-Van Beuningen, Rotterdam, December 16, 1990–February 17, 1991. Rotterdam, 1990. [The exhibition traveled to the Museum of Fine Arts, Boston, January 15–April 12, 1992; Kimbell Art Museum, Fort Worth, May 9–August 2, 1992; and Pierpont Morgan Library, New York, September 11–November 29, 1992.]

Rouart and Orienti 1970
Denis Rouart and Sandra Orienti. *Tout l'oeuvre peint d'Édouard Manet.* Paris, 1970.

Rouart and D. Wildenstein 1975
Denis Rouart and Daniel Wildenstein. *Édouard Manet: Catalogue raisonné.* 2 vols. Lausanne, 1975.

Rouen 1999
Autour de Claude-Joseph Vernet: La Marine à voile de 1650 à 1890. Exh. cat. edited by Claude Pétry. Musée des Beaux-Arts, Rouen, July 20–September 14, 1999. Rouen, 1999.

Rouen and Le Mans 2001
Trésors cachés: Chefs-d'Oeuvre du Cabinet d'Arts Graphiques du Château de Versailles. Exh. cat. by Xavier Salmon. Musée des Beaux-Arts, Rouen, March 9–May 15, 2001; and Musée de Tessé, Le Mans, June 22–September 2. Paris, 2001.

Roux 1931–55
Marcel Roux. *Inventaire du fonds français: Graveurs du XVIIIᵉ siècle.* 8 vols. Département des Estampes, Bibliothèque Nationale, Paris. Paris, 1931–55.

Roworth 1989
Wendy Wassyng Roworth. "Salvator Rosa's Self-Portraits: Some Problems of Identity and Meaning." *Seventeenth Century* 4, no. 2 (Autumn 1989), pp. 117–48.

Roy 1929a
Maurice Roy. "Les Jehan Cousin, I. Les Deux Jehan Cousin." In *Artistes et monuments de la Renaissance en France: Recherches nouvelles et documents inédits*, vol. 1, pp. 1–43. Paris, 1929.

Roy 1929b
Maurice Roy. "Les Jehan Cousin, II. Les Tapisseries de Saint-Mammès de Langres: Compositions authentiques de Jehan Cousin Père." In *Artistes et monuments de la Renaissance en France: Recherches nouvelles et documents inédits*, vol. 1, pp. 44–55. Paris, 1929.

Royalton-Kisch and Ekserdjian 2000
Martin Royalton-Kisch and David Ekserdjian. "The *Entombment of Christ*: A Lost Mantegna Owned by Rembrandt?" *Apollo* 151 (March 2000), pp. 52–56.

Ruland 1876
[Carl Ruland.] *The Works of Raphael Santi da Urbino as Represented in the Raphael Collection in the Royal Library at Windsor Castle, Formed by H.R.H. the Prince Consort, 1853–1861, and Completed by Her Majesty Queen Victoria.* N.p., 1876.

Saccomani 1980
Elisabetta Saccomani. "Domenico Campagnola: Gli anni della maturità." *Arte veneta* 34 (1980), pp. 63–77.

Saint Louis 1961
"A Galaxy of Treasures from St. Louis Collections." City Art Museum of St. Louis, January 18–February 12, 1961. [Exh. cat. published in *Bulletin* (City Art Museum of St. Louis) 44, no. 4 (1961).]

Saint Louis 1962
"Collector's Choice: V." City Art Museum of St. Louis, 1962.

Salerno 1963
Luigi Salerno. *Salvator Rosa.* Collana d'arte del Club del Libro 5. Milan, 1963.

Salerno 1988
Luigi Salerno. *I dipinti del Guercino.* Rome, 1988.

Salvaing 1996
Jean Salvaing. "Le Domaine de la Présidente du XVIᵉ au XXᵉ siècle et ses possesseurs." *Cahier* (Société Archéologique, Scientifique et Littéraire de Béziers), no. 2 (1996), pp. 40–45.

Sand, *Lettres*, 2005 (ed.)
George Sand. *Nouvelles Lettres d'un voyageur.* Paris, 1877. 2005 ed., edited by E. Sourian. Paris, 2005.

Sandoz 1974
Marc Sandoz. *Théodore Chassériau, 1819–1856: Catalogue raisonné des peintures et estampes.* Paris, 1974.

Sandoz 1977
Marc Sandoz. *Jean-Baptiste Deshays, 1729–1765.* Paris, 1977.

Sandoz 1986
Marc Sandoz. *Cahiers Théodore Chassériau.* Vol. 2, *Portraits et visages dessinés par Théodore Chassériau.* Paris, 1986.

Sandrart 1675–79
Joachim von Sandrart. *Teutsche Academie der edlen Bau-, Bild- und Mahlerey-Künste.* 2 vols. Nuremberg, 1675–79.

San Francisco and Williamstown 2006–7
Claude Lorrain: The Painter as Draftsman. Drawings from the British Museum. Exh. cat. by Richard Rand, with contributions by Antony Griffiths and Colleen M. Terry. California Palace of the Legion of Honor, San Francisco, October 14, 2006–January 14, 2007; and Sterling and Francine Clark Art Institute, Williamstown, Massachusetts, February 3–April 29. New Haven and Williamstown, 2006.

Sapori 1974–76
Giovanna Sapori. "Percorso di Raffaellino del Colle."

Annuario dell'Istituto di Storia dell'Arte, 1974–75/1975–76, pp. 167–92.

Savage 1922
Spencer Savage. "The Discovery of Some of Jacques Le Moyne's Botanical Drawings." *Gardeners' Chronicle*, 3rd ser., 71 (1922), p. 44.

Savage 1923
Spencer Savage. "Early Botanical Painters: No. 3, Jacques Le Moyne de Morgues." *Gardeners' Chronicle*, 3rd ser., 73 (1923), pp. 148–49.

Sawicka and Sulerzyska 1960
Stanislawa Sawicka and Teresa Sulerzyska. *Straty w rysunkach z Gabinetu Rycin Biblioteki Uniwersyteckiej, 1939–1945 / Les Pertes de dessins au Cabinet des Estampes de la Bibliothèque de l'Université de Varsovie.* [In Polish, with summary in French.] Acta Bibliothecae Universitatis Varsoviensis / Prace Biblioteki Uniwersyteckiej w Warszawie 3. Warsaw, 1960.

Schapelhouman 1987
Marijn Schapelhouman. *Nederlandse tekeningen omstreeks 1600 / Netherlandish Drawings, circa 1600.* Catalogus van de Nederlandse tekeningen in het Rijksprentenkabinet, Rijksmuseum, Amsterdam 3. The Hague, 1987.

Schatborn 1981
Peter Schatborn. "Van Rembrandt tot Crozat: Vroege verzamelingen met tekeningen van Rembrandt." *Nederlands kunsthistorisch jaarboek* 32 (1981), pp. 1–54. Issue titled *Verzamelen in Nederland.*

Schatborn 2005
Peter Schatborn. "Dans l'atelier de Rembrandt." In Stefaan Hautekeete, *Les Dessins de Rembrandt et ses élèves, appartenant à la collection de Jean de Grez, Musées Royaux des Beaux-Arts de Belgique–Bruxelles,* pp. 8–16. Exh. cat. Musées Royaux des Beaux-Arts de Belgique, Brussels, July 8–September 30, 2005. Brussels, 2005.

Schiff 1973
Gert Schiff. *Johann Heinrich Füssli, 1741–1825.* 2 vols. Oeuvrekataloge Schweizer Künstler 1. Zurich and Munich, 1973.

Schilling 1973
Edmund Schilling. *Katalog der deutschen Zeichnungen: Alte Meister.* 3 vols. Städelsches Kunstinstitut, Frankfurt-am-Main. Munich, 1973.

Schmitz 1998
Erik Schmitz. "The Landscape Rembrandt Knew: The Countryside around Amsterdam in the Mid-Seventeenth Century." In Amsterdam and Paris 1998–99, pp. 42–68.

Schnapper 1973
Arthur Schnapper. "Louis de Silvestre: Tableaux de jeunesse." *La Revue du Louvre et des musées de France* 23, no. 1 (1973), pp. 21–26.

Schulz 1974
Wolfgang Schulz. *Lambert Doomer: Sämtliche Zeichnungen.* Disegno, Studien zur Geschichte der europäischen Handzeichnung 2. Berlin, 1974.

Schulze Altcappenberg 1995
Hein-Th. Schulze Altcappenberg. *Die italienischen Zeichnungen des 14. und 15. Jahrhunderts im Berliner Kupferstichkabinett: Kritischer Katalog.* Berlin, 1995.

G. Schwartz 1985
Gary Schwartz. *Rembrandt: His Life, His Paintings. A New Biography with All Accessible Paintings Illustrated in Colour.* London, 1985.

G. Schwartz 2006
Gary Schwartz. *Rembrandt's Universe: His Art, His Life, His World.* London, 2006.

M. Schwartz 1959
Marvin D. Schwartz. "'Contrasts in Landscape' at Wildenstein's." *Apollo* 70 (November 1959), p. 136.

Scrase 1991
David Scrase. "A Drawing by Francesco Menzocchi Acquired by the Fitzwilliam Museum." *Burlington Magazine* 133 (November 1991), pp. 773–76.

Il Seicento lombardo 1973
Il Seicento lombardo. 3 vols. [Vol. 1], *Saggi introduttivi,* Milano, Palazzo Reale, Pinacoteca Ambrosiana; [vol. 2], *Catalogo dei dipinti e delle sculture,* Milano, Palazzo Reale; [vol. 3], *Catalogo dei disegni, libri, stampe,* Milano, Pinacoteca Ambrosiana. Milan, 1973. [Repr., 1991.]

Sensier 1881
Alfred Sensier. *La Vie et l'oeuvre de J. F. Millet.* Edited by Paul Mantz. Paris, 1881.

Shearman 1965
John Shearman. *Andrea del Sarto.* 2 vols. Oxford, 1965.

Shearman 1972
John Shearman. *Raphael's Cartoons in the Collection of Her Majesty the Queen, and the Tapestries for the Sistine Chapel.* London, 1972.

Shearman 2003
John Shearman. *Raphael in Early Modern Sources (1483–1602).* 2 vols. Römische Forschungen der Bibliotheca Hertziana 30, 31. New Haven, 2003.

Shoolman Slatkin 1976
Regina Shoolman Slatkin. "Abraham Bloemaert and François Boucher: Affinity and Relationship." *Master Drawings* 14, no. 3 (Autumn 1976), pp. 247–60.

Shoolman Slatkin 1980
Regina Shoolman Slatkin. "French Drawings: Two Exhibitions at the National Gallery." *Drawing* 1, no. 5 (January–February 1980), pp. 110–13.

Sievers 2000
Ann H. Sievers, with Linda Muehlig and Nancy Rich, with contributions by Kristen Erickson and Edward J. Nygren. *Master Drawings from the Smith College Museum of Art.* New York, 2000.

Signac 1911/1978
Paul Signac. *D'Eugène Delacroix au Néo-Impressionnisme.* New ed. Petite Bibliothèque d'art moderne. Paris, 1911. 1978 ed.: Edited by Françoise Cachin. Collection Savoir. Paris, 1978.

Široká 1995
Eva Jana Široká. "Northern Artists in Italy, ca. 1565–85: Hans Speckaert as a Draughtsman and a Teacher." 3 vols. Ph.D. diss., Princeton University, 1995.

Široká 1997
Eva Jana Široká. "Hans Speckaert as a Draughtsman and a Teacher." *Bolletino d'arte,* suppl. no. 100 (1997), *Fiamminghi a Roma, 1508–1608: Atti del convegno internazionale, Bruxelles, 24–25 febbraio 1995,* edited by Nicole Dacos, pp. 133–48.

Smith 1996
Jeffrey Chipps Smith. "Imhoff." In *The Dictionary of Art,* edited by Jane Turner, vol. 15, pp. 144–45. New York, 1996.

Smyth 1971
Hugh Craig Smyth. *Bronzino as Draughtsman: An Introduction; with Notes on His Portraiture and Tapestries.* Locust Valley, N.Y., 1971.

Sotheby's 1957
Catalogue of Drawings of Landscapes and Trees by Fra Bartolommeo. Sotheby's, London, sale cat., November 20, 1957. [Preface and catalogue entries by Carmen Gronau.]

Spear 1982
Richard E. Spear. *Domenichino.* 2 vols. New Haven, 1982.

Spike 2002
John T. Spike. "A Rediscovered Modello for the Caprara Altarpiece by Annibale Carracci." *Studi di storia dell'arte,* no. 13 (2002), pp. 251–58.

Stampfle 1991
Felice Stampfle, with Ruth S. Kraemer and Jane Turner. *Netherlandish Drawings of the Fifteenth and Sixteenth Centuries and Flemish Drawings of the Seventeenth and Eighteenth Centuries in the Pierpont Morgan Library.* New York and Princeton, 1991.

Starcky 2000
Laure Starcky. *Les Peintures françaises: Catalogue sommaire illustré.* Musée Magnin, Dijon. Paris, 2000.

Stechow 1932
Wolfgang Stechow. *Apollo und Daphne.* Studien der Bibliothek Warburg 23. Leipzig, 1932.

Stein 2000
Perrin Stein. "Copies and Retouched Drawings by Charles-Joseph Natoire." *Master Drawings* 38, no. 2 (Summer 2000), pp. 167–86.

Stephan 1996
Susanne Stephan. "Narrenbühne auf dem Zeichenblatt: Das Pulcinellentheater des Giandomenico Tiepolo." *Die Weltkunst* 66, no. 18 (September 15, 1996), pp. 2128–30.

Stratis 1994
Harriet K. Stratis. "Beneath the Surface: Redon's Methods and Materials." In Chicago, Amsterdam, and London 1994–95, pp. 354–77, 427–31.

Strauss and Van der Meulen 1979
Walter L. Strauss and Marjon van der Meulen. *The Rembrandt Documents.* New York, 1979.

Street 1972
Leonora Street. "La vendita Ellesmere di disegni dei Carracci." *Arte illustrata,* no. 50 (September 1972), pp. 355–58.

Stuttgart 1979–80
Zeichnung in Deutschland: Deutsche Zeichner, 1540–1640. 2 vols. Exh. cat. by Heinrich Geissler. Graphische Sammlung, Staatsgalerie, Stuttgart, December 1, 1979–February 17, 1980. Stuttgart, 1979–80.

Sumowski 1979–92
Werner Sumowski. *Drawings of the Rembrandt School.* 10 vols. New York, 1979–92.

Sumowski 2002
Werner Sumowski. "Rembrandt and the Village of Sloten." Translated by Russell Stockman. *Master Drawings* 40, no. 3 (Fall 2002), pp. 239–42.

Tabarant 1931
Adolphe Tabarant. *Manet: Histoire catalographique.* Paris, 1931.

Tabarant 1947
Adolphe Tabarant. *Manet et ses oeuvres.* Paris, 1947.

Tanzi 1985
Marco Tanzi. "Qualche aggiunta al Malosso e alla sua cerchia." *Prospettiva,* no. 40 (January 1985), pp. 82–85.

Tanzi 1992
Marco Tanzi. "Microstorie malossesche: Pratica di bottega e problemi di committenza." In *Dal disegno all'opera compiuta: Atti del convegno internazionale, Torgiano, ottobre–novembre 1987,* edited by Mario Di Giampaolo, pp. 105–7. Perugia, 1992.

Terme 1921
Pierre Terme [pseud.]. *Mon Languedoc.* Paris, 1921.

Terme 1922
Pierre Terme [pseud.]. *Les Servantes du feu: Images et recueillement.* Paris, 1922.

Ternois 1954
Daniel Ternois. "Un Album de dessins au château de Chatsworth: Jacques Callot paysagiste." *Gazette des beaux-arts,* 6th ser., 43 (March 1954), pp. 151–64.

Ternois 1962a
Daniel Ternois. *L'Art de Jacques Callot.* Paris, 1962.

Ternois 1962b
Daniel Ternois. *Jacques Callot: Catalogue complet de son oeuvre dessiné.* Paris, 1962.

Ternois 1992
Daniel Ternois. "Les Deux Langages de Jacques Callot." In Nancy 1992, pp. 33–48.

Ternois 1993
Daniel Ternois. "Dessins de Jacques Callot: Quelques Attributions récentes et leurs enseignements; ses méthodes de travail, son atelier, ses continuateurs." In *Jacques Callot (1592–1635): Actes du colloque organisé par Le Service Culturel du Musée du Louvre et la ville de Nancy, à Paris et à Nancy, les 25, 26 et 27 juin 1992,* edited by Daniel Ternois, pp. 357–98. Paris, 1993.

Thiem 1977
Christel Thiem. *Italienische Zeichnungen, 1500–1800.* Graphische Sammlung, Staatsgalerie, Stuttgart. Stuttgart, 1977.

Thomas Le Claire Kunsthandel 1989
Thomas Le Claire Kunsthandel. *Meisterzeichnungen, 1500–1900.* Thomas Le Claire Kunsthandel 6. Hamburg, 1989.

Thomson 1995
Richard Thomson. *Edgar Degas: Waiting.* Getty Studies on Art. Malibu, 1995.

Thuillier 1978
Jacques Thuillier. "Gericault et sa légende." In Grunchec 1978, pp. 5–9.

Thuillier 1996
Jacques Thuillier. "Pierre Brébiette dessinateur: Essai de chronologie." In *Hommage au dessin: Mélanges offerts à Roseline Bacou,* edited by Maria Teresa Caracciolo, pp. 274–323. Rimini, 1996.

Tietze and Tietze-Conrat 1944
Hans Tietze and Erika Tietze-Conrat. *The Drawings of the Venetian Painters in the Fifteenth and Sixteenth Centuries.* New York, 1944.

Tokyo and Kyoto 1980
Fragonard. Exh. cat. by Denys Sutton. [In English and Japanese.] National Museum of Western Art, Tokyo, March 18–May 11, 1980; and Kyoto Municipal Museum, May 24–June 29. Tokyo, 1980.

Tongiorgi Tomasi 1993
Lucia Tongiorgi Tomasi. *I ritratti di piante di Iacopo Ligozzi.* Ospedaletto, 1993.

Tonkovich 2002
Jennifer Tonkovich. "Claude Gillot and the Theater, with a Catalogue of Drawings." Ph.D. diss., Rutgers, State University of New Jersey, 2002.

Tonkovich 2005
Jennifer Tonkovich. "Claude Gillot's Costume Designs for the Paris Opéra: Some New Sources." *Burlington Magazine* 147 (April 2005), pp. 248–52.

Tonkovich 2006
Jennifer Tonkovich." A New Album of Theater Drawings by Claude Gillot." *Master Drawings* 44, no. 4 (Winter 2006), pp. 464–86.

Toronto 2000
A Dream of the Past: Pre-Raphaelite and Aesthetic Movement Paintings, Watercolours and Drawings from the Lanigan Collection. Exh. cat. University of Toronto Art Centre, April 8–September 22, 2000. Toronto, 2000.

Toronto and New York 1985–86
Italian Drawings from the Collection of Duke Roberto Ferretti. Exh. cat. by David McTavish. Art Gallery of Ontario, Toronto, October 26, 1985–January 5, 1986; and Pierpont Morgan Library, New York, February 14–April 20. Toronto, 1985.

Toronto, Ottawa, San Francisco, and New York 1972–73
French Master Drawings of the Seventeenth & Eighteenth Centuries in North American Collections / Dessins français du 17ᵉᵐᵉ et du 18ᵉᵐᵉ siècles des collections américaines. Exh. cat. by Pierre Rosenberg. Art Gallery of Ontario, Toronto, September 2–October 15, 1972; National Gallery of Canada, Ottawa, November 3–December 17; California Palace of the Legion of Honor, San Francisco, January 12–March 11, 1973; and New York Cultural Center, April 4–May 6. Toronto, 1972.

Toulouse 1992
Le Dessin baroque en Languedoc et en Provence. Exh. cat. by Jean Penent et al. Musée Paul Dupuy, Toulouse, 1992. Toulouse, 1992.

Tournus 2005
Greuze et l'affaire du Septime Sévère. Exh. cat. Musée Greuze, Tournus, June 25–September 18, 2005. Paris and Tournus, 2005.

Tours and Toulouse 2000
Les Peintres du Roi, 1648–1793. Exh. cat. Musée des Beaux-Arts, Tours, March 18–June 18, 2000; and Musée des Augustins, Toulouse, June 30–October 2. Paris, 2000.

Trent 2006
Romanino: Un pittore in rivolta nel rinascimento italiano. Exh. cat. Castello del Buonconsiglio, Trent, July 29–October 29, 2006. Cinisello Balsamo, 2006.

Tümpel 1993
Christian Tümpel. "Jordaens: A Protestant Artist in a Catholic Stonghold. Notes on Protestant Artists in Catholic Centres." In Antwerp 1993, vol. 1, pp. 31–37.

Turner 1999
Nicholas Turner. *Italian Drawings in the Department of Prints and Drawings in the British Museum.* [Vol. 6], *Roman Baroque Drawings, c. 1620 to c. 1700.* 2 vols. London, 1999.

Turner 2000
Nicholas Turner. *Federico Barocci.* Paris, 2000.

Van Tuyll 2000
Carel van Tuyll van Seeroskerken. *The Italian Drawings of the Fifteenth and Sixteenth Centuries in the Teyler Museum.* Haarlem, Ghent, and Doornspijk, 2000.

Udine and Bloomington 1996–97
Giandomenico Tiepolo, maestria e gioco: Disegni dal mondo. Exh. cat. by Adelheid M. Gealt and George Knox. Castello di Udine, September 14–December 31, 1996; and Indiana University Art Museum, Bloomington, January 15–March 9, 1997. Milan, 1996.

Uwins 1858/1978
Thomas Uwins. *A Memoir of Thomas Uwins, R.A., . . . with Letters to His Brothers during Seven Years Spent in Italy, and Correspondence with the Late Sir Thomas Lawrence, Sir Charles L. Eastlake, A. E. Chalon, R.A., and Other Distinguished Persons.* Edited by Sarah Uwins. 2 vols. London, 1858. Repr., Biographies of British Artists. East Ardsley, 1978.

Vaccaro 2002
Mary Vaccaro. *Parmigianino: The Paintings.* Turin, 2002.

Valentiner 1932
Elisabetta Valentiner. "Hans Speckaert: Ein Beitrag zur Kenntnis der Niederländer in Rom um 1575." *Städel-Jahrbuch* 7–8 (1932), pp. 163–71.

Valéry 1938
Paul Valéry. *Degas, danse, dessin.* Paris, 1938.

Vancouver, Ottawa, and Washington 1988–89
Master Drawings from the National Gallery of Canada. Exh. cat. by Marie-Nicole Boisclair et al. Vancouver Art Gallery, September 13–November 20, 1988; National Gallery of Canada, Ottawa, December 9, 1988–February 12, 1989; and National Gallery of Art, Washington, D.C., March 5–May 21. Washington, D.C., 1988.

Van Gogh, *Letters,* 2000 (ed.)
Vincent Van Gogh. *The Complete Letters of Vincent Van Gogh: With Reproductions of All the Drawings in the Correspondence.* 3 vols. 3rd ed. Boston, 2000.

Vasari 1568 (1966–87 ed.)
Giorgio Vasari. *Le vite de' più eccellenti pittori, scultori e architettori nelle redazioni del 1550 e 1568.* 3 vols. 2nd ed. Florence, 1568. 1966–87 ed.: Edited by Rosanna Bettarini; commentary by Paola Barocchi. 6 vols. Florence, 1966–87.

Vasari 1568 (1912–14 ed.)
Giorgio Vasari. *Le vite de' più eccellenti pittori, scultori e architettori nelle redazioni dell 1550 e 1568.* 3 vols. 2nd ed. Florence, 1568. 1912–14 ed.: *Lives of the Most Eminent Painters, Sculptors, & Architects.* Translated by Gaston du C. De Vere. 10 vols. London, 1912–14.

Vecce 1995
Leonardo da Vinci: Libro di pittura. Edizione in facsimile del Codice Urbinate lat. 1270 nella Biblioteca Apostolica Vaticana. Critical transcription by Carlo Vecce. Introduction by Carlo Pedretti. 2 vols. Florence, 1995.

Venice 1955
Giorgione e i Giorgioneschi. Exh. cat. edited by Pietro Zampetti. Palazzo Ducale, Venice, June 11–October 23, 1955. Venice, 1955.

Venice 1962
Canaletto e Guardi: Catalogo della mostra dei disegni. Exh. cat. edited by Karl Theodore Parker and James Byam Shaw. Fondazione Giorgio Cini, Venice, 1962. Cataloghi di mostre 16. Venice, 1962.

Venice 1965a
Disegni veneti del Museo di Budapest. Exh. cat. edited by Iván Fenyő. Fondazione Giorgio Cini, Venice, 1965. Cataloghi di mostre 22. Venice, 1965.

Venice 1965b
Mostra dei Guardi. Exh. cat. edited by Pietro Zampetti. Palazzo Grassi, Venice, June 5–October 10, 1965. Venice, 1965.

Venice 1982
Canaletto: Disegni, dipinti, incisioni. Exh. cat. edited by Alessandro Bettagno. Fondazione Giorgio Cini, Venice, July 17–October 30, 1982. Grafica veneta 3. Venice, 1982.

Venice 1992
Leonardo & Venice. Exh. cat. edited by Giovanna Nepi Sciré and Pietro C. Marani. Palazzo Grassi, Venice, March 23–July 5, 1992. Milan, 1992. [Italian ed., *Leonardo & Venezia.* Milan, 1992.]

Venice 1993
Francesco Guardi: Vedute, capricci, feste. Exh. cat. edited by Alessandro Bettagno. Fondazione Giorgio Cini, Venice, August 28–November 21, 1993. Cataloghi di mostre 51. Milan, 1993.

Venice 2004
Tiepolo: Ironia e comico. Exh. cat. edited by Adriano Mariuz and Giuseppe Pavanello. Fondazione Giorgio Cini, Venice, September 3–December 5, 2004. Cataloghi di mostre 62. Venice, 2004.

Venturi 1927
Adolfo Venturi. "Giorgione." *Vita artistica* 2 (July 1927), pp. 125–32.

Venturi 1928
Adolfo Venturi. *Storia dell'arte italiana.* Vol. 9, pt. 3. Milan, 1928.

Versailles 1963
Charles Le Brun, 1619–1690: Peintre et dessinateur. Exh. cat. by Jacques Thuillier and Jennifer Montagu. Château du Versailles, July–October 1963. Versailles, 1963.

Versailles 2004
Esquisses, pastels et dessins de François Boucher dans les collections privées. Exh. cat. by Françoise Joulie. Musée Lambinet, Versailles, October 12, 2004–January 9, 2005. Paris and Versailles, 2004.

Versailles, Munich, and London 2002–3
Madame de Pompadour et les arts. Exh. cat. edited by Xavier Salmon. Musée National des Châteaux de Versailles et de Trianon, February 14–May 19, 2002; Kunsthalle der Hypo-Kulturstiftung, Munich, June 14–September 15; and National Gallery, London, October 16, 2002–January 12, 2003. Paris, 2002.

Viard, Decron, and Wu 1994
Georges Viard, Benoît Decron, and Fang-Cheng Wu. *La Cathédrale Saint Mammès de Langres: Histoire, architecture, décor.* Langres, 1994.

Vienna 1985
Albrecht Dürer und die Tier- und Pflanzenstudien der Renaissance. Exh. cat. by Fritz Koreny. Graphische Sammlung Albertina, Vienna, April 18–June 30, 1985. Munich, 1985.

Vigne 1995
Georges Vigne. *Dessins d'Ingres: Catalogue raisonné des dessins du Musée de Montauban.* Paris, 1995.

Viroli 2000
Giordano Viroli. *I Longhi, Luca, Francesco, Barbara: Pittori ravennati (sec. XVI–XVII).* Ravenna, 2000.

Vogl 1987
Alphons Vogl. *Der Bilderzyklus "Der Triumph der Kirche" von Otto van Veen.* Schriften aus dem Institut für Kunstgeschichte der Universität München 19. Munich, 1987.

Vollard 1918
Ambroise Vollard. *Tableaux, pastels & dessins de Pierre-Auguste Renoir.* Paris, 1918.

Vollard 1919
Ambroise Vollard. *La Vie & l'oeuvre de Pierre-Auguste Renoir.* Paris, 1919.

Vollard 1924
Ambroise Vollard. *Degas, 1834–1914.* Artistes d'hier et d'aujourd'hui. Paris, 1924.

Volle 1979
Nathalie Volle. *Jean-Simon Berthélemy, 1743–1811: Peintre d'histoire.* Paris, 1979.

Le Voyage au Maroc 1992
Eugène Delacroix. *Le Voyage au Maroc.* Edited by Maurice Arama, Maurice Sérullaz, and Arlette Sérullaz. 6 vols. Paris, 1992.

Wagner 1971
Helga Wagner. *Jan van der Heyden, 1637–1712.* Amsterdam, 1971.

Washington 1978–79
Hubert Robert: Drawings and Watercolors. Exh. cat. by Victor Carlson. National Gallery of Art, Washington, D.C., November 19, 1978–January 21, 1979. Washington, D.C., 1978.

Washington 1984
James McNeill Whistler at the Freer Gallery. Exh. cat. by David Park Curry. Freer Gallery of Art, Washington, D.C., May 11–November 5, 1984. Washington, D.C., and New York, 1984.

Washington 1984–85
Degas: The Dancers. Exh. cat. by George T. M. Shackelford. National Gallery of Art, Washington, D.C., November 22, 1984–March 10, 1985. Washington, D.C., 1984.

Washington 1999–2000
The Drawings of Annibale Carracci. Exh. cat. by Daniele Benati et al. National Gallery of Art, Washington, D.C., September 26, 1999–January 9, 2000. Washington, D.C., 1999.

Washington 2002
The Flowering of Florence: Botanical Art for the Medici. Exh. cat. by Lucia Tongiorgi Tomasi and Gretchen A. Hirschauer. National Gallery of Art, Washington, D.C., March 3–May 27, 2002. Washington, D.C., 2002.

Washington and Chicago 1973–74
François Boucher in North American Collections: 100 Drawings. Exh. cat. by Regina Shoolman Slatkin. National Gallery of Art, Washington, D.C., December 23, 1973–March 17, 1974; and Art Institute of Chicago, April 4–May 12. Washington, D.C., 1973.

Washington and New York 1986–87
The Age of Bruegel: Netherlandish Drawings in the Sixteenth Century. Exh. cat. by John Oliver Hand et al. National Gallery of Art, Washington, D.C., November 7, 1986–January 18, 1987; and Pierpont Morgan Library, New York, January 30–April 5. Washington, D.C., and Cambridge, 1986.

Washington and other cities 1962–63
Old Master Drawings from Chatsworth: A Loan Exhibition from the Devonshire Collection. Exh. cat. National Gallery of Art, Washington, D.C., October 28–November 25, 1962; Pierpont Morgan Library, New York; Museum of Fine Arts, Boston; Cleveland Museum of Art; National Gallery of Canada, Ottawa; Art Institute of Chicago; and California Palace of the Legion of Honor, San Francisco. Exhibition circulated by the Smithsonian Institution, 1962–63. Washington, D.C., 1962.

Washington and other cities 1969–70
Old Master Drawings from Chatsworth: A Loan Exhibition from the Devonshire Collection. Exh. cat. by James Byam Shaw. National Gallery of Art, Washington, D.C., November 2–30, 1969; Philadelphia Museum of Art; Pierpont Morgan Library; Art Gallery of Toronto; and other venues. Exhibition circulated by the International Exhibitions Foundation, 1969–70. [Washington, D.C., 1969.]

Washington and Paris 1982–83
Claude Gellée dit Le Lorrain, 1600–1682. Exh. cat. by H. Diane Russell. National Gallery of Art, Washington, D.C., October 17, 1982–January 2, 1983; and Galeries Nationales du Grand Palais, Paris, February 16–May 16. Paris, 1983. [English ed., *Claude Lorrain, 1600–1682.* Washington, D.C., 1982.]

Washington and Parma 1984
Correggio and His Legacy: Sixteenth-Century Emilian Drawings. Exh. cat. by Diane DeGrazia, with an essay by Eugenio Riccòmini. National Gallery of Art, Washington, D.C., March 11–May 13, 1984; and Galleria Nazionale, Parma, June 3–July 15. Washington, D.C.,

1984. [Italian ed., *Correggio e il suo lascito: Disegni del Cinquecento emiliano.* Parma, 1984.]

Washington, Cambridge, and New York 1978–79
Drawings by Fragonard in North American Collections. Exh. cat. by Eunice Williams. National Gallery of Art, Washington, D.C., November 19, 1978–January 21, 1979; Fogg Art Museum, Harvard University, Cambridge, Massachusetts, February 16–April 1; and Frick Collection, New York, April 20–June 3. Washington, D.C., 1978.

Washington, New York, Minneapolis, and Malibu 1981–82
French Master Drawings from the Rouen Museum: From Caron to Delacroix. Exh. cat. by Pierre Rosenberg and François Bergot. National Gallery of Art, Washington, D.C., August 2–September 13, 1981; National Academy of Design, New York; Minneapolis Institute of Arts; and J. Paul Getty Museum, Malibu, California. Exhibition circulated by the International Exhibitions Foundation, 1981–82. Washington, D.C., 1981.

Washington, Paris, and Berlin 1984–85
Watteau, 1684–1721. Exh. cat. by Margaret Morgan Grasselli and Pierre Rosenberg. National Gallery of Art, Washington, D. C., June 17–September 23, 1984; Galeries Nationales du Grand Palais, Paris, October 23, 1984–January 28, 1985; and Schloss Charlottenburg, Berlin, February 22–May 26. Paris, 1984. [English ed., Washington, D.C., 1984.]

Watson 1950
F. J. B. Watson. "Some Unpublished Canaletto Drawings of London." *Burlington Magazine* 92 (November 1950), pp. 315–19.

Wegner 1970
Wolfgang Wegner. "Bemerkungen zum Werke des Meisters von Liechtenstein." *Wallraf-Richartz-Jahrbuch* 32 (1970), pp. 263–68.

Wegner 1973
Wolfgang Wegner. *Die niederländischen Handzeichnungen des 15.–18. Jahrhunderts.* 2 vols. Katalog (Staatliche Graphischen Sammlung München) 1. Berlin, 1973.

Weinglass 1982
David H. Weinglass, ed. *The Collected English Letters of Henry Fuseli.* Millwood, N.Y., 1982.

Weitzenhoffer 1986
Frances Weitzenhoffer. *The Havemeyers: Impressionism Comes to America.* New York, 1986.

Welcker 1933
Clara J. Welcker. *Hendrick Avercamp, 1585–1634, bijgenaamd "De Stomme van Campen" en Barent Avercamp, 1612–1679, "Schilders tot Campen."* Zwolle, 1933.

Welcker 1979
Clara J. Welcker. *Hendrick Avercamp, 1585–1634, bijgenaamd "De Stomme van Campen" en Barent Avercamp, 1612–1679, "Schilders tot Campen."* Edited by D. J. Hensbroeck-Van der Poel. Doornspijk, 1979.

West Palm Beach 1969
Old Master Drawings from the Collection of Mr. and Mrs. Lester Francis Avnet. Norton Gallery and School of Art, West Palm Beach, February 1969. Exhibition circulated by the American Federation of Arts, 1969–70. New York, 1969.

Whistler 1888/1908
James McNeill Whistler. *Mr. Whistler's "Ten O'Clock."* London, 1888. Repr., Jamaica, N.Y., 1908.

B. E. White 1996
Barbara Ehrlich White. *Impressionists Side by Side: Their Friendships, Rivalries, and Artistic Exchanges.* New York, 1996.

C. White and Crawley 1994
Christopher White and Charlotte Crawley. *The Dutch and Flemish Drawings of the Fifteenth to the Early Nineteenth Centuries in the Collection of Her Majesty the Queen at Windsor Castle.* Cambridge, 1994.

Whiteley 1983
J. J. L. Whiteley. "London: French Art, 1750–1850." *Burlington Magazine* 125 (August 1983), pp. 506, 509.

Whiteley 1998
J. J. L. Whiteley. *Claude Lorrain: Drawings from the Collections of the British Musem and the Ashmolean Museum.* London, 1998.

Whitney 1997
Wheelock Whitney. *Géricault in Italy.* New Haven, 1997.

A. Wildenstein 1992–98
Alec Wildenstein. *Odilon Redon: Catalogue raisonné de l'oeuvre peint et dessiné.* 4 vols. Paris, 1992–98.

G. Wildenstein 1923
Georges Wildenstein. "L'Inventaire après décès de Claude Gillot." *Bulletin de la Société de l'Histoire de l'Art Français,* 1923, pp. 114–20.

G. Wildenstein 1933
Georges Wildenstein. *Chardin.* Paris, 1933.

G. Wildenstein 1963
Georges Wildenstein. *Chardin.* Zurich, 1963.

G. Wildenstein 1964
Georges Wildenstein. *Gauguin.* Vol. 1, *Catalogue.* Paris, 1964.

G. Wildenstein 1969
Georges Wildenstein. *Chardin: Catalogue raisonné.* Revised by Daniel Wildenstein. Oxford, 1969.

Wilhelm 1951
Jacques Wilhelm. "François Le Moyne et Antoine Watteau." Translated by Liselotte Moser. *Art Quarterly* 14, no. 3 (Autumn 1951), pp. 216–30.

Winkler 1963
Friderich Winkler. "The Anonymous Liechtenstein Master." *Master Drawings* 1, no. 2 (Summer 1963), pp. 34–38.

Winterthur 1953
Théodore Géricault, 1791–1824. Exh. cat. by Pierre Dubaut. Kunstmuseum Winterthur, August 30–November 8, 1953. Winterthur, 1953.

Witcombe 1989
Christopher L. C. Ewart Witcombe. "Raffaellino del Colle and Giulio Romano's *Holy Family with Saints* in S. Maria dell'Anima." *Gazette des beaux-arts,* 6th ser., 114, (September 1989), pp. 51–62.

Wolk-Simon 1991
Linda Wolk-Simon. "A New Drawing by Raffaellino del Colle and an Old Attribution Reconsidered." *Master Drawings* 29, no. 3 (Autumn 1991), pp. 301–6.

Wolk-Simon 1994
Linda Wolk-Simon. "Drawings by Raphael and His School in Stockholm and Some Related Sheets." [Review of *Rafael: Teckningar,* by Börje Magnusson; exh. cat., Nationalmuseum, Stockholm, 1992.] *Master Drawings* 32, no. 4 (Winter 1994), pp. 393–96.

Wood 1998
Christopher Wood. *Burne-Jones: The Life and Works of Sir Edward Burne-Jones (1833–1898).* New York, 1998.

Woodward 1996
David Woodward. *Catalogue of Watermarks in Italian Printed Maps, ca. 1540–1600.* Chicago, 1996.

Wurzbach 1906–11
Alfred von Wurzbach. *Niederländisches Künstler-Lexikon.* 3 vols. Vienna, 1906–11.

Zahn 1923
Leopold Zahn. *Die Handzeichnungen des Jacques Callot, unter besonderer Berücksichtigung der Petersburger Sammlung.* Munich, 1923.

Zampetti 1968
Pietro Zampetti. *L'opera completa di Giorgione.* Milan, 1968.

Zerner 1969
Henri Zerner. *École de Fontainebleau: Gravures.* Paris, 1969.

Zerner 1996a
Henri Zerner. *L'Art de la Renaissance en France: L'Invention du classicisme.* Paris, 1996.

Zerner 1996b
Henri Zerner. "Le Portrait, plus ou moins." In *Géricault* 1996, vol. 1, pp. 321–36.

Zimmermann 1991
Michael F. Zimmermann. *Les Mondes de Seurat: Son Oeuvre et le débat artistique de son temps.* Antwerp and Paris, 1991.

Zurich and Tübingen 1994–95
Degas: Die Portaits. Exh. cat. by Felix Baumann and Marianne Karabelnik, with contributions by Jean Sutherland Boggs et al. Kunsthaus Zürich, December 2, 1994–March 5, 1995; and Kunsthalle Tübingen, March 18–June 18. London, 1994.

Zvereva 2005
Alexandra Zvereva. "La Collection de portraits au crayon de Catherine de Médicis: Reconstitution et analyse socio-culturelle." 2 vols. Ph.D. diss., Université Paris IV-Sorbonne, Paris, 2005.

Index

Photograph Credits